Provisional Cities

This book considers the provisional nature of cities in relation to the Anthropocene – the proposed geological epoch of human-induced changes to the Earth system. It charts an environmental history of curfews, admonitions and alarms about dwelling on Earth. 'Provisional cities' are explored as exemplary sites for thinking about living in this unsettled time. Each chapter focuses on cities, settlements or proxy urbanisations, including past disaster zones, remote outposts in the present, and future urban fossils. The book explores the dynamic, changing and contradictory relationships between architecture and the global environmental crisis and looks at how to reposition architectural and urban practice in relation to wider intellectual, environmental, political and cultural shifts. The book argues that these rounder and richer accounts can better equip humanity to think through questions of vulnerability, responsibility and opportunity that are presented by immense processes of planetary change. These are cautionary tales for the Anthropocene. Central to this project is the proposition that living with uncertainty requires that architecture is reframed as a provisional practice. This book would be beneficial to students and academics working in architecture, geography, planning and environmental humanities as well as professionals working to shape the future of cities.

Renata Tyszczuk is an academic and artist whose work explores the relationship between global environmental change and provisionality in architectural thinking and practice. She is Senior Lecturer in Architecture at the University of Sheffield, UK. In 2013 she was awarded a British Academy Mid-Career Fellowship for her research on Provisional Cities.

Studies in Architecture Series

Series Editor: Eamonn Canniffe, Manchester School of Architecture, Manchester Metropolitan University, UK

The discipline of Architecture is undergoing subtle transformation as design awareness permeates our visually dominated culture. Technological change, the search for sustainability and debates around the value of place and meaning of the architectural gesture are aspects which will affect the cities we inhabit. This series seeks to address such topics, both theoretically and in practice, through the publication of high-quality original research, written and visual.

For a full list of titles in this series, please visit www.routledge.com/architecture/series/ASHSER-1324

Other titles in this series

The City Crown
Bruno Taut
Edited by Matthew Mindrup and Ulrike Altenmuller-Lewis

Phenomenologies of the City
Studies in the History and Philosophy of Architecture
Edited by Henriette Steiner and Maximilian Sternberg

From Formalism to Weak Form: The Architecture and Philosophy of Peter Eisenman
Stefano Corbo

Forthcoming titles in this series

On Surface and Place
Between Architecture, Textiles and Photography
Peter Carlin

Architecture, Death and Nationhood
Monumental Cemeteries of Nineteenth-Century Italy
Hannah Malone

Reconstruction and the Synthesis of the Arts in France, 1944–1962
Nicola Pezolet

Provisional Cities
Cautionary Tales for the Anthropocene

Renata Tyszczuk

LONDON AND NEW YORK

First published 2018
by Routledge
2 Park Square, Milton Park, Abingdon, Oxon OX14 4RN

and by Routledge
711 Third Avenue, New York, NY 10017

Routledge is an imprint of the Taylor & Francis Group, an informa business

© 2018 Renata Tyszczuk

The right of Renata Tyszczuk to be identified as author of this work has been asserted by her in accordance with sections 77 and 78 of the Copyright, Designs and Patents Act 1988.

All rights reserved. No part of this book may be reprinted or reproduced or utilised in any form or by any electronic, mechanical, or other means, now known or hereafter invented, including photocopying and recording, or in any information storage or retrieval system, without permission in writing from the publishers.

Trademark notice: Product or corporate names may be trademarks or registered trademarks, and are used only for identification and explanation without intent to infringe.

British Library Cataloguing-in-Publication Data
A catalogue record for this book is available from the British Library

Library of Congress Cataloging-in-Publication Data
Names: Tyszczuk, Renata, author.
Title: Provisional cities : cautionary tales for the anthropocene /
Renata Tyszczuk.
Description: First Edition. | New York : Routledge, [2018] | Series: Studies in architecture series | Includes bibliographical references and index.
Identifiers: LCCN 2017023085 | ISBN 9781472426109 (hardback) |
ISBN 9781315602769 (ebook)
Subjects: LCSH: Urban geography. | Cities and towns. |
Nature–Effect of human beings on.
Classification: LCC GF125 .T97 2018 | DDC 307.76–dc23
LC record available at https://lccn.loc.gov/2017023085

ISBN: 978-1-472-42610-9 (hbk)
ISBN: 978-1-315-60276-9 (ebk)

Typeset in Sabon
by Out of House Publishing

 Printed in the United Kingdom by Henry Ling Limited

For my sons, Tomasz, Łukasz and Staś.

Contents

Prologue: Cautionary tales   viii

Introduction: Provisional cities   1

1   Fossil traces   20

2   Disaster zone   48

3   Proving ground   76

4   Proxy world   113

5   Bounded planet   148

6   Monster Earth   195

7   Temporary home   223

Epilogue: Precautionary tales   255

Bibliography   266
List of illustrations   290
Acknowledgements   295
Index   297

Prologue
Cautionary tales

An.thro.po.ce.no.pho.bia

noun

Definition:

a fear of, or anxiety about the *Anthropocene* – the new epoch of human making; also harbouring a fear of the excessive deliberations about either human epochal prowess, or human frailty.

Origin:

a portmanteau term derived from *Anthropocene* and *phobia*.

Possible synonyms:

Holocenophilia, derived from the Holocene – the official geological epoch of the last 11,700 years, often associated with a nostalgia for clement, warm and relatively stable times.

Usage:

'She found that the frequent references to a new epoch brokered by a novel sense of human calamity and talk of an "apocalypse that was already here and now" induced in her a kind of *Anthropocenophobia*. She was aware of an unfolding global catastrophe – who wasn't? She didn't care what it was called, whether it was a good or a bad *Anthropocene*, whether it was about saving business-as-usual or this-changes-everything. She simply found it frightening: fear of human hubris, fear of human vulnerability; fear, in fact, that in spite of all the epochal talk, nothing would make a difference. The sky would just keep on falling.'

The Anthropocene, or, colloquially, 'the Age of Humans', is the name proposed for the geological epoch or story we are supposed to have stumbled into.[1] It has superceded the 'safe' and relatively stable Holocene world that we are familiar with.

The Anthropocene announces a catastrophe. It introduces humanity as an Earth-altering force of geological scale, like an asteroid strike or an ice age. It is identified by the vast geomorphic transformations of the Earth's surface, including rapid urbanisation, the acidification of oceans, the relentless destruction of biota, and by massive disruptions to the Earth system. And, 'we're making Earth wobble a little'.[2]

The Anthropocene tale, now unfolding in real time, was anticipated by many auguries of human-induced environmental change and extinction events. It is attended by longstanding insecurities and anxieties about unpredictable and unstable futures. It is unsettling. The Anthropocene, this book suggests, is a cautionary tale of its own making. It is a fearsome story told to try to make sense of the calamity-ridden world we find ourselves in.

The Anthropocene Working Group (AWG) of the Subcommission on Quaternary Stratigraphy has been gathering evidence on whether or not the Anthropocene should be formalised as an epoch and, if so, when it began. As of August 2016, the majority opinion of the AWG is that we are indeed in the Anthropocene Epoch of the Quaternary Period of the Cenozoic Era of the Phanerozoic Eon. The AWG has explored multiple possible markers for the Anthropocene, among them signs of human impact on the planet that will linger long after we are gone. These range from radiation traces from nuclear tests, a layer of technofossils (human-made materials such as concrete and plastic), to the future fossils of the bones of the domestic chicken, the world's most populous bird species, that proliferate in landfills and waste heaps around the globe.[3] Whether or not the term is formally adopted, human impact on the Earth promises to be even more 'stratigraphically significant', and hence even more frightening, in the future.[4] The advent of the Anthropocene is presented by many as an emergency, imperilling the 'safe operating space for humanity with respect to the Earth system'.[5] Concerns over dramatic and irreversible transformations of the Earth's systems generate a sense of urgency, panic, even tragedy, that a once hospitable planet may no longer offer the shelter that humans have long taken for granted. At the same time, there is a good deal of caution at the changes that Anthropocene thinking carries with it. Along with an imperative to intervene more in Earth systems in a bid to sustain a more Holocene-like state, and to do so quickly and effectively, there is an agonising lack of understanding as to how to go about it. The challenges of inhabiting and acting in a world without precedent can easily turn such anxieties into an *Anthropocenophobia*.[6]

Anthropocene rock

Anthropocene rock is a warning and a provocation. The geologic story of the boundary conditions of this frightening new epoch has become entangled with humanity's story – as historian Dipesh Chakrabarty puts it, 'the contingent history of our falling into the Anthropocene'.[7] By identifying the Anthropocene as but one more stratum – Anthropocene rock – in a long and turbulent Earth history, the human species is thrown into a strange historicity. This is a geological transition event, layered among other events; a possible trace in some future rocks that may or may not be legible to a post-human observer. Along with increasing alarm at the prospect of widespread anthropogenic planetary transformation, the Anthropocene announces a 'crisis of agency'.[8] For just at the moment when humans are called on to recognise their planetary-scaled agency, they are also made aware of their limited capacity to do anything at all. Furthermore, naming a geological epoch after *anthropos* – some kind of unitary human – might reinforce the presumption that everything is configured around 'us humans' and 'our time', just as we have started to question humanity's exaggerated sense of its own place in the world. It also elides the ethical problem of the power differentials between different groups of humans, and the intellectual problem of (always artificial, but fiercely guarded) disciplinary divisions. Furthermore, it flattens out – perhaps disastrously – the complexities in human relationships with the non-human natural world. Many of the Anthropocene's detractors agree that 'the idea of the Anthropocene is arrogant, universalist and capitalist-technocratic'.[9] A common position is that it is 'a reflection and reinforcement of the anthropocentric actionable world view that generated "the Anthropocene" – with all its looming emergencies – in the first place'.[10] There are many alternative names offered to account for the complexity of an epoch of geopolitical and ecological turmoil, among them 'Urbanthropocene', 'Capitalocene', 'Chthulucene', 'Ecocene', 'Plasticene', even 'Unforgiveable-crimescene' or 'Obscene'.[11] Still, as Raj Patel notes:

> Herein lies the danger. We're surrounded by catastrophic narratives of almost every political persuasion, tales that allow us to sit and wait while humanity's End Times work themselves out. The Anthropocene can very easily become the Misanthropocene.[12]

This naming and renaming indicates that we are still short of a word or two to describe the present predicament, in which human actions are dislodging the ground and upending the sky. Fearful and uncertain times may indeed require a new lexicon.[13] In the meantime, the Anthropocene has become a catch-all for the perils associated with the present day. Along with warnings regarding imminent climatic tipping points and predictions of catastrophe, there are concerns that time is running out for the countermeasures that might still be taken (ranging from local adaptation to planetary-scale geoengineering) and a host of anxieties about societal breakdown and wars over resources. In short, there is plenty to be fearful of. If the Anthropocene is a cautionary tale of its own making, its product is *Anthropocenophobia*. The Anthropocene brings with it fear and foreboding that the world (as we know it) is ending; that the sky will keep falling.

Cautionary world

The Anthropocene is presented here as a cautionary tale in a heuristic sense, in order to explore both its potential and its pitfalls when thinking about the future. Cautionary tales are meant to warn us against acts of transgression or recklessness. They are the 'be careful what you wish for' or 'don't go into the woods' narratives familiar from fairy tales; or the didactic nursery stories about instructions unheeded, risks recklessly taken, such as Heinrich Hoffmann's *Der Struwwelpeter* (1845) and the 'awful warnings' of 'bad behaviour' in Hilaire Belloc's *Cautionary Tales for Children* (1907). They usually narrate the crossing of some boundary and the unsettling of the status quo – with painful results. Cautionary tales expose the dangers, taboos and prohibitions of certain courses of action. Indulging in a forbidden act – carelessly or deliberately – leads their protagonists to an unpleasant fate. The cautionary tale often achieves a creeping horror by placing grizzly events in banal, domestic settings. As in a nightmare, the comfortable world we know suddenly becomes hostile and strange. Remember '*George, who played with a Dangerous Toy and suffered a Catastrophe of Considerable Dimensions*'?[14]

Ecological crisis narratives are cautionary tales *par excellence*. They render the familiar uncanny and make (planetary) home unhomely; they threaten obscure and dreadful punishments for deeds we barely understand. The more sophisticated our climate models get, the more we learn to think not of singular catastrophes, but of cascading and erratic chains of destruction – and the more paranoia clouds our planetary future. Stories of disruption and disbelief, like the tale of 'Chicken Licken', place us in a world in which the sky is always – impossibly, vertiginously – already falling. In an uncertain and fearsome world, then, cautionary tales are here to stay. And we should be ready for the stories – like the events they are preparing us for – to become stranger. The playwright Steve Waters observed:

> If we reach for genre is that simply a way of making it precedented? The genres we keep reaching for – cautionary tales, dystopic tales, apocalyptica, tragedy – flow in and out of our ways of reading the very unprecedented nature of the unrepresentable thing before us – an undiscovered country from which no traveller returns, right? It's a bit like the Lisbon earthquake. It's a bit like the Cold War. Maybe we don't have the equipment.[15]

The Anthropocene presents itself as the pre-eminent cautionary tale. After all, it warns of an unprecedented existential threat: human-induced human species demise. How might the Anthropocene be enlisted in fabulating narratives that will help carry the human species beyond the confines of a reactionary and anxious culture?[16] What is the point of cautionary tales in an unsettled world?

Cautionary tales are terrifying and didactic; they are rescue vessels, meant to steer us away from the rocks. But they also have an unsavoury aspect, in that they dwell luridly on gore and misfortune. They can be seen as smug, having an element of *schadenfreude*, or even a traumatising effect that baffles action: what is too awful to face, we will repress, and it will haunt us. They often take an alienating tone of rebuke – they imply a listener in need of correction, a criminal, or even a pre-criminal of sorts, chastised before she's had a chance to do anything wrong. There are many versions of the Anthropocene cautionary tale. It is like other cautionary tales in that it, too, is terrifying: a shock tactic intended to prompt human society to purposeful action. And, like other cautionary tales, it carries the risk of being immobilising rather than galvanising.

However, the Anthropocene is different from other cautionary tales in so far as it isn't simply a fable. It isn't just about an avoidable hypothetical future; it is also the story of an unavoidable catastrophe that is already happening. The unfolding disaster in some ways *is* the narrative: written on the Earth in a script of tsunamis, wildfires, garbage gyres and coal-seam gas leaks. The Anthropocene is thus also a story about inhabiting this disaster, adjusting ourselves to its shocks, and shifting away from a worst-case future. It transpires as an unsettling of entrenched conventions of thought and behaviour – liberal individualism, consumer capitalism, short-termism. It draws attention to complicated human and nonhuman relations and dangerous practices we take for granted. It gives us a sense of a longer 'now' and an uncertain 'what next?' Whereas in most cautionary tales all that is required for a good ending is prudence, temperance and obedience on the part of the individual, in the case of the Anthropocene it requires the transformative collective will of a whole society to take responsibility for the disaster of its own making.

The story to end all stories

The Anthropocene is a story about how human societies have affected the planet so drastically that it has been shunted into a new geological epoch. It is also the site of speculation about the residues (and the absences) that humans will leave behind. Rising oceans, toxic water, species extinctions, nuclear landscapes, climate change: many of the planetary changes that are seen as constituting proof of the Earth's shift from the Holocene to the Anthropocene are signposts to a future in which the planet may no longer be able to sustain human life. The Anthropocene concept is perhaps 'the ultimate eschatological narrative, a doomsday device ticking down to an apocalyptic end'.[17] It evokes the prospect of human extinction and therefore a world from which any experiencing, knowing, perceiving subject is absent. In other words, the Anthropocene story is one that does away with narrative, human narrative and the human altogether – *it is the story to end all stories.*

The Anthropocene story is riddled with paradoxes: a boundary event which can only be identified through catastrophic transgression of that boundary; a geological stratum named after humans for which there will be no human witnesses; a post-human Earth where all traces of imagining it have been erased. It tells a story of loss sedimented into future strata. Cormac McCarthy's novel *The Road* evokes the anxieties of our planetary predicament – not only the disappearance of a familiar physical world, home, or refuge, but also the language to describe it: 'The world shrinking down about a raw core of parsible entities. The names of things following those things into oblivion. Colours. The names of birds. Things to eat.'[18]

We live precariously on a perilously disturbed planet. The Earth's inherent changeability has always been a challenge to human habitation: 'instability and upheaval, rhythmical movement and dramatic changes of states are ordinary aspects of the Earth's own history.'[19] Comet and asteroid strikes or massive volcanic eruptions like those that have disrupted Earth's story in the past may happen again, with effects far more catastrophic than the worst-case scenarios of anthropogenic climate change. Indeed, the activities of the human species would be vanishingly insignificant compared with planetary dynamics, were it not for the emerging evidence that the former is capable of nudging the latter into greater and more chaotic extremes than ever before considered. 'The Earth,' writes philosopher Bruno Latour, 'has become once again... an agent of... our common *geostory*.' He continues, 'The problem becomes for all of us in philosophy, science or literature, how do we tell such a story.'[20] The story we seem intent on ending (badly) is the human one. For now we have the prospect of increasingly violent geophysical phenomena meeting vulnerable populations; and disasters are always socially produced and inequitably distributed.

Predictions vary wildly as to the consequences of the present epoch of human activity, and of our ability to alter our present course. There are quarrels over a 'good' or 'bad' Anthropocene.[21] Optimists call for a transition to a radically new stewardship of the Earth, founded in the sustainable use of resources. Pessimists anticipate runaway climate change, mass extinctions, and a brutally reduced human population. A few highly speculative technofixes have been mooted to stabilise the Earth system through sophisticated geoengineering. To many, however, such scientific utopianism is pure hubris – more frightening even than pursuing our present course unreflectively. It is clear that, if there is no undoing of the disastrous human incursions and impacts, the toxic chemical transformations of the oceans and atmosphere, and the human imperative to accumulate and consume, then we will need to find ways of coping with, shaping, and enduring an Anthropocene that can't be unmade. Inhabiting the disaster with ethical commitment rather than belatedly worrying about trying to stop it happening may be the best we can do. The writer Rebecca Solnit offers an alternative to the certainty of optimism or pessimism in times of despair, where hope, 'is not about what we expect. It is an embrace of the essential unknowability of the world, of the breaks with the present, the surprises'.[22]

Cassandra scientists

What I hope is that the term 'Anthropocene' will be a warning to the world.[23]

For atmospheric chemist Paul Crutzen, who is credited with popularising the term, 'Anthropocene' was intended as a way of sounding the alarm. Crutzen's key research statements are watersheds in the long-drawn-out cautionary tale of the 20th and 21st centuries. His research in the 1970s led to the discovery of the ozone hole over the Antarctic, demonstrating the damage effected by human activities – specifically, at that time, the use of chlorofluorocarbons (CFCs) in fridges and aerosol sprays – on an indispensable part of the Earth system. In the 1980s Crutzen co-authored a text on 'nuclear winter', arguing that the aerosols and gases produced in nuclear explosions could 'change the heat and radiative balance and dynamics of the Earth and the atmosphere'.[24] This idea gripped the collective imagination with enough force to encourage other theorists in their turn to address environmental issues at the planetary scale. The corollary to Crutzen's announcement of the Anthropocene in 2000 were his more recent contributions to the debate on geoengineering, the last-ditch attempts to counter human-activated catastrophe with man-made technological fixes.

Crutzen has spent a good deal of time worrying about what humans are doing to the Earth (and themselves in the process). The Anthropocene is more than a convenient framework for organising the concerns of Earth systems scientists. It is a shock tactic – an attempt to re-energise the stalled debate on environmental issues and to galvanise action. If Earth systems scientists such as Crutzen are easily placed in the cultural tradition of the prophet, this comes with its own risks.[25] Bruno Latour coined the term 'Cassandra scientists' for those Earth systems experts whose warnings are unheeded, even ridiculed.[26] Cassandra – the princess in Ancient Greek mythology blessed with the gift of prophecy and cursed not to be believed – is a resonant archetype for the group of researchers whose models and experiments have consistently predicted large-scale environmental catastrophe in the near future.

In *The Shock of the Anthropocene*, Christophe Bonneuil and Jean-Baptiste Fressoz contend that the 'grand narrative of the Anthropocene' has placed *anthropos* in two mutually antagonistic roles: the uninformed mass of humanity that has inadvertently acquired geological agency, and the small elite group of scientists, the 'ecological vanguard of the world', who have revealed a dangerous and uncertain planetary future.[27] The prophetic narrative that warns of 'a dishevelled planet and its errant humanity' is a burden that Earth systems scientists are keen to share.[28] Will Steffen and his colleagues assert: 'We are the first generation with the knowledge of how our activities influence the Earth system, and thus the first generation with the power and the responsibility to change our relationship with the planet.'[29] However, Bonneuil and

Fressoz write: 'This story of awakening is a fable.'[30] In other words, we have entered the Anthropocene in spite of consistent warnings.

This is by no means the first moment when humans have worried about what they are doing to the Earth – cautionary tales abound. There have been multiple warnings, oracles, prophecies, forecasts, model predictions, scenarios, visions and stories. The mid-20th century introduced decades of concern about human degradation of the Earth and awareness of global ecological disturbances. Notable texts include William Vogt's *Road to Survival* and Henry Fairfield Osborn's *Our Plundered Planet*, both from 1948; Rachel Carson's *Silent Spring*, 1962; and Barry Commoner's *The Closing Circle*, 1971. The Union of Concerned Scientists was formed in 1969, 'calling for scientific research to be directed away from military technologies and toward solving pressing environmental and social problems'.[31] It followed the example of the *Bulletin of the Atomic Scientists*, established by scientists of the Manhattan Project in 1945.[32] Their symbolic Doomsday Clock, which first appeared on the cover of the magazine in 1947 set to 11:53 pm, was advanced to 11:57 pm on 22 January 2015. The world was in trouble: 'Humanity's failure to reduce global nuclear arsenals as well as climate change prompted the *Bulletin of the Atomic Scientists* to advance their warning about our proximity to a potentially civilisation-ending catastrophe.'[33]

On 26 January 2017, the existential threat was deemed to have become even more serious and the clock was advanced by a further 30 seconds. The scientists cited continued failure to curb nuclear proliferation, to act on climate change and the political rhetoric of the newly inaugurated US president, Donald J. Trump, as reasons for the move.[34] The world was now two and a half minutes from doomsday. James Hansen's seminal article on global warming, written with a team of NASA researchers in 1981, and his congressional testimony in 1988 had established him as the world's most prominent 'worried scientist'.[35] In the run-up to the 2015 United Nations Climate Change Conference (COP 21), Hansen and 16 other climate researchers expressed their alarm at major ice sheet melt in both Greenland and Antarctica, predicting increased storminess and exponential sea level rise 'of at least Eemian proportions'.[36] The study's scenario indicated that coastal cities on the planet could have only a few more decades of habitability left. In these scientists' view, we are past 'the era in which humans have contributed to global climate change', which may have begun a thousand years ago or more. We are now in 'a fundamentally different phase, a Hyper-Anthropocene… initiated by explosive 20th-century growth of fossil fuel use'.[37]

The roster of the concerned includes Martin Rees, Baron Rees of Ludlow, the British Astronomer Royal. Rees's book title makes clear his gloomy outlook: *Our Final Hour: A Scientist's Warning: How Terror, Error, and Environmental Disaster Threaten Humankind's Future in this Century – on Earth and Beyond*. He is worried about all kinds of existential risk, and gives humankind 50-50 odds of surviving to the end of the 21st century. He warns:

> Our increasingly interconnected world is vulnerable to new risks, 'bio' or 'cyber', terror or error. The dangers from 21st-century technology could be graver and more intractable than the threat of nuclear devastation that we faced for decades. And human-induced pressures on the global environment may engender higher risks than the age-old hazards of earthquakes, eruptions and asteroid impacts.[38]

In other words, humans are the catastrophe. Owen Gaffney and Will Steffen have announced that the exceptional regime change of the planet we call home can be represented by an 'Anthropocene equation' – where the rate of change of the Earth system is fundamentally a function of humanity. The usual drivers of change: astronomical and geophysical forcings (the Sun, asteroids, currents) and internal dynamics (for example, the evolution of cyanobacteria) are considered negligible by comparison.[39] Human 'forcing' could lead to abrupt changes in the Earth system lasting for millions of years. In the short term, however, this could trigger societal collapse and remove humans from the equation altogether. Their intention is that 'formalising the Anthropocene mathematically brings home an entirely new reality'.[40] The Earth is no longer shaping its own worlds: it has been usurped by hybrid human-technological systems as the dominant planetary geomorphic force. What the long cautionary tale of human entanglements with dynamic Earth processes tells us is that the prospect of a planet gone awry needs to be taken seriously. Even in a system as ancient, as complex, and as endlessly changeable as Earth's planetary processes, the activities of humans over the past century represent a threat of unprecedented magnitude. This is a cautionary tale we would do well to heed.

The sky is falling

The Anthropocene is a time full of fears of a falling sky. Cosmic impacts have been significant in shaping the history of life on Earth and on rare occasions have collided with human history.[41] Indeed, fears of cosmic catastrophe go back to ancient times. Tales of falling skies, evil comets, burning asteroids and crashing meteors are also stories about the very real dangers of living as a quarrelsome species on a disaster-prone planet. Science-fiction writer Bruce Sterling's sardonic pronouncement about the future evokes a perfect storm of prediction, demographics, urbanisation and climate change: 'The Future is About Old People in Big Cities Afraid of the Sky.'[42] It bears remembering that there is a weirdness in the human experience of the sky above our heads – the changing and unpredictable maelstrom of weather and atmosphere – which undermines any global project for climate preservation, manipulation and control, or even any promise of good behaviour. Our hopes and fears, our predictions and even our prejudices can't stop the sky from falling. And then, there are always so many other things – more immediate-feeling, more concrete things – for us to be getting on with.

'Chicken Licken' or 'Chicken Little', the fable about a chicken which runs around panicking that the sky is falling, is now so familiar that the phrase 'the sky is falling' has passed into the English language as shorthand for a hysterical or mistaken belief that disaster is imminent. Hence its ready connotation with Anthropocene crisis narratives – shrill pronouncements of runaway, unprecedented, or catastrophic climate change.[43] The label 'Chicken Little' is often attached to environmental extremists or 'eco-loons' and global-warming alarmists or 'warmists' – with little distinction made between the two. In Margaret Atwood's version of the fable, however, the activist Chicken Little argues with her detractors: '"The sky is falling" is a metaphor, said Chicken Little huffily. It's true that the sky really is falling, but the falling of the sky represents all sorts of other things that are falling as well. Falling down, and falling apart. You should wake up!'[44]

We could also take heed of the words of Chief Vitalstatistix, a character in the comic book series *Asterix the Gaul*, whose rallying cry was: 'We have nothing to fear but the sky falling on our heads.' Although this joke is at the superstitious Gauls' expense, the comic punch line is rooted in historical accounts of this widespread ancient fear and linked to a comet impact in Europe during the Iron Age. The perpetual fear that the sky might fall is not entirely misplaced. Atwood's plucky Chicken Little and the fearless chief remind us that in a world of falling skies, it is important to be alive to fear, but not ruled by it.

'A big chunk of nature falls in the middle of the city,' writes philosopher Michel Serres in *The Natural Contract*, in his retelling of the story of the philosopher Anaxogoras, who was put on trial for suggesting that the Sun was a burning stone larger than the Peloponnese. Anaxogoras was also reputed to have foreseen the fall of a meteorite that landed near Aegospotami (modern northwestern Turkey) in 467 BC. The meteorite was, for him, evidence of the Sun falling apart. Serres connects this story to the myth of Tantalus, a king condemned to eternal punishment who, in some versions, waits for a delicately balanced rock to fall on his head. Serres considers the implications of humanity as a geological force, but also suggests it was always going to be too late to renegotiate a contract with nature:

> So, the stone falls on the city, the earth quakes and thus shakes our walls and our constructed certainties; nature bursts in on the citizen, who believes only in the assurances provided by human labour and by the political order or police... We ought to admire the madness or wisdom of our ancestors the Gauls, who feared, it is told, that the sky would fall on their heads: indeed, that could happen this morning, unannounced, and what's more it will surely happen some fine morning. Their madness or wisdom is just like ours, alive and brief, the eternal anguish of the king in hell, threatened by the rock.[45]

For Serres, nature is not the reliable and stable background to human activity, but is instead prone to catastrophe. Perhaps the Anthropocene is the epoch where the sky is always falling. Indeed, for Davi Kopenawa, shaman of the Yanomami people of the Amazon, who are tasked with holding up the sky, we live in the time of the 'falling sky'.[46] And if we humans have tumbled into the Anthropocene, return passage to a safe Holocene epoch is impossible. Thinking about 'falling into the Anthropocene' prompts reconsideration of the increasingly unruly aspects of a disastrously anthropogenic world. The catastrophe of the Anthropocene connects us to the Earth's cosmic irruptions. The question arises as to how humanity might live more responsibly while shaping Anthropocene rock and Anthropocene sky. It alerts us to 'living with Earth and cosmic processes... in the context of a deep, elemental underpinning that is at once a source of profound insecurity'.[47] Perhaps this *Anthropocenophobia* can help us to acknowledge the complexity of the human condition, which, despite its fundamentally earthbound nature, remains ungraspable and incalculable. In a world beyond our control, confronting our intractable fears is important. The Anthropocene sky will keep on falling whatever we do. This novel sense of fearfulness won't diminish the range of challenges we face, but it may help us respond to them in more just, considerate and purposeful ways.

Cautionary tales for the Anthropocene

The Anthropocene is a cautionary tale that invites us into a world that is fractured rather than whole, surprising rather than certain, and changeable rather than enduring.

Prologue: Cautionary tales xvii

There will never be a unifying narrative made from the array of signals emerging from a world falling apart. Nor will there be a foolproof guide as to what to do about it. Instead there will be multiple stories told about this unsettling juncture as well as numerous pathways to consider – interactions that are mutually shaping and futures that are inescapably bound to a restless home planet.

Cautionary tales for the Anthropocene remind us that we live with and are part of an earth-shattering-sky-falling nature. We are afraid of the future with good reason. We need cautionary tales, and not just for sounding the alarm or announcing the end of the world. They can also be about taking stock. They can help us to acknowledge the complexity of the human condition, bound up as it is with cosmic upheavals, planetary-scale adjustments, resource poverty, inadequate evacuation plans, and infrastructure breakdown. These are also stories of trial and error that can be absorbed and learned from. Cautionary tales for the Anthropocene might invoke an ethos of reckoning with non-human agency – for we need to be prepared for a surprising Earth. But they also reveal the provisionality of our knowledge about, and relationship with, the world. Cautionary tales also allow for human emotions and aptitudes

Figure 0.0 The Comet of 1618 over Augsburg; from *Iudicium Astrologicum*, by Elias Ehinger (publisher: Johann Schultes, ca. 1621?)
Source: Beinecke Rare Book & Manuscript Library, Yale University

to be explored: fear and distress, certainly, but also wit, humour, and ingenuity in the face of disaster. Perhaps the Anthropocene cautionary tale can help us to reappraise responsibility and grasp it on a different scale; to confront the fact of a turbulent planet, and brace ourselves for an uncertain future.

Notes

1. Paul J. Crutzen and Eugene Stoermer, 'The Anthropocene', *International Geosphere-Biosphere Programme Newsletter* 41 (2000): 17–18; Paul J. Crutzen, 'Geology of mankind', *Nature* 415 (January 2002): 23.
2. Owen Gaffney, '15 ways you know you're in the Anthropocene', The Huffington Post (29 August 2016), www.huffingtonpost.com/owen-gaffney/15-ways-you-know-youre-in_b_9764330.html; Scientists have suggested that the loss of mass from Greenland and Antarctica's rapidly melting ice sheets could be causing the eastward shift of the spin axis, Earth's 'wobble'; see NASA, 'NASA study solves two mysteries about wobbling Earth' (8 April 2016), www.nasa.gov/feature/nasa-study-solves-two-mysteries-about-wobbling-earth
3. Damian Carrington, 'The Anthropocene epoch: scientists declare dawn of human-influenced age", *The Guardian* (29 August 2016), www.theguardian.com/environment/2016/aug/29/declare-anthropocene-epoch-experts-urge-geological-congress-human-impact-earth?CMP=Share_iOSApp_Other
4. Elizabeth Kolbert, 'Enter the Anthropocene – age of man', *National Geographic Magazine* (March 2011), ngm.nationalgeographic.com/2011/03/age-of-man/kolbert-text
5. Johan Rockström *et al.*, 'A safe operating space for humanity', *Nature* 461 (September 2009): 472–75.
6. Renata Tyszczuk, 'Anthropocenophobia. The stone falls on the city', *Harvard Design Magazine* 42 (2016).
7. Dipesh Chakrabarty, 'The climate of history: Four theses', *Critical Inquiry* 35 (Winter 2009): 219–20.
8. Renata Tyszczuk, 'Architecture of the Anthropocene: The crisis of agency', *Scroope* 23 (Summer 2014): 67–73.
9. Robert Macfarlane, 'Generation Anthropocene: How humans have altered the planet for ever', *The Guardian* (1 April 2016), www.theguardian.com/books/2016/apr/01/generation-anthropocene-altered-planet-for-ever
10. Eileen Crist, 'On the poverty of our nomenclature', *Environmental Humanities* 3 (2013): 129–147.
11. On 'Urbanthropocene see Timothy W. Luke, 'Urbanism as cyborganicity: Tracking the materialities of the Anthropocene', in *New Geographies 06: Grounding Metabolism*, eds. Daniel Ibenez and Nikos Katsikis (Harvard University Press, 2014): 38–51. On Capitalocene, see Bruno Latour, 'Anthropology at the time of the Anthropocene – a personal view of what is to be studied' (lecture, Washington DC, December 2014), www.bruno-latour.fr/sites/default/files/139-AAA-Washington.pdf; see also Donna Haraway, 'Anthropocene, Capitalocene, Plantationocene, Chthulucene: making kin', *Environmental Humanities* 6 (2015): 159–65. On Ecocene, see Rachel Armstrong, 'Transitioning towards the Ecocene', in *Built to Grow: Blending Architecture and Biology*, eds. Barbara Imhof and Petra Gruber (Basel: Birkhauser, 2016): 11–13. On Plasticene see Christina Reed, 'Plastic Age: How it's reshaping rocks, oceans and life', *New Scientist* (28 January 2015), www.newscientist.com/article/mg22530060-200-plastic-age-how-its-reshaping-rocks-oceans-and-life/. On Misanthropocene, see Elizabeth Kolbert, 'Out Loud: The Misanthropocene', podcast on The New Yorker online (29 December 2013), www.newyorker.com/culture/culture-desk/out-loud-the-misanthropocene. On Unforgiveable-crimescene and Obscene see Kathleen Dean Moore, 'Anthropocene is the wrong word', *Earth Island Journal* (Spring 2013), www.earthisland.org/journal/index.php/eij/article/anthropocene_is_the_wrong_word/
12. Raj Patel, 'Misanthropocene', *Earth Island Journal* (Spring 2013), www.earthisland.org/journal/index.php/eij/article/misanthropocene/
13. Among these, Robert Macfarlane's crowdsourced Anthropocene glossary launched with 'Desecration phrasebook: A litany for the Anthropocene', *New Scientist* (15 December

Prologue: Cautionary tales xix

2015), www.newscientist.com/article/mg22830523-200-desecration-phrasebook-a-litany-for-the-anthropocene/; see also cultural anthropologists Cymene Howe and Anand Pandian's online project, 'Lexicon for an Anthropocene yet unseen', www.culanth.org/fieldsights/803-lexicon-for-an-anthropocene-yet-unseen; see also the Bureau of Linguistical Reality, a public participatory artwork by Heidi Quante and Alicia Escott, bureauoflinguisticalreality.com

14 Hilaire Belloc, *Cautionary Tales for Children: Designed for the Admonition of Children Between the Ages of Eight and Fourteen Years* (London: Eveleigh Nash, 1907).
15 Steve Waters, talk at *Culture and Climate Change: Narratives* launch event, Free Word Centre (June 2014).
16 Etienne Turpin, 'Who does the Earth think it is, now?' in *Architecture in the Anthropocene: Encounters Among Design, Deep Time, Science and Philosophy*, ed. Etienne Turpin (Ann Arbor, Michigan: Open Humanities Press, 2013: 7.
17 Cary Wolfe and Claire Colebrook, 'Is the Anthropocene… a doomsday device?', (12 January 2013), in conversation for the Anthropocene Project HKW, www.hkw.de/en/programm/projekte/veranstaltung/p_83894.php
18 Cormac McCarthy, *The Road* (New York: Alfred A. Knopf, 2006): 75. See also Bradon Smith, 'Words after things: narrating the ends of worlds' in *Culture and Climate Change: Narratives*, eds. J. Smith, R. Tyszczuk and R. Butler (Cambridge: Shed, 2014): 58–68.
19 Nigel Clark, *Inhuman Nature: Sociable Life on a Dynamic Planet* (London: Sage, 2011): xii.
20 Bruno Latour, 'Agency at the time of the Anthropocene', *New Literary History* 45 (2014): 1–18; 3; emphasis in original.
21 Clive Hamilton, 'The Theodicy of the "Good Anthropocene"', *Environmental Humanities* 7 (2015): 233–238.
22 Rebecca Solnit, *Hope in the Dark: Untold Histories, Wild Possibilities* (New York: Nation Books, 2004): 136.
23 Paul Crutzen cited in Elizabeth Kolbert, 'Enter the Anthropocene – age of man', *National Geographic Magazine* (March 2011); ngm.nationalgeographic.com/print/2011/03/age-of-man/kolbert-text
24 Paul J. Crutzen and John W. Birks, 'The atmosphere after a nuclear war: Twilight at noon', *Ambio* 11 (1982): 114–125; 123.
25 Lynda Walsh, *Scientists as Prophets: A Rhetorical Genealogy* (New York: Oxford University Press, 2013).
26 Bruno Latour, 'War and peace in an age of ecological conflicts', lecture prepared for the Peter Wall Institute, Vancouver (23 September 2013), published in *Revue Juridique de l'Environnement* 1 (2014): 51–63.
27 Christophe Bonneuil and Jean-Baptiste Fressoz, *The Shock of the Anthropocene*, trans. David Fernbach (London: Verso, 2016): 79–80.
28 Christophe Bonneuil and Jean-Baptiste Fressoz, *The Shock of the Anthropocene*, trans. David Fernbach (London: Verso, 2016): 80.
29 Will Steffen *et al.*, 'The Anthropocene: From global change to planetary stewardship', *Ambio* 40 (2011): 739–761; 757.
30 Christophe Bonneuil and Jean-Baptiste Fressoz, *The Shock of the Anthropocene*, trans. David Fernbach (London: Verso, 2016): xiii.
31 Union of Concerned Scientists, www.ucsusa.org/about-us#.V5Ycz06J-qA
32 *Bulletin of the Atomic Scientists*, thebulletin.org
33 Megan Gannon, 'Doomsday Clock set at 3 minutes to midnight', *Scientific American* (24 January 2015), www.scientificamerican.com/article/doomsday-clock-set-at-3-minutes-to-midnight/
34 Lawrence M. Krauss and David Titley, 'Thanks to Trump, the Doomsday Clock advances towards midnight', *The New York Times* (26 January 2017), www.nytimes.com/2017/01/26/opinion/thanks-to-trump-the-doomsday-clock-advances-toward-midnight.html?partner=IFTTT&_r=0; see also Sarah Karacs, 'Doomsday Clock: humanity might be edging closer to its end', CNN (1 February 2017); edition.cnn.com/2017/01/26/world/doomsday-clock-2017/index.html
35 James Hansen *et al.* (J. D. Johnson, A. Lacis, S. Lebedeff, P. Lee, D. Rind, and G. Russell), 'Climate impact of increasing atmospheric carbon dioxide', *Science* 213 (1981): 957–966. See also R. A. Kerr, 'Hansen vs. The World on the greenhouse threat: Scientists like the attention the greenhouse effect is getting on Capitol Hill, but they shun the reputedly unscientific

way their colleague James Hansen went about getting that attention', *Science* 244. 4908 (1989): 1041–1043.
36 James Hansen *et al.*, 'Ice melt, sea level rise and superstorms: evidence from paleoclimate data, climate modelling, and modern observations that 2 C global warming is highly dangerous', *Atmospheric Chemistry and Physics*, Discussion paper 15: 20059–20179 (2015): 20119. A later peer-reviewed version was published as James Hansen *et al.*, 'Ice melt, sea level rise and superstorms: evidence from paleoclimate data, climate modelling, and modern observations that 2 C global warming could be dangerous', *Atmospheric Chemistry and Physics* 16 (2016): 3761–3812; www.atmos-chem-phys.net/16/3761/2016/acp-16-3761-2016-discussion.html
37 James Hansen *et al.*, 'Ice melt, sea level rise and superstorms: evidence from paleoclimate data, climate modelling, and modern observations that 2 C global warming is highly dangerous', *Atmospheric Chemistry and Physics*, Discussion paper 15: 20059–20179 (2015): 20118.
38 Martin Rees, *Our Final Hour: A Scientist's Warning: How Terror, Error, and Environmental Disaster Threaten Humankind's Future in This Century – On Earth and Beyond* (New York: Basic Books, 2003).
39 Owen Gaffney and Will Steffen, 'The Anthropocene equation', *The Anthropocene Review* (February 2017): 1–9.
40 Owen Gaffney and Will Steffen, 'Introducing the terrifying mathematics of the Anthropocene', The Conversation (10 February 2017), theconversation.com/introducing-the-terrifying-mathematics-of-the-anthropocene-70749
41 Mike Davis, 'Cosmic dancers on history's stage? The permanent revolution in the Earth sciences', *New Left Review* 217 (1996): 48–84.
42 Bruce Sterling and John Lebkowsky, State of the World (2012); www.well.com/conf/inkwell.vue/topics/430/Bruce-Sterling-and-Jon-Lebkowsky-page01.html; rs.resalliance.org/2014/03/17/old-people-in-big-cities-afraid-of-the-sky/; For full transcript of Bruce Sterling's Closing Remarks at SXSW Interactive 2014 in Austin, Texas on 11 March see: pastebin.com/LYZvU0GL
43 Renata Tyszczuk, 'Cautionary Tales: The sky is falling! The world is ending!' in *Culture and Climate Change: Narratives*, eds. Joe Smith, Renata Tyszczuk, and Robert Butler (Cambridge: Shed, 2014): 45–57.
44 Margaret Atwood, 'Chicken Little goes too far', *The Tent* (London: Bloomsbury, 2006).
45 Michel Serres, *The Natural Contract* (Ann Arbor: University of Michigan Press, 1995): 72.
46 Davi Kopenawa and Bruce Albert, *The Falling Sky: Words of a Yanomami Shaman*, trans. Nicholas Elliott and Alison Dundy (Cambridge, MA: Harvard University Press, 2013). As noted in Bruce Albert's introduction, Kopenawa's shamanic prophecies have a surprising parallel in current discourses around climate change and the Anthropocene.
47 Nigel Clark, *Inhuman Nature: Sociable Life on a Dynamic Planet* (London: Sage, 2011): xiv.

Introduction
Provisional cities

This is a book of cautionary tales about provisional cities. It is an incomplete account of the ways in which our ideas about cities have come under pressure – and sometimes been transformed – in extraordinary times. The advent of the Anthropocene has made questions of planetary settlement more urgent. It has also exposed the thought that any possible answer to these questions is provisional. This is a book, therefore, about unsettlement.

The Anthropocene is a geological epoch of devastating human-induced changes to Earth systems – changes which, in geological terms, are manifesting as catastrophes on a par with volcanism, glacial cycles and asteroid strikes. This book is part of a bloom of simultaneous responses to the Anthropocene thesis. However, it is distinctive in its imaginative focus on cities and settlements, and in its specific mode of inquiry: that is, stories. It is about the capacity for stories about the Anthropocene unsettlement to transform and shape reality. Stories have agency: deployed effectively, 'stories undo stories'. Storytelling is, among other things, the high-stakes 'battle' between 'unjust narratives and just ones, disabling imaginaries and enabling ones'.[1]

The Anthropocene yokes together geological time with human history – and reveals the surprising mutability of both. It is therefore both geostory and cautionary tale. This book is not about cataloguing the various threats to human settlements and habitation, or proposing solutions to living more sustainably and securely in cities around the world – many good books of these types already exist. Instead it is something more tentative and more provisional: a study of how *storying* can help make sense of and assemble the realities we are dwelling in now. For ultimately, it is difficult to understand the story we are in. And yet the Anthropocene story offers the potent prospect of working *with* the unavoidable catastrophe rather than running for cover. Importantly for humanity, this cautionary tale offers the possibility of changing its own story.

This book starts from the assumption that the anthropogenic impacts on Earth systems are not simply the concern of science, scientific authority, and experts. They circulate in our social and cultural life, as a tangled and complicated set of tales, scenarios, proxies, networks, equations, models and conversations, which together have contributed to narratives of the Anthropocene. This book is caught somewhere between interpreting the past, surveying the here-and-now, and imagining the future. The Anthropocene is a planetary condition within which new 'settlements', and new modes of settlement, will need to be negotiated. It is an event that can only be fully apprehended through consideration of the deep time of planetary processes. Terrestrial futures will bear scant evidence of contemporary human activity and its distinctive detritus. What we might consider our most lasting constructions of steel and stone will either be erased altogether or squeezed into thin layers of rock. Geological time frames may remind us that all human settlement is provisional, but global urban practices and contemporary geopolitics continue to show little recognition of the precarious interdependence of human and non-human worlds, their radical instability, their capacity to surprise. If the Anthropocene is showing us that everything – even our most enduring symbols of mastery and permanence, from the dome of the Capitol Building to the temples of Angkor Wat – is actually provisional, how can stories about settlement and unsettlement help us to meet and to cope with this new ontological and philosophical crisis? The Anthropocene, understood as a cautionary tale, may yet have the potential to help us embark on alternative trajectories.

This is not to denounce cities, but to recognise that the history of cities – in all their incarnations: garden cities, ecocities, sustainable cities, resilient cities, smart cities, and so on – sees one grand narrative replacing the next, and that ultimately they are all provisional. 'Provisional cities' is by no means a unifying term. The book addresses a wide array of sites, with divergent scales, times and scope: from past disaster zones to remote outposts in the present to future urban fossils. What links them is their precariousness, tentativeness, temporariness – their ephemeral stability with respect to Earth inhabitation. If *un*settlements – from tent cities to megalopolises – are stories about a planetary humanity, can they also be stories about how we have created, and how we might survive, the Anthropocene? Stories have the capacity to construct systems for acknowledging radical transformation and coping with instability, forging dynamic narratives about humanity's provisional relation to its planetary home. For, 'provisionality is not something to be overcome, a structural vulnerability, but rather *the underlying condition of the world*'.[2] The Anthropocene story – or geostory – might allow for immersion in the world as it is, prone to rapid abrupt change, violent disruptions, sudden storms and perils. Perhaps it can help us cope with the idea that stability is transient and that we are always on unsure ground. The tricky thing is that humanity needs to learn to trust its own footing on this precarious ground – to inhabit the cautionary tales of its own making.

Holocene disruptions

This book is written during a time of disorientating and abrupt climate change, in what is increasingly being understood as the last years of a period of *relative* stability – the Holocene epoch. The unstable concept of the Anthropocene designates a move beyond the geologic conditions characteristic of the Holocene, and a shift into a novel epoch whose signature is irreversible human impact on Earth and life processes.[3] The unusually settled climate of the Holocene, which began with the ending of the last glacial epoch, 11,700 years ago, has also accompanied the approximately 10,000-year-long history of agricultural civilisations and city-building. Present generations of rapidly urbanising humans are thus likely to be living through the next shift in Earth epochs. As the academic and writer Jeremy Davies explains:

> The Holocene matters because it is the only geological epoch so far in which there have been symphony orchestras and hypodermic needles, moon landings and gender equality laws, patisseries, microbreweries, and universal suffrage – or, to put it plainly, the agricultural civilisations that eventually made all of those things

possible. With its demise, the civilised rights and pleasures previously confined to the Holocene will have to negotiate radically changed ecological conditions if they are to endure, let alone if they are to be extended more generously to more people. That is the political problem of the Anthropocene.[4]

The Anthropocene, therefore, Davies concludes, 'asserts the pressing need to re-imagine human and non-human life outside the confines of the Holocene'.[5] The problem, however, is that no one knows how to live in anything but the Holocene. The Anthropocene has been proposed as a new epoch on the geologic time scale to recognise the shift in the functioning of the Earth system to a 'no-analogue state'.[6] This temporal moment, understood in terms of Earth strata, coincides with the particular historical juncture that has seen predictions of human-induced climatic tipping points and extinction events expressed as a transgression of 'planetary boundaries'.[7] In addition to the build-up of greenhouse gases, the new stratum could be defined by human landscape transformations exceeding natural sediment production (such as urbanisation and industrialised agriculture); by accumulated technofossils (plastics and concretes); by the acidification of oceans; by the relentless destruction of biota, and, above all, by radical instability.

When understood in the context of deep Earth history, the scale of devastation observed indicates a transition to a new epoch in planetary time – comparable to the transition from the Pleistocene to the Holocene, which saw a 5°C change in global average temperature and a 120-metre change in sea levels. The reason we understand the inception of the Anthropocene not just as change but as *catastrophic* change is that we are witnessing irreversible alterations unprecedented in the past 11,700 years. In other words, the particular moment we are now living can only be interpreted on the geologic time scale – any smaller scale of temporal reference cannot capture its uniqueness.

It could be argued that anthropogenic climatic disruptions will turn out to be just one more hazard for Earth's inhabitants in a sequence that stretches over millennia, from plague and pestilence to the prospect of nuclear annihilation. Can it really get worse then it has already been? For humans – urban or otherwise – and our companion species, the answer appears to be a resounding yes. What climate records show, in addition to the connection between CO_2 levels and global temperatures, is that the last glaciation was a time of frequent and traumatic climate swings, and of dwindling itinerant human populations that only just made it through. Humans only settled down when the climate did, building villages, towns and cities, and inventing all the basic technologies – agriculture, metallurgy, writing. Until the climate cooperated, the exceptional ingenuity claimed by the human species was not enough to help them embark on agriculture and city building.[8] In other words, the entire human history of urbanisation might be seen as coinciding with 'a fluke in Earth history'.[9] Moreover it is the construction and maintenance of cities (and the survival of their human inhabitants) that is now understood as responsible, directly or indirectly, for most of the Earth system changes associated with the Anthropocene: CO_2 emissions, changed patterns of erosion and sedimentation, and biodiversity loss. The provisional making of cities and settlements continues to be bound up in the notion of a threshold between the Holocene and the Anthropocene.

The Anthropocene thesis entails the idea that continuing to live in the Holocene is no longer an option. The Anthropocene thus unsettles any preconceptions we might have about modes of habitation and settlement on Earth. It suggests that we can no longer hope either to remain settled or to return to a settled state after only a brief interlude of crisis. Yet if we accept the idea of 'living in the Anthropocene' – even temporarily, or for this moment in time – in what sort of time and what sort of space do we find ourselves? A new epoch, by definition, is marked by a lasting geological signature. Only the most radical changes in the Earth's 4.6 billion year history have been inscribed in its geological strata thus far. The Anthropocene thesis suggests that future rocks will bear witness to geomorphic transformations of our time; the result of human activities now taking place at an unprecedented scope and planetary scale. 'The notion of the Anthropocene, then, vividly captures the folding of the human into the air, into the sea, the soil and DNA,' wrote the academic Ben Dibley.[10] Indeed as science writer Oliver Morton notes:

> It may seem nonsense to think of the (probably sceptical) intelligence with which you interpret these words as something on a par with plate tectonics or photosynthesis. But dam by dam, mine by mine, farm by farm and city by city it is remaking the Earth before your eyes.[11]

Geophysical and ecological changes at the global scale, from climate change to biodiversity loss, alongside rapid urbanisation and economic globalisation, seem to indicate that humanity should prepare itself for sudden and unpredictable change. Projections show that the greatest risks will be borne by the most economically and geographically vulnerable communities. There is also a growing interest in planetary-scale responses, with private enterprise proposing a number of more-or-less fantastical, often highly intrusive, geoengineering fixes. Some commentators, such as Mark Lynas in *The God Species*, argue for taking renewed control of the planet through climate engineering and biotechnology, with a view to managing Earth's systems in an artificial but Holocene-like state. Others argue for reigning in technological intervention and trying instead to restore balance – a kind of return to nature. The urgent need to reduce the vulnerabilities of large human populations in rapidly changing environments has, paradoxically, tended to obscure the philosophical and cultural shifts that are inevitably bound up with the more scientific-technical adjustments to 'living in the Anthropocene'. This book seeks to address this omission *within the gap* – the interval, or hiatus – we now appear to be inhabiting; the hinge between Holocene and Anthropocene. If the advent of the Anthropocene is being announced as a planetary emergency, it is also an opportunity for reflection.

Planet of cities in planetary crisis

The Anthropocene is a story unfolding on the planetary scale. It thus calls up the many different ways that the planetary has been refigured through the idea of the city: from Isaac Asimov's sci-fi planet-city of Trantor, and Constantinos Doxiadis's Ecumenopolis that covered the globe, through to the experimental cities of planetary consciousness such as Arcosanti and Auroville. The planet-city dyad is also expressed in the cosmopolitanism of Immanuel Kant (via the Stoics) and the cosmopolitics of Isabelle Stengers and Bruno Latour, who each combine *cosmos* with *polis* – the root of both politics and the city. The story of Earth is, increasingly, a story of cities: humanity inhabits an urbanised and urbanising planet. The accelerated growth of settlements,

Introduction: Provisional cities 5

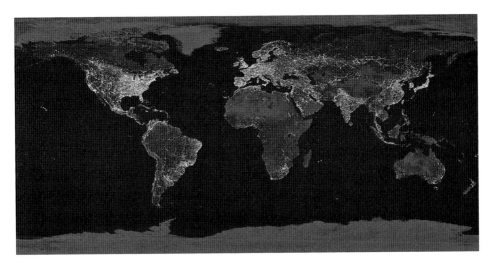

Figure 0.1 'Night Lights 2012'; the image of the Earth at night is a composite assembled from data acquired by the Suomi National Polar-orbiting Partnership (Suomi NPP) in April 2012 and October 2012
Source: NASA Earth Observatory image by Robert Simmon, using Suomi NPP VIIRS data provided courtesy of Chris Elvidge (NOAA National Geophysical Data Center)

cities, megacities, is considered the most characteristic geophysical feature of the so-called Anthropocene-in-the-making. As the philosopher Michel Serres notes, 'When it is unevenly distributed, skyrocketing demographic growth becomes concentrated and stuck together in giant units, colossal banks of humanity, as powerful as oceans, deserts or ice caps, themselves stockpiles of ice, heat, dryness, or water'.[12] The Anthropocene is identified by the ecological disturbances and environmental destruction associated with the processes of urbanisation, resulting from transport, sanitation and waste, manufacturing, energy production and consumption, engineered and agronomic systems. These go beyond mere surface inscriptions; they go deep in their disruption to Earth systems processes. As the site of 'urban disturbances' – or urban–driven evolution, from the level of the urban ecosystem to the planetary scale – the Anthropocene is evidenced by modifications of habitat and new biotic interactions between plant and animal populations.[13] Whether drawing attention to an 'urban age',[14] the 'age of humans', or indeed the 'urbanthropocene',[15] we are, in effect, describing a planet of cities in planetary crisis.

The majority of the world's population live in or rely on cities. Cities have become an increasingly dominant land-use and resource-use, with dependencies, relations and impacts that spread out from their hinterlands across the globe. The dominant patterns of this 'planetary urbanization' show no sign of slowing down.[16] These include energy-intensive developments, suburban sprawl, disconnected infrastructures and speculator-led construction. And it is well understood that it is the wasteful ways in which cities have expanded, the persistence of carbon-fuelled economic systems, and the exploitation of resources, that have led to the present crisis. Conversely, it is also clear that the impacts of escalating crises – financial, democratic, environmental – are concentrated in cities. Nevertheless, in 2012 the UN Habitat report stated that 'Cities can offer remedies to the worldwide crises – if only we put them in better positions to respond to the challenges of our age, optimising resources and harnessing the potentialities of the future'.[17]

Up to a point. 'Our heavily urbanised planet,' the writer and academic Nigel Clark reminds us, 'is also a chronically turbulent one.'[18] There is every reason to feel uneasy about the future prospects of an urbanised planet, not least because of the growing awareness of the limits of human agency – that is, the capacity to act, or make a difference, in a warming and unstable world. With crisis inevitable, strategies of adaptation and mitigation are now a priority for cities, governments and markets. The task of urban planners, architects and engineers has been to prepare cities, settlements and infrastructures for unpredictable conditions. Their focus has been on the capacity of settlements to adapt to climate change and of ways to 'design in' resilience. Recent proposals for future cities have therefore emphasised flexibility – amphibious constructions, hybrid ecologies, ecosystem engineering and smart technologies. They have also imagined security, in the form of physical barriers, strategies of managed retreat, and proposals for colonising subterranean spaces, the sea, or the sky.

But in spite of all these innovations that claim a degree of preparedness for living with uncertainty, the conventions of urban design and planning have, in practice, changed little. They remain rigid and reactionary. While tensions persist between the upheavals effected by top-down city planning and the incremental change of bottom-up approaches, democratic paths to decision-making in cities remain elusive. It seems unlikely that urban planning – at either the imaginative or administrative levels – will suddenly acquire the necessary agility, worldwide and simultaneously, to preempt the coming crisis. As the writer Mike Davis observes, even if global agreement were possible, achieving worldwide adaptation to climate change along with poverty alleviation and the assisted migration of peoples 'would command a revolution of almost mythic magnitude'.[19] The task implies a more equitable redistribution of income and power unprecedented in human history. In his view, no person or organisation is capable of coping with the problems facing a rapidly urbanising planet:

> No one. Not the UN, the World Bank, the G20: no one has a clue how a planet of slums with growing food and energy crises will accommodate their biological survival, much less their aspirations to basic happiness and dignity.[20]

The Anthropocene describes the collision between the industrial civilisation of cities and the Earth's geo and biospheres. The catastrophe of RMS *Titanic* in 1912 – the crash of a mobile, state-of-the-art, miniature techno-city with a 10,000-year-old piece of Greenland ice – presents an allegorical forewarning of the Anthropocene. It seems an 'ideal Anthropocene tale', one that is 'compressed between technological optimism and natural catastrophism'.[21] But it also indicates that the human catastrophe cannot be avoided simply with better engineering, improved management and a bit more foresight. For it is also a tale about the social relationships inscribed in the ship, and in the shipwreck: there were not enough lifeboats, but there were some for first-class passengers. If the tendency of Anthropocene discourse is to underline that in terms of the planetary crisis 'we are all in the same boat', the narrative also reveals again and again that we are not all in it in the same way.[22]

Anthropoceneries

> Corporate-owned seed and genetically engineered fish, plastic-laden oceans and soil-burdened rivers, disappearing animal beings and evolving machine intelligence, rising seas and retreating ice fields, drought-stricken regions and inundated coastal zones, last gasps of going-extinct charismatic megafauna and rapid blooms of post-antibiotic microbial diseases, continental urban sprawls and minuscule remote wilderness, light-polluted night and exhaust polluted day.[23]

Entry into the Anthropocene comes with an array of warnings not to hope to keep things the way they are. We have already failed; and delusions to the contrary may lead us into further harm. Timothy W. Luke's catalogue of 'anthropoceneries' of the 'urbanthropocene' draws attention to the damage already done. The Anthropocene thesis is a thought experiment: as ontologically unsettling to established world views as it will be in the most practical sense to great tranches of the urbanised human population. The cautionary tale of the Anthropocene ushers in a series of unsettlements, temporal, spatial, political and conceptual. The Anthropocene demands a stretching of the imagination backwards and forwards over timescales much vaster than we usually think in, and over incommensurable negotiations and arrangements of settlements. It forces us to inhabit not merely a lifetime or a generation, but 'deep time'. Disorienting as this is, it is also an invitation to extend our sense of responsibility; to redouble our efforts for social and environmental justice, not just for present-day Earth inhabitants but for those who come after us – including generations of humans who will be living in a world we can't imagine, on terms with 'nature' that we can barely begin to comprehend. Valued ways of living will have to be renegotiated in the face of radically changed environmental conditions. Most of these changes have not been forced on us yet; but if we have the capacity to anticipate them, we also, arguably, have the obligation to brace ourselves for the coming confrontation.

The Anthropocene idea arrives in an era of ambivalence about humans' extraordinary capability to influence the planet we inhabit. But nature and the Earth are not simply benevolent entities at the mercy of a power-crazed humanity. If the Anthropocene is a cautionary tale – a warning against the hubris of exaggerating the reach of human agency – it also draws attention to a collective disavowal of the power wielded by the non-human and more-than-human – even what might be called cosmic agency. In the Anthropocene, we are increasingly being made aware of the forces that threaten to wash, irradiate, or blow us into oblivion. This might be expected to alert us to a diminishing human agency and a decentring of the human. For in a worst-case scenario, regardless of what humans do next, it is possible that the Earth might undergo extreme volcanic events or be hit by an asteroid. Researchers in disaster studies tell us that when it comes to the next hurricane, earthquake or eruption, it is not a case of *if*, but *when*. As the philosopher Georges Bataille reminded us, 'the ground we live on is little other than a field of multiple destructions'.[24] We dwell between catastrophes, between the perturbations of the atmosphere, hydrosphere, biosphere, heliosphere, cryosphere, lithosphere – air, water, life, sun, ice and rock. Volcanic eruptions, earthquakes, tsunamis, floods, hurricanes and typhoons are the norm rather than the exception. Moreover, it is now a familiar observation that there is no such thing as a 'natural disaster'. The degree of urbanisation over the last 250 years is exceptional in the relatively short history of the human species – and with this astounding amount of city-building has come the increased vulnerability of large numbers of urban populations to natural hazards.

The megacities and the vast urban conglomerations of today might be posited as the inevitable end product of the Holocene. Yet urban restlessness resists categorisation. As the urban commentator AbdouMaliq Simone observes, cities are rather worlds of 'constant rehearsal and revision, improvisation and experimentation, planning and anticipation'.[25] The dramatic technological and social changes in metropolitan regions in the last century have been surprising, even overwhelming, but as the urbanist Edward Soja observes, 'It is almost surely too soon to conclude with any confidence that what happened to cities in the late 20th century was the onset of a revolutionary change or just another minor twist on an old tale of urban life'.[26] The philosopher Zygmunt Bauman warns of attempts to forecast what will become of cities: 'Whether cautious or reckless, radical or ambivalent, partisan or uncommittal, there was hardly a single prognosis that has not been dismissed by some other writers…'[27] When it comes to cities, therefore, we should continue to be cautious about predictions of the future. Cities are inherently unstable, unpredictable and averse to smooth functioning. And there are plenty of tales about troubled cities – failed projects, disappeared neighbourhoods, dysfunctional politics, disjunctions and upheavals – that jostle with predictions of growth and development. Discordant stories about city-dwelling are in step with the general state of alarm about the sustainability of cities. Whether as an issue arising out of the inevitable ecological impacts of cities, or as recognition of the increasing stresses of urban population expansion without the requisite economic and infrastructural underpinnings on water, energy, transport services – there are plenty of things that need sorting out in cities. Burgeoning cities around the world, we are repeatedly told, are poised on the brink of *a planetary state of emergency*, and yet make few concessions to the calamities that threaten to engulf them. This book about provisional cities touches on what it means to dwell within an unfolding disaster of human making, a world without stability – and yet continue to attempt the fiction of a settled life.

This book does not intend to veer between warnings of apocalypse and calls for adaptation – as if it were a straightforward matter to build better, smarter, stronger, catastrophe-proof cities. Recent years have provided access to difficult new knowledge about potentially abrupt climate change and cataclysmic Earth processes that are likely to undermine all the best-laid plans. Any projects to accommodate a rapidly urbanising population must therefore take into account the certainty of intermittent catastrophe, but also, beyond this, the possibility that the relatively stable conditions – both political and physical – so relied on by contemporary humans and so conducive to their constructions, could disappear with very little warning. The Anthropocene and its anthropoceneries thus provoke thinking about what abrupt and irreversible climate change would mean for some of the more settled ideas about human settlement.

Fear and trembling

> As cities collapse and grow desolate when there is an earthquake and man erects his house on volcanic land only in fear and trembling and only briefly, so life itself caves in and grows weak and fearful when the *concept-quake* caused by science robs man of the foundation of all his rest and security, his belief in the enduring and eternal.[28]

The trouble with science, according to Friedrich Nietzsche, was that it was fundamentally unsettling. His neologism 'concept-quake' – *Begriffsbeben* – plays on the enduring metaphor of an earthquake to express the radical sense of contingency provoked by the discoveries of 19th-century scientific empiricism. The coining of the 'Anthropocene' neologism marks an equally momentous epochal crisis. This epoch-naming brings with it its own concept-quake whereby confidence in the stability and permanence of the world, its institutions and constructions, is shattering. At the same time, the advent of the Anthropocene signals *a planetary crisis of agency*. As Bruno Latour puts it: 'How can we simultaneously be part of such a long history, have such an important influence, and yet be so late in realising what has happened and so utterly impotent in our attempts to fix it?'[29]

Nietzsche's metaphor is still apt for a world that recognises its existence as increasingly contingent and precarious. The Anthropocene arrives at a particular juncture when information from Earth sciences research, philosophical enquiry on human and non-human relations, and a focus on ethico-political issues arising from ecological predicament coalesce – with the common theme of a volatile, unpredictable cosmos. Anthropogenic climate change and the concomitant disruption of Earth processes is ontologically scary. It is both intensely local – as when a place we know intimately and depend upon (or else a place remote from us but that looms large in our fantasies, a kind of global 'unreal estate',[30] like Venice, or New Orleans) is threatened – and massively distributed in time and space. It provokes a reflection on our place on Earth and in the cosmos: what is the human, what is society, what is Earth; what does it mean to exist at all?[31] The Anthropocene thesis provokes the question: what does all of this mean for the settled Holocene life we have taken for granted? There is much to unsettle us and keep us awake in the night.

In his reading of Søren Kierkegaard's *Fear and Trembling*, Jacques Derrida writes, 'We tremble in that strange repetition that ties an irrefutable past (a shock has been felt, a traumatism has already affected us) to a future that cannot be anticipated; anticipated but unpredictable;… apprehended precisely *as* unforeseeable, unpredictable; approached *as* unapproachable.'[32] Living within an unfolding disaster, in a Holocene world that is ending, provokes 'a deep shuddering of temporality'.[33] The philosopher Timothy Morton's term *hyperobjects* denotes some of the characteristic entities of the Anthropocene. 'For it is gigantic non-human beings –radioactive materials, global warming, the very script of the layers in Earth's crust that opens the Anthropocene – who bring about the end of the world.'[34] These harbingers of the Anthropocene are met with opposition: 'The panic and denial and right-wing absurdity about global warming are understandable,' writes Morton. 'Hyperobjects pose numerous threats to individualism, nationalism, anti-intellectualism, racism, speciesism, anthropocentrism, you name it. Possibly even capitalism itself.'[35] Morton observes that recognition of the crisis alerts us not only to our potential physical destruction (via storm, flood, fire, or drought) but points to the metaphysical evaporation of our 'world'. For Morton, the contemporary condition is a 'fundamental shaking of being, a *being-quake*'.[36]

In *The Natural Contract*, Michel Serres describes our planetary condition as 'living in a permanent earthquake':

> For, as of today, the Earth is quaking anew: not because it shifts and moves in its restless, wise orbit, not because it is changing, from its deep plates to its envelope of air, but because it is being transformed by our doing… We are disturbing the Earth and making it quake! Now it has a subject once again.[37]

Serres invites coming to terms with cosmic processes that have gone on from way before, and will continue long after, our species' constructions – and with utter indifference to them. Before cities could even be imagined, the planet went through periodic upheavals and constructions of its own. Any consideration of cities and settlements may therefore need to touch on those lithic architectures – the geophysical forms of earthly mobility and place-making, such as plate-tectonics, seismic upheavals and eruptions, that are beyond the scope of human involvement. To think of provisional cities, landscapes, infrastructures and settlements that are open to being reworked and reconfigured as a result of convulsive Earth systems suggests, paradoxically, the reinstantiation of foundational 'ground' as an unstable present. We might also need to uncover stories about cities that allow for the imagination of worlds indifferent and incomprehensible to humans.

The Anthropocene story offers insights into the work of researchers in the geophysical sciences, in their discoveries of a turbulent world. As philosopher Graham Harman observes, 'The history of the universe is packed with numerous fateful revolutions: the emergence of the heavier elements from hydrogen; the birth of solar systems; the break-up of Pangaea into multiple continents; the emergence of multicellular life...'[38] Thinking about the Anthropocene invites consideration of both scientific accounts and philosophical deliberations about the ways in which the Earth is changing, and the ways humans and the worlds they inhabit are changing, or failing to change, with it. It alerts us to 'living with Earth and cosmic processes... in the context of a deep, elemental underpinning that is at once a source of profound insecurity'.[39] The Earth wobbles, leaving humanity unsteady and wavering. The Anthropocene story involves the being-quake, the concept-quake, as well as the just plain scary earthquake – how should humans act when they have so little stability on offer?

The Anthropocene and other tales

The shared vocabularies of loss, catastrophe, cataclysm, disaster and crisis, along with the compulsion to story across times and places, are two key features of Anthropocene unsettlement. In the face of events that are unpredictable, and incommensurable with our day-to-day lives, we fashion tales of the destruction and/or the improbable endurance of cities and city dwellers. Cities in trouble are a ceaseless spur to storytelling. Stories have accompanied cities through frequent disasters, for example, in the chain of dire warnings that is Mike Davis's *Dead Cities: And Other Tales*. In a book ostensibly about American West Coast urbanism, Davis weaves together tales of asteroid impacts, mass extinctions, Victorian disaster fiction, planetary gravitational imbalances and anthropogenic climate change. Scary stories about cities and their uncertain futures in what is being termed the Anthropocene might perhaps offer at once a more provocative and more attentive engagement with present conditions. They may be what allows us finally to face up to, and grapple with, the prospect of irreversible changes in the Earth system. Cautionary tales have steered us through the fears and paranoias of the last century of anthropogenic calamity, confronting the unknowable and thinking the unthinkable. We have turned to stories to work through the consequences of pollution and toxicity, confront nuclear threats and the Cold War, deal with environmental distresses and imbalances, and imagine life in the aftermath of devastation. Cautionary tales allow us to rehearse, if not avoid, a distorted future world of our own making: a world in which there may or may not be room for our own species.

In the early 21st century, we are steeped in stories of the destruction of habitats, cities and infrastructures, either because of humans, or in spite of humans. These are all cautionary tales for the Anthropocene. In 1886, the same year that the Holocene was officially approved as the 'wholly recent' geological epoch, Richard Jefferies published *After London*, where he imagined the collapse of civilisation, with London engulfed in a poisonous miasma after some mysterious cataclysmic event. In J.G. Ballard's novel *The Drowned World* (1962), flora and fauna reached colossal sizes after the world warms dramatically, a previously temperate London now so hot as to be uninhabitable as the Earth regresses to earlier climatic conditions. 'A Fable for Tomorrow', the innocently titled prologue in Rachel Carson's *Silent Spring* (1962), warns about contamination by pesticides and nuclear fallout by weaving a poetic narrative about seasonal dysfunction and desolation in an everyday American town. Environmental apocalypse was imagined in the New York of Harry Harrison's novel *Make Room! Make Room!* (1966) and also in the film it inspired, *Soylent Green* (1973), which reveals the macabre solution to a resource-stricken city where most human beings are considered 'surplus'. The annihilation of the world's cities in the worst-case scenarios of nuclear war, developed by Herman Kahn with the RAND Corporation, set the scene for Stanley Kubrick's apocalypse satire *Dr Strangelove* (1964). Cormac McCarthy's *The Road* (2006), adapted into an eponymous film (2009), is a vision of utter ecological devastation that reduces the few survivors to scavenging or cannibalism. Jeff Nichols's film *Take Shelter* (2011), set in small-town Ohio, explores a construction worker's premonitions of an apocalyptic storm that results in compulsive yet seemingly pointless shelter building. The prophetic visions of this 'modern-day Noah' are dismissed by his family and friends as the product of inherited mental illness – they thus 'safely annexe the apocryphal storm as a symptom of his psychological turmoil'.[40] There is no reassurance of safety from the storm in the film – instead it augurs the kind of unsettlement and uncertainty we may need to get used to. Such cautionary tales negotiate the discord between the actual and the (im)possible, and test the pragmatic, moral, physical and psychological consequences of certain courses of action. They compel us to imagine how things could be – disastrously – otherwise than the more or less stable state we have always known. Cautionary tales can be a strategy for dealing with a contingent, turbulent, uncertain future of humanity's own making.

The United Nations' Intergovernmental Panel on Climate Change (IPCC) reports have consistently warned of possible devastating impacts of anthropogenic climate change. And with each report, real events are catching up with the worst-case scenarios. In 2007, *The Independent* offered five different scenarios for the world in the year 2100, warming in one degree increments between 2.4° and 6.4°. It didn't look good:

+6.4°: Most of life is exterminated
Warming seas lead to the possible release of methane hydrates trapped in sub-oceanic sediments: methane fireballs tear across the sky, causing further warming. The oceans lose their oxygen and turn stagnant, releasing poisonous hydrogen sulphide gas and destroying the ozone layer. Deserts extend almost to the Arctic. 'Hypercanes' (hurricanes of unimaginable ferocity) circumnavigate the globe, causing flash floods which strip the land of soil. Humanity reduced to a few survivors eking out a living in polar refuges. Most of life on Earth has been snuffed out, as temperatures rise higher than for hundreds of millions of years.[41]

12 Introduction: Provisional cities

From the data-driven scenarios and decadal timescales of IPCC reports through to examples in mainstream media (*The Day After Tomorrow*, 2004; *The Age of Stupid*, 2009), the contemporary imagining of possible futures has been dominated by doom and gloom, a realised eschatology of global environmental change – now culminating in the Anthropocene. Recent utopian designs for urban futures are likewise influenced by a pessimistic futurology, inherited from the 1970s' worst-case scenarios of *Limits to Growth* and *A Blueprint for Survival*. In the early 21st century, back-to-basics survival manuals proliferate alongside exuberant technofantasies of massive-scale geoengineering. Indeed, these are two sides of the same ecotopian/eschatological coin. We live in an uncertain world fraught with potential danger and imminent collapse. Each year of the present century has brought more examples of extreme weather, epic floods, seismic unrest, typhoons, pestilence, and war. Fear and foreboding are appropriate responses. We have cautionary tales of grim futures in abundance.

Various titles on the bookshelves add to the increasing array of future disaster tales warning of climate change: of a world that is 'post-apocalyptic', 'post-human' or 'without us', along with user manuals for coping with 'the end of the world as we know it'. Long-form investigative journalism has likewise been a source of dire warnings, as in Elizabeth Kolbert's *Field Notes from A Catastrophe* (2006) and her more recent book *The Sixth Extinction: An Unnatural History* (2014). James Lovelock's *Revenge of Gaia* (2006) describes bleak scenes of dwindling human populations struggling to reach a suitable habitat in the Arctic circle. Alan Weisman's *The World Without Us* (2007) predicts the gradual deterioration and destruction of human artefacts, and nature's eventual reclamation of urban environments, after an unnamed cataclysm (many scenarios are possible) that wipes out our species. He lingers aesthetically on the absurd spectacle of our artefacts of convenience – the stainless steel saucepans with their plastic handles, the cars, the bridges – surviving the creatures who made them. Bill McKibben's *Eaarth: Making a Life on a Tough New Planet* (2010) offers a vision of total ecological devastation, arguing that we are already two decades too late to avoid a cruelly inhospitable future.

Many narratives about anthropogenic climate change have been framed in apocalyptic terms. If they offer any consolation, it is in the form of a call to arms, explicit or implied: we must try to stop this inhospitable future from happening. If recent decades have taught us anything, however, it is that humans do not seem built to pivot easily toward coordinated action – and certainly not at the expense of short-term profit and convenience – to avert disaster. Or at least, we do not seem inclined to be frightened into it. Tales of unmitigated doom and gloom may therefore have been of little effectiveness; or even have further embedded inaction. As the writer Frederick Buell warns, we need to be wary of the 'domestication within crisis' and instead find ways of 'dwelling actively within… crisis'.[42] For cautionary tales to be effective, then, it seems they cannot merely spell out imminent disaster. They must offer the possibility of inhabiting the prevailing doom and gloom more purposefully; of doing something with it. Even if it is the *story to end all stories*, the Anthropocene offers the prospect of working with and within the story *as it unfolds*.

A thousand and one cautionary tales

> They still hung suspended between catastrophe and paradise, spinning bluely in space like some terrible telenovela. Scheherazade was Earth's muse, it seemed; it

was just one damn thing after another, always one more cliffhanger, clinging to life and sanity by the skin of one's teeth...[43]

2312, Kim Stanley Robinson's tale of cosmic inhabitation, posits the troubled planet as a planet-sized cautionary tale – 'some terrible telenovela' – which, since it is in the reader's future, might still suggest the possibility of evasive action. Of course, our oldest stories indicate that humanity has always been susceptible to catastrophe – especially wherever we concentrate and settle. Biblical, mythical, and historical accounts (confirmed by recent scientific findings) indicate ancient cities' extreme vulnerability to flood, drought, and plague, as well as to an intermittently shaking ground. The masonry quilt of Jerusalem's old walls shows repeated damage and repair; it tells a story of destructions wrought not only by humans but by earthly tremors. The collapse of ancient urban civilisations is regularly attributed to climatic and geophysical disruptions.[44] But the current situation is different: the shifts in Earth systems we are experiencing now are rare enough in the Earth's 4.6 billion-year history; in the span of *human* history, they are without precedent. The potential for the sudden and catastrophic dislodgement of our settlements has never been greater; and yet we remain remarkably stubborn in how we build and how we live, ranging busily over our planetary-scaled construction site as if nothing had ever changed and never will. Why are severe warnings being ignored?

Stories about cities are often stories about devastation – cyclones, earthquakes, floods, plagues, tyranny, class warfare – but they are also, usually, stories of endurance. Cities have the capacity to bounce back and cling on. Alongside narratives of folly and avoidable calamity there are tales of improbable survival. Making it through to the next retelling is something cities do well. Telling stories to survive, just as Scheherazade does in *One Thousand and One Nights*, is a constant theme for cities and city dwellers. Like the stories she tells, forestalling the cataclysm each night with an embroidery of complications, stories told about cities undergo myriad retellings generating further stories, alarming and compelling in equal measure. *One Thousand and One Nights* was also a favourite book of Cold War strategist and futurist Herman Kahn and is discernible in the scenarios of his experimental epic narrative *On Thermonuclear War*, published in 1960. Kahn's storytelling impulse ranges from quirky asides through details of the 'unthinkable', such as lists of casualties of hypothetical nuclear war, to detailed analyses of the pageantry of World Wars I through to VIII. The book's structure of nested stories promised to continue – no matter what – with no end to the scenarios. A journalist remarked at the time, 'Herman Kahn may feel that, by inventing one scenario after another, he is holding back the changes that would seal our doom'.[45] Scheherazade is still Earth's muse. Cities, like stories, are provisional and open to constant revision and reinvention. Cities are unfinished stories. They prompt the question: 'What next?'

The Anthropocene is the story of the human species' changing attachment to Earth. It veers between precarious inhabitation and ruthless opportunism on a stranger-than-fiction planet. With our accidental and unsettling advance into the Anthropocene, fearsome stories with the planetary at stake – the earth-shattering, sky-falling and world-ending variety – have renewed poignancy. Catastrophic events bring incommensurable times and scales into collision: geological time folding into the gestures and routines of everyday social life, the global invading the local, planetary energy bearing down on a city. Cautionary tales that evoke the cosmic dimensions of planetary inhabitation are ripe for retelling. They draw attention to the transformative power of stories – where things might change, or remain the same... or else... What stories can be told about an Anthropocene epoch in the making? How can they help with inhabiting the Anthropocene in more just, considerate and purposeful ways?

Anthropocene unsettlements

This book sets out to comprehend the Anthropocene through the narratives that were the making of it. It presents a series of essays about Anthropocene unsettlements. It has charted an environmental history full of curfews, admonitions and alarms about dwelling on Earth – the multiple warnings that announced that widespread environmental disarray was linked with human activity. These were accounts steered by frequent surprises and disasters; that revealed the restless and turbulent conditions of the Earth. This story of getting to the Anthropocene is not simply a rebuke to humans about *not* heeding warnings. It is much more complex and messy. It is a story of trial and error, and more error. It concerns geopolitical struggles, alternative paths that might have been taken, and others that were considered and abandoned. The book recognises the futility of attempts to frame the Anthropocene in terms of a unifying planetary history.[46] Instead it posits 'provisional cities' as exemplary sites for the Anthropocene. Each chapter focuses on cities, settlements and urbanisation in different states of crisis and disruption, real or hypothetical. The writing touches on these sites' inevitable entanglements with history, geology, and different (often incommensurable) ways of thinking what it is to be human; what it is to inhabit this fragile-resilient Earth.

Chapter 1, *Fossil traces*, reviews the stratigraphic case for the Anthropocene, and considers the implications for humanity's planetary future. The present day is still officially within the Holocene epoch. This chapter projects imaginatively millions of years into the future to uncover and contemplate the fossil traces that may remain as evidence of human societies' disfigurement of the planet they have always depended upon. It reflects on the Anthropocene as a site of unparalleled human-induced 'unconformity' in Earth's systems, and also of human impasse. It explores how the most significant yet provisional human artefacts – cities – might be inscribed in the archive of deep time.

Chapter 2, *Disaster zone*, traces the existential and ontological threads of current thinking about catastrophic upheavals back to the Lisbon earthquake of 1755. The 18th century also saw the beginning of the modern period and is considered by some to be the start of humanity's fossil-fuelled trajectory towards its final geological inscription. Recent narratives of the Anthropocene as 'a disaster read in the rocks' can be compared with the philosophical impact of the Lisbon earthquake on European society, in terms of the scale of cultural shift required to respond to increasingly volatile urban conditions.

Chapter 3, *Proving ground*, looks at the history of test sites for warfare and civil defence in the nuclear age, and the roles of military-scientific strategies and technological infrastructures in rehearsing the mass destruction of cities. The Cold War introduced the possibility of an age that could destroy itself, feeding an apocalyptic imaginary that has informed thinking about the Anthropocene. The development of emergency scenarios, proving grounds and test cities was part of an elaborate system of preparedness that was not just technological but narratological. The construction of bomb sites and testing of bombs necessitated the construction of nuclear fictions. These rehearsals for the end of the world, fuelled by horror at its very possibility, served, ironically, to bring that scenario closer.

Chapter 4, *Proxy world*, travels to the ends of the Earth in pursuit of an experimental, inhospitable, off-limits site: a place that is beyond the pale of most human practices of inhabitation, and yet one of the most intensely monitored on Earth. Antarctica accommodates research laboratories that are world observatories, fragile spaceship-like bubbles of habitability that appear as clumsy scars on the landscape they are there to document. It has been the key warning site for the Anthropocene: ozone holes; glacial melt; ice-shelf collapse. Antarctica stands in for all the places we can't reach or don't understand – it is the most extraterritorial and extraterrestrial place on Earth.

Chapter 5, *Bounded planet*, explores the ways in which planet Earth has been conceived of as a spaceship, conveying our species through the cosmos and providing a 'life support' system subject to strict boundaries and limits – including, perhaps, a limited carrying capacity. The notion of Spaceship Earth helped to establish the idea that humanity's home planet was a temporary and fragile biospheric environment that would need our careful attention to maintain. This idea was important to the popular environmentalist movements of the 1960s and 70s and has inspired contemporary thinking on 'planetary boundaries' – an accessory concept to the Anthropocene. 'Spaceship Earth' also inspired ideas for space colonies – closed, Earth-like environments, which would allow humanity – or a select minority – to escape this planet and its troubles altogether.

Chapter 6, *Monster Earth*, addresses geoengineering: the range of ambitious and often disturbing schemes currently under consideration for global-scale, technology-driven interventions into Earth's complex systems. Mostly speculative, but increasingly within our technological grasp, geoengineering is a process of intentional Earth-alteration that reifies the entire planet as an object of experimentation and control. It is presented as the technological fix that can save humanity from the environmental crisis that our species engineered in the first place. It also puts us at risk by sustaining a dream of human mastery of the environment in the face of increasing evidence that Earth has the capacity to humble humanity at a stroke, even to our destruction.

Chapter 7, *Temporary home* discusses the precarious contemporary condition of human unsettlement. Tent cities across the world are strained to bursting as we attempt to contain large-scale geopolitical upheavals which, increasingly, show signs of having ecological origins. Citizens are stranded in the wreckage of cities devastated by flooding, earthquakes and drought, unable to rebuild, unable to move on. In the context of a climate that humans are actively changing, catastrophic environmental change and unsettlement may well become more familiar in the future, as the so-called Anthropocene epoch unfolds. It suggests inhabiting this crisis – the transition or interval between the Holocene and the Anthropocene – with a renewed sense of responsibility and hospitality, an attentiveness to the limits of human agency, and a spirit of cooperation without which it will be difficult to endure.

Cautionary tales for the time-being

One of the most intriguing things about the Anthropocene warning is that it is provisional. As a proposed geological term naming a stratum of the Earth, it may not meet the stringent requirements of stratigraphers. Even if it is formally adopted,

'Anthropocene' already has the potential to be superceded by the next geological epoch-naming. As a *story* called 'the Anthropocene', it is a container for divergent narratives of a radically uncertain future; for we have no real idea of what is going to happen next or how we should respond. In other words, this moment of paradoxical hubris – of proposing to name a geological boundary event for *anthropos*, that may only be legible in the world after humans – may well be short-lived.

While the Anthropocene thesis has been a success insofar as it it has provoked widespread debate, in the longer term it just might not catch on, or there might be some better ideas on the horizon. It remains to be seen whether it will be accepted as an official geological term or consigned to the same heap as other words that have attempted to describe the planetary force of humans – for example, 'noosphere', 'anthropozoic' and 'anthrocene'.[47] It is as yet a nascent concept. It is also one that has its own end in sight: a term with obsolescence built in. And one with such wide-ranging implications, for human life and for the planet we call home. It is also remarkably accommodating of interdisciplinary analysis. This scientific proto-concept has strayed into areas beyond geology and stratigraphy, prompting innovations of social, cultural, political and philosophical thought about dynamic Earth processes and the humans who are vulnerable to them. As one review of the new epoch-naming puts it: 'The Anthropocene appears as a rough place-holder for an undefined and arguably unprecedented historical condition underpinned by environmental uncertainties, which demand critical re-assessments of how material engagements take form, hold fast, and/or break apart in space and through time.'[48] Regardless of the eventual decision (to be delivered by one particular discipline – geology), the deliberations of an Anthropocene epoch offer an opportunity to revise our terms. This geological boundary-crossing creates the space to hesitate, to pay attention, and to rethink human-planetary engagement, *for the time being*.

The Anthropocene warning nevertheless comes with its own pitfalls and faultlines. It troubles the identification and articulation of a world whose social, political and physical parameters are changing faster than our capacity to process change. It evokes the sense of present precariousness, even impasse. Yet the Anthropocene is as much a provocation as it is a lament. It suggests an experimental and transformative approach to Earth pasts, presents and futures that simultaneously demands the exercise of caution. As a cautionary tale in and of itself, it administers 'a massive jolt to the imagination'[49] that prompts the need to think again and act differently. The Anthropocene may well be the brief moment in time where it is still possible to talk *as if* what we do now might matter and could make a difference to the future. It may be the last time we are able to talk about the future at all. For, in the grandest of narratives, we may have already and unwittingly written ourselves out of the story. Telling stories that matter, even if they are scary ones, is therefore the theme of this book.

Like all discussions of the Anthropocene, this book offers only a provisional investigation. It is an invitation to unexpected futures and changing stories. It asks that we try to imagine how we might yet get to grips with the Holocene-Anthropocene interim for our cities in the making. Stories about Anthropocene unsettlements reveal a complicated history of humans as inventive, negligent, recalcitrant, misguided, and imperilled. Paradoxically, stories about the Anthropocene can open up less anthropocentric ways of understanding materiality, making visible the eternal but often ignored proximity of the geological and non-human and human life. As the geographer Doreen Massey reflects, 'bearing in mind the movement of the rocks, both space and landscape could be imagined as provisionally intertwined simultaneities of ongoing, unfinished, stories'.[50] Anthropocene tales are not merely human. They are imagined through intimacy with incalculable temporalities, frighteningly dynamic entities and ecological precariousness. This book asks what narratives are needed in this provisional time of human settlement – tentatively termed the Anthropocene – to equip humanity to thrive, or at least survive, in a future that is uncertain. Isabelle Stengers' *In Catastrophic Times* reflects on tangled histories of scientific projects gone awry: 'What is proper to every event is that it brings the future that will inherit from it into communication with a past narrated differently.'[51] Tuning into the catastrophic world we are living in now through the idea of the Anthropocene suggests that it is no longer possible to expect to maintain the status quo, nor is it any longer viable to treat the world simply as a resource for human use. The Anthropocene is an uncanny tale that sets both its tellers and its listeners adrift – unsettled, yet somehow still 'at home'. For the time being, this book argues, we still need cautionary tales.

Notes

1 Victor E. Taylor and Richard Kearney, 'A conversation with Richard Kearney', *Journal for Cultural and Religious Theory*. 6.2 (Spring 2005): 17–26; 21.
2 Renata Tyszczuk, 'On constructing for the unforeseen' in *Culture and Climate Change: Recordings*, eds. Robert Butler, Eleanor Margolies, Joe Smith and Renata Tyszczuk (Cambridge: Shed, 2011): 23–27.
3 Jan Zalasiewicz, Mark Williams, A. Smith, T. L. Barry, A. L. Coe, P. R. Bown, P. Brenchley, *et al*. 'Are we now living in the Anthropocene?', *GSA Today* 18.2 (2008): 4–8.
4 Jeremy Davies, *The Birth of the Anthropocene* (Oakland CA: University of California Press, 2016): 5.
5 Jeremy Davies, *The Birth of the Anthropocene* (Oakland CA: University of California Press, 2016): 209.
6 Paul J. Crutzen and Will Steffen, 'How long have we been in the Anthropocene era? An editorial comment', *Climatic Change* 61 (2003): 251–257; 253.
7 Johan Rockström *et al.*, 'A safe operating space for humanity,' *Nature* 461 (September 2009): 472–75.
8 Elizabeth Kolbert, *Field Notes from a Catastrophe: A Frontline Report on Climate Change* (London: Bloomsbury, 2007): 187.
9 Evan Eisenberg, *The Ecology of Eden: Humans, Nature and Human Nature* (London: Picador, 1998): 433; see also Nigel Clark, 'Turbulent prospects: sustaining urbanism on a dynamic planet' in *Urban Futures: Critical Commentaries on Shaping the City*, eds. Malcolm Miles and Tim Hall (London and New York: Routledge, 2003): 182–193; 190.
10 Ben Dibley, 'The shape of things to come': Seven theses on the Anthropocene and attachment', *Ecological Humanities* 52 (May 2012); www.australianhumanitiesreview.org/archive/Issue-May-2012/dibley.html
11 Oliver Morton, 'The Anthropocene: A man made world; Science is recognizing humans as a geological force to be reckoned with', *The Economist* (26 May 2011).
12 Michel Serres, *The Natural Contract* (Ann Arbor: University of Michigan Press, 1995): 17.
13 Marina Alberti, Cristian Correa, John M. Marzluff, Andrew P. Hendry, Eric P. Palkovacs, Kiyoko M. Gotanda, Victoria M. Hunt, Travis M. Apgar, YuYu Zhou, 'Global urban signatures of phenotypic change in animal and plant populations', *Proceedings of the National Academy of Sciences of the United States of America (PNAS)* (2017).
14 Ricky Burdett and Deyan Sudjic (eds.) *The Endless City* (Phaidon Press, 2008); Ricky Burdett and Deyan Sudjic (eds.), *Living in the Endless City* (Phaidon Press, 2011).
15 Timothy W. Luke, 'Urbanism as cyborganicity: Tracking the materialities of the Anthropocene', in *New Geographies 06: Grounding Metabolism*, eds. Malcolm Miles and Tim Hall (Harvard University Press, 2014): 38–51.

16 Neil Brenner and Christian Schmid, 'Planetary urbanization,' in *Urban Constellations*, ed. Matthew Gandy (Berlin: Jovis, 2012): 10–13; and *Implosions/Explosions: Towards a Study of Planetary Urbanization*, ed. Neil Brenner (Berlin: Jovis, 2013).
17 UN Habitat, *State of the World's Cities 2012/2013: Prosperity of Cities* (New York: Earthscan, Routledge, 2013): v.
18 Nigel Clark, 'Turbulent prospects: sustaining urbanism on a dynamic planet' in *Urban Futures: Critical Commentaries on Shaping the City*, eds. Malcolm Miles and Tim Hall (London and New York: Routledge, 2003): 182–193; 182.
19 Mike Davis, 'Who will build the ark?', *New Left Review* 61 (Jan–Feb 2010): 29–45; newleftreview.org/II/61/mike-davis-who-will-build-the-ark.
20 Mike Davis, 'Who will build the ark?', *New Left Review* 61 (Jan–Feb 2010): 29–45; newleftreview.org/II/61/mike-davis-who-will-build-the-ark.
21 Marco Armiero, 'Of the Titanic, the Bounty, and other shipwrecks', *intervalla* 3 (2015).
22 Rob Nixon, 'The Anthropocene: the promise and pitfalls of an epochal idea', The Edge Effects (6 November 2014); edgeeffects.net/anthropocene-promise-and-pitfalls/
23 Timothy W. Luke, 'Urbanism as cyborganicity: tracking the materialities of the Anthropocene', in *New Geographies 06: Grounding Metabolism*, eds. Daniel Ibenez and Nikos Katsikis (Harvard University Press, 2014): 38–51; 49.
24 Georges Bataille, *The Accursed Share*, 1 (New York: Zone Books, 1991): 23.
25 AbdouMaliq Simone, 'Ghostly cracks and urban deceptions: Jakarta' in *In the Life of Cities*, ed. Mohsen Mohstafavi (Zurich: Lars Muller Publishers, 2012): 105–119; 107.
26 Edward W. Soja, *Postmetropolis: Critical Studies of Cities and Regions* (London: Blackwell, 2000): xii.
27 Zygmunt Bauman, 'City of Fears, City of Hopes' (London: Goldsmiths' College, Centre for Urban and Community Research, 2003): 4–5.
28 Friedrich Nietzsche, 'On the uses and disadvantages of history for life', in *Untimely Meditations*, trans. R.J. Hollingdale, (Cambridge: Cambridge University Press, 1983):120.
29 Bruno Latour, 'Agency at the time of the Anthropocene', *New Literary History* 45 (2014): 1–18; 2.
30 Vladimir Nabokov, *Speak, Memory: An Autobiography Revisited* (Vintage International, 1989): 40.
31 Timothy Morton, *Hyperobjects: Philosophy and Ecology after the End of the World* (Minneapolis and London: University of Minnesota Press, 2013): 15.
32 Jacques Derrida, *The Gift of Death, Second Edition & Literature in Secret*, trans. David Wills (Chicago: University of Chicago Press, 2008): 55.
33 Timothy Morton, *Hyperobjects: Philosophy and Ecology after the End of the World* (Minneapolis and London: University of Minnesota Press, 2013): 16.
34 Timothy Morton, 'Ecology without the present', *The Oxford Literary Review* 34.2 (2012): 229–238; 232.
35 Timothy Morton, *Hyperobjects: Philosophy and Ecology after the End of the World* (Minneapolis and London: University of Minnesota Press, 2013): 21.
36 Timothy Morton, *Hyperobjects: Philosophy and Ecology after the End of the World* (Minneapolis and London: University of Minnesota Press, 2013): 19; 94.
37 Michel Serres, *The Natural Contract* (Ann Arbor: University of Michigan Press, 1995): 86.
38 Graham Harman, *Guerrilla Metaphysics: Phenomenology and the Carpentry of Things* (Chicago and La Salle, Illinois: Open Court, 2005): 243.
39 Nigel Clark, *Inhuman Nature: Sociable Life on a Dynamic Planet* (London: Sage, 2011): xiv.
40 Agnes Wooley, '"There's a storm coming!": reading the threat of climate change in Jeff Nichols's *Take Shelter*', *Interdisciplinary Studies in Literature and Environment* 21.1 (Winter 2014).
41 Mark Lynas, 'Global warming: the final warning. According to yesterday's UN report, the world will be a much hotter place by 2100. This will be the impact …', *The Independent* (3 February 2007); worldnewstrust.com/global-warming-the-final-warning-mark-lynas741.
42 Frederick Buell, *From Apocalypse to Way of Life: Environmental Crisis in the American Century* (London: Routledge, 2003): 205–206.
43 Kim Stanley Robinson, *2312* (London, Orbit, 2013): 305. Copyright © 2012 by Kim Stanley Robinson. Used by permission of Orbit, a division of the Hachette Book Group USA Inc. All rights reserved.

44 *Sustainability or Collapse?: An Integrated History and Future of People on Earth*, eds. Robert Costanza, Lisa J. Graumlich and Will Steffen (Cambridge MA and London: MIT Press, 2007).
45 William McWhirter, 'I am one of the 10 most famous obscure Americans', *Life* (12 June 1968); see also Sharon Ghamari-Tabrizi, *The Worlds of Herman Kahn: The Intuitive Science of Thermonuclear War* (Cambridge MA. And London, England: Harvard University Press, 2005): 204.
46 On the IHOPE initiative (Integrated History and Future of People on Earth) see Libby Robin and Will Steffen, 'History for the Anthropocene', *History Compass* 5.5 (2007): 1694–1719.
47 On the 'Anthropozoic era' see Antonio Stoppani, Corso di Geologia (1873. On 'noosphere' see V. Vernadsky, 'The biosphere and the noosphere', *American Scientist* 33 (1945): 1–12 On 'anthrocene' see Andy Revkin, *Global Warming: Understanding the Forecast* (Abbeville Press, 1992); see also Will Steffen *et al.*, 'The Anthropocene: conceptual and historical perspectives' *Philosophical Transactions of the Royal Society A* 369 (2011): 842–867; 842.
48 Elizabeth Johnson *et al.*, 'After the Anthropocene: politics and geographic inquiry for a new epoch', *Progress in Human Geography* (2014): 1–18; 2.
49 Robert McFarlane, 'Generation Anthropocene: how humans have altered the planet forever', *The Guardian*, (1 April 2016); www.theguardian.com/books/2016/apr/01/generation-anthropocene-altered-planet-for-ever
50 Doreen Massey, 'Landscape as a provocation: reflections on moving mountains', *Journal of Material Culture* 11.1–2 (2006):, 33–48.
51 Isabelle Stengers, *In Catastrophic Times: Resisting the Coming Barbarism*, trans. Andre Goffey (Open Humanities Press, 2015): 39.

1 Fossil traces

DANGER: construction site

The Anthropocene thesis is the proposition that we are entering or have already entered a new geological epoch in the Earth's 4.6 billion year history: one in which human agency can be compared to a determining planetary force. It announces the end of geologic conditions characteristic of the 10,000 to 12,000 years since the end of the last glacial epoch and the move into a novel epoch in which human activities are pushing the Earth system out of the late Quaternary pattern into a 'no-analogue state'.[1] An Anthropocene epoch would terminate the Holocene, the postglacial epoch of agriculture and cities. If the Anthropocene thesis announces the role that human societies are playing in this drastic Earth-changing, it is also a story that speculates on the fossil traces that humans will leave behind. It anticipates how cities are being recomposed into the geological stratum of a Holocene-Anthropocene transition.

Geology, 'is a science of vast durations, slow movements and inhuman scale'.[2] The Anthropocene, potentially the latest addition to the geologic time scale (GTS) represents both a break in and a continuation of millions of years of deep history. In 2008, the Stratigraphy Commission of the Geological Society of London agreed to consider the possible formalisation of the term *Anthropocene* as a unit on the GTS.[3] The Anthropocene Working Group (AWG), convened by the geologist Jan Zalasiewicz, was initiated as part of the Subcommission on Quaternary Stratigraphy. Its task was to gather evidence for the new epoch.[4] Members of the AWG (which in addition to stratigraphers has included botanists, zoologists, atmospheric and ocean scientists as well as science journalists and historians) announced at the time: 'We have entered a distinctive phase of Earth's evolution that satisfies geologists' criteria for its recognition as a distinctive stratigraphic unit, to which the name Anthropocene has already been informally given.'[5] They set a target date of 2016 to present their findings to the International Commission on Stratigraphy (ICS) and the International Union of Geological Sciences, the timekeepers of geology. In 2016 the AWG stated their support for formally defining a new epoch with 'distinctive attributes'.[6]

The GTS is not amended lightly, however. The AWG's recommendations are just the first step in an arduous process which includes a global quest for an appropriate site for a 'golden spike' – an actual physical point marking the geological evidence for a Holocene-Anthropocene transition. In making its assessment, the AWG considered various human-induced disruptions to the Earth system and their possible legacy in the rocks. It analysed changes in land use, monoculture and intensive agriculture practices, deforestation, resource extraction; combustion of carbon-based fuels and attendant emissions; the depositing of nuclear and chemical wastes; species extinction patterns and population growth; and the large-scale geomorphic transformations of the Earth's surface in the construction of cities and infrastructures. The AWG is concerned with what all these changes will mean for the geological stratification of the Earth. They have acknowledged that the abrupt and catastrophic transformations of the lithosphere indicated in this proposed epoch are rare in the Earth's 4.6 billion year history. The dominant anthropogenic forces shifting the Earth system – including warming, acidification, nitrate concentrations and species extinctions – are continuing on an upward curve.[7] Human impacts on the Earth thus promise to be even more stratigraphically significant in the future. The Anthropocene is different from all other epochs: not only since humans may already be living within it, but because observable human perturbations are ongoing and may continue for millennia to come.

The start date of the Anthropocene – stratigraphically speaking – is as yet uncertain. It is clear that the most profound anthropogenic alterations to Earth systems and processes have occurred since the Industrial Revolution, and intensified with the 'Great Acceleration' in the years after World War II.[8] From a geological perspective, only episodes of exceptional violence are likely to leave any lasting traces in the rocks. The widespread crisis that the human species now faces is considered to be on par with the last mass extinction 65 million years ago, caused by an asteroid impact – an event that marks the K-T or Cretaceous-Tertiary boundary.[9] The article by Earth system scientist Paul Crutzen and Eugene Stoermer that introduced the Anthropocene thesis in 2000 lists all the things that humans usually worry about, before trumping them with the notion that humanity itself is commensurate, in its impact, with the gravest of 'natural' disasters:

> Without major catastrophes like an enormous volcanic eruption, an unexpected epidemic, a large scale nuclear war, an asteroid impact, a new ice age, or continued plundering of Earth's resources by partially still primitive technology… mankind will remain a major geological force for many millennia, maybe millions of years to come.[10]

The profound changes to the functioning of the Earth system promise devastating effects on a planet of cities far into the future. Where humans and their resources cluster, sites of volatility and vulnerability come into being. The identification of the Anthropocene positions humans as the fossil-fuelled driving force of change, capable of epochal shifts, but at the same time undermines all human constructions by anticipating their eventual fossilisation. The Anthropocene thesis also confronts the possibility of the end of this trajectory: that of humanity's fossil-fuelled demise.

The idea that human impact on Earth is akin to a geological force is not new. As Jan Zalasiewicz and colleagues have noted, 'The term Anthropocene is the latest iteration of a concept to signal the impact of collective human activity on biological, physical and chemical processes at and around the Earth's surface'.[11] In 1873, the Italian geologist Antonio Stoppani described human activities as 'a new telluric force that for its strength and universality does not pale in the face of the greatest forces of the globe', and coined the term 'Anthropozoic era'.[12] The Russian mineralogist Vladimir Vernadsky introduced the notion of the 'biosphere' in the 1920s. His later, related concept of the 'noosphere' emphasised the growing human effect on the Earth's biogeochemical cycles.[13] In 1992, science journalist Andy Revkin, surveying the growing human impacts on Earth, had speculated that future Earth scientists might name a post-Holocene era 'for us', identifying 'a geological age of our own making'.[14] What is distinctive about the Anthropocene concept is the idea of *rupture* – that human activities have influenced a rapid transition to a new geological epoch.[15] As the academic Clive Hamilton writes:

> The Earth has now crossed a point of no return; its great cycles have changed, the chemical compositions of air and ocean have been altered in ways that cannot be undone except on a millennial timescale. In short, the Earth system is now operating in a different mode and nothing humans can do now, even ending the burning of fossil fuels in short order, can turn the geological clock back to the Holocene.[16]

If the geological clock cannot be turned back, it is the problem of going forward in time that has dominated discussions of the Anthropocene. The question of what residues – or *fossil traces* – the human species will leave behind in a post-human world has been a prominent theme in academic and popular science writing on the Anthropocene. Jan Zalasiewicz describes the criteria that enable researchers to link the fossilised remains of species with geological epoch-making events: 'A biostratigrapher wishes upon any species the life of the wilder kind of Romantic poet: early brilliant success, a worldwide reach, and then a sudden death.'[17] Zalasiewicz notes that the human species is looking increasingly likely to meet these criteria. The stratigraphic Anthropocene introduces speculation on the human through consideration of the traces (or lack of) that humanity will leave behind in the rocks. The imagination of fossil traces millions of years from now stands in for evidence in the geological record of the impacts of human societies on Earth processes. The Anthropocene is where the human meets geology. The fossil traces of human impact might be identified as much by the marks left by the subways, sewers and landfills of megacities as in signs of possible extinctions in the rocks – even our own. Thinking through the Anthropocene is thus disruptive of understandings of geology, of the human, and of human habitation on Earth.

Anthropocene unconformities

The proposal for an Anthropocene epoch was initiated in the Earth system science community in 2000.[18] Since then it has provoked an integration of the approaches of Earth system sciences and stratigraphy.[19] It is challenging many areas of research into Earth's future. The term has worked its way beyond the disciplinary boundaries of geology, stratigraphy, Earth system sciences and natural sciences. It has migrated into public and policy discourses. It has also established a presence in the arts, humanities, and social sciences. It has prompted a questioning of what it means to live in the present epoch. Thinking about the Anthropocene challenges the fixity of concepts of humanity and nature, and therefore what it means to be 'of this Earth'. As Bruno Latour asks, 'What is the exact *shape of the Earth* or, more exactly, what is the Earth that is now facing us?'[20] The Anthropocene geostory does away with the dominant narrative of progress, the old plot devices of agency and control, and the usual protagonists and antagonists of human/non-human, nature/culture and other binaries. The emergence of the Anthropocene concept acts as a break with the 'old paradigm' ways of analysis and prediction.[21] It is also part of a challenge to 'figure out… how to *maintain our Earthling status* in its various entanglements'.[22] There is no obvious route to getting to grips with the Anthropocene thesis and its manifold implications. Earth system science, which itself represents a paradigm shift in the Earth and life sciences,[23] introduces the Anthropocene as 'the *very recent rupture* in Earth history arising from the impact of human activity on the Earth system as a whole'.[24] The idea of the Anthropocene as *rupture* thus invites new understandings of the human relationship to the Earth.

The Anthropocene announces the meshing of inhuman and human forces in a configuration of mutual threat. Declaring the Anthropocene means crediting human agency with the capacity to reshape the planet at the very moment we are beginning to question an anthropocentric view of the world. To reflect on the present epoch is to tremble, paradoxically, at humanity's power to disrupt, and at our vulnerability to disruption. For if humans are named as the driving force of geological change, capable of epochal shifts, this summons a time when everything human-made will be subsumed in the rocks, leaving only a fossilised trace. The Anthropocene invites renewed contemplation of lithic and corporeal entanglements that both outlast and elude us. Thinking geologically binds together incommensurable times and scales and incompatible materials and things. Jan Zalasiewicz reads the planet's story 'in a pebble' limned by disaster and flourishing.[25] For stone is the foundation of the mundane, it endures the Earth's recurrent cataclysms and is an 'active partner in the 'shaping of worlds'.[26] Stone, for philosopher Jeffrey Jerome Cohen, has an 'ardour for unconformity, stone sediments contradiction… It offers a stumbling block to anthropocentrism and a spur to ceaseless story'.[27]

An aporia between rock strata is termed an 'unconformity'. It is the lithic manifestation of 'missing time', a hiatus in sedimentary geological records that helps geologists to determine where epochs begin and end. More generally, unconformity is the scientific term for the inscrutability of the lithic: elementary transformations whereby ocean floors become deserts, or the bones of plain-dwelling dinosaurs are lifted to the roof of the world. The geological record is a millefeuille of rifts, schisms, lacunae. The academic Bronislaw Szerszynski likens the geological concept of the Earth to a great stone book which records its own history.[28] The Anthropocene might one day be read in the geological record in numerous possible unconformities: unusual layers of sediment marking the deposition of building rubble, metal oxides, radioactive material, plastic pollution in hurricane and earthquake zones, and the changing distribution and extinction of species. In short, the Anthropocene unconformity is likely to bear traces of large-scale human impacts on the Earth.

On Friday 11 March 2011, the Tōhoku earthquake and ensuing tsunami triggered the meltdown of three nuclear reactors in the Fukushima Daiichi power plants. The lubricating layer of clay sediments on the bordering Pacific plate allowed it to slide 30–50 metres under the Eurasian plate that houses the Japanese island of Honshu. It was the largest fault slip ever recorded.[29] The resulting earthquake moved Honshu 2.4 m east and shifted the Earth on its axis by estimates of between 10 cm and 25 cm. At least 16,000 people died; 129,225 buildings totally collapsed, a further 254,204 buildings 'half collapsed', and another 691,766 buildings were partially damaged; 4.4 million households in northeastern Japan were left without electricity and 1.5 million without water. Entire coastal regions were devastated, and nuclear radiation and other pollutants were widely dispersed across agricultural and residential areas. The event went down as the costliest disaster in world history.

24 *Fossil traces*

The disaster in Japan also drew attention to the vulnerability of anthropogenically modified strata to tremors and tsunami incursions. The Japanese geologists who studied the quake identified a geomorphological phenomenon called 'jinji unconformity' or 'jinji discontinuity'. The Japanese word *jinji* is a combination of two *kanji* characters – '*jin*' meaning human being, and '*ji*' meaning 'natural'. It refers to the stratigraphic boundary or threshold that separates the sedimentary layers of predominantly human-made deposits from earlier strata.[30] In the UK this boundary is often referred to as 'rock head'. The Japanese geologists noted extensive fluidisation, liquefaction and subsidence in this boundary, resulting in the widespread dispersal of contaminated materials.[31] Jinji unconformity is a term put forward to define the diachronous base layer of the Anthropocene. In the case of the Tōhoku triple-disaster, seismic tremors, tsunami incursions and nuclear meltdown converged on the artificial structure of reclaimed land with devastating consequences. The stratigraphic configuration is at once natural, cultural, and technological. The significance of this boundary 'emerges from the mixture, rather than the division, of geological and human'.[32] And like the Anthropocene itself, the jinji unconformity is 'in ongoing boundary formation mode'.[33]

The jinji or Anthropocene unconformity is thus a porous interface between different imaginaries, geological and cultural. As the Anthropocene gains acceptance in a number of disciplines, it promises to alter more than the nomenclature in geology textbooks. If the Anthropocene is a cautionary tale of human making, it also introduces doubt as to where to begin – what to say or what to do to avoid the coming catastrophe. The mounting evidence that humanity is doggedly, wilfully undermining itself leaves us at a loss. Yet this loss might create space – some necessary wiggle-room for our cornered species. By asserting the centrality of human presence in the Anthropocene, we are simultaneously unsettling long-entrenched human-centred modes of thinking and doing. Anthropocene unconformities – in all their dimensions – are frightening. But they might also act as necessary signposts for the unavoidable move from the relative stability of the Holocene to an unprecedented state of human-geophysical instability.

Missing time

> The result, therefore, of our present enquiry is, that we find no vestige of a beginning, –no prospect of an end.[34]

The Scottish geologist James Hutton introduced the concept of deep time. Hutton's *Theory of the Earth* (1788) illustrated the instability of the planetary lithosphere by identifying long cycles of geological succession and upheaval that resemble the cycles in a living system.[35] Hutton presented the terrestrial system as a 'machine of a peculiar construction'. His theory depended on geological unconformities – gaps in the rock record that separated epochs, and thus revealed Earth's history to be, not a gradual decline into ruin, but a cycle of deposition, uplift and displacement. Unconformities – the discontinuities and breaks in the geological record that recognise missing time – are the very foundations of geology.

Hutton had found striking evidence for his theories of geological unconformity in 1788 at Siccar Point on the east coast of Scotland. At Siccar Point, the 425-million-year-old Silurian Greywacke strata, tilted to a near vertical, are overlayed by a

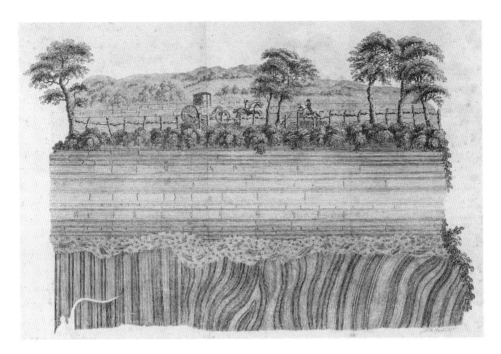

Figure 1.1 Hutton's Unconformity; engraving after a drawing by John Clerk of Eldin (1787) of the unconformity at Jedburgh in James Hutton, *Theory of the Earth*, Volume I, Plate III (1795)
Source: Cambridge University Library

horizontal 345-million-year-old stratum of Devonian (Old Red Sandstone) rocks. The feature, later named 'Hutton's Unconformity', formed when the crustal fragments that would become Scotland collided and fused – a result of the tortuous movement of the Earth's tectonic plates over millions of years. John Playfair, Hutton's colleague, wrote of the experience of seeing this evidence of geological unconformity:

> We felt necessarily carried back to a time when the schistus on which we stood was yet at the bottom of the sea, and when the sandstone before us was only beginning to be deposited, in the shape of sand or mud, from the waters of the supercontinent ocean... The mind seemed to grow giddy by looking so far back into the abyss of time.[36]

Hutton's theory met with resistance because it broke with established scientific views on geological formation and Earth chronology. Science at the time conformed to an intergenerational estimate of the beginning of time from the biblical record of the Creation: Earth was deemed to be 6,000 years old, with each day of creation correlating to a thousand years of human history. Hutton's theory conflicted with the then-prevailing theory of catastrophism, which understood transformations in the Earth only as a result of major, rapid, catastrophic events and which could therefore be related to biblical stories of cataclysm, as in for example, Noah's flood.

Hutton's vision of a vast, non-instrumentalised Earth, shaped by slow-moving forces and random chance, eventually came to be known as uniformitarianism. It was popularised by Charles Lyell in *Principles of Geology* (1830–1833). In the 19th century, the emerging science of geology was keen to distance itself from catastrophism's 'unscientific' biblical accounts of Earth history, and was therefore reluctant to accept that a transition from one period in Earth history to the next could be due to some sudden convulsion. Lyell wrote:

> Yet many geologists, when they behold spoils of the land heaped in successive strata, and blended confusingly with the remains of fishes, or interspersed with broken shells and corals, imagine that they are viewing the signs of a turbulent instead of a tranquil and settled state of the planet. They read in such phenomena the proof of chaotic disorder, and reiterated catastrophes, instead of indications of a surface as habitable as the most delicious and fertile districts now tenanted by man.[37]

Yet evidence of 'reiterated catastrophes' – for example asteroid strikes – interrupting the gradual, drawn-out changes on Earth has challenged uniformitarian-inclined views. The GTS now includes several transitions from one era or epoch to the next marked by cataclysmic events and the ensuing mass extinctions of dominant species. Humans struggle to relate to deep time, with its long caesurae and its sudden ruptures and discontinuities. Human history is a mere blip in Earth history. It is not easy for the human mind to conceive of epoch after epoch heaped up in the rock strata, one on top of the next. Deep time is so radically destabilising of conventional timescales, so insistent on long-term cycles, that it upsets other notions of time, making it hard to conceive of them simultaneously. As the philosopher Timothy Morton observes: 'Geological time, emerging for humans since the advent of modernity, is an abyss whose reality becomes increasingly uncanny, not less, the more scientific instruments are able to probe it.'[38] Hutton's deep time chronology displaced divinity and humanity from Earth's history. It also bifurcated Earth and human history. And as the scientist Stephen Jay Gould has observed: 'Hutton's rigidity is both a boon and a trap. It gave us deep time, but we lost history in the process. Any adequate account of the Earth requires both.'[39]

In geological terms, the move into the Anthropocene, occurring over an extremely short period, registers as a rupture or regime shift. The Anthropocene is catastrophism all over again. It is riddled with unconformities. With the advent of the new epoch the catastrophe of human time confronts missing time: the quotidian activities of human life are placed in the context of immeasurable and surprising time signatures. Entering into the abyss of missing time in the Anthropocene means being shaken, not only by attempts to contemplate Earth processes with durations exceeding human comprehensibility, but also by the realisation of humans' capacity for generating upheavals of geological magnitude. It is not surprising that all certainties – and interpretive tools – founder.

The advent of the Anthropocene is a provocation to engage with very different temporalities from those in which we normally operate. It demands the simultaneous conceptualisation of both human and geologic timescales. Even if it were possible in the future to recognise minuscule remnants of anthropogenic interventions on Earth, the immediacy and particularity of human life events would fail to register in the midst of evidence of planetary-scale mobilisations of species and rock in geological strata. About one kilometre to the west of Siccar Point, the ruins of St Helen's Romanesque chapel reveal a tell-tale jumble of grey and red rocks hewn from Hutton's unconformity. The story of the Silurian and Devonian rocks weaves across millions of years of formation and erosion, yet includes a brief instance of construction and ruination: from long processes of sedimentation on the ocean floor to the transience of chapel walls, millions of years and no time at all. The rock is laid down, squeezed, pushed, contorted, trammelled, hewn, split, carried, arranged, propped, carved, repaired, cemented, destroyed, eroded – by non-human and human activity. The ruined chapel's stratigraphic hodge-podge of memories, distances and temporalities – human, geological, planetary – are impossible to reconcile even as they leave a record of human time as a reassembly of deep time.

The notion of the Anthropocene as both ungrounding humanity from, and entangling us in, Earth systems processes recalls Michel Serres' topological image of spacetime as a mixture folding in upon itself and constantly changing consistency: 'Time enters into the dough, a prisoner of its folds, a shadow of its folding over.'[40] In this image of the dough of history, it is as if time and space are endlessly re-gathering and mixing, so that what was near is dispersed, and what was previously unimaginably distant is brought into proximity. The Anthropocene thus suggests an experimental relation to temporality: a thinking through the anomalies, curiosities, ruptures and unconformities within the multiple unfoldings of missing time.

Our world has ended

Results of AWG Vote (35 members):

> *Is the Anthropocene stratigraphically real?*
> **For: 34**; Against: 0; Abstain: 1.
> *Should the Anthropocene be formalised?*
> **For :30**; Against: 3; Abstain: 2.
> *Hierarchical level of the Anthropocene?* Era: 2; Period: 1.5; **Epoch: 20.5**; Subepoch: 1; Age: 2; Sub-age: 0; None: 1; Uncertain: 3; Abstain: 4.
> *Base/beginning of the Anthropocene?*
> ~7 Ka: 0; ~3 Ka: 1.3; 1610 Orbis: 0; ~1800: 0; **~1950: 28.3**; ~1964: 1.3; Diachronous: 4; Uncertain: 0; Abstain: 0.
> *Global Standard Stratigraphic Age (GSSA) .v. Global Boundary Stratotype Section and Point (GSSP)?*
> **GSSP: 25.5**; GSSA: 1.5; Uncertain: 8.
> *What is the primary signal?*
> Aluminium: 0;, Plastic: 3; Fuel ash particles: 2; Carbon dioxide concentration: 3; Methane concentration: 0; Carbon isotope change: 2; Oxygen isotope change: 0; Radiocarbon bomb spike: 4; **Plutonium fallout: 10**; Nitrate concentration/nitrogen isotope change: 0; Biostratigraphic: extinction/assemblage change: 0; Other (lead, persistent organic pollutants, technofossils): 3; Uncertain: 2; Abstain: 6.[41]

In 2016 the AWG voted on the Anthropocene epoch, in time to take its recommendations on a potential new geological time interval to the 35th International Geological Congress.[42] They agreed that the Anthropocene was 'stratigraphically real' and should be formalised. For the time being, however, we are still officially living in the Holocene epoch of the Quaternary period, Cenozoic era and Phanerozoic eon. In *Principles of Geology* Charles Lyell had characterised this epoch as 'recent', as evidenced in rock strata that contained fossil assemblages of 'the shells of the present seas and lakes, and the remains of animals and plants now living on the land'.[43] These 'recent formations' were coincident with the time during which Earth had been 'tenanted by man'. The French palaeontologist Paul Gervais gave the epoch the name Holocene in 1867. It was formally acknowledged at the Third International Geological Congress in Bologna in 1885 as the chronostratigraphic division that followed the Pleistocene epoch. Holocene comes from the Greek words *holos* ('whole') and *kainos* ('recent'), referring to the fact that this epoch was considered the most recent division of Earth history. The preceding epoch of the Quaternary was the Pleistocene, starting about 2.588 Ma (millions of years before the present), characterised by oscillation between glacial and interglacial periods. The Holocene, by contrast, is a period of unusually stable climate. It follows the last glaciation and started around the time that humans started clearing forests for agriculture, approximately 11,700 years ago. The start of the official process for 'naming the Anthropocene' in 2008 prompted Mike Davis's plaintive farewell to the Holocene: 'Our world... has ended.'[44] But if the Holocene epoch – the world as we know it – is over, when did the Anthropocene begin?

The AWG of the Stratigraphy Commission has been considering what the perceived global-scale human impacts on Earth systems mean for the geological stratification of the Earth. Chronostratigraphy, or rock-time, insists that identification of the beginning of the Anthropocene requires precise chronostratigraphic data. These must conform to several criteria, such as physical character (lithostratigraphy), fossil content (biostratigraphy), chemical properties (chemostratigraphy), magnetic properties (magnetostratigraphy), as well as patterns within rock-time related to sea level change (sequence stratigraphy) and more recent technofossils (technostratigraphy). In the 1970s a 'golden spike', or Global Boundary Stratotype Section and Point (GSSP), was introduced to mark the threshold between epochs. It is awarded by the International Commission of Stratigraphy. The golden spike is ceremoniously driven into a rock face (or ice core) between two types of strata, marking the interface between two different epochs. It can take decades to find irrefutable evidence in the strata. In 2009, when the Holocene was finally awarded its golden spike – located in an ice core 1,492 metres below the surface of Greenland – the AWG had already begun the search for possible times and locations for the spike to mark the transition to the Anthropocene. The quest to identify the point in time and rock when humans became a geological force continues. Insertion of the Anthropocene into the geologic time scale will depend on recognition of a suitable global event horizon discernible in the rocks. The distinct magnetic, chemical, palaeontological, technological or climatic signals between the Holocene and Anthropocene that will need to be detected worldwide will be expected to simultaneously mark the boundaries between both the time units of geochronology and their equivalent time–rock units of chronostratigraphy.[45] The Anthropocene has not yet earned its golden spike. The typical predicament faced by geologists is inverted: while the ties between human activity and Earth system changes are well documented, the Anthropocene is not yet legible in the sedimentary rock record and won't be for some time. Time-rock takes its time.

In 2014 the Anthropocene Working Group offered four key time periods as potential placement for the base of the Anthropocene: the pre-Industrial Revolution, the Industrial Revolution, the mid-20th century age, and the future.[46] These time periods neatly map on to Will Steffen, Crutzen and McNeill's earlier proposal in their 2007 *Ambio* paper. These are the 'pre-Anthropocene', followed by three stages of the Anthropocene proper: 'The Industrial Era (ca. 1800–1945): Stage 1'; 'The Great

Acceleration (1945– ca. 2015): Stage 2'; 'Stewards of the Earth System? (ca. 2015–?): Stage 3'.[47] Crutzen and Stoermer had originally suggested locating the start of the new epoch in the second half of the 18th century, to coincide with the invention of the steam engine. The technological harnessing of fossil fuels as a source of energy is understood to have marked the beginning of an uninterrupted rise in atmospheric CO_2, methane and nitrous oxide levels.[48]

The period of more gradual human-induced change that preceded the Industrial Revolution has been characterised as the 'Palaeoanthropocene', suggesting humans as an integral part of the Earth system with a long history of Earth modification.[49] The palaeoclimatologist William Ruddiman put forward an 'early Anthropocene' hypothesis arguing that as a result of the agricultural revolution and deforestation around 5,000 years ago, humans had already caused emission of sufficient greenhouse gases to modify the Earth's climatic trajectory.[50] Other researchers have proposed that collective human endeavour unintentionally altered climatic conditions from at least the Middle Ages, and perhaps centuries earlier. More recently, geographers Simon Lewis and Mark Maslin argued that the start date of the Anthropocene could coincide with the European colonisation of the New World.[51] The demographic collapse of the Amerindian population – from between 54–61 million in 1492 to around 6 million in 1650 – caused urban and agricultural retreat and the subsequent reforestation of more than 60 million hectares. This in turn reduced the carbon concentration in the atmosphere to around 272 ppm (though still within the general Holocene range of 260 to 284 ppm).[52] However, Clive Hamilton has argued that suggestions of an early Anthropocene indicate a grave misreading:

> By treating the new epoch as a continuation of landscape or ecosystem change going back centuries or millennia, they divorce it from modern industrialisation and the burning of fossil fuels. In this way they deny that the Anthropocene represents a rupture in Earth history, and deprive it of its dangerous quality.[53]

More appropriately dangerous, perhaps, is the most recent recommendation by the AWG of the nuclear age as the marker for the start of the Anthropocene. Jan Zalasiewicz and colleagues proposed to date the Anthropocene to the precise moment of 16 July 1945, 05:29:45 (local time), when the first atom bomb was exploded at Alamogordo, New Mexico.[54] 'The Bomb' marks the beginning of the nuclear age and the global spread of artificial radionuclides, as a result of the extensive atmospheric nuclear weapon testing that followed the Alamogordo test. It is widely accepted that the period since World War II will be marked by a clear increase in radioactivity and a global distribution of nuclear detritus.[55] Ice cores and speleothems show a significant radiocarbon signal dating from the mid 1950s. This period, referred to by Will Steffen as the 'Great Acceleration', also designates the dramatic increase in population growth, consumption and technological development, and is described as ushering in a time when human activities go from merely influencing to dominating the global environment.[56]

The mid-20th century thus presents both an appropriately momentous stratigraphical signal and a significant enough leap in humans' destructive capabilities to warrant consideration for the inception of the Anthropocene. However, in *The Shock of the Anthropocene*, Bonneuil and Fressoz warn against marking this as the start date, for it 'masks deeper causes and processes [and] obscures the major rupture, both environmental and civilisational, of the entry into thermo-nuclear society based on fossil fuels'.[57] Other researchers point to the diachronous character of the physical strata of the Anthropocene, arguing that the onset and impact of geological processes are spread out over time, so that it is impossible to impose onto them a precise, globally synchronous date or instantaneous time.[58] However, what appears as diachronous in terms of human timescale might be considered as synchronous on a geological timescale and still have some relevance to definitions of chronostratigraphic units. With its claims to deep-time future fossils, based on recent events that may yet prove insignificant, the Anthropocene is difficult to formalise in terms of the geologic time scale. The geologist Jay Quade speculates on a more conspicuous 'Cenozoic- Anthropozoic' or 'C-A' boundary event between eras rather than epochs – a stratigraphic marker horizon which would 'be akin to – if not bigger than – the Permian-Triassic mass extinction 250 million years ago and the Cretaceous-Tertiary extinction that cleared out the dinosaurs and led to the Age of Mammals – and us.'[59] The Anthropocene epoch may yet unfold into a period, an era or an eon of unknown duration.

However, even if the stratigraphic proofs required for altering geological timekeeping are not yet inscribed in the rocks, the Anthropocene thesis has implications for geology in terms of Earth systems sciences. Jan Zalasiewicz, convenor of the AWG, points out: 'The Anthropocene is not about being able to detect human influence in stratigraphy, but reflects a change in the Earth system.'[60] For the Earth system scientists who proposed the Anthropocene, the key point is that the dynamic between humankind and the Earth has been fundamentally altered. Most importantly, as Paul Crutzen and Will Steffen observe: 'The Earth currently operates in a state without previous analogy.'[61] Whether or not we have officially entered a new geological epoch matters less than acknowledging that we live in a world without precedent.

The collision of histories

One of the most difficult reframings that the infant Anthropocene presents to geologists is its vanishingly short time frame compared with the unfathomable eons and more manageable epochs and ages across which they are accustomed to ranging. If the marker for this epoch were to land somewhere in the 18th century, the Anthropocene would then be only 250 years or so in the making. Alternatively, if it is dated to the period after World War II it will have lasted less than 100 years. Whichever way you look at it, the Anthropocene is a renegade and juvenile epoch. Even the Holocene epoch has so far lasted only around 11,700 years, where an average epoch counts 13 million years. The nomenclature of the GTS has been evolving for only 200 years, from the period of geologists' first forays into deep time and the realisation of the enormity of that time encapsulated in Hutton's unconformities. It was, however, only in the 20th century that the GTS and its boundary changes were understood as reflecting not simply epochs and eons of otherwise immeasurable time, but fundamental and cataclysmic changes in the Earth's climate state.[62] And it is *now* – in what is being called the Anthropocene – that geologic history has become entangled with human history, the planetary is mixed up with the global, and species thinking has collided with critiques of capital. The historian Dipesh Chakrabarty has written of the profound challenges to writing history in the time of the Anthropocene:

> At the same time, the story of capital, the contingent history of our falling into the Anthropocene, cannot be denied by recourse to the idea of species, for the

Anthropocene would not have been possible, even as a theory, without the history of industrialisation. How do we hold the two together as we think the history of the world since the Enlightenment? ... The crisis of climate change calls for thinking simultaneously on both registers, to mix together the immiscible chronologies of capital and species history. This combination, however, stretches, in quite fundamental ways, the very idea of historical understanding.[63]

In this reading, incommensurable chronologies must somehow be wrestled into parallel. The challenge is to reconfigure a historical understanding of the human species that can hold together things, states and arrangements that are radically dissimilar and temporally discontinuous: political regimes, cultural orders, metabolisms, tectonic upheavals, energy cycles. The Anthropocene names the intersection of human history and geological time; in the same moment, it supercedes the concept of *nature* as a stable non-human background to human-made history. The history of industrialisation since the late 18th century – including deforestation, resource extraction, combustion of carbon-based fuels and attendant emissions, extinction, population growth, and the accelerated construction of cities and infrastructures – has the potential for multiple indicators of the human transformation of Earth systems. Yet the list of irreversible human impacts on Earth and life processes is uncomfortably close to a roll call of human achievements, including all the things that have been the sum and substance of human 'progress' and 'modernity'. The Anthropocene expresses a historical paradox: it comes about as the result of the urge to appropriate, redistribute and exploit the world's resources with the promise of boundless progress; at the same time, it calls for nothing less than the derailment of this so-called 'progress'. For all that we insist that the Anthropocene is singular and exceptional, we nevertheless cannot help trying to understand it from within a progressivist view of history, in which the past serves chiefly as a source of lessons for the future, and time is a one-directional acceleration – toward betterment, or disaster. As Bonneuil and Fressoz contend in *The Shock of the Anthropocene*, 'The new teleology of ecological reflexivity and collective learning replaces the old teleology of progress. Such heralding of the end of modernisation is in fact a new modernist fable.'[64]

It is, as the philosopher Isabelle Stengers puts it, 'a little as if we were suspended between two histories'.[65] The 'first history' is the familiar one of global growth and progress; the second, the intangible one that we have recently embarked on, but do not yet know how to respond to. Moreover, the 'second history' is defined by 'an intrusion' that she names, following Lovelock, *Gaia*:

> We all know that something is in the process of intruding into our history that was neither anticipated nor prepared for, that was wished for by no one, including of course those who have been struggling against capitalism's hold ... No one is ready for what's coming. It is beyond all of us.[66]

According to Stengers, the significance of Gaia's intrusion is occluded because the 'first history' makes it seem as if this were only a 'crisis' to be surmounted, like so many others before it. For the Earth has long been considered as either a resource to be exploited or an entity that needs protecting. Stengers asks that we consider the Earth anew, as a fearful power that might destroy us in the future.[67] Caution is called for in any attempt to come to terms with the telluric power that human activities have roused, but have so far seemed oblivious to. The new state of the Earth system will bring a disorder that will render the Earth less habitable to humans, yet in the 4.6-billion-year history of the Earth this will scarcely matter. For, as Stengers reminds us, even if we can invoke a transformed Earth 'as having been put in play by our histories', we are nevertheless dealing with an Earth that is indifferent to us and our histories:

> Of the Earth, the present subject of our scenarios, we can presuppose a single thing: it doesn't care about the questions we ask about it. What we call a catastrophe will be, for it, a contingency. Microbes will survive, as well as insects, whatever we let loose. In other words, it is only because of the global ecological transformations we can provoke, which are potentially capable of putting in question the regimes of terrestrial existence we depend on, that we can invoke the Earth as having been put in play by our histories. From the viewpoint of the long history of the Earth itself, this will be one more 'contingent event' in a long series.[68]

Anticipatory geology

Stratigraphy is a mode of reading the past in the layers of rock. To posit the Anthropocene is to project the imagination into a future past world. It is to attempt to read in advance what is not yet inscribed in the Earth's crust: the fossilised traces of a vanished humanity. Clive Hamilton argues that this calls for 'a new kind of 'anticipatory geology'.[69] The Anthropocene is a proleptic undertaking: geologists, accustomed to digging deep into the past, are charged with finding evidence that will be stratigraphically significant deep in the future.

Antonio Stoppani's 1870s proclamations of the 'Anthropozoic era' went hand in hand with his imagination of a 'strange intelligence' studying a post-human geology: 'Let us admit, though eccentric it might be, the supposition that a strange intelligence should come to study the Earth in a day when human progeny ... has disappeared completely.' He speculates that the 'future geologist, wishing to study our epoch's geology, would end up narrating the history of human intelligence.'[70] Charles Lyell had described a similar 'intelligent being' in his *Principles of Geology*. This future surveyor of Earth would 'soon perceive that no one of the fixed and constant laws of the animate and inanimate world was subverted by human agency'; and that 'whenever the power of the new agent was withheld, even for a brief period, a relapse would take place to the ancient state of things'.[71] Lyell further argued: 'Now, if it would be reasonable to draw such inferences with respect to the future, we cannot but apply the same rules of induction to the past.'[72] With the advent of the Anthropocene thesis, Lyell's well-known dictum 'The present is the key to the past' is neatly revised. For it is becoming clear that the future is the key to the present.

A key event in the process of formalising the Anthropocene was a meeting for members of the AWG organised by the Geological Society in 2011 at Burlington House, London. Will Steffen reports:

> As speaker after speaker demonstrated via observations that the imprint of the human enterprise was already clear in many stratigraphic features of Earth, the mood changed to one of excitement. Participants began to put themselves into the positions of geologists centuries or millennia in the future, looking back on this remarkably sharp and profound period of environmental change and speculating on what they would actually find in the stratigraphic record.[73]

This thought experiment is the foundation of the stratigraphic Anthropocene. It asks, if future geologists studied the Earth, what traces of present-day upheavals might they find in the rocks? Jan Zalasiewicz of the AWG has also written a fictional narrative, *The Earth After Us*. In this popular science work, the Earth is described as a 'strata machine' and Zalasiewicz re-enacts the thought experiments that the Stratigraphy Commission are confronted with through a fictional excursion into a post-human future.[74] For Zalasiewicz, the Earth's 'treasury of strata' offers 'countless narrative possibilities'.[75] Engaging with hybrid genres of discovery, and tropes of lost worlds and end times, Zalasiewicz describes the future 'geologists' as 'storytellers'. It is the slippage between the business of collecting empirical evidence and that of conveying the imaginary that is of interest. This device is reminiscent of both Voltaire's *Micromégas*, and Lyell's thought experiment in *Principles of Geology*. In Zalasiewicz's story, alien scientist-explorers visit the Earth 'one hundred million years from now'. This is a time span that, looking backwards, is roughly equivalent to the one that separates humans from the 'heyday of the dinosaurs'. Looking forwards, 'Geologically, it is the near future. Cosmologically, we are almost there.'[76] Zalasiewicz's explorers probe the fossilised remnants of cities and settlements found in what he calls the 'Human Event Stratum', revealing:

> ... compressed outlines of concrete buildings, some still cemented hard, some now decalcified and crumbly; of softened brick structures; of irregular patches of iron oxides and sulphides representing former iron artefacts from automobiles to AK-47s; of darkened and opaque remnants of plastics; of white, devitrified fragments of glass jars and bottles; of carbonised structures of shaped wood; of outlines of tunnels and pipes and road foundations; of giant middens of rubble and waste.[77]

The collapsing of human, post-human, imaginary and geological chronologies in the Anthropocene thought experiment is complicated and contradictory. What makes it all the more perplexing is that stratigraphers are attempting to simultaneously observe and anticipate fossil traces and their anthropogenic causes in the geological record, for Anthropocene rock to be admissible as primary evidence of human geomorphic agency. The identification of human influence and domination of Earth processes requires humans to recognise in advance forces of a magnitude and timescale that are difficult to comprehend, let alone control.[78] As Zalasiewicz's account augurs,

> technological and natural processes have already become so inextricably interlinked that our actions now will literally be raising mountain belts higher, or lowering them, or setting off volcanoes (or stifling them), or triggering new biological diversity (or suppressing it) for many million years to come.[79]

The chemical pollutants and radioactive waste that humans have accumulated over the past 200 years and buried deep in the ground will also leave a geological signal that stretches into the distant future. Geologists – adhering to what Bronislaw Szerszynski calls 'geology's semiotic character' – talk about the Anthropocene in terms of signals laid down for future geologists.[80] Their temporal dilemma has a striking precedent. In 1991 a group of interdisciplinary experts in the US took part in an elaborate thought experiment about the future warnings of nuclear waste, condensed into a report titled 'Ten Thousand Years of Solitude'.[81] They were tasked with devising messages to future beings to prevent them from intruding on a subterranean storage facility for radioactive waste, the Waste Isolation Pilot Plant (WIPP), proposed for construction in the New Mexico desert. The half-life of plutonium-239 is around 24,100 years, while the written history of humanity is about 5,000 years old. The challenge was to devise a system of signs that could survive catastrophic phases of an unknown planetary future and communicate danger to unknown future readers of the signs. The concern was that the stored waste could be discovered by accident in a remote future. In 2010, the documentary film *Into Eternity* about Onkalo, the world's first nuclear waste repository for the final disposal of spent nuclear fuel, built deep in the bedrock in Finland, drew on the WIPP report for its narrative.[82] It recognised the impossibility of leaving legible warning signs to a post-human world. Given human-scale temporal elasticities and limits of signification, how can we know what all this Earth-changing and ground-making means for a future that is not ours?

Anticipatory geology deploys an inverted forensic imaginary. In the context of humanitarian crises, the architect Eyal Weizman has shown how forensics requires both fieldwork – the scientific tools of investigation – and a forum – the persuasive presentation of an argument.[83] But in the Anthropocene, the forensic imaginary precedes the evidence. Researchers in the geological sciences are urged to review evidence of the human-made catastrophe of the Anthropocene *as if* at the scene of a future crime. Instead of engaging in their usual practice of recording and interpreting the accumulated layers and rocks of a past world they are being asked to speak for rocks that have not yet fully materialised. The testimony and evidence of the Anthropocene is involved in geological processes that will take thousands if not millions of years. Stratigraphy is a science and practice that, like forensics, usually follows the evidence, but it is now immersed in the speculative world of conjectures, in 'pre-crime' and the rhetorical upside-down world of the thought experiment.

Humans have never witnessed a new geological era, let alone *been* the geophysical force that, like asteroid impacts and volcano eruptions, might extinguish or redirect planetary life. With the customary hubris of the narcissistic naming and re-naming of Earth strata after humans, the Earth-rock ironically meets its maker. The presumption that everything can be configured around human time, human witnessing and human prognostics has also laid the groundwork for writing the human species out of the picture. The Anthropocene reminds us of previous extinctions by naming our own, confronting us with the image of human as fossil. It also occludes – leaving much out of the story. The Anthropocene nevertheless invites an extension of the fossil spectrum to take in the arche-fossil and the technofossil. The philosopher Quentin Meillassoux's concept of the 'arche-fossil' reveals 'not just materials indicating the traces of past life... but materials indicating the existence of an ancestral reality or event'.[84] The ancestral trace travels to a past where both humanity and life are absent. It can also travel to a future. The arche-fossil pertains to contingency and possibility, and 'every discourse whose meaning includes a temporal discrepancy between thinking and being'.[85] Anthropocene rock folds in temporal co-existence and non-existence in its intertwined strata. The dominant narratives of the Anthropocene deal with the more predictable and readable geological impacts. Yet at the same time epochal imaginings have invited humans to begin to sense a world without humans. As the cultural theorist Claire Colebrook reminds us,

> We imagine a viewing or reading in the absence of viewers or readers, and we do this through images in the present that extinguish the dominance of the present. The figure of a frozen Sydney opera house, a London where Trafalgar Square is desolate, layers of rock distorted through a camera lens that is not the point of view of any body, an underwater Manhattan, or a sunlight so bright it would destroy the eye – all these experiments strive to image a world *as image* (as referential) but not referential *for* any body. These images cannot be sustained, and are unsustainable; they – like the thought of extinction itself – will always be *for us*, and are always co-opted by the narrative lures they fragment. They nevertheless indicate an era or epoch that has begun to sense, if not have a sense of, a world without bodies.[86]

Figure 1.2 Construction of the Metropolitan Railway, the world's first underground railway. Illustration shows the trench and partially completed cut-and-cover tunnel close to King's Cross Station, London. The railway opened in 1863. (Photographed by Topical Press, January 1862 – December 1862; 2 February 1861. *The Illustrated London News*, page 99; author: Percy William Justyne)

Source: London Transport Museum collection

Urban stratum

In chronostratigraphy – the science of dating rock strata – cities find themselves in the 'novelty' category of geological phenomena and strata in the making.[87] The built environment comprises an amalgam of modified, fragmented and morphed geological materials such as sand, gravel, limestone, mudstone, oil shale, coal and mineral spoil, together with novel composite materials as well as plastics, metal alloys, and glass. Cities and towns tend to rest on the compacted materials of earlier settlements and their anthropogenic deposits, along with the substantial subsurface constructions of foundations, pilings and pipelines in a layer several metres thick. The British Geological Survey maps represent these collectively as 'artificial deposits' – a novel 'made ground' that complements the 'worked ground' of pits and quarries.[88] Artificial or 'made ground' constructed from accumulated societal spoils, discards, and rubbish tends to be unstable. If cities are made of and on geology, in the Anthropocene condition they also make geology. The impacts of global urbanisation and urban processes can be measured in energy-intensive technological systems, extraction of resources, deposition of waste, conversion of land use, damming of rivers, consumption of fossil fuels with attendant carbon emissions, ocean acidification, and biodiversity loss. These impacts are significant drivers of what is identified as the unfolding Anthropocene, or even the 'urbanthropocene', and their traces will linger long into future epochs. Jan Zalasiewicz has argued that, even in a hundred million years, records of human existence will remain on Earth in a layer he calls the 'urban stratum'. Sustained contemplation of the urban stratum, one thin leaf between numberless geological pasts and futures, unsettles the usual privileges afforded to human artefacts for inscription within the archive of deep time.

The accelerated growth of cities is perhaps the most characteristic geophysical feature of the so-called Anthropocene in the making, and yet in some ways it is the most transient. The surface constructions and infrastructure of cities, including road and electricity networks, may be the most visible sign of human influence on Earth from space, but they are also the most susceptible to forces of erosion.[89] The remnants of cities found in the urban stratum will likely be the trace fossils made up of the subways, sewers, conduits and infrastructures presently below ground – preserved in the rock record like a giant footprint or burrow. The generation of resources on a massive scale, necessary to sustain the clustered human life of cities, will also likely leave its trace in Anthropocene strata. The global perturbation of the nitrogen cycle caused by broadacre cropping will be hard to detect, but the scale of 21st-century industrial agriculture will remain in the fossilised evidence of monocultures, which will contrast starkly with the varied pollen record of complex ecosystems such as rainforests. Plant and animal species shifting their ranges as a result of urbanisation and climate transition may also leave a significant trace; as might the new cocktail of organisms in the seas – the result of the use of ballast water in the global shipping trade. The increased acidity of the oceans and resultant coral bleaching might register in the future as reef gaps. The rise of plastics – seemingly indispensable to city life – could be another key geological indicator for the Anthropocene. In 2015, the cumulative amount of plastics produced was of the order of 5 billion tons – 'enough to wrap the Earth in a layer of cling film', with the amount projected by 2050 being 'enough to wrap six layers of cling film around the planet'.[90] Or to put it another way, by 2050 there may be more plastic than fish in the ocean, by weight.[91] The widespread distribution of plastics in terrestrial and marine realms as artefacts, fragments and microplastics, and their preservation potential in sedimentary deposits, make for a distinctive stratal component of Anthropocene rock.

Although the start date of the Anthropocene is open to debate, the most profound alterations to geologically significant systems and processes have certainly occurred since the Industrial Revolution, and intensified with the nuclear age. Anticipating traces of nuclear tests or invasive species, many stratigraphers think there is compelling evidence for an epoch-making time-rock boundary. The last mass extinction event 65 million years ago that marks a major boundary in geological time, the K-T or Cretaceous-Tertiary boundary, as well as the end of the Mesozoic era, was identified by reef gaps, the end of the dinosaurs, plesiosaurs, pterosaurs and ammonites. It was also marked by a 'golden spike' or 'indelible extraterrestrial signature'[92] of iridium-rich dust from an asteroid impact, which spread all over the globe. The current widespread impact of human fossil-fuelled activities, coinciding with fundamental changes in Earth systems, has put many species on an extinction trajectory and is thus expected to leave as significant a trace in the rocks. As the palaeontologist Anthony Barnosky has stated, 'we are the asteroid'.[93]

What will remain of this planet of cities? What might be considered the most permanent and stable constructions and achievements of human societies will probably be the most transient. Zalasiewicz's view, Elizabeth Kolbert reports, is that, 'the sculptures and the libraries, the monuments and the museums, the cities and the factories – will be compressed into a layer of sediment not much thicker than a cigarette paper'.[94] Cities have a good chance of leaving a recognisable trace of species activity in the rocks, but only if they are destroyed quickly. If left to the gradual forces of erosion, cities and settlements will turn to sand, leaving insignificant mineral remains. However, if sea level rises are rapid, as anticipated with the destruction of the West Antarctic ice sheet, coastal cities could quickly sink beneath ocean waters. Our drowned cities,' Zalasiewicz writes, '…would begin to be covered by sand, silt, and mud, and take the first steps towards becoming geology. The process of fossilisation will begin.'[95] Coastal cities such as Venice, Amsterdam, Shanghai, New Orleans and Lagos, sited on land vulnerable to sudden sea level rise and prone to processes of sedimentation rather than erosion, thus have a good chance of fossilisation.

Megacities are the giant technofossil assemblages of the future. They have their FAD, or 'first occurrence datum' in geological terminology, in 19th-century London – the first city of one million inhabitants. Megacities have now developed in Europe (Moscow, London, Paris), Asia (Shanghai, Beijing, Tokyo, Seoul, Mumbai), Africa (Cairo, Lagos) and the Americas (Mexico City, New York City, Sao Paulo), totalling 27 metropolitan centres, each housing over 10 million inhabitants.[96] The building and maintenance of megacities (and the provisioning of their human inhabitants) has been responsible, directly or indirectly, for many of the other changes associated with the Anthropocene, such as greatly increased CO_2 emissions, changed patterns of erosion and sedimentation, and biodiversity loss. Their spread has been effectively instantaneous from a geological perspective, and the accelerating growth of megacities in the latter part of the 20th century has occurred mainly on subsiding coastal plains and river deltas, which also means that their preservation potential as fossils is high. In terms of both present lived experience and future fossil traces, then, the megacity is the site par excellence of the 'Great Acceleration' that has characterised the post-industrial period. London has especial geological significance as a possible location for a 'golden spike' (GSSP) in a stratum that will be recognisable across the globe as marking the base of the Anthropocene. The London Underground has been proposed as a useful datum for 'defining the origins of this behavioural and community complexity', since metro systems are 'a particular style of human trace fossil associated with the mass movement of people (and ideas)'.[97] The division between Proterozoic and Phanerozoic eons is marked by the burrows of a wormlike creature and the emergence of newly complex animal behaviour. In similar vein, the Anthropocene could be marked by the human burrowing evident in mega-urban habitats.[98] The golden spike could be instated, for example, at Baker Street, Euston Square or Farringdon, the original stations of the Metropolitan Line – the world's oldest underground or metro line, constructed between 1861 and 1863. Potential stratigraphic markers in the 20th century are derived from the accelerated global industries, technologies and urbanisations that have affected people all over the world. These include alterations in sediment dynamics from dam-building, the intensification of mining activities and resource extraction, and especially radionuclide fallout from nuclear tests. Such markers are tied not only to the 'Great Acceleration' but also to the overwhelming destruction of cities. An even more compelling and more dangerous marker for the base of the Anthropocene may, however, lie unforeseen in the future.

The Anthropocene is catastrophic in its relationship to the past and the future. The fossil fuel technologies of industrial capitalism that construct and expand our urban centres are founded on the catastrophic events of a deep past. Extractive technologies release the residues of previous extinction events – oil, gas, coal – these are 'stores of energy that have accumulated over millions of years'.[99] Their burning contributes to the present catastrophic period. The geographer Gavin Bridge calls them 'geological subsidies to the present day'. He quotes from Italo Calvino's short story, 'The Petrol Pump', where the 'rotating drill pushes in an instant from one millennium to the next as it cuts through the sedimentary rocks of the Pliocene, the Cretaceous, the Triassic'. The extraction of fossil energies 'compresses time', it is 'a transfer of geological space and time that has underpinned the compression of time and space in modernity'. But extractive technologies are not just portals to thinking in deep time but to acknowledging the present-day spaces of habitation and inequality – whether in urban centres or remote mining outposts – that go with the expansionary dynamics of capitalist industries and the 'insatiable drive toward the end of the Earth that has seen the extractive frontier constantly redefined'.[100]

The naming of the urban stratum serves as a warning. It draws attention to the catastrophic temporalities of our economies of consumption and extraction – accelerating emissions, fossil energies that cannot be replaced and toxic wastes that need to be quarantined for thousands if not millions of years. It challenges us to rethink the urban in terms of the inevitability of epoch-making ruptures and disruptions. Predicting the future fossil traces that our own radically unstable moment might leave behind invites us to imagine the unimaginable: the end of the human species. In so doing we necessarily focus on urban centres, for the devastation to the human species wrought by this anthropogenic planetary change is likely to be catalysed by and concentrated in, cities. The stratigraphic version of the Anthropocene anticipates the end of cities and societies and the inscription of their demise in a fossil record that may one day be read by someone, but not by us. It is dominated by imaginaries of drowned, deserted, sedimented and ultimately fossilised human settlements – wafer-thin layers in the ground of a post-human future.

But if the story of the future of cities finds its apogee in stratification, it simultaneously draws attention to the fragility, impermanence and unruliness of urban life. Human societies inhabit seemingly irreconcilable temporalities. The plethora of possible fossil traces of an urban stratum will not offer an account of living in the Anthropocene. They will reveal the present crisis in its deep time context; the human-sized lives we now live will not be legible. Much of what we presently hold dear seems puny in the face of such planetary crisis. And if we are to take effective evasive action, it will necessarily involve cooperation, and shifts in priorities, on scales that are hard to imagine. Defensive modes of urban planning that aim at shifting risk conditions cannot stop the future happening. Future-oriented discussions around the Anthropocene have tended to focus on the residues and debris that human impacts will leave behind in the strata, and not with the question of how our species may actually survive and cope with the next round of upheavals on this volatile Earth. The threshold of the Anthropocene warns repeatedly of the need to contend with the intensities, inconsistencies and potentialities of a dynamic Earth that is marked by impermanence and change.

Figure 1.3 Cut-and-cover construction at Praed Street, Paddington, London, during the building of the Metropolitan Railway's Kensington extension. A steam crane or 'steam navvy', with vertical boiler, complex gearing and crude shelter, stands midground left. The workmen seem to have stopped work to pose for the camera (unknown photographer, circa 1866)

Source: London Transport Museum collection

Figure 1.4 Building the District Railway in front of Somerset House, London, in 1869. Construction of a cut-and-cover cutting; most of the workmen are staring at the photographer. Victoria Embankment was opened on 13 July 1870; the railway from Westminster to Blackfriars on 30 May 1870 (unknown photographer, 1869)
Source: London Transport Museum collection

The story in the rocks

> The people of Israel chant psalms before the dismantled Wailing Wall: of the temple, not one stone remains standing on another. What did the wise Thaleäes see, do, and think, by the Egyptian pyramids, in a time as remote for us as the time of Cheops was for him? Why did he invent geometry by this pile of stones? All Islam dreams of travelling to Mecca where, in the Kaaba, the Black Stone is preserved. Modern science was born, in the Renaissance, from the study of falling bodies: stones fall to the ground. Why did Jesus establish the Christian Church on a man called Peter? I am deliberately mixing religion with science in these examples of inauguration.[101]

In Michel Serres' *Statues*, significant human history is presented as an archaeology of stones. Serres' series of petrifications not only offers the lithic as the foundation of inaugural stories but asks why these 'silent things' – rocks and stones – have not been interrogated for their part in the story. In his retelling of the 'Myth of Sisyphus' in the same volume, Serres wryly observes that despite the 'perpetual fall of the rock

... no one ever speaks of it'. Everyone is concerned with Sisyphus's labour to the point of condemning it as an absurd struggle, despite the fact that the myth points so explicitly to the endurance of the rock. Serres' reflection on things, or what he called 'pragmatogony', seeks to counter the usual inattentiveness to their mute presence – here, the stones and rocks. To be able to think with the rock – the province of geology – might reveal that rocks and humans are linked in a much more complex history.[102] Stories of rocks are inevitably about the human and the geologic bound together. Thus, in spite of its unfathomable temporality, the geologic posits an intimate spur to storying. The story in the rocks, however, is a cautionary one.

The Anthropocene names a threshold or unconformity in deep time that announces the impossibility of distinguishing life from non-life, biological from geological, humans from rock. At the same time it announces a crisis of the *anthropos*. With its challenge to think with the rocks, the Anthropocene has ushered in a speculative geology and geophysics and a convergence of diverse fields of enquiry.[103] While the speculative dimension of geology privileges certain technologies of inscription and anticipation, it also simultaneously unsettles them. As Serres might ask, what would the rocks say?

The Anthropocene thesis continually undermines itself. It needs a rupture marker or boundary scar (of cataclysmic proportions) with the Holocene to assert its existence: an existence that corresponds also to the potential non-existence of humankind in the future. Humanity's advance into the Anthropocene epoch thus puts it in a paradoxical situation, since almost all of its political and ethical systems and representational constructions have been developed to deal solely with the here and now. The Anthropocene announces the geological agency of humans and at the same time heralds the demise of an epoch – the Holocene – of relative climate stability, which allowed contemporary social formations and institutions to be constructed. If the world *as we know it* has ended, how can we even begin to think about how we might respond and be responsible in a future world? How is it possible to give an account of *the future* if it depends on descriptions of a past that has not yet occurred? What does it mean to have developed institutions, materials, industries, technologies and activities that, even once we are gone, have consequences that promise to be highly disruptive for a future far longer than all of human history? The Earth system is charting a new course never experienced before – and certainly not by humans. Nigel Clark argues that this requires a novel negotiation with strata:

> The question that arises from trying to think the social and the political *stratigraphically*, then, is not so much whether we – or at least the most heavy-handed of us – ought to abstain from geological agency. It is how we, collectively and heterogeneously, might negotiate more carefully, more judiciously, more generatively with strata.[104]

The Anthropocene tells us that we dwell in catastrophe and on made ground that is unstable. The Anthropocene construction site presents an aporetic world of our constant dismantling, making, and remaking. Human perceptions of time are challenged, traditions are called into question, and the unsynchronised simultaneities of planetary and human forces unfold side by side. Entering the Anthropocene, we find ourselves in a site that is both out of time and out of place, untimely and displaced. It is a place where current practices of inhabitation must be considered not as sedimented but instead as unconformities with challenging consequences for and beyond ourselves. Facing up to the difficulties and paradoxes of the incipient Anthropocene might propel us to think beyond disciplinary limits. The present moment – of being in between epochs – requires a new responsiveness: to immiscible chronologies; to a complex folded dynamic terrain; to the irreversibility of Earth processes at least partly of our own making. The Anthropocene unsettlement suggests that adjustments in our thinking and our institutions are required. This is not a question of how to engage authoritatively with a world that we have already made, but how to take part with a good deal more humility or 'groundedness' in the process of remaking the world we are living in now. The Anthropocene in its unconformities may unsettle us for a little while yet.

Watch your step.

Notes

1 Paul J. Crutzen and Will Steffen, 'How long have we been in the Anthropocene era? An editorial comment' *Climatic Change* 61 (2003): 251–257; 253. See also Will Steffen *et al.*, *Global Change and The Earth System A Planet Under Pressure*, The IGPB Series (Berlin, Heidelberg, New York: Springer, 2004): 262.
2 Jeffrey Jerome Cohen, *Stone: An Ecology of the Inhuman* (Minneapolis and London: University of Minnesota Press, 2015): 27.
3 Jan Zalasiewicz, Mark Williams, A. Smith, T. L. Barry, A. L. Coe, P. R. Bown, P. Brenchley, *et al.* 'Are we now living in the Anthropocene?' *GSA Today* 18.2 (2008): 4–8. This paper by 21 members of the Geological Society of London was followed by two collections of essays: Jan Zalasiewicz, Mark Williams, Alan Haywood and Michael Ellis. 'The Anthropocene: A New Epoch of Geological Time?', *Philosophical Transactions of the Royal Society A: Mathematical, Physical and Engineering Sciences* 369.1938 (13 March 2011): 835–41; and C.N. Waters, J.A. Zalasiewicz, M. Williams, M.A. Ellis and A.M. Snelling, *A Stratigraphical Basis for the Anthropocene*, Special Publications, 395 (London: Geological Society, 2014).
4 Subcommission on Quaternary Stratigraphy, Anthropocene Working Group; quaternary.stratigraphy.org/workinggroups/anthropocene/
5 Jan Zalasiewicz, Mark Williams, A. Smith, T. L. Barry, A. L. Coe, P. R. Bown, P. Brenchley, *et al.* 'Are we now living in the Anthropocene?', *GSA Today* 18.2 (2008): 4–8.
6 Colin N. Waters *et al.* 'The Anthropocene is functionally and stratigraphically distinct from the Holocene', *Science* 351 (8 Jan 2016): 6269.
7 Clive Hamilton, 'The Anthropocene as rupture', *The Anthropocene Review* 3. 2 (2016): 93–106.
8 J. R. McNeill and Peter Engelke, *The Great Acceleration: An Environmental History of the Anthropocene since 1945* (Cambridge, Mass.: Harvard University Press, 2016).
9 Anthony D. Barnosky *et al.*, 'Has the Earth's sixth mass extinction already arrived?', *Nature* 471 (2011): 51–57.
10 P.J. Crutzen and E.F Stoermer, 'The "Anthropocene"', *IGBP [International Geosphere-Biosphere Programme] Newsletter* 41 (2000): 17–18.
11 J. Zalasiewicz *et al.*, 'Stratigraphy of the Anthropocene', *Philosophical Transactions of the Royal Society A* 369 (2011): 1036–1055; 1037.
12 Antonio Stoppani, 'First period of the Anthropozoic era', an excerpt from Corso di Geologia (1873), trans. Valeria Federighi; Etienne Turpin and Valeria Federighi (eds.). See also 'A new element, a new force, a new input: Antonio Stoppani's Anthropozoic', in *Making the Geologic Now: Responses to Material Conditions of Everyday Life*, eds. Elizabeth Ellsworth and Jamie Kruse (New York: Punctum Books, 2013): 34–41; 36.
13 V. Vernadsky, 'The biosphere and the noosphere', *American Scientist* 33 (1945): 1–12. See also Will Steffen *et al.*, (2011), 'The Anthropocene: conceptual and historical perspectives', *Philosophical Transactions of the Royal Society A*, 369 (2011): 842–867; 842.
14 Andy Revkin, *Global Warming: Understanding the Forecast* (Abbeville Press, 1992).

15 Clive Hamilton, 'The Anthropocene as rupture', *The Anthropocene Review* 3.2 (2016): 93–106.
16 Clive Hamilton, 'The Anthropocene as rupture', *The Anthropocene Review* 3.2 (2016): 93–106.
17 Jan Zalasiewicz, *The Earth After Us: What Legacy will Humans Leave in the Rocks?* (Oxford: Oxford University Press, 2009): 102.
18 P.J. Crutzen and E.F. Stoermer, 'The "Anthropocene"', *IGBP [International Geosphere-Biosphere Programme] Newsletter* 41 (2000): 17–18. See also P. Crutzen, 'Geology of mankind', *Nature* 413 (2002): 23.
19 W. Steffen et al., 'Stratigraphic and Earth system approaches to defining the Anthropocene', *Earth's Future*, 4 (2016): 324–345.
20 Bruno Latour, 'Facing Gaia, six lectures on the political theology of nature', The Gifford Lectures on Natural Religion (Edinburgh, 2013). See also Bruno Latour, 'War and peace in an age of ecological conflicts' in *Revue Juridique de l'Environnement* 1 (2014): 51–63 (written originally as a lecture at the Peter Wall Institute for Advanced Studies, Vancouver, 23 September 2013).
21 Jill Bennett, Living in the Anthropocene: *100 Notes, 100 Thoughts: Documenta Series 53* (Hatje Cantz Verlag, 2012)
22 Jane Bennett, 'Afterword: Earthling, now and forever?' in *Making the Geologic Now: Responses to Material Conditions of Contemporary Life*, eds. Elizabeth Ellsworth and Jamie Kruse (Brooklyn, NY: Punctum Books, 2012): 244–246; 245.
23 C. Hamilton and J. Grinevald, 'Was the Anthropocene anticipated?', *The Anthropocene Review* 2.1 (2015): 59–72.
24 Clive Hamilton, 'The Anthropocene as rupture', *The Anthropocene Review* 3.2 (2016): 93–106.
25 Jan Zalasiewicz, *The Planet in a Pebble: A Journey into Earth's Deep History* (Oxford: Oxford University Press, 2010).
26 Jeffrey Jerome Cohen, *Stone: An Ecology of the Inhuman* (Minneapolis and London: University of Minnesota Press, 2015): 14.
27 Jeffrey Jerome Cohen, *Stone: An Ecology of the Inhuman* (Minneapolis and London: University of Minnesota Press, 2015): 6.
28 Bronislaw Szerszynski, 'The end of the end of nature; the Anthropocene and the fate of the human', *Oxford Literary Review* 34.2 (2012): 165–184.
29 Frederick M. Chester et al., 'Structure and composition of the late-boundary slip Zone for the 2011 Tohoku-Oki Earthquake', *Science*, 342.6163 (2013).
30 Hisashi Nirei et al., 'Classification of man-made strata for assessment of geopollution', *Episodes* 35.2 (2012): 333–336.
31 Hisashi Nirei et al., 'Classification of man-made strata for assessment of geopollution', *Episodes* 35.2 (2012): 333–336.
32 Matt Edgeworth, Dan deB Richter, Colin Waters, Peter Haff, Cath Neal and Simon James Price, 'Diachronous beginnings of the Anthropocene: The stratigraphic bounding surface between anthropogenic and non-anthropogenic deposits,' *The Anthropocene Review* 2.1 (2015): 33–58; 51.
33 Matt Edgeworth, Dan deB Richter, Colin Waters, Peter Haff, Cath Neal and Simon James Price, 'Diachronous beginnings of the Anthropocene: The stratigraphic bounding surface between anthropogenic and non-anthropogenic deposits,' *The Anthropocene Review* 2.1 (2015): 33–58; 51.
34 James Hutton, 'Theory of the Earth; or an investigation of the laws observable in the composition, dissolution and restoration of land upon the globe', *Transactions of the Royal Society of Edinburgh* 1 (1788): 96.
35 James Hutton, 'Theory of the Earth; or an investigation of the laws observable in the composition, dissolution, and restoration of land upon the globe', *Transactions of the Royal Society of Edinburgh* 1 (1788): 209–304.
36 John Playfair, 'Hutton's Unconformity'. *Transactions of the Royal Society of Edinburgh* V.III (1805).
37 Charles Lyell, *Principles of Geology, Being an Attempt to Explain the Former Changes of the Earth's Surface, by Reference to Causes Now in Operation*, I (London: John Murray, 1830): 190.

38 Timothy Morton, 'Ecology without the Present', *The Oxford Literary Review* 34.2 (2012): 229–238; 233.
39 Stephen Jay Gould, *Time's Arrow, Time's Cycle* (Cambridge, MA, 1987): 97.
40 Michel Serres, *Rome: The Book of Foundations* (1983), trans. Felicia Mc Carren (Stanford: Stanford University Press,1991): 81.
41 'Media note: Anthropocene Working Group (AWG)', press release, University of Leicester (August 2016); www2.le.ac.uk/offices/press/press-releases/2016/august/media-note-anthropocene-working-group-awg
42 35th International Geological Congress, Cape Town, South Africa (27 August – 4 September 2016); www.35igc.org
43 Charles Lyell, *Principles of Geology, Being an Attempt to Explain the Former Changes of the Earth's Surface, by Reference to Causes Now in Operation*, Volume I (London: John Murray, 1830): 160.
44 Mike Davis, 'Living on the ice shelf': humanity's meltdown', TomDispatch (26 June 2008); www.tomdispatch.com/post/174949
45 J. Zalasiewicz *et al.*, 'Stratigraphy of the Anthropocene', *Philosophical Transactions of the Royal Society A* 369 (2011): 1036–1055; doi:10.1098/rsta.2010.0315.
46 Colin N. Waters, Jan A. Zalasiewicz, Mark Williams, Michael A. Ellis and Andrea M. Snelling, 'A stratigraphical basis for the Anthropocene?' in *A Stratigraphical Basis for the Anthropocene*, eds. C.N. Waters, J.A. Zalasiewicz, M. Williams, M.A. Ellis and A.M. Snelling, Special Publications, 395 (London: Geological Society, 2014).
47 W. Steffen, P.J. Crutzen and J.R. McNeill, 'The Anthropocene: are humans now overwhelming the great forces of nature?' *Ambio* 36.8 (2007): 614–621.
48 Paul Crutzen and Will Steffen, 'How long have we been in the Anthropocene era?', *Climatic Change* 61.3 (2003): 251–257.
49 Stephen F. Foley *et al*, 'The Palaeoanthropocene – the beginnings of anthropogenic environmental change', *Anthropocene* 3 (2013): 83–88.
50 W. F. Ruddiman, 'The Anthropogenic greenhouse era began thousands of years ago', *Climatic Change* 61 (2003): 261–293. See also W. Ruddiman, M.C. Crucifix and F. Oldfield, 'The early-Anthropocene hypothesis', *The Holocene* 21.5 (2011): 713–879; and W. Ruddiman, 'The Anthropocene', *Annual Review of Earth & Planetary Science* 41 (2013): 45–68.
51 Simon L. Lewis and Mark A. Maslin, 'Defining the Anthropocene', *Nature* 519 (12 March 2015): 171–180.
52 J. Zalasiewicz *et al*, 'Colonization of the Americas, "Little Ice Age" climate, and bomb-produced carbon: Their role in defining the Anthropocene', *The Anthropocene Review* 2.2 (2015): 117–127.
53 Clive Hamilton, 'The Anthropocene as rupture', *The Anthropocene Review* 3.2 (2015): 93–106.
54 Jan Zalasiewicz *et al.*, 'When did the Anthropocene begin?' A mid-twentieth century boundary level is stratigraphically optimal', *Quaternary International* 383 (2015): 196–203.
55 Colin N. Waters, Jan A. Zalasiewicz, Mark Williams, Michael A. Ellis and Andrea M. Snelling, 'A stratigraphical basis for the Anthropocene?' in *A Stratigraphical Basis for the Anthropocene*, eds. C.N. Waters, J.A. Zalasiewicz, M. Williams, M.A. Ellis and A.M. Snelling, Special Publications, 395 (London: Geological Society, 2014). See also J. Zalasiewicz, M. Williams and C.N. Waters, 'Can an Anthropocene series be defined and recognized?', in *A Stratigraphical Basis for the Anthropocene*, eds. C.N. Waters, J.A. Zalasiewicz, M. Williams, M.A. Ellis and A.M. Snelling, Special Publications, 395 (London: Geological Society, 2014).
56 Paul Crutzen and Will Steffen, 'How long have we been in the Anthropocene era?', *Climatic Change* 61.3 (2003): 251–257.
57 Christophe Bonneuil and Jean-Baptiste Fressoz, *The Shock of the Anthropocene*, trans. David Fernbach, (London: Verso, 2016): 17.
58 Matt Edgeworth, Dan deB Richter, Colin Waters, Peter Haff, Cath Neal and Simon James Price, 'Diachronous beginnings of the Anthropocene: The stratigraphic bounding surface between anthropogenic and non-anthropogenic deposits', *The Anthropocene Review* 2.1 (2015): 33–58; 51.
59 Andy Revkin, 'An Anthropocene journey', *Anthropocene* (October 2016); www.anthropocenemagazine.org/anthropocenejourney/. See also Jay Quade, Jordan Abell, Mary

Stiner, William McIntosh and Sileshi Semaw, 'The earliest Anthropocene and the "Age of Garbage"', abstract, 24th Biennial Meeting of the American Quaternary Association; biology.unm.edu/fasmith/2016AMQUA/amquafiles/AMQUA_2016_Abstracts.pdf
60 Jan Zalasiewicz, response to Adrian J. Ivakhiv's 'Against the Anthropocene' blog post (7 July 2014); blog.ubv.edu. See also Christophe Bonneuil and Jean-Baptiste Fressoz, *The Shock of the Anthropocene*, trans. David Fernbach, (London: Verso, 2016): 14.
61 Paul Crutzen and Will Steffen, 'How long have we been in the Anthropocene era?' *Climatic Change* 61 (2003): 251–257; 253.
62 M. Williams and J. Zalasiewicz, 'Enter the Anthropocene: an epoch of geological time characterised by humans', *Open University Geological Society Journal*, 30 (2010): 31–34.
63 Dipesh Chakrabarty, 'The Climate history: four theses', *Critical Inquiry* (Winter 2009): 197–222. French translation: 'Le climat de l'histoire: quatre the ses', La Revue Internationale 5 (Paris: January-February 2010): 22–31. Also carried in *Eurozine* (30 October 2009).
64 Christophe Bonneuil and Jean-Baptiste Fressoz, *The Shock of the Anthropocene*, trans. David Fernbach (London: Verso, 2016): 78.
65 Isabelle Stengers, *In Catastrophic Times: Resisting the Coming Barbarism*, trans. Andre Goffey (Open Humanities Press, 2015): 17.
66 Isabelle Stengers, 'History through the middle: between macro and mesopolitics – an interview with Isabelle Stengers, 25 November 2008', with Brian Massumi and Erin Manning, INFLeXions 3 – Micropolitics: Exploring Ethico-Aesthetics (October 2009); www.inflexions.org/n3_stengershtml.html; accessed 1 September 2013.
67 Isabelle Stengers, *In Catastrophic Times: Resisting the Coming Barbarism*, trans. Andre Goffey (Open Humanities Press, 2015).
68 Isabelle Stengers, *The Invention of Modern Science* (University of Minnesota Press, 2000): 144.
69 Clive Hamilton, 'The Anthropocene as rupture', *The Anthropocene Review* 3.2 (2016): 93–106.
70 Antonio Stoppani, an excerpt from Corso di Geologia (1873), eds. Etienne Turpin and Valeria Federighi, 'A new element, a new force, a new input: Antonio Stoppani's Anthropozoic,' in *Making the Geologic Now: Responses to Material Conditions of Everyday Life*, eds. Elizabeth Ellsworth and Jamie Kruse, (New York: Punctum Books, 2013): 40.
71 Charles Lyell, *Principles of Geology, Being an Attempt to Explain the Former Changes of the Earth's Surface, by Reference to Causes Now in Operation* I (London: John Murray, 1830): 163–164.
72 Charles Lyell, *Principles of Geology, Being an Attempt to Explain the Former Changes of the Earth's Surface, by Reference to Causes Now in Operation* I (London: John Murray, 1830): 164.
73 Will Steffen, 'Commentary: Paul J. Crutzen and Eugene F. Stoermer, '"The Anthropocene" (2000)' in *The Future of Nature*, eds. Libby Robin, Sverker Sörlin, Paul Warde (New Haven and London: Yale University Press, 2013): 486–490; 488–489.
74 Jan Zalasiewicz, 'Buried treasure', *New Scientist* 158.2140 (27 June 1998). See also Jan Zalasiewicz, *The Earth After Us: What Legacy will Humans Leave in the Rocks?* (Oxford: Oxford University Press, 2008).
75 Jan Zalasiewicz, *The Earth After Us: What Legacy will Humans Leave in the Rocks?* (Oxford: Oxford University Press, 2008): 17–18.
76 Jan Zalasiewicz, *The Earth After Us: What Legacy will Humans Leave in the Rocks?* (Oxford: Oxford University Press, 2008): 7.
77 Jan Zalasiewicz, *The Earth After Us: What Legacy will Humans Leave in the Rocks?* (Oxford: Oxford University Press, 2008): 189.
78 Mark Williams, Jan Zalasiewicz, Alan Haywood and Mike Ellis (eds.), theme issue 'The Anthropocene: a new epoch of geological time?', *Philosophical Transactions of the Royal Society A* 369.1938 (2011): 833–1112; rsta.royalsocietypublishing.org/content/369/1938.
79 Jan Zalasiewicz, *The Earth After Us: What Legacy will Humans Leave in the Rocks?* (Oxford: Oxford University Press, 2008): 240. See also Jan Zalasiewicz, Mark Williams, Alan Haywood and Mike Ellis, 'Introduction: The Anthropocene: a new epoch of geological time?', *Philosophical Transactions of the Royal Society A* 369.1938 (2011): 835–841.

80 Bronislaw Szerszynski, 'The end of the end of nature; the Anthropocene and the fate of the human', *Oxford Literary Review* 34.2 (2012): 165–184; 169.
81 Gregory Benford, Craig W. Kirkwood, Harry Otway and Martin J. Pasquatelli, *Ten Thousand Years of Solitude? On Inadvertent Intrusion into the Waste Isolation Pilot Project Repository*, Los Alamos National Laboratory, New Mexico (1990); www.wipp.energy.gov/PICsProg/PICs_tech_concept.htm. See also Peter C.Van Wyck, *Signs of Danger: Waste Trauma and Nuclear Threat*, (University of Minnesota Press, 2005).
82 Michael Madsen, dir., *Into Eternity* (2010) follows the construction of the Onkalo waste repository at the Olkiluoto Nuclear Power Plant on the island of Olkiluoto, Finland.
83 Eyal Weizman, 'Forensic architecture: notes from fields and forums', '100 Notes – 100 Thoughts' *dOCUMENTA* 13.62.
84 Quentin Meillassoux, *After Finitude: An Essay on the Necessity of Contingency* (Bloomsbury London: Continuum, 2008): 22.
85 Quentin Meillassoux, *After Finitude: An Essay on the Necessity of Contingency* (Bloomsbury London: Continuum, 2008): 112.
86 Claire Colebrook, *Death of the PostHuman, Essays on Extinction* 1 (Ann Arbor: Open Humanities Press with Michigan Publishing – University of Michigan Library, 2014): 28.
87 J. Zalasiewicz *et al.*, 'Stratigraphy of the Anthropocene', *Philosophical Transactions of the Royal Society A* 369 (2011): 1036–1055; doi:10.1098/rsta.2010.0315.
88 S. J. Price, J.R. Ford, A. H. Cooper and C. Neal, 'Humans as major geological and geomorphological agents in the Anthropocene: the significance of artificial ground in Great Britain', *Philosophical Transactions of the Royal Society A* 369 (2011): 1056–1084; doi:10.1098/rsta.2010.0296.
89 Elizabeth Kolbert, 'Enter the Anthropocene – age of man', *National Geographic Magazine* (March 2011).
90 Jan Zalasiewicz *et al.*, 'The geological cycle of plastics and their use as a stratigraphic indicator of the Anthropocene', *Anthropocene* 13 (2016): 4–17; 5.
91 'The new plastics economy: rethinking the future of plastics', World Economic Forum report (January 2016): 14.
92 Mike Davis, 'Cosmic dancers on history's stage? The permanent revolution in the Earth sciences', *New Left Review* 217 (1996): 48–84; 55.
93 Anthony Barnosky quoted in Andrew Luck-Baker, 'Leaving our mark: what will be left of our cities?' BBC News Science and Environment (1 November 2012); www.bbc.co.uk/news/science-environment-20154030. See also Anthony D. Barnosky *et al.*, 'Has the Earth's sixth mass extinction already arrived?', *Nature* 471 (3 March 2011): 51–57.
94 Jan Zalasiewicz as paraphrased in Elizabeth Kolbert, *The Sixth Extinction: An Unnatural History* (London: Bloomsbury Publishing, 2014): 105.
95 Jan Zalasiewicz, *The Earth After Us: What Legacy will Humans Leave in the Rocks?* (Oxford: Oxford University Press, 2008): 84–85.
96 M. Williams, J.A. Zalasiewicz, C.N. Waters and E. Landing, 'Is the fossil record of complex animal behaviour a stratigraphical analogue for the Anthropocene?' in *A Stratigraphical Basis for the Anthropocene*, eds. C.N. Waters, J.A. Zalasiewicz, M. Williams, M.A. Ellis and A.M. Snelling, Geological Society, London, Special Publications, 395 (2014): 143–148; 147.
97 M. Williams, J.A. Zalasiewicz, C.N. Waters and E. Landing, 'Is the fossil record of complex animal behaviour a stratigraphical analogue for the Anthropocene?' in *A Stratigraphical Basis for the Anthropocene*, eds. C.N. Waters, J.A. Zalasiewicz, M. Williams, M.A. Ellis and A.M. Snelling, Geological Society, London, Special Publications, 395 (2014): 143–148; 146.
98 M. Williams, J.A. Zalasiewicz, C.N. Waters and E. Landing, 'Is the fossil record of complex animal behaviour a stratigraphical analogue for the Anthropocene?' in *A Stratigraphical Basis for the Anthropocene*, eds. C.N. Waters, J.A. Zalasiewicz, M. Williams, M.A. Ellis and A.M. Snelling, Geological Society, London, Special Publications, 395 (2014): 143–148; 146.
99 Gavin Bridge, 'The Hole world: scales and spaces of extraction', *New Geographies 2: Landscapes of Energy* (Graduate School of Design, Harvard University, 2009): 43–48; 48.

100 Gavin Bridge, 'The Hole world: scales and spaces of extraction', *New Geographies 2: Landscapes of Energy* (Graduate School of Design, Harvard University, 2009): 43–48.
101 Michel Serres, *Statues: Le second livre des fondations* (Paris: Éditions François Bourin, 1987): 213. See also Bruno Latour, *We Have Never Been Modern*, trans. Catherine Porter (Cambridge MA: Harvard University Press, 1993): 82–83.
102 Émilie Hache and Bruno Latour, 'Morality of moralism?: An exercise in sensitization', trans Patrick Camilier, in *Common Knowledge* 16.2 (Spring 2010): 311–330.
103 Nigel Clark, 'Rock, life, fire: speculative geophysics and the Anthropocene', *Oxford Literary Review* 34.2 (December 2012).
104 Nigel Clark, 'Politics of strata', *Theory, Culture & Society* 34.2-3 (2017): 211-231.

2 Disaster zone

CAUTION: *falling objects*

On the morning of 1 November, All Saints' Day, 1755, at about 9:50 am, the world ended in Lisbon.[1] The city was rocked by three huge tremors that opened giant fissures in the ground, destroying countless buildings, including most of the churches, monasteries, convents, and the royal palace. The earthquake caught a large proportion of the populace worshipping in the churches, which collapsed onto congregations.[2] Day turned into the darkness of night as a cloud of suffocating dust rose from the ruins.[3] Fires swept through the city, ignited, according to some accounts, by toppling altar candles[4] and stoked by deserters, plunderers and soldiers.[5] The survivors struggled to reach the waterfront where they were met with the terrifying sight of a withdrawing sea exposing a world littered with the tangled debris of shipwrecks. The tsunamis that followed surged up the river Tagus and overwhelmed the city. Those lucky enough to be spared by the water likely perished in the fires, which raged in the city for over a week.[6] The combined destruction of the city by earthquake, water and fire offered, 'such a Spectacle of Terror and Amazement, as well as the Desolation to Beholders, as perhaps has not been equaled since the Foundation of the World!'[7] Many believed, as one eyewitness wrote in a letter from Lisbon, that the 'dissolution of the world was at hand.'[8] His testimony continues:

> … one was struck with horror in beholding dead bodies by six or seven in a heap, crush'd to death, half buried and half burnt; and if one went through the broad places or squares, nothing to be met with but people bewailing their misfortunes, wringing their hands, and crying the world is at an end.[9]

From its epicentre below the ocean off the coast of southern Portugal, the earthquake sent a series of tidal waves. Damage was caused throughout Portugal, southern Spain and North Africa. Devastation and extensive loss of life occurred along the coasts of the Iberian peninsula, western Morocco, and the Madeira and Azores islands. The earthquake was felt as far away as Great Britain, Holland and Germany. As Immanuel Kant wrote: 'History has no precedent for so widespread a disturbance of water and a large part of the Earth observed in the space of a few minutes.'[10] Cities far and wide felt the force of the tremors. Voltaire's 'Poem on the Lisbon Disaster, An inquiry into the Maxim: "Whatever is, is right"', drew attention to the widespread devastation and unwarranted human suffering caused by the earthquake:

> Women and children heaped up mountain high,
> Limbs crushed which under ponderous marble lie;
> Wretches unnumbered in the pangs of death,
> Who mangled, torn, and panting for their breath,
> Buried beneath their sinking roofs expire,
> And end their wretched lives in torments dire.[11]

We owe much of our current way of thinking about disasters – and about the Anthropocene as the quintessence of human disasters – to the story of the Lisbon quake. The destruction wrought by earthquake, tsunami and fires sent shock waves across Europe. Those who registered the shock in their writings included Voltaire, Rousseau, Kant, Goethe and Kleist. For the rest of the 18th century, mentions of 'the Earthquake' in European writings were understood to mean the Lisbon event. T. D. Kendrick's introduction to his historical account, *The Lisbon Earthquake*, ponders the essential human fear of a shaky ground.

> For, truly, an earthquake *is* a terrifying thing, even without a death-roll and destruction. Almost all the ordinary actions of our lives demand as an essential prerequisite that the ground should remain firm and motionless under our feet and beneath the foundations of our houses.[12]

This echoes the philosopher Edmund Husserl's account of Earth as an unshakeable ark, whereby the primary experience of the Earth is understood 'as a supportive and sustaining ground – as the resting point from which we register the movement and thingness of all other things'.[13] When the Earth moves, it undermines not just the structures perched on its surface, but our confidence in the intelligibility of the world. Fear of the impending Anthropocene and the perils of a changing planet are related, both causally and conceptually, to an enduring fear of an Earth that moves beneath our feet. The Lisbon earthquake is the key event that introduces the unsettling dimensions of thought that run through the Anthropocene. For the Lisbon earthquake was a double destabilising shock: the jolt of earthly dynamics governed by random chance, and the impact of a human-inflicted disaster.

The Lisbon earthquake is often presented as the first 'modern' disaster in that it prompted philosophers to seek rational, non-divine explanations for natural catastrophes. The concept of an ultimately beneficent and divinely created natural order was shaken by the earthquake, which generated much discussion as to the natural or supernatural character of the event. Was it an act of God or an act of Earth? Referring to the debates of Voltaire and Rousseau on the earthquake, Eyal Weizman reflects that 'we can see the Lisbon event as perhaps the first message from the Anthropocene… In this conception, human action and what insurance companies still call "acts of god" are entangled on a planetary-scale construction site'.[14] Lisbon's destruction was not simply that of a city; it elicited a widely felt and profound sense of human disintegration in the face of cosmic upheavals. The exposure of the city to the terrifying forces of the Earth provoked speculation on the efficacy of human control in the face of disaster and its consequences. Lisbon, which in the 18th century stood for 'disaster', also became 'the precursor of a definitively modern form of urban renewal'.[15]

Walter Benjamin's 1931 radio broadcast 'The Lisbon Earthquake' was part of a series for children on disasters: an earthquake, a volcanic eruption, a fire, a flood, and a train wreck. Benjamin asserts the singularity of the earthquake: not a 'disaster like a thousand others', but 'remarkable, even unique'. He credits the Lisbon earthquake with inspiring the beginnings of the science of seismology. Scientific descriptions of the quake and a nascent understanding of the forces of a moving Earth – tectonics, fault lines, and tremors – were synthesised from eyewitness accounts and observations. And alongside this new geophysical curiosity, nascent insights into the psychology and philosophy of disaster also stirred. Lisbon's earth-shattering event was a spur to thinking in both the natural and human sciences. It set the epistemological conditions for 'thinking the Anthropocene'. It also rehearsed the upheavals the Anthropocene is certain to bring – upheavals to ground on which our very survival depends, and to the assumptions on which so many human activities and ambitions rest.

In *The Natural Contract*, Michel Serres summoned a seismic imaginary to describe urban conglomerations as 'enormous and dense tectonic plates of humanity' capable of shifting planetary processes: 'the albedo, the circulation of water, the median temperature, and the formation of clouds or wind…'[16] This description anticipated the Anthropocene thesis in framing humanity as a geological force. The rhetorical question of the Anthropocene Working Group (AWG) is: 'Are humans now overwhelming the great forces of nature?'[17] One might reply that a major earthquake cannot fail to remind us of the opposite. Nigel Clark's *Inhuman Nature* foregrounds human 'susceptibility to the Earth's eventfulness… our all-too-human exposure to forces that exceed our capacity to control or even make full sense of them'.[18] To date, however, most discussions of the Anthropocene have tended to focus on Earth's susceptibility to human eventfulness.

The Lisbon event is a warning not to forget the consequences of our much-discussed eventfulness in the Anthropocene epoch. Any damage humans may manage to wreak on Earth's systems will be paid back with interest. The horrifying singularity of the Lisbon event resonates as a cautionary tale for the Anthropocene: a reminder that all bets are off in the context of our increasingly volatile earthly conditions. In their attempts to come to grips with the Lisbon earthquake, our ancestors set in motion a complex interplay between cultural, philosophical and geophysical processes that continues to trouble us today. The Anthropocene brings with it further insights into the earth-moving, sky-falling, world-ending potentialities in a human-natural-planetary hybrid system. As the growing instability of Earth's systems makes itself felt, we can learn from the Lisbon earthquake to expect cultural, philosophical and political aftershocks. In many ways, therefore, the Anthropocene as a disaster zone is Lisbon, all over again.

Lisbon swallowed up

Lisbon's utter destruction horrified the rest of Europe. It is estimated that between 10,000 and 100,000 people died in the disaster, crushed by collapsing buildings, drowned in the ensuing tsunami, or burnt in the fires that consumed the city. With fire, water and shaking earth descending in close succession on this national capital and stronghold of the Inquisition, could this mean Lisbon had incurred God's particular wrath? The irony of an earthquake striking on All Saints' Day, at a time when the worshipping faithful congregated in churches, was not lost on survivors or observers.

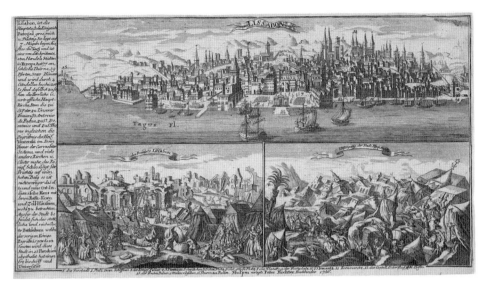

Figure 2.1 Lisbon 1756 (*Lissabon / Das ruinirte Lissabon / Untergang der Stadt Mequinetz*; print of original etching and engraving; published by Paul Emanuel Richter, Stolpe, 1756). Design in three compartments; the upper a view of Lisbon from the river Tagus; lower left: Lisbon in ruins after the earthquake of 1755, agitated figures by tents in the foreground, a double hanging in the background at centre; lower right: the fall of Meknes from the effects of the Lisbon earthquake, buildings, figures and camels toppling into the ground

Source: © The Trustees of the British Museum

It underlined the dread associated with disasters that humans can neither predict nor control. Voltaire's 'Poem on the Lisbon Disaster' questioned Gottfried Wilhelm Leibniz's notion of a benevolent deity supervising the 'best of all possible worlds'. In the philosopher Theodor Adorno's view, 'The earthquake of Lisbon sufficed to cure Voltaire of the theodicy of Leibniz'.[19] Voltaire was palpably disillusioned with the notion that Lisbon's suffering could be part of God's greater purpose. If 'what is, is right'? Voltaire had asked, 'could it really have been worse without Lisbon swallowed up by the Earth?'[20]

Lisbon was the focus of attention for the 'whole of the relevant civilised world'.[21] At the time of the earthquake, with an estimated population of 275,000, Lisbon was the fourth largest city in Europe – after London, Paris and Naples – and famous for its wealth. A powerful and cosmopolitan capital bustling with commerce, it had amassed capital through exploration and colonisation: 'it was staggeringly rich, rich in the almost fabulous contents of its palaces and churches, rich in the great stores of bullion and jewels and costly merchandise in its wharves and business premises, rich in its tremendous commercial importance.'[22] While the number of human casualties is impossible to establish from the historical record, we know exactly what goods and property were lost thanks to the meticulous inventories made by Lisbon's merchants. The royal archives disappeared altogether, along with records of the explorations of Vasco da Gama and other early navigators. But documents made after the disaster

52   Disaster zone

record the loss of staggering amounts of gold and silver, the destruction of hundreds of paintings, including works by Titian, Correggio and Rubens, rare books and manuscripts, as well as valuable furniture, tapestries and ornaments from homes, churches and palaces.[23] Voltaire's caustic observation was that only the merchants of the prosperous city would be able to give an accurate account of their losses:

> All the losses have been exaggerated. The hundred thousand men who perished in Lisbon have already been reduced to twenty-five thousand; they will probably soon be reduced to ten or twelve thousand. Only merchants know the precise amount of their losses, for they know the quantity of their goods, and kings never know the number of their men.[24]

Apart from the original brief notices in Lisbon's newspaper, the *Gazeta*, the first printed eyewitness account – a pamphlet in the form of a letter to a friend – appeared over a month later, on 20 December.[25] It exaggerated the horrors of the destruction of the 'wicked city'. The dissemination of news and reports reversed the path of the seismic waves: information came from outside Lisbon first, and only later from the epicentre of destruction.[26] Reports on the warning signs, symptoms and consequences of the earthquake gradually reached the *Gazeta*: the red and sulfurous river water, the lakes that rose and fell strangely, the dust which made the sun grow pale, the submerged rocks which suddenly became visible, the waters of the ocean that grew and receded, even the sudden appearance of comets crossing the night skies. The translation of the sudden and violent event into news was slow and difficult. Inevitably there was little news coming out of Lisbon, and it was precisely this absence that provoked amongst contemporaries the feeling of impending doom. 'The silence of Lisbon' was the condition that both authorised and generated all sorts of terrifying projections and alarmist discourse.[27] In the weeks and months that followed, numerous accounts of the disaster were published all over Europe. These ranged from eyewitness accounts, cathartic testimony and apocalyptic sermons through to scientific and philosophical explorations, as well as fanciful tales and make-believe. The Lisbon disaster also coincided with the rapid expansion of publishing, and contributed to it by becoming an international media sensation. Among the accounts is a passage in Giacomo Casanova's *Memoirs*: imprisoned in Venice at the time, he described the large master beam in his prison cell moving 'as if turning upon itself', though the tremor did not, as he had hoped, cause a collapse of the Doge's palace.[28]

In the aftermath, this single event was said to have convulsed western civilisation more than any since the fall of Rome.[29] The cataclysm helped bring forth the rational-sceptical Enlightenment subject, but the birth was a traumatic one. In Lisbon in 1755 many kinds of authority – divine, political, philosophical or scientific – met their most radical challenge.

Aftermath and aftershocks

> In short, Lisbon is a Heap of Ruins and its Inhabitants are the most unhappy Wretches upon the face of the Earth![30]

The world had ended. Heaps of smouldering ruins and rotting corpses filled what remained of the city. Sixteen days after the earthquake, the ruins were still so hot from fires that baskets used to carry rubble and rubbish would ignite.[31] There was a desperate scramble to leave the city. Terrified refugees fled to the fields surrounding Lisbon without their effects, as most material goods and possessions had been consumed by the fires. An eyewitness reported, 'hardly anything is left to cover people's nakedness and they live in tents in the fields'.[32] Lisbon suffered over 500 aftershocks in the ensuing months.[33] Few people dared to live in what remained of their ruined dwellings for fear of further collapse, and for the most part the population shifted from the centre of the city to temporary settlements in the open spaces to the east and west of the destroyed area, such as the parish of Santa Isabel, which accommodated a refugee population of 25,000, and the settlements of Belem and Ajuda on the high ground encircling the city. Makeshift dwellings were made from carpets and canvas sails; huts and barracks of salvaged timber were erected for growing streams of homeless refugees. It is estimated that 9,000 temporary wooden buildings were assembled in the six months after the quake.[34] The royal court was also 'encamped', accommodated in a huge complex of tents and wooden pavilions in the hills of Ajuda, 'none of the royal palaces being fit to harbour them'.[35]

The restoration of the city was undertaken under the authority of Sebastião José de Carvalho e Mello, the Portuguese Secretary of State and Conde de Oeiras, later elevated to the rank of Marquis of Pombal. When the King had despairingly asked, 'What can be done?', in the aftermath of disaster, Pombal's pragmatic response had been, 'Bury the dead and feed the living'.[36] In the aftermath of the earthquake, Pombal took charge of the relief and reconstruction efforts, setting up office in his carriage among the ruins. Under Pombal's authority, everything possible was done to confirm Lisbon's ability to survive and recover – even if the King himself, obviously shaken by the events, chose never again to leave his tent city outside Lisbon's walls.

There was no doubt that Lisbon should be rebuilt. According to one eyewitness, 'The whole city is one continued heap of rubbish and ruins; and not withstanding that, they talk of nothing but rebuilding it'.[37] Pombal organised the military and immediately appointed special magistrates for each of the 12 wards or *barrios* of the city to implement the government's emergency directions. He swiftly organised the disposal of corpses at sea to prevent an outbreak of the plague. The next urgent matter was to ensure food supplies, which he dealt with by taking control of any surviving stores and ships' cargoes. The military also requisitioned wagons, and established routes through the ruins for supplies. Food distribution centres, camp kitchens and ovens were constructed; millers and bakers and cooks were prevented from leaving the city, and fish was sold free of duty. Pombal also demanded that trading and businesses, such as banking and exchange, should continue as far as possible. Hospitals and shelter services for the wounded were established. All available supplies of wood were commandeered to construct temporary shelters for the homeless. Land rents were controlled and laws were passed which forbade landlords from evicting tenants from any habitable dwellings.

The city was placed under strict disciplinary control. Refugees were forbidden from venturing too far from the city and a pass system was instituted to regulate those coming and going. Gallows were erected as warnings against looting and at least 34 people were executed in the immediate aftermath of the earthquake.[38] One observer reported a much higher number, noting that 'there were above eighty bodies hanging upon gibbets round about the city'.[39] Among the reported scenes of anarchy, brutality, pillaging, villainy and rape, there were also accounts of kindness displayed by a 'compassionate and resolute people'.[40] Pombal's authoritative responses to the disaster are considered an early model of state-directed reconstruction.[41] Pombal, still known at the time as the Conde de Oeiras, took the credit for everything:

> ... everything written, ordered, or done in the name of His Most Faithful Majesty in respect of burying the dead, restoring morale, collecting provisions, calling in troops, dealing with looting, providing protection against African pirates, stopping and controlling refugees, maintaining a strict military discipline, protecting nuns, averting God's wrath, preserving the King's person, punishing traitors, suppressing Jesuits, restoring commerce, encouraging the arts, clearing the ruins, planning and rebuilding the city, all this, we are told, was in the greater part due to the foresight wisdom and authority of the Conde de Oeiras.[42]

The *Providencias*, a 1758 record of Pombal's actions and principal directives, are a consistent set of documents beginning on 1 November 1755.[43] They leave no room for doubt that Pombal was in complete command of disaster management from day one. Pombal dealt with one crisis after another with a series of decisive actions. The city's cultural and scientific institutions prepared a questionnaire, now known as the 'Marquis de Pombal Inquiry'. It is considered a landmark in the history of modern seismology. The questionnaire consisted of 13 questions, such as: How long did the earthquake last? How many shocks were felt? What kind of damage was caused? Did animals behave strangely? What happened in the wells and water holes? The bishops were asked to forward the questionnaire to all the parishes in Portugal, for the recording of observations was to be as wide and as detailed as possible. The resulting report gathered data on seismic propagation, soil liquefaction, movement of buildings and resultant damage, and obstacles to recovery. Its findings are still relevant to disaster planning today. Accounts of the foreshocks, it seemed, would allow for more preparedness in future: for if only they had known in advance what it meant to sense a rumbling and shuddering of the earth, or for earthworms to leave the soil, as had been reported in Cadiz, the devastation might have been reduced. The Pombal Inquiry turned the Lisbon earthquake into a historical and scientific object of research, the basis for future policy and urban design.

Pombal's emergency response was from the first focused on comprehensive reconstruction. He wanted the new Lisbon to be protected, to whatever degree might be possible, from the social, political and physical consequences of any future disaster. His work in the aftermath of the earthquake included ensuring that the weekly paper, *Gazeta de Lisboa*, was published on 5 November, just four days after the catastrophe, and that it thereafter never missed an edition. He understood the media's role in restoring a semblance of normal life, by providing news about the world beyond, as well as dispelling rumours and false speculation about Lisbon's state of devastation. Pombal was explicit in his support for natural explanations of the earthquake. These ranged from strict Aristotelian doctrine through to modern explosive and electrical theories on the causes of earthly tremors. He strove to underplay any claims of metaphysical significance in the period when aftershocks continued to feed fears of impending doom. For the government in Lisbon the question of divine or natural causes could not remain abstract: it had direct political consequences.[44] Many theologians had taken Lisbon as a commandment to return to a theocentric view of nature from which society had started to stray. The greed and licentiousness of the wealthy city was used to explain the devastation as divine punishment, and they argued that the earthquake portended apocalypse. Pombal held the Jesuits responsible for the most alarmist preaching and prophesying. He singled out Gabriel Malagrida, the Italian Jesuit priest who had questioned Pombal's directives for the reconstruction of Lisbon. Malagrida had instead urged for a regimen of prayer and penitence, scourging and fasting in preparation for the millennium, delivered in countless sermons in the aftermath of the earthquake. In 1756 he published a pamphlet outlining his views.[45] He insisted that this period of aftershocks was not the time for reconstruction and rebuilding because 'the Lord is still shaking the Earth' with the object of extracting penitence:

> Learn, O Lisbon, that the destroyers of our houses, palaces, churches, and convents, the cause of the death of so many people and of the flames that devoured such vast treasures, are your abominable sins, and not comets, stars, vapours and exaltations, and similar natural phenomena. Tragic Lisbon is now a mound of ruins.[46]

Pombal and Malagrida disagreed fundamentally in their interpretations of the disaster and, therefore, on how to respond. In the summary of the philosopher Susan Neiman, 'Pombal wished to save citizens from sickness and famine; Malagrida wished to save souls from hell. Each worked under the shadow of a ticking clock.'[47] In 1758, Pombal gave permission for a day long *auto-da-fé* in the centre of Lisbon, appeasing calls from the church for a cleansing sacrifice of sinners. After a failed assassination attempt on King José I, Pombal seized the opportunity to marginalise the influence of the church by arresting and executing Malagrida and several other Jesuit clerics on charges of conspiracy. After Malagrida's trial and execution, the Jesuit order was sent into exile, their property was confiscated by the crown, and the rule of the Inquisition ended in Portugal. Pombal could now continue with the rebuilding of Lisbon.

> The King seems determined to build *Lisbon* again in the same place, and the militia around the country are now clearing the streets. But this must be a Work of Time.[48]

On 29 November, a detailed survey of the ruins was ordered to prevent future litigation over property site and size. The army was mobilised to enforce the rebuilding work in the city where 'scarce one house of this vast city is left habitable'.[49] Military engineers controlled debris disposal and salvage operations, decided the sites of rubble dumps, and levelled the squares. Lime kilns for mortar and ovens for bricks were set up, and debris salvaged and sorted for use in reconstruction. In total about 1,000 properties were restored in the first year. As it had been decided that Lisbon should be rebuilt to a master plan, all unauthorised building in the ruined areas was stopped. By the end of November 1755, plans for the reconstruction of the city were taking shape. It was generally held that the narrowness of the streets had contributed to the destruction of the city[50] and that the passages, filling up with falling rubble, had made escape and emergency response difficult.[51]

The pragmatic and rationalist approach of military engineering was a significant element in Pombal's urban strategy, focused not only on protection from future disaster, but convenience for citizens and the expediency of trade.[52] General Manuel da

Maia, the royal engineer-in-chief, was responsible for the conceptual development of plans for the city's reconstruction.[53] By 1756 in the *Dissertação* addressed to King José, he presented five detailed options for the city's reconstruction. One option was to rebuild the old city as it was before the earthquake using salvaged materials. The next two plans proposed widening certain streets, or reducing the heights of buildings to two storeys, still on the old city plan. The fourth option proposed razing the entire Baixa quarter and 'laying out new streets without restraint'. The fifth called for a new capital city to be built to the west of the old city near Bélem. Pombal selected the fourth, 'clean slate' option, and a team of military engineers set to work on six further plans. The final plan consisted of a regular grid pattern with standardised lots, large wide avenues, and involved a realignment of the squares and streets by 13 degrees to maximise sunlight. The waterfront area was levelled, creating the new lower town. It became known as 'Baixa Pombalina'.

The construction of new dwellings involved prefabrication and standardisation of materials: chiefly, ironwork, wooden joints, and tiles. The buildings were among the earliest seismically protected constructions involving a wooden frame called the *gaiola*, or 'cage', providing flexibility for future shocks. Soldiers marched around scale models of the constructions to simulate the tremors of an earthquake. The centrepiece of the rebuilt city was the new square, Praça de Commércio. Its name reflected not only its funding but also Pombal's vision for Lisbon's future as a revived centre of commerce. In 1775, three days of celebrations marked the dedication of the square and the unveiling of an equestrian statue of King José. It was important that Lisbon's new architecture gave the impression of prosperity, so elaborate canvas and wooden scenery was erected to mask the still-unfinished reconstruction work.

The Lisbon earthquake did not simply mark the destruction of an important city, but also the violent exposure of a frail humankind to the recalcitrant forces of the Earth. It was an event so earth-shattering that it had reduced conceptual and physical constructions alike to rubble. The organisation and delineation of disaster in the wake of Lisbon was achieved through preparation for the philosophical, theological and practical management of earthquakes throughout Europe. The political handling of the Lisbon event was the precursor to a distinctly modern form of urban renewal and disaster preparedness. It is considered the first modern disaster insofar as the state took on the responsibility for mobilising the emergency response and for developing and implementing a comprehensive plan for reconstruction.[54] The French academic Marie-Hélène Huet argues that the 'state of emergency' so characteristic of late Western culture has its origins in 'a pervasive anxiety about catastrophic events now freed from their theological meanings and worsened by human failures'. After Lisbon, she suggests, disaster became a 'properly human concern'.[55]

Ever since Lisbon, European societies have expected coordinated state response in times of disaster, and are less inclined to attribute them to a cosmic impulse to punishment. Lisbon marks the severing of moral meaning from nature, and, with it, the rise of impersonal, accidental evil in our view of natural calamities. But this shift has not solved the problem of human vulnerability to momentous geophysical instability. In the increasingly calamitous conditions of an anthropogenically altered world, concern is rising over the levels of preparedness and security among vulnerable populations. As Susan Neiman observes:

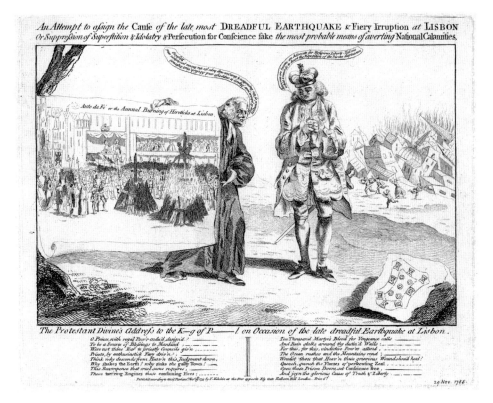

Figure 2.2 'An Attempt to assign the Cause of the late, most Dreadful Earthquake & Fiery Irruption at Lisbon Or Suppression of Superstition & Idolatry & Persecution for Conscience sake the most probable means of averting National Calamities'; 'A goose of old did save a State'; etching and engraving of a satirical print published by Thomas Kitchin, London, 29 November 1755
Source: © The Trustees of the British Museum

Natural disaster is the object of attempts at prediction and control, not of interpretation… None of the questions that tormented Europeans reflecting on Lisbon was ever directly answered or even directly rejected… Theory proceeded much as Pombal did. It focused on eradicating those evils that could be reached by human hands… But in proceeding as if questions were settled that were simply left hanging, theory left residues that cloud our attempts to eradicate evils today.[56]

The best of all possible worlds

With its intricate mix of myth, fable and history, Voltaire's satirical narrative *Candide, ou l'Optimisme*, published in 1759, in the midst of the turmoil of the Seven Years' War, was a cautionary tale on the current state of the world. The headline-grabbing destruction of Lisbon provided a significant episode in the novel.

> Scarcely had they set foot in the city, still weeping over the death of their benefactor, than they felt the earth quake beneath their feet. In the port a boiling sea rose up and smashed the ships lying at anchor. Whirlwinds of flame and ash covered the streets and public squares: houses disintegrated, roofs were upended upon foundations, and foundations crumbled...
> 'The end of the world is come!' Candide shouted.[57]

Candide's philosophy master Pangloss reassures him that things could not be otherwise: 'all this is the best there could be; for if there is a volcano under Lisbon, then it couldn't be anywhere else.' He continues, 'For it is impossible that things could be placed anywhere except where they are. For all is well.' Voltaire was as horrified by the earthquake as by the purges that followed. The Inquisition's response to the calamity had been that of an *auto-da-fé*, designed to prevent the wrath of God and further catastrophe. Sinners and heretics were rounded up for public execution in what remained of the city's squares. Inevitably, Candide and Pangloss get caught up in the disaster and its philosophical and theological repercussions. And while Pangloss is being hanged for heresy, the earth shakes again:

> Terrified, confounded, thoroughly distraught, all bleeding and trembling, Candide reflected to himself: 'If this is the best of all possible worlds, then what must the others be like?'[58]

In the aftermath of Lisbon, no one could doubt the uselessness of humans when it came to facing the threatening forces of the Earth. In one of his lectures on Leibniz, the French philosopher Gilles Deleuze stated that philosophy was untenable after Lisbon. Referring to *Candide*, Voltaire's satirical take on Leibniz's optimism, he argues, 'the problem of good and evil cannot be posed as it was a century before. I believe this is the end of the blessed and the damned... After 1755, the problem will be posed differently.'[59] Lisbon's disaster was not just a terrifying convulsion of the Earth in which humans had got caught up to devastating effect, but it shattered a way of making sense of such events.[60] And it has been troubling us ever since. Thank goodness, then, for the human capacity for satire and irony, as the writer Julian Barnes notes in his reflection on *Candide*:

> The world is not reformed by the end of *Candide*, and cultivating one's garden protects no one from an army of Bulgars. Satire is not about 'finding a solution', doesn't spring from a worked-out strategy for the micro-managed moral rehabilitation of humanity; rather, it is the necessary expression of moral rage. Satirists are by nature pessimists; they know that the world changes all too slowly. If satire worked – if the hypocrite and liar, publicly chastised, reformed themselves – then satire would no longer be needed. 'But to what end,' Candide muses, 'was the world formed?' Martin replies: 'To make us mad.' Satire is one response to, and outlet for, this *cosmic madness*.[61]

The Lisbon earthquake showed all too well the workings of a violent recalcitrant world and the fallibility of humans, confirming an emerging tenet of Enlightenment thought and political practice. Responses to the event heralded the end of theological interpretations of disaster. But they also challenged the idea of a purely 'natural' disaster, since the enquiries that preceded and informed reconstruction revealed many ways in which the Lisboans had unknowingly participated in their own destruction. This raised questions about the role of the city or the state in minimising such destruction in the future. In short: after Lisbon, disaster became politicised.[62]

According to Jean-Jacques Rousseau, lessons could be learnt from overcrowded, vulnerable Lisbon on how to construct cities better *and* think about them better. Rousseau's 'Letter to Voltaire on Optimism' of August 1756 was a challenge to Voltaire's refutation of metaphysical optimism.[63] Rousseau makes it clear that there has perhaps never been a natural disaster – that all disasters owed their destructive capacity to man's inability to comprehend the physical world and take its violent nature into account.[64] He defends the underlying goodness of the natural world. The real problem is that 'The new men – "free, perfected and corrupted" – have built far from Eden' a precarious city that prioritises ostentation over survival.

> Without leaving your chosen subject of Lisbon, you must acknowledge, for example, that it was not nature that piled up there twenty thousand houses of six or seven floors each; and that if the inhabitants of this great city had been spread out more evenly and had lived in less massive buildings, the destruction would have been a lot less, and perhaps insignificant.[65]

In Rousseau's analysis, the earthquake's catastrophic aftermath was inevitable for such a packed, congested and shoddily built city. Moreover, many inhabitants had been reported as initially reluctant to flee and leave their material possessions behind.

> How many poor creatures died in this disaster because one wanted to go back for his clothes, another for his papers, a third for his money? Can't you see that the physical existence of a human being has become the least important part of themselves, and that it seems to be scarcely worth saving it when one has lost all the rest?[66]

Rousseau observed that earthquakes also took place in desert regions, but such occurrences were not deemed newsworthy because they did not affect an urban elite. Rousseau is outspoken on the bias of the discussion – as if earthquakes only happened to city dwellers:

> You would have wanted the earthquake to occur in the distant reaches of some desert rather than in Lisbon. Is there any reason to think earthquakes don't occur in deserts? But we don't discuss them, because they do no harm to city dwellers, the only human beings to whom we attribute any significance. It's true they don't do much harm to animals and the savages who live scattered through those inaccessible zones, and who don't worry about their roofs falling in or their houses being undermined.[67]

Rousseau's letter to Voltaire on the Lisbon earthquake has been identified as 'the first truly social scientific view of disaster' and an early attempt to conceptualise vulnerability.[68] As Marie-Hélène Huet writes, 'Soon after Rousseau, acts of God would be relegated to the vocabulary of insurance companies, and the Revolution would give the concept of "risk" its first legal definition'.[69] Lisbon established the city as a disaster zone.[70] Thereafter it was impossible to speak of disaster without reference to its regulation and management. Lisbon's misfortune is a cautionary tale that has resonated across subsequent centuries of civic attempts to protect inhabitants against catastrophe. Systematic scientific investigation of physical phenomena such as earthquakes has enabled the development of practical measures – systems of levees and military defence, improved building codes, insurance schemes, early warning systems and ever-improving methods of earthquake prediction. However, none of these systems of security can prevent disaster – they can only ameliorate the impact. The extent to which all such systems are haunted by their insufficiency has been brought home in recent years by an escalating series of disasters. It is little wonder that anxiety – for many of us, an anxiety more disabling than galvanising – attends the prospect of bigger disasters to come.

Since Lisbon, we have been acutely aware of the risk to people in cities from episodic planetary turbulence. Like Rousseau before him, Nigel Clark observes that, 'cities amplify the risks of geological unrest by concentrating human beings and by stacking these populations in heavy, brittle structures'.[71] Humans gather in large numbers for protection, for convenience, for commerce – and for the pursuit of complex societal projects. But when disaster strikes, the very infrastructure that supports our collective life can become a lethal threat. In recent years, the impacts of environmental crises and extreme events on densely packed and precariously sited cities around the world have been harder to dismiss. In spite of the provisions of early warning systems, seismic safety codes, risk registers and plans for civil emergencies, cities built to accommodate the mass of humans on a dynamic planet will always be the places that are most susceptible to planetary disruptions. These disruptions must, inevitably, have economic and political dimensions, too – since an urban population without infrastructure can't maintain its normal economic activities, and since the disruptions to the Earth system that so disproportionately burden cities are intimately intertwined with industry and its political interests. In the context of rapidly accelerating urbanisation and the complex interweaving of weather, lives, infrastructures and economies, it is often the fissures between governments and civil society that are made more evident when disaster strikes.

The consequences of disasters are always geographically, historically, politically and socially uneven. 'They tear at the fabric of our economies, our democracies, and our citizenship.'[72] Social justice post-disaster, is about coming to terms with and exposing the 'built-in' systematic vulnerabilities and accumulated crises of poor governance. It is also an opportunity for 'rethinking resilience' beyond an emphasis on physical or personal robustness, as the academic Bronwyn Hayward argues in her discussion of the aftermath of the Christchurch, New Zealand earthquakes of 2011. This involves expanding the political imagination about the resilience of cities, to include 'ideas of compassion experienced as shared vulnerability, and political resistance forged in ongoing, collective struggles for social justice and alternative visions of hope'.[73] The writer and campaigner Paul Chatterton has shown in his discussion of New Orleans post-Hurricane Katrina that the collective injury of abandonment and institutional failure in the wake of the disaster hardened into a trauma around which the politics of reconstruction is tortuously bent. In this sense therefore, the city is an 'unfinished story' about the right to define and shape the future city in the midst of environmental and social crisis.[74] It is also an unfinishable story. In anticipating the accumulation

Figure 2.3 'Ruins of Lisbon as appeared immediately after the Earthquake and Fire of the 1st Novbr 1755'; 'The Patriarchal Square'; print of an etching and engraving after Jacques Philippe Le Bas, published by Robert Sayer, London, 1757–1760
Source: © The Trustees of the British Museum

of disasters that will characterise the Anthropocene, we may need to acknowledge that many of the adaptive strategies for our present-day cities and infrastructures are experiments, necessarily precarious and provisional.[75] Rousseau urged humility and caution in the wake of the Lisbon event. Quoting Cicero in his letter to Voltaire, he warned: 'The world is a hotel in which we stay for a few nights; we have no permanent residence here.'[76]

The Earth trembles

Kant published three essays on the Lisbon catastrophe in 1756.[77] It was his ambition to present the best available knowledge on the physical causes of earthquakes, along with his reflections on the moral and practical lessons that might be drawn from the event in Lisbon. The first essay focused on the physical dynamics of earthquakes and offered reassurance that earthquakes would not happen in Prussia.[78] Kant insisted that the Lisbon earthquake should not be viewed as an evil inconsistent with God's existence and the perfection of the world, nor as an act of divine vengeance for the sinful behavior of Lisboans. Instead he argued that earthquakes have physical causes and that we should respond not with fear but, rather, with careful thought about how

Figure 2.4 'Ruins of Lisbon as appeared immediately after the Earthquake and Fire of the 1st Novbr 1755'; 'St Roch's Tower commonly call'd the Patriarch's Tower'; print of an etching and engraving after Jacques Philippe Le Bas, published by Robert Sayer, London, 1757–1760
Source: © The Trustees of the British Museum

best to control and adapt to their effects – for example through appropriate urban planning.

> We dwell peacefully on ground whose foundations are shaken from time to time. Without concern, we build over cavities whose supports sometimes sway and threaten to collapse.[79]

Kant urges humans to make use of the knowledge we gain from such terrible catastrophes. He warns the 'unhappy survivors of Lisbon' not to build again along the length of the Tagus, which, according to him, indicates the direction along which earthquakes naturally occur in Portugal.

> The catastrophe at Lisbon thus seems to have been exacerbated by its position along the banks of the Tagus. And for this reason, any town or country where earthquakes have been experienced several times, and where their direction can be known from [previous] experiences, should not be laid out in a direction that is the same as the earthquakes.[80]

Kant expands on the embryonic fault theory that was developing in the wake of Lisbon. He understood earthquakes to be caused by explosive reactions of materials compressed in extensive caverns below the Earth's surface, and therefore to be connected with volcanic activity, magnetism and atmospheric changes. As part of his explanation, he included instructions for a simple experiment to make a miniature earthquake that could demonstrate the general laws of earthquakes and the 'subterranean conflagrations' that were their cause:

> It is now time to say something about the cause of earthquakes. It is easy for a natural philosopher to reproduce their manifestations. One takes twenty-five pounds of iron filings, an equal amount of sulphur, and mixes it with ordinary water, buries this paste one or one-and-a-half feet underground and compresses the earth firmly above it. After several hours, a dense vapour is seen rising; the earth trembles, and flames break forth from the soil.[81]

The terrors of a hostile Earth are here reduced, thanks to an empiricist spirit and some commonly available materials, to manageable dimensions. In his second essay Kant was keen to point out that his report was 'not a history of the instances of misfortune that people have suffered as a result of it, nor a list of the cities and their inhabitants destroyed under the debris'. He acknowledges the phenomenological horror of the experience of natural disaster, before excluding it from his purview.

> All the terrible things the imagination can conceive have to be taken together to understand even to a small extent the horror people must experience when the Earth moves under their feet, when everything around them crashes to the ground, when a body of water moved in its foundations completes their misfortune through flooding, when the fear of death, the despair at having lost all one's earthly goods, and finally the sight of other people in misery must dishearten even the most courageous. A narrative of such events would be moving, and it would, since it has such an effect on the heart, perhaps also have the effect of improving the latter. But I shall leave this story to more skilful hands. Here I shall only describe the work of nature, and the most remarkable natural circumstances that accompanied the terrible event together with its causes.[82]

Leaving the story of the disaster 'to more skilful hands', Kant confines himself to scientific observation. He reports that the earthquake was preceded by vapour rising into the air, which turned red and made the torrential rains that followed blood red as well. He attributes these phenomena to the mass release of iron compounds from the Earth in the conflagration that caused the earthquake. He goes on to describe the tsunami and aftershocks, their connection with the seasons, and their influence on the atmosphere. In Kant's view it is a moral and ontological error on the part of man to view himself, rather than nature, as the object of God's actions:

> We demand that the Earth's surface should be so constituted that one might wish to live on it forever. In addition, we imagine that we would better regulate everything to our advantage, if fate had asked for our vote on this matter. Thus we wish to have e.g. the rain in our power so that we could distribute it over the whole

year in accordance with our convenience and so could always enjoy pleasant days between the dull ones.[83]

There are, according to Kant, examples of more appropriate ways of dwelling and constructing in the world. 'The inhabitants of Peru', for example, 'live in houses built with mortar only up to a low height and the rest consists of reeds. Man must learn to adapt to nature but wants nature to adapt to him.'[84] He concludes by offering reflection that the world was not made for human advantage in spite of human tendency to imagine it so. Kant's natural world is God's creation, and is inherently inconstant: 'man is not born to build everlasting dwellings on this stage of vanity.'[85]

Kant wrote his final essay at a time when Lisbon was still experiencing aftershocks that continued to generate anxiety in the destroyed city and across the world. Kant reports that 'the fire of the subterranean vaults has not yet subsided', and the 'disorder in the atmosphere has altered the seasons in half of the world'.[86] He recounts and critiques various popular theories about the earthquake. Some declare 'without reflection or understanding' that 'the Earth has shifted its position and come closer to the Sun', while others 'bring comets back into play'.[87] His focus is on refuting superstitious explanations, including invidious astrological conjunctions. He also criticises proposals by contemporary naturalists to attempt to control earthquakes, for example by boring through the Earth's crust to release built-up gases. He closes with a warning against such geoengineering fantasies:

> From the Prometheus of modern times, Herr Franklin[88], who sought to disarm the thunder, to that man who sought to extinguish the fire in Vulcan's workshop, all such endeavours are proofs of the boldness of man, allied with a capacity which stands in a very modest relationship to it, and ultimately they lead him to the humbling reminder, which is where he ought properly to start, that he is never anything more than a human being.[89]

Kant's final words link projects of human hubris with the inescapable humility of humans. He underlines the disproportion between the audacity of humans and their actual abilities and casts doubt on how much faith should be placed in the human capacity to strive beyond its physical limits. Kant's essays reveal the tension between the limited, humble, earthbound nature of human beings and their status as moral beings whose proper concerns transcend the earthly realm. In researching his trilogy of essays, Kant synthesised reports of the terrestrial and atmospheric phenomena observed across Europe in the days before and after the earthquake, with a diligence and breadth of vision that led the philosopher Walter Benjamin to credit him with originating the science of seismology.[90] Georg Gerland, who founded the International Seismological Association in 1901, praised Kant's essays as the 'first truly scientific treatment of an earthquake', thanks in part to the omission of 'doubtless exciting, but seismologically irrelevant trappings'.[91] Implied in this praise is the idea that a focus on the victims' plights would have been a distraction. As the historian Deborah Coen observes, 'Kant brought Europe into the modern age of science by producing an account of disaster in which the human victims fell silent'.[92] Kant's writings on Lisbon informed his lectures on 'physical geography' as part of his programme of constructing science as 'pragmatic cosmopolitan knowledge' – a view which has had lingering influence in the environmental sciences. '[Geography] teaches us to recognise the workshops of nature in which we find ourselves – nature's first laboratory and its tools and experiments.'[93] Subsequent centuries of environmental thought have never quite escaped the tension between the technical mastery and critical humility that emerged with this view.

An anxiety about an Earth that moves beneath us is a central motif in Kant's philosophy. The earthquake continued to resonate in Kant's formulation of the sublime in his later *Critique of Judgment* (1790). As the writer Gene Ray puts it: 'The sublime moves the mind like the tremors or deep shudders of an earthquake.'[94] For Kant, the subject confronts that which is 'excessive for the imagination': an excess experienced as 'an abyss… in which it fears to lose itself'.[95] The Earth's terrors affirm the blind forcefulness of nature relative to the puny human subject, temporarily paralysing thought. The subject responds, however, with a swell of will and the application of the human faculty of super-sensible reason. In this way, the sublime is a provocation: it reminds humans of physical vulnerability, only to call forth their most transcendent mental faculties, thus reminding them that they are made, intellectually, in God's image. Kant's notion of the sublime therefore allows the unruly and disruptive forces of the Earth to be harnessed as an aesthetic encounter, albeit uneasily. To those persistent fears of a dynamic Earth that haunt the Kantian sublime we can also add the contemporary fear – characteristic of the Anthropocene – that it is human activities that are contributing to the destruction of our Earthly home.

Dis-astered

Cosmic – 'sky-falling' and 'world-ending' – phenomena such as meteors, tsunamis and earthquakes have always terrified humans. Meteors and comets were known as 'disasters': literally a fallen, dysfunctional, or evil star (*dis-astron*).[96] As Marie-Hélène Huet notes, 'the word is thus directly related to disorders of uncommon magnitude: the destruction, despair, and chaos resulting from the distant power of cosmic agencies.'[97] To be 'dis-astered', as in the French expression *désastré* or Italian *dis-astrato*, is to 'have been disowned by the stars that ensure a safe passage through life'.[98] The 'wider "dis-aster" of Lisbon' thus signals 'not only the falling away of firm ground underfoot, but the loss of a divine guiding star'.[99] It is in this doubled sense of calamity – the changed relation of humans to Earth and life processes, and the uprooting of existing conceptual frameworks – that the Anthropocene is also understood as a *dis-aster*. And, according to Jan Zalasiewicz, the Anthropocene portends not only an 'Earthly disaster' but a 'cosmic tragedy':

> … conserving living organisms is far more important than conserving fossils…
> The Earth, in sustaining and harbouring these organisms, is by far the most complex and valuable object in space for many, many billions of miles in any direction. It would be not merely an Earthly disaster if its surface was converted to the kind of wasteland that appeared after the Permian-Triassic or Cretaceous-Tertiary boundary extinction events. It would be a cosmic tragedy, one in which the injuries sustained would not heal for millions of years.[100]

The Anthropocene is the disaster to end all disasters. It represents the human destruction of something that does not belong to us – a thing whose value, quite aside from its transient instrumentalisation, exceeds all human scales of calculation.

The Anthropocene is also the story to end all stories. In *The Writing of the Disaster* Maurice Blanchot asks, 'How does one write disaster?' He recalls the literal meaning of *dis-aster* as 'being separated from the star' and 'the decline which characterises disorientation'.[101] Blanchot suggests that knowledge of disaster is itself disastrous, insofar as it destroys notions of identity, unity and temporality; and also because disaster erases stories, which carry and safeguard cultural meaning. For Blanchot, the rupture with sense that ensues with disaster is paradoxically generative: it demands change and inevitable restart – for better or for worse, but with a reminder: '… under a well-disposed sky and upon the Earth that sustains us… There the cosmic order still subsists, but as an arrogant, impatient, discredited reign.'[102] Blanchot goes further and postulates *all* writing as disaster, that is, as absence, violence, rupture and fragment: 'There is disaster only because, ceaselessly, it falls short of disaster.'[103] In other words, disaster is narratable. The philosopher Richard Kearney interprets Blanchot's 'writing of disaster' as a 'struggle between story and unstory'. Kearney observes: 'This is indeed storytelling in straits, but it is storytelling nonetheless.'[104]

The Lisbon earthquake is the anterior disaster to the Anthropocene. Marie-Hélène Huet's *Culture of Disaster* approaches disaster as both premise and condition for modern thought, and links this intimately to the 1755 earthquake.[105] There had been other enormous disasters in the 17th and 18th centuries – notably the plague in Marseille in 1720, and the earthquake that had destroyed Port Royal, Jamaica in 1692 – but none had been as shocking as Lisbon. None had caused lasting, discernible, conceptual damage.[106] As conviction grew that the calamity had not been caused by the wrath of God, a new dual understanding of disaster emerged as both the 'workings of a violent universe' and 'human-engineered calamity'.[107] Lisbon marked a shift in the debate: from the divine origin of disasters to concern about their unpredictable unfolding. Thereafter the responsibility for disasters fell more on humans and less on nature.[108] A number of writers seeking to understand the cataclysmic human brutality of the 20th century – nuclear war, totalitarianism, the Holocaust – have drawn connections back to the conceptual devastation of the Lisbon disaster. In *Evil in Modern Thought* Susan Neiman takes the intellectual reactions to Lisbon and Auschwitz as 'a way of locating the beginning and end of the modern'.[109] She proceeds with caution, knowing that 'comparing Lisbon to Auschwitz can seem not mistaken but monstrous', as if disregarding the role, in the latter catastrophe, of human agency and intent. Her point is rather that the two events 'stand as symbols of the breakdown of the world views of their eras'.[110] For 'each case shattered what had allowed those who lived through it to negotiate their ways through the world'.[111] And, 'In both cases, the events themselves created boundaries between what could and what could not be thought'.[112] In *Negative Dialectics*, Theodor Adorno writes,

> The earthquake of Lisbon sufficed to cure Voltaire of the theodicy of Leibniz, and the visible disaster of the first nature was insignificant in comparison with the second, social one, which defies human imagination as it distills a real hell from human evil.[113]

Adorno, writing under the heading 'After Auschwitz', suggests that philosophy is devastated by the disaster, and that it is unthinkable to make sense of, narrate, dramatise or exploit the horrific events: only silence is possible. Adorno reformulates the Kantian sublime as a traumatic undermining of the individual ego, a loss of the ground beneath one's feet: *Erschütterung*. Gene Ray explains this as a 'tremor or shudder of what is beyond imagination and conventionalised experience – the shock waves of traumatic occurrence'.[114] There is no longer the possibility of redemption through any kind of rational explanation. The trauma is of human-made disaster: 'the abomination of the death camps radically eclipses the catastrophe of Lisbon, because it is a disaster of our own making.'[115] If humankind lost faith in the world at Lisbon, after Auschwitz it lost faith in itself.[116] We are no longer perturbed quite as much by nature's cosmic upheavals as we are by the violence we bring upon ourselves. Following Adorno, Gene Ray presents the changing imaginary of disaster as a fable of human calamity:

> Once upon a time, encounters with the power or size of nature defeated the imagination and moved us to terror and awe. After Auschwitz, however, we have had to recognise such sublime effects among our own responses to this demonstrated human potential for systematic and unbounded violence. After this history, human-inflicted disaster will remain more threatening, more sublime, than any natural disaster.[117]

The thematic of the *human-inflicted* disaster has persisted through the various perceived threats of the 20th and 21st centuries, from the Cold War threat of nuclear annihilation, through the nuclear accidents at Chernobyl and Fukushima, to the AIDS pandemic, international terrorism, and anthropogenic climate change. The Anthropocene disaster is conceived of as a rupture with all previous manifestations of disaster, along with the destruction of any vestige of human capacity to make sense of them. As Timothy Morton writes:

> The worry is not whether the world will end, as in the old model of the *dis-astron*, but whether the end of the world is already happening, or whether perhaps *it might already have taken place*. A deep shuddering of temporality occurs.[118]

The disaster of the Anthropocene is that it is a disaster of human making on a planetary scale. The cautionary tale of Lisbon *dis-astered* revealed the limits of human civilisation in protecting itself from calamity – and even, perhaps, its deep implication in its own dis-astering. The Lisbon quake was the event that spurred humankind to take responsibility for its own affairs, demanding an ambivalent mixture of rational mastery and cautious humility that might yet still prove insufficient. For our species, it was the sense of vulnerability, rather than the certainty of domination, that provided the impetus to rise above the threatening forces of the Earth. If our attempts to take responsibility for the world have left it in disarray, the question arises as to what actions might be prudent in preparing for disaster and catastrophe in the cities and settlements of today, and what interventions may only make things worse. The time and place of the Anthropocene is not simply about how we prepare for and respond to disasters or about how and where we build settlements and with what adjustments. It is about how to inhabit a world where, we now know, our species has been active in accumulating disasters. The challenge of the Anthropocene lies in acknowledging our implication in our own endangerment, and in the vandalisation of a planet we have not long called home, in a way that spurs us to protective action rather than to further reckless exploitation, or disabling panic.

68 *Disaster zone*

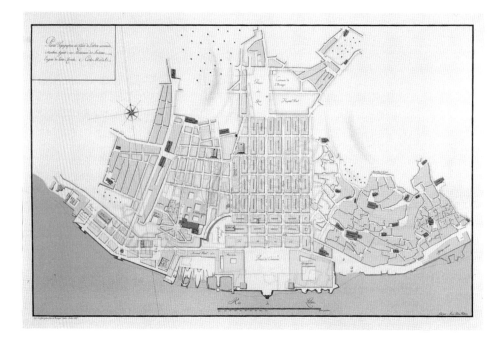

Figure 2.5 A Topographical Plan of Lisbon ruined by the earthquake of 1755 with superimposed reconstruction project of Eugénio dos Santos Carvalho and Carlos Mardel, 12 June 1758 (Coloured lithograph by João Pedro Ribeiro, 1947)
Source: Museu de Lisboa

Living in an earthquake

> The Earth quakes constantly but so slightly that we do not sense it.[119]

Around 500,000 earthquakes are detected each year with current instruments, but only about 100,000 of these can be sensed by humans. Most earthquakes take place in a 40,000 km-long horseshoe-shaped seismic zone along the Pacific Plate boundary, known as the Pacific Ring of Fire. The Earth sciences have helped us to understand the deep workings of this turbulent planet, and have suggested that such catastrophes and convulsions as the Lisbon earthquake – capable of upsetting all human creations and constructions – are but the minor readjustments of a planet in constant motion. But in spite of our better scientific understanding of the shaky ground that we dwell on, for the most part we have continued to presume (or, rather, hope blindly for) the solidity and stability of the Earth beneath our feet. And we are not much better now then we were in the aftermath of Lisbon's disaster at making sense of it all. Recent narratives around the Anthropocene have resonance with the impact of the Lisbon earthquake in terms of the scale of the cultural shift involved in readjusting to increasingly volatile earthly conditions. The destabilising concept of the Anthropocene also augurs a shift. We are starting to acknowledge the earth-moving, sky-falling effects of a human-natural-planetary hybrid system and the cultural, philosophical and political aftershocks. After all, it is when the Earth fails us in its presumed, eternal role as nurturer that it appears to us afresh, all itself, unruly – refusing to be instrumentalised. Michel Serres recounts his personal experience of an earthquake that not only shakes the ground beneath his feet but also unravels familiar world connections and conditions:

> All of a sudden the ground shakes off its gear: walls tremble, ready to collapse, roofs buckle, people fall, communications are interrupted, noise keeps you from hearing each other, the thin technological film tears, squealing and snapping like metal or crystal; the world, finally, comes to me, resembles me, all in distress. A thousand useless ties come undone, liquidated, while out of the shadows beneath unbalanced feet rises essential being, background noise, the rumbling world...[120]

The Earth is astonishingly good at unleashing primordial forces of destruction and pulling the ground out from under our feet. Nigel Clark draws attention to the 'radical asymmetry' of realities beyond 'the reach of negotiation': 'the impression that deep-seated forces of the Earth can leave on social worlds is out of all proportion to the power of social actors to legislate over the lithosphere.'[121] The Anthropocene epoch-in-the-making marks a growing recognition of humankind as an unpredictable geological and geomorphic force. At the same time, intractable seismic, volcanic, meteoric, atmospheric and other earth-moving, earth-shattering and earth-changing forces attest to the limits of the human. Humans may be newly and inadvertently powerful in terms of planetary dynamics but still powerless in the face of geophysical forces. As Clark writes: 'Whatever we have made or unmade of our world, in this sense, we remain partially under the sway of forces beyond our control, and even beyond our influence.'[122] Our own interventions into Earth's systems have forced a confrontation with a geologic materiality and temporality far beyond the human scale. Our social, political and communal life in future will need to be responsive to the unpredictability and increasing hostility of our earthly home; we will need to prepare for living in a permanent state of earthquake.

While most earthquakes are caused by movement of the Earth's tectonic plates, human activity is also known to produce earthquakes. The 2008 Sichuan earthquake, which resulted in 69,227 fatalities, is now considered the first known human-made earthquake. The Zipingu Dam, in the Sichuan Province of China, was built near a fault line, and the pressure of water in the dam probably accelerated the rate of movement of the fault and increased the power of the earthquake. Other human activities, such as drilling, boring and mining, are also thought to contribute to earth tremors. Some researchers are exploring whether anthropogenic global warming has increased seismic activity, on the basis of the possibility that melting glaciers and rising sea levels disturb the balance of pressure on Earth's tectonic plates, thus causing an increase in the frequency and intensity of earthquakes. The rapid growth of megacities such as Mexico City, Tokyo and Tehran in areas of seismic activity is another major cause for concern. It is becoming clear that the violence done by earthquakes – of any magnitude – is exacerbated by planetary-scale engineering, massive city and infrastructure constructions, and the high-risk conditions in which nuclear power is generated. Disasters waiting to happen are multiple, cascading, hybrid and exceedingly dangerous, like the more recent triple-disaster of the Tōhoku earthquake, tsunami and nuclear fire. Humans are literally destabilising the lithosphere beneath their feet.

Uncontrollable earthly calamities, constellated with the unintended consequences of human actions, will always threaten the fragile order we create. The Anthropocene ushers in a new kind of planetary turbulence: a confusion of human and non-human capabilities, actions, and consequences. In the Anthropocene disaster zone, what does a renewed sense of implication in earth-changing mean for humans? The Anthropocene is a dis-astering idea that might yet provoke attention – not only to the physical vulnerabilities inherent in human settlements, but to the political, philosophical and social upheavals that disaster entails. Dwelling on a planet capable of taking us by surprise, we confront the necessity of openness to the Earth's intrinsic instability. Nigel Clark writes: 'the disaster is a moment that calls for an audacious response. If it is not to be a prelude to despair, the disaster must be an incitement to risk-taking, improvisation and experiment.'[123] The Anthropocene disaster zone calls urgently for alternative ways of framing, anticipating and responding to catastrophes. It demands, on pain of annihilation, that human societies learn to live more skilfully and more provisionally with the increasingly unruly elements of a disastrously anthropogenic world.

Keep looking ahead.

Notes

1 Immanuel Kant, 'History and natural description of the most noteworthy occurrences of the earthquake that struck a large part of the Earth at the end of the year 1755', (1756) trans. Olaf Reinhardt in *Natural Science, The Cambridge Edition of the Works of Immanuel Kant*, ed. Eric Watkins (Cambridge: Cambridge University Press, 2012): 337–364; 344; Immanuel Kant fixed the time of the Lisbon earthquake at 9:50 am.
2 Thomas Chase in *The Lisbon Earthquake of 1st November 1755: Some British Eye-Witness Accounts*, ed. Judite Nozes (Lisbon: British Historical Society of Portugal, 1987):39–60; 55. See also 'Letter Lisbon Harbour, Nov.19 1755' in *The Lisbon Earthquake of 1st November 1755: Some British Eye-Witness Accounts*, ed. Judite Nozes (Lisbon: British Historical Society of Portugal, 1987): 71–73; 71.
3 Thomas Downing Kendrick, *The Lisbon Earthquake* (London: Methuen & Co., 1956): 24.
4 '(1755) An Account…' in *The Lisbon Earthquake of 1st November 1755: Some British Eye-Witness Accounts*, ed. Judite Nozes (Lisbon: British Historical Society of Portugal, 1987): 71–73; 23.
5 Thomas Chase in *The Lisbon Earthquake of 1st November 1755: Some British Eye-Witness Accounts*, ed. Judite Nozes (Lisbon: British Historical Society of Portugal, 1987): 39–60; 57.
6 'Letter Lisbon Harbour, Nov. 19 1755' in *The Lisbon Earthquake of 1st November 1755: Some British Eye-Witness Accounts*, ed. Judite Nozes (Lisbon: British Historical Society of Portugal, 1987): 71–73; 72; see also Thomas Downing Kendrick, *The Lisbon Earthquake* (London: Methuen & Co., 1956): 31.
7 '(1755) An Account…' in *The Lisbon Earthquake of 1st November 1755: Some British Eye-Witness Accounts*, ed. Judite Nozes (Lisbon: British Historical Society of Portugal, 1987): 17–28; 17.
8 'Letter Lisbon, Nov. 19' in *The Lisbon Earthquake of 1st November 1755: Some British Eye-Witness Accounts*, ed. Judite Nozes (Lisbon: British Historical Society of Portugal, 1987): 80.
9 'Letter Lisbon, Nov. 19' in *The Lisbon Earthquake of 1st November 1755: Some British Eye-Witness Accounts*, ed. Judite Nozes (Lisbon: British Historical Society of Portugal, 1987): 81.
10 Immanuel Kant, 'History and natural description of the most noteworthy occurrences of the earthquake that struck a large part of the Earth at the end of the year 1755', (1756) trans. Olaf Reinhardt in *Natural Science, The Cambridge Edition of the Works of Immanuel Kant*, ed. Eric Watkins (Cambridge: Cambridge University Press, 2012): 337–364; 345.
11 Voltaire, 'Poem on the Lisbon disaster' in *Candide and Related Texts*, ed. David Wootton (Indianapolis: Hackett Publishing Company, 2000): 99–108; 104; this translation is a

reproduction of *Voltaire, Works*, trans. Tobias Smollett and others) (London: J. Newbery, 1761–1765).
12 Thomas Downing Kendrick, *The Lisbon Earthquake* (London: Methuen & Co., 1956): 22–23.
13 Nigel Clark, *Inhuman Nature: Sociable Life on a Dynamic Planet* (London: Sage, 2011): 5.
14 Eyal Weizman, 'Matters of calculation: the evidence of the Anthropocene', Eyal Weizman in conversation with Heather Davis and Etienne Turpin in *Architecture in the Anthropocene: Encounters Among Design, Deep Time, Science and Philosophy* (Ann Arbor, MI: Open Humanities Press, 2013): 63–81; 64.
15 Nigel Clark, 'Geo-politics and the disaster of the Anthropocene' in *Disasters and Politics: Materials, Experiments, Preparedness*, eds. Manuel Tironi, Israel Rodríguez-Giralt and Michael Guggenheim (Chichester: John Wiley & Sons, 2014): 19–37; 20.
16 Michel Serres, *The Natural Contract* (Ann Arbor: University of Michigan Press, 1995): 16.
17 Will Steffen, Paul J. Crutzen and John R. McNeill, 'The Anthropocene: are humans now overwhelming the great forces of nature?', *Ambio* 36.8 (December 2007): 614–621.
18 Nigel Clark, *Inhuman Nature: Sociable Life on a Dynamic Planet* (London: Sage, 2011): xiv.
19 Theodor Adorno, *Negative Dialectics* (London: Routledge,1973): 361.
20 Voltaire, 'Poem on the Lisbon disaster' in *Candide and Related Texts*, ed. David Wootton (Indianapolis: Hackett Publishing Company, 2000): 99–108.
21 Thomas Downing Kendrick, *The Lisbon Earthquake* (London: Methuen & Co., 1956): 25.
22 Thomas Downing Kendrick, *The Lisbon Earthquake* (London: Methuen & Co., 1956): 28.
23 Thomas Downing Kendrick, *The Lisbon Earthquake* (London: Methuen & Co., 1956): 32.
24 Voltaire, letter to Jean-Robert Tronchin, in *Correspondance*, ed. Theodore Besterman (Paris: Bibliotheque de la Pléiade, 1978). See also Marie-Hélène Huet, *The Culture of Disaster* (Chicago and London: The University of Chicago Press, 2012): 40.
25 Thomas Downing Kendrick, *The Lisbon Earthquake* (London: Methuen & Co., 1956): a summary of the first published description appeared in a pamphlet from Coimbra dated 20 December 1755: 'Carta em que hum amigo dá noticia a outro do lamantavle successo de Lisboa.'
26 Anne Saada and Jean Sgard, 'Tremblements dans la presse', in *The Lisbon Earthquake of 1755: Representations and Reactions*, eds. E.D. Braun and John B. Radner (Oxford: Voltaire Foundation, 2005): 208–224. See also Anne Saada, 'Le désir d'informer: le tremblement de terre de Lisbonne, 1755' in *L'invention de la catastrophe au XVIIIe siècle. Du châtiment divin au désastre naturel*, eds. A.-M. Mercier-Faivre and C. Thomas (Genève: Droz, 2008): 208–230.
27 Anne Saada, 'Le désir d'informer: le tremblement de terre de Lisbonne, 1755' in *L'invention de la catastrophe au XVIIIe siècle. Du châtiment divin au désastre naturel*, eds. A.-M. Mercier-Faivre and C. Thomas (Genève: Droz, 2008): 208–230; 225.
28 Jean-Paul Poirier, *Le Tremblement de terre de Lisbonne* (Paris: Odile Jacob, 2005): 77.
29 Susan Neiman, *Evil in Modern Thought: An Alternative History of Philosophy* (Princeton and Oxford: Princeton University Press, 2002): 240; following Thomas Downing Kendrick, *The Lisbon Earthquake* (London: Methuen & Co., 1956): 122.
30 'A Particular Account…' in *The Lisbon Earthquake of 1st November 1755: Some British Eye-Witness Accounts*, ed. Judite Nozes (Lisbon: British Historical Society of Portugal, 1987): 89.
31 Fowke, A Genuine Letter in *The Lisbon Earthquake of 1st November 1755: Some British Eye-Witness Accounts*, ed. Judite Nozes (Lisbon: British Historical Society of Portugal, 1987): 63–67.
32 'Letter Lisbon Harbour, Nov.19 1755' in *The Lisbon Earthquake of 1st November 1755: Some British Eye-Witness Accounts*, ed. Judite Nozes (Lisbon: British Historical Society of Portugal, 1987): 71–73; 72.
33 Thomas Downing Kendrick, *The Lisbon Earthquake* (London: Methuen & Co., 1956): 41.
34 Thomas Downing Kendrick, *The Lisbon Earthquake* (London: Methuen & Co., 1956): 39.
35 'Letter from Abr. Castres' in *The Lisbon Earthquake of 1st November 1755: Some British Eye-Witness Accounts*, ed. Judite Nozes (Lisbon: British Historical Society of Portugal, 1987): 33–35; 34.
36 Thomas Downing Kendrick, *The Lisbon Earthquake* (London: Methuen & Co., 1956):.45.

72 Disaster zone

37 'Letter "Bellem, Nov. 20, 1755"' in *The Lisbon Earthquake of 1st November 1755: Some British Eye-Witness Accounts*, ed. Judite Nozes (Lisbon: British Historical Society of Portugal, 1987): 31.
38 Antonio Pereira de Figueiredo, *A narrative of the earthquake and fire of Lisbon by Antony Pereira, of the Congregation of the Oratory, an eye-witness thereof. Illustrated with notes. Translated from the Latin* (London: G. Hawkins, 1756).
39 Thomas Chase in *The Lisbon Earthquake of 1st November 1755: Some British Eye-Witness Accounts*, ed. Judite Nozes (Lisbon: British Historical Society of Portugal, 1987): 39–60; 57.
40 James O'Hara in *The Lisbon Earthquake of 1st November 1755: Some British Eye-Witness Accounts*, ed. Judite Nozes (Lisbon: British Historical Society of Portugal, 1987): 83–85; 84.
41 Russell R. Dynes, 'The dialogue between Voltaire and Rousseau on the Lisbon earthquake: the emergence of a social view,' *International Journal of Mass Emergencies and Disasters* 18.1 (March 2000): 106.
42 Thomas Downing Kendrick, *The Lisbon Earthquake* (London: Methuen & Co., 1956): 43–44; Antonio Pereira de Figueiredo's history of the Lisbon earthquake of 1761.
43 Thomas Downing Kendrick, *The Lisbon Earthquake* (London: Methuen & Co., 1956): 46: 'Memorias das principes Providencias que se derao no Terremoto, que padeceo a Corte de Lisboa no anno de 1775... por Amador Patricio de Lisboa.'
44 Susan Neiman, *Evil in Modern Thought: An Alternative History of Philosophy* (Princeton and Oxford: Princeton University Press, 2002): 248.
45 Thomas Downing Kendrick, *The Lisbon Earthquake* (London: Methuen & Co., 1956): 87–88: Gabriel Malagrida, 'Juizo da verdadeira causa do terremoto (An opinion on the true cause of the earthquake)'.
46 Thomas Downing Kendrick, *The Lisbon Earthquake* (London: Methuen & Co., 1956): 137; cf. Gabriel Malagrida.
47 Susan Neiman, *Evil in Modern Thought: An Alternative History of Philosophy* (Princeton and Oxford: Princeton University Press, 2002): 249.
48 Fowke, A Genuine Letter in *The Lisbon Earthquake of 1st November 1755: Some British Eye-Witness Accounts*, ed. Judite Nozes (Lisbon: British Historical Society of Portugal, 1987): 63–67.
49 'Letter "Lisbon, Nov. 19"' in *The Lisbon Earthquake of 1st November 1755: Some British Eye-Witness Accounts*, ed. Judite Nozes (Lisbon: British Historical Society of Portugal, 1987): 79–82; 79.
50 'Letter "Lisbon, Nov. 19"' in *The Lisbon Earthquake of 1st November 1755: Some British Eye-Witness Accounts*, ed. Judite Nozes (Lisbon: British Historical Society of Portugal, 1987): 79–82; 80.
51 Thomas Chase in *The Lisbon Earthquake of 1st November 1755: Some British Eye-Witness Accounts*, ed. Judite Nozes (Lisbon: British Historical Society of Portugal, 1987): 39–60; 55.
52 Helena Murteira, 'City-making in the Enlightenment: the rebuilding of Lisbon after the earthquake of 1755', *E.A.R. Edinburgh Architecture Research* 29 (2004): 19–22.
53 John R. Mullin, 'The reconstruction of Lisbon following the earthquake of 1755: a study in despotic planning', *Planning Perspectives* 7.2 (April 1992): 157–179.
54 Russell R. Dynes, 'The Lisbon earthquake in 1755: the first modern disaster' in *The Lisbon earthquake of 1755. Representations and reaction*, eds. Theodore E. D. Braun and John B. Radner (Oxford: SVEC, The Voltaire Foundation, 2005): 34–49; 46, 48.
55 Marie-Hélène Huet, *The Culture of Disaster* (Chicago and London: The University of Chicago Press, 2012): 7.
56 Susan Neiman, *Evil in Modern Thought: An Alternative History of Philosophy* (Princeton and Oxford: Princeton University Press, 2002): 250.
57 Voltaire, *Candide and Other Stories*, trans. Roger Pearson (London: Everyman's Library, 1992): 11–12.
58 Voltaire, *Candide and Other Stories*, trans. Roger Pearson (London: Everyman's Library, 1992): 14.
59 Gilles Deleuze, course on Leibniz, Vincennes-St. Denis, Paris (7 April 1987). See also Marie-Hélène Huet, *The Culture of Disaster* (Chicago and London: The University of Chicago Press, 2012): 49. For a full transcript of the lecture see www.webdeleuze.com/php/texte.php?cle=147&groupe=Leibniz&langue=

60 Nigel Clark, *Inhuman Nature: Sociable Life on a Dynamic Planet* (London: Sage, 2011): 90. See also Susan Neiman, *Evil in Modern Thought: An Alternative History of Philosophy* (Princeton and Oxford: Princeton University Press, 2002): 246.
61 Julian Barnes, 'A candid view of Candide', *The Guardian* (1 July 2011) www.theguardian.com/books/2011/jul/01candide-voltaire-rereading-julian-barnes.
62 Marie-Hélène Huet, *The Culture of Disaster* (Chicago and London: The University of Chicago Press, 2012).
63 Jean-Jacques Rousseau, 'Letter to Voltaire on Optimism, 18 August 1756', in *Candide and Related Texts*, ed. David Wootton (Indianapolis: Hackett Publishing Company, 2000): 108–122.
64 Marie-Hélène Huet, *The Culture of Disaster* (Chicago and London: The University of Chicago Press, 2012): 54.
65 Jean-Jacques Rousseau, 'Letter to Voltaire on Optimism, 18 August 1756', in *Candide and Related Texts*, ed. David Wootton (Indianapolis: Hackett Publishing Company, 2000): 108–122; 110–111.
66 Jean-Jacques Rousseau, 'Letter to Voltaire on Optimism, 18 August 1756', in *Candide and Related Texts*, ed. David Wootton (Indianapolis: Hackett Publishing Company, 2000): 108–122; 111.
67 Jean-Jacques Rousseau, 'Letter to Voltaire on Optimism, 18 August 1756', in *Candide and Related Texts*, ed. David Wootton (Indianapolis: Hackett Publishing Company, 2000): 108–122; 110–111.
68 Russell R. Dynes, 'The dialogue between Voltaire and Rousseau on the Lisbon earthquake: the emergence of a social view,' *International Journal of Mass Emergencies and Disasters* 18.1 (March 2000): 97–115; 106.
69 Marie-Hélène Huet, *The Culture of Disaster* (Chicago and London: The University of Chicago Press, 2012): 53.
70 Marie-Hélène Huet, *The Culture of Disaster* (Chicago and London: The University of Chicago Press, 2012): 7.
71 Nigel Clark, 'Turbulent prospects: sustaining urbanism on a dynamic planet' in *Urban Futures: Critical Commentaries on Shaping the City*, eds. Malcolm Miles and Tim Hall (London and New York: Routledge, 2003): 182–193; 190.
72 Bronwyn Hayward, 'Rethinking resilience: reflections on the earthquakes in Christchurch, New Zealand, 2010 and 2011', *Ecology and Society* 18.4 (2013): 37.
73 Bronwyn Hayward, 'Rethinking resilience: reflections on the earthquakes in Christchurch, New Zealand, 2010 and 2011', *Ecology and Society* 18.4 (2013): 37.
74 Paul Chatterton, 'The urban impossible: A eulogy for the unfinished city', *City*, 14.3 (2010): 234–244.
75 Renata Tyszczuk, 'Future Worlds – to-ing and fro-ing', in *Atlas: Geography, Architecture and Change in an Interdependent World*, eds. R. Tyszczuk, J. Smith, N. Clark and M. Butcher (London: Black Dog Publishing 2012): 132–139; 137.
76 Jean-Jacques Rousseau, 'Letter to Voltaire on Optimism, 18 August 1756', in *Candide and Related Texts*, ed. David Wootton (Indianapolis: Hackett Publishing Company, 2000): 108–122; 118.
77 The first essay was published in two instalments on 24 and 31 January 1756 in *Wochentliche Konigsbergische Frag – und Anzeigungs-Nachrichten*. The second essay is the most detailed and was published as an independent piece by Johan Heinrich Hartung's press in Konigsbeg dated 21 February 1756; it was advertised in the 11 March 1756 issue of *Konigsbergische Frag – und Anzeigungs-Nachrichten*. The final essay was published in the 10 and 17 April 1756 issues of the same Konigsberg weekly paper.
78 Immanuel Kant, 'On the causes of earthquakes on the occasion of the calamity that befell the western countries of Europe towards the end of last year', trans. Olaf Reinhardt in *Immanuel Kant, Natural Science*, ed. Eric Watkins (Cambridge: Cambridge University Press, 2012): 327–336; 332.
79 Immanuel Kant, 'On the causes of earthquakes on the occasion of the calamity that befell the western countries of Europe towards the end of last year', trans. Olaf Reinhardt in *Immanuel Kant, Natural Science*, ed. Eric Watkins (Cambridge: Cambridge University Press, 2012): 327–336; 330.

80 Immanuel Kant, 'On the causes of earthquakes on the occasion of the calamity that befell the western countries of Europe towards the end of last year', trans. Olaf Reinhardt in *Immanuel Kant, Natural Science*, ed. Eric Watkins (Cambridge: Cambridge University Press, 2012): 327–336; 331.

81 Immanuel Kant, 'On the causes of earthquakes on the occasion of the calamity that befell the western countries of Europe towards the end of last year', trans. Olaf Reinhardt in *Immanuel Kant, Natural Science*, ed. Eric Watkins (Cambridge: Cambridge University Press, 2012): 327–336; 332.

82 Immanuel Kant, 'History and natural description of the most noteworthy occurrences of the earthquake that struck a large part of the Earth at the end of the year 1755', (1756) trans. Olaf Reinhardt in *Natural Science, The Cambridge Edition of the Works of Immanuel Kant*, ed. Eric Watkins (Cambridge: Cambridge University Press, 2012): 337–364; 342.

83 Immanuel Kant, 'History and natural description of the most noteworthy occurrences of the earthquake that struck a large part of the Earth at the end of the year 1755', (1756) trans. Olaf Reinhardt in *Natural Science, The Cambridge Edition of the Works of Immanuel Kant*, ed. Eric Watkins (Cambridge: Cambridge University Press, 2012): 337–364; 359.

84 Immanuel Kant, 'History and natural description of the most noteworthy occurrences of the earthquake that struck a large part of the Earth at the end of the year 1755', (1756) trans. Olaf Reinhardt in *Natural Science, The Cambridge Edition of the Works of Immanuel Kant*, ed. Eric Watkins (Cambridge: Cambridge University Press, 2012): 337–364; 360.

85 Immanuel Kant, 'History and natural description of the most noteworthy occurrences of the earthquake that struck a large part of the Earth at the end of the year 1755', (1756) trans. Olaf Reinhardt in *Natural Science, The Cambridge Edition of the Works of Immanuel Kant*, ed. Eric Watkins (Cambridge: Cambridge University Press, 2012): 337–364; 363.

86 Immanuel Kant, 'History and natural description of the most noteworthy occurrences of the earthquake that struck a large part of the Earth at the end of the year 1755', (1756) trans. Olaf Reinhardt in *Natural Science, The Cambridge Edition of the Works of Immanuel Kant*, ed. Eric Watkins (Cambridge: Cambridge University Press, 2012): 337–364; 368.

87 Immanuel Kant, 'History and natural description of the most noteworthy occurrences of the earthquake that struck a large part of the Earth at the end of the year 1755', (1756) trans. Olaf Reinhardt in *Natural Science, The Cambridge Edition of the Works of Immanuel Kant*, ed. Eric Watkins (Cambridge: Cambridge University Press, 2012): 337–364; 368.

88 Benjamin Franklin (1706–1783) was an American politician and physicist. His main scientific work was concerned with studies of electrical phenomena, which included lightning.

89 Immanuel Kant, 'Continued observations on the earthquakes that have been experienced for some time' (1756), trans. Olaf Reinhardt in *Natural Science, The Cambridge Edition of the Works of Immanuel Kant*, ed. Eric Watkins (Cambridge: Cambridge University Press, 2012): 365–373; 373.

90 Walter Benjamin's talk, broadcast by the Berliner Rundfunk, is printed in *Gesammelte Schriften 7*, eds. Rolf Tiedemann and Hermann Schweppenhäuser (Frankfurt/Main: Suhrkamp Verlag): 220–226; in English as 'The Lisbon Earthquake', trans. Rodney Livingstone, in *Selected Writings* 2, eds. Michael W. Jennings, Howard Eiland, and Gary Smith (Cambridge, Mass.: Belknap/Harvard University Press, 1999): 536–540; 538.

91 Deborah Coen, *The Earthquake Observers: Disaster Science from Lisbon to Richter* (The University of Chicago Press, 2013): 7.

92 Deborah Coen, *The Earthquake Observers: Disaster Science from Lisbon to Richter* (The University of Chicago Press, 2013): 8.

93 Immanuel Kant, Physiche Geographie, cf. Deborah Coen, *The Earthquake Observers: Disaster Science from Lisbon to Richter* (The University of Chicago Press, 2013): 8.

94 Gene Ray, 'Reading the Lisbon earthquake: Adorno, Lyotard, and the contemporary sublime', *The Yale Journal of Criticism* 17.1 (2004): 1–18; 11.

95 Immanuel Kant, Critique of Judgment, cf. Gene Ray, 'Reading the Lisbon earthquake: Adorno, Lyotard, and the contemporary sublime', *The Yale Journal of Criticism* 17.1 (2004): 1–18; 10.

96 Timothy Morton, *Hyperobjects: Philosophy and Ecology after the End of the World* (Minneapolis and London: University of Minnesota Press, 2013): 16.

97 Marie-Hélène Huet, *The Culture of Disaster* (Chicago and London: The University of Chicago Press, 2012): 4.

98 Marie-Hélène Huet, *The Culture of Disaster* (Chicago and London: The University of Chicago Press, 2012): 3.
99 Nigel Clark, *Inhuman Nature: Sociable Life on a Dynamic Planet* (London: Sage, 2011): 89.
100 Jan Zalasiewicz, *The Earth After Us: What Legacy will Humans Leave in the Rocks?* (Oxford: Oxford University Press, 2009): 240.
101 Maurice Blanchot, *The Writing of Disaster*, trans. Ann Smock (University of Nebraska Press: Lincoln, 1986): 2.
102 Maurice Blanchot, *The Writing of Disaster*, trans. Ann Smock (University of Nebraska Press: Lincoln, 1986): 55.
103 Maurice Blanchot, *The Writing of Disaster*, trans. Ann Smock (University of Nebraska Press: Lincoln, 1986): 41.
104 Richard Kearney, *On Stories* (Abingdon: Routledge, 2002): 22.
105 Marie-Hélène Huet, *The Culture of Disaster* (Chicago and London: The University of Chicago Press, 2012): 2.
106 Susan Neiman, *Evil in Modern Thought: An Alternative History of Philosophy* (Princeton and Oxford: Princeton University Press, 2002): 241.
107 Marie-Hélène Huet, *The Culture of Disaster* (Chicago and London: The University of Chicago Press, 2012): 2.
108 Marie-Hélène Huet, *The Culture of Disaster* (Chicago and London: The University of Chicago Press, 2012): 9.
109 Susan Neiman, *Evil in Modern Thought: An Alternative History of Philosophy* (Princeton and Oxford: Princeton University Press, 2002): 2.
110 Susan Neiman, *Evil in Modern Thought: An Alternative History of Philosophy* (Princeton and Oxford: Princeton University Press, 2002): 8.
111 Susan Neiman, *Evil in Modern Thought: An Alternative History of Philosophy* (Princeton and Oxford: Princeton University Press, 2002): 239.
112 Susan Neiman, *Evil in Modern Thought: An Alternative History of Philosophy* (Princeton and Oxford: Princeton University Press, 2002): 239.
113 Theodor Adorno, *Negative Dialectics* (London: Routledge, 1973): 361.
114 Gene Ray, 'Reading the Lisbon Earthquake: Adorno, Lyotard, and the Contemporary Sublime,' *The Yale Journal of Criticism* 17.1 (2004): 1–18; 13.
115 Nigel Clark, *Inhuman Nature: Sociable Life on a Dynamic Planet* (London: Sage, 2011): 96.
116 Susan Neiman, *Evil in Modern Thought: An Alternative History of Philosophy* (Princeton and Oxford: Princeton University Press, 2002): 250.
117 Gene Ray, 'Reading the Lisbon Earthquake: Adorno, Lyotard, and the Contemporary Sublime,' *The Yale Journal of Criticism* 17.1 (2004):1–18; 1.
118 Timothy Morton, *Hyperobjects: Philosophy and Ecology after the End of the World* (Minneapolis and London: University of Minnesota Press, 2013): 16; emphasis in original.
119 Jeffrey Mehlman, *Walter Benjamin for Children: An Essay on his Radio Years* (Chicago and London: University of Chicago Press, 1993): 30; Walter Benjamin, 'The Lisbon Earthquake'.
120 Michel Serres, *The Natural Contract* (Ann Arbor: University of Michigan Press, 1995): 124.
121 Nigel Clark, *Inhuman Nature: Sociable Life on a Dynamic Planet* (London: Sage, 2011): xvi.
122 Nigel Clark, 'Ex-orbitant globality', *Theory, Culture and Society* 22.5 (2005): 165–185; 14.
123 Nigel Clark, 'Geo-politics and the disaster of the Anthropocene' in *Disasters and Politics: Materials, Experiments, Preparedness*, eds. Manuel Tironi, Israel Rodríguez-Giralt and Michael Guggenheim (Chichester: John Wiley & Sons, 2014): 19–37; 22.

3 Proving ground

WARNING: radiation risk

A layer of radioactive materials deposited in soils across the globe since 1945 as a result of nuclear weapons deployment and testing marks a decisive geological moment of Earth transformation in the Anthropocene. The period after World War II is referred to as the 'Great Acceleration' – or second phase of the Anthropocene – and is characterised by dramatic increases in population growth, industrialisation, urbanisation, consumption and technoscientific development.[1] It marks the moment, many commentators argue, that human activities go from merely influencing to dominating the planetary environment.[2] It is a juncture now seen as most likely to meet the demand for a geosynchronous marker in the stratigraphic formalisation of the Anthropocene.

The 'Great Acceleration' coincides with the nuclear age, the space race, and the rise of global environmentalism. But the acceleration trajectory has a sense of finality in the nuclear age, 'an age or epoch that opens the possibility of destroying its own epochal limit'.[3] Nuclear-age humanity evinces an extraordinary belief in unending technological progress, even while living everyday life in and around the technological infrastructures of prospective human extinction. We pursue progress as if compulsively, in the face of growing evidence that what we are advancing toward is our own species' demise. The nuclear age has so far unfolded as a series of rehearsals for the end of the world. Nuclear weapons are amassed under the banner of ultimate deterrence – a war waged against the future, whose casualties will be everyone. It is in this sense, that the Great Acceleration can be seen as a dry run for the catastrophic environmental change that may escalate yet more in the future. In both cases a stricken future is accelerating towards humanity – a humanity abetting that acceleration.

The Cold War period was marked by the development of an elaborate apparatus of emergency. This included: the setting-up of the first 'think tank', the RAND corporation (which stood for 'Research ANd Development' of military strategy) in 1948; the development of emergency scenarios; the founding of new proving grounds and test sites for warfare and civil defence; the widespread diffusion of surveillance technologies by the military-scientific complex; and the establishment of regimes of urban securitisation in the name of preparedness for nuclear disaster. Between July 1945 and September 1992, the United States conducted 1,149 nuclear detonations (including the 35 detonations of Operation Plowshares and 24 joint US–UK nuclear tests). The Japanese artist Isao Hashimoto's animated map of 'Nuclear explosions 1945–1998' displays the planetary politics and temporal disjunctions of the nuclear age. For if the imaginary of global nuclear war presents it as the ultimate disaster, brutal and sudden and to be deterred, Hashimoto's video shows that, for over six decades of the 20th century, nuclear war had been raging all along, in proving grounds and test sites around the world.[4]

The test sites built in the Nevada desert in the 1950s under the rubric of 'civil defence' against the power of atomic weapons were part of a concerted effort to engage US citizens in imagining collectively the worst-case scenarios of physical destruction. In other words, the US state sought to prepare its citizens for nuclear apocalypse. The test cities and irradiated atolls of the nuclear imagination relied on the construction of fictions. These nuclear fictions had an astounding and unpredictable acceleration of their own. They came to pass as a frenzied surge: from the inauguration of weapons of mass destruction, through rehearsals of cities under attack and civil defence programmes,[5] to scenarios of total war and the vainglorious ruses of nuclear deterrence, to warnings of doom that brought environmental and then energy issues to attention, to the secret burial and commemoration of nuclear waste, and the controversies around nuclear futures. Current imaginings of future planetary contamination, of exclusion zones and of struggles to survive in a post-apocalyptic, post-human world continue to have much in common with those of the Cold War. If we want to understand the failure of all attempts so far to disarm the world; or if we want to trace, in the Cold War arms race, an important antecedent to the technoscientific 'fixes' currently being proposed for an ailing planet; we need to understand the strange dialectic that fuelled the development of costly and polluting nuclear weapons: one of terrorised inevitability, on the one hand, and scientistic triumphalism on the other.

> Your first thought upon awakening be: 'Atom'. For you should not begin your day with the illusion that what surrounds you is a stable world.[6]

The historian Gunther Anders' *Commandments in the Atomic Age* signals a wake-up call. The thermonuclear anxiety of the Cold War was a harbinger of one of the key motifs of the Anthropocene thesis: the human reduced to a fossil trace. Imaginings of nuclear apocalypse inhabit the same narrative territory as other world-ending scenarios like the impact of giant asteroids, the sixth mass species extinction, and, most recently, climate change. Apocalypse has two meanings: it can indicate both revelation and the end of times. The Anthropocene thesis resonates with both meanings. As *the story to end all stories* it reveals humans and their terrifying capabilities as they are now, but also telegraphs their future extinguishment.

Test cities

> Suppose we considered the war itself as a laboratory?[7]

About 90 miles southwest of Salt Lake City lie the vast unknown expanses of the Dugway Proving Ground. Missing on maps and shrouded in official secrecy and Cold War myths, this 800,000-acre area of salt flats and non-arable land was the environmental testbed for dangerous and toxic chemical, biological and incendiary warfare experiments – or, as Mike Davis has called it, 'the devil's own laboratory'.[8] Government scientists tested poison gas, phosgene, cyanogen, hydrogen cyanide, and other deadly airborne agents at Dugway, and also developed anthrax. Rumours persist that some areas will need to remain quarantined 'for at least 1,000 years'.[9] In 1943, the Chemical Warfare Corps of the US Army and the Standard Oil Development Company started constructing 'enemy villages' under the instructions of the National Defense Research Committee (NDRC).[10] Their purpose was to test the impact of the latest incendiary bombs on urban areas. Such devices were central to the indiscriminate counter-civilian Allied campaign intent on total devastation of enemy cities.[11] The test cities were detailed reproductions of typical housing found in the industrial districts of German and Japanese cities.

The remnants of 'German village', as it is labelled on declassified US military maps, are all that remain of the larger 'composite German/Japanese doomtown'.[12] The surviving double tenement block – known as Building 8100 – is typical of the *Mietskasernen* or 'rent barracks' of working-class housing in 1940s Berlin, considered at the time to be the densest slums in Europe. The creation of the enemy villages involved meticulous research and careful imitation. The expatriate German architects Erich Mendelsohn and Konrad Wachsmann and the Czechoslovakian architect Antonin Raymond, an expert in Japanese construction, were employed as consultants in the design of the replica houses. Members of the Authenticity Division of RKO film studios and set designers who had worked on wartime films were hired to design appropriate furniture and fittings. Building materials were carefully sourced: Douglas fir and loblolly pine replaced the European spruce normally used in German construction, and either original hard-packed rice straw *tatami* or imitation mats made from thistle were used in the Japanese-type buildings. The forms of typical Berlin rooftops and those of factory cities on the Rhine were replicated with examples of tile-on-batten and slate-over-sheathing roofs, in order to test different possibilities of penetration and intensity of fires in target buildings. The moisture content of wood and other materials in the different enemy climates was mimicked in order to carefully calibrate the 'ignition time' of each structure.

It took only 44 days to complete the six apartment blocks of German Village and the 12 double apartments of the Japanese counterpart. Their construction was speeded up by the wholesale conscription of inmates from the Utah State prison as labour. It took hardly any time to destroy the enemy village. The entire complex was fire-bombed with the newly invented incendiary devices of napalm (AN-M69) and thermite (AN-M60). It was then completely reconstructed at least three times between May and September 1943. The predictable weak spots were the timber-framed attics for German housing and the *tatami* floors of Japanese dwellings. In an authoritative post-war report, Horatio Bond, the NDRC's chief incendiary expert, underscored Allied frustration at the difficulty of real-life incendiary attacks: 'Berlin was harder to burn than most of the other German cities. There was better construction and better "compartmentation".'[13] He insisted on the calculus of destruction: 'This is a story about the destruction of cities. I must emphasise that it was not hit-or-miss. The amount of destruction to both cities and industries could be calculated in advance.'[14] Operation Gomorrah, the firebombing raid on Hamburg in 1943 in the early hours of July 27, is described by W. G. Sebald in harrowing detail:

> At one-twenty am, a firestorm of an intensity that no one would ever before have thought possible arose. The fire now rising two thousand metres into the sky, snatched oxygen to itself so violently that the air currents reached hurricane force, resonating like mighty organs with all their stops pulled out at once. The

fire burned like this for three hours. At its height, the storm lifted gables and roofs from buildings, flung rafters and entire advertising billboards through the air, tore trees from the ground, and drove human beings before it like living torches... When day broke, the summer dawn could not penetrate the leaden gloom above the city... Horribly disfigured corpses lay everywhere... the remains of families consisting of several people could be carried away in a single laundry basket.[15]

The devastation of city burning in Germany was a prelude to what Mike Davis has called the 'B-29 autos-da-fé' inflicted on Japanese cities, which by the end of the war left approximately one million Japanese people dead.[16] Japan's vulnerability to incendiary attack, because of its 'paper cities' – ephemeral constructions of paper and wood – was well understood by military strategists. By the end of the war, US military statisticians calculated that between 50 and 90 per cent of the populations in nearly 70 cities under attack had been killed.[17] The US Air Force bombing raids on Tokyo began on 9 March 1945. Two thousand tons of napalm and magnesium incendiaries were dropped in the dense pattern devised at the Dugway proving grounds to maximise both temperature and fire spread. An estimated 100,000 people were killed and an area of nearly 16 square miles was completely destroyed. When the macabre success of the raid was reported in the US press in May 1945, few complained. But there was more to come. General Henry 'Hap' Arnold had argued that 'three or four cities must be saved intact from the B-29s['regular operations]' as unspoiled targets for the new weapon'.[18]

At 05:29:21 (plus or minus 2 seconds) US time on 16 July 1945, the 'new weapon' was tested at the Alamagordo Bombing and Gunnery range, New Mexico. This was the Trinity test, the result of the Manhattan Project. The 'Gadget' device exploded with an energy equivalent to around 20 kilotonnes of TNT (84 TJ). Less than a month later, on 6 August 1945, 'Little Boy' was dropped on Hiroshima, followed three days later by 'Fat Man' on Nagasaki. The benign names attached to these weapons of such extraordinary destruction attracted barely any comment. The atomic bombs that destroyed the cities and caused the mass extermination of civilians were listed as 'tests' by the US Department of Energy. In the view of Susan Neiman, treating living cities as the laboratory of atomic warfare was a definitive ontological break for humanity: it 'disturbed the order of the universe, for it... had exceeded every prior limit to destruction and made complete and total destruction of life itself an ever-present possibility'.[19] The chronological marker 'After Hiroshima' makes immediate and intuitive sense: living in cities will never be the same. In his book *Survival City*, Tom Vanderbilt writes, referring to Adorno's doubt about the possibility of poetry 'after Auschwitz': 'If one could not write poetry after Auschwitz... then after Hiroshima, one could no longer speak of cities.' Once cities were conceived of as prime targets for this modern warfare, it was but a short step to the contemplation of the total erasure of a city, and an even shorter step to identify *all* cities as vulnerable to nuclear extinguishment. Vanderbilt continues, 'In one stroke, the concept of what it meant to live in a city, the parameters of security and the contours of daily life, had been fundamentally reordered. Over every city hovered the ghostly afterimage of Dead City.'[20]

In a culture of acceleration one war is but a proving ground for the next bigger event. The 'economic instinct' of the war effort seemed to demand that such expensively manufactured and stringently tested devices be put to use, regardless of the outcomes.[21] And as the historian Gunther Anders argues, 'Nagasaki syndrome' ensured that what had been done once could be repeated, with ever fewer reservations in each successive case.[22] The sixth day of August had been only a rehearsal for the ninth. Atrocities occurred because they could; because they had occurred before. As Zygmunt Bauman writes, 'once a contraption allowing the separation of technological capacity from moral imagination is put in place, it becomes self-propelling, self-reinforcing and self-reinvigorating'.[23] Moreover, for Anders, it is in the relatively new phenomenon of the 'hiatus (*Diskrepanz*) separating the human powers of creation and imagination that the contemporary variety of evil sets its roots'.[24] The moral calamity of our time 'does not grow from our sensuality or perfidity, dishonesty or licentiousness, nor even from exploitation – but from a *deficit of imagination*'.[25] The French philosopher Jean-Pierre Dupuy refers to this discrepancy as an irreducible gap: 'beyond certain thresholds our power of making and doing infinitely exceeds our capacity for feeling and imagining.'[26]

'I write to frighten you,' declared Harold C. Urey, a Manhattan Project scientist and member of the Federation of Atomic Scientists, in an open letter to the American public on 5 January 1946 in *Collier's* magazine. 'I'm a frightened man myself. All the scientists I know are frightened – frightened for their lives– and frightened for *your* life.' He followed with a frank account of the annihilation wrought by an atomic explosion:

> In an [atomic] explosion, thousands die within a fraction of a second. In the immediate area, there is nothing left standing. There are no walls. They are vanished into dust and smoke. There are no wounded. There are not even bodies. At the centre, a fire many times hotter than any fire we have known has pulverised buildings and human beings into nothingness.[27]

Later that same year, John Hersey's ethnographic account *Hiroshima*, written from the perspective of six survivors of the nuclear bomb, was published in *The New Yorker* on 31 August 1946. Hersey's vivid essay brought home the ways in which the mundane contingencies of everyday life had determined the fate of the city's inhabitants. From their stories it was clear that any notion of preparedness for such an attack was futile – survival depended simply on place and time: whether one was at home or on the way to work, still in bed or having breakfast, in one part of the city or another. Hersey's essay recounted the horrors of nuclear war in intricate detail. Scientific exactness and lyrical detail sit morbidly side-by-side in his narrative:

> He was the only person making his way into the city; he met hundreds and hundreds who were fleeing, and every one of them seemed to be hurt in some way. The eyebrows of some were burned off and skin hung from their faces and hands. Others, because of pain, held their arms up as if carrying something in both hands. Some were vomiting as they walked. Many were naked or in shreds of clothing. On some undressed bodies, the burns had made patterns – of undershirt straps and suspenders and, on the skin of some women (since white repelled the heat from the bomb and dark clothes absorbed it and conducted it to the skin), the shapes of flowers they had on their kimonos.[28]

By the time Hersey's account was published, the meaning of 'Hiroshima' was already becoming established as shorthand for the vulnerability of the American city – and New York City in particular – to nuclear disaster. Imaginings of New York under attack had appeared in evening editions of newspapers immediately after the bombing of the Japanese city, on 7 August 1945.[29] A book by Manhattan Project scientists, *One World or None* (1946), had also included a hypothetical description of an A-bomb exploded over Manhattan.[30] In a curious inversion of nuclear perpetrator to nuclear victim, 'Hiroshima' soon stood for New York City itself, as presented in a 1950 special issue of *Collier's*, 'Hiroshima USA', illustrated with mushroom clouds and detonations superimposed on views of Manhattan.[31] In a further twist, these depictions of nuclear clouds were also eerily prescient of the architects Buckminster Fuller and Shoji Sadao's emergency *Dome over Manhattan* project of 1960, which encapsulated a two-mile diameter section of midtown Manhattan in a climate-controlled transparent dome. Fuller offered backhanded reassurances about this city of last resort: 'The established cities will probably not adopt the doming until environmental and other emergencies make it imperative.' Throughout the Cold War, a stream of news reports and magazine articles, civil defence pamphlets, comics, films and TV shows continued to imagine the destruction of New York City. The imagery of nuclear attack and nuclear cataclysm centred on New York became ubiquitous. The repeated imaginary destruction and survival of the city remains a leitmotif of American popular culture.[32] The city was already implicated in the ominous code-name for wartime atomic tests, so it is no small irony that the Manhattan Project should be revisited on its namesake, to be destroyed again and again.

Figure 3.1 Project for a geodesic dome over Manhattan, R. Buckminster Fuller, with Shoji Sadao, 1960
Source: Estate of R. Buckminster Fuller

82 *Proving ground*

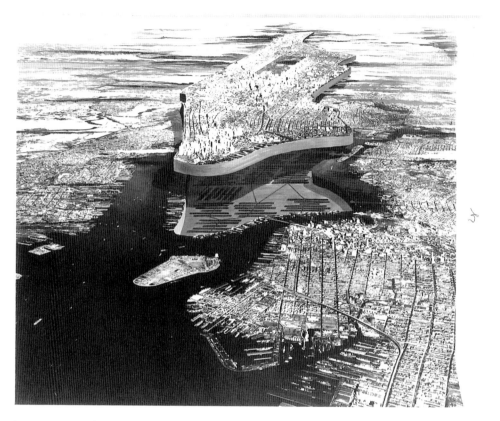

Figure 3.2 Manhattan Shelter Study, by Guy B. Panero Engineers, 1958 (image by Federal Civil Defense and Preparedness Agency under contract No. CD-SR-58-42)
Source: FEMA US Fire Administration, National Emergency Training Center Library

Doom town

I will show you fear in a handful of dust.[33]

The early 1950s saw the development and testing of thermonuclear or hydrogen bombs with yields several hundred times greater than the atomic bomb that had destroyed Hiroshima.[34] Unleashing destructive power on this scale required a great deal of open space, and isolation. The Nevada Test Site is a remote 1350-square-mile territory encircled by desert hills, 65 miles northwest of Las Vegas. Now labelled as an Environmental Research Park and renamed the Nevada National Security Site, it remains out of bounds, an arid landscape with only the craters of past bombs and the occasional collapsing structure to break up the expanses of dust. Between 1951 and its final decommissioning, the Test Site was the place for 'rehearsing the end of the world over and over again'.[35] There were 923 nuclear detonations in total at the site. These tests mingled the fascinating terror of human-made stars – created and extinguished in a moment[36] – with the horrifying apparatus of war, including military exercises, mock-cities tested to destruction, and pigs dressed in military uniforms and exposed to 37-kiloton blasts.[37] With payloads of this size, no amount of geographic isolation could ever contain the fallout completely. An official report states baldly that: 'Any person living in the contiguous United States since 1951 has been exposed to radioactive fallout, and all organs and tissues of the body have received some radiation exposure.'[38] The atmospheric tests that were intended to prepare America for the event of hypothetical thermonuclear war were rehearsals conducted with actual weapons that unleashed real effects. But the damage has been largely invisible, the victims unacknowledged. In this sense, the Nevada test programme is an unstated war; one 'that has been going on all along'.[39] In 1963 the Limited Test Ban forbade atmospheric nuclear testing and the tests moved underground, but the colossal explosions continued to vent leaked radiation into the atmosphere. Throughout its history, the Nevada Test Site has been shrouded in obscurity, as have the effects of radioactive fallout from its tests on exposed humans. The full story may never surface, but as journalist Rebecca Solnit writes of her tour of the facility: 'I remembered to be afraid of the dust…'[40]

The 'doom towns' of the Nevada Test Site were part of an imaginary war waged against the material technologies of everyday life. 'Doom Town' was the test city built for Operation Doorstep, an FCDA civil defence test done in conjunction with the 16-kiloton shot Annie on 17 March 1953. It was one in a chain of 11 nuclear detonations planned by the Atomic Energy Commission that year, known as the Upshot-Knothole series. The idea was to create an accurate simulation – 'to show the people of America what might be expected if an atomic burst took place over the doorsteps of our major cities'.[41] Doom Town was on the small side. It consisted of just two houses and eight shelters. The houses were typical American colonial two-storey, centre-hall, wood-framed dwellings, with freshly painted white clapboard exteriors. They were designed with input from the American Association of Architects. One house stood at 3,500 feet and the other at 7,500 feet from ground zero. Doom Town included 50 numbered automobiles of various types, colour and operating conditions – all of them contemporary models circa 1946–1953 – strewn across the desert parking lot. Unlike the empty Dugway enemy villages, Doom Town was occupied. Fifty mannequins were brought in to inhabit the city and its environs, and arranged in domestic tableaux eerily reminiscent of 1950s sitcoms and interiors magazines. The mannequins were dressed in the latest outfits made from the latest fabrics and materials – 'today's wearing apparel' – donated by J.C. Penney, a Las Vegas department store. With exuberant mercantile curiosity, the store manager speculated: 'The outcome of this test is unpredictable, but the results of the evaluation may be a powerful factor in deciding fashion trends in the years to come.'[42] A journalist, writing at the time, was similarly enthused by the prospect of bespoke nuclear attire:

> All known varieties of American clothing, excepting a mink coat, have been placed on the mannequins, and it is possible that out of the evaluation tests may come civil defence warnings as to how to dress in these atomic times.[43]

After the blast, J.C. Penney's advertisements include an ominous series of 'before and after' mannequin portraits, first published in the *Las Vegas Review Journal* on 3 April 1953. A photograph of each mannequin, carefully poised, was shown alongside one of their 'injured' – or ominously missing – counterparts. The surviving 'Doom-Town dummies' were taken to Los Angeles for radiation testing.[44] In April 1953 some of them were put on display in a civil defence exhibition in Pershing Square, Los Angeles, where they were on view for three days next to a stand with an F-84 Thunderjet. The exhibit recreated the interior of the test houses as discovered in the aftermath of the blast, with the original mannequins adopting the 'positions in which they were found'. Though one imagines that visitors' only defence against panic would have been an attitude of salacious detachment, such exhibits were at least *supposed* to deliver shocks of the salutary kind. The 1953 civil defence film *Operation Doorstep* challenged citizens to prepare actively for nuclear cataclysm, as if it were like any other civic duty: 'Or will you, like a mannequin, just sit and wait?'[45]

Two years later, on 5 May 1955, Doom Town was recreated for the staged destruction of another 'typical American community' by the FCDA 29-kiloton Apple-2 shot. The site was given a new moniker, 'Survival City'. Under the title 'Cue for Survival', or 'Operation Cue', some surviving buildings were improved and an assortment of new buildings was constructed and fitted out. The stated goal of the test was to observe how houses, shelters, power lines, a radio tower, metal buildings, food, clothing, and people would survive at various distances from a nuclear blast.[46] The test city was again populated with compliant citizen mannequins – 75 of them, dressed again in the latest fashions from J.C. Penney. Operation Cue's purpose was the demonstration and evaluation of not just the effects of nuclear detonation on the materials and artefacts of American cities, but also the capabilities of civil defence organisations to respond with prompt rescue and recovery operations for any survivors. The detonation was scheduled for a live broadcast with approximately 6,000 spectators 6 miles away, and army troops in tanks and trenches positioned between 2 to 3 miles from the epicentre of the blast. Footage of the preparations, blast and aftermath was used in several civil defence public information films, including *Operation Cue*.[47] Photographs of the destroyed site and 'surviving' mannequins were published in *Life* magazine. They show elegantly composed desert vistas with collapsed buildings, twisted pylons, dented cars, and leaning mannequins. Shattered interiors reveal table settings knocked askew, broken furniture, and battered, dismembered dummies in scorched and tattered clothing awkwardly contorted amongst the debris. The images are accompanied by morbidly informative captions: 'Scorched, male mannequin in suit of dark fabric indicates a human would be burned but alive'; 'Burned up except for face, this mannequin ... was 7,000 feet [one and a quarter miles] from blast'; 'Unburned, a lady mannequin with wig askew is wearing light-coloured dress which absorbs less heat'; 'Fallen mannequin in house 5,500 feet from bomb is presumed dead.'[48]

More extensive testing-to-destruction, on the architecture, engineering, building technologies and materials for future cities, was carried out at Area 5 of the Nevada Proving Grounds, also known as Frenchman's Flat. Nuclear-proofing cities to withstand shock waves and firestorms required blasting a full range of urban infrastructures, bridges, railroad equipment, electric power substations, underground shelters, field fortifications, military structures and vehicles, mines, as well as artificial forests of coniferous trees, military equipment and weapons, and field medical equipment.[49] The aim was to establish a 'vulnerability scale' in order to predict the behaviour of structures for a test city or hypothetical target complex, including airfield, shipyard, factories, petroleum refinery and a built-up urban area.[50] *Let's Face It*, a civil defence film from 1955, incorporated footage from the test cities at the Nevada Test Site along with civil defence manoeuvres.[51] It enumerated the concerns such tests were determined to respond to: the durability and safety of modern structures, possible damage to industry and transportation infrastructure, and the dangers of radioactive fallout. The next best thing to actual destruction of a city, it seems, was using real weapons to destroy a fake city, assembled from fragments of suburbia and the discontinuous elements of urban infrastructure placed at critical points from ground zero. These were 'representative units of a test city', assembled,

> with steel and stone and brick and mortar, with precision and skill – as though it were to last a thousand years. But it's a weird, fantastic city. A creation right out of science fiction. A city like no other on the face of the Earth. Homes, neat and clean and completely furnished, that will never be occupied. Bridges, massive girders of steel spanning the empty desert. Railway tracks that lead to nowhere. For this is the end of the line.

Every part of this 'weird, fantastic city' was given over to the simultaneous and antithetical objectives of destruction and survival. Every material and structural sacrifice was meticulously calibrated for recording blast phenomena in this carefully orchestrated nuclear fiction:

> Every brick, beam, and board will have its story to tell. When pieced together these will give some of the answers, and some of the information we need to survive in the nuclear age ... Every bit of twisted steel makes its contribution. Blackened ruins and ashes of a structure add another chapter. The shattered wreckage of a dwelling offers an eloquent testimonial. Piece by piece, like the parts of a jigsaw puzzle, our story is assembled, analysed and evaluated. Then the facts are made available to you through your local civil defence programme.[52]

The blast-coping architectural profile that emerged after years of testing was predictably far removed from the generic suburban dwellings of white clapboard houses that had been tested to destruction on the site.[53] The tests had shown conclusively how timber splintered, brick contorted, windows were structural weak spots as well as apertures for radioactive particles and dangerous debris, and furnishings and textiles were lethal fire hazards. Not surprisingly, recommendations for shelters emphasised the austere and cave-like properties of constructions capable of withstanding a nuclear bomb: windowless, featureless, sealed bunkers of reinforced concrete, preferably located underground. In other words, 'home' was not safe; and the only place that might be safe in no way resembled 'home'.

The findings of the Doom Town tests at the Nevada Proving Grounds made their way into numerous fallout shelter guidebooks, radiological defence engineering manuals, Cold War civil defence exercises, and public information films. The macabre, almost gloating tones in which this footage was so often mediated to the public raises the question: was unsettling people, rather than educating them, the point all along? The idea that home might not be a haven – and the feeling of 'unsettlement', in every sense, that attends this idea – is ripe with the potential for political and commercial instrumentalisation. Rebecca Solnit, looking back on the nuclear heyday across a gap of half a century, reflects:

> Radiation can make cells lose their memory, and loss of memory seems to be one of the cultural effects of the bombs too, for Americans forget that bomb after

bomb was being exploded here. Or perhaps people never forgot we were testing bombs, rehearsing the end of the world, but learned it so well and so deeply that bomb-makers no longer needed to terrorise children with bomb drills, or adults with civil defence scenarios and mushroom clouds on TV.[54]

Along with billowing mushrooms clouds, Operation Doorstep footage showing the disintegration of a typical house at the Nevada Test Site has become visual shorthand for an apocalyptic atomic age. Lasting just over two seconds and shown in stop-motion for full effect, it shows the house illuminated by the explosion before the siding bursts into smoke and flame, the house leans away from the force of the blast's shock wave, and then breaks loose of its foundations in a whirlwind of debris. But not all of Doom Town's buildings were destroyed in the tests. Over 60 years later, although the sites of the detonations are still too radioactive to yet allow visitors, various structures survive. Two of them are houses: one just over a mile away and another a mile and a half from ground zero. On the nearest house, its basic frame intact, the paint has been blasted off, the shutters torn away, the chimney twisted, the windows shattered and the interior ripped apart. The mannequin inhabitants are long gone. As tourism to the renamed Nevada National Security Site booms, there is a fresh incentive to preserve the remaining houses and structures as spectacles – a neat inversion of their previous purpose, to be spectacularly destroyed. The political meaning of this site may change, but its anthropogenic toxicity endures: dust blown across the desert will remain radioactive for thousands of years.

Data from the test cities informed thousands of hypothetical survival cities as everyday life came to be structured around the technological and psychological infrastructures of annihilation. Beginning in 1954, the annual rehearsals for World War III, as 'Operation Alert' or 'OPAL' tests, engrossed numerous cities across America. In *The Imaginary War*, Guy Oakes describes them as 'an elaborate national sociodrama that combined elements of mobilisation for war, disaster relief, the church social, summer camp and the county fair'.[55] Each city, its businesses and institutions, along with the agencies of federal government, was expected to test its warning signals, emergency plans and evacuation drills for survival, by following the scenario of the protocol for 'target cities' under imaginary nuclear attack. These dramatic rehearsals of preparedness involved the 'fiction of telescoping' – concentrating a potentially drawn-out relief operation into a few hours or a weekend of simulation.[56] The events were supported by concerted press coverage, public relations exercises, and the careful management of public information. This included scripted radio broadcasts and commissioned films of the exercises, such as *Operation Alert* (1956). The whole enterprise was designed not only as a full-scale test of national preparedness, but as a demonstration (and foregone conclusion) of 'nuclear crisis mastery'. This ritualised national simulation took place within the framework of the Cold War conception of nuclear reality as a survivable and necessary state. In the protocol of the 1956 exercise, for example, the US would be victim to 124 nuclear strikes, including five hydrogen bombs hitting New York City. But all would be well. The message was simple: the exercise of managerial rationality could reduce nuclear disaster to a simple set of surmountable problems. It just needed a proper rehearsal.

The nuclear city crisis was acted out in Operation Alert and re-enacted in the civil defence film of the same title. *Operation Alert* presents a homogeneous, white, middle-class, well-dressed, immaculately coiffed, compulsively tidy and well-ordered society taking part in the scripted operation – indeed not so different from the mannequins in test cities that had also rehearsed nuclear attack. The film details faultless, uneventful evacuations, displays of carefully coordinated community spirit, and dutifully emptied towns awaiting destruction. Requests for emergency assistance in the aftermath of the attack are handled serenely and dispassionately. There is no sign of panic, malfunction, breakdown. No one is affected by fear or anxiety. Everyone performs their tasks according to plan. All that dealing with fallout requires, it seems, is good housekeeping. The post-attack world is reassuringly indistinguishable from the immaculate pre-attack city. Not a messy mundane world at all, but a perfectly functioning, well-engineered, resilient system. In this fantasy of nuclear crisis, the accelerated return to 'business as usual' is expertly controlled and the public are reassured that America has indeed a blueprint for survival.

These large scale civil defence rehearsals can be understood as a collective exercise in 'mortgaging the future' – a postponement of catastrophe through a negotiation between knowledge of existing horrors and a dreaded future recast as manageable.[57] One of the most paradoxical fictions of the nuclear age was the promotion and continued prescription of civil defence at a time when it was discussed in official government and scientific circles as irrelevant to survival in the event of total war. In the 1950s it was already widely understood that any meaningful protection from nuclear attack was impossible, and any civic guidelines for survival would therefore be woefully inadequate if not altogether farcical. In 1964, with the development of the H-bomb, the civil defence film *Operation Cue* was updated, in recognition that with a 20-megaton blast, structures within a mile of ground zero would be 'obliterated' with no prospect of survival. A disclaimer was added at the start: 'Therefore while *Operation Cue* was valuable for research and test purposes, it does not reflect the full severity of today's larger thermonuclear weapons with their associated fallout hazard.'[58] The civil defence programme was nevertheless maintained as an elaborate illusion deemed necessary to create popular tolerance for the strategy of nuclear deterrence – presented as the only means of forestalling nuclear annihilation.[59] At the time, the US and USSR had locked each other into a strategy summarised by the acronym MAD, that is, 'Mutually Assured Destruction'. Everyday life had become caught up in the imagination of nuclear apocalypse, with its wide-ranging cultural, environmental and social effects. As a result of purposeful steps by political and military leaders the city dwellers of East and West found themselves living as if in a doomed narrative.

Doomsday scenarios

> War is a terrible thing; but so is peace. The difference seems to be a quantitative one of degree and standards.[60]

Herman Kahn's *On Thermonuclear War* (1960) is a strange and lyrical text exploring the US military principle of 'deterrence' by thinking through to their logical conclusions a variety of nuclear war scenarios. It addresses itself to 'the problem of avoiding disaster and buying time, without specifying the use of this time'.[61] Kahn's response to the widespread anxiety about possible world annihilation was a rational, calm and informative description of exactly what nuclear cataclysm might look like – and an assessment of the prospects of humanity in its aftermath. The book is an agglomeration of matter-of-fact calculations, graphs and data on the effects of global

Figure 3.3 'Operation Doorstep'; four mannequins in damaged living room, Nevada Test Site
Source: Nevada Test Site; National Nuclear Security Administration (NNSA), DOE

Figure 3.4 'Operation Doorstep'; damaged wooden bedroom with mannequin, Nevada Test Site
Source: Nevada Test Site; National Nuclear Security Administration (NNSA), DOE

Figure 3.5 'Operation Doorstep'; vehicle No. 40, and other vehicles at the Nevada Test Site
Source: Nevada Test Site; National Nuclear Security Administration (NNSA), DOE

nuclear cataclysm, including anticipated human casualties (or 'megadeaths' as he called them), the genetic effects of radiation, and protracted years of recovery. The quantitative projections were accompanied by dispassionate and objective advice. Kahn considered Nevil Shute's book *On the Beach*, which described inevitable extinction following fallout from thermonuclear war, as 'interesting but badly researched'.[62] The imagined devastation of 'Tragic but Distinguishable Postwar States' in one of Kahn's tables calculates that 160 million dead would require 100 years of economic recuperation. The caption asks bleakly: 'Will the survivors envy the dead?'[63] Kahn insisted that thermonuclear war would be but a temporary interlude and a survivable future, and not the utter annihilation of the human species. Even Armageddon, he argued, must have a sequel.

Kahn was keen to avoid the 'tit-for-tat exchange' of city destruction.[64] In an 'urban country' such as the United States,[65] he argued that it was important to understand the enemy's capacity to launch ferocious, tactical and escalating attacks on American cities: 'If you destroy Moscow, I will destroy New York, Washington, Los Angeles, Philadelphia and Chicago. If you destroy Leningrad, I will destroy Detroit, Pittsburgh, San Francisco, New Orleans and Miami.'[66] Kahn's 'counterforce' theory was aimed at diminishing the prospect of total destruction. It relied on active and passive defence to avoid the targeting of civilian centres, and included retaliatory threats but also shelters and anti-contamination measures.[67] He was as concerned with the survival of production capacity and capital after the destruction of the '53 Standard Metropolitan Areas'.[68] He reasoned: 'Most important of all, sober study shows that *the limits on the magnitude of the catastrophe seem to be closely dependent on what kinds of preparations have been made, and on how the war is started and fought.*'[69] An important part of the plan for preparedness was to exploit any warning of attack on cities through swift evacuation. As part of enhancing the credibility of America's nuclear threat, Kahn therefore insisted on the importance of investing in civil defence. He contemplated the possibility of regular mass evacuations for city dwellers, and was keen to use mineshafts as evacuation centres. He employed engineer Robert Panero to produce one such scheme for fallout shelters in the rock below Manhattan: The Manhattan Shelter Study.[70] Yet so much depended on managing and assuaging the doomsday anxiety of the civilian population. Kahn was aware of this as a liability: 'During the last few years New Yorkers have exhibited an attitude which might be called a "prime-target-fixation syndrome". This is an expression of apathy or fatalism often found among those who believe that their city or location would constitute a prime target in the event of a nuclear attack.'[71] In international conflict the doomsday gap was just as problematic as the missile or shelter gap. New Yorkers, it seems, were expected to learn to live intimately with the bomb, if not to love it.

> Assume that for say $10 billion we could build a device whose only function is to destroy all human life.[72]

The most notorious technological fixes from *On Thermonuclear War* were the Doomsday Machine and its refinements, the Doomsday-in-a-Hurry Machine and the Homicide Pact Machine.[73] For Kahn, the description of 'these idealised (almost caricaturised) devices', were a necessary response to the extreme suicidal brinkmanship of MAD.[74] The hypothetical Doomsday Machine was a stockpile of hydrogen bombs controlled by a massive computer connected to 'hundreds of sensory devices all over the United States'. When the computer sensed imminent and intolerable danger from a Soviet attack, it would detonate the bombs, causing total destruction. The calculative disposition of the ultimate deterrent device made world annihilation a credible proposition. He added a salutary caveat: 'it might not be possible to destroy groups of especially well-prepared people.' He was also sanguine about the effects of the Machine on the Earth's structural integrity: 'The mechanism used would most likely not involve the breaking up of the Earth, but the creation of really large amounts of radioactivity or the causing of major climatic changes, or, less likely, the extreme use of thermal effects.'[75] The desirable characteristics for the Doomsday Machine were listed as: '1. Frightening; 2. Inexorable; 3. Persuasive; 4. Cheap; 5. Nonaccident prone; 6. Controllable.' The first five characteristics could be met by the ultimate deterrent – no problem. The only one that proved elusive was the sixth characteristic: 'Controllable.' Herman Kahn's proposals were later parodied in Stanley Kubrick's 1964 *Dr Strangelove or: How I Learned to Stop Worrying and Love the Bomb*. The story of out-of-control and uncontrollable nuclear war hurrying to an inevitable end is brought to a head with Dr Strangelove's exasperated response to the USSR ambassador: 'The whole point of the Doomsday Machine is lost if you keep it a secret. Why didn't you tell the world, eh?'

According to Kahn, in a world imperilled as never before, 'thinking the unthinkable' was the only way to prepare for the vicissitudes of all-out nuclear confrontation. Kahn's scenario techniques were originally developed at RAND to model the effects of nuclear war.[76] They combined game theory, nuclear war strategy and systems theory. They involved writing multiple histories of the future – or the future-now – that involved detailed analysis of contemporary concerns and trends combined with imaginative storytelling. The outcomes of the many possible conjectures – optimistic and catastrophic – could then be assumed to approximate actual world events. Kahn was inspired to use the term 'scenarios' – originally a term drawn from Baroque theatre – by Hollywood screenwriters.[77] He considered scenarios, or 'modern-day myths', to be a compelling way to demonstrate threats and opportunities, as well as a means of anticipating them. Like the fairy tales and cautionary tales of popular fiction, scenarios could warn their audience of danger but, as Kahn pointed out, could also reassure: 'Remember, it's only a scenario.'[78] The scenarios were primarily intended to stimulate thinking about the future, and Kahn and his team of storytellers were adept at devising different frameworks and categories for conjectures about political, social, economic and cultural change that ranged from 'an extreme efflorescent society' to 'catastrophic worlds'.

> Prophets of doom have multiplied remarkably in the past few years. It used to be commonplace for men to parade city streets with sandwich boards proclaiming "The End of the World Is at Hand!" They have been replaced by a throng of sober people, scientists, philosophers, and politicians, proclaiming that there are more subtle calamities just around the corner.[79]

Doomsday scenarios developed at RAND were not limited to nuclear catastrophe. The connections explored between national security and the Earth's vulnerability included dire warnings of population pressure, environmental degradation and the spread of disease. The 'scenario' method was deployed in the writing of such publications such as Paul Ehrlich's *The Population Bomb* (1968), the Club of Rome-sponsored *World Dynamics* (1971), and *Limits to Growth* (1972), the latter hastily published in time for the Stockholm UN 'Earth Summit' conference. These publications were based upon, or strongly influenced by, system dynamics approaches to questions of human survival. *Limits to Growth* included a series of 'World Models' based upon the scary predictions and shaky prognostics of complex computer calculations.[80] Ehrlich's apocalyptic narrative predicted the 'Four Horsemen of Apocalypse – disease, famine, war and death', but it also included scenarios such as 'Eco-Catastrophe', which included projections of riots and national emergency. It is not surprising that the catastrophic futurology of publications like *Limits to Growth* and *Blueprint for Survival*[81] were accused of generating 'doomsday syndrome' – a disabling state of pessimism that allowed lazy science and panic to prevail over rational solutions.[82] These became set texts for environmentalism, and their inherent catastrophism has strongly influenced the formation of discourses around global environmental change. They are attention-grabbing, and rightly so – but the problem of public resistance to these narratives *because* of their intense pessimism has not yet been solved. And as extreme narratives like these have come to dominate, they have squeezed out more ordinary, but no less dramatic, accounts of adaptation and resilience – accounts which might prove more effective in mobilising calls for political accountability, both national and international, in this turbulent moment of planetary inhabitation.

Herman Melville's *Moby-Dick* inspired the 1967 *Star Trek* episode 'The Doomsday Machine', in which the crew of the Enterprise had to hunt down and destroy a planet-eating artificial organism/machine.[83] The machine recalls the whale's 'monomaniac incarnation of all those malicious agencies' that haunt the human psyche.[84] Captain

92 *Proving ground*

Kirk describes the Doomsday Machine as the ultimate weapon, but one that was never meant to be used and gives the example of the 20th century's H-bomb. Until recently, the archetypal doomsday machine was a world-ending nuclear payload. But in recent years the Anthropocene has emerged as another doomsday device – this one made by humans, not deliberately, but as a ghastly accident of our relentless will toward 'progress'.[85] Humanity's compulsion to master the Earth is also the force that has allowed it to encounter its own spectacular capacity to destroy life. The Anthropocene narrative is a warning, a portent of doom, and even a bluff. It informs humanity of the ultimate inscription of the end of human time as a judgement or a reckoning. It encounters a counter-narrative of doomsaying as a 'counterforce' of how things could have been otherwise – if humanity had been better prepared. It therefore challenges humanity to imagine its own devastation, and be prompted to act to avoid it, rather than passively allow it to unfold. If the Anthropocene is a doomsday device, will we finally be prompted to do something about it? As a form of deterrence, perhaps the Anthropocene and its implicitly inward-looking and human-centred narrative is simply a way of buying time. The Anthropocene thesis faces at least one serious obstacle, however, in capturing humanity's collective imagination: the problem of cataclysm burnout. In a culture replete with doomsday scenarios, there is always the danger that humanity has already learnt to stop worrying and has come to feel at home with, if not love, the bomb.

Plowshares

> And he shall judge among the nations, and shall rebuke many people: and they shall beat their swords into plowshares, and their spears into pruning hooks: nation shall not lift up sword against nation, neither shall they learn war any more. (Isaiah 2:3-5)

Operation Plowshares was the Atomic Energy Commission's project, running from 1957–1975, to develop a plan for the use of doomsday weapons for peaceful construction purposes.[86] The project formally began at the Department of Energy's Lawrence Livermore Radiation Laboratory in Berkeley, California in July 1957, and was announced to the public in June 1958. In 1958, after calls for a ban on weapons testing from concerned scientists, the Soviet Union and the US entered a three-year moratorium, which meant that testing could only resume on 1 September 1961. Among the opponents of the freeze on nuclear tests and advocates of 'peaceful nuclear explosions' was Edward Teller, 'the father of the hydrogen bomb' and one of the founders of the Livermore Radiation Laboratory. Teller's 1962 *Legacy of Hiroshima*, written to express his misgivings over a test ban treaty, included a chapter on 'How to Be an Optimist in the Nuclear Age'. In this he described the 'exciting possibilities' enabled by peaceful nuclear explosions in the Plowshares programme, from the 'geographical engineering' of harbours and canals to modifications of the climate. Teller was determined to continue nuclear testing and showed contempt for the precautions that opponents of nuclear tests were calling for. 'To be an optimist,' wrote Teller, 'requires courage, but to be an optimist in the nuclear age demands even more: It demands imagination.'[87] Teller's 'imagination,' however, seems a perilously selective faculty – fixated on utopian visions of progress; blind to the catastrophic risks that would attend the smallest misstep in their execution.

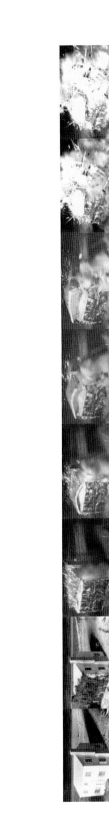

Figure 3.6 (**a, b, c, d, e, f, g, h**) 'Operation Doorstep'/'Upshot-Knothole Annie'; Nevada Proving Grounds, 17 March 1953; complete destruction of House No 1 located 3,500 feet from ground zero. The time from the first to last picture was 2.33 seconds. The camera was completely enclosed in a 2-inch lead sheath as a protection against radiation. The only source of light was that from the bomb

Source: Nevada Test Site; National Nuclear Security Administration (NNSA), DOE

Plowshares intended to highlight the potential of the 'peaceful atom' and develop a climate of world opinion more favourable to further weapons development and testing. It sought legitimation at a time when the enterprise of testing was under threat. Plowshares was thus a matter of both science and politics, both a 'legitimate experimental programme' and a 'Cold War boondoggle'.[88] It countered the plodding caution of testing naysayers with an appeal to the geophysical sublime, promising massive earthmoving feats among other achievements. The Plowshares project was an explicit geoengineering effort that offered to literally 'move mountains' in the name of human progress. However, it gave scant attention to the possible consequences, and its proponents were unprepared for the inevitable literal and political 'fallout'.[89] A 1968 film, *Excavating with Nuclear Explosives*, introduced the project:

> Excavations of new harbours, big dams, canals, passes through rugged terrain – these and other massive, imaginative Earth-moving projects may soon be ours, created in seconds with the tremendous energy of the peaceful atom …It is a deliberate, careful, scientific programme.[90]

Plowshares PR domesticated nuclear explosive power as a 'proven tool and a proven technology'.[91] The cognitive dissonance of this is self-evident. As the academic and writer Joseph Masco observes, 'the repeated invocation of care in planning, of rigorous scientific judgment, and good governance was at odds with the radical nature of the project'.[92] For it was intended that 'the tremendous energy of the peaceful atom' would be put to use on public works of enormous scale, beyond the highly controlled and isolated setting of the test sites. The project's intended activities fell into two categories. The first was harnessing the explosive power of nuclear weapons for excavations, including such tasks as excavating harbours, canals, lakes, cuts through mountains, and open pit quarries. This included the long-term goal of using nuclear explosions to excavate a new Atlantic-Pacific canal through Central America – an alternative Panama canal. The second category was the use of nuclear weapons to blow open large cavities in underground rock formations, to be used for storage, underground laboratories and the detection of new radioactive isotopes. In addition, the underground explosions could be used to unlock natural gas reserves – a kind of nuclear or pre-hydraulic 'fracking'. The 1973 AEC promotional film *Plowshares* promised that nuclear explosions would make the Earth profitable – unlocking its energy, and reengineering its geography:

> Some will be dramatic in their effect as nuclear explosions move huge masses of earth in excavation jobs, reshaping the geography of the land in dimensions never before possible, to meet the needs of man, needs he can see as he struggles against the geography nature has pitted against him.[93]

To test the possible uses of nuclear explosives on a planetary-scale construction site, the US detonated 35 devices of various sizes over the 15-year period of Operation Plowshares; most were conducted at the Nevada Test Site. A number of distinct projects were planned as part of the programme. Project Chariot was to involve using multiple thermonuclear explosions to excavate a deep-water harbour at Cape Thompson, Alaska, and dig a channel to connect the harbour to the ocean for use in shipment of resources from coal and oil fields. The chosen site was Orgotoruk Creek, located in the traditional hunting grounds of the indigenous Inupiat people. A base camp was set up at Orgotoruk for preliminary field tests for an environmental study – now considered the first *de facto* environmental impact statement.[94] Chariot was eventually scrapped because of mounting concerns over the radiation-related health risks to the Inupiat peoples from strontium-90 entering the foodchain, and predictions on the environmental degradation from fallout.[95] Plowshares had to retreat from considering Alaska as a 'test site' for dangerous technologies, although other AEC projects continued to do so. Plowshares continued, however, with other tests, such as Project Gnome, devised to study isotopes and energy production, and provide seismic measurements. Its 3-kiloton explosion excavated a cavern in a salt bed near Carlsbad, New Mexico. Project Ditchdigger was intended to test the feasibility of building sea-level canals. The preparations included surveying for potential environmental impacts and conducting high-explosive tests to understand variables involved in working with different types of soil. Project Sedan was another experiment to determine the feasibility of using nuclear explosions for large excavation projects, such as harbours and canals. Sedan's controlled explosion on 7 June 1962 at the Nevada Test Site created an enormous crater. It remains the leading attraction for recreational tours of the Test Site, even though external radiation surrounding the crater remains above normal background levels.

> The 100-kiloton nuclear explosion excavated more than 6 million cubic yards of earth in a matter of seconds. The result was a crater more than 1,200 feet in diameter, the length of four football fields and 325 feet deep, the height of a 32-storey building. Created in less time than it takes to describe it.[96]

The fallout from Operation Plowshares tests was much higher than anticipated.[97] Concerns about the negative impacts from Project Plowshare's 27 nuclear projects, including nuclear contamination, eventually led to the programme's termination, due in large part to public opposition. The identified consequences of the 'peaceful nuclear explosions' included tritium-contaminated water and radioactive material being injected into the atmosphere before underground testing had been mandated by treaty. The public had also become concerned that the earth-moving tests could trigger earthquakes or create foul groundwater, or that radioactive gases could escape from excavated cavities. Operation Plowshares remains as a record of the audacious attempt to terraform the Earth through the force of nuclear explosions. When they said they would move mountains, they meant it. As Edward Teller announced: 'If your mountain is not in the right place, drop us a card.'[98] The nuclear detonations were conceived as 'tests' but were deliberate planetary-scale industrial events intended to continue nuclear exploitation and bolster extractive economies. They were unapologetically profit-driven and neglectful of the consequences. The Project Chariot controversy was revisited in 1992, after documents revealed that, before abandoning the Chariot camp at Orgotoruk, US government scientists had illegally buried nuclear waste at the site.[99] The Plowshares project of thermonuclear, planetary-scale earthworks is a cautionary tale about efforts to consciously control and re-engineer the Earth, with potentially devastating human consequences. The cumulative effects of human attempts to transform the face of the Earth by dint of their technological prowess, also perpetuate the notion of nature as entirely separate from humanity. It thus carries important lessons for the technocratic solutions mooted for 'environmentally

Silent spring and nuclear winter

> There was once a town in the heart of America where all life seemed to live in harmony with its surroundings ... Then a strange blight crept over the area and everything began to change.[101]

'A Fable for Tomorrow', the opening chapter of Rachel Carson's *Silent Spring* (1962), presented a doomsday scenario of environmental collapse as a subverted fairy tale. An earlier draft had begun: 'Once upon a time...' It tells of a fictional any-town in an idyllic rural setting which is destroyed one year by a mysterious chemical threat – a dust that falls from the sky. This could so easily be the story of a town caught in the grim aftermath of nuclear fallout, choked by irradiated dust like that which blows across the Nevada Test Site. Carson could rely on her readers picking up the comparison. Her cautionary tale reworked the then-ubiquitous imaginary scenario of the nuclear devastation of an all-American doomtown. Her purpose was to bring home to her readership the less visible threat posed by environmental pollutants of industrial origin.

> The roadsides, once so attractive, were now lined with browned and withered vegetation as though swept by fire. These, too, were silent, deserted by all living things... In the gutters under the eaves and between the shingles of the roofs, a white granular powder still showed a few patches; some weeks before it had fallen like snow upon the roofs and the lawns, the fields and streams.[102]

Like Hershey's *Hiroshima*, Carson's work was initially published in *The New Yorker*. Appearing at the height of the Cold War, a month before the Cuban Missile Crisis, it linked prevailing fears of nuclear aggression and the resulting radioactive fallout to a growing public awareness of the effects of herbicides and pesticides. Carson's fable was based on extensive research into DDT (dichlorodiphenyltrichloroethane) and other pesticides, offshoots of chemical warfare research. The contaminations wrought by fallout and pesticides, 'chemical fallout', were revealed as a series of complex linkages leading from atmospheric testing through systems of production and consumption to the vulnerable, intimate spaces of the human body itself:

> In this now universal contamination of the environment, chemicals are the sinister and little recognised partners of radiation in changing the very nature of the world – the very nature of its life. Strontium-90, released through nuclear explosions into the air, comes to earth in rain or drifts down as fallout, lodges in soil, enters into the grass or corn or wheat grown there, and in time takes up its abode in the bones of a human being, there to remain until his death.[103]

The nuclear, chemical and technological arsenal that mid-century America had at its disposal was also an omnipresent threat – to its own citizens, to the rest of the world's population, and to nature in all its variety. Living with that threat was the price the citizenry paid for dominance over the environment at every scale. Carson laid bare the connections between fantasies of infinite consumption and progress, the profit motive, and the potential (or actual, already unfolding) devastation of our planetary home. And ordinary people were implicated in this, she suggested, because of the stories they chose to tell themselves, and allowed others to tell them. In the shadow of the bomb, for example, the poisonous gardening practices of American suburbanites could be understood as waging miniature war against insect enemies:

> Manufacturers offer us do-it-yourself booklets on how to kill bugs. With push-button ease, one may send a fog of dieldrin into the most inaccessible nooks and crannies of cabinets, corners, and baseboards.[104]

Silent Spring's stern warnings and urgent call to action represented a shift from Carson's previous writing. The book shocked and appalled, and sold in great numbers, becoming a defining text for the environmental movement. It offered a framework for understanding the fragile interdependencies of humans and their bio-chemical-technological infrastructures; it also recognised the role of culture, of collective story-telling, in creating humanity's future. *Silent Spring* was significant in mapping out an alternative narrative for post-war acceleration, not as a route to progress, but as a toxic trajectory hurtling towards doomsday: 'The road we have long been travelling is deceptively easy, a smooth superhighway on which we progress with great speed, but at its end lies disaster.'[105] Carson's recognition of the massive scale of environmental changes wrought by humans anticipated present-day debates around the Anthropocene. *Silent Spring* concludes with a vision of a future Earth purged, through human recklessness, of all organic life: 'No witchcraft, no enemy action had silenced the rebirth of new life in this stricken world. The people had done it themselves.'[106]

If Carson's vision of Earth disrupted was a birdless, cropless spring brought about by lethal synthetic chemicals, the 1980s brought an irradiated version of this doomed season: nuclear winter. The 'nuclear winter' hypothesis brought the prospect of environmental collateral damage of nuclear war to a planetary scale. It combined the wholesale destruction of total war wrought on cities across the globe with the dangerous after-effects of nuclear blasts: smothering pollution and devastating climate change. 'Nuclear winter' was different from the visions of nuclear cataclysm that had preceded it because it did not require a planet-smashing bomb to bring about a planetary-scale ending of life. Humans, animals and plants need not be atomised in a chain of blasts; instead, they might be suffocated by a planet-wide blanket of dust and soot or suffer from cold and starvation. The nuclear winter hypothesis was accompanied by the idea that nuclear cataclysm might be imbricated with the more mundane phenomena of turbulent weather and food shortages. In 1982 Paul Crutzen and John Birks forecast that a nuclear war could propel enough smoke and dust into the atmosphere causing darkening of the skies and enough hydrocarbons and oxides of nitrogen to cause dangerous levels of air pollution, potentially causing crop failure.[107] And since these latter phenomena would not be localised the way a bomb blast would be expected to be, there might be no 'winners' in even a small-scale nuclear war. The scientist and educator Carl Sagan announced 'The Nuclear Winter' hypothesis in an eponymous 1983 article for *Parade* magazine, a Sunday supplement that reached an audience of an estimated 20 million readers:

> In a 2-megaton explosion over a fairly large city, buildings would be vapourised, people reduced to atoms and shadows, outlying structures blown down like matchsticks and raging fires ignited. And if the bomb were exploded on the ground, an enormous crater, like those that can be seen through a telescope on the surface of the Moon, would be all that remained where midtown once had been. There are now more than 50,000 nuclear weapons, more than 13,000 megatons of yield, deployed in the arsenals of the United States and the Soviet Union – enough to obliterate a million Hiroshimas.

The TTAPS group, who proposed the theory, had used computer models to project the future of the Earth's atmosphere in the aftermath of a nuclear war.[108] They predicted that the resulting dust and smoke from nuclear firestorms incinerating cities could blanket the entire planet, reducing sunlight penetration and causing plummeting temperatures and the eventual demise of life on Earth.[109] As Sagan warned, '…the cold, the dark and the intense radioactivity, together lasting for months, represent a severe assault on our civilisation and our species …. There is little question that our global civilisation will be destroyed.'[110] So much for the world ending with a massive bang: the nuclear winter scenario concretised the by now familiar notion that post-World War III humanity might very well end with a long-drawn-out whimper.[111]

Sagan's series of dire warnings echo the predictions of the aftermath of nuclear war by the fictional USSR Ambassador in *Dr Strangelove*: who compared the surface of the Earth to a pock-marked Moon and warned of a Doomsday shroud wrapping the Earth for 93 days. But the sky-falling and world-ending threat of the bomb had a cosmic counterpart: the asteroid. Among the spurs for the nuclear winter hypothesis was a 1980 article by Luis and Walter Alvarez and associates on the Cretaceous-Tertiary (K-T) extinction event caused by the impact of an asteroid 65 million years ago. They had reported finding a distinctive geological layer of clay at the K-T boundary that contained enormous levels of the element iridium – a composition characteristic of extraterrestrial bolides rather than terrestrial rocks.[112] They further hypothesised that the main cause of the mass extinction was not the asteroid impact, nor even the immediate aftermath, but the ensuing 'impact winter'. Dust and debris from the impact would have darkened the skies, blocking the Sun, suppressing photosynthesis and reducing Earth surface temperatures. These climatic malfunctions were thought to have caused the mass extinction of dinosaurs, ammonites and countless other species whose fossil record coincided with the K-T boundary. Diverse plant communities in forests were wiped out and marine ecosystems collapsed, remaining in a depleted state for millions of years: 'the desolate post-impact sea has been dubbed the "Strangelove ocean"'.[113]

The 'nuclear winter' scenario – a narrative that ushered in the notion of global atmospheric politics – rapidly became one of the key catastrophe narratives of the environmental movement. As a historian of the Cold War, Jacob Darwin Hamblin comments, 'nuclear winter was an end-of-the-world story that fit the times'.[114] It had enormous political import in undermining the Reagan administration's claims that the US would 'prevail' in the event of nuclear war. As such, this was an idea with powerful enemies. In the scientific and political controversy that followed, environmentalists were painted as monomaniacal doomsayers and the predictions were roundly dismissed as flawed science. Warnings of cataclysm proved easy to ignore or ridicule when months and years passed and the initiating events did not take place. It is hard to persuade people that the sky is *about to* fall. If the idea failed to gain the necessary traction to change military-industrial practices, however, it nevertheless continued to haunt the cultural imaginary. Environmental doomsday scenarios of the nuclear age bolstered a belief in the extraordinary human capability to change the environment on a vast scale – and also gave powerful testimony to the catastrophic consequences. Hamblin sums up the conundrum: 'Through science, humans tried to harness the power of nature against their foes. Perhaps in the process, they discovered they were arming nature against themselves.'[115] The discovery of human incrimination in horrific seasonal dysfunction – silent spring and nuclear winter – was evidently a painful one – too painful, perhaps, to be confronted. Possibly the very scale of the projected devastations suffocated thought; paralysed action. Perhaps the heady cocktail of ambiguous effects that characterised the post-war psyche was overwhelming – fantasies of total domination jostling with a barely suppressed panic about annihilating force turned back on its wielder. However it came about, it is clear that popular scepticism thwarted, and continues to work against, the possibility of collective response to a planetary-scale threat.

Inadvertent intrusion

> There is no *away* to which we can meaningfully sweep the radioactive dust. Nowhere is far enough or long-lasting enough. What must happen instead is that we must care consciously for nuclear materials… The future of plutonium exerts a causal influence on the present, casting its shadow backward through time. All kinds of options are no longer thinkable without a deliberate concealment of the reality of radioactive objects.[116]

As philosopher Timothy Morton observes, the pernicious and invisible threat of environmental contamination by nuclear materials, along with accumulating heaps of nuclear waste, pose enormous challenges – ones dealt with through fictions that condone ignorance of the threats. The US Department of Energy's (DOE) nuclear waste burial programme originated in 1955, at the time of the escalation of atmospheric nuclear testing and research into the use of nuclear energy. But it took over 40 years for the disposal project to come into effect. The site eventually confirmed as a permanent geological repository for high-level radioactive transuranic waste was 42 km east of Carlsbad, New Mexico, deep in the desert's 250-million-year-old sedimentary salt layer. The DOE started construction on the Waste Isolation Pilot Plant (WIPP) in 1979. Transuranic waste is produced during nuclear fuel assembly and reprocessing, nuclear weapons research, production, and clean-up. It generally consists of protective clothing, tools and equipment contaminated with radioactive materials that remain unsafe for approximately 24,000 years – the half-life of plutonium. In his history of WIPP, *Signs of Danger*, Peter C. Van Wyck argues that the project is symptomatic of a 'perilous deficit in contemporary ecological thought and practice'. He writes:

> It became clear to me that the reason we end up with a spectacular nuclear dump in the desert is not because it will do the job required of it or because it's just a good idea, but precisely because no one in charge could think of any other way to think about the problem. Inertia, in other words.[117]

Congress authorised the opening of WIPP in 1992 and decided on a cap of 175,000 cubic metres of nuclear waste to be stored there. Transportation of waste to the site from various US nuclear testing facilities started in 1999 with a shipment from the Los Alamos National Laboratory. The transuranic (TRU) waste accumulated at the Nevada Test Site comes from nuclear weapons production, research, and development since the 1940s, and includes such materials as laboratory clothing, rubber gloves, tools, glove boxes, glassware, piping, air filters, plastics, wood, metals, soil and solidified waste water sludges contaminated with transuranic materials. But the Nevada site also stores waste from nuclear weapons research at the Lawrence Livermore National Laboratory in California. The latter was moved from California to Nevada in a series of shipments from the 1970s to the 1990s, for temporary storage at the Radioactive Waste Management Site, Area 5.[118] As of February 2014, 48 shipments of nuclear waste from the Nevada Test Site had been delivered to WIPP, with about 70 more scheduled for the future.[119]

It is expected that some time in 2035 the vaults – caverns carved out of rock salt 650 metres underground – will be filled to capacity and sealed up. At this point, the US government is planning to construct monuments or 'permanent markers' to serve as a warning to future generations about the hazards of the site. These warnings will need to last at least 10,000 years, or 300 generations. This is the approximate time that allows the radioactive materials to be considered relatively safe, and has been considered to be within the bounds of comprehensibility. It is also roughly equivalent to the time of the Holocene, going the other way, or at least the development of urbanisation as currently understood. For the most part the issue of nuclear waste has been approached as a technical problem; and yet it inevitably calls up the intractable issues of language, culture and history. The whole venture, as Van Wyck explains:

> is an enormous wager that hinges on making waste safe – through burial – then making it dangerous again – through signification. And in it must persist the groundless hope that the semiotic decomposition of the sign will take place at a slower rate than the nuclear decomposition of the waste itself.[120]

In 1991 the DOE convened a panel of experts to design a system of warnings meant to dissuade the next 300 generations or so from digging, drilling, excavating, inhabiting or planting the ground. Drawn from the fields of material science, architecture, environmental design, anthropology, linguistics, archaeology, astronomy, and geomorphology, they faced an impossible design task: the permanent markers should exist longer than any human monument or semiotic system has ever survived; they must communicate warnings to future societies, whether illiterate or unthinkably technologically advanced, avoiding slippage or decay of meaning; and they must repel curiosity rather than attract it. Their report, 'Expert Judgment on Markers to Deter Inadvertent Intrusion into the Waste Isolation Pilot Plant' (1993), makes for bizarre reading.[121] Their recommendations included a massive warning landscape, graphic images of human faces contorted with horror, terror, or pain inspired by Edvard Munch's *Scream*, and cautions in numerous languages to aid decoding, like the Rosetta stone. They envisioned information rooms like a menacing visitors' centre, with star charts, maps of nuclear disposal sites around the world, and diagrams of the facilities; and the institution of an 'atomic priesthood' to pass down warnings through the ages. Among the proposals for 'permanent markers' were a 'Landscape of Thorns' with giant stone shards protruding from the ground; 'Menacing Earthworks' with jagged lightning-shaped mounds radiating out of a square; 'Black Hole', a black masonry slab to stand for 'an immense nothing; a void; land removed from use with nothing left behind; a useless place'; and 'Forbidding Blocks,' an arrangement of irregular boulders imitating an (un)ideal city, 'set in a grid, defining a square, with 5-feet wide 'streets' running both ways. You can even get 'in' it, but the streets lead nowhere, and they are too narrow to live in, farm in, or even meet in.' The main worry was that 120th-century visitors would not be able to parse 21st century signs of danger. 'What will be the world view of someone contemplating the WIPP site in 12000 AD?' asks another DOE commissioned report, 'Ten Thousand Years of Solitude? On Inadvertent Intrusion into the Waste Isolation Pilot Project Repository.'[122] Yet concerns about predicting the future reveal much more about contemporary anxieties, ideas of risk and the pathologies of threat.[123] Consider this scenario, from 'Ten Thousand Years of Solitude?':

> TDY1142 released her sleeping cocoon and mumbled to her dressing robot, 'Something blue'. Then 'news on'. The announcer's image materialised above the kitchen table. 'Good morning. In the top of the news today: The City Builders have discovered some prehistoric ruins at 2100 feet while moving south toward the Mexican isthmus. Following the disastrous release of the common cold last year from other ruins, they are proceeding with caution...[124]

If the city builders of the future have to proceed with caution, so do the nuclear waste facility engineers of today and tomorrow. The entire project of WIPP is built around scenarios: probabilities of inadvertent or deliberate intrusion to the site; versions of terrestrial and extraterrestrial future societies; geological transformations to the salt layer; transportation accidents. A WIPP report states that, 'The probability of inadvertent intrusion into the WIPP repository over the next 10,000 years lies between 1 and 25 per cent.'[125] In scenario planning, the endless iteration of multiple storylines fanning out from the present holds open the possibility – hopeful, yet threatening – that one of them might just turn out to be true. However, the sheer scale of the enterprise confronts the human inability to imagine geology and climate, let alone human futures, 10,000 years from now. This is a project about exceeding, impossibly, unimaginably, the limits of the human:

> Everything about the WIPP and the monument operates in a complex relation to a limit. At the limit of civilisation; its place is the desert – the other American wilderness. At the limit of history; its time is the deep future. At the limit of meaning; its witness is unknown, abstract and indeterminate. At the limit of the symbolic; auguring the *language* of the future is a dizzying confrontation with the aporias that obtain when one steps outside of the frame of the present. At the limit of technology; the ability to engineer materials for this unprecedented duration is and remains hypothetical at best.[126]

Not only is it impossible to predict future geology, there is no guarantee of stability, either above ground or below ground. An explosion and fire at the plant in 2014 resulted in a radiation leak, and suspension of waste disposal operations at the site. The incident was reported in an article in the *Bulletin of the Atomic Scientists*: 'Wastes containing plutonium blew through the WIPP ventilation system, travelling 2,150 feet to the surface, contaminating at least 17 workers and spreading small amounts of radioactive material into the environment.'[127] The year-long investigation into the accident concluded that the rupture of a single drum of nuclear waste, 68660, was caused by the use of the wrong brand of cat litter (organic sWheat Scoop® in place of inorganic) sparking a chemical reaction and explosion.[128] The highly absorbent litter material is routinely used for soaking up liquid nuclear waste in the drums. This accident, caused by human error, has brought into focus the problem of whether or not WIPP could ever be considered safe. It also drew renewed attention to a problem that had been long avoided: what to do with a mounting stockpile of spent fuel from US commercial reactors, currently stored at reactor sites?[129] As Van Wyck cautions, 'nuclear materials stand in relation to their containment only very imperfectly – there is always leakage'.[130] While engineers, geophysicists and government agencies attempt to sort things out, the shipping of further nuclear waste to WIPP has been suspended, and plans to store spent nuclear fuel there thrown into doubt. There is nowhere, it seems, for nuclear waste to go. Yet leaving it in place in shallow burial runs the risk of spreading radioactive contamination into water, soil, air and DNA. In short, the current strategy gradually consigns the entire USA to the status of waste repository. Nuclear energy has long been promoted as a safe, clean energy source, but the problem of storing the accumulated waste – transmuted uranium, toxic plutonium, strontium, caesium – to accommodate half-lives of 24,000 years or more has not been solved, and may never be solved. The nuclear past and its permanent, if invisible, markers are still here. As Van Wyck asserts, it is 'a past that *actually* persists in the form of a threat to the present'.[131] The pervasive and cumulative effects of the nuclear complex live on in a proliferation of toxic futures that continue to dictate the geopolitical landscape. This is a cautionary tale in the sense that it urges caution; but not one in which there is hope of avoiding the danger completely. The apocalyptic disaster has already occurred. The doomsday future is already here.

No apocalypse

> I wanted to begin as quickly as possible with a warning in the form of a dissuasion: watch out don't go too fast.[132]

This cautionary note appears at the beginning of 'No Apocalypse, Not Now', Jacques Derrida's 1984 analysis of the first Reagan administration's rhetoric surrounding nuclear proliferation, deterrence, and war. Derrida confronts the issue of acceleration – or the 'economy of speed' – as a predicament, though a productive one: 'the nuclear age allows us to think through this aporia of speed (ie, the need to move both slowly and quickly).' His ironic response to this predicament is a volley of 'nuclear aphorisms' or 'tiny inoffensive missiles: in a discontinuous more or less haphazard fashion'. He writes 'full speed ahead, seven missiles, seven missives', taking as a literary model the seven letters of the Apocalypse of John. These quick-fire assertions paradoxically aim to slow down thinking and encourage reflection. His cautions for the nuclear age suggest a way of approaching the different temporalities of annihilation refigured in the Anthropocene, as well as a coming-to-terms with the human compulsion to narrate the end of the world. For Derrida, our speculations of nuclear war could be construed as a fable, which either makes a place for the occurrence of nuclear war or prevents it (through 'fabulously textual' deterrents and precautions) from taking place altogether:

> In our techno-scientifico-militaro-diplomatic incompetence we may consider ourselves, however, as competent as others to deal with a phenomenon whose essential feature is that of being *fabulously textual*, through and through. Nuclear weaponry depends, more than weaponry in the past, it seems, upon structures of information and communication, structures of language, including non-vocalisable language, structures of code and graphic decoding. But the phenomenon is fabulously textual also to the extent that, for the moment, a nuclear war has not taken place: one can only talk and write about it.[133]

In the same way, it is possible only to talk and write about either the survival of cautionary markers at WIPP or the projected fossilisations of the Anthropocene – for these too are 'fabulously textual' phenomenona that have not yet happened. The fabulous textuality of the nuclear age was, for Derrida, a cause for concern: 'The growing multiplication of the discourse – indeed, of the literature – may constitute a process of fearful domestication, the anticipatory assimilation of that unanticipatable entirely other.'[134] He asks the reader to consider the fact that, while 'nuclear war is for the time being a fable', at the same time, the reality of the stockpiling of nuclear materials is happening everywhere. Moreover, the fable of nuclear war *constructs* the reality of the nuclear age: 'the fright of imaginary anticipation' is such that the 'hypothesis of total nuclear war conditions every discourse and all strategies'.[135] Nuclear apocalypse is made real through an array of nuclear fictions. The nuclear age is here presented as an 'absolute epoch' in which 'the movement of its inscription is the very possibility of its effacement'.[136] The inscription of the Anthropocene, too, is a portent of its own demise. If the Anthropocene imaginary transpires as *the story to end all stories*, it also demands an awareness of and a reckoning with the proliferation of a *fabulous textuality*.

The nuclear age also draws attention to the idea of witnessing so prominent in the Anthropocene – that is, the modes of revealing or reporting by which humans or approximate humans are capable of seeing and surveying the Earth beyond apocalypse. This is the witnessing of the doomed survivor or distant observer – the fieldworker, travel writer, forensic geologist or alien explorer – wandering and interpreting a diminished world. It transpires as a contemplation of a world of waste, missing information, dwindling resources, destruction and impoverishment – a point of view familiar to us, in all its fabulous estrangement, from the genre of post-apocalyptic literature. And as Claire Colebrook observes, 'From *Mad Max* to *The Road* we project this scene into a possible future, forgetting that fragmented humans ranging across a depleted Earth that is dominated by terror, anarchy, fragmented technologies and alien systems is a fairly accurate picture of the present'.[137] An imagined human-witnessing of the end of time underscores the difficulty of thinking a world beyond humans. The Anthropocene epoch conjures a territory that has annihilated all the (human) means by which it might be comprehended. At the same time, this witnessing at a distance of a post-human Earth reveals an essential paradox. That same detached ability to witness and measure which has enabled the discourses around ecology, environmentalism and the Anthropocene, has also enabled the destructive distancing from the fact of human dependence on Earth systems that fuels anthropogenic devastation.

What does it mean to live amid an unfolding apocalypse of human making? The sense of an apocalypse is perhaps most chillingly felt in the creating of exclusion zones around sites of nuclear disaster: those around the Chernobyl Nuclear Power Plant and the Fukushima Daiichi Nuclear Power Plant. These exclusion zones realise one kind of cautionary tale in which humanity's pact with a dangerous technology leads to devastation. In their witnessing of the aftermath, they also draw attention to the diverging stories humans tell themselves, post-disaster. After the 1986 meltdown and fire in one of the four nuclear reactors, the Chernobyl facility was encased in a concrete shell – the 'sarcophagus' – and a 30-km exclusion zone was created. In addition to the 31 plant operators and firemen that died in the immediate aftermath of the explosion, the accident is thought to have caused the death of thousands more, though exact figures are not available. Estimates of eventual fatalities from radiation sickness range between 4,000 (World Health Organisation) and 200,000 (Greenpeace).[138] Around 330,000 inhabitants were evacuated from the affected area, leaving Pripyat a ghost town. The surrounding villages soon disappeared in encroaching undergrowth. The ruins of the city are now familiar through photographs. Tourist visits to the zone have increased since its depiction in computer games, and it has served as inspiration for Alan Weisman's *The World Without Us*. The legacy of the accident includes increased incidence of thyroid cancers and genetic mutations, as well as expensive clean-up operations and futile remediation programmes for a site that will be affected by radiation for 48,000 years. The Chernobyl exclusion zone remains a poisoned landscape, with significant levels of radioactive caesium-137, strontium-90 and plutonium isotopes still polluting the ground. Yet it is also a nature reserve for endangered species: among them the European bison and Przewalski's horse.[139] For a single site to be both ground zero for the worst nuclear accident on record and Europe's largest wildlife refuge is an astonishing dissonance. The appearance of thriving wildlife and a buoyant wilderness, obviously aided by the removal of humans as key predator and disruptor, nevertheless obscures the invisible dangers of species mutations, toxic soils, and dramatically reduced survival rates.[140] Such ambivalences make for confusing agendas, as in for example, the pro-nuclear environmentalist Mark Lynas, who has descanted on 'How a Nuclear Disaster Can Be Good For Ecology'.[141] The danger here is the production of consoling versions of apocalypse: the idea that ecosystems can flourish again once domineering humans and industrial modernity are removed from the equation.[142]

The triple-disaster in Japan in 2011 – the Tōhoku earthquake and tsunami, and the consequent explosion of the Fukushima Daiichi Nuclear Power Plant – carried echoes of different types of catastrophe: Lisbon's earthquake and tsunami, the industrial-technological disaster of Chernobyl, and the annihilating disaster of Hiroshima. The destruction at the power plant reawakened post-Chernobyl nuclear phantasms and generated widespread anxiety over nuclear fallout. The 12-km exclusion zone around the Japanese power plant went into effect on 22 April 2011 – Earth Day. In total 80,000 people were evacuated after the disaster. Namie, a small city of 21,000 inhabitants in Fukushima Prefecture, is now synonymous with the world's worst nuclear disaster since Chernobyl. Like the city of Pripyat, it is a nuclear ghost town, gradually being reclaimed by nature. The secrecy and lack of data surrounding the disaster exacerbate concern about its recurrence, and also about the extent of the danger posed by endlessly circulating radioactive materials from the explosion. Namie's displaced citizens have demanded long-term health monitoring programmes and guidelines, and have named these after the books used to monitor the health of the atomic bomb survivors in Hiroshima and Nagasaki – *hibakusha* (explosion-affected people). There seems to be little prospect of return to the affected areas, and hardly any news about the decontamination and clean-up operations. All anyone can do is wait for the exclusion zone to be redrawn. Nevertheless, abandoned cities like Namie and other zones of 'no-return' near the Fukushima Daiichi plant, can now be visited courtesy of Google's Street View cars.[143] This presents another kind of redemption post-disaster, and another way of rehearsing, aesthetically, an idea that seems to stymie the faculty of reason: that some day, the planetary environment may cease to be hospitable to humans. Alternately viewed as wildlife refuges or toxic wastelands, cultural curiosities or tourist attractions, or places to be cordoned off and erased from thought – nuclear exclusion zones are weirdly interchangeable in their adaptations and cultural uses. We are yet to witness an exclusion zone on a planetary scale, though it is a plausible possibility for Earth's near future. Our capacity to avoid annihilation may well depend on our ability to imagine it, and to face up to our imaginings with collective effort. The atomic age has furnished us with a demonstration of the destructive, consequence-blind, iterative logic of our dreams of infinite domination and progress. This is a cycle in which every unthinkable atrocity, once thought and done, is the proving ground for the next. Scientists and philosophers warned for decades against the fantasy of a nuclear war that one side could possibly 'win'. If this is an impossible fiction for nuclear cataclysm, we should be alert to parallels in our disregard for the toxic fallout of extractive-driven industry and agriculture; and in the present-day global standoff over the setting of caps on carbon emissions. On a planet as small as Earth, with the human capacity for interference grown so large, there can be no winning and losing sides – only cooperation, or destruction. When the nuclear age ushered in the Anthropocene, it also equipped it with a ready-made warning: a humanity willing to conspire in 'fearful domestication' of its possible apocalyptic futures is complicit in bringing them about.

Adjust your speed.

Notes

1 J. R. McNeill and Peter Engelke, *The Great Acceleration: An Environmental History of the Anthropocene since 1945* (Cambridge, Mass.: Harvard University Press, 2016). See also W. Steffen, J. Grinevald, P. Crutzen, and J. McNeill, 'The Anthropocene: conceptual and historical perspectives', *Philosophical Transactions of the Royal Society A: Mathematical, Physical and Engineering Sciences* 369.1938 (2011): 842–867.
2 Paul Crutzen and Will Steffen, 'How long have we been in the Anthropocene era?', *Climatic Change* 61.3 (2003): 251–257.
3 Claire Colebrook, 'Not symbiosis, not now: why anthropogenic change is not really human', *The Oxford Literary Review* 34.2 (2012): 185–209; 206.
4 Joseph Masco, 'Terraforming planet Earth: the age of fallout' in *The Politics of Globality since 1945: Assembling the planet*, eds. Rens van Munster and Caspar Sylvest (London & New York: Routledge, 2016): 44–70; 66. Hashimoto's video animation is available online at www.ctbto.org/specials/1945-1998-by-isao-hashimoto/
5 On Cold War civil defence exercises as rehearsals see Guy Oakes, *The Imaginary War: Civil Defense and American Cold War Culture* (New York and Oxford: Oxford University Press, 1994); and Tracy C. Davis, *Stages of Emergency: Cold War Nuclear Civil Defense* (Durham, N.C.: Duke University Press, 2007).
6 Gunther Anders, 'Commandments in the Atomic Age' in *Burning Conscience: The Case of the Hiroshima Pilot Claude Eatherley, told in his Letters to Gunther Anders* (New York: Monthly Review Press, 1961): 11–20; 11.

7 Thomas Pynchon, *Gravity's Rainbow* (Vintage, 2013): 57.
 8 Mike Davis, 'Berlin's skeleton in Utah's closet', in *Dead Cities and Other Tales* (New York: The New Press, 2002): 65–83. See also Tom Vanderbilt, 'Survival city: this is only a test', *Survival City: Adventures Among the Ruins of Atomic America* (New York: Princeton Architectural Press, 2002: 68–95.
 9 Mike Davis, *Dead Cities and Other Tales* (New York: The New Press, 2002): 82.
10 Standard Oil Development Company, 'Design and Construction of Typical German and Japanese Test Structures at Dugway Proving Grounds, Utah' (27 May 1943) was the source for Mike Davis's essay in *Dead Cities and Other Tales* (New York: The New Press, 2002).
11 Mike Davis refers to Vera Brittain's *Massacre by Bombing* as the only significant example of public dissent to Churchill's strategy, *Dead Cities and Other Tales* (New York: The New Press, 2002): 70.
12 Mike Davis, *Dead Cities and Other Tales* (New York: The New Press, 2002): 65.
13 *Fire and the Air War: A Compilation of Expert Observations on Fires of the War Set by Incendiaries and the Atomic Bombs, Wartime Fire Fighting, and the Work of the Fire Protection Engineers Who Helped Plan and the Destruction of Enemy Cities and Industrial Plants,*. ed. Horatio Bond (Boston: National Fire Protection Association International, 1946): 86-243. See also Mike Davis, *Dead Cities and Other Tales* (New York: The New Press, 2002): 72–73.
14 *Fire and the Air War: A Compilation of Expert Observations on Fires of the War Set by Incendiaries and the Atomic Bombs, Wartime Fire Fighting, and the Work of the Fire Protection Engineers Who Helped Plan and the Destruction of Enemy Cities and Industrial Plants,*. ed. Horatio Bond (Boston: National Fire Protection Association International, 1946): 21. See also Tom Vanderbilt, *Survival City: Adventures Among the Ruins of Atomic America* (New York: Princeton Architectural Press, 2002): 59.
15 W. G. Sebald, *On the Natural History of Destruction* (New York: Random House, 2003): 26–28.
16 Mike Davis, *Dead Cities and Other Tales* (New York: The New Press, 2002): 78.
17 Jacob Darwin Hamblin, *Arming Mother Nature: The Birth of Catastrophic Environmentalism* (Oxford, New York: Oxford University Press, 2013): 5.
18 Michael Sherry, *The Rise of American Air Power* (New Haven; Yale University Press, 1987) :255. See also Tom Vanderbilt, *Survival City: Adventures Among the Ruins of Atomic America* (New York: Princeton Architectural Press, 2002): 73.
19 Susan Neiman, *Evil in Modern Thought: An Alternative History of Philosophy* (Princeton and Oxford: Princeton University Press, 2002): 251.
20 Tom Vanderbilt, *Survival City: Adventures Among the Ruins of Atomic America* (New York: Princeton Architectural Press, 2002): 74.
21 Zygmunt Bauman, 'A natural history of evil' in *Collateral Damage Social Inequalities in a Global Age*, ed. Zygmunt Bauman (Cambridge: Polity Press, 2011): 128–149; 141.
22 Gunther Anders, in Zygmunt Bauman, 'A natural history of evil' in *Collateral Damage Social Inequalities in a Global Age*, ed. Zygmunt Bauman (Cambridge: Polity Press, 2011): 128–149; 142.
23 Zygmunt Bauman, 'A natural history of evil' in *Collateral Damage Social Inequalities in a Global Age*, ed. Zygmunt Bauman (Cambridge: Polity Press, 2011): 128–149; 145.
24 Zygmunt Bauman, 'A natural history of evil' in *Collateral Damage Social Inequalities in a Global Age*, ed. Zygmunt Bauman (Cambridge: Polity Press, 2011): 128–149; 146.
25 Gunther Anders, 'Wenn ich verzweifelt bin, was geh't mich an? (1977)' in French translation, 'Et si je suis désespéré, que voulex-vous que j'y fasse?' (Éditions Allia, 2007): 65–66. See also Zygmunt Bauman, 'A natural history of evil' in *Collateral Damage Social Inequalities in a Global Age*, ed. Zygmunt Bauman (Cambridge: Polity Press, 2011): 128–149; 146.
26 Jean-Pierre Dupuy, *A Short Treatise on the Metaphysics of Tsunamis*, trans. M.B. DeBevoise (Michigan State University Press, 2015): 47.
27 Harold C. Urey, '"I'm a Frightened Man", *Collier's* (5 January 1946): 18. See also Guy Oakes, *The Imaginary War: Civil Defense and American Cold War Culture* (New York and Oxford: Oxford University Press, 1994): 44.
28 John Hersey, *Hiroshima* (New York: Knopf, 1946): 39. In the same year, the essay 'Hiroshima' from *The New Yorker* (31 August 1946), was published as a book and broadcast on ABC radio in four 30-minute episodes.

29 The New York daily newspaper *PM* carried the story 'Here's what could happen to New York in an atomic bombing' (7 August 1945). See also Mick Broderick and Robert Jacobs, 'Nuke York, New York: nuclear holocaust in the American imagination from Hiroshima to 9/11', *The Asia-Pacific Journal*, 10.11.6 (12 March 2012).
30 Philip Morrison, 'If the bomb gets out of hand', in *One World or None: A Report to the Public on the Full Meaning of the Atomic Bomb*, eds. Dexter Masters and Katherine Way (New York: Federation of Atomic Scientists, 1946). See also Mick Broderick and Robert Jacobs, 'Nuke York, New York: nuclear holocaust in the American imagination from Hiroshima to 9/11', *The Asia-Pacific Journal*, 10.11.6 (12 March 2012).
31 John Lear, 'Hiroshima USA: can anything be done about it?', *Collier's* (5 August 1950): 11–15. See also Robert S. Richardson, 'Rocket blitz from the Moon', *Collier's* (23 October 1948): 24–25; 44–46; both issues were illustrated by Chesley Bonestell.
32 Mick Broderick and Robert Jacobs, 'Nuke York, New York: nuclear holocaust in the American imagination from Hiroshima to 9/11', *The Asia-Pacific Journal*, 10.11.6 (12 March 2012). See also Max Page, *The City's End: Two Centuries of Fantasies, Fears and Premonitions of New York's Destruction* (Yale University Press, 2008).
33 TS. Eliot, The Waste Land (Faber and Faber) in Rebecca Solnit, *Savage Dreams: A Journey into the Landscape Wars of the American West* (Berkeley and Los Angeles: University of California Press, 1999): 4.
34 From 1946 to 1956, 14 series of atmospheric weapons tests were held at two test sites – the Marshall Islands in the Western Pacific Ocean and at the Nevada Test Site.
35 Rebecca Solnit, *Savage Dreams: A Journey into the Landscape Wars of the American West* (Berkeley and Los Angeles: University of California Press, 1999): 5; Solnit gives an account of a series of springtime visits to the Peace Camp, the site of anti-nuclear activism adjacent to the Nevada Test Site, between 1988–1991.
36 Rebecca Solnit, *Savage Dreams: A Journey into the Landscape Wars of the American West* (Berkeley and Los Angeles: University of California Press, 1999): 43–44.
37 There were experiments with non-human subjects at the Nevada Test Site: sheep, rabbits and pigs confined in pens at various distances from ground zero. The pigs were dressed in military uniforms to test the effects of a blast on fabrics next to skin: 'Project 8.5, Thermal Radiation Protection Afforded Test Animals by Fabric Assemblies'. See Lynn Eden, *Whole World on Fire: Organizations, Knowledge, and Nuclear Weapons Devastation* (Cornell University Press, 2004): 162.
38 'A Feasibility Study of the Health Consequences to the American Population From Nuclear Weapons Test Conducted by the United States and Other Nations,' Department of Health and Human Services (DHHS), Centres for Disease Control and Prevention (CDC) and the National Cancer Institute (NCI), (2001); the report concludes that atmospheric testing between 1951 and 1963 produced 11,000 cancer deaths and somewhere between 11,300 and 212,000 thyroid cancers among US citizens; see Joseph Masco, *The Nuclear Borderlands: the Manhattan Project in Post-Cold War New Mexico* (Princeton and Oxford: Princeton University Press, 2006): 302–303.
39 Rebecca Solnit, *Savage Dreams: A Journey into the Landscape Wars of the American West* (Berkeley and Los Angeles: University of California Press, 1999): 2.
40 Rebecca Solnit, *Savage Dreams: A Journey into the Landscape Wars of the American West* (Berkeley and Los Angeles: University of California Press, 1999): 4.
41 Lynn Eden, *Whole World on Fire: Organizations, Knowledge, and Nuclear Weapons Devastation* (Cornell University Press, 2004): 166.
42 Hillman R. Lee, a J. C. Penney store manager, quoted in John Wills, *US Environmental History: Inviting Doomsday* (Edinburgh: Edinburgh University Press, 2013): 54.
43 Bob Considine quoted in John Wills, *US Environmental History: Inviting Doomsday* (Edinburgh: Edinburgh University Press, 2013): 54.
44 *Los Angeles Mirror (*1 April 1953); for news reports on mannequins being dressed and on display at the J.C. Penney store before the 17 March 1953 detonation and their subsequent fate, see the blog of artist Rachele Riley, research for www.evolution-of-silence.net: blog.racheleriley.com/update-on-the-annie-test-mannequins/
45 Operation Doorstep (US Federal Civil Defense Administration, 1953); archive.org/details/28072OperationDoorstep

46 Operation Cue (US Federal Civil Defense Administration), *Cue for Survival: Operation Cue, AEC Nevada Test Site, May 5, 1955* (Washington, DC: US Government Printing Office, 1955) archive.org/details/Operatio1955
47 Operation Doorstep (US Federal Civil Defense Administration, 1953); archive.org/details/Operatio1955
48 Ben Cosgrove, 'The haunted desert: aftermath of a Nevada A-bomb test', *Time magazine* (30 May 2012); photos by Loomis Dean, 'From an atomic bomb Test in the Nevada desert, 1955', LIFE.com; time.com/3675016/nevada-a-bomb-test/
49 Lynn Eden, *Whole World on Fire: Organizations, Knowledge, and Nuclear Weapons Devastation* (Cornell University Press, 2004): 150.
50 Lynn Eden, *Whole World on Fire: Organizations, Knowledge, and Nuclear Weapons Devastation* (Cornell University Press, 2004): 151.
51 *Let's Face It* (US Federal Civil Defense Administration, 1955), Project 95-1-54, unclassified video; US Department of Energy; archive.org/details/FederalCivilDefenseAdministrationletsFaceIt
52 Transcribed from Operation Doorstep (US Federal Civil Defense Administration, 1953), Project 95-1-54, unclassified video; US Department of Energy; archive.org/details/FederalCivilDefenseAdministrationletsFaceIt
53 Tom Vanderbilt, *Survival City: Adventures Among the Ruins of Atomic America* (New York: Princeton Architectural Press, 2002): 85.
54 Rebecca Solnit, *Savage Dreams: A Journey into the Landscape Wars of the American West* (Berkeley and Los Angeles: University of California Press, 1999): 6–7.
55 Guy Oakes, *The Imaginary War: Civil Defense and American Cold War Culture* (New York and Oxford: Oxford University Press, 1994): 84.
56 Guy Oakes, *The Imaginary War: Civil Defense and American Cold War Culture* (New York and Oxford: Oxford University Press, 1994): 85
57 Tracy C. Davis, *Stages of Emergency: Cold War Nuclear Civil Defense* (Durham, N.C.: Duke University Press, 2007): 98.
58 Operation Cue (US Federal Civil Defense Administration, 1964); archive.org/details/71662OperationCue1964RevisionHD
59 Guy Oakes, *The Imaginary War: Civil Defense and American Cold War Culture* (New York and Oxford: Oxford University Press, 1994): 166.
60 Herman Kahn, *On Thermonuclear War* (New Brunswick NJ: Transaction Publishers, 2007): 28.
61 Herman Kahn, *On Thermonuclear War* (New Brunswick NJ: Transaction Publishers, 2007): 7.
62 Herman Kahn, *On Thermonuclear War* (New Brunswick NJ: Transaction Publishers, 2007): 9.
63 Herman Kahn, *On Thermonuclear War* (New Brunswick NJ: Transaction Publishers, 2007): 20.
64 Herman Kahn, *On Thermonuclear War* (New Brunswick NJ: Transaction Publishers, 2007): 13.
65 Herman Kahn, *On Thermonuclear War* (New Brunswick NJ: Transaction Publishers, 2007): 76.
66 Herman Kahn, *On Thermonuclear War* (New Brunswick NJ: Transaction Publishers, 2007): 168.
67 Herman Kahn, *On Thermonuclear War* (New Brunswick NJ: Transaction Publishers, 2007): 16.
68 Herman Kahn, *On Thermonuclear War* (New Brunswick NJ: Transaction Publishers, 2007): 75–83.
69 Herman Kahn, *On Thermonuclear War* (New Brunswick NJ: Transaction Publishers, 2007): 10–11.
70 Manhattan Shelter Study (Guy B. Panero Engineers, 1958); see also atomic-skies.blogspot.co.uk/2013/09/rock-to-hide-me.html
71 Herman Kahn, Hudson Institute, *Nonmilitary Defense Policies: A Context, Reappraisal, and Commentary*, I (Harmon-on-Hudson: Hudson Institute, 1964); 18 July 1964. See also Mick Broderick and Robert Jacobs, 'Nuke York, New York: nuclear holocaust in the American imagination from Hiroshima to 9/11', *The Asia-Pacific Journal*, 10.11.6 (12 March 2012).

72 Herman Kahn, *On Thermonuclear War* (New Brunswick NJ: Transaction Publishers, 2007): 145.
73 Herman Kahn, *On Thermonuclear War* (New Brunswick NJ: Transaction Publishers, 2007): 145.
74 Herman Kahn, *On Thermonuclear War* (New Brunswick NJ: Transaction Publishers, 2007): 145.
75 Herman Kahn, *On Thermonuclear War* (New Brunswick NJ: Transaction Publishers, 2007): 145, note 3.
76 Herman Kahn originally developed his scenario method with the RAND Corporation and later at the Hudson Institute in the 1960s. Kahn and Anthony J. Wiener's study *The Year 2000: A Framework for Speculation* (1967) established the scientific and political use of scenario techniques and the emerging practices of futurology.
77 Herman Kahn, *World Economic Development: 1979 and Beyond* (London: Croom Helm, 1979): 112.
78 Herman Kahn, *World Economic Development: 1979 and Beyond* (London: Croom Helm, 1979): 112.
79 John Maddox, *The Doomsday Syndrome* (New York: McGraw-Hill, 1972). See also sociologist Hilary Rose's response to the Maddox critique, 'Doomsday gloom and optimism', *The Times* (3 September 1971).
80 The *Limits to Growth* report was covered in the environment section of *Time* magazine on 24 January 1972 and illustrated by the 'Projection for Disaster' graph with the caption: 'Adapted from the computer output chart in the *Limits to Growth* report'.
81 Edward Goldsmith and Robert Allen, *A Blueprint for Survival* (Penguin Books, 1972); originally published as a special issue of the *Ecologist* magazine, January 1972.
82 John Maddox, editor of *Nature*, in 'Doomsday gloom and optimism', *The Times* (3 September 1971): 5. See also John Maddox, *The Doomsday Syndrome* (New York: McGraw-Hill, 1972); Jacob Darwin Hamblin, *Arming Mother Nature: The Birth of Catastrophic Environmentalism* (Oxford, New York: Oxford University Press, 2013): 170–171.
83 'The Doomsday Machine', *Star Trek*, episode 35 (20 October 1967); the writer of the episode, Norman Spinrad, recalls: 'The original idea, which was complicated, is maybe a machine, but it's maybe an artificial organism, to serve the same purpose. Then you have the question, "When does an artificial organism become a machine and when does a machine become an artificial organism?"' www.startrek.com/article/doomsday-more-with-norman-spinrad-part-1
84 Herman Melville, *Moby-Dick; or the Whale* (New York: Harper & Brothers, 1851): 203.
85 This is also the topic of 'Is the Anthropocene a Doomsday Device?', dialogue between Carey Wolfe, Department of English, Rice University, Houston and Claire Colebrook, Department of English, Penn State University, University Park; introduction: Cecelia Watson (Max-Planck-Institut für Wissenschaftsgeschichte, Berlin) – Haus der Kulturen der Welt (12 January 2013); www.hkw.de/en/programm/projekte/2014/anthropozaen/anthropozaen_2013_2014.php
86 Executive Summary Plowshare programme; US Department of Energy; www.osti.gov/opennet/reports/plowshar.pdf
87 Scott L. Kirsch, *Proving Grounds: Project Plowshare and the Unrealized Dream of Nuclear Earthmoving* (New Brunswick: Rutgers University Press, 2005): 40.
88 Scott L. Kirsch, *Proving Grounds: Project Plowshare and the Unrealized Dream of Nuclear Earthmoving* (New Brunswick: Rutgers University Press, 2005): 41.
89 Joseph Masco, 'Terraforming planet Earth: the age of fallout' in *The Politics of Globality since 1945: Assembling the Planet*, eds. Rens van Munster and Caspar Sylvest (London & New York: Routledge, 2016): 44–70; 58.
90 See *Nuclear Excavation, Excavating with Nuclear Explosives – Technology Status Report Plowshare Program* (United States Atomic Energy Commission, 1968); www.youtube.com/watch?v=ZGXS_Qgfqno
91 *Plowshare* (United States Atomic Energy Commission, 1973); www.youtube.com/watch?v=ZGXS_Qgfqno
92 Joseph Masco, 'Terraforming planet Earth: the age of fallout' in *The Politics of Globality since 1945: Assembling the Planet*, eds. Rens van Munster and Caspar Sylvest (London & New York: Routledge, 2016): 44–70; 58.

110 Proving ground

93 *Plowshare* (United States Atomic Energy Commission, 1973); www.youtube.com/watch?v=ZGXS_Qgfqno.
94 Published by the AEC as Environment of the Cape Thompson Region Alaska in 1966; see Dan O'Neill, *The Firecracker Boys: H-Bombs, Inupiat Eskimos, and the Roots of the Environmental Movement* (Perseus, 2007): 293.
95 See Dan O'Neill, 'How Alaska escaped nuclear excavation', *Bulletin of Atomic Scientists* 45.10 (December 1989): 28–37.
96 *Plowshare* (United States Atomic Energy Commission, 1973); www.youtube.com/watch?v=ZGXS_Qgfqno.
97 B. C. Hacker, 'Fallout from Plowshare Peaceful Nuclear Explosions and the Environment 1956–1973', Organization of American Historians Annual Meeting, Lawrence Livermore National Laboratory, Washington DC (30 March – 2 April 1995; e-reports-ext.llnl.gov/pdf/401977.pdf ; accessed from US Department of Energy website: www.osti.gov/home/
98 Edward Teller quoted in *Anchorage Daily Times* (26 June 1959); cf. Dan O'Neill, *The Firecracker Boys: H-Bombs, Inupiat Eskimos, and the Roots of the Environmental Movement* (Perseus, 2007): 96.
99 Dan O'Neill, *The Firecracker Boys: H-Bombs, Inupiat Eskimos, and the Roots of the Environmental Movement* (Perseus, 2007): 302.
100 Paul J. Crutzen, 'Geology of mankind', *Nature* 415 (2002): 23.
101 Rachel Carson, *Silent Spring* (London: Hamish Hamilton, 1963): 3.
102 Rachel Carson, *Silent Spring* (London: Hamish Hamilton, 1963): 4.
103 Rachel Carson, *Silent Spring* (London: Hamish Hamilton, 1963): 5.
104 Rachel Carson, *Silent Spring* (London: Hamish Hamilton, 1963): 144.
105 Rachel Carson, *Silent Spring* (London: Hamish Hamilton, 1963): 226.
106 Rachel Carson, *Silent Spring* (London: Hamish Hamilton, 1963): 4.
107 Paul J. Crutzen and John W. Birks, 'The atmosphere after a nuclear war: twilight at noon', *Ambio* 11 (1982): 114–125; reprinted in *The Aftermath: The Human and Ecological Consequences of Nuclear War*, ed. Jeannie Peterson (Oxford: Pergamon, 1983): 73–96.
108 The nuclear winter hypothesis was outlined in the article by the group known as TTAPS (the initials of its five authors, Turco, Toon, Ackerman, Pollack and Sagan); Richard P. Turco, professor of atmospheric science at the University of California, Owen Brian Toon and James B. Pollack, both of the National Aeronautics and Space Administration's Ames Research Centre, Thomas P. Ackerman of Pennsylvania State University and Carl Sagan, professor of astrophysics at Cornell University. R.P. Turco *et al.*, 'Nuclear winter: global consequences of multiple nuclear explosions', *Science* 222.4630 (23 December 1983).
109 The TTAPS group sequenced three models – a nuclear war scenarios model, a particle microphysics model, and a one-dimensional radiative-convective climate model. Their models predicted that even limited nuclear wars could inject enough dust and soot into the stratosphere to adversely affect global climate. See R.P. Turco *et al.*, 'Nuclear winter: global consequences of multiple nuclear explosions', *Science* 222.4630 (23 December 1983). A companion article by Paul Ehrlich and colleagues argued that dark and cold could combine to cause the death of much unprotected life and deal a blow to food production that could cause massive starvation. See Paul Ehrlich *et al.*, 'Long-term biological consequences of nuclear war,' *Science* 222.4630 (23 December 1983). Carl Sagan also authored another article on the topic: 'Nuclear war and climate catastrophe: some policy implications', *Foreign Affairs* 62.2 (1983): 257–292.
110 Carl Sagan, 'Nuclear winter', *Parade* (30 October 1983).
111 'This is the way the world ends / This is the way the world ends / This is the way the world ends / Not with a bang but a whimper', T.S. Eliot, 'The Hollow Men' (Faber and Faber). Also quoted on the title page of Nevil Shute's *On the Beach* (Heinemann, 1957).
112 L.W. Alvarez, W. Alvarez, F. Asaro and H.V. Michel, 'Extraterrestrial cause for the Cretaceous-Tertiary extinction', *Science* 208.4448 (1980): 1095–1108.
113 See Chapter IV 'The Luck of the Ammonites' in Elizabeth Kolbert, The Sixth Extinction: An Unnatural History (London: Bloomsbury Publishing, 2014): 87.
114 Jacob Darwin Hamblin, *Arming Mother Nature: The Birth of Catastrophic Environmentalism* (Oxford, New York: Oxford University Press, 2013): 241.

115 Jacob Darwin Hamblin, *Arming Mother Nature: The Birth of Catastrophic Environmentalism* (Oxford, New York: Oxford University Press, 2013): 251.
116 Timothy Morton, *Hyperobjects: Philosophy and Ecology after the End of the World* (Minneapolis and London: University of Minnesota Press, 2013): 120.
117 Peter C. Van Wyck, *Signs of Danger: Waste Trauma and Nuclear Threat* (Minneapolis and London: University of Minnesota Press, 2005): x.
118 Planning for DOE Transuranic Waste Shipments from The Nevada Test Site to The Waste Isolation Processing Plant, www.state.nv.us/nucwaste/yucca/wippfact.htm
119 Shipment and Disposal Information, Waste Isolation Pilot Plant (US Department of Energy; www.wipp.energy.gov/shipments.htm
120 Peter C. Van Wyck, *Signs of Danger: Waste Trauma and Nuclear Threat* (Minneapolis and London: University of Minnesota Press, 2005): xvi.
121 Kathleen M. Trauth, Stephen C. Hora and Robert V. Guzowski, '*Expert Judgment on Markers to Deter Inadvertent Intrusion into the Waste Isolation Pilot Plant*' (DOE, Sandia National Laboratories, 1993).
122 Gregory Benford, Craig W. Kirkwood, Harry Otway and Martin J. Pasqualetti, '*Ten Thousand Years of Solitude? On Inadvertent Intrusion into the Waste Isolation Pilot Project Repository*', Los Alamos National Laboratory, New Mexico (1990).
123 Peter C. Van Wyck, *Signs of Danger: Waste Trauma and Nuclear Threat* (Minneapolis and London: University of Minnesota Press, 2005).
124 Gregory Benford, Craig W. Kirkwood, Harry Otway and Martin J. Pasqualetti, '*Ten Thousand Years of Solitude? On Inadvertent Intrusion into the Waste Isolation Pilot Project Repository*', Los Alamos National Laboratory, New Mexico (1990): iii; www.wipp.energy.gov/PICsProg/PICs_tech_concept.htm
125 Gregory Benford, Craig W. Kirkwood, Harry Otway and Martin J. Pasqualetti, '*Ten Thousand Years of Solitude? On Inadvertent Intrusion into the Waste Isolation Pilot Project Repository*.' Los Alamos National Laboratory, New Mexico (1990): 36.
126 Peter C. Van Wyck, *Signs of Danger: Waste Trauma and Nuclear Threat* (Minneapolis and London: University of Minnesota Press, 2005): 26.
127 Robert Alvarez, 'The WIPP problem, and what it means for defense waste disposal', *Bulletin of the Atomic Scientists* (23 March 2014); thebulletin.org/wipp-problem-and-what-it-means-defense-nuclear-waste-disposal7002#.UzBYydcs1FA; accessed 15 July 2014.
128 Waste Isolation Pilot Plant Technical Assessment Team Report (17 March 2015); energy.gov/em/downloads/technical-assessment-team-report.
129 In 2010, the DOE mothballed plans to develop Yucca Mountain in Nevada, which since 1987 had been designated as the future site of an underground repository.
130 Peter C. Van Wyck, *Signs of Danger: Waste Trauma and Nuclear Threat* (Minneapolis and London: University of Minnesota Press, 2005): 19.
131 Peter C. Van Wyck, *Signs of Danger: Waste Trauma and Nuclear Threat* (Minneapolis and London: University of Minnesota Press, 2005): 123.
132 Jacques Derrida, 'No apocalypse, not now (full speed ahead, seven missiles, seven missives)', trans. Catherine Porter and Philip Lewis, *Diacritics* 14.2 (Summer 1984): 20–31; 21.
133 Jacques Derrida, 'No apocalypse, not now (full speed ahead, seven missiles, seven missives)', trans. Catherine Porter and Philip Lewis, *Diacritics* 14.2 (Summer 1984): 20–31; 23.
134 Jacques Derrida, 'No apocalypse, not now (full speed ahead, seven missiles, seven missives)', trans. Catherine Porter and Philip Lewis, *Diacritics* 14.2 (Summer 1984): 20–31; 23.
135 Jacques Derrida, 'No apocalypse, not now (full speed ahead, seven missiles, seven missives)', trans. Catherine Porter and Philip Lewis, *Diacritics* 14.2 (Summer 1984): 20–31; 23.
136 Jacques Derrida, 'No apocalypse, not now (full speed ahead, seven missiles, seven missives)', trans. Catherine Porter and Philip Lewis, *Diacritics* 14.2 (Summer 1984): 20–31; 27.
137 Claire Colebrook, 'Not symbiosis, not now: why anthropogenic change is not really human', *The Oxford Literary Review* 34.2 (2012): 185–209; 203.
138 Robin McKie, 'Chernobyl 25 years on: a poisoned landscape', *The Guardian* (27 March 2011); www.theguardian.com/world/2011/mar/27/chernobyl-disaster-anniversary-japan
139 Selah Hennessy, 'Chernobyl zone – Europe's largest wildlife refuge?' (25 April 2011), Russia Watch Voice of America; blogs.voanews.com/russia-watch/2011/04/25/nuclear-zone-turns-into-wildlife-refuge/

140 Mark Kinver, 'Chernobyl not a wildlife haven', BBC News (14 August 2007),; news.bbc.co.uk/1/hi/sci/tech/6946210.stm
141 Mark Lynas, 'How a nuclear disaster can be good for ecology' (7 June 2011), www.marklynas.org/2011/06/how-a-nuclear-disaster-can-be-good-for-ecology/
142 Toby Goaman-Dodson, 'Zone of exclusion' in *Anticipatory History*, eds. Caitlin de Silvey, Simon Naylor and Colin Sackett (Axminster: Uniform Books, 2011): 71.
143 David McNeill, 'Google Street View sends cameras into Namie, an abandoned town in Fukushima where once 21,000 people lived', *The Independent* (27 March 2013); www.independent.co.uk/news/world/asia/google-street-view-sends-cameras-into-namie-an-abandoned-town-in-fukushima-where-once-21000-people-lived-8552039.html

4 Proxy world

DANGER: *thin ice*

Antarctica is a proxy world. It stands in for all the places we can't reach or don't understand – the most extraterritorial and extraterrestrial place on Earth. The sparse and relatively recent human history of Antarctica makes it an important place to think about the Anthropocene. It is a continent 'still wrapped in the Ice Age'.[1] This most uninhabitable place is also a vantage point from which to contemplate the possible future of an uninhabitable Earth. Antarctica has been the key site for global environmental change research since the International Geophysical Year (IGY) in 1957, which saw the establishment of international year-round research stations and the commencement of several long-term studies of the region. Since that time, ideas of an austral *terra incognita* – pristine environment, absolute wilderness, last outpost – are giving way to an awareness of Antarctica's dynamism and restlessness, its minute responsiveness to changes far away. Antarctica is both the experimental ground and the advanced warning system for global environmental change. Though few will ever see Antarctica, all of humanity is likely to see the effects of changes to its remote ice caps. Significant temperature increases in both the oceans and the atmosphere are threatening to melt the Antarctic ice sheet, ultimately as a result transforming coastlines and affecting weather patterns around the world.

The word proxy comes from the Latin *procuratio* – meaning administration, management and stewardship. It brings the sense of the direction of affairs for another entity. There are two kinds of proxies in scientific discourse. One is a transposition of measurements, in which one physical quantity is used as an indicator of the value of another. For example, in palaeoclimatology, the study of past climates, climate proxies are preserved physical characteristics of the past that stand in for the direct measurements no human could take at the time. These include data from ice cores, tree rings, boreholes, corals, lake and ocean sediments, and carbonate speleothems. The other sense of a proxy is that of the illustration, model, diagram, and scientific parable – a means of demonstrating a phenomenon to audiences unable to see it in nature for themselves. One example is John Tyndall's 'carefully orchestrated' and 'impressive' ice shows at London's Royal Institution in 1857 and 1859, designed to demonstrate the movement of glaciers and the atmospheric absorption of solar heat. Tyndall's public performances of the science '…had to make these phenomena visible to his audience'. He used models of ice blocks and lenses to demonstrate the process of regelation, along with projections onto a screen from a spectrophotometer to show the infrared absorption of different gases. Tyndall was creating plausible and enticing proxies in order to communicate complex scientific knowledge to his audience.[2] 'The bearing of this experiment upon the action of planetary atmospheres is obvious,' Tyndall claimed of his demonstrations, establishing an experimental basis for what later became known as the planetary greenhouse effect.[3] He later elaborated on his findings with the idea that changes in the amount of the radiatively active constituents of the atmosphere 'may have produced all the mutations of climate which the researches of geologists reveal'.[4]

Antarctica works as a proxy in both senses – as an indicator of changes in the world and as a story or model of disruption. Just as the ice core is a proxy for global environmental change, Antarctica is a proxy for all that lies north of it: what happens to this ice continent affects the rest of the world. This place is key to deepening understanding of the past dynamics of planetary climate, in order to more accurately predict its future. In Antarctica, divergent trajectories cohere and collide. Humanity's ambition for Antarctica is that it represents a symbol of both science and peace – as enshrined in the 1959 Antarctic Treaty – and a refiguring of the utopian as international and ecological. It is an experimental site for ascertaining species extinctions, testing international laws, and living within planetary boundaries. Antarctica is the principal location for the vast exercise of measuring the Earth, with remote sensing monitoring of the atmosphere, deep seas, and the integrative environmental analysis of climate change modelling.

Antarctica is acknowledged as being the site of important indicators in the disturbance of global climate systems. Disruptions to global climate register at the boundaries of the coldest regions first. Over the last 50 years, annual mean temperatures on the Antarctic Peninsula have risen by almost 3°C, making the Antarctic one of the fastest-warming regions in the world. As a result, significant impacts have been seen on the Antarctic Peninsula, in the retreating of glaciers, reduction in snow cover, and the collapse of regional ice shelves. According to glaciologist Robert Bindschadler, 'You might say ice sheets are the "canaries in the coal mine" of climate science. And right now the canaries are chirping an alarm.'[5] With the discovery of the ozone hole above Antarctica in 1985, followed by NASA satellite images in 2002 that documented the collapse of the Antarctic Peninsula Larsen B ice shelf, the region has been increasingly prominent in our awareness of the global climate catastrophe. Indeed, the catastrophe of Antarctic ice sheet melt acts as a proxy of the catastrophe that might be visited on the rest of the world. As Jan Zalasiewicz of the Anthropocene Working Group (AWG) warns:

> If the delicately poised West Antarctic Ice Sheet were to slide suddenly into the sea, as the ice sheets of North America did 10,000 years ago, many coastal cities would be plunged underwater, and in a geological instant would be carried into the realm where fossilisation begins.[6]

Teetering between a deep geologic past and an uncertain planetary future, Antarctica is an important placeholder for the Anthropocene. The Anthropocene thesis suggests that 'the Earth has now left its natural geological epoch, the present interglacial state called the Holocene' and furthermore that human activities are 'pushing the Earth into planetary *terra incognita*'.[7] Antarctica is already a destabilising place for humans: it offers an uncanny experience of space and time, sensory extremes, days and nights that last for months, and physical dangers that test our survival skills to the limit. As the historian Stephen Pyne observes, Antarctica's isolation and its uncannily 'abiotic, acultural' barrenness make it similar to extraterrestrial spaces such as the deep seas and outer space.[8] Antarctica's *terra incognita* thus works as the analogue for outer space: for Mars, the Moon, and more distant worlds. It is not only 'a constituent of an ice regime broadcast throughout the solar system',[9] but a cryospheric record of Earth's climatic and geological past.

Terra incognita

Antarctica has long stood for the geographical, spatial, and cultural ends of the Earth. In the 4th century BC, Aristotle could only guess at the existence of another and equivalent icy region to the Arctic on the other side of the world. This hypothetical place was named for what it was not: *Ant-arctica*. In the 2nd century AD, Ptolemy's *Geographia* postulated that the lands in the northern hemisphere should be balanced by lands in the south. *Terra Australis Incognita*, a hypothetical southern continent, appeared on maps between the 16th and 18th centuries. Francesco Roselli's 1508 world map depicted a large southern landmass, '*Antarcticus*'; while Abraham Ortelius's 1570 map showed '*Terra Australis Nondum Cognita*' ('The Southern Land Not Yet Known'). A speculative outline of the southernmost land surrounded by mythical sea creatures appears also in Matteo Ricci's 1602 map of the world, which drew on observations made by Chinese astronomers of lunar shadows.[10] Myths and speculation about the unknown southern land abounded. It was not until the 19th century that its existence could be verified.

In his first voyage of exploration, made between 1768 and 1771 in HMS *Endeavour*, Captain James Cook was under orders to observe and record the transit of Venus, and to discover and claim for Britain the elusive southern land – the place that 18th-century Europeans imagined to be the ends of the Earth. Cook's 'secret instructions' from the Admiralty were that any uninhabited lands he might find (designated in law at the time as *terra nullius*, or 'nobody's land') he should 'take possession [of] for his Majesty by setting up proper marks and inscriptions as first discoverers and possessors'.[11] On his second voyage of 1772–1775, Cook crossed the Antarctic circle and circumnavigated Antarctica with the ships *Resolution* and *Adventure*. However, despite reaching the frozen ocean, Cook was unable to find land. The antipodean land imagined by the ancients, he decided, lay 'where the sea is so pestered with ice that the land is thereby inaccessible'. Deterred by the thick pack ice from sailing further, Cook predicted that *terra australis* would never be discovered. 'The risque one runs in exploring a coast, in these unknown and icy seas, is so very great, that I can be bold enough to say that no man will venture further than I have done; and the lands which may lie to the South will never be explored.'[12]

The Antarctic continent was likely first sighted in January 1820 by a Russian expedition led by Admiral Fabian Gottlieb Thaddeus von Bellinghausen in the *Vostok* and *Mirnyi*. A year later an American sealer, Captain John Davis, is supposed to have been the first person to set foot on the continent, going ashore at Hughes Bay on the Antarctic Peninsula. Cook's account of the rich marine life in *A Voyage towards the South Pole* had provoked a rush of whalers and sealers to the subpolar regions, as well as inspiring further voyages of discovery, and the concomitant political and economic rivalry for the resources he had observed. The industrial exploitation of the region was spurred by the development of metal-hulled ships and food preserved in cans. As the architect Sam Jacob has observed, 'the continent only enters the human world as fact, rather than speculation, supposition or myth, after the Industrial Revolution'.[13] In other words: the discovery, exploitation and appropriation of Antarctica coincides with one of the key time markers suggested for the base of the Anthropocene.

Early expeditions to Antarctica had only managed to survey the coastline. In 1841, James Clark Ross's British expedition to find the South Magnetic Pole sailed in HMS *Terror* and HMS *Erebus* through the pack ice of what is now known as the Ross Sea, and discovered Cape Adare. Ross, who had expected only ice, was astounded to find a spectacular mountainous landscape. A small party alighted on the rocks, planted a flag, and carried out a ceremony, taking possession of the lands in the name of Queen Victoria. Ross continued south to McMurdo Bay (named later, after Archibald McMurdo, his lieutenant on the *Terror*), now the site of McMurdo, the largest Antarctic research station, and then found Ross Island, as well as an enormous wall of ice in the Ross Sea now known as the Ross Ice Shelf. Two visible volcanic peaks were named after his ships. Marie-Hélène Huet notes, 'The ships' names may have seemed especially appropriate for the volcanoes: one was extinct, while the other – *Erebus* – actively spewed fire and fumes over the desolate landscape.'[14] Apart from the islands round the edge, pillaged by sealers, Antarctica remained largely untouched until the end of the 19th century because of its hostile environment, its lack of resources, and its isolation. It endured, however, as a potent *terra incognita* in the imagination. Polar narratives, real and fictional, dwelt on isolation in empty oceanic space, floating mysteries of ice and fog, Antarctic mirages and spectres. These were 'interpretations that built on ideas of disaster as the extreme limit of human encounters with inhuman space'.[15] The reclusive horror fiction writer H.P. Lovecraft strikes an ominous note on the perils of Antarctica:

> I am forced into speech because men of science have refused to follow my advice without knowing why. It is altogether against my will that I tell my reasons for opposing this contemplated invasion of the Antarctic – with its vast fossil hunt and its wholesale boring and melting of the ancient ice caps. And I am the more reluctant because my warning may be in vain.[16]

Antarctica, like the Arctic, was the apogee of hostile terrain – both spatial and psychological. Voyages of conquest to the poles were driven by a competitive desire for a sense of global mastery, but were far more likely to be met with disaster and disappointment. Science fiction tales of horror and discovery by the likes of Edgar Allan Poe, Jules Verne and H.P. Lovecraft mingled in the popular imagination with real accounts of polar exploration.[17] There are tales of woe like the mysterious disappearance of Captain Sir John Franklin's 1845 expedition to the North Pole with the *Terror* and *Erebus* – the same ships used in Ross's expedition. The early-20th-century race to the poles, with its multiple simultaneous expeditions and fierce rivalries, took on an aura of heroic fascination, even when journeys ended in disaster. The stories include the compelling adventures of Ernest Shackleton's *Endurance* and *Nimrod* expeditions, tales of triumph like Roald Amundsen's expertly planned *Fram* expedition – the first to reach the South Pole – and also of adversity like Scott's *Discovery* expedition, and even more so the ill-fated *Terra Nova* expedition, which saw the entire South Pole party die of exhaustion and cold after learning that Amundsen had beaten them to their goal.

In order to be sure he had set foot on the South Pole, Amundsen paced a grid of 12 miles across around the projected spot of his calculations, and planted the Norwegian flag square in the middle of it.[18] Scott had only disappointment when he reached the Pole on 17 January 1912, discovering Amundsen had reached it weeks earlier. 'Great God! This is an awful place and terrible enough for us to have laboured to it without the reward of priority.'[19] Amundsen's party may have been the first people to stand in real life at 90°0'S, but Jules Verne's fictional Captain Nemo beat them to it. In *Twenty Thousand Leagues Under the Seas*, published in 1870, Nemo lists all the explorers (including Ross), along with the latitudes reached, who had to that date ventured near the Pole without reaching that coveted destination. Nemo's supranational identity and the global hypermobility of his craft the *Nautilus*, with its motto, *mobilis in mobile*, announced his freedom to navigate and possess the very remotest reaches of the world. Antarctica, however, is always a negotiation with something it is not; as Verne's stunt with an inverted flag recognises. Performing a symbolic act of possession, Nemo unfurls a vast black banner emblazoned with a big 'N' at the South ('S') Pole:

> 'I, Captain Nemo, on this 21st day of March, 1868, have reached the South Pole on the ninetieth degree; and I take possession of this part of the globe, equal to one-sixth of the known continents.'
> 'In whose name, Captain?'
> 'In my own, sir!'
> Saying which, Captain Nemo unfurled a black banner, bearing an 'N' in gold quartered on its bunting. Then, turning towards the orb of day, whose last rays lapped the horizon of the sea, he exclaimed:
> 'Adieu, sun! Disappear, thou radiant orb! rest beneath this open sea, and let a night of six months spread its shadows over my new domains!'

The US Flag was planted at the South Pole in 1956. The US Amundsen-Scott South Pole Station now marks the spot – or almost. The original research station was built in 1956 by Seabees (US Naval Construction Forces) during Operation Deep Freeze in time for the IGY, and was the first permanent human structure at the South Pole. The Amundsen-Scott Station has been continuously occupied since it was built, but it has also been demolished, rebuilt, expanded, relocated, and upgraded several times. The station currently lies within 100 metres of the Geographic or Terrestrial South Pole, though as it is located on a moving glacier, it is being carried towards the Pole at a rate of about 10 metres per year. Google's Street View now allows access to a 360-degree panorama of the Geographic South Pole marker, surrounded by the flags of the 12 original signatories of the 1959 Antarctic Treaty. The South Magnetic Pole, the South Geomagnetic Pole and the South Pole of Inaccessibility are all in different locations, which feels appropriate, since the goals of polar exploration have always been imaginary: 'The poles exist only in their scientific and cartographic representations, and they are multiple – geographic, magnetic, geomagnetic, each indeterminate and mobile.'[20] And in blizzard whiteout it is difficult to be certain of anything.

Antarctica's coastlines were still traced by question marks on a map in a 1966 atlas, and accurate mapping of Antarctica was only finally achieved at the end of the 20th century, with the aid of satellite imagery.[21] In *Apollo's Eye*, Denis Cosgrove connects three strategic spatial metaphors in his history of global visions: the *encirclement* of the globe expressed in Cook's circumnavigation of the seas; the interior *penetration*

118 *Proxy world*

of continental and telluric space in 19th-century explorations and the axial *advance* to the polar ends of the Earth, achieved in the early 20th century.[22] The poles, he observes, 'represent the final ends of the Earth, global destinations of ultimate inaccessibility..'.[23] Whereas in previous ages the conquest of Antarctica's white space on the map promised global mastery, we have learned to regard the poles with a new anxiety:

> Even today, with azimuthal maps of polar regions a standard feature of any atlas and with the white expanses of frozen ocean and continental Antarctica inescapable features of space photographs of the Earth, there seems to be an unwillingness to contemplate these regions without anxiety; they remain *eschatological ends of the Earth*, whence ozone depletion or ice-sheet meltdown threatens life across the globe.[24]

Antarctica has remained on the edges of human concern, remote, impenetrable and unknown – planted with the occasional flag, to be swallowed soon enough by accumulating ice like any other human detritus; the permanent home of incomprehensible, implacable, overweening Nature. For centuries, Antarctica's inaccessibility and cartographic strangeness warned of a decidedly off-limits environment. As a site for scientific investigation, it remains as inhospitable and remote a place as can be imagined, and as exacting a laboratory as it could be. Moreover, it has always been the exploitation of resources, the mining of coal and burning of oil, that has driven and updated our knowledge about Antarctica. The irony is that it is not possible to learn more about the region without being part of its destruction. As we enter the unchartered territory of the Anthropocene, Antarctica figures as the uncanny space, *terra incognita*, for thinking the 'eschatological ends of the Earth'.

Ship shape

> The *Belgica* appeared small, but she seemed well adapted to the prospective work, and above all, she was filled brim full with good food – such delicacies as only a Belgian could select. I am sure as we penetrate the white antarctic she will seem large enough; she will afford us a safe home and many, very many, comforts, as comforts go in the polar regions.[25]

The first habitation in Antarctica was a ship. The Belgian Antarctic Expedition party, led by Baron Adrien de Gerlache, inadvertently spent the winter in their steam ship the *Belgica*, while trapped in sea ice from 28 February 1898 through to 14 March 1899. The ship had been equipped with a research laboratory, and enough provisions for one year. Among the members of the expedition were the future heroes of polar exploration, Frederick A. Cook, Henryk Arctowski and Roald Amundsen. As the ship drifted hopelessly with the ice, Cook observed that some consolation could be found in the occasional nautical observations of their position, granted by a glimpse of the Sun: 'Today we know the exact spot on which we are being thrown about,' he writes. 'In reality, however, we are as hopelessly isolated as if we were on the surface of Mars, and we are plunging still deeper and deeper into the white antarctic silence.'[26] By March 1898, Cook's mood in the journals is desolate: 'We are imprisoned in an endless sea of ice, and find our horizon monotonous. We have told all the tales, real and imaginative, to which we are equal. Time weighs heavily upon us as the darkness

Figure 4.1 View looking towards the Discovery Hut, with sailing ship '*Discovery*' moored behind; British National Antarctic Expedition, 1901–04 (photographer: Herbert Ponting)
Source: Scott Polar Research Institute, University of Cambridge

advances.'[27] By 19 May, the Sun disappeared below the horizon for the start of the long Antarctic night – it would not be seen again for another 63 days. Cook was also a doctor, and his account details the challenges of venturing so far south – anaemia, malnourishment, scurvy, lethargy, depression and paranoia bloomed in the confines of the ship and the small 'village' of 'outhouses, sledges, sounding machines... strewn on the pack [ice]'.[28] Importantly, however, Cook lived to tell the tale. After almost a year trapped in the ice, the crew of the *Belgica* repurposed the ship and dynamited trenches through the sea ice, escaping just in time to avoid the onset of the next winter.

Carsten Borchgrevink, leading the 1899 British-financed *Southern Cross* expedition, was the first to intentionally overwinter on the Antarctic mainland. He built a refuge, the first permanent structure and land base on the continent, at Cape Adare. From here he could conduct meteorological and magnetic observations and collect specimens of Antarctic rock. Built to last, 'Borchgrevink's hut,' approximately 6.4 m x 5.4 m, was prefabricated in Norway by Strømmen Traevarefabrikk from seasoned Baltic pine, with tongue and groove interior panelling, layers of sealskin, and papier maché insulation. Most of the early constructions in the region were simple shelters built by gangs of sealers dropped on the beaches for short stays, and the whaling stations on South Georgia, all since subsequently abandoned. The earliest constructions on the Antarctic mainland were the cairns, and the pre-fabricated timber huts, shelters and research bases of the heroic age: Discovery Hut on Ross Island at Hut Point, 1902; Shackleton's Hut of 1908; and Scott's Hut at Cape Evans built in 1911. Scott's Hut was the largest at 15 m x 7.6m, with double-planked inner and outer walls, insulated with seaweed sewn into a quilt. It had a stable area for the expedition horses and a porch and corridor for storing equipment, fuel cans and seal blubber. The hut was divided into different sections by partitions created from boxes of supplies, and areas were set aside for the officers, for the scientists and their laboratories, and for the lower-ranking members of the expedition, according to naval practice – keeping everything ship-shape was the order of the day. A tin of Huntley & Palmers' biscuits remains frozen onto the table at Scott's abandoned hut. As the writer Sarah Moss points out, these ship's biscuits are emblematic of the frozen chapter of imperial exploration, and have become fetishes of these early polar explorers' daring. For Scott, however, they were simply the 'currency of survival': 'Truly awful outside the tent. Must fight it out to the last biscuit, but can't reduce rations.'[29]

The 20th and 21st centuries have seen a proliferation of scientific outposts in Antarctica. The population of the continent now oscillates between approximately 1,000 people in the winter and 4,000 in the summer. While the latest research stations are described as 'space-age architecture'[30], they have much in common with whaling stations, mining camps and oil rigs, and also with the original huts of the heroic age. As the author Francis Spufford observes, 'In effect, exploring the interior of Antarctica *was* a space programme, 1900-style; a venture into a white space on the map that was so inhospitable to life, you had to take along every scrap of food and fuel and equipment you needed, and every night retreat into a capsule of the warmer climate you came from.'[31] The inhabitation of Antarctica remains provisional, strictly limited by finite resources and challenging logistics, galvanised by the necessity of functioning in extremes of climate, 'at the edge of the possibilities of civilisation'. Provisions, materials, fuel and labour are all shipped from elsewhere. The research stations have been established as self-contained temporary communities set up for global science and monitoring programmes, or as bases for NASA astronaut training camps on 'analogue missions'. NASA's Mars programme prepares astronauts to cope with months of isolation, confinement, and an extreme environment (identified with the acronym ICE) – on the actual ice of Antarctica. As astronaut Cristina Hammock Koch explains: '[This] means going months without seeing the Sun, with the same crew, and without shipments of mail or fresh food.' She continues: 'The isolation, absence of family and friends, and lack of new sensory inputs are all conditions that you must find a strategy to thrive within.'[32]

The research stations provide basic accommodation, laboratories and workshops, along with canteens, washing facilities, and spaces for sport and leisure. They maintain satellite links for the transmission of research data and communications, and serve as bases for aircraft, ship and field operations in the region. Sam Jacob traces in the modern architecture of Antarctica the 'idea of the primitive hut': 'Within this landscape, each station acts as a shelter, a bubble containing and enabling society to formulate specific outposts of culture, behaviour and knowledge.' This holds as true for today's 'space-age' research stations as it did for the 'heroic age' huts of wood, paper and seaweed. Jacob observes: 'the history of Antarctic architecture seems a hyper-accelerated history of architecture itself, progressing from the hut to the space station in just over a hundred years.'[33] They remain, however, in some senses, primitive huts.

Halley is the British Antarctic Survey's most isolated year-round research station, established in 1956 for the IGY and providing an unbroken record since that date of meteorological and atmospheric data. It is one of only two research stations in Antarctica sited on a floating ice shelf – the Brunt Ice Shelf, situated 75 degrees south at the edge of the southern auroral zone, and 700 miles from the nearest human settlement. It is now in its sixth incarnation. Each station, in turn, has been buried by blizzards and snowdrifts and has also needed to be relocated to adjust for the slide of the ice shelf towards the Weddell Sea. Halley VI opened in 2012 and was hailed as the first fully relocatable polar research station in the world. In December 2016 it was announced that it would be relocated 23 km across the ice, upstream of a previously dormant ice chasm that had begun to show signs of growth in 2012.[34] Designed by Hugh Broughton Architects and AECOM Engineers, it consists of a series of modules elevated on ski-equipped, jackable legs, to prevent it being buried in the snow. Hugh Broughton cites Thunderbird 2 International Rescue's transporter as an influence; there are echoes, too, of Archigram's Walking City.[35] The new modular station was designed to be self-sufficient, to withstand freezing winter temperatures of -55°C, and to have minimal impact on Antarctica's pristine environment. Around 16 staff inhabit the station in the Antarctic winter, and 70 in the summer. New supplies and provisions, logistics staff, research scientists and technicians arrive annually on RRS *Ernest Shackleton*. It departs again in February, removing summer staff and waste, and leaving a small group behind for overwintering. In 2017, the British Antarctic Survey decided not to overwinter at Halley because of concerns about the instability of the ice, particularly as a result of a new crack.[36] The station was shut down as a precautionary measure: if the ice shelf fractured during the Antarctic winter of 24-hour darkness, extremely low temperatures and frozen sea, evacuation of personnel would be extremely difficult. On 30 July 2014, Halley VI suffered a 19-hour electrical breakdown in winter temperatures of -32°C. The inhabitants were unharmed, but research activities were suspended for some time afterward.[37] This incident is a reminder of the extensive life-support technology required to survive in a 'primitive hut' in a hostile world, and it underscores the impossibility of survival – at least in our current state of technological development – without the assistance of fossil fuels. Halley VI's vulnerability illustrates philosopher Peter Sloterdijk's observation about the space station: 'it represents a model for being in a world condemned to artificiality.'[38]

There is a city on Antarctica, or at least an approximate city. The US McMurdo Station, the largest continent's largest research base, was raised in 1956 on the volcanic rock of Ross Island, on the shore of McMurdo Sound. The base maintains a quasi-military social order inherited from its previous incarnation as a naval base: 'McMurdo was officially designated as a ship, its residents ate in a galley and, like a submarine on Cold War missile control, it was powered by a small nuclear reactor, known affectionately to locals as 'Nukey-Poo'.[39] An extensive clean-up operation in the 1970's shipped 12,200 tons of radioactive soil and rock back to the US for disposal.[40] McMurdo functions as a logistics base for much of the Antarctic continent. It has an airport and transport interchange, from which the snow road to the South Pole departs – the McMurdo South Pole Highway. McMurdo accommodates over 1,000 people in the summer in temporary buildings: 'Dorms', 'Inns' and 'Hotels'. McMurdo dwarfs the other, more remote US bases in Antarctica, which are dependent upon it to function. It supplies them with energy and manages their waste, and they share the

122 *Proxy world*

Figure 4.2 The 'Tenements' – bunks in Winterquarters Hut of Lt Henry Bowers, Apsley Cherry-Garrard, Captain Oates, Cecil Meares and Dr Atkinson; 9 October 1911; British Antarctic Expedition 1910–13 (photographer: Herbert Ponting)
Source: Scott Polar Research Institute, University of Cambridge

use of the roads and tunnels, planes, tractors, helicopters and building materials that cluster around McMurdo, all pointing to an ongoing, unfinished project of urbanisation at the ends of the Earth.

A National Science Foundation (NSF) information guide makes McMurdo's cosmopolitan aspirations explicit: 'You will find that McMurdo Station resembles an urban centre in its population diversity and hectic pace. Like major cities, McMurdo serves as an international centre where people of different backgrounds meet and exchange ideas.'[41] However, most sources describe McMurdo less grandly. Plonked down in the pristine grandeur of the Antarctic wilds, this outpost of human 'civilisation' strikes many visitors with its banal, very human, ugliness. In his memoir of working as a contractor at McMurdo, *Big Dead Place* (2005), Nicholas Johnson describes the corporate bureaucracy and mundane routines of the population of researchers and support workers, from 'dishwashers and mechanics, to hairdressers and explosives-handlers'. McMurdo's architecture resembles a suburban office park; its streets are loud with traffic noise and cluttered with shabby infrastructure:

> McMurdo lies in the shadow of Mount Erebus, a smouldering volcano encrusted with thick slabs of ice. To make room for McMurdo a ripple of frozen hills on the edge of Ross Island have been hacked away to form an alcove sloped like the back of a shovel, and then affixed with green and white cartridges with doors and

windows. Silver fuel tanks sparkle on the hillside like giant watch batteries. As if unloosed from a specimen jar, a colony of machines scours the dirt roads among the simple buildings, digesting snow and cargo dumped by the wind and planes, rattling like cracked armour and beeping loudly in reverse ... In the distance, framed by ratty utility poles and twisted electrical lines, the gleaming mountains of the Royal Society Range spill glaciers that glow like molten gold onto the far rim of the frozen white sea. Near Castle Rock, skiing toward Mount Erebus, in the middle of nowhere, you can stop at the bright red emergency shelter that looks like a giant red larva and call your bank to dispute your credit card fees.[42]

When Werner Herzog arrived at McMurdo to film his 2007 documentary film *Encounters at the End of the World*, he, too, was disappointed to find McMurdo 'like an ugly mining town, filled with caterpillars and noisy construction sites'. In voiceover he observes that this is probably close to what a future space settlement would look like – not some sublime, high-tech encounter with an alien landscape, but a blot upon it.[43] Herzog interviews a selection of McMurdo's 'full-time travellers', 'part-time workers' and 'professional dreamers'. These are people who, as Stefan Pashov, 'philosopher, forklift driver' observes, 'have this intention to jump off the margins of the map'. They include maintenance workers, researchers, volcanologists, ecologists, glaciologists, biologists, zoologists – in different ways, in Herzog's view, all attempting to escape from life elsewhere. For Herzog, even the research station has too much of the human world about it – 'From the very first day, we just wanted to get out of this place'. But first he requires survival training. This includes taking part in the 'bucket-head whiteout' scenario, in which everyone wears a bucket on their head to simulate vision restrictions in a blizzard. Interviews at McMurdo and its surrounding research bases and field camps are intercut with archive footage of the heroic era – the evacuation and breaking up of the ice-bound *Endurance*; the interior of Shackleton's Discovery Hut ('like an extinct supermarket') – and, of course, with images of the enigmatic desolation of the Antarctic landscape. Gazing on the white wastes, Herzog worries about a time when we will need to make artificial snow; he follows this immediately with an interview with a canteen worker, demonstrating the McMurdo galley's ice cream-maker:

> This is Frosty Boy... It's the equivalent of ice cream in the States, and it's a really big hit... And it has the texture of ice cream but it's not quite ice cream. There's a lot of crises that happen in McMurdo when the Frosty Boy runs out. It's bad news. Word circulates everywhere throughout McMurdo when Frosty Boy goes down... It's really good stuff.[44]

It may be that the Antarcticans relish such insignificant crises because they domesticate this whole wild and precarious venture. Perhaps they are a comforting distraction from the far more significant dangers that are only ever a few equipment failures away. Tweeting from the malfunctioning, winter-bound Halley VI station, engineer Anthony Lister joked, 'Got internet, lots of @Yorkshire Tea and a big kettle. Really, what more do you actually need?'[45] Yet even an ironic performance of frontier stoicism affirms a frontier mentality, in which the project of domesticating wild nature all too often instrumentalises and besmirches it. Naming their backyard nuclear reactor 'Nukey-Poo' might have made its presence less nerve-racking to residents of McMurdo. It did not, however, stop it from leaking and malfunctioning, and eventually having to be removed.

Herzog's *Encounters* presents a parable on the inevitable end of humanity with the Frosty Boy crisis as yet another episode in a tale of recurring catastrophes. From Frosty Boy it is a short conceptual step, in Herzog's mind, to humanity's eventual extinction. Our dependence on technology makes us vulnerable; our love of comfort makes us ignore the plainest warnings about our precarious position.

> Human life is part of an endless chain of catastrophes, the demise of the dinosaurs being just one of these events. We seem to be next. And when we are gone what will happen thousands of years from now in the future? Will there be alien archaeologists from another planet trying to find out what we were doing at the South Pole?[46]

Herzog's narrative that imagines these archaeologists' excavations goes with footage of descending into tunnels deep below the South Pole station carved from snow and ice, at -70°C: 'the place has outlived all the large cities in the world.' He finds various artefacts, a whole frozen sturgeon, a can of Russian caviar and other trinkets and mementos framed by a garland of popcorn – all placed in carved-out shelves in the ice walls, and preserved frozen by the extremely cold and dry air. He recognises this as remnants of human presence on the planet. The South Pole's 'obituary to civilisation' could so easily be an obituary for the Holocene. The Anthropocene presents us with the notion that the apocalypse we fearfully wait for, or hope to avoid, is already here. It is an 'end of the world' that we are *all* encountering – with all the banal unconcern of daily life on a provisional Antarctic research settlement. An 'end of the world' which is more like the series of accommodations, disjunctions, frustrations, and localised disorders in which humans working in Antarctica go about their everyday lives.

Ice ages

> Antarctica, it was slowly discovered, was quite unlike the Arctic. Northern hemisphere assumptions foundered on a very different, southern reality: a continent at the pole, an ice age in action, the cold core of Earth's atmosphere, the engine of global climate. Antarctica was Louis Agassiz's dream – or nightmare – discovered on our planet in our own time. It is where nine-tenths of the world's land ice resides.[47]

In 1840 Louis Agassiz published *Études sur les glaciers*, the work in which he laid out his theory of ice ages. The study of geologic ice is intimately connected with the study of rocks. Geologists had turned up evidence that the past few million years, during which the ice sheets cycled back and forth through growth and decline, had been an unusual time in the Earth's history. Phenomena such as erratics, moraines and striations came to be associated with the advance and retreat of glaciers, and these ideas were popularised by Agassiz with his notion of an 'Ice Age' – as Stephen Pyne describes it, 'an almost Noachian Deluge of glacial ice across Europe'.[48] Charles Darwin's *On the Origin of the Species* incorporated Agassiz's theory, and speculated on the vast migrations that he supposed the advance and retreat of the glaciers must have necessitated. The Pleistocene epoch, proposed by Charles Lyell in 1839, which lasted from about 2,588,000 to 11,700 years ago, accommodated this recent period of repeated glaciations and, towards its end, the emergence and survival of *Homo sapiens* – the only extant human species. The Holocene epoch is the name given to the most recent of the interglacial spells – one whose end, in turn, is announced with the advance of the Anthropocene and its urban-age humans. It is to Antarctica, a Pleistocene relic, that *anthropos* still turns, in order to think through the implications of a changed climatic future.

A remarkably prescient fiction story appears in a 1911 issue of the *South Polar Times*, the shipboard scrapbook newspaper of which Ernest Shackleton was the founding editor, that had, of course, the 'largest circulation of any periodical within the Antarctic circle'.[49] It describes the extinction of humanity due to climate change triggered by the melting of the Antarctic ice following industrial exploitation. 'Fragments of a Manuscript Found by the People of Sirius When They Visited the Earth During the Exploration of the Solar System' was written by George Clarke Simpson, meteorologist on the *Terra Nova* expedition of 1910–1913, and later director of the Meteorological Office (Met Office).[50] Simpson's science fiction story describes the disruptions of climate change and the melting of the Antarctic ice following industrial exploitation. 'I know not why I write,' begins the last living human being and narrator of the tale, 'for there will be none to read; but the history of the human race since the dawn of civilisation has been written, and I feel impelled to set down the manner of the end.'[51] The story describes Antarctica's role in producing drinking water, the 'elixir of life', through freezing and thawing cycles: 'The ice-bound shores of McMurdo Sound became the centre of the world. From it flowed the life-giving fluid which alone sustained the human race.'[52] Simpson's research as a meteorologist concerned the study of climate during the ice ages. Like many others of the time, he was convinced that the prehistoric ice ages held the key to understanding human evolution, and therefore to understanding our species' future. Simpson's tale, and the 'people' or extraterrestrials that visit a future Earth to find evidence of the 'last man', anticipate the foundational thought experiment of the Anthropocene, and Zalasiewicz's alien forensic geologists' survey of urban fossils. The challenges of imagining a post-human Earth seem to have been suited to the huddled privations of Antarctic overwintering.

In the 1930s, Admiral Richard Byrd's US expeditions introduced an era of intensive mechanisation and utopian speculation to Antarctica that are generally held to mark the end of the heroic age of Antarctic exploration. Byrd flew in the 'Floyd Bennett', a 1928 Ford 4-AT-B Tri-Motor Airplane, over the South Pole on 28–29 November 1929. The flights during his first expedition of 1928–1930 provided extensive meteorological and magnetic observations. Byrd established aerial reconnaissance, the pattern of polar logistics, and aerial photography as a basis for cartography. This was the 'Conquest of Antarctica by Air' as hailed in a *National Geographic* special issue from 1930.[53] Byrd considered Antarctic discovery to be 'one of the great *undone* tasks of the world'.[54] He led several Antarctic expeditions including the vast US military exercise Operation Highjump in 1946–1947, which involved 4,700 men, 13 ships and 33 aircraft.

For Byrd, Antarctica was also the ideal site for a new kind of settlement, and in the 1930s he advocated permanent colonisation as a way to secure national possession. His US research base of 83 people, of which 42 overwintered, was conceived as a small-town utopia and named 'Little America'. Referred to by Byrd as a 'colony', it was a collection of huts built from boxes, crates, and 'odds and ends of lumber', connected by underground tunnels, and connected to Washington DC by a radio tower.[55] These structures soon proved, however, to be 'temporary colonisations', because it turned out that 'each iteration of the encampment had to be abandoned and rebuilt with the shifting ice'.[56] Byrd's intention had been to institute a way of life, a model society: 'a 20th-century City on the Ice'. Byrd's thoroughly modern utopia took its inspiration from the American frontier, which he saw as being a lost site of authenticity and industriousness.[57] 'I wanted to create a single attitude,' Byrd wrote, 'a single state of mind – unfettered by the trivial considerations of civilisation.' The challenge of thriving in such extreme conditions would be salutary for a decadent culture. The blankness of the polar wastes was, for Byrd, a political tabula rasa: 'The Antarctic is a new world for all of us which requires its own standards'.[58]

It might have been the need to test out this 'single attitude' that inspired Byrd, during his second expedition of 1933–1935, to overwinter solo at the Bolling Advance Weather Base, a tiny hut for meteorological readings on the Ross Ice Barrier, 120 miles from Little America base camp. *Alone*, Byrd's account of his four solitary months there, was published in 1938 and inspired several Antarctic fictions.[59] He writes that he named one corner of the shack 'Palm Beach' and the other 'Malibu' – 'to make the relatively distant reaches more attractive'.[60] Byrd experienced his isolation as remote in both space and time: 'Out there on the South Polar barrier, in cold and darkness as complete as that of the Pleistocene, I should have time to catch up, to study and think and listen to the phonograph.'[61] And he notes, 'At times I felt as if I were the last survivor of an ice age, striving to hold on with the flimsy tools bequeathed by an easy-going temperate world.'[62] Byrd's desolate surroundings suggested to him a future inhospitable to humanity, when the ice sheets of a new glacial period would return. 'This is the way the world will look to the last man when it dies.'[63] Byrd adopts the vantage point of the sole inhabitant of the Earth, the 'last man' witnessing the death throes of a planet. Looking back in order to look forward and then back again, the geological past is summoned in a future vision that anticipates the intensity of the future-orientated 'end of the world as we know it' witnessing of the Anthropocene.

> Now, against the cold the explorer has simple but ample defences. Against the accidents which are the most serious risks of isolation he has inbred resourcefulness and ingenuity. But against darkness, nothing much but his own dignity.[64]

Byrd's auto-experiment in ice age living was as much a test of the dignity of modern civilisation as a trial of coping with the exigencies of ice. He was a frozen modern-day Robinson Crusoe in a frozen laboratory. Byrd was eventually rescued from Advance Base when his increasingly confused radio communications back to base camp had indicated something was not right. His underground hut had been badly ventilated and the lanterns and stove had gradually been poisoning him with carbon monoxide. In some aspects, *Alone* resembles the more famous Antarctic memoir of Apsley Cherry-Garrard of the *Terra Nova* expedition, *The Worst Journey in the World*.[65] It also, however has echoes of Henry David Thoreau's *Walden*.[66] In Byrd's narrative the apocalyptic mode mingles with the pastoral – for a story of the last human is also a story about a return to an undisturbed world. In place of the tranquil verdure that Thoreau had portrayed in his life on Walden Pond, however, Byrd substitutes the strangeness and deprivations of the Pleistocene.

During the Holocene, the sole surviving species of the genus *Homo* has not had to endure the climatic extremes that severely tested its ancestors over the preceding two-and-a-half million years. If present-day transformations count as an epoch-level shift and announce the end of the relatively stable Holocene interglacial, we may well be the 'last humans' of the Holocene – equipped, as Byrd was, only with 'flimsy tools'. By current indications, however, an anthropogenically climate-changed future won't deliver us back into a Pleistocene-like ice age. The nearest analogue for predicted atmospheric compositions, temperatures and tipping points is the mid-Pliocene. The Anthropocene therefore announces a no-analogue state in human history: conditions that none of our species has ever experienced. The renewed calls to rescue and survive in the Anthropocene refer back to imagined ice-age struggles, the heroic agency of rescue and survival, but also instigate new fantasies, the dreams and nightmares of technoscientific fixes, neoliberal management regimes and lifeboat ethics. But the Anthropocene also calls time on laments for a lost world, or for the last human. For all that there is pathos in current visions of a depopulated planet – an Earth 'after us' – there is also a dawning de-anthropocentrism: an awareness that the world may never have been about us, or for us, at all.

Figure 4.3 Little America IV, Austral Summer 1946–1947; an aerial view of Little America IV, established at the Bay of Whales, during Operation Highjump, a US Navy operation that commenced August 1946 and ended in late February 1947 (photograph by: US Navy, NSF)

Source: United States Antarctic Program, National Science Foundation (NSF)

I.G.Y. (what a beautiful world)

I.G.Y. – the titular initials in Donald Fagen's 1980s pop song – stand for 'International Geophysical Year'. This global event, which took place between 1957 and 1958, expressed an emerging ambition for synoptic scientific research that would encapsulate the Earth and outer space. The song presents a retro-futuristic technological utopia, a 'streamlined world' of plenty, perfect weather and marvellous spandex clothing for everyone, all brought about by science. The mood of mingled optimism and trepidation that characterised the IGY is conveyed by the headline-grabbing launch of Sputnik I in October 1957. Sputnik had made the most far-fetched visions of the future seem possible. It had also set off the 'Space Race', with all the militarism and paranoia that this entailed. The IGY's project of international scientific cooperation cannot be separated from the Cold War – a period in which the military involvement in scientific research increased significantly. The IGY and Sputnik had opened the door to a vast array of planetary-scale projects that made the Earth a laboratory. In terms of both its geopolitical and geophysical legacies, the IGY has been considered as important for the 20th century as *Endeavour*'s tracking of the transit of Venus was for the 18th.[67]

The IGY was a successor to the two International Polar Years in 1882–1883 and 1932–1933, with renewed focus on the geophysical exploration of Antarctica. The idea for the IGY had been hatched at a gathering of scientists held by US physicist James Van Allen, which included Sydney Chapman and Lloyd V. Berkner.[68] Berkner later wrote of the new perspectives that the IGY offered on the Earth, 'it is like coming from outer space and finding a new planet'.[69] The IGY's purpose was to understand apparently disparate planetary phenomena as a 'single physical system'. It instigated a 'global observatory' – an examination of the whole Earth, from the Arctic to Antarctic, from the upper atmosphere to the depths of the oceans. The project had to coordinate more than 60,000 scientists in about 4,000 research stations engaged in observing, collecting and processing large sets of data about Earth geophysical processes. A total of 67 nations took part in the IGY, and 12 nations established over 40 different research stations in Antarctica. If the ambition was to provide a 'synoptic portrait' of the Earth in scientific terms, the same idea had inspired military planners, in whose hands the term 'synoptic' meant control, manipulation and domination of whole physical systems.[70] The IGY provided the arena for highly speculative planetary modification schemes – with the aim not only of predicting weather events, but of gaining an unprecedented degree of mastery over the Earth.[71]

The IGY gave rise to the representation of Antarctica as laboratory: a continent belonging to science. The unpopulated and remote region had been earmarked as the perfect proving ground for nuclear weaponry after the war. The IGY agenda was weighted towards the study of the upper atmosphere, solar activity, cosmic rays, the aurora, ionospheric physics and geomagnetism. Antarctica was the best place to observe these enigmatic phenomena. Antarctica was allied to those other geophysical unknowns studied in the IGY, interplanetary space and the depths of oceans. The founding of the rocketry programme and the creation of the National Aeronautics and Space Administration (NASA) were paralleled by experiments with remote sensing probes in the deep oceans. And Antarctica was not only the testing ground for new technologies, it also 'became a point of departure for the study of planets'. As Stephen Pyne explains: 'Its cold lithic plate, simplified geomorphology, and hostile atmosphere made it a natural terrestrial analogue for planets and moons composed of rock and ice.'[72]

The IGY counts among its achievements the detection of radiation belts surrounding Earth, the discovery of mid-ocean submarine ridges (important in the development of plate tectonics theory) and the launching of artificial satellites for outer space Earth-monitoring as well as mapping the thickness of the Antarctic ice sheet. It also raised the geopolitical stakes of geophysics, as the superpowers raced to collect data of strategic military importance. Operation Argus was a series of high-altitude bomb tests designed to create artificial auroras to test for Earth's radiation belts (later called 'Van Allen belts'). Walter Sullivan, a journalist reporting on the IGY for *The New York Times*, wrote of Operation Argus: 'It has been said that geophysics is a science "in which the Earth is the laboratory and nature conducts the experiments." In this case the space surrounding this planet was the laboratory, but the experiment was conducted by man.'[73] The energies of the blasts produced by humans were shown to have had long-lasting effects on the Earth's magnetic field. Humans were now capable of far-reaching experiments – with the Earth and its surrounding space as a laboratory. Oceanographer Roger Revelle's 1957 paper with chemist Hans Suess announced that the ocean surface layer had limited ability to absorb carbon dioxide, indicating the rise in levels of atmospheric CO_2. Their work had built on several studies of ocean chemistry and contamination from nuclear tests such as those conducted at Bikini Atoll. It introduced the notion that humans might be altering climate on a planetary scale:

> Human beings are now carrying out a large-scale geophysical experiment of a kind that could not have happened in the past nor be reproduced in the future. Within a few centuries we are returning to the atmosphere and oceans the concentrated organic carbon stored in sedimentary rocks over hundreds of millions of years.[74]

Revelle made this observation with no apparent sense of panic. He understood the 'experiment' rather as benign and progressive, and was interested in finding out more about the geophysical processes involved: 'An opportunity exists during the International Geophysical Year to obtain much of the necessary information.' The IGY did yield an indication that all was not well – and that, intentionally or otherwise, humans were capable of initiating changes to physical systems. Hired by Revelle at the Scripps Institution of Oceanography in California, Charles David Keeling started taking carbon dioxide measurements both in Antarctica and at a station on top of Mauna Loa mountain in Hawaii. His aim was to establish a reliable 'baseline' CO_2 level that could be checked over the following decades with continuous data collection. The line describing the increasing concentration of carbon dioxide in the Earth's atmosphere since 1958 is now known as the 'Keeling Curve'.[75] IGY research projects tracked the dynamics of the planet's hydrosphere, atmosphere and lithosphere, identified cycles and reservoirs of the Earth's main chemical components, and began to decipher the complex external forcings and internal feedback effects that orchestrate periodic shifts in major Earth systems. Developments in the Earth sciences from the 1950s on radically undermined assumptions of a stable and rigid world, revealing a turbulent geophysical system highly susceptible to human influence. The last half-century of development in the Earth sciences has been described as a 'permanent revolution'.[76]

130 *Proxy world*

Describing the shift to an 'open system' view, Mike Davis observes that 'the biggest step for the Earth sciences has not been the admission of an occasional catastrophe or two, but rather the acceptance that terrestrial events, at a variety of time-scales, form a meaningful continuum with extraterrestrial processes'.[77]

The planetary imaginary fostered by the IGY's 'global observatory' established Earth not only as an artefact, but also as a system that could be manipulated. Data collected by satellites in Earth orbit or projected through future-oriented climate modelling have been prominent in rendering Earth intelligible as a planetary system in which all human and non-human processes are interlinked. These novel monitoring technologies, with their origins in the military and strategic requirements of the Cold War, have also been integral to understanding the disruptions to Earth systems in the Anthropocene. In other words, we now know that 'the world is ending' because of the technologies we developed to end the world. Ecological precarity is ever more visible; this does not make the fact of it new. The challenge of the Anthropocene is grappling with a reality that humans have long had a part in creating, but are only just beginning to understand.

Ice core

> Here is the dust and music
> Of your brief cities;
> Here is the ash and smoke;
> Here are your traffic jams
> And vapour trails;
> Here are your holidays in the sun
> And your masterpieces
> And your pop songs.[78]
> – Nick Drake, 'The Ice-Core Sample'

Ice cores from Antarctica and Greenland hold the story of how the climate and atmosphere have changed over the last 800,000 years. Bubbles of atmosphere are trapped between falling snowflakes and act as tiny receptacles for sequentially entombed ancient air. Year after year, as snow falls and settles on the surface of an ice sheet, it is compacted by the weight of new snow falling on top of it and is transformed into solid ice over decades. Over hundreds of years these layers of snow stack up to form an ice archive of deep time. By analysing the layers in ice cores, researchers can gauge the composition of the Earth's atmosphere over time; isotopes of water enable an estimate of global temperatures, while analysis of particles indicates wind patterns, speeds and global distribution. As the writer Heather Frazer has commented, an ice core 'may hold atmospherically transported Saharan dust, tropical methane, and pollen spores from all over the planet'.[79] It is a record, not only of many times, but of many places – and yet a reminder that the Earth is, in an important sense, one single place. The atmospheric history contained in ice cores includes an indication of how industrialisation has reconfigured atmospheres, the global circulation of CO_2, the spread of ash from major volcanic eruptions (Vesuvius, Krakatoa, Tambora), and the accelerated history of atmospheric fallout – all of which can be read through spectral traces. Humankind's influence on the atmosphere and on important biogeochemical cycles has left an imprint in the library of ice, alongside the disruptions caused by volcanoes and meteors. Between archived atmospheres and projected futures, a whole complex infrastructure of ice-coring comes into play. Regarding 'the geopolitical relations of cold', geographer Kathryn Yusoff observes:

> the locations of ice core geographies are multiple: field, drill site, freezer, ship, cold storage, laboratory, chemical analysis, General Circulation Models (GCMs), scientific papers, political briefings, policy documents, public spaces. In this sense, ice cores are spacio-temporal envelopes, archiving global atmospheres over nearly one million years, atmospherically constituting many disparate places and events in one.[80]

Ice core technology was originally developed for military-drilling machines during the Cold War. The first attempts to extract ice cores occurred in 1956, as part of one of the large-scale IGY ecological studies. The first palaeoclimate data came from an ice core drilled between 1963–1966 at Camp Century in Greenland. The core was 1,390 m deep and covered 120,000 years of snowfall. Camp Century was an American military base constructed eight metres beneath the surface of the ice – ostensibly for research and ice-construction testing. It was however an elaborate cover for the US Army's 'Iceworm' nuclear missile project, proliferating silently beneath the ice sheet. Known as 'the city under the ice', it was powered by the world's first mobile nuclear generator. Its 3-km network of tunnels housed laboratories, missile-launch facilities, a shop, a hospital, a cinema, a chapel and accommodation for 200 soldiers. The camp was abandoned in 1967 along with its infrastructure – and its biological, chemical and radioactive waste – and it was assumed that it would be 'preserved for eternity' by accumulating snow and ice.[81] However, melting ice cover threatens to expose the hazardous waste by 2090, introducing the prospect of 'an entirely new form of political dispute resulting from climate change'.[82]

While the oldest Greenland ice cores go back 240,000 years, Dome C in Antarctica currently yields records of around 800,000 years. The search is on to find 'Oldest-Ice' – a 1.5-million-year ice core in the Antarctic ice sheet that could help explain the role of greenhouse gases in the mid-Pleistocene Transition (MPT). The MPT, which occurred between 1.2 million and 900,000 years ago, was a switch in the cyclicity of glacial and interglacial changes that is seen by scientists as the 'most important and enigmatic time interval in the more recent climate history of our planet'.[83] Ice cores provide the most reliable and detailed record of climate variations over very long periods, covering multiple glacial periods ('ice ages') and interglacials. Data from ice cores retrieved in Greenland and Antarctica has provided evidence of an integrated Earth system with enormous implications for the planet's future. As the science historian Spencer Weart reflects:

> This work fulfilled the old dream that studying the different climates of the past could be almost like putting the Earth on a laboratory bench, switching conditions back and forth and observing the consequences.[84]

The story told by the ice cores is one of a febrile, restless Earth. Ice records hold signatures of sudden transformations, dramatic reversals and abrupt, zigzagging changes in climate. These changes have taken place over decades rather than millennia. As glaciologist Richard Alley observes: 'For most of the last 100,000 years, a crazily jumping climate has been the rule, not the exception.'[85] Elizabeth Kolbert emphasises, 'It is our own relatively static experience of climate that has come to look exceptional.'[86] In such shifts, temperatures of climatic regions were shown to jump by several degrees Celsius, not over centuries or millennia but in a few years or decades – 'almost no time in geological terms, and not much time in human terms'.[87] Ice core records have shown that the Earth is drawing closer to the temperature peaks of the last interglacial, when sea levels were about 15 feet higher than they are today. Studies of ice have further revealed that the global climate system is *inherently* chaotic and unstable, and therefore all the more susceptible to human and more-than human 'forcings'.[88] Will Steffen explains: 'Societies can have little or no warning that a forcing factor is approaching such a threshold, and by the time that the change in Earth system functioning is observed, it will likely be too late to avert the major change.'[89]

In the 1980s and 1990s, ice core data from both Antarctica and Greenland established abrupt climate change as a disturbing past reality in relation to the disturbing future prospects presented in climate models. It thus brought a new sense of urgency to scientific and public debates about the climate crisis. Wallace S. Broecker's 1987 article for *Nature*, 'Unpleasant Surprises in the Greenhouse?' announced: 'What these records indicate is that Earth's climate does not respond to forcing in a smooth and gradual way. Rather it responds in sharp jumps which involve large-scale reorganisation of Earth's system.' He cautioned against being 'lulled into complacency by model simulations that suggested a gradual warming over a period of about 100 years', like those of earlier climate change theories. Rather, humanity should prepare itself for 'unpleasant surprises'.[90] Broecker calls for a serious revision of our approach to environmental governance that would better allow us to respond to such 'surprises'. Like Revelle and Suess before him, he describes an experiment of vast scale conducted by humans, but now asks that the experimenters be wary:

> The inhabitants of planet Earth are quietly conducting a gigantic environmental experiment. So vast and so sweeping will be the consequences that, were it brought before any responsible council for approval, it would be firmly rejected. Yet it goes on with little interference from any jurisdiction or nation.[91]

Research shows that, in the non-linear dynamics of complex physical systems, small stimuli could have enormous impact, even though it is impossible to anticipate the critical thresholds of such 'tipping points'. Broecker warns: 'The palaeoclimate record shouts to us that, far from being self-stabilising, the Earth's climate system is an ornery beast which overreacts even to small nudges.'[92] He advances the theory that the dramatic swings in climate in the past were triggered by the shutdown or restarting of the 'conveyor belt' of ocean circulation. In other words, global warming can potentially produce global freezing. An exaggerated version of this theory was explored in the 'instantaneous ice age' plot of the film *The Day After Tomorrow* (2004). At the beginning of the film, an ice core drilling team on Antarctica's 'Larsen B' ice shelf are stranded when the section they are standing on breaks off. What follows in the movie is even worse; but even if the science in the film becomes increasingly fanciful, its opening visual metaphor is a compelling one. In the ice – in meticulously drilled, sub-zero-archived cores of it; and in its dramatic, sudden collapses – we can read the signs of a disaster we will be hard-pressed to keep up with. The Larsen B ice shelf did in fact partially collapse, in late 2000 – and, as Yusoff has observed, this event was the 'catalyst to activate (turn up the heat) on' the cool facts previously revealed by the ice core samples. The abruptness of climate change, its unpredictability, remained for most of the world a scientific abstraction until the ice put on a live, full-scale demonstration. At that point, Yusoff notes: 'Glacial became a fast word. Ice was moving faster than the models (and continues to do so). The world gained scientific traction as a model of the world.'[93]

In 1999 the Vostok record was retrieved – an ice core of 3,623-m depth, stopping just short of the Vostok subglacial lake. The Vostok core charted four full cycles of glacial and interglacial periods over 420,000 years. Its visual signature was a rhythmic sawtooth graph recording the ice ages. It showed that the composition of the atmosphere had changed in step with the movement of the ice sheets and with temperature. Even more significantly, it indicated that the present-day levels of greenhouse gases were unprecedented. As Will Steffen recalls:

> To me the Vostok core was the most beautiful piece of evidence of the Earth as a single system... For the first time we saw this beautiful rhythmic pattern, how the Earth as a whole operated. You saw temperature, you saw gases, you saw dust all dancing to the same tune, all triggered by the Earth's orbit around the Sun... but still a mystery, it couldn't explain the magnitude of those swings.[94]

The Vostok ice core first established the long, relatively stable Holocene as a unique and striking feature of Earth's climate, coming at the end of a series of dramatic swings. 'The Holocene, which has already lasted 11 kyr, is, by far, the longest stable warm period recorded in Antarctica during the past 420 kyr.'[95] And this has had 'possibly profound implications for evolution and the development of civilisations'.[96] In the article in which Crutzen and Stoermer introduced the Anthropocene thesis, they dated it to the latter part of the 18th century. They have since revised this, but the initial decision was guided by evidence from the ice: 'this is the period when data retrieved from glacial ice cores show the beginning of a growth in the atmospheric concentrations of several "greenhouse gases" in particular CO_2 and CH_4.'[97] An ice core has since been used to define the GSSP for the Pleistocene–Holocene boundary: 'Borehole NGRIP2, located in the central Greenland ice sheet at 75.108 N, 42.328 W. The Pleistocene–Holocene boundary is at 1,492.45 m depth.'[98] Ice cores from this location are archived in below zero conditions at the University of Copenhagen. Ice cores are also thought to have the potential to define the Holocene–Anthropocene boundary.[99] However, with the extensive wasting of ice thanks to global temperature increases – and with the greatest increases occurring in the polar regions – the potential that ice formed a little over half a century ago will be preserved for possible future extraction is now uncertain. The changes to the ice sheets associated with the Anthropocene may thus also affect geological record-keeping.

The Holocene, if left to its own devices, might just have been another unremarkable interglacial. The Holocene is only uniquely identified as an 'epoch' because it was named as such by the 19th-century geologists who recognised themselves as living through it. As palaeoclimatologist Eric Wolff writes: 'It would have ended conceptually by the next glacial inception, and, by analogy, as with its start... would probably have been defined by an abrupt climate cooling seen in a Greenland ice core.'[100] From a complex systems perspective, the Anthropocene is conceived as a gathering

134 *Proxy world*

of momentum away from Holocene relative stability, at a geologically instantaneous rate, towards an alternative, and unknown, state of the Earth system, 'a planetary *terra incognita*'.[101] And yet, Nigel Clark warns:

> Whatever 'we' do, ice cores and other proxies of past climates profess to us, our planet is capable of taking us by surprise. With or without the destabilizisng surcharge of human activities, the conditions most of us take for granted could be taken away, quite suddenly, and with very little warning.[102]

The Anthropocene might be about millennial timescales, such as those associated with significant changes in the polar ice, and the even longer timescales associated with the recovery of mass extinctions of biological species – events through which a catastrophe too slow to be seen is made intelligible in the rocks. But it is also about the potential for the climate to suddenly switch to a new state with very little warning. Such abrupt changes, driven by Earth system feedbacks, may, in turn, drive further disruptions and geologically significant global changes. In other words, the Anthropocene invites attentiveness to critical actions or forcing activities taking place over short time durations, as well as on geological time scales. It is uncertain whether the transition to the Anthropocene will be gradual, or whether there will yet be sudden shifts comparable to those that have marked epochal boundaries in the past. Either way, traces of the Anthropocene, like the dust in ice cores, may well linger in proxies that in the future will represent the upheavals and instabilities of today.

Ozone hole

> On page four of my daily newspaper, I learn that the measurements taken above the Antarctic are not good this year: the hole in the ozone layer is growing ominously larger… The same article mixes together chemical reactions and political reactions. A single thread links the most esoteric sciences and the most sordid politics, the most distant sky and some factory in the Lyon suburbs, dangers on a global scale and the impending local elections or the next board meeting. The horizons, the stakes, the time frames, the actors – none of these is commensurable, yet there they are, caught up in the same story.[103]

The story of the ozone hole opens the discussion in Bruno Latour's *We Have Never Been Modern*. In Latour's analysis, the ozone debate, like global warming, reveals the construction of hybrid systems that mix politics, science, technology, and nature. The dramatic discovery of the thinning of the ozone layer over Antarctica, made around the time of the nuclear winter controversy in the 1980s, drew attention to the vulnerability of the global atmosphere in relation to ordinary, everyday human activity: it linked casual use of hairspray or deodorant to global catastrophe. 'The story of the ozone layer teaches important lessons,' writes the ecosocialist Ian Angus. 'In particular, it illustrates what Earth system scientists mean when they say that in the Anthropocene human activity is *overwhelming the great forces of nature* with potentially catastrophic results. The ozone crisis was the first major demonstration of that, the first near-catastrophe of the Anthropocene.'[104] The idea of a hole in the ozone layer had already been speculated on by UCLA physicist Gordon MacDonald in his 1968 warning essay on geophysical warfare, 'How to Wreck the Environment'.[105] But it was information publicised in the 1980s about the thinning of the Earth's protective membrane that successfully captured the attention of the lay public. The news of an invisible fissure in the atmosphere finally marked, for many, a looming anthropogenic catastrophe.

Ozone is what gives the stratosphere its 'upside-down character', to use Oliver Morton's phrase.[106] It absorbs ultraviolet radiation, heating the top of the stratosphere. The ozone layer is distributed through the stratosphere. It protects the Earth's surface from harmful forms of ultraviolet radiation despite only being a tiny component of the very thin upper air. It was not until the 1980s, however, that the ozone layer came to be considered fragile. Understanding dawned along with new realisations that human activity might be significantly affecting the functioning of the Earth system. The ozone hole was flagged as an example of destruction through anthropogenic activity in Crutzen and Stoermer's 2000 Anthropocene article. Indeed, it had been Crutzen's research in the 1970s into ozone depletion that had helped to establish human activity as a threat to the protective ozone layer.

The cautionary tale of the ozone hole begins in the 1930s, when, at the request of General Motors (GM), the American chemist and engineer Thomas Midgley – who had already added lead to petrol to combat engine knocking in motor vehicles – turned his attention to refrigeration. The task was to improve the safety of domestic and industrial fridges, and to find a non-toxic refrigerant for GM's Frigidaire line of home refrigerators. Midgley's team is reputed to have synthesised the chemical compound of Freon, the first chlorofluorocarbon (CFC), in just three days. They thought CFCs would be ideally suited for use in refrigeration devices because they are stable and non-flammable. Indeed Midgley was keen to demonstrate the safety of CFCs by inhaling a lungful and then blowing out a candle.[107] It took less than two years to move from invention – of what was deemed an incredibly safe product – into industrial production. The period after World War II saw increased sales in refrigerators and air-conditioning units, and a marked acceleration in the use of CFCs. By the 1970s, approximately 750,000 tons of CFC compounds were being emitted into the global atmosphere annually.[108] The problem, unknown to Midgley and his team, was that CFCs only broke down in the Earth's upper atmosphere, where their chemical reactions eroded the protective layer of ozone. The loss of ozone – and the resultant increase in harmful ultraviolet radiation reaching the Earth's surface – has been linked to elevated levels of skin cancer, terrestrial plant damage, and dwindling levels of oceanic plankton populations. Midgley's is a cautionary tale of the unintended consequences of scientific innovation. The environmental historian John McNeill has observed that Midgley 'had more impact on the atmosphere than any other single organism in Earth history'.[109]

The Global Atmospheric Ozone Monitoring Network of the World Meteorological Organisation (WMO) dates back to the 1957 International Geophysical Year.[110] The issue of ozone depletion had been raised by studies of supersonic transport (SST) systems, and the release of nitrogen oxides in jet exhaust into the stratosphere in the 1970s. This was linked to research on aerosols in the aftermath of nuclear war, with the modelling of dust clouds from volcanic eruptions and NASA observations of storms on Mars.[111] Paul Crutzen's research in 1970–71 warned that increases in nitrogen oxides in the upper atmosphere could deplete the ozone layer and expose Earth to increased ultraviolet radiation. In 1973 James Lovelock published an analysis of atmospheric data collected on a British-led expedition to Antarctica, in which the staying power and global reach of CFCs was highlighted: he found them in every sample, 'wherever and whenever they were sought'.[112] In the same year, research by the chemists Mario Molina and Frank Rowland established that the ozone layer was in trouble. They found that CFC molecules reaching the stratosphere would break down, releasing chlorine and, in the process, destroying ozone. They therefore argued that CFCs should be banned in order to protect life on Earth.[113] In 1974, Crutzen developed a model, based on the research of Molina and Rowland, of the potential ozone depletion resulting from continued use of CFCs.[114] The results showed that up to 40 per cent of ozone would be depleted if the use of CFCs continued at 1974 rates. In 1976, the scientific community requested a ban on CFCs, but with limited success. The chemical companies that made CFCs, among them DuPont, resisted any restrictions or regulations, demanding actual proof of damage and arguing that 'ozone depletion figures to date are computer projections based on a series of uncertain assumptions'.[115] Although the CFC-ozone reaction could be demonstrated under laboratory conditions, finding evidence of ozone depletion in the stratosphere was another matter. It wasn't until the mid-1980s that *in situ* studies in Antarctica, supported by satellite data, established that the ozone layer was thinning much faster than anyone had expected.

The 'ozone hole' was discovered in 1985 by three researchers from the British Antarctic Survey who were recording ozone data in Antarctica for their work on weather forecasting.[116] Their measurements at Halley Bay Observatory showed that the ozone layer was thinning rapidly during the southern hemisphere's spring (September to November). When the springtime values of ozone levels between 1954 and 1984 were plotted against the CFC concentrations in the atmosphere, they revealed the contours of a 'hole'. As one of the researchers explains, 'In retrospect, that was a really good thing to call it, because an ozone hole must be bad. Almost automatically, it meant that people wanted something to be done about it. The hole had to be filled.'[117] The explanation for the hole was that CFCs adhere particularly well to ice crystals. Earlier satellite data underwent subsequent review and the 'ozone hole' situation became sufficiently obvious to become a global concern. As the academic Paul N. Edwards observes, 'The terrifying metaphor of a "hole" in the protective ozone "shield" constituted a crisis sufficient to galvanise the international community.' It led to the development of the 'Protocol on Substances that Deplete the Ozone Layer', agreed in Montreal, Canada, on 16 September 1987. The Protocol was designed to plug the hole and restore the ozone layer. After several revisions, the Montreal Protocol resulted in a complete ban on CFCs and other ozone-destroying gases. In 2003, the then United Nations Secretary-General Kofi Annan termed the Montreal Protocol 'perhaps the single most successful international environmental agreement to date'.[118]

In 1992, one year after the Mount Pinatubo volcanic eruption had delivered excess sulfate aerosols into the atmosphere, catalysing further ozone-destroying chemical reactions, the amount of ozone contained in the stratosphere as a whole dropped to the lowest of any time on record. 1993 and 1994 were even worse. NASA's Ozone Hole Watch continues to monitor the hole with daily updates. In 2015 the ozone hole mean recorded by NASA was 25.6 million km^3.[119] The stratosphere is still losing ozone, although the rate of depletion has slowed. In other words, the ozone hole is still growing. The ozone layer is expected to start to regenerate in 2025, and researchers are optimistic that it will return to 1980 levels between 2050 and 2070. The ozone crisis has not gone away. As Frank Biermann argues in his proposal for Earth system governance in the Anthropocene: 'In the case of stratospheric ozone depletion, we have already had a "near miss", that is, a sudden transition in a tipping element of the Earth system that was only recognised at a late stage in the process.'[120]

The ozone hole episode as a 'near miss' of the Anthropocene, establishes Antarctica as the site of planetary-scale human catastrophes. It is the remote place where invisible damage is given greatest visibility, whether in data retrieved from ice cores, or in satellite maps revealing a cascade of ice melt, or in the plotting of the ozone hole. As Michel Serres observes, we are increasingly troubled by a dynamic nature that encompasses the whole planet: 'it tears a round hole in the ozone layer, it exposes the world to great dangers.'[121] The 20th century saw the rise of global networks and institutions for policy-making and commentary, particularly within the United Nations, in response to planetary-scale issues. These produced landmark publications such as the Brundtland Report of 1987. The UN also brokered international agreements, including the Montreal Protocol on ozone depletion in 1987 and the Kyoto Protocol on climate change in 1997, which arose out of the UN Conference on Environment and Development in 1992. The planetary institutions and protocols of the United Nations are no longer a given in the Anthropocene. They require renewed attention in tandem with unfolding narratives about present dangers. The Anthropocene warning is

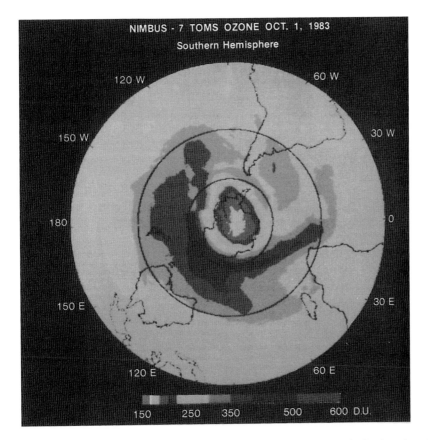

Figure 4.4 Ozone Hole, 1983; first space-based view of the ozone hole, data from TOMS (Total Ozone Mapping Spectrometer)
Source: NASA Goddard Space Flight Center

an appeal for a way of coming to terms with the myriad disturbances of place, time and scale.

Peaceful purposes

In 1493, one year after Christopher Columbus reached the 'New World', the Treaty of Tordesillas was concluded between the warring Spain and Portugal. The Treaty agreed that 'a boundary or straight line be determined and drawn north and south, from pole to pole, on the said ocean sea, from the Arctic to the Antarctic pole … at a distance of three hundred and seventy leagues west of Cape Verde Islands' – to divide the oceans (and lands) between them. The geographical divisions of the Treaty included those places as yet undiscovered and unknown, nevertheless brought under one regulatory regime in the name of peace. In *Mare Liberum* (1602), writing on behalf of Dutch trading ambitions, Hugo Grotius argued against such imperial claims to exclusive jurisdiction over the high seas and undiscovered territories. The final words of *Mare Liberum* appeal to 'the common benefit of humankind' (that is, not just Spain and Portugal). The ongoing tension between state-ruled territories and the terrestrial commons of humankind is central to international law regarding trade, resource exploitation, and environmental stewardship. Grotius's intellectual arguments underpin the modern concept of the 'freedom of the seas'. This idea or its close variants have been encoded in the United Nations Convention on the Law of the Sea (UNCLOS) in 1957, the Antarctic Treaty (1961), and the Outer Space Treaty (1967). As the academic Elizabeth DeLoughrey explains: 'Extraterritorial spaces, such as the high seas, Antarctica, and outer space, are imaginatively, historically, and juridically interconnected.'[122] The Antarctic Treaty, catalysed by post-World War II military and territorial expansion in the southern continent, promoted a 'peaceful global commons' – a concept derived from the Law of the Sea, and subsequently adopted by the Outer Space Treaty.[123]

Article I of the Antarctic Treaty provides:

1. Antarctica shall be used for peaceful purposes only. There shall be prohibited, *inter alia*, any measures of a military nature, such as the establishment of military bases and fortifications, the carrying out of military manoeuvres, as well as the testing of any type of weapons.
2. The present Treaty shall not prevent the use of military personnel or equipment for scientific research or any other peaceful purpose.[124]

On 1 December 1959, the Antarctic Treaty was signed in Washington by the 12 countries whose scientists had been active in and around Antarctica during the IGY of 1957–58. At the end of World War II, territorial claims had acquired a new urgency, and seven nations had more or less occupied Antarctica.[125] The Antarctic Treaty was a way of making Cold Peace out of Cold War.[126] It entered into force in 1961 and has since been acceded to by many other nations. The total number of parties to the Treaty is now 50. The treaty covers the area south of 60°S latitude. Its aims are simple, yet unique in international relations: to enable international scientific cooperation, to set aside disputes over territorial sovereignty, to demilitarise Antarctica, to establish it as a zone free of nuclear tests and the disposal of radioactive waste, and to ensure that it is used *for peaceful purposes only*.[127]

The Protocol on Environmental Protection to the Antarctic Treaty (Madrid Protocol) was ratified in 1991, bringing new significance to the concept of peaceful global commons as spaces to be nourished, protected, and used for the benefit of all humankind – including future generations. It has stalled mining in Antarctica and banned industrial research or exploitation for 50 years, until its review in 2048.[128] Military activity is similarly prohibited. The continent has been placed under ecological quarantine and continues to be protected from human settlement, except in restricted ways at the year-round research stations. However, sovereign claims on the continent have never disappeared. Maps of Antarctica resemble a pie chart with overlapping sectors representing rival claims such as those of Argentina, Chile and Great Britain. The Treaty of Tordesillas has been invoked by Chile as justification for claiming sovereignty over Antarctica, with lines being drawn south from Chile's eastern and western boundaries in a triangular claim over the remote and barely habitable land. Great Britain's claim is based on Cook's 1772 expedition. Argentina and Chile have both attempted to create a 'citizenship' of Antarctica to substantiate their claims, and have both established small civilian settlements. In 1978 Emilio Marcos Palma was the first person to be born in Antarctica. His mother had been airlifted to Esperanza Base in order to complete her pregnancy. The base on the Antarctic Peninsula is in a sector of Antarctica subject to rival claims by Argentina, Great Britain and Chile. Chile argues that it was the first to 'colonise' Antarctica, having established a tiny Antarctic 'city', Villa Las Estrellas, complete with families, a school, sports hall, post office, bank, church and civil registry. In January 2016, journalist Simon Romero wrote:

> Fewer than 200 people live in this outpost founded in 1984 during the dictatorship of General Augusto Pinochet, when Chile was seeking to bolster its territorial claims in Antarctica. Since then, the tiny hamlet has been at the centre of one of Antarctica's most remarkable experiments: exposing entire families to isolation and extreme conditions in an attempt to arrive at a semblance of normal life at the bottom of the planet.[129]

The Antarctic Treaty System remains silent on the issue of human settlement. And yet, with increasing human activity in the Antarctic, and the influx of tourists on luxury cruises, its stations, cities and settlements may need to play an increasingly important custodial role. The era of mounting concerns about global environmental change has simultaneously seen a new intensification of national-interest rivalries, in which the world's least explored continent is becoming increasingly territorialised in a race for strategic minerals and resources. Great Britain is planning to claim sovereign rights over an area that covers more than a million square kilometres of the remote seabed off Antarctica.[130] This claim would ignore the Antarctic Treaty, which specifically states that no new claims shall be asserted on the continent. Antarctica is neither battle-free nor pristine. Neither, for that matter, is outer space.

The Outer Space Treaty 1967 established all of outer space as an international commons by describing it as the 'province of all mankind' and forbidding states from claiming territorial sovereignty.[131] Its concepts and some of its provisions were modelled on its predecessor, the Antarctic Treaty. Like the Antarctic Treaty, it was intended to prevent a new form of colonial competition over this new zone of human exploration, and to avoid the conflict and self-seeking exploitation that might otherwise ensue. The context for it was the combination of anxiety and excitement about the space race during the Cold War. As John F. Kennedy had announced in 1960, 'Control of space will be decided in the next decade. If the Soviets control space, they can control Earth, as in past centuries the nation that controlled the seas dominated the continents.'[132] In the 21st century, our increasing global reliance on space systems means that establishing dominance and control in space is more urgent than ever. Satellites are used for photo reconnaissance, targeting, communications, weather forecasting, early warning systems, and intelligence-gathering. 'Peaceful purposes', the central principle of the space law regime, has been interpreted as allowing for defence and intelligence-related activities in pursuit of national security and other goals.[133] With the rise of commercial activities and private interests in space, a complex and contested politics has emerged. The Space Treaty regime is confronted with issues around expanding space activities and protecting the space environment, increased militarisation and weaponisation, property rights debates, launches, telecommunications, commercial remote sensing, Earth observations, the dangers of orbital debris, as well as astronaut codes of conduct.[134]

The utopian and dystopian possibilities of the exchange between Antarctic and extraterrestrial politics are central to Kim Stanley Robinson's novels, *Antarctica* and the *Mars* Trilogy. Robinson establishes the parallels between Martian and Antarctic inhabitation in his *Mars* Trilogy: *Red Mars*, *Green Mars*, and *Blue Mars*, published in the early 1990s.[135] Like NASA's astronauts, Robinson's Mars colonists live in the Dry Valleys of Antarctica for more than a year in preparation for the harsh and isolated environment of their Martian settlement. Mars appears to them 'like Antarctica but even purer', and threats to the utopian principles of the 'Mars treaty' in the novel echo those of the 'fragile and idealistic' Antarctic Treaty on which it is based. The implications of the scenarios that Robinson establishes are not only that Antarctic and outer space communities can never be closed systems, but also that the utopian values of the Antarctic-like treaties are precarious and impossible to maintain without conflict.

In *Green Mars*, Robinson uses the collapse of the unstable West Antarctic Ice Sheet and the consequent global sea level rise as a plot device: the climate change catastrophe diverts the attention of Earth's political authorities away from suppressing a Martian revolution, allowing the rebels to establish Mars as an independent new world. Robinson's pacified Mars is thereafter the proxy through which to rethink the organisation of the Earth: 'We exist for Earth as a model or experiment. A thought experiment for humanity to learn from,' says Maya, one of the characters. 'A real experiment,' responds another character, Nadia.[136] The same could be said of Antarctica. As Stephen Pyne reflects, 'Though *terra Antarctica* seems to possess what people and nations believe it to have, its greatest asset is not any resource it possesses but the stripped and reradiated revelations it makes about those who stare into it.'[137]

The planetary-scale operations of the IGY were key to establishing the new scientific and juridical regimes of the extraterritorial spaces of the deep seas, outer space and Antarctica in the 20th century. Human activities in the Antarctic region have intensified in the 21st century, bringing new challenges to the governance system and the environmental protection obligations set out under the Madrid Protocol. Although the continent is preserved from legal claims and resource exploitation until 2048, the advance of research programmes has been escalating in the southern polar regions. Antarctica continues to be the site of experimentation and testing, not only in the arena of science but in terms of global politics and laws. However, ice and politics are both unstable. Like the ice sheet, geopolitical unity could disintegrate unexpectedly.

The remit of what we have called 'environmentalism' has begun to change as we realise the scale of the changes ushered in by the Anthropocene: we have begun to understand ourselves, not just as potential stewards (or damagers) of a fragile planet, but as very vulnerable and dependent parts of a rapidly destabilising Earth system. In other words, the Anthropocene concept recognises the role of humans in the *destabilisation* of the Earth system and not just the human impacts on the environment that have been the focus of environmentalism. The Anthropocene also announces a fundamental change in the context within which international law operates. For this context has been predicated on stability – both in terms of the conscious objective of 'stability' in the geopolitical sense, and in the general assumptions about human experience that were made in relatively stable Holocene conditions, and that may not apply any more, or into the future. For example, coastlines are assumed to define the contours of a nation and also determine the maritime zones in the Law of the Sea; but future sea level rises may bring increasing uncertainty to coastal geographies. If the international legal order continues to aspire to stability under changing conditions, it will need to evolve new legal axioms better able to cope with the challenges augured by the shift from the Holocene to the Anthropocene.

The Anthropocene thesis emerges from the ambition of integrated Earth sciences. It proceeds from a conception of a whole Earth with interdependent dynamic properties: lithosphere, hydrosphere, atmosphere, cryosphere, biosphere. Yet it also brings with it the possibility – even the likelihood – of catastrophes on a large enough scale to fracture imaginaries of global unity, stability and holism. A politics of globality is obviously an urgent concern, but it cannot be assumed as a given; it is, instead, part of a bigger ongoing experiment in planetary-scale rifts and estrangements. International law has taken the conditions of the Holocene for granted – relying on assumptions that its stable conditions will continue indefinitely.[138] The profoundly different conditions of the Anthropocene, call for more than an amendment to the rules. We may need to find wholly new ways of navigating this climatic and geopolitical *terra incognita*. Antarctica, the site of intensifying experiments in Anthropocene living, is no longer a forbidding and pristine wasteland, nor even simply a fragile place to be conserved and protected. Rather, it reveals itself as a strange, contested, experimental place – part of a dynamic and unsettled Earth system that humans not only inhabit by proxy but can transform 'without ever leaving home'.[139] Among other things, this *terra incognita* may yet be an important source of fresh thinking about governance in the Anthropocene.

Be prepared for heavy weather.

Notes

1 Walter, Sullivan, *Quest for a Continent: The Story of the Antarctic* (New York: McGraw Hill, 1963): 1.
2 Hildegard Diemberger, Kirsten Hastrup, Simon Schaffer *et al.* (Charles F. Kennel, David Sneath, Michael Bravo, Hans-F. Graf, Jacqueline Hobbs, Jason Davis, Maria Luisa Nodari, Giorgio Vassena, Richard Irvine, Christopher Evans, Marilyn Strathern, Mike Hulme, Georg Kaser, and Barbara Bodenhorn), 'Communicating climate knowledge: proxies, processes, politics', *Current Anthropology* 53.2 (April 2012): 226–244; 231.

3 John Tyndall, 'On the transmission of heat of different qualities through gases of different kinds', *Proceedings of the Royal Institution* 3 (London, 1859): 155–158. Extract in *The Future of Nature*, eds. Libby Robin, Sverker Sörlin, Paul Warde (New Haven and London: Yale University Press, 2013): 296–302. See also Mike Hulme, 'On the origins of the greenhouse effect: John Tyndall and the interrogation of nature', *Weather* 64.5 (2009): 121–123.
4 John Tyndall, 'The Bakerian Lecture: On the absorption and radiation of heat by gases and vapours, and on the physical connexion of radiation, absorption, and conduction', *Philosophical Transactions of the Royal Society of London* 151 (1861): 1–36; 29.
5 Robert Bindschadler quoted in 'David Herring, 'Time on the Shelf', NASA Earth Observatory (12 July 2005); earthobservatory.nasa.gov/Features/TimeShelf/time_shelf4.php
6 Jan Zalasiewicz, 'Buried treasure', *New Scientist* 158.2140 (27 June 1998).
7 Will Steffen, Paul J. Crutzen and John R. McNeill, 'The Anthropocene: are humans now overwhelming the great forces of nature?', *Ambio* 38 (2007): 614–21; 614.
8 Stephen J. Pyne, 'The extraterrestrial Earth: Antarctica as analogue for space exploration', *Space Policy* 23 (2007): 147–149; 147.
9 Stephen J. Pyne, *The Ice* (London: Weidenfeld & Nicolson, 2003): 6.
10 Matteo Ricci, 'Kunyu Wanguo Quantu (A Map of the Myriad Countries of the World) 1602'. See also Renata Tyszczuk, 'Mappa Mundi', in *Atlas: Geography, Architecture and Change in an Interdependent World*, eds. Renata Tyszczuk, Joe Smith, Nigel Clark and Melissa Butcher (London: Black Dog Publishing, 2012): 10–14;13.
11 Stephen J. Pyne, *The Ice* (London: Weidenfeld & Nicolson, 2003): 328.
12 James Cook, *A Voyage Towards the South Pole and Round the World: Performed in His Majesty's Ships the Resolution and Adventure, in the Years 1772, 1773, 1774 and 1775*, 1st edition, 2 volumes (London, 1777).
13 Sam Jacob, 'High tech primitive: the architecture of Antarctica' in *Ice Lab: New Architecture and Science* Arts Catalyst exhibition catalogue, ed. Sandra Ross (London: The British Council, 2013): 54–75; 57–58.
14 Marie-Hélène Huet, *The Culture of Disaster* (Chicago and London: The University of Chicago Press, 2012): 171.
15 Marie-Hélène Huet, *The Culture of Disaster* (Chicago and London: The University of Chicago Press, 2012): 11.
16 H.P. Lovecraft, *At the Mountains of Madness* (1931) (CreateSpace Independent Publishing Platform, 2016): 4.
17 Edgar Allan Poe, The Narrative of Arthur Gordon Pym of Nantucket (New York: Harper & Brothers, 1839) and Jules Verne, The Sphinx of the Ice Fields *(Le Sphinx des Glaces)* (Pierre-Jules Hetzel, 1897).
18 Sarah Moss, *Scott's Last Biscuit: The Literature of Polar Exploration* (Oxford: Signal Books, 2006):19-21.
19 Sarah Moss, *Scott's Last Biscuit: The Literature of Polar Exploration* (Oxford: Signal Books, 2006): 107.
20 Denis Cosgrove, *Apollo's Eye: A Cartographic Genealogy of the Earth in the Western Imagination* (Baltimore, Maryland: John Hopkins University Press, 2001): 216.
21 Denis Cosgrove, *Apollo's Eye: A Cartographic Genealogy of the Earth in the Western Imagination* (Baltimore, Maryland: John Hopkins University Press, 2001): 216-220.
22 Denis Cosgrove, *Apollo's Eye: A Cartographic Genealogy of the Earth in the Western Imagination* (Baltimore, Maryland: John Hopkins University Press, 2001): 207.
23 Denis Cosgrove, *Apollo's Eye: A Cartographic Genealogy of the Earth in the Western Imagination* (Baltimore, Maryland: John Hopkins University Press, 2001): 217.
24 Denis Cosgrove, *Apollo's Eye: A Cartographic Genealogy of the Earth in the Western Imagination* (Baltimore, Maryland: John Hopkins University Press, 2001): 220.
25 Frederick A. Cook, *Through the First Antarctic Night 1898–1899: A Narrative of the Voyage of the "Belgica" Among Newly Discovered Lands and Over an Unknown Sea About the South Pole* (New York: Doubleday, Page and Company, 1909): 5.
26 Frederick A. Cook, *Through the First Antarctic Night 1898–1899: A Narrative of the Voyage of the "Belgica" Among Newly Discovered Lands and Over an Unknown Sea About the South Pole* (New York: Doubleday, Page and Company, 1909): 173.

27 Frederick A. Cook, *Through the First Antarctic Night 1898–1899: A Narrative of the Voyage of the "Belgica" Among Newly Discovered Lands and Over an Unknown Sea About the South Pole* (New York: Doubleday, Page and Company, 1909): 231.
28 Frederick A. Cook, *Through the First Antarctic Night 1898–1899: A Narrative of the Voyage of the "Belgica" Among Newly Discovered Lands and Over an Unknown Sea About the South Pole* (New York: Doubleday, Page and Company, 1909): 369.
29 Sarah Moss, *Scott's Last Biscuit: The Literature of Polar Exploration* (Oxford: Signal Books, 2006): x.
30 Sandra Ross, 'Introduction', in *Ice Lab: New Architecture and Science* Arts Catalyst exhibition catalogue, ed. Sandra Ross (London: The British Council, 2013): 5.
31 *The Ends of the Earth: An Anthology of the Finest Writing on the Arctic and the Antarctic*, Volume 2 'The Antarctic', ed. Francis Spufford (London: Granta Books, 2007): 1.
32 Monica Edwards, 'Antarctica provides ICE to study behavior effects in astronauts', (19 December 2016); blogs.nasa.gov/analogsfieldtesting/2016/12/19/antarctica-provides-ice-to-study-behavior-effects-in-astronauts/
33 Sam Jacob, 'High tech primitive: the architecture of Antarctica' in *Ice Lab: New Architecture and Science* Arts Catalyst exhibition catalogue, ed. Sandra Ross (London: The British Council, 2013): 54–75; 66–67.
34 British Antarctic Survey, 'Relocation of Halley Research Station', press release (6 December 2016); www.bas.ac.uk/media-post/relocation-of-halley-research-station/
35 Sam Jacob, 'High tech primitive: the architecture of Antarctica' in *Ice Lab: New Architecture and Science* Arts Catalyst exhibition catalogue, ed. Sandra Ross (London: The British Council, 2013): 54–75; 69.
36 British Antarctic Survey, 'Halley Research Station Antarctica to close for winter', press release (16 January 2017); www.bas.ac.uk/media-post/halley-research-station-antarctica-to-close-for-winter/
37 'Antarctic Halley Station lost power and heat at -32 C', BBC News online, 7 August 2014; www.bbc.co.uk/news/uk-england-cambridgeshire-28687841
38 Peter Sloterdijk, 'Foreword to the theory of spheres' in *Cosmograms*, eds. M. Ohanian and J.C. Royaux (New York: Lukas and Sternberg, 2005): 223–240; 236.
39 *The Ends of the Earth: An Anthology of the Finest Writing on the Arctic and the Antarctic*, Volume 2 'The Antarctic', ed. Francis Spufford (London: Granta Books, 2007): 11.
40 Owen Wilkes and Robert Mann, 'The story of Nukey-Poo', *Bulletin of the Atomic Scientists* (October 1978): 32–36.
41 'Your Stay at McMurdo Station, Antarctica', prepared by Antarctic Support Associates for the National Science Foundation (NSF, 1995); www.nsf.gov; archived at passporttoknowledge.com/lfa/background/NSF/mc-stay.html
42 Nicholas Johnson, *Big Dead Place: Inside the Strange And Menacing World of Antarctica* (Los Angeles: Feral House, 2005): 10–11.
43 *Encounters at the End of the World*, directed by Werner Herzog (Chatsworth: Image Entertainment, 2008).
44 *Encounters at the End of the World*, directed by Werner Herzog (Chatsworth: Image Entertainment, 2008).
45 Anthony Lister, @AntAntarctic (7 August 2014), twitter.com; twitter.com/AntAntarctic/status/497074688921993216?ref_src=twsrc%5Etfw
46 *Encounters at the End of the World*, directed by Werner Herzog (Chatsworth: Image Entertainment, 2008).
47 Tom Griffiths, 'Commentary: Wallace S. Broecker, "Unpleasant surprises in the greenhouse?" (1987) J. R. Petit, J. Jouzel, D. Raynaud et al., "Climate and atmospheric history of the past 420,000 years from the Vostok Ice Core, Antarctica" (1999)', in *The Future of Nature*, eds. Libby Robin, Sverker Sörlin, Paul Warde (New Haven and London: Yale University Press, 2013): 359–362; 361.
48 Stephen J. Pyne, *The Ice* (London: Weidenfeld & Nicolson, 2003): 279.
49 A.B. Armitage, *Two Years in the Antarctic: being a narrative of the British National Antarctic Expedition*, (London, 1905): 90–91; cf. Tony White, *Shackleton's Man Goes South* (London: Science Museum, 2013): 33.
50 Tony White, *Shackleton's Man Goes South* (London: Science Museum, 2013): 68–69.

51 G.C. Simpson, *South Polar Times*, Vol. III part II (September 1911): 75; cf. Tony White, *Shackleton's Man Goes South* (London: Science Museum, 2013): 35.
52 G.C. Simpson, *South Polar Times*, Vol. III part II (September 1911): 75; cf. Tony White, *Shackleton's Man Goes South* (London: Science Museum, 2013): 36.
53 Richard E. Byrd, 'The conquest of Antarctica by air', *National Geographic* 58 (1930): 127–225.
54 Richard E. Byrd, *Little America* (New York and London: G. P. Puttnam's Sons, 1930): 392.
55 Richard E. Byrd, *Little America* (New York and London: G. P. Puttnam's Sons, 1930): 155.
56 Elena Glasberg, *Antarctica as Cultural Critique: The Gendered Politics of Scientific Exploration and Climate Change* (New York: Palgrave Macmillan, 2012): xv–xvi.
57 Stephen J. Pyne, *The Ice* (London: Weidenfeld & Nicolson, 2003): 102.
58 Richard E. Byrd, *Little America* (New York and London: G. P. Puttnam's Sons, 1930):192-193.
59 Alone was a direct influence on Don L. Stuart's (John Wood Campbell) short story 'Who Goes There?' (1938) and H.P. Lovecraft's novella At the Mountains of Madness (1939). Campbell's story was adapted as a 1982 film by director John Carpenter: *The Thing*.
60 Richard E. Byrd, *Alone* (London: George Putnam and Sons, 1938); cf Sarah Moss, '"I dread getting up": Richard Byrd alone in the Antarctic', *Scott's Last Biscuit. The Literature of Polar Exploration* (Oxford: Signal Books, 2006): 85–91; 87.
61 Richard E. Byrd, *Alone* (London: George Putnam and Sons, 1938); cf Sarah Moss, '"I dread getting up": Richard Byrd alone in the Antarctic', *Scott's Last Biscuit. The Literature of Polar Exploration* (Oxford: Signal Books, 2006): 85–91; 85–86;
62 Richard E. Byrd, *Alone* (London: George Putnam and Sons, 1938); cf Sarah Moss, '"I dread getting up": Richard Byrd alone in the Antarctic', *Scott's Last Biscuit. The Literature of Polar Exploration* (Oxford: Signal Books, 2006): 85–91; 87.
63 Richard E. Byrd, *Alone* (London: George Putnam and Sons, 1938); cf Sarah Moss, '"I dread getting up": Richard Byrd alone in the Antarctic', *Scott's Last Biscuit. The Literature of Polar Exploration* (Oxford: Signal Books, 2006): 85–91; 86.
64 Richard E. Byrd, *Alone* (London: George Putnam and Sons, 1938); cf Sarah Moss, '"I dread getting up": Richard Byrd alone in the Antarctic', *Scott's Last Biscuit. The Literature of Polar Exploration* (Oxford: Signal Books, 2006): 85–91; 86.
65 Apsley Cherry-Garrard, *The Worst Journey in the World* (London: Chatto and Windus, 1922).
66 Henry D. Thoreau, *Walden; or, Life in the Woods* (Boston: Ticknor and Fields, 1854).
67 Stephen J. Pyne, 'The extraterrestrial Earth: Antarctica as analogue for space exploration', *Space Policy* 23 (2007): 147–149.
68 Jacob Darwin Hamblin, *Arming Mother Nature: The Birth of Catastrophic Environmentalism* (Oxford, New York: Oxford University Press, 2013): 90. See also Walter Sullivan, *Assault on the Unknown: The International Geophysical Year* (London: Hodder and Stoughton Limited, 1961): 20–24.
69 Lloyd V. Berkner, 'International Geophysical Year' (Industrial College of the Armed Forces, Publication L, 59–97, 1959): 4; cf. Stephen J. Pyne, *The Ice* (London: Weidenfeld & Nicolson, 2003): 115.
70 Jacob Darwin Hamblin, *Arming Mother Nature: The Birth of Catastrophic Environmentalism* (Oxford, New York: Oxford University Press, 2013): 135.
71 J. R., Fleming, *Fixing the Sky: The Checkered History of Weather and Climate Control* (Columbia University Press, New York, 2010).
72 Stephen J. Pyne, *The Ice* (London: Weidenfeld & Nicolson, 2003): 243.
73 Walter Sullivan, 'US atom blasts 300 miles up mar radar, snag missile plan; called "Greatest experiment"' *The New York Times* (19 March 1959): 1; cf. Jacob Darwin Hamblin, *Arming Mother Nature: The Birth of Catastrophic Environmentalism* (Oxford, New York: Oxford University Press, 2013): 122.
74 R. Revelle and H.E. Suess, 'Carbon dioxide exchange between atmosphere and ocean and the question of an increase of atmospheric CO_2 during the past decades', *Tellus* 9 (1957): 18–27; 19.
75 Charles David Keeling, 'The concentration and isotopic abundances of carbon dioxide in the atmosphere', *Tellus* 12 (1960): 200–203.
76 Mike Davis, 'Cosmic dancers on history's stage? The permanent revolution in the Earth sciences', *New Left Review* 217 (1996): 48–84.

77 Mike Davis, 'Cosmic dancers on history's stage? The permanent revolution in the Earth sciences', *New Left Review* 217 (1996): 48–84.
78 Nick Drake, 'The ice-core sample', *Farewell Glacier* (Bloodaxe Books, 2012): 45. Reproduced with permission of Bloodaxe Books.
79 Heather Frazer, 'Icy demands: coring, curating and researching the GISP2 ice core' in *Bipolar*, ed. Kathryn Yusoff (London: the Arts Catalyst, 2007): 40.
80 Kathryn Yusoff. 'Navigating the Northwest Passage' in *Envisioning Landscapes, Making Worlds: Geography and the Humanities*, eds. S. Daniels, D. DeLyser, J.N. Entrikin and D. Richardson (New York and London: Routledge, 2011): 299–310; 303.
81 Jon Henley, 'Greenland's receding icecap to expose top-secret US nuclear project', *The Guardian* (27 September 2016); www.theguardian.com/world/2016/sep/27/receding-icecap-top-secret-us-nuclear-project-greenland-camp-century-project-iceworm
82 William Colgan et al. (W., H. Machguth, M. MacFerrin, J. D. Colgan, D. van As and J. A. MacGregor), 'The abandoned ice sheet base at Camp Century, Greenland, in a warming climate', *Geophysical Research Letters* 43 (2016): 8091–8096.
83 European Geosciences Union (EGU), 'Oldest ice core: finding a 1.5 million-year record of Earth's climate', ScienceDaily; www.sciencedaily.com/releases/2013/11/131105081228.htm; accessed 8 October 2016. For the paper see H. Fischer, et al. (J. Severinghaus, E. Brook, E. Wolff, M. Albert, O. Alemany, R. Arthern, C. Bentley, D. Blankenship, J. Chappellaz, T. Creyts, D. Dahl-Jensen, M. Dinn, M. Frezzotti, S. Fujita, H. Gallee, R. Hindmarsh, D. Hudspeth, G. Jugie, K. Kawamura, V. Lipenkov, H. Miller, R. Mulvaney, F. Pattyn, C. Ritz, J. Schwander, D. Steinhage, T. van Ommen, F. Wilhelms), 'Where to find 1.5 million yr old ice for the IPICS "Oldest Ice" ice core', *Climate of the Past Discussions* 9.3 (2013): 2771.
84 Spencer Weart, 'The Discovery of Global Warming'; www.aip.org/history/climate/cycles.htm#N_51_; rise and fall of greenhouse gases that matched the rise and fall of temperature. See also Spencer Weart, *The Discovery of Global Warming* (Cambridge MA: Harvard University Press, 2003).
85 R.B. Alley, *The Two Mile Time Machine: Ice Cores, Abrupt Climate Change and Our Future* (Princeton NJ: Princeton University Press, 2000): 120.
86 Elizabeth Kolbert, 'The Climate of Man – I', *The New Yorker* (25 April 2005); www.newyorker.com/magazine/2005/04/25/the-climate-of-man-i
87 Ian Angus, *Facing the Anthropocene: Fossil Capitalism and the Crisis of the Earth System* (New York: Monthly Review Press, 2016): 69.
88 Nigel Clark, *Inhuman Nature: Sociable Life on a Dynamic Planet* (London: Sage, 2011): xi.
89 Will Steffen et al., *Global Change and the Earth System: A Planet under Pressure*, Global Change – The IGBP Series (Berlin: Springer, 2004): 235.
90 Wallace S. Broecker, 'Unpleasant surprises in the greenhouse?', *Nature* 328 (1987): 123–126.
91 Wallace S. Broecker, 'Unpleasant surprises in the greenhouse?', *Nature* 328 (1987): 123–126.
92 Wallace S. Broecker, 'Ice cores: cooling the Tropics', *Nature* 376 (20 July 1995): 212–213.
93 Kathryn Yusoff. 'Navigating the Northwest Passage', in *Envisioning Landscapes, Making Worlds: Geography and the Humanities*, eds. S. Daniels, D. DeLyser, J.N. Entrikin and D. Richardson (New York and London: Routledge, 2011): 299–310; 305.
94 Will Steffen cf. Tom Griffiths, 'Commentary: Wallace S. Broecker, "Unpleasant surprises in the greenhouse?" (1987) J. R. Petit, J. Jouzel, D. Raynaud et al., "Climate and atmospheric history of the past 420,000 years from the Vostok Ice Core, Antarctica" (1999)', in *The Future of Nature*, eds. Libby Robin, Sverker Sörlin, Paul Warde (New Haven and London: Yale University Press, 2013): 359–362; 361.
95 J. R. Petit, J. Jouzel, D. Raynaud, *et al.*, 'Climate and atmospheric history of the past 420,000 years from the Vostok Ice Core, Antarctica' (1999)' in *The Future of Nature*, eds Libby Robin, Sverker Sörlin and Paul Warde (New Haven and London: Yale University Press, 2013): 348–358; 355.
96 J.R. Petit, J. Jouzel, D. Raynaud *et al.*, 'Climate and atmospheric history of the past 420,000 years from the Vostok Ice Core, Antarctica', *Nature* 399 (1999): 429–436; reprinted in *The Future of Nature*, eds Libby Robin, Sverker Sörlin and Paul Warde (New Haven and London: Yale University Press, 2013): 348–358; 356.
97 P.J. Crutzen and E.F Stoermer, 'The "Anthropocene"', *IGBP [International Geosphere-Biosphere Programme] Newsletter* 41 (2000): 17–18.

146 *Proxy world*

98 Mike Walker *et al.* (S. Johnsen, S. O. Rasmussen, T. Popp, J.-P. Steffensen, P. Gibbard, W. Hoek, J. Lowe, J. Andrews, S. Björck, L. C. Cwynar, K. Hughen, P. Kershaw, B. Kromer, T. Litt, D. J. Lowe, T. Nakagawa, R. Newnham and J. Schwander), 'Formal definition and dating of the GSSP (Global Stratotype Section and Point) for the base of the Holocene using the Greenland NGRIP ice core, and selected auxiliary records', *Journal of Quaternary Science* 24 (2009): 3–17; 11.
99 Eric W. Wolff, 'Ice sheets and the Anthropocene', in *A Stratigraphical Basis for the Anthropocene*, eds. C.N. Waters, J.A. Zalasiewicz, M. Williams, M.A. Ellis and A.M. Snelling, Geological Society, London, Special Publications, 395 (2014): 255–263.
100 Eric W. Wolff, 'Ice sheets and the Anthropocene', in *A Stratigraphical Basis for the Anthropocene*, eds. C.N. Waters, J.A. Zalasiewicz, M. Williams, M.A. Ellis and A.M. Snelling, Geological Society, London, Special Publications, 395 (2014): 255–263; 256.
101 Will Steffen, Paul J. Crutzen and John R. McNeill, 'The Anthropocene: are humans now overwhelming the great forces of nature?', *Ambio* 38 (2007): 614–21; 614.
102 Nigel Clark, *Inhuman Nature: Sociable Life on a Dynamic Planet* (London: Sage, 2011): xi.
103 Bruno Latour, *We Have Never Been Modern*, trans. Catherine Porter (Cambridge MA: Harvard University Press, 1993): 1.
104 Ian Angus, *Facing the Anthropocene: Fossil Capitalism and the Crisis of the Earth System* (New York: Monthly Review Press, 2016): 79; emphasis in text.
105 Oliver Morton, *The Planet Remade: How Geoengineering Could Change the World* (London: Granta, 2015): 136. See also Jacob Darwin Hamblin, *Arming Mother Nature: The Birth of Catastrophic Environmentalism* (Oxford, New York: Oxford University Press, 2013): 159–160.
106 Oliver Morton, *The Planet Remade: How Geoengineering Could Change the World* (London: Granta, 2015): 48.
107 Ian Angus, *Facing the Anthropocene: Fossil Capitalism and the Crisis of the Earth System* (New York: Monthly Review Press, 2016): 81.
108 John R. McNeill, *Something New Under the Sun: An Environmental History of the Twentieth Century* (London: Penguin Books, 2000): 113.
109 John R. McNeill, *Something New Under the Sun: An Environmental History of the Twentieth Century* (London: Penguin Books, 2000): 111.
110 Global Atmospheric Ozone Monitoring Network: Global Atmosphere Watch (GAW), World Meteorological Organization (WMO); public.wmo.int/en/bulletin/global-atmospheric-ozone-monitoring
111 Paul N. Edwards, *A Vast Machine: Computer Models, Climate Data, and The Politics of Global Warming* (Cambridge: MIT Press, 2010): 381.
112 J.E. Lovelock, R. J. Maggs and R.J. Wade, 'Halogenated hydrocarbons in and over the Atlantic', *Nature* 241 (1973): 194–96.
113 Mario J. Molina and F. S. Rowland, 'Stratospheric sink for chlorofluoromethanes: chlorine atom-catalysed destruction of ozone', *Nature* 249 (1974): 810–812. See also Ian Angus, *Facing the Anthropocene: Fossil Capitalism and the Crisis of the Earth System* (New York: Monthly Review Press, 2016): 82–83.
114 Paul J. Crutzen, 'Estimates of possible variations in total ozone due to natural causes and human activities', *Ambio* 3.6 (1974): 201–210. See also Christian Schwägerl, *The Anthropocene: The Human Era and How it Shapes Our Planet*, trans. Lucy Renner Jones (Santa Fe & London: Synergetic Press, 2014): 5.
115 Ian Angus, *Facing the Anthropocene: Fossil Capitalism and the Crisis of the Earth System* (New York: Monthly Review Press, 2016): 84. See also Sharon Roan, *Ozone Crisis: The 15-year Evolution of a Sudden Global Emergency* (New York: John Wiley, 1990): 96.
116 J. C. Farman, B.G. Gardiner and J.D. Shanklin, 'Large losses of total ozone layer in Antarctica reveal seasonal ClO_x/NO_x interaction', *Nature* 315 (May 1985): 207–210.
117 Jonathan Shanklin, interview in documentary, '*The Antarctic Ozone Hole: From Discovery to Recovery, a Scientific Journey*', United Nations Environment Programme (UNEP) Division of Technology Industry and Economics (DTIE), (2011); www.unpe.org/ozoneaction ; cf. Seth Denizen, 'Three holes in the geological present' in *Architecture in the Anthropocene: Encounters Among Design, Deep Time, Science and Philosophy*, ed. Etienne Turpin (Ann Arbor: Open Humanities Press, 2013): 29–46; 34.

118 United Nations Environment: 'Key achievements of the Montreal Protocol to date'; www.unep.org/ozonaction/Portals/105/documents/Ozone_Day_2012/Key%20achievements%20of%20the%20Montreal%20Protocol%202012%20low%20res.pdf
119 Ozone Hole Watch; National Aeronautics and Space Administration Goddard Space Flight Center. The mean ozone hole size for 7 September–13 October 2015; ozonewatch.gsfc.nasa.gov/
120 Frank Biermann, *Earth System Governance: World Politics in the Anthropocene* (Cambridge, MA: MIT Press, 2013): 6.
121 Michel Serres, *The Natural Contract* (Ann Arbor: University of Michigan Press, 1995): 63.
122 Elizabeth DeLoughrey, 'Satellite planetarity and the ends of the Earth' in *Public Culture* 26.2 73 (2014): 257–280; 260.
123 Jackson N. Maogoto, 'The Military ascent into space: from playground to battleground – the new uncertain game in the heavens', bepress Legal Series. Working Paper 1347 (5 May 2006); law.bepress.com/expresso/eps/1347
124 The Antarctic Treaty, December 1, 1959, 1 U.S.T. 794, T.I.A.S. No. 4780, 402 U.N.T.S. 71 (effective 23 June 1961); Secretariat of the Antarctic Treaty, www.ats.aq/documents/ats/treaty_original.pdf; British Antarctic Survey: The Antarctic Treaty www.bas.ac.uk/about/antarctica/the-antarctic-treaty/the-antarctic-treaty-1959/
125 Christy Collis and Klaus Dodds 'Assault on the unknown: the historical and political geographies of the International Geophysical Year (1957–8)', *Journal of Historical Geography* 34.4 (2008): 555–573; 558.
126 Stephen J. Pyne, Chapter 8: 'The Cold Peace: The Geopolitics of Antarctica', *The Ice* (London: Weidenfeld & Nicolson, 2003): 323–378; 347.
127 Christy Collis and Klaus Dodds 'Assault on the unknown: the historical and political geographies of the International Geophysical Year (1957–8)', *Journal of Historical Geography* 34.4 (2008): 555–573; 563.
128 British Antarctic Survey: Protocol on Environmental Protection to the Antarctic Treaty; www.bas.ac.uk/about/antarctica/the-antarctic-treaty/environmental-protocol/protocol-on-environmental-protection-to-the-antarctic-treaty-1991/
129 Simon Romero, 'Antarctic life: no dogs, few vegetables and a 'little intense" in the winter', *International New York Times* (6 January 2016); www.nytimes.com/2016/01/07/world/americas/chile-antarctica-villa-las-estrellas.html?_r=0 ; accessed 20 September 2016.
130 Owen Bowcott, 'Britain to claim more than 1m sq km of Antarctica', *The Guardian*, (17 October 2007); www.theguardian.com/news/2007/oct/17/antarctica.sciencenews
131 The Outer Space Treaty's full title reads, 'Treaty on Principles Governing the Activities of States in the Exploration and Use of Outer Space, including the Moon and Other Celestial Bodies' (27 January 1967); history.nasa.gov/1967treaty.html
132 John F. Kennedy, 'If the Soviets control space – they can control the Earth', from 'Missiles and Rockets' (10 October 1960): 12–13; www.jfklink.com/speeches/joint/app17_missile-sandrockets.html
133 Jackson Maogoto, 'The Military ascent into space: from playground to battleground – the new uncertain game in the heavens', bepress Legal Series. Working Paper 1347 (5 May, 2006); law.bepress.com/expresso/eps/1347
134 Joanne Irene Gabrynowicz, 'The international space treaty regime in the globalization era', *Ad Astra, The Magazine of the National Space Society* 17. 3 (Autumn 2005): 30–31.
135 Kim Stanley Robinson, *Red Mars*, (New York: Bantam Books, 1993); *Green Mars* (New York: Bantam Books, 1995); *Blue Mars* (New York: Bantam Books, 1996).
136 Kim Stanley Robinson, *Green Mars* (New York: Bantam Books, 1995): 376. See also *Green Planets: Ecology and Science Fiction*, eds. Gerry Canavan and Kim Stanley Robinson (Middletown, CT: Wesleyan, 2014). Kim Stanley Robinson visited Antarctica in 1995 while on the National Science Foundation's Artists and Writer's Program; see also Kim Stanley Robinson, *Antarctica* (New York: Bantam, 2002).
137 Stephen J. Pyne, *The Ice* (London: Weidenfeld & Nicolson, 2003): 378.
138 Davor Vidas, 'The Anthropocene and the International Law of the Sea' *Philosophical Transactions of the Royal Society A* 369 (2011): 909–925.
139 *The Ends of the Earth: An Anthology of the Finest Writing on the Arctic and the Antarctic*, Volume 2 'The Antarctic', ed. Francis Spufford (London: Granta Books, 2007): 14.

5   Bounded planet

WARNING: *no trespassing*

The most familiar images of humanity's home planet are the NASA photographs taken by astronauts: 'Earthrise', by the Apollo 8 crew on 24 December 1968; and the 'Blue Marble', or 'Whole Earth', taken from Apollo 17 on 7 December 1972. These images, endlessly reproduced on T-shirts, news media backdrops and the cover of the *Whole Earth Catalog*, now evoke both the space age and the counter-cultural ecology movements of the mid-to-late 20th century. They have become so ubiquitous it is easy to forget their impact when they were first released. Half a millennium earlier, Copernicus had decentred humanity's planetary home in the cosmos. Still, Earth had remained the only vantage point from which to observe, lopsidedly, the cosmic void. Its distances had been the greatest ever traversed. This was the case until the Apollo missions removed to the Moon and looked back at home – a small, cloud-whorled sphere on an infinite black ground.

These images introduced a conception of the Earth as a limited, bounded, integrated whole; one that required nothing from the bigger universe but motion and solar radiation to give rise to, and sustain, all life. This went hand in hand with a shift in scientific thinking about Earth's macro processes – they were being reconceived as a complex and interdependent set of 'life-support systems'. The NASA photographs were useful analogies for this shift. The ecologist Howard Odum wrote in 1971, 'We can begin a systems view of the Earth through the macroscope of the astronaut high above the Earth.'[1] James Lovelock's work with NASA on the detection of life on Mars had led him to the conception of the Earth as a living superorganism – 'Gaia'. He too referred to the experience of an astronaut: 'When I first saw Gaia in my mind, I felt as an astronaut must have done as he stood on the moon, gazing back at our home the Earth.'[2] Gaia was 'symbiosis as seen from space'.[3]

A systems view of the Earth promoted a holistic view of dynamic interactions between the biosphere, hydrosphere, atmosphere, geosphere, pedosphere and cryosphere. Yet the global visions made possible by astronautic photography also distanced humans from the Earth: 'Apollo's eye,' Denis Cosgrove observes, is 'synoptic and omniscient, intellectually detached'.[4] From detachment, it is a small step to instrumentalisation; from a dream of omniscience, less exalted but perhaps more dangerous fantasies of the bureaucratic mastery of Earth's 'systems' can flow. As Kathryn Yusoff points out, images of a 'static rounded Earth did much to calcify concepts of dynamic Earth systems'.[5] Seeing our life-support system, our only known home, as a blue marble in the void could have humbled or overwhelmed us. For the most part, however, this vision only bolstered our sense of control: 'Whole Earth gave us the illusion of the Earth as a discrete artefact, which could be managed and encoded into systems or geoengineered.'[6]

Perhaps the most powerful expression of the Earth as a fragile discrete artefact was the notion of Spaceship Earth, which in the 1960s became a rallying call for the environmental movement. It offered not only a way of expressing humanity's common interest in understanding the global environment as a system of sustenance, but also a way of signalling its predicament. But the metaphor of Spaceship Earth was troubling: it offered little room for deviating from a pre-ordained course. As Oliver Morton observes:

> The metaphor of the spaceship plays up holism and hides the contingency of the Earth system. It implies that there is a single ship-shape way that the Earth should run. It encourages the notion that there is a fixed limit to the Earth's carrying capacity, just as there is a fixed complement for a vessel – an argument that has been used to justify brutal ideas about population control. And it can be used to divide humans into officers, crew and supercargo.[7]

Earth systems sciences presented the Earth as a graspable, monitorable and manageable entity. They had developed in tandem with military-industrial research on capsule living in submarines, nuclear shelters and spaceships. The imaginary of the sealed cabin of the spacecraft, a compact shelter in a vast and hostile environment, also evoked (at least for American thinkers) the self-reliant homesteading of the frontier – an analogy that should have troubled some 'Spaceship Earth' thinkers more than it appears to have done. If the home planet was bounded, and full to capacity, then it could also be imagined as a lifeboat or forward base for resettlement projects and space cities in a boundless universe. Spaceship Earth helped to establish the planet as a temporary biospheric environment and opened up the prospect of leaving Earth – and its troubles – behind altogether.[8]

The Brundtland Report, *Our Common Future* – issued by the UN World Commission on Environment and Development in 1987, and the document which introduced 'sustainable development' to policy discourse – opens by invoking the Apollo images of the Earth:

> In the middle of the 20th century, we saw our planet from space for the first time. Historians may eventually find that this vision had a greater impact on thought than did the Copernican revolution of the 16th century, which upset the human self-image by revealing that the Earth is not the centre of the universe. From space, we see a small and fragile ball dominated not by human activity and edifice but by a pattern of clouds, oceans, greenery, and soils. Humanity's inability to fit its activities into that pattern is changing planetary systems, fundamentally. Many such changes are accompanied by life-threatening hazards. …This new reality, from which there is no escape, must be recognised – and managed.[9]

This imperative ushered in an era of technoscientific management. The musings on the view of the Earth from space imply that the only way to properly observe 'Spaceship Earth' is from within a well-operated 'Earth Spaceship'. 'Earth Observations' is a website operated by NASA that offers interactive visualisations of a vast collection of data sets on weather phenomena, forestation, land and ocean temperature, population density, and so on. With each set imposed on the same identical world map, and viewable at different points in time, 'Earth Observations... help you picture climate and environmental changes as they occur on our home planet'.[10] But the sophisticated instantaneous mapping of data made possible by such programs runs the risk of confusing knowledge with control. Philosopher Peter Sloterdijk describes this de-terrestrialised, macroscopic vision as 'an inverted astronomy' that sees humans 'looking down from space onto the Earth rather than from the ground up into the skies'.[11]

Today our 'inverted astronomical' gaze – trained on data beamed from remote sensing devices in space, and also on the simulated 'globes' of terrestrial data visualisation – is registering far-reaching changes in the Earth. With the advent of the Anthropocene, the Earth's 'pattern of clouds, oceans, greenery, and soils' is understood as significantly more disturbed than it has been for tens of thousands of years. We are coming to understand that human activity is changing planetary systems, as only vast cosmic phenomena have ever changed it before. The Brundtland Commission had defined 'sustainable development' as 'development that meets the needs of the present without compromising the ability of future generations to meet their own needs'. Recent thinking suggests this must be redefined for a new era of Earth stewardship in the Anthropocene, as: 'development that meets the needs of the present while safeguarding Earth's life-support system, on which the welfare of current and future generations depends.'[12]

The line of thinking that describes humanity's home planet as limited and bounded and has emphasised preservation of its life-support systems has, since the widespread emergence of environmental concerns in the 1960s, consistently warned of the dangers of transgressing boundaries. The 'planetary boundaries' hypothesis, developed at the Stockholm Resilience Centre, is the latest incarnation of this thinking, and its rise to prominence coincides with our entry into the Anthropocene epoch. But the image of the 'fragile Earth' that dominated the environmental movement in the late 20th century is also being challenged by new indications that Earth is far more resilient than the human species. The Earth has been a habitable planet for about four billion years, enduring enormous climatic changes and asteroid impacts, recovering, realigning, adapting. To characterise it as 'fragile' may be a misprision. All the same, its long-term habitability for humans is now in doubt. In recent decades, humanity has responded to the new data about our planet's precarity – not in itself, perhaps, but as a home for our species – with two main lines of enquiry: visions of the Earth as a (possibly 'steerable', possibly 'reparable') spaceship; and dreams of spaceships as tiny surrogate Earths. The problem of ongoing human survival, in a delicate craft that places a thin protective skin between us and annihilation, is common to both. As is the problem of who, exactly, we are talking about when we talk about the 'we' who must survive.

Astronautics

> Earth is the cradle of humanity, but one cannot live in the cradle forever.[13]

Astronautics in the Anthropocene is marked by the curious interplay of boundedness to and detachment from the Earth. The Russian rocket scientist Konstantin Tsiolkovsky was a pioneer of astronautic theory and practice who created the mathematical formula

Bounded planet 151

Figure 5.1 'Earthrise' (24 December 1968); astronaut photograph from Apollo 8 mission
(NASA image AS08-14-2383)
Source: Earth Science and Remote Sensing Unit, NASA Johnson Space Center

for propelling an object into orbit around the Earth. His cradle metaphor reveals what drove his innovative anthropocosmism: the unsettling (in all senses) conviction that planet Earth was outgrowing its usefulness as humanity's home. Tsiolkovsky is credited with laying the foundations of the science of astronautics, put forward in *Free Space*, his monograph from 1883, developed in *Dreams of Earth and Sky* (1895) and his space fantasy *Beyond the Planet Earth* (1920), and later codified in his 1926 treatise, *Sixteen Stages of Space Exploration*. His proposals for extending human life beyond Earth included designs for space elevators, jet-propelled spaceships, space stations, air locks and pressurised space suits, multi-stage rockets or 'rocket trains', the use of liquid hydrogen and liquid oxygen as rocket fuel, gyroscopic stabilisation, as well as the closed-cycle biological systems supporting space colonies and cities in space. All of these proposals later inspired Sergei Korolev, Chief Designer of the Soviet space programme, who was responsible for the launch of Sputnik. In *The Aim of Astronautics* (1929), Tsiolkovsky described an artificial vessel for extended dwelling in space that included details of a complex life-support system. Ultimately, in his view,

152 *Bounded planet*

Figure 5.2 'The Blue Marble' or 'Whole Earth' (7 December 1972); astronaut photograph from Apollo 17 mission (NASA image AS17-148-22727)
Source: Earth Science and Remote Sensing Unit, NASA Johnson Space Center

astronautics was a matter of species survival: 'Man must at all costs overcome the Earth's gravity and have, in reserve, the space of at least the solar system. All kinds of danger lie in wait for him on the Earth.'[14] Tsiolkovsky was haunted by the prospect of planetary-scale disaster: a flood, an earthquake, an asteroid impact, a resource war, an exploding Earth, an extinguished Sun, or one of any 'numerous other terrible dangers' was sure to do for an earthbound humanity in the end.[15] Astronautics, he reasoned, could provide a means of escape. But on what time scale? And for how many of us? And what quality of life might the survivors expect to enjoy, after evacuating Earth? Between the reality of a 1920s *terra firma* and an eventual self-sustaining exocolony among the stars lay a lot of hard terrain still to be traversed – a terrain fraught with technical, political and ethical challenges in which humanity is yet to prove itself competent.

Sputnik, Earth's 'fellow traveller', in the form of the first artificial Earth satellite, was launched into orbit on 4 October 1957 during the IGY. It was the size of a basketball, weighed approximately 83 kg, and took 96 minutes to orbit the Earth on an elliptical trajectory. The launch had originally been planned to coincide with the 100th anniversary of Tsiolkovsky's birth in September that year, but was delayed. Propelled into space with a kerosene-powered rocket, the little beeping satellite also launched what has since come to be known as the 'Sputnik crisis' – a period of fear and uncertainty among the US public caused by the perceived technological gap between the rival superpowers. Less than a month later, Sputnik 2 was fired into space carrying the first cosmonaut – Laika, a stray dog from Moscow. Spurred into competitive action, the US launched the unmanned *Explorer* satellite in 1958. The achievement of photographing the Earth from space could not be far behind – and in fact, the first such photographs, hazy and low-res, were taken in 1959 by the NASA satellite, *Explorer 6*, which was collecting data on nuclear radiation. The next images to follow did not get public release: they were spy satellite images taken of the Soviet Union, Asia and the poles. No sooner did humanity get an eye in space than we used it to surveil our own kind.

The era of 'inverted astronomy' had begun. Earth had sat for its portrait, and the ontological shock was palpable – indeed, to some contemporary thinkers, deeply disturbing. In *The Conquest of Space and the Stature of Man*, written in 1963, Hannah Arendt argued that humanity was inconceivable outside the range of its terrestrial habitat.[16] She pointed out that the epistemology of science had long rehearsed the extraterrestrial vantage point – or 'Archimedean point' – realised in her time by the satellites, turning their mechanical (and soon to be human) eyes on a radically defamiliarised Earth. She felt we ought to receive this 'achievement' with ambivalence.

> It was precisely by abstracting from these terrestrial conditions, by appealing to a power of imagination and abstraction that would, as it were, lift the human mind out of the gravitational field of the Earth and look down upon it from some point in the universe, that modern science reached its most glorious and, at the same time, most baffling achievements.[17]

However, the launch of Sputnik also encapsulated, in Arendt's view, the threat of 'Earth alienation' that science posed to the 'common-sense experiences of Earthbound creatures'.[18] For the Earth, she wrote, 'is the very quintessence of the human condition'. The philosopher Martin Heidegger was also concerned that the modern planetary imagination signalled a technologically induced expulsion from our earthly home. He was disturbed by the first photographic images of the Earth from the distance of the Moon – taken by the satellite *Lunar Orbiter 1* in August 1966 when it was surveying the Moon for Apollo landing sites:

> I do not know whether you were frightened but I at any rate was frightened when I saw pictures coming from the Moon to the Earth. We don't need any atom bomb. The uprooting of man has already taken place. The only thing we have left is purely technological relationships. This is no longer the Earth on which man lives.[19]

Sputnik, primitive and brave, had emitted a steady radio beep or 'chirrup' which the nervous US had tried to decode. In fact, its only use to Soviet researchers was the information it conveyed about the ionosphere. The first artificial satellite was relatively insignificant as an instrument for gathering Earth or space data. The more elaborate biotelemetry developed for Sputnik 2, however, was capable of transmitting data that signalled Laika's distress in the overheating capsule. Subsequent satellites would be equipped to tell ever more elaborate stories, not only about the status of their astronauts-cosmonauts, but also about the Earth and its physical layers. Emerging alongside this growing body of information about the home planet was a heightened sense of responsibility toward it, and of dependence upon its ecosystems. Awareness of Earth as a life-support system grew at precisely the time technical know-how was turned to the problem of the physical vulnerability of passengers in tiny space capsules. It was inevitable that the idea of the spaceship as a surrogate Earth would emerge – a home-from-home for pioneering space travellers. In 1961 Yuri Gagarin's spaceflight, *Poyekhali!—Let's go!* – launched the Space Age proper. In the same year Gherman Titov, another Soviet cosmonaut, was the first human to spend 24 hours in space. He orbited the planet 17 times in his tiny, high-tech bubble, sleeping and suffering space sickness, before returning to Earth. In 1963 the first woman, and first civilian, a textile-factory assembly worker and expert sky-diver called Valentina Tereshkova, completed 48 orbits of the Earth in three days. But closed-system technologies were being developed at the time to sustain vulnerable lives in cramped conditions in an inhospitable environment for far longer periods of time. Since the International Space Station (ISS) launched in 1998, it has been continuously inhabited. Astronauts-cosmonauts trained in the constant monitoring of life-support systems and bodily functions, readied with a thousand contingency plans for as many potentially fatal emergencies, spend long enough in this strange environment for it to become routine. They tweet from space, answer emailed questions, shoot comedy videos of themselves brushing their teeth and washing their hair, performing David Bowie's 'Space Oddity' and snacking on space-lettuce. They trust a thin skin of metal and glass to cocoon them safely within the boiling, freezing, annihilating depths of space. They always, as is essential within an 'inverted astronomy', have Earth in view.

The German philosopher Hans Blumenberg's notion of 'astronoetics' explores the desire to travel to the stars, and the 'wondering' that this has entailed, since long before the conditions of astronautics – its marvels, its discomforts and disappointments – were possible. In 1958 Blumenberg had answered a call to intellectuals to respond to the Soviet Union's launch of Sputnik – described as the false comet (*falsche Komet*) or chirruping artificial moon (*piepende Kunstmond*). He presented a research proposal seeking funding for theoretical investigations on the as yet unseen 'dark side of the Moon', which, he suggested would be published in a new journal, *Current Topics on Astronoetics*.[20] The possibility of humans actually reaching the moon seemed a distant prospect, so astronoetics might have been conceived as the only – for the time being – viable means of travelling to the stars. Yet in answering the question 'What is Astronoetics?', Blumenberg insists that astronautics does not render astronoetics irrelevant. Rather, astronoetics persists as a 'thoughtful consideration' of space travel:

> 'Astronoetics' is called so not as an alternative to 'astronautics' – to think of instead of actually travelling somewhere. 'Astronoetics' also names the thoughtful consideration of whether, and if so just what sense it would make, to travel there. It could be that even after a successful round-trip, the question whether the effort had been worthwhile could not be decided.[21]

Blumenberg observed that astronoetics coupled with astronautics might encourage a new kind of geocentrism. Humanity and planet Earth may have been decentred in the cosmos, but this does not change the fact that Earth is our home. As the philosopher Karsten Harries puts it, 'Not just astronautics but science has left us behind... by the same token it has both left us at home and left us our home'.[22] Astronoetics makes possible – and necessary – an ethical challenge to astronautics. It addresses those 'left at home' demanding renewed consideration of human inhabitation of the Earth, and challenging our fantasies of escaping Earth and its planetary limits.

Up to the Moon or back down to Earth? In July 1969, the writer Kurt Vonnegut was hired by CBS as a commentator for their coverage of the Apollo 11 Moon mission. However, his broadcast commentary got cut off when he suggested on air that Earthbound social improvements might have been a better way to spend the money. According to Vonnegut, the space programme had cost $33 billion. He later expanded on his views in an article for *The New York Times Magazine*:

> Earth is such a pretty blue and pink and white pearl in the pictures NASA sent me. It looks so *clean*. You can't see all the hungry, angry Earthlings down there– and the smoke and the sewage and trash and sophisticated weaponry.[23]

Vonnegut punctures, in salutary fashion, narratives of human ingenuity and innovation: 'Most of the true tales of masterfulness in new environments with new technologies have been cruel or greedy.' Human history on Earth has so far been of 'tremendous messes to be cleaned up, ravaged landscapes dotted by shattered Earthlings and their machines. Stupid.'[24] He quotes Arthur C. Clarke, following Tsiolkovsky: '"The Earth is our cradle, which we are about to leave... And the solar system will be our kindergarten."' Vonnegut points out: 'Most of us will never leave this cradle, of course, unless death turns out to be a form of astronautics.'[25] In the decades since Vonnegut set out his objections to dreams of abandoning Earth, the idea has continued to exert a fascination for many. Yet the Challenger and Columbia shuttle disasters, and the near catastrophe of the Apollo 13 mission, were sobering reminders of technology's fallibility; and if Virgin Galactic's recent 'in-flight anomaly'[26] was illustrative, it seems even brief, recreational space flight for non-specialists is still some time off. Outside the sphere of small-scale commercial speculation, political and economic pressure have somewhat curtailed our spacefaring aspirations. Humanity comes crashing down back to earth and reaches more tentatively for the stars.

In *The Natural Contract*, Michel Serres describes an 'astronaut humanity' cast off from the familiar moorings of Earth only to find itself tethered in more complicated and stranger ways to its home planet: 'by the totality of our knowledge, the sum of our technologies, the collection of our communications; by torrents of signals, by the complete set of imaginable umbilical cords, living and artificial, visible and invisible, concrete or purely formal.'[27] For the Earthbound, including those living in what Serres considers the extraterrestrial world of cities, astronoetics remains a necessary complement to astronautics in the Anthropocene.

Spaceship Earth

> I've often heard people say, 'I wonder what it would feel like to be on board a spaceship,' and the answer is very simple. What *does* it *feel* like? That's all we have ever experienced. We are all astronauts.[28]

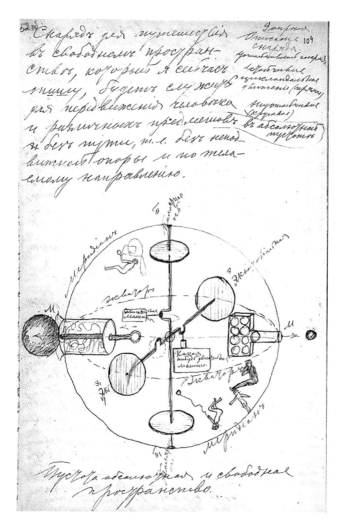

Figure 5.3 'Free Space' (9 March 1883); manuscript: sketch of cross-section of jet-propelled spaceship. Right: Cannon firing spherical projectiles and propelling the vehicle through space with its recoil (reaction). Centre: Gyroscopes, the revolving of which can change the position (orientation) of the spaceship in space

Source: KE Tsiolkovsky Archive; Russian Academy of Sciences

The audacious redefinition of humanity's home planet as spaceship was allegedly introduced by Buckminster Fuller in a discussion about the US space rocket programme in 1951.[29] In 1969, he published *Operating Manual for Spaceship Earth: A Bold Blueprint for Survival that Diagnoses the Causes of Environmental Crisis*. In Fuller's view, Spaceship Earth has a limited 'carrying capacity'[30] in terms of both resources and space. The need to optimise the management of these things is therefore high. Among the dangers to the equilibrium of Spaceship Earth, Fuller lists poverty, economic inequality, pollution, energy over-consumption, and war. The only escape route from

Bounded planet 157

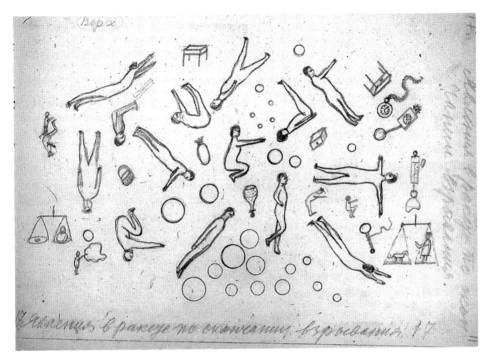

Figure 5.4 Drawing of people and objects floating around weightless in space; from Konstantin Tsiolkovsky's 1933 paper 'Album of Space Travel'
Source: KE Tsiolkovsky Archive; Russian Academy of Sciences

environmental disaster is, therefore, to develop scientific and technological regimes of efficiency and self-sufficiency. In Fuller's terms this requires acknowledging, first, that 'we are all astronauts'.

Spaceship Earth is 'an integrally designed machine which to be persistently successful must be comprehended and serviced in total'. For its intelligent and somewhat technologically adept passengers, this shouldn't be a problem – except that there is 'no instruction book' for this complex craft.[31] Fuller asserts that humankind will have to 'discover retrospectively' its 'forward capabilities' – learning all by itself 'how to operate and maintain Spaceship Earth and its complex life-supporting and regenerating systems'.[32] Fuller's book nevertheless offers an 'operating manual' of sorts. It begins with the origins of the astronautical point of view, with an account of the links between seafaring, international trade, and governance. He draws on his own training in the US Navy, including 'the powerfully effective forecasting arts of celestial navigation, pilotage, ballistics, and logistics'. He also suggests we recover lost competencies: 'the long-range, anticipatory design science governing yesterday's naval mastery of the world from which our present day's general systems theory has been derived.'[33] Fuller's veneration of a bloody and exploitative period in human 'progress' might give some cause for concern. Yet he does at least address the political dimension of our present dilemma: 'Despite our recently developed communications intimacy and popular awareness of total Earth we, too, in 1969 are as yet politically organised entirely in the terms of exclusive and utterly obsolete sovereign separateness.'[34] Fuller referred to the function of a 'trim tab' – a miniature rudder – in nautical design, as a metaphor for how individuals could make a difference in the world and change the course of humanity. With its image of subtle action provoking a substantial shift, the trim tab, according to Fuller, 'demonstrates the principle of self-regenerative amplification, on which the original cybernetic experience is based and from which the feedback control system is derived, namely how one navigates a ship.'[35] 'Call me Trim-Tab' was Fuller's imperative, echoing another mariner of a distinctly internationalist-idealist bent.[36]

Like Ishmael, Fuller was all for ship-shape hierarchies: keeping Spaceship Earth on a steady course into the future would necessarily fall to an intellectual elite of 'planners, architects and engineers', aided by the principles of good management and a state-of-the art computer to monitor Earth's systems. For the computer, Fuller argued, was capable of 'bringing all of humanity in for a happy landing'.[37] There is already a glimpse of Fuller's particular take on Earth stewardship in his conception of the computer as an extension of human intelligence in his technopolitical treatise, *Nine Chains to the Moon* (1938). Drawing on emerging theories of cybernetics, Fuller had described a superorganism, 'Phantom Captain', which maintains and guides the technobiological body. Without this captain, 'the mechanism becomes inoperative and very quickly disintegrates into basic chemical elements'.[38] Fuller returned to these notions of a super-consciousness in describing Spaceship Earth as an intricate cybernetic machine, managing a complex of life-support and maintenance systems, and equipped with intelligent operators with an inbuilt drive to learn and to optimise.

The best individuals among our species – the self-improving operators of a complex machine – have, in Fuller's view, a clear 'responsibility of making humanity comprehensively and sustainably successful'.[39] And success consists in efficiency. The successful operation of Spaceship Earth would be measurable in the 'increase the performance per pound of the Earth's resources'. Fuller's vision was of a coordinated world that could meet the needs of all of humanity, regardless of which political system prevailed in this region or that.[40] Humans could live within their limits, he believed, if they would only anticipate them and work with them, through innovations in design and technology. In 1950 Fuller had made detailed designs of geodesic domes, including a proposal for a vast structure to enclose New York City that would be capable of withstanding a super hurricane (see Figure 3.1).[41] He claimed at the time, 'The broad ramifications of the potential significance of geodesic structures… could function as an economic and social Noah's Ark'.[42] By the time he wrote *Spaceship Earth*, Fuller was convinced that the 'physical resources of the Earth can support all of a multiplying humanity at higher standards of living than anyone has ever experienced or dreamed'.[43] Recognising our limitations, of space and of resources, and the interdependence of all parts within the whole, did not, for Fuller, mean disregarding the needs of the many for the First World few. With Spaceship Earth conceived as humanity's ark, continued industrial development could be supported through the careful conservation of resources, along with mastery of the necessities for survival.

> We have thus discovered also that we can make all of humanity successful through science's world engulfing industrial evolution provided that we are not so foolish as to continue to exhaust in a split second of astronomical history the orderly energy savings of billions of years' energy conservation aboard our Spaceship Earth.[44]

Spaceship Earth's 'savings account' or 'storage battery' was made up of the fossil fuels accumulated over billions of years beneath the Earth's surface. These were deposited through the action of dynamic Earth processes: 'photosynthesis and progressive, complex, top soil fossilisation buried ever deeper within Earth's crust by frost, wind, flood, volcanoes, and earthquake upheavals.'[45] Humanity's first task was to curtail the reckless expenditure of this resource; its next, to harness other forms of readily available energy. But only by understanding the dynamic Earth systems that converted biological matter into oil, sunlight into food, and other deep processes, would humanity 'progressively harness ever more of the celestially generated tidal and storm generated wind, water, and electrical power concentrations'.[46] There was urgency in Fuller's writing: the window of time available for taking control of this complex craft and learning to steer it with no instruction manual appeared to him perilously narrow.

In the 1960s and 1970s, there was no shortage of attempts to provide operating manuals for Spaceship Earth. For Kenneth Boulding, himself an economist, the solution, unsurprisingly, took economic form. In his 1966 article 'The Economics of the Coming Spaceship Earth',[47] he proposed a 'spaceman economy' or 'closed economic system', with an ethic of responsible, cooperative management of the Earth, as opposed to the 'cowboy economy' or 'open system' that had prevailed to date:

> For the sake of picturesqueness, I am tempted to call the open economy the 'cowboy economy', the cowboy being symbolic of the illimitable plains and also associated with reckless, exploitative, romantic, and violent behaviour, which is characteristic of open societies. The closed economy of the future might similarly be called the 'spaceman' economy, in which the Earth has become a single spaceship, without unlimited reservoirs of anything, either for extraction or pollution, and in which, therefore, man must find his place in a cyclical ecological system which is capable of continuous reproduction of material form even though it cannot escape having inputs of energy.'[48]

The limited spaceship offers access to the frontiers of the future. In the spaceship economy, informed by notions of scarcity, the primary concern is the control of reserves, or 'stock maintenance'. This relies on a strict economy of circulation, a precise technology of energy and information flows and continuous material exchange and renewal. This line of thinking was influential in the development of ecological economics, and in the notion of an ecological footprint. Another guide to political and economic survival was provided by British economist Barbara Ward. Her 1966 book *Spaceship Earth* warns that the whole world is vulnerable to planet-scaled catastrophe:

> This space voyage is totally precarious. We depend upon a little envelope of soil and a rather larger envelope of atmosphere for life itself. And both can be contaminated and destroyed.[49]

Ward uses the notion of a fragile spaceship as an allegory for global interdependence. According to her, it is the United Nations that promise the unified, harmonious management of the planet's carrying capacity.[50] Ward's work had also previously inspired US ambassador Adlai Stevenson's 1965 address to the UN:

160 *Bounded planet*

> We travel together, passengers on a little spaceship, dependent on its vulnerable reserves of air and soil; all committed for our safety to its security and peace; preserved from annihilation only by the care, the work, and, I will say, the love we give our fragile craft.[51]

The UN repaid Ward's faith in their effectiveness by rapidly taking up 'Spaceship Earth' and the idea of coordinated Earth stewardship into their discourse. For the inaugural Earth Day event in 1971, Secretary-General U Thant wished: 'May there be only peaceful and cheerful Earth Days to come for our beautiful Spaceship Earth as it continues to spin and circle in frigid space with its warm and fragile cargo of animate life.'[52]

Inherent in the 'Spaceship Earth' metaphor, in all its iterations, is the idea of central coordination. In all the prominent expositions of this idea, this involved elaborate technoscientific intervention, and this, too, became part of real-world environmental management policies in the mid to late century. Computer models of natural and industrial flows of energy and materials were ordered, for example – so as to make an inventory of Earth's cargo and 'objectively' determine its carrying capacity. But alongside these morally neutral technocratic interventions, a more disturbing tendency was on the rise: a return to alarmist Malthusianism among such writers as Garrett Hardin and Paul Ehrlich. These writings were intended to play on popular First World fears. The title of Paul Ehrlich's *The Population Bomb* (1968), deliberately evoked the threat of the nuclear arms race (one of its covers showed a cartoon bomb with the words 'The Population Bomb Keeps Ticking'). In Ehrlich's view, the 'good ship Earth'[53] was on the verge of sinking. Ehrlich's particular interpretation of the idea of a limited 'carrying capacity' was very much focused on the number of 'passengers' in the 'ship' rather than on how resources might be distributed between them; his proposals included a strict and sinisterly pragmatic triage system for the classification of nations.[54] Ehrlich later developed this thinking with co-writer Richard Harriman, taking inspiration from the spaceship metaphor in their book *How to be a Survivor: A Plan to Save Spaceship Earth* (1971). The first Earth Day, 22 April 1970, was the impetus for their book. It took Adlai Stevenson's 'little spaceship' UN address for its epigraph. They claimed the book to be 'a step toward the development of a survival manual for Spaceship Earth'.[55] It opened with an account of the Apollo 13 disaster in the chapter 'Spaceship in Trouble':

> That very same April a much larger spaceship was also in trouble. Its life-support systems were malfunctioning, it was running out of vital supplies, and half of its overcrowded passengers were hungry. But on this spaceship there had been no emergency planning; indeed there was not even any crew… That spaceship was, and is, the Spaceship Earth.[56]

Ehrlich and Harriman argued that the life-support systems of the little Earth craft were inadequate to cope with the rapidly increasing number of passengers. Their assertion that 'The people who bear the responsibility for saving Spaceship Earth are the first-class passengers'[57] is followed up with a chilling suggestion for the 'Department of Population and Environment' to be instituted, and given 'broad' but unspecified 'powers to maintain the QOL (quality of life)'.[58]

This 'survival of the first-class passengers' view was not limited to writers who anticipated humanity's future unfolding on Earth. In Garrett Hardin's 1972 science-fiction parable, *Exploring New Ethics for Survival: The Voyage of the Spaceship Beagle*, humanity's only hope of survival is a transfer to a small raft of near-Earth exocolonies for the lucky few. However, these fortunate passengers are doomed to repeat their species' errors and calamities in their hygienic new home before finally evolving into the rationality – and the brutally pragmatic 'lifeboat ethics' – necessary, in Hardin's vision, for the species to attain a stable growth rate. It was impossible to expect any kind of stability from the changeable, argumentative and fickle passengers – in other words, 'the real problem of a spaceship is its people'.[59] One of the measures taken by the ship's custodians along the way is forcing the population to choose one of three biblical plagues – famine, war, or pestilence – to be visited upon them to reduce population. The perceived threat of overpopulation on Earth was, of course, what prompted Hardin to imagine the tale of the unruly passengers of the *Spaceship Beagle*. He addressed this more explicitly in a 1976 article, 'Carrying Capacity as an Ethical Concept', in which he ventriloquised, apparently without irony, a vengeful Old Testament God: 'Thou shalt not exceed the carrying capacity.'[60] In his essay 'Lifeboat Ethics: The Case Against Helping the Poor' (1974), Hardin argues that the issue of survival on Earth depends solely on 'carrying capacity' (as measured in human passengers) and not on the technopolitical interventions of a steering elite. The latter would always be hobbled by human nature, anyway. The perennial problem with the spaceship, he argues, is the issue of good governance:

> A true spaceship would have to be under the control of a captain, since no ship could possibly survive if its course were determined by committee. Spaceship Earth certainly has no captain; the United Nations is merely a toothless tiger, with little power to enforce any policy upon its bickering members.[61]

The UN Stockholm Conference of the Environment in 1972 – the first 'Earth Summit' and a landmark event in the history of environmental politics – was the occasion through which the UN set the international institutional framework and standards for managing the 'whole Earth'. It comprised a suite of systems-based ecological paradigms, monitoring networks and scientific stewardship. In effect this meant computer-aided steering for Spaceship Earth. The data-driven agenda is encapsulated in the so-called 'doomsday report' commissioned in time for the conference, *The Limits to Growth: A Report for the Club of Rome's Project on the Predicament of Mankind* (1972), which brought to prominence the use of computer simulation using feedback-based 'world-models' as a mainstay of policy-making.[62] The systems dynamics WORLD3 model discussed in the report built on Jay Forrester's WORLD1 and WORLD2 published as *World Dynamics* (1971), and was based on his study of cities, *Urban Dynamics* (1969).[63] Forrester had scaled up his conception of the management of urban systems to offer computer-based techniques for governing Earth. WORLD3's attempts to visualise the 'predicament of mankind' via the entangled processes of pollution, world population, industrialisation, food production and resource depletion produced alarming graphs of an imminent catastrophe allied with the exponential growth of an unconstrained world. It projected visions of humanity locked into trajectories of worst-case scenarios and predicted that business-as-usual would breach planetary limits leading to 'a rather sudden and uncontrollable decline in both population and industrial capacity'.[64] Understanding the Earth as limited and vulnerable had justified calls for technological and economic restraint. The solution proposed was that humanity must 'begin a controlled, orderly transition from growth to global equilibrium'.[65] The WORLD3 model remained blind, however, to the cultural, social and political dimensions of global interdependency – indeed anything deemed irrelevant or inadmissible to the computer's calculations.

The French cultural theorist Paul Virilio commented on the Stockholm conference in his 1976 work *L'insecurité du territoire*, presenting it as part of the mechanisms deployed in the expansion of US economic systems after World War II under the guise of peace. Virilio advised that the 'coming together of the international experts, as in Stockholm, has, perforce, no meaning… the statistical curves can soar vertiginously toward the end of the planet, and after? Thought is dried up.'[66] Graphs such as those of the *Limits to Growth* report were emblematic of the deployment of a 'constant ascent of statistics toward planetary death'. In the same essay Virilio draws attention to, 'The exploitation of the malaise of man *vis-à-vis* his environment (maladjustment, new urban situation, pollution, insecurity, desocialisation, overpopulation, etc.)', whereby this malaise 'tends to replace the contempt for the milieu by the fear of it'.[67] What was at stake in Stockholm was the controlled management of life in that milieu. The figure of Spaceship Earth collapsed world crises into the operations of a complex machine.

To coincide with the UN Stockholm conference, Barbara Ward and René Dubos co-authored a book on environmental protection and efficient resource management: *Only One Earth: The Care and Maintenance of a Small Planet*. Like Fuller's work before it, it imagined the development of a technical reference manual that could guide humanity in 'accept[ing] responsibility for stewardship of the Earth'. Ward and Dubos introduced the idea of a planetary system and argued that: 'This techno-economic environment is as much a fact about planetary society as the air over the nations or the seas that wash their shores.'[68] The vision of Earth as a single, integrated system – the Apollo's-eye-view – merged with the 'one boat' motif of the 1972 UN conference to arrive at the conviction that all of humanity are confined to a common vessel, and share a common fate – sink or swim – within absolute limits.[69] In the last quarter of the century, it was becoming clear that the mission of human technological innovation was to sustain vulnerable lives in an inhospitable environment, thanks to properly functioning life-support systems – whether on Earth or in space. As expressed by Frank Borman, commander of the Apollo 8 mission:

> Of all the accomplishments of technology, perhaps the most significant one was the picture of the Earth over the lunar horizon. If nothing else, it should impress our fellow man with the absolute fact that our environment is bounded, that our resources are limited, and that our life-support system is a closed cycle. And, of course, when this space station Earth is viewed from 240,000 miles away, only its beauty, its minuteness, and its isolation in the blackness of space are apparent. A traveller from some far planet would not know that the size of its crew is already too large and threatening to expand, that the breathing system is rapidly becoming polluted, and that the water supply is in danger of contamination with everything from DDT to raw sewage. The only real recourse is for each of us to realise that the elements we have are not inexhaustible. We're all in the same spaceship.[70]

A striking reminder of human precariousness on Spaceship Earth had been the near-catastrophe of the Apollo 13 mission to the Moon in April 1970: 'Hey, we've got a problem here.' Following an explosion in an oxygen tank that severely damaged the *Odyssey* command module's electrical systems, the astronauts maintained air and water supplies through makeshift repairs, improvising with equipment, power and oxygen from the lunar landing module, *Aquarius*. Mission control in Houston devised a strategy to use the lunar module – which had an independent life-support apparatus – as a lifeboat. 'The story of the ill-fated mission is worth remembering and retelling' wrote the ecosystems ecologist Eugene Odum, 'for its relevance to our predicament here on "Spaceship Earth".' He continued, 'Our global life-support system that provides air, water, food, and power is being stressed by pollution, poor management, and population pressure. It is time to heed the early warning signs…'[71] Because the astronauts returned safely to Earth, despite failing to reach their goal and land on the Moon, the Apollo 13 mission has mostly been described as a 'successful failure'.

Spaceship Earth had become something of a watchword, for the metaphor drew attention to the dire consequences of failure and operator error on board any spaceship – especially when there was no manual, no crew and no lifeboats.

We still don't have a well-proven operating or survival manual for planet Earth. Nonetheless, geologist Richard Alley has recently claimed that 'science offers us an operators' manual. [And] if we approach Earth as if we have an Operators' Manual, we can avoid climate catastrophes, improve energy security, and make millions of good jobs.'[72] If only it were so simple. It is not possible to imagine a singular guide to best planetary practice. But if humanity cannot create a manual for coordinated stewardship of the Earth in time to avoid catastrophe, the question arises as to whether it might do better elsewhere.

In the 1972 film *Silent Running*, the space freighter *Valley Forge* carries a precious cargo of plants, housed within a large glass geodesic dome and tended by robots and an astronaut-botanist, Freeman Lowell.[73] Earth, we learn, is an endangered planet. Its plant life is extinct and it has become one massive city, its dense population sustained through artificially manufactured nutrients. The spaceship, its journey and its mission are a 'provisional solution'.[74] Its artificial environment compensates for a damaged Earth, its voyage is uncertain, and its cargo at risk. Ground control sends instructions to terminate the mission and destroy the domes on the fleet of freighters. Lowell rebels: he blows up the spaceship and jettisons the last biodome allowing it to drift precariously into space. The twinned ideas – 'Earth as vulnerable spaceship' and 'spaceship as surrogate Earth' – emerged simultaneously in the culture in the last quarter of the 20th century, as different responses to the same problem: the fragility of survival in an inhospitable environment. Those who favoured staying on Earth turned their thoughts toward ecology and resource management. But there were those who believed, and still believe, that the future of the human species depends on leaving Earth behind. In their view, humanity's efforts should be trained along this technologically intensive and highly speculative route – if only because it seemed a better bet than the degraded alternative.

Goodbye Earth!

> 'Is the surface of a planet really the right place for an expanding technological civilisation?'[75]

In 1969, the year of the Apollo 11 mission to the Moon, Gerard O'Neill, a physics professor at Princeton University, challenged his students with that question. In an interview with O'Neill for the *CoEvolution Quarterly*, Stewart Brand neatly summarises the episode:

> So, as I understand it, the question was asked, and the implied answer was, 'No, the planet's surface is not the right place.' And the implied next question is, 'Where, then?' And then the answer was inside-out planets.[76]

O'Neill had reasoned that humankind had the technical and scientific capability not only to explore space but to establish space colonies in the process. He took his inspiration from Tsiolkovsky's vision of 'cities in space'. Tsiolkovsky's *Beyond the Planet Earth* had speculated about 'mansion-conservatories' in geosynchronous orbit in space, a milieu awash with 'a thousand times more energy than the Earth… it only remains to fill it with dwellings, greenhouses – and people'.[77]

At the World Future Society convocation of 1975, O'Neill claimed that, through colonising space, 'we can not only benefit all humankind but also spare our threatened planet and permit its recovery from the ravages of the industrial revolution'.[78] O'Neill's *inside-out planets* were to be self-sustaining environments within cylinders generating their own gravity, constructed from materials mined from the Moon and asteroids, and with the potential to harness an unlimited supply of solar energy. Their purpose was two-fold: to relieve the Earth of the burden of overpopulation and resource scarcity, and to allow for the continued expansion of a technological civilisation predicated on unlimited economic and technological growth. As O'Neill explained, 'The steady-state society, ridden with rules and laws, proposed by the early workers on the limits of growth was, to me, abhorrent'.[79] According to O'Neill, space colonies could potentially house communities of up to a million like-minded people in an enclosed system of manufactured landscapes of mountains, lakes, rivers, forests, all populated by animals. This was an inverted astronomy that looked down on an artificial Earth within an inverted pretend planet. O'Neill's ideas eventually found patronage with Stewart Brand. Brand used the royalties from the *Whole Earth Catalog* for a research fund, the Point Foundation, and funded the conference on space colonisation at Princeton University in 1975.[80] O'Neill was also supported by NASA's Ames Research Centre for studies on 'space settlements' and 'space resources' in 1975 and 1977.'[81] At their request, he had judiciously avoided the term 'space colonies'. The NASA space settlements site states,

> These free-space settlements could be wonderful places to live; about the size of a California beach town and endowed with weightless recreation, fantastic views, freedom, elbow-room in spades, and great wealth.[82]

Issac Asimov was among those thinkers who championed space colonisation at the time. In 1974, he had written a short book warning of overpopulation and resource scarcity: *Earth Our Crowded Spaceship*.[83] In 1976 he reasoned, 'Colonies, whether they are on the Moon or in near space, would fulfil functions that are now fulfilled by cities on the surface of the Earth.'[84] And in a short essay, 'The Next Frontier?', based on the NASA Ames study on space settlements, he imagined what life would be like on Torus L-5 ('a world, but it's also a town of 10,000') for the 'hardworking pioneers' and 'alumni of Earth':

I wasn't very hungry but it seemed polite to have a frankfurter and milkshake. They were dispensed by token-operated machines. 'Did you like it?' asked Fenton. 'Oh, yes,' I said cautiously. (Good enough, but I was used to better on Earth.)[85]

In 1975 O'Neill had presented his ideas on space colonisation to the US House of Representatives Committee on Science and Technology, arriving with NASA-produced visualisations, a short film and a large model.[86] The Moon landing, he opined, should be considered a 'prospecting survey' for space colonisation rather than simply a scientific expedition. Space colonies, he argued, were essential to US economic and resource security because of their access to an 'inexhaustible source of energy'.[87] Humanity was poised on the 'threshold of a new frontier'. O'Neill insisted that the technological capability existed and it was only a matter of time before 'that frontier can be exploited for all of humanity, and its ultimate extent is a land area many thousands of times that of the entire Earth'.[88]

In *The High Frontier: Human Colonies in Space*, a book he wrote in 1976, O'Neill argues that colonising space could solve Earth's immediate energy crisis and relieve the planet's longer-term problem with overcrowding, while providing 'the opportunity for increased human options and diversity of development'.[89] O'Neill reasoned that colonisation of the new world had already brought humankind to the limits of the Earth and therefore the high frontier of space was the next logical place for expansion and exploration. His book ties the frontier myth essential to the American way of life to the biblical story of Noah's Ark. O'Neill's space colonies require a selective and smooth-functioning ecosystem, put together like 'Noah's passenger list, two by two… Perhaps, too, we can find less annoying scavengers than the housefly, and can take along the useful bees while leaving behind wasps and hornets.'[90] O'Neill's space habitats had a hand-picked guest list, free unlimited solar energy, a balmy climate and optimum farming conditions; all in an environment modelled on the 'prettier areas of Old Earth'.[91]

The High Frontier is interspersed with fictional letters from space, the diary accounts of Edward and Jennie, US space pioneers. The space passenger liners, the *Konstantin Tsiolkovsky* and the *Robert H. Goddard*, that carry them to the new colonies are named after space visionaries. Their first space community consists of 10,000 people on Bernal Alpha, a sphere 500 metres in diameter, with a Hawaiian climate and 'Canaveral time'. Plentiful supplies of fresh fruit and vegetables 'in season all the time' are grown in agricultural cylinders. Amid such abundance, only 'first-generation immigrants are likely to get 'island fever'. The space community has a 'vacation atmosphere', with 'flying people' and 'low-gravity swimming'.[92] In the final letter, Edward and Jennie describe their plans for a homesteading venture to an asteroid belt in a 'wagon train' of five specially kitted-out craft. The letter is written to their son Stephen, whose nursery on board the spacecraft will double as a storm shelter for protection from cosmic rays and solar flares during the eight-month journey.

> We've got food on board for two years, if we have to stretch it, lots of seeds, fish, chickens, pigs and turkeys. To get things started once we arrive, we've sunk about $50,000 in a stock of prefabricated spheres and cylinders, aluminised plastic for mirrors, chemicals for crop-growing, and a lot of equipment…[93]
>
> We've got a whole world to build here, Stephen, so grow up fast and get in on the construction![94]

O'Neill's imagination of space settlements is like Hardin's in that it imitates 'the American way of life' in its affluent suburban iteration – albeit with even more containment and enhanced control over the environment. O'Neill's imagining of the continuation of modern industrial civilisation in space habitats reveals its limitations – as idyllic as its creator intends it to be, it comes across as a sanitised and impoverished version of the lives left behind. Despite this, or perhaps because of it, the idea gained considerable purchase in the zeitgeist. In 1975, Stewart Brand presented O'Neill's ideas in an issue of *CoEvolution Quarterly*, a journalistic offshoot of the *Whole Earth Catalog* that took its title from Paul Ehrlich's coevolution thesis. In 1977, he published *Space Colonies*.[95] The book included the contents of previous *CoEvolution Quarterly* issues on space colonisation alongside readers' responses and further invited commentary from prominent public figures. Brand was excited about a new cultural conversation created around the questions of space colonisation:

> O'Neill's scheme invites you to give your imagination a space colony ... of one million inhabitants, each of whom has five acres of 'land' ... Have you any thoughts about how to organise its economy, politics, weather, land use, education, culture? Any thoughts about how to organise your life to get there?[96]

Among those promoting the idea of space colonies were Buckminster Fuller, Lynn Margulis, Carl Sagan, astronaut Rusty Schweickart and the architect Paolo Soleri. Among those resistant to or at least critical of the idea of space colonisation were Ken Kesey, Lewis Mumford, E.F. Schumacher, Dennis Meadows, the poet Wendell Berry and Garrett Hardin. For Paolo Soleri, founder of the experimental town of Arcosanti, who coined the term 'arcology' – a fusion of architecture and ecology,[97] space migration was an inevitable part of humanity's future. It was a way of bringing about his vision of densely populated ecologically low-impact human habitats. These cities in space or arcologies would be 'the best defence against the squalor of the lifeboat theory and the carrying capacity "miscalculations"':

> To this end there is no escaping the need for a more reverential, urbane, civilised sense of the human experiment and, ultimately, the need for the eschatological vision of a universe in the process of self-divinisation, the Urban Effect.[98]

John Todd, co-founder of the New Alchemy institute and co-designer of the Ark experimental bioshelter project on Prince Edward Island, Canada, offered the more pragmatic observation that ecological systems were difficult to replicate in closed environments and that current understanding of whole systems when compared to nature's complexity was 'primitive'. 'When I read of schemes to create living spaces from scratch upon which human lives will be dependent for the air they breathe, for extrinsic protection from pathogens and for biopurification of wastes and food cultures,' he wrote, 'I begin to visualise a titanic-like folly born of an engineering world view.' He went on to warn: 'In space there are no doors to open or neighbouring ecosystems to correct our mistakes.'[99] To Paul and Anne Ehrlich, it seems, lack of neighbours might have been part of the attraction; space colonisation offered to them the prospect of reducing population density on Earth so that 'it might even make war obsolete'.[100] Neo-Malthusian Garrett Hardin, however, had his doubts. His contribution recalls the problems he imagined on *Spaceship Beagle*, with its lifeboat model for selection and governance, and he concludes that the project of space colonisation was doomed to failure:

> The principal attraction of the space colony proposal is that it apparently permits us to escape the necessity of political control. But, as we have just seen, this is only an apparent escape. In fact, because of the super-vulnerability of the spaceship to sabotage by tribal action, the most rigid political control would have to be instituted from the outset in the selection of the inhabitants and in their governance thereafter.[101]

The San-Francisco architecture and media collective Ant Farm (founded by Chip Lord and Doug Michels) ridiculed the proposals for space colonies, with their 'Hawaiian climate in one [module] and New England in the other, with the usual traffic of surfboards and skis between them', comparing them to 'LSD fantasies of the late Sixties'.[102] John Holt reminded readers that artificial environments will in the final analysis be rather 'large containers floating in space'. The sales talk might promise luxury interiors, to rival cruise ships and Las Vegas lobbies, but they would more likely be 'like military barracks or troopships'; certainly they would be 'crowded'.[103] Steve Baer, alternative technology inventor, also recognised the less-than ideal environment of space frontier outposts, his imagination transported him to an entirely different experience:

> Once on board, in my mind's eye I don't see the landscape of Carmel-by-the-Sea as Gerard O'Neill suggests... Instead, I see acres of air-conditioned Greyhound bus interior, glinting, slightly greasy railings, old rivet heads needing paint – I don't hear the surf at Carmel and smell the ocean – I hear piped music and smell chewing gum. I anticipate a continuous vague low-key airplane fear.[104]

Lewis Mumford's letter of response was even more ascerbic:

> Dear Stewart Brand,
>
> If you were familiar with my analysis of 'The Pentagon of Power', you would know that I regard space colonies as another pathological manifestation of the culture that has spent all of its resources on expanding the nuclear means for exterminating the human race. Such proposals are only technological disguises for infantile fantasies.[105]

Wendell Berry, the poet and environmental activist, observed that the 'salesman' O'Neill 'faithfully utters every shibboleth of the cult of progress.' Moreover he thought O'Neill's ideas were at root conventional in their 'reliance on technical and economic criteria'. They were also sinisterly 'superbly attuned to the wishes of the corporation executives, bureaucrats, militarists, political operators, and scientific experts' – 'the chief beneficiaries of the forces that have produced our crisis'.[106] Berry recognised O'Neill as the inheritor of a 19th-century 'frontier mentality': one of 'spatial and mental boundlessness', the 'limitless[ness] of physical resources and human possibility', the 'breathless viewing of conjectural vistas' – and blind to the 'tragedy of that mentality'.[107] O'Neill's was an idea of 'moral bewilderment': in claiming concern for the Earth's environment he proposed 'a plan to strip-mine the Moon'.[108] E.F. Schumacher responded with sarcasm, 'Yes, Stewart, I'm all for it.' He continued: 'I am prepared to nominate, free of charge, at least 500 people for immediate emigration.' For each emigrant Schumacher was prepared 'to donate $1,000 for the furtherance of the work that really needs to be done; namely, the development of technologies by which ordinary, decent, hardworking, modest and all-too-often-abused people can improve their lot' – a job that would be made a great deal easier with his 'nominees' out of the way. He borrows a cautionary *post scriptum* from the ancient Chinese philosopher Lao Tzu:

> P.S. 'As for those who would take the whole world to tinker with as they see fit, I observe that they never succeed.'[109]

Hubristic tinkering with the whole world was, however, for Brand the entire point: 'If built, the fact of space colonies will be as momentous as the atomic bomb,' he enthused.[110] 'If we can learn to manage large complex ecosystems in the space colonies, that sophistication could help reverse our destructive practices on Earth.' Moreover, he was prepared for the experiment to fail:

> And if we fail, if our efforts to impersonate evolution in space repeatedly run amok, then we will have learnt something as basic as Darwin about our biosphere – that we cannot manage it, that it manages us, that we are in the care of wisdom beyond our knowing (true anyway).[111]

Brand had already anticipated that the outcome of efforts to manage ecosystems in space 'run amok' would be only to discover what was already known – that back on Earth, the biosphere could not be managed. But he felt it was worth trying. The biosphere of the Earth was the only known life-support system capable of self-maintenance and endurance. And Brand argued that it was imperative to know whether or not humans could leave, and live beyond, Earth – or if not, then learn to be more responsible. 'The success of space colonies', he argued, 'would bring needed whole-system sophistication.' And on the other hand, 'their failure would bring needed whole-system humility'.[112] Ultimately, however, Brand's countercultural ideals when channelled into technocratic fantasies 'were easily redirected toward cynical ends'.[113] Speculation on space settlements had established that there was little difference in the exploitation or colonisation of either planetary surfaces or interplanetary space. The bounded horizons of inside-out planets tended to invite not only a prospecting mentality and frontier expansionism but concomitant neoliberal techniques of power, politics and governance. O'Neill himself conceded that the first colonies would be 'more like a Texas-tower oil rig, or a construction camp on the Alaska pipeline, or like Virginia City, Nevada, in about the year 1875', rather than 'a utopian paradise or a laboratory for sociological experiments'.[114] Colonising a planet or homesteading on an asteroid might have the advantages of mineral resources on the doorstep, but in any case the habitable environments created would be little more than grounded spacecraft. Away from Earth, the life-support systems needed to keep a colony going would always be akin to those of a spaceship – whatever the scale of the enterprise. Before anyone could say, '*Goodbye Earth!*' it was clear a successful simulation needed to be achieved on *terra firma*.

Figure 5.5 Toroidal Colony, population: 10,000; construction along the Torus rim; 'Stanford Torus' based on the 1975 NASA Ames/Stanford University Summer Study (art work by Don Davis, 1975; NASA ID Number AC75-1886)
Source: NASA Ames Research Center

Biosphere 2

Why not build a spaceship like the one we've been travelling on?'[115]

Biosphere 2 was an experiment to recreate the Earth's biosphere in a great domed habitat. The Earth systems research facility was built in the Arizona desert between 1987 and 1991 by Space Biosphere Ventures.[116] It was the initiative of scientist and entrepreneur John P. Allen, and presented as a possible solution to the 'potentially debilitating conditions of an overburdened planet'. These included the 'burdens of population explosion, agricultural stress on the environment, technological paralysis, [and] mineral and fossil fuel depletion'.[117] Biosphere 2 was simultaneously a proxy space settlement and analogue for the Earth. It conceived of the natural environment as a life-support system that could be operated in direct analogy to a spaceship. In this sense, it was a literal embodiment of the Spaceship Earth idea.

Biosphere 2's designers took their cues from existing human-designed self-sufficient ecological systems like submarines, nuclear shelters, and space capsules.[118] In 1962 Russian scientist Yevgeny Shepelev had survived 24 hours in a metal container,

170 *Bounded planet*

Figure 5.6 Interior view, Toroidal Colony, population: 10,000; 'Stanford Torus' based on the 1975 NASA Ames/Stanford University Summer Study (art work by Don Davis 1975; NASA ID Number AC75-2621)
Source: NASA Ames Research Center

breathing only oxygen produced by 45 litres of *Chlorella* algae.[119] In the Bios-3 experiment in Krasnoyarsk, Siberia, in 1972, researchers survived for six months in an artificial ecosystem without the need for external inputs of water or oxygen.[120] Biosphere 2 was by far the most complicated of these artificial ecosystem experiments, aiming for a complex interdependence between humans, habitats, farming technologies, and nature. Its living laboratory was deliberately designed as an analogue for Biosphere 1 – the Earth.[121]

> In a sense, because of the accelerating and uncontrolled drive of humankind's technical development, Biosphere I has been the subject of large-scale, although always partial, human experiments with no *control* biosphere by which to assess the results. Biospheres II, III, IV...n... will be of inestimable value in understanding the operation of our present biosphere.[122]

Biosphere 2 was intended as a 'control biosphere' and also a rehearsal space for testing out ways to survive the 'Inevitable Doom of Biosphere 1'. John Allen and Mark Nelson anticipated a number of possible world-ending threats: increased radiation from a

Figure 5.7 Bernal Sphere Colony, population: 10,000; construction crew at work on the colony; the Bernal Sphere is a point design with a spherical living area (art work by Don Davis, 1976; NASA ID Number AC76-1288)

Source: NASA Ames Research Center

swelling Sun; catastrophic cosmic impacts from 'planetisimals, comets and meteors'; the consequences of the hostile use of technology, such as 'nuclear winter'; and/or increasing human impact 'on the grand cycles and mechanisms of the biosphere'. Biosphere 1's prospects were bleak: 'It is doomed to die within a small fraction of life of the cosmos unless it can birth offspring that can escape to other stars.'[123] Biosphere 2 was conceived as a space-age Noah's Ark, permanently escaping the crisis situation that had inspired its invention. As the children's book on the project, *Glass Ark*, put it: 'The day draws nearer when humans will be able to pack their bags, microbes, tissue cultures, and animal companions, and set out for the space frontier.'[124] Biosphere 2 was a space in which to gather together a representative, harmonious sample of the Earth's life forms, in anticipation of life after Earth. An Earth in miniature, with its mix of biospherics and astronautics, the project always explicitly aimed at rehearsing for space colonisation:

> ... biospherics opens up, together with astronautics, the ecotechnical possibilities, even the historic imperative, to expand Earthlife into the solar system and beyond that to the stars and then in time's good opportunity to the galaxies...[125]

Biosphere 2 was thus a 'prototype for a space colony' to settle 'sustainable communities' on Mars.[126] The terrestrial experiment was to 'provide both the first model and the data... that will allow the successful building and operation of the Mars settlement.'[127] But the ecological aspect of the project was not to be forgotten – rather, the two (apparently antithetical) goals of human potential – 'to serve as steward to the biosphere here on Earth, and to assist its spread and evolution through space' – would supposedly be equally furthered by the Biosphere 2 experiment.[128] Nevertheless, Biosphere 2's inventors very clearly had the Earth marked down as either a temporary way station or the grave of humans and our companion species: 'Biosphere I must disappear sooner or later unless it can participate in sending forth offspring biospheres to populate other regions of the cosmos.'[129]

Biosphere 2's mooring was a three-acre patch of desert, 30 km north of Tucson, Arizona, purchased for the purpose in 1984. The first test module and greenhouses were built in 1986 and the final complex was completed in 1991. The glass enclosure was transparent and airtight. Its steel 'spaceframes' were inspired by the geodesic structures of Buckminster Fuller and designed by one of his collaborators, Peter Pearce.[130] The whole construction was 'designed to last for a hundred-year period without major repairs, barring catastrophes' – a space industry standard.[131] As one commentator noted, Biosphere 2's 'striking edifice' simultaneously suggested 'visions of a NASA moon base, a countercultural commune, a Mesopotamian ziggurat, a climatronic greenhouse, a Mayan ruin and a sci-fi hideout.'[132]

On 26 September 1991, the eight Biospherians entered Biosphere 2 for the start of their two-year 'Mission 1'. Wearing specially designed jumpsuits and the focus of intense media attention, they looked just like astronauts walking to the launch pad. Passing through the airlock doors, they were sealed inside the glass enclosure, where every aspect of their life and environment would be monitored. In addition to the eight humans, Biosphere 2's 'spaceship' was inhabited by 3,800 carefully selected animal and plant species. It was organised into seven biomes: 'large-scale complexes of life communities, soils and climates in characteristic geographic positions' including a savannah, a mangrove-marsh, an ocean with coral reef, a tropical rainforest, a desert, an area of intensive agriculture and a 'micropolis', a miniature city for the eight Biospherians.

> The intensive agriculture biome musters a fish-rice-azolla aquaculture zone; a small goat, pig and chicken ranch; a tiny herb garden; a miniaturised fruit orchard; a legume and tuber plot; and a diverse grain farm in 18 fields. Rotating through three crops a year, this zone supposedly mimics subtropical regions with high humidity and temperate ranges from 65°F winter lows to 85°F summer highs. In fact, there is no direct analogue of this agricultural region anywhere in the world. Instead, the mix of foods represents the flow of products made available by global food commerce; this biome emulates, through intensive on-site production, what the average suburban consumer can feed on after extensive car trips to the supermarket in a US or European city.[133]

Here, then, was Earth in miniature – specifically, the Earth as experienced by its tourist-consumer 'first-class passengers'. As with the fictional exocolonial ships imagined by Hardin and O'Neill, Biosphere 2 was patterned on a life of suburban abundance that approximated the American dream. The aesthetic and cultural dimensions of the experiment cannot be overlooked. Although the complex required a vast infrastructure of machines, turbines, ventilators, pumps, cables, and monitoring and regulation systems in order to run, these were concealed beneath an Edenic surface – gleaming steel-framed curves of glass; miniature coral reef; graceful rows of fruit trees. If the presiding objective was really to maximise humanity's chances of living for a long time in a constructed environment, then clinging to the living standards, and even the aesthetic principles, of First-World Earth life might be conceived as an indulgence – or a dangerous distraction. As with the arms race, however, the non-lethal tech race was presented to the public as being as much about preserving a 'way of life' as it was about preserving life *tout court*. As Timothy Luke contends, in a world so exploited by the interests of 'transnational corporate capitalist society... the "environment" is becoming a Denature'. Biosphere 2 was imitating the 'space of surveillance, management and production which is now the Earth's biosphere'.[134]

The Biospherians had to be multi-taskers: they were to be 'their own plumbers, electricians and tailors' and had also 'been trained to be good observers and researchers, as well as competent farmers and computer users'.[135] If this sounded like a tall order, they were, unlike the inhabitants of Biosphere 1 and Spaceship Earth, at least provided with a 'rough draft of an operating manual.'[136] The manual was influenced by the new disciplines of 'biospherics', drawing on Vernadsky's 'biosphere' concept, Lovelock's Gaia theory, and its integrated counterpart 'biotechnics', directed toward the cybernetic construction of a technosphere that could 'stand in' for the geophysical and climatic functioning of the planet.[137] Although Biosphere 2 was presented as a 'closed system', information was allowed to come and go. In addition to the flow of data, the Biospherians were allowed to communicate with mission control, with their loved ones, and with a similar 'closed system' experiment taking place simultaneously in Antarctica. The Biospherians, interviewed after the fact, reported that only one thing in Biosphere 2 was more precious to them than the ability to communicate – the private bedrooms. Crucially, the complex was also supplied externally with energy. In a letter published in the 1996 issue of the journal *Nature*, Eugene P. Odum opined that, 'the most important result of the first Biosphere-2 experiment' was the

174 *Bounded planet*

information on the energy consumption costs of the artificial life-support systems. Their 'complex pumping and filtering machinery' demanded a great deal of electricity generated from non-renewable fossil fuel sources. Calculating at the then-average cost of 10 cents per kilowatt-hour for private electricity use, Odum pointed out:

> If the crew of eight people had to pay the utility bills at these residential rates, their monthly bill would be more than $150,000. At anywhere near this cost, very few of the billions of people on Earth could ever afford to live in domed cities.[138]

Biosphere 1 had taken billions of years to provide a habitat that worked for humans – was it at all reasonable to expect an artificially created techno-ecological-human system to work in just two? When the Biospherians emerged in 1993 after two years, 'They had orange skin from the high levels of beta-carotene in their diet. They had since become acclimated to oxygen levels that initially found them with symptoms of high-altitude sickness. And they hadn't carried cash in two years.'[139] The experiment had run into all sorts of trouble. Among the documented problems of the artificial environment of Biosphere 2 were harvest failures, food shortages, reduced oxygen, a decline in pollinating insects, loss of species, and a plague of ants. In effect, Biosphere 1 had had to bail out Biosphere 2.

The second Biosphere 2 experiment of 1994 was even more shortlived. Space Biosphere Ventures were facing significant money troubles and in 1993 the billionaire financier of the project, Ed Bass, hired Steve Bannon (appointed White House strategist in 2016) as CEO of Biosphere 2.[140] The project folded following disputes about financial management and the direction of research, and all closed system experimentation ceased. The complex reverted to a more conventional research facility and education centre. It has been owned since 2007 by the University of Arizona. But throughout its time as Biosphere 2, there was always the problem of the 'confused tangle of duplicities' – commercial, scientific, and political – within which it struggled to justify its existence:

> Organised as a scientific simulation of the Earth, it has operated mainly as another roadside attraction in the greater Tucson area leisure industry ... Supposedly designed to be a credible scientific project, it has mostly functioned as a media event and technoscience soap opera. Funded initially as a private venture capital exercise to the tune of $150 million, it openly survived by huckstering other products to the consuming public – science shows, motel facilities, restaurant meals, T-shirts — in order to keep its doors open.[141]

This was a 'Human Experiment' – to quote the titles of a couple of books on Biosphere 2 – in more ways than one.[142] Some of the most informative of the official findings of Biosphere 2 were with regards to it as an ICE (Isolated Confined Environment) experiment – in particular, the psychological effects of the confinement on the mission crew, the interpersonal relations that emerged, and the influence that these had on the completion of overall mission objectives.[143] This experiment in cabin ecology, which slipped more readily into cabin fever than the participants might have hoped, went on to inspire the reality TV show *Big Brother*. As Jane Poynter, one of the Biospherians, recalls, 'When things started going wrong, it wasn't because of the science, because of the technology, it was because the human relations broke down.'[144] In other words, just as in Garrett Hardin's *Spaceship Beagle*, the problem was the people. It would seem that higher-order social needs are neglected when survival itself is a struggle. Eugene P. Odum, who was present during the press interviews of the Biospherians, commented: 'As with the Apollo 13 flight to the Moon, survival becomes the mission when life-support is in question.'[145]

The Biosphere 2 experiment revealed that it was not possible for the biospheric environment to be self-controlled and human-controlled at the same time. In order for Biosphere 2 to test its function as a self-organising, self-regulating whole system, it would have required humans to have relinquished control and for the experiment to have run its course – possibly at the expense of its human inhabitants. Conversely, with humans attempting to manage every aspect of the environment, the biomes that had been planned as self-sufficient ecosystems quickly veered into imbalance. And so did the human relations. Ultimately, Biosphere 2 failed to establish itself as the model of post-terrestrial human survival. If it is unsuitable as a blueprint for the future, then it must be salvaged as a cautionary tale. As Donella Meadows commented in 1994 on the lesson from the Biosphere 2 experiment:

> Science and technology are welcome and wonderful, but they are not the answers to our problems. The more we focus on them, the more we avoid the real and crucial challenges before us – challenges of human relations, human communications, human organisation. It's not the planet that's out of control, it's us. It's not the biosphere we have to understand and manage. It's ourselves.[146]

Biosphere 2 had been created in response to a vision of a doomed Biosphere 1. As the Earth scientist Sabine Höhler notes, 'This modern ark was designed not only as a space of storage to wait out the ecological catastrophe, but also as a frontier vehicle that would transport the earthly habitat to formerly uninhabitable regions in the universe.'[147] Biosphere 2 was predicated on a view of Earth denigrated by rash experimentation that carried echoes of Revell and Suess's announcement in the 1950s of the 'large-scale geophysical experiment' carried out by human beings. The controlled experiment of Biosphere 2 – which re-cast Earth as something that could be managed and manoeuvred – had also anticipated Latour's observation of the 'worldwide lab'. Biosphere 2 was a miniature laboratory, a grounded 'Spaceship Earth'. In the Anthropocene, the Earth itself – already in the process of being anthropogenically re-engineered – has become one giant biospheric experiment.

Planetary boundaries

> Our planet's ability to provide an accommodating environment for humanity is being challenged by our own activities. The environment – our life-support system – is changing rapidly from the stable Holocene state of the last 12,000 years, during which we developed agriculture, villages, cities, and contemporary civilisations, to an unknown future state of significantly different conditions. One way to address this challenge is to determine 'safe boundaries' based on fundamental characteristics of our planet and to operate within them.[148]

The Anthropocene thesis has brought new prominence to the risk and actuality of transgressing safe planetary boundaries identified with a stable Holocene state of the

Earth system. The 'planetary boundaries' hypothesis, first proposed in 2009 by Johan Rockström and colleagues at the Stockholm Resilience Centre, and updated in 2015, has become an influential framework for discussing global environmental problems and solutions.[149] Following the convention established by the *Limits to Growth* report, planetary boundaries mark the precautionary limits for critical Earth system processes. With its foundation in complex systems theory, resilience thinking and ecological economics, 'planetary boundaries' identifies nine global biophysical limits to human development, which, if exceeded, could spell catastrophe for humans and for other life on Earth. These are: climate change; ocean acidification; stratospheric ozone depletion; biogeochemical nitrogen and phosphorus cycle levels; global freshwater use; land system change; biodiversity loss; chemical pollution; and atmospheric aerosol loading. Rockström *et al.* have estimated that humanity has already transgressed three planetary boundaries: for climate change, rate of biodiversity loss, and changes to the global nitrogen cycle. They further warn that transgressing these interdependent boundaries will have catastrophic consequences.[150]

Humans are accused of imperilling 'the safe operating space for humanity with respect to the Earth system' and implored not to overstep 'planetary boundaries' newly calibrated to maintain a 'desirable' Holocene-like state for as long as possible.[151] Rockström *et al.* argue that the environmental conditions of the Holocene are preferable to those of an unknown and potentially inhospitable future Anthropocene. The Holocene is the devil we know. It is, indeed, the *only* state that humans know – although it may now be starting to fray. According to its proponents, the value in the 'planetary boundaries' hypothesis is that it allows access to thinking about anthropogenic Earth systems change – a phenomenon whose underlying patterns are so complex that they are hard to observe, comprehend and respond to. While there is widespread intellectual awareness that Earth's systems are becoming dangerously unstable, things generally *appear* to be continuing in reasonably harmonious fashion – until suddenly, disastrously, they are not:

> There is little doubt… that the complexities of interconnected slow and fast processes and feedbacks in the Earth system provide humanity with a challenging paradox. On the one hand, these dynamics underpin the resilience that enables planet Earth to stay within a state conducive to human development. On the other hand, they lull us into a false sense of security because incremental change can lead to the unexpected crossing of thresholds that drive the Earth system, or significant sub-systems, abruptly into states deleterious or even catastrophic to human well-being. The concept of planetary boundaries provides a framework for humanity to operate within this paradox.[152]

The 'planetary boundaries' project follows a persistent line of thought that frames environmental crises as a management problem – how to maintain a limited and fragile Earth as an operable Biosphere. With its emphasis on a 'safe operating space for humanity', and its concerns over the 'carrying capacity' of the Earth, planetary boundaries thinking is related to Spaceship Earth thinking. Although more tentative in its language and in its conclusions than its 1960s and 1970s precedents, the planetary boundaries hypothesis has renewed discussions on appropriate stewardship of Earth systems in the 21st century. And, like the Spaceship Earth metaphor, planetary boundaries thinking reveals the same blurred lines between ideas of stewardship and operational procedures.

> Although we present evidence that three boundaries have been overstepped, there remain many gaps in our knowledge. We have tentatively quantified seven boundaries, but some of the figures are merely our first best guesses. Furthermore, because many of the boundaries are linked, exceeding one will have implications for others in ways that we do not as yet completely understand. There is also significant uncertainty over how long it takes to cause dangerous environmental change or to trigger other feedbacks that drastically reduce the Earth system, or important sub-systems, to return to safe levels.[153]

As a 'first best guess' the planetary boundaries hypothesis suggests 350 parts per million (ppm) as the safe planetary 'carrying capacity' for atmospheric carbon dioxide – the measureable parameter for the Earth system process of climate change. On 10 May 2013, the daily-average measured atmospheric concentration of carbon dioxide at the Earth Systems Research Laboratory, Mauna Loa Observatory, Hawaii was recorded as exceeding 400 ppm. At the start of the Industrial Revolution (and the proposed origins of the Anthropocene), atmospheric CO_2 was at 280 ppm. The last time CO_2 levels hit 400 ppm was in the Pliocene (between 2.6 and 5.3 million years ago), when the Earth was around four degrees hotter and the oceans up to 40 metres higher than at present. The only major national newspaper in the UK to carry the story on its front page was *The Independent* – the *Financial Times* reported on corrupt banking practices, while the *Daily Mail* covered the sale of drugs on Amazon.[154] The transgression of the symbolic ceiling of 400 ppm, long considered a figure of great jeopardy, came and went. One possible conclusion to draw from this is that cautionary tales of eco-catastrophe are in fact becoming less impactful the more frequent these disasters become – as if we were suffering, collectively, from a kind of catastrophe fatigue. If this is the case, it is important, because powerful interest groups invested in preserving the economic status quo – even at the expense of our planetary future – might be inclined to treat apparent public indifference as *carte blanche*.

The planetary boundaries framework raises important questions about relationships between the authority of scientific research, social meaning and political agency. It has been adopted as a key framework in the United Nations Global Sustainability deliberations, featuring prominently at the Planet Under Pressure conference in London, and also in the 'Welcome to the Anthropocene' opening of the UN Rio+20 Summit in 2012. There were criticisms of its effectiveness as a rallying point for coordinated climate action. In 2012, US environmental think tank the Breakthrough Institute cautioned against uncritical acceptance of the planetary boundaries framework. Its report pointed out the 'arbitrary nature of identifying non-threshold planetary boundaries and assigning them quantitative limits'.[155] They argued that six of the supposed planetary boundaries could not be considered global but only regional or local; and that there was no compelling evidence that transgressing these six 'non-threshold boundaries' would necessarily diminish human welfare.

The Breakthrough Institute's ecomodernist approach drew attention to the choices and ingenuity humans possess to both adapt to and change their surrounding environments, insisting that people can and must 'trade off' between alternative goals and courses of action. They warned that 'attempts to depoliticise [trade-off decisions]… with reference to scientific authority is dangerous, as it precludes democratic resolution of… [public] debates, and limits, rather than expands, the range of available choices and opportunities'.[156] This challenged Rockström et al.'s claims that planetary boundaries are 'non-negotiable' or that they can 'exist irrespective of peoples' preferences, values, or compromises based on political and socioeconomic feasibility'.[157] Instead, they suggested that the complex societal challenges of planetary stewardship mean that 'no global boundary can be meaningfully determined.'[158]

The notion of a 'safe and just space for humanity' has introduced a critique – or at least a substantial amendment – of the planetary boundaries thesis – rooted in human needs.[159] This has recognised the issue of global responsibilities in the face of resource constraints and has made explicit the link between environmental degradation and human deprivation. Adding social considerations to the planetary boundaries picture might help in achieving climate justice – the extension of equal rights to people of all regions, whose needs will be very different if climate change follows present projections – and greater equity in the distribution of global resources. The issue of planetary boundaries cannot be detached from a fraught international and domestic politics of growth incentives, competing economic interests, territorial rights, and global and regional obligations regarding pollution and the use of natural resources. So far, the planetary boundaries framework has provoked a concerted scientific effort to define global limits, as well as a call to action in line with UN Sustainable Development Goals.[160] But the corresponding thresholds and targets that might be needed for implementation at regional and local scales remain harder to define.

There is growing recognition of the need to develop and strengthen those frameworks capable of meeting the political challenges of maintaining Earth systems in socially desirable states.[161] Models for addressing this are proposed in such terms as 'planetary stewardship',[162] 'Earth system governmentality',[163] and 'global Earth system governance'.[164] Rockström is keen to promote the idea of planetary stewardship, or joint governance at the planetary scale, through research and policy collaborations such as the Earth League and Future Earth.[165] His vision is to 'launch an Apollo type endeavour – which starts now – of addressing exactly this integrated science for transition to global sustainability'.[166] Apollo – all-seeing, synoptic eye in space and symbol for American achievement – may or may not prove an apt mascot for the endeavour Rockström proposes. His account of historical precedents implies straightforward progress from 'growth without limits' via the 'limits to growth' agenda through to current paradigms of 'growth within limits'.[167] It assumes there are no limits to human ingenuity and innovation. In support of this vision, Steffen and his colleagues assert that: 'Effective planetary stewardship must be achieved quickly, as the momentum of the Anthropocene threatens to tip the complex Earth system out of the cyclic glacial-interglacial pattern during which *Homo sapiens* has evolved and developed.' As difficult as such stewardship may be to achieve, in its absence 'the Anthropocene threatens to become for humanity a one-way trip to an uncertain future in a new, but very different, state of the Earth System'.[168]

Planetary boundaries thinking, it is argued, is one of the perspectives needed to 'strengthen the universal relevance' of United Nations Sustainable Development Goals and help 'mobilise new agents of change such as businesses, cities, civil society'. 'Beyond cockpitism' is the motto here, which recognises that top-down steering by governments and intergovernmental organisations alone cannot address global problems.[169] To date, however, there is no successful model for coordinated Earth stewardship and no precedent for effective governance at a planetary scale. This is partly because doing so would require facing – more directly than the First World has yet proven comfortable with – the problem of the global wealth gap. As Mike Davis has pointed out, in the case of climate diplomacy, while a common interest is assumed, there are few examples in history for the kind of solidarity needed to deal with the 'dramatically unequal impacts' of climate change. These will continue to be most severe for the world's poorest and most vulnerable people. Also adopting spaceship terminology, but to challenge spaceship thinking, Davis argues, 'there is no planetary shortage of "carrying capacity" if we are willing to make democratic public space, rather than modular, private consumption, the engine of sustainable equality'.[170] And he is concerned about the abandonment of global mitigation in favour of selective adaptation:

> instead of galvanising heroic innovation and international cooperation, growing environmental and socio-economic turbulence may simply drive elite publics into more frenzied attempts to wall themselves off from the rest of humanity. Global mitigation, in this unexplored but not improbable scenario, would be tacitly abandoned – as, to some extent it already has been – in favour of accelerated investment in selective adaptation for Earth's first-class passengers. The goal would be the creation of green and gated oases of permanent affluence on an otherwise stricken planet.[171]

Davis warns of a return to the disturbing lifeboat ethics of the 1970s, promoted among others by Garrett Hardin and Paul Ehrlich, and revived more recently by James Lovelock.[172] In the absence of an 'operating manual' for a way of steering the Earth system back towards Holocene-like conditions, we may need to imagine ways to navigate a turbulent Anthropocene instead. These conditions may require new political thinking, as much as new technological thinking. Hardin argued that the problem was that a spaceship needs a captain – but it may be that no hypothetical autocrat, however competent, could do the job. After all, the planet is not a machine. Earth's systems cannot be controlled as if a maintenance engineer were to simply adjust a planetary thermostat, or as if a captain were able to set the ship on a pre-determined course to safety. Furthermore, not only are humans never really in control of Earth systems, there is an unevenness in their relationships with the Earth: they need it; it doesn't rely on them. As Nigel Clark contends, 'we are gifted into an atmosphere, a biosphere, a hydrosphere, a lithosphere – substrata on which we remain utterly and unilaterally dependent'. Furthermore, 'these pre-existing organisations of the elements retain a capacity to withdraw the support and substance they provide'.[173] While the Anthropocene brings with it renewed anxiety that the Earth has been forced into a state of disequilibrium and turbulence that only seems to be getting worse, it is important to acknowledge that this is nevertheless part of the ordinary workings of planetary existence, rather than a digression in the solar system. The continued inhabitation of humans on a surprising, indifferent, at times inhospitable Earth calls for an ethical and political framework that works beyond notions of planetary limits managed by benign husbandry, ingenious human agency or cybernetic stewardship. It also needs to acknowledge the radical asymmetry of the relationship between the frailty of human existence and the cosmic strangeness of the Earth.

Forward base

> Mars would also provide an excellent forward base for exploring and mining the asteroid belt, and developing whole new industries. A self-sustaining Mars colony would serve as a 'lifeboat' in the event of a global catastrophe on Earth. In coming centuries, our civilisation faces small but persistent threats from comet and asteroid impacts, world wars, global pandemics and climatic upheavals, any of which could wipe out all humanity. An outpost on Mars would keep the flame of human culture alight even in the worst-case scenario.[174]

A new generation of privately funded spaceships, arks and lifeboats is being planned by those intent on dispensing with planetary boundaries altogether and re-embarking for the *terra incognita* of outer space. Against a backdrop of 'persistent threats' to Earth, the ambitions of the private spaceflight industries, collectively known as NewSpace, conjure up the heroic eras of polar exploration and the push into the American West. Space Exploration Technologies (SpaceX), the inventor and entrepreneur Elon Musk's commercial rocket business, has a contract with NASA to ferry astronauts and cargo to the International Space Station (ISS). Their Dragon cargo capsule delivered the first experimental space farm chamber 'Veggie' to the ISS in April 2014.[175] SpaceX is also developing its own Mars transporter with a view to establishing a colony of 80,000 people on Mars.[176] Golden Spike has ambitions to send astronauts back to the Moon, while the Shackleton Energy Company plans to join it there for some lunar mining. Planetary Resources Inc's stated aim with its asteroid mining plans is to 'expand Earth's natural resource base', while B612's mission is to launch an infrared telescope that will be 'ever vigilant for dangerous asteroids hurtling toward Earth'.[177] Virgin Galactic has allied with Scaled Composites to build SpaceShipTwo, a passenger spaceplane to take tourists 70 miles above the Earth for short flights. The goal of increasing human presence in space features prominently in NewSpace discussions. Hence the obsession with Mars: the red planet is considered humanity's next outpost: it is relatively close, reasonably well-researched and deemed sufficiently Earth-like. The Mars One mission intends to finance its colonisation of Mars with a reality TV show following the first settlers.[178] NASA's partnerships with commercial enterprises mean it is also making preparations for 'pioneering Mars'. Its latest report, 'NASA's Journey to Mars: Pioneering next steps in Space Exploration', declares: 'Like the Apollo programme, we embark on this journey for all humanity. Unlike Apollo, we will be going to stay.'[179] Its plans for Mars colonies describe three stages: Earth Reliant, Proving Ground, and Earth Independent.

In the 2014 film *Interstellar* the astronaut character Cooper describes the human mission on Earth: humans are, 'explorers, pioneers, not caretakers'. Later in the film, the character Professor Brand announces, 'We're not meant to save the world. We're meant to leave it.'[180] With unbounded technological optimism, projects for establishing space colonies claim that they will mine the solar system to supply vital minerals and energy to our overtaxed planet, but also that the solutions they develop to sustain life off-planet will prove useful in supporting sustainable living on Earth. They are also presented as a means of developing technologies, plans and safeguards for inhabiting an increasingly unstable and dangerous Earth. However, in focusing 'beyond Earth', there is a danger that such projects are leaving the Earth behind in more ways than one. The real-life company Icarus Interstellar is busy designing 'a spaceship that would sustain human life in the event of global catastrophe'. This long-term project is dedicated to achieving interstellar flight by the year 2100, working to an aerospace industry thought experiment standard of 100 years.[181] They are also thinking way beyond the next three generations, and have set themselves the challenge of staying in space for a very long time: 'if there was to be some sort of apocalypse – some sort of nuclear war, some sort of flood, meteorite coming down to rain down on us – this would be our little lifeboat.'[182] The fully self-sustaining spacecraft will include a complex ecosystem, simulated gravity propulsion system, and a habitat for humans. Its component project, Persephone, concerns the design and engineering of a 'living' interior for 50–100 (highly skilled) people.

These mobile cities in space are being conceived from the ground up, literally: they depend on the development of synthetic soils, purpose grown for an unknown space environment. Persephone is imagined as an 'open' system that resists entropic decay and which may need to 'feed' on space 'junk', asteroids and the electromagnetic spectrum, so that the living system supporting the interstellar crew 'does not grind to an energetic halt'.[183] Persephone's developers claim the project is of direct relevance to the 21st-century challenges of coping with the growth of terrestrial megacities. Their infrastructures and technologies, it suggests, need to be adaptable and dynamic: 'the building industry, utilities and energy companies necessarily lag behind the physical demands of a growing city and where inflexible infrastructures become inadequate or inappropriate then urban decay sets in with crime, homelessness, waste and resource management issues, traffic congestion etc.'[184]

In a similar vein, the Lifeboat Foundation is currently developing programmes to prevent existential events ('shields') as well as programmes to preserve civilisation ('preservers'). One of these is the ARK I project, a space settlement for 1,000 inhabitants, powered by the Sun and auxiliary nuclear fission plants and consisting of four large wheels of 150m radius rotating at 2.4427 revolutions per minute to produce artificial gravity. ARK I plans are for initial orbit around the Earth at a height of 400 km. For sustenance, its inhabitants would rely on the re-supply of provisions from the Earth as well as ARK I's own greenhouse environment. The plan is that ARK I would eventually grow and move further away from Earth, harvesting bulk materials – metals, oxygen, hydrogen, silicon, and carbon – from the Moon or near-Earth objects such as asteroids along the way. With its marketing drawn almost word for word from NASA's space settlements website,[185] ARK I's adventure into the solar system promises weightless recreation, zero-g construction possibilities, custom living, reliable solar energy, and a great view:

> Space colonisation is, at its core, a real estate business. The value of real estate is determined by many things, including 'the view'. Any space settlement will have a magnificent view of the stars at night. Any settlement on the Moon or Mars will also have a view of unchanging, starkly beautiful, dead-as-a-doornail, rock-strewn surface. However, settlements in Earth orbit will have one of the most stunning views in our solar system – the living, ever-changing Earth.[186]

ARK I is promoted with no sense of irony as the 'ultimate gated community'. In a world of fraught class relations and geopolitical turbulence, it offers an air-tight solution: 'Those who can't get along can be separated by millions of miles of hard vacuum, which in some cases seems necessary. All entry into a space settlement must be through an airlock, so controlling immigration should be trivial.'[187] These planetary exit schemes might seem at best irrelevant, if not so disturbing when considering both the potentially vast resources and labour that would need to be deployed in their execution – diverting these things from pressing earthly matters in the process. Perhaps the best escape from a troubled world and its less illustrious inhabitants is offered by arch-parodists The Yes Men, with their 'SurvivaBalls'. Their modular outfits are wearable arks – a 'gated community for one'.[188]

All these 'forward base' projects have failed to address an obvious question: what happens to the rest of us – the majority of humanity who will be left behind on Earth? Will future generations be abandoned to degraded soils, flooded cities, giant rodents, meteorite showers, resource wars, deadly pandemics on an Earth in terminal decline? It is perhaps small consolation for the terrestrial 99 per cent that interstellar space flight and the elite exit route will not be viable for at least the next century. And that is just in terms of working out how to 'get there'. NASA claims, 'We are developing the capabilities to get there, land there and live there' – 'there' being Mars.[189] Earth has long been the testing ground for Mars missions with its proxy landscapes and analogue space cities, those of the Nevada desert or Antarctica's Dry Valleys. A critical aspect of NASA's Mars mission is not just to develop adequate life-support systems along with sustainable food supplements for its long-duration space pioneers but also the necessary 'countermeasures' for associated psychological risks. These include devising 'meaningful work', and modifications to space habitats to include space gardening – maintenance of 'a little piece of Earth'.[190] NASA's Hi-Seas (Hawaii Space Exploration Analog and Simulation) eight-month mission in a dome on top of Mauna Loa recently tested the use of VR environments to help combat the anticipated isolation of sojourning on Mars.[191] But other concerns that hinder interplanetary missions include the potential cross-contamination of Mars and Earth, and the changing planetary protection requirements of Special Regions that seek to manage a pristine Martian environment.[192] If the planetary protection measures instigated by the Outer Space Treaty are to be respected, it could mean that Mars is off-limits forever.[193] More immediate plans from the Inspiration Mars Foundation involve sending a middle-aged couple on a round trip to Mars, ingeniously insulated for the voyage by their provisions and excrement.[194] Even with the planets in optimal alignment, the voyage could take up to two years. Biosphere 2 'astronauts' Jane Poynter and Taber McCallum, with their two-year long experience of ICE, are possible candidates for the mission, currently scheduled for 2018, or failing that, 2021. Meanwhile, Valentina Tereshkova has stated that she is ready to make a one-way trip to Mars.[195] The rest of astronaut-humanity, however, is not going anywhere anytime soon. For our next century of space exploration, historian Stephen Pyne suggests learning from the previous century of experience in Antarctica – the *terra incognita* that already serves as an extraterrestrial Earth. He cautions:

> If, then, after a century of sustained contact, remote bases remain just that, remote bases, not preludes to mass migration and settlement; if social interest lies almost exclusively in scientific discovery and national prestige, not in a broad spectrum engagement with the culture; if such earthly sites demand endless and costly support, unable to grow food crops or even to extract freshwater from sea or ice without imports of oil; if left to their own devices residents sink into semi-hibernation and ritual rather than bustle and bubble over with new ideas; if we can

do no more than this with our own planet's polar regions, where we can actually breathe unaided, then why should we assume that a lunar base or an outpost on Mars should be different?[196]

The Earth ark

The original ark, Earth, does not move.[197]

Edmund Husserl described the primary experience of Earth as an ark – a primordial and foundational ground that is both sustaining and supporting. But the Earth does indeed move and, furthermore, the supportive ground has become destabilised by our deepening knowledge of human-induced environmental crisis. The ground humans have always relied on has been pulled literally and metaphorically from under our feet. If, in the Anthropocene, provisionality is now the new ground condition, this situation calls for both acknowledging the turbulence of the planetary ark and for preserving human solidarity in the face of convergent planetary crises. The Anthropocene is playing out as a planetary shipwreck – a disaster to end all disasters. If the Earth is a ship, it may already be sinking.

Figure 5.8 Apollo 1 astronaut pre-flight training, Ellington Air Force Base Houston, Texas (June 1966; NASA image: S66-51583)
Source: NASA Johnson Space Center

At the end of *The Natural Contract*, Michel Serres invokes the image of a sailor casting off – about to embark on a complex and entangled endeavour, buffeted by turbulent waters, on an uncertain voyage. The sailor's governance of a boat, he suggests, is about staying afloat in all weathers: not simply relying on maps, instruments and instructions, but paying attention to a changing world. For Serres, this means living on constant shipwreck alert:

> To cast off means that the boat and its sailors entrust themselves to their technologies and their social contract, for they leave the port fully armed, head to toe, with proud yards and boom aimed toward the future... I have no more gear on my craft... I have gone naked. Reduced to bare leftovers. I am even missing much of the indispensable baggage for living comfortably. I live in shipwreck alert. Always in dire straits, untied, lying to, ready to founder.[198]

For a model of the world, philosopher Peter Sloterdijk has also resorted to the boat – the biblical ark, and its updated form, the spaceship. And for Sloterdijk, the city is a 'landed ark', a 'survival ship' no longer an offering to the 'waters of catastrophe, instead anchoring itself obstinately on the Earth's surface'.[199] In Sloterdijk's 1993 essay, 'In the Same Boat', the allegorical model of 'being-in-the-same-boat' stands in for 'a cybernetical theory of the human *experimentum mundi*' – Ernst Bloch's term for a worldly construction site.[200] In his second volume of *Spheres*, Sloterdijk suggests that all ark narratives are characterised by selectivity: the chance of survival is offered only to those that have acquired one of the few boarding passes.[201] Noah's ark denotes both the 'ontology of enclosed space' and the essential site of selection and coevalness of post-flood creatures. The ark provides the only possible 'atmosphere' for its inhabitants, ensuring all of the requirements of a habitat that must preserve life, as against the jeopardy of the monstrous ocean. Moreover, the ship offers an ecological model for relating to the future, for it is always 'engaged with the prevailing winds'.[202]

Sloterdijk's bounded ark might be reconfigured as a Holocene world buffeted by the Anthropocene storm. In Sloterdijk's more recent engagement with Buckminster Fuller's notion of Spaceship Earth, on the occasion of COP 15, the spaceship replaces the ark or boat as the contemporary model for the planetary whole – a whole that binds humans and the Earth together in a complex symbiosis. While Fuller's astronauts journeyed for two million years 'not even knowing they were on board a ship', Sloterdijk points out that 'Human being-in-the-world... turns out actually to be being-on-board on a cosmic vehicle prone to faults'.[203] In what comes across as a reworking of Fuller's self-identification as 'Trim-Tab', Sloterdijk proposes anthropotechnics as a means of surviving a turbulent world: a transformation of the human condition through the cultivation of tech-driven alliances of networks, humans and non-humans.

When Mike Davis asks, 'Who will build the Ark?',[204] he suggests that we 'must start thinking like Noah'. Brought up to date, 21st-century Noah displays an improvisatory agency that involves practices, materials, technologies and desires that diverge from 'business as usual' constructions:

> Since most of history's giant trees have already been cut down, a new ark will have to be constructed out of materials that a desperate humanity finds at hand in insurgent communities, pirate technologies, bootlegged media, rebel science and forgotten utopias.[205]

For Davis, construction of the planetary ark is about salvaging goods from a planetary shipwreck. It is not about planetary-scale triage or even about expert management. It is about tackling the challenges facing the whole planet, rather than focusing on a few privileged countries or social groups. This also means resisting a future in which 'designers are just the hireling imagineers of elite alternative existences.'[206] Moreover, Davis observes, 'The city is our ark in which we might survive the environmental turmoil of the next century'.[207] His focus is on reconstructing the social and physical infrastructures of cities. For he contends that, in the future, it is the cities of the Anthropocene that will remain the 'ground zero of convergence' between the processes of disordering and inhabiting crises of human making.[208]

The Anthropocene may already be here. Even if returning to a benevolent Holocene were possible, there always remains the possibility for the world – as planet and as spaceship – to be periodically shaken by unpredictable cataclysm. As Bruno Latour frets: 'But who will answer if earthlings begin to panic and report: "Houston, we have a problem."'[209] The Earth has never been a safe place. In a renewed conception of the Earth as a shipwrecked ark or precarious spaceship – perhaps one that is already foundering – there is no obvious technical fix and, furthermore, there is no ground control. Steering such a Spaceship Earth through the Anthropocene presents an astronaut-humanity with a radically different state of affairs from anything it has faced before. An inverted astronomy on a bounded planet meets its own potential for cataclysm. The Earth is not an artefact that is manageable, nor is it a system that is controllable. Rebuilding the shipwrecked Earth ark is a project beyond mere technical know-how or technological stewardship – it is also a project of ethical imagination.

But who will rebuild the Earth ark? For the not-so-foreseeable future humans are stranded on Earth. And the Earth is far from ship-shape. Whether living on shipwreck alert or already living in the condition of shipwreck, the human is bound together with the non-human. Entry into the Anthropocene prompts renewed attention to earthly conditions and a keen awareness of a more-than-human agency that can fling humanity off-course. It is a jolt to a revived sense of humility or groundedness. It is also a cue to reimagining life on Earth 'beyond the confines of the Holocene'. That is, if we are going to bother rebuilding the ark at all.

Know your limits.

Notes

1 H.T. Odum, *Environment, Power and Society* (New York: Wiley Interscience, 1971): 11.
2 James Lovelock, *The Ages of Gaia* (New York: W.W. Norton & Co., 1988): 205.
3 A phrase used by Lynn Margulis and attributed to a student of hers, Gregory Hinkle. Lynn Margulis and Dorion Sagan, *Slanted Truths: Essays on Gaia, Symbiosis and Evolution* (New York: Copernicus, Springer-Verlag, 1997): xxii.
4 Denis Cosgrove, *Apollo's Eye: A Cartographic Genealogy of the Earth in the Western Imagination* (John Hopkins University Press, 2001): 2.
5 Kathryn Yusoff, 'Excess, catastrophe, and climate change', *Environment and Planning D: Society and Space* 27 (2009): 1010–1029; 1017.
6 Kathryn Yusoff, 'Excess, catastrophe, and climate change', *Environment and Planning D: Society and Space* 27 (2009): 1010–1029; 1017.
7 Oliver Morton, *The Planet Remade: How Geoengineering Could Change the World* (London: Granta, 2015): 77.
8 Sabine Höhler, *Spaceship Earth in the Environmental Age, 1960–1990* (London: Pickering & Chatto, 2015): 107.

186 Bounded planet

9 UN World Commission on Environment and Development: Our Common Future (1987); www.un-documents.net/ocf-01.htm
10 NASA Earth Observations (NEO); neo.sci.gsfc.nasa.gov/about/
11 Peter Sloterdijk, 1990; cf. Wolfgang Sachs, *Planet Dialectics: Explorations in Environment and Development* (London: Zed Books, 1999).
12 David Griggs *et al*, 'Sustainable development goals for people and planet', *Nature* 495 (21 March 2013): 305–307.
13 Konstantin Tsiolkovsky from a letter written in 1911; www.nasa.gov/audience/foreducators/rocketry/home/konstantin-tsiolkovsky.html.
14 Konstantin Tsiolkovsky, 'The aims of astronautics' (1929) in *The Call of the Cosmos*, trans. X. Danko, ed. V. Dutt (Moscow: Foreign Languages Publishing House, 1960): 333–372; 370.
15 Konstantin Tsiolkovsky, 'The aims of astronautics' (1929) in *The Call of the Cosmos*, trans. X. Danko, ed. V. Dutt (Moscow: Foreign Languages Publishing House, 1960): 333–372; 370–372.
16 Hannah Arendt, 'The conquest of space and the stature of man' (1963), *The New Atlantis* 18 (Autumn 2007): 43–55; www.thenewatlantis.com/docLib/TNA18-Arendt.pdf
17 Hannah Arendt, 'The conquest of space and the stature of man' (1963), *The New Atlantis* 18 (Autumn 2007): 43–55; 48; www.thenewatlantis.com/docLib/TNA18-Arendt.pdf
18 Hannah Arendt, 'The conquest of space and the stature of man' (1963), *The New Atlantis* 18 (Autumn 2007): 43–55; 49; www.thenewatlantis.com/docLib/TNA18-Arendt.pdf
19 '"Only a God can save ss": *Der Spiegel*'s interview with Martin Heidegger' (September 1966), trans. in Maria P. Alter and John D. Caputo, *Philosophy Today XX* (4/4) (1976): 267–285; also in Richard Wolin, *The Heidegger Controversy: A Critical Reader* (MIT Press, 1993): 91–115; 105–106.
20 Karsten Harries, 'Epilogue: astronautics and astronoetics', *Infinity and Perspective* (Cambridge MA: The MIT Press, 2001): 318–331; Harries quotes from Hans Blumenberg in *Die Vollzahligkeit der Sterne* (*The Full Complement of the Stars*) 2nd edition. (Frankfurt am Main: Suhrkamp, 1997).
21 Hans Blumenberg, cf. Karsten Harries, *Infinity and Perspective* (Cambridge MA: The MIT Press, 2001): 320.
22 Karsten Harries, *Infinity and Perspective* (Cambridge MA: The MIT Press, 2001): 325.
23 Kurt Vonnegut, 'Excelsior! We're going to the Moon! Excelsior!', *The New York Times Magazine* (13 July 1969): 9–11; reprinted in *Wampeters, Foma and Granfalloons (Opinions) (1974)* (New York: Dell, 1985): 77–89; 83.
24 Kurt Vonnegut, 'Excelsior! We're going to the Moon! Excelsior!', *The New York Times Magazine* (13 July 1969): 9–11; reprinted in *Wampeters, Foma and Granfalloons (Opinions) (1974)* (New York: Dell, 1985): 77–89; 80.
25 Kurt Vonnegut, 'Excelsior! We're going to the Moon! Excelsior!', *The New York Times Magazine* (13 July 1969): 9–11; reprinted in *Wampeters, Foma and Granfalloons (Opinions) (1974)* (New York: Dell, 1985): 77–89; 84.
26 Ian Sample and Juliette Garside, 'Some Virgin Galactic seatholders ask for refund on tickets after crash', *The Guardian* (5 November 2014); www.theguardian.com/science/2014/nov/05/virgin-galactic-seatholders-ask-for-refund-on-tickets
27 Michel Serres, *The Natural Contract* (Ann Arbor: University of Michigan Press, 1995): 122.
28 Richard Buckminster Fuller, *Operating Manual for Spaceship Earth* (1969) (Lars Müller Publishers, 2008): 55–56; emphasis in original. © 2008 The Estate of R. Buckminster Fuller.
29 R. Buckminster Fuller, *Your Private Sky - R. Buckminster Fuller: The Art of Design Science*, eds. Joachim Krausse and Claude Lichtenstein (Lars Müller Publishers, 1999): 11.
30 The concept of 'carrying capacity' is used by ecologists to define the maximum number of representatives of a given species that a habitat can support without permanently corrupting the environment and endangering the life of the species. It is closely linked to the notion of sustainable development and the discourse around ecological limits.
31 R. Buckminster Fuller, *Operating Manual for Spaceship Earth* (Lars Müller Publishers, 2008): 60. © 2008 The Estate of R. Buckminster Fuller.
32 R. Buckminster Fuller, *Operating Manual for Spaceship Earth* (Lars Müller Publishers 2008): 61. © 2008 The Estate of R. Buckminster Fuller.

33 R. Buckminster Fuller, *Operating Manual for Spaceship Earth* (Lars Müller Publishers, 2008): 22. © 2008 The Estate of R. Buckminster Fuller.
34 R. Buckminster Fuller, *Operating Manual for Spaceship Earth* (Lars Müller Publishers, 2008): 31. © 2008 The Estate of R. Buckminster Fuller.
35 R. Buckminster Fuller, *Your Private Sky - R. Buckminster Fuller: Discourse*, eds. Joachim Krausse and Claude Lichtenstein (Lars Müller Publishers, 2001): 18.
36 R. Buckminster Fuller, 'Introduction', *Operating Manual for Spaceship Earth* (Lars Müller Publishers, 2008): 11.
37 R. Buckminster Fuller, *Operating Manual for Spaceship Earth* (Lars Müller Publishers, 2008): 138. © 2008 The Estate of R. Buckminster Fuller.
38 R. Buckminster Fuller, *Nine Chains to the Moon* (1938) (Carbondale, Illinois: Southern Illinois University Press, 1963): 18–30.
39 R. Buckminster Fuller, *Operating Manual for Spaceship Earth* (Lars Müller Publishers, 2008): 130. © 2008 The Estate of R. Buckminster Fuller.
40 R. Buckminster Fuller, *Operating Manual for Spaceship Earth* (Lars Müller Publishers, 2008): 133. © 2008 The Estate of R. Buckminster Fuller.
41 'Factors of stress calculations of structure for New York City', 'Project Noah's Ark /2' (dated 22 August 1950); facsimile in R. Buckminster Fuller, *Your Private Sky - R. Buckminster Fuller: Discourse*, eds. Joachim Krausse and Claude Lichtenstein (Lars Müller Publishers, 2001): 177–225; 224–225.
42 'Noah's Ark/2 p. 176; Project Noah's Ark /2' (dated 22 August 1950); facsimile in R. Buckminster Fuller, *Your Private Sky - R. Buckminster Fuller: Discourse*, eds. Joachim Krausse and Claude Lichtenstein (Lars Müller Publishers, 2001): 177–225.
43 R. Buckminster Fuller, 'A citizen of the 21st century looks back' (1969) in *Utopia or Oblivion - The Prospects for Humanity* (Lars Müller Publishers, 2008): 33.
44 R. Buckminster Fuller, *Operating Manual for Spaceship Earth* (Lars Müller Publishers, 2008): 128. © 2008 The Estate of R. Buckminster Fuller.
45 R. Buckminster Fuller, *Operating Manual for Spaceship Earth* (Lars Müller Publishers, 2008): 128. © 2008 The Estate of R. Buckminster Fuller.
46 R. Buckminster Fuller, *Operating Manual for Spaceship Earth* (Lars Müller Publishers, 2008): 129. © 2008 The Estate of R. Buckminster Fuller.
47 Peder Anker, 'The ecological colonization of xpace', *Environmental History*, 10.2 (April 2005): 239–268; and Peder Anker, Chapter 6, 'The ecological colonization of space' in *From Bauhaus to Ecohouse: A History of Ecological Design* (Baton Rouge: Louisiana State University Press, 2010).
48 Kenneth E. Boulding, 'The economics of the coming Spaceship Earth' in *Environmental Quality in a Growing Economy*, Essays from the Sixth RFF Forum on Environmental Quality held in Washington DC, 8-9 March 1966, ed. Henry Jarrett (Baltimore: Johns Hopkins University Press, 1966).
49 Barbara Ward, *Spaceship Earth* (New York: Columbia University Press, 1966): 15.
50 Barbara Ward, *Spaceship Earth* (New York: Columbia University Press, 1966).
51 Adlai E. Stevenson, US ambassador to the United Nations, last major speech, to the Economic and Social Council of the United Nations, Geneva, Switzerland, 9 July 1965; *Adlai Stevenson of the United Nations*, eds. Albert Roland, Richard Wilson and Michael Rahill (1965): 224. Quoted in Garrett Hardin, *Exploring New Ethics for Survival: The Voyage of the Spaceship Beagle* (New York: The Viking Press, 1972): 17.
52 U Thant, cf. Felix Dodds, Michael Strauss and Maurice Strong, *Only One Earth: The Long Road via Rio to Sustainable Development* (London and New York: Routledge, 2012): 5.
53 Paul R. Ehrlich, *The Population Bomb* (1968; New York: Ballantine, 1969): 132.
54 Paul R. Ehrlich, *The Population Bomb* (1968; New York: Ballantine, 1969): 159.
55 Paul R. Ehrlich and Richard L. Harriman, 'Spaceship in trouble', *How to be a Survivor: A Plan to Save Spaceship Earth* (London: Ballantine Books, 1971): 2.
56 Paul R. Ehrlich and Richard L. Harriman, 'Spaceship in trouble', *How to be a Survivor: A Plan to Save Spaceship Earth* (London: Ballantine Books, 1971): 1.
57 Paul R. Ehrlich and Richard L. Harriman, *How to be a Survivor: A Plan to Save Spaceship Earth* (London: Ballantine Books Ltd., 1971): 58.

188 Bounded planet

58 Paul R. Ehrlich and Richard L. Harriman, *How to be a Survivor: A Plan to Save Spaceship Earth* (London: Ballantine Books, 1971): 67.
59 Garrett Hardin, *Exploring New Ethics for Survival: The Voyage of the Spaceship Beagle* (New York: The Viking Press, 1972): 92.
60 Garrett Hardin, 'Carrying capacity as an ethical concept', in *Lifeboat Ethics: The Moral Dilemmas of World Hunger*, eds. George Lucas Jr. et al. (New York: Harper & Row, 1976): 134.
61 Garrett Hardin, 'Lifeboat ethics: the case against helping the poor', *Psychology Today* 8.4 (September 1974): 38–43.
62 Donella H. Meadows et al., *The Limits to Growth: A Report for the Club of Rome's Project on the Predicament of Mankind* (New York: Universe Books, 1972).
63 Jay W. Forrester, *World Dynamics* (Cambridge, MA: Wright-Allen Press, 1971).
64 Donella H. Meadows et al., *The Limits to Growth* (New York: Signet, 1972): 29.
65 Donella H. Meadows et al., *The Limits to Growth* (New York: Signet, 1972): 188.
66 Paul Virilio, 'The suicidal state', in *The Virilio Reader*, trans. James Der Derian, Michael Degener and Lauren Osepchuk, ed. James Der Derian (Malden, MA: Blackwell, 1998): 42. Originally published in Paul Virilio, *L'insecurité du territorire* (1976; Paris: Galilée, 1993).
67 Paul Virilio, 'The suicidal state', in *The Virilio Reader*, trans. James Der Derian, Michael Degener and Lauren Osepchuk, ed. James Der Derian (Malden, MA: Blackwell, 1998): 41.
68 Barbara Ward and René Dubos, *Only One Earth: the Care and Maintenance of a Small Planet* (Middlesex: Penguin Books Ltd, 1972): 261.
69 Sabine Höhler, '"The real problem of a spaceship is its people" Spaceship Earth as ecological science fiction' in *Green Planets: Ecology and Science Fiction*, eds. Gerry Canavan and Kim Stanley Robinson (Middletown, CT: Wesleyan University Press, 2014): 99–114.
70 Frank Borman, cf. David Oates, *Earth Rising: Ecological Belief in an Age of Science* (Corvallis, OR: Oregon State University Press, 1989): 12.
71 Eugene.P. Odum, 'Prologue: The flight of Apollo 13', *Ecology and our Endangered Life-support Systems* (Sundarland, MA: Sinauer Associates, 1989): 1.
72 earththeoperatorsmanual.com/about_the_program#sthash.pJV1h4bu.dpuf
73 *Silent Running*, directed by Douglas Trumbull (Universal, 1972).
74 Sabine Höhler, *Spaceship Earth in the Environmental Age, 1960–1990* (London: Pickering & Chatto, 2015): 28.
75 Gerard O'Neill cf. Stewart Brand '"Is the surface of a planet really the right place for an expanding technological civilization?" Interviewing Gerard O'Neill' in *Space Colonies, A Co-Evolution Book Published by the Whole Earth Catalog with Penguin Books*, ed. Stewart Brand (1977): 22–30; 22.
76 Stewart Brand '"Is the surface of a planet really the right place for an expanding technological civilization?" Interviewing Gerard O'Neill' in *Space Colonies, A Co-Evolution Book Published by the Whole Earth Catalog with Penguin Books*, ed. Stewart Brand (1977): 22–30; 22.
77 Konstantin Tsiolkovsky, *Beyond The Planet Earth*, cf. Gerard K. O'Neill, *The High Frontier: Human Colonies in Space* (London: Jonathan Cape, 1977): 60.
78 Gerard K. O'Neill, 'The high frontier' in *Space Colonies, A Co-Evolution Book Published by the Whole Earth Catalog with Penguin Books*, ed. Stewart Brand (1977): 8–11; 8.
79 Gerard K. O'Neill, *The High Frontier: Human Colonies in Space* (London: Jonathan Cape, 1977): 236.
80 For the conference proceedings see Gerard K. O'Neill, A-III. The Colonization of Space, Appendix A, Proceedings of the Princeton Conference on the Colonization of Space, May 10, 1974, in Space Manufacturing Facilities (Space Colonies), Proceedings of the Princeton/AIAA/NASA Conference May 7–9, 1975 and the Princeton Conference on the Colonization of Space, May 10, 1974, ed. Jerry Grey (New York: American Institute of Aeronautics and Astronautics, Inc., 1977); www.nss.org/settlement/manufacturing/spacemanufacturing01.htm
81 The term 'space colony' was officially abjured by the US State Department because of its associations with earthly colonisations. For the NASA Ames Research Centre studies see 'Space Settlements - A Design Study' (1975) settlement.arc.nasa.gov/75SummerStudy/Design.html; and 'Space Resources and Space Settlements' (1977); settlement.arc.nasa.gov/spaceres/index.html

Bounded planet 189

82 NASA, 'Space Settlements: spreading life through the solar system'; settlement.arc.nasa.gov
83 Isaac Asimov, *Earth: Our Crowded Spaceship* (Greenwich, CT: Fawcett Publications, 1974).
84 Isaac Asimov in 'Five noted thinkers explore the future', *National Geographic* 150.1 (July 1976): 68–74; 73.
85 Isaac Asimov, 'The next frontier?' *National Geographic* 150.1 (July 1976): 76–89; 83.
86 Gerard K. O'Neill, 'Space Colonization and Energy Supply to the Earth. Testimony of Dr. Gerard K. O'Neill, Professor of Physics, Princeton University, Princeton New Jersey Before the Sub-Committee on Space Science and Applications of the Committee on Science and Technology United States House of Representatives. July 23, 1975'; settlement.arc.nasa.gov/ONeill1975Testimony.pdf; A shorter version of the testimony was included in *Space Colonies, A Co-Evolution Book Published by the Whole Earth Catalog with Penguin Books*, ed. Stewart Brand (1977): 12–21. The artists who provided the visualisations were Donald Davis and Frank Guidice from the NASA-Ames laboratory.
87 Gerard K. O'Neill, 'Testimony'; 168; settlement.arc.nasa.gov/ONeill1975Testimony.pdf
88 Gerard K. O'Neill, 'The high frontier' in *Space Colonies, A Co-Evolution Book Published by the Whole Earth Catalog with Penguin Books*, ed. Stewart Brand (1977): 8–11; 8.
89 Gerard K. O'Neill, *The High Frontier: Human Colonies in Space* (London: Jonathan Cape Ltd, 1977): 19.
90 Gerard K. O'Neill, *The High Frontier: Human Colonies in Space* (London: Jonathan Cape Ltd, 1977): 49.
91 Gerard K. O'Neill, *The High Frontier: Human Colonies in Space* (London: Jonathan Cape Ltd, 1977): 5–51; 99.
92 Gerard K. O'Neill, *The High Frontier: Human Colonies in Space* (London: Jonathan Cape Ltd, 1977): 177–184.
93 Gerard K. O'Neill, *The High Frontier: Human Colonies in Space* (London: Jonathan Cape Ltd, 1977): 204.
94 Gerard K. O'Neill, *The High Frontier: Human Colonies in Space* (London: Jonathan Cape Ltd, 1977): 207.
95 *Space Colonies, A Co-Evolution Book Published by the Whole Earth Catalog with Penguin Books*, ed. Stewart Brand (1977).
96 Stewart Brand in *Space Colonies, A Co-Evolution Book Published by the Whole Earth Catalog with Penguin Books*, ed. Stewart Brand (1977): 5.
97 Paolo Soleri, *Arcology: The City in the Image of Man* (Cambridge, MA: MIT Press, 1974).
98 Paolo Soleri in *Space Colonies, A Co-Evolution Book Published by the Whole Earth Catalog with Penguin Books*, ed. Stewart Brand (1977): 56–60; 60.
99 John Todd in *Space Colonies, A Co-Evolution Book Published by the Whole Earth Catalog with Penguin Books*, ed. Stewart Brand (1977): 48–49.
100 Paul and Anne Ehrlich in *Space Colonies, A Co-Evolution Book Published by the Whole Earth Catalog with Penguin Books*, ed. Stewart Brand (1977): 43.
101 Garrett Hardin in *Space Colonies, A Co-Evolution Book Published by the Whole Earth Catalog with Penguin Books*, ed. Stewart Brand (1977): 54.
102 Ant Farm in *Space Colonies, A Co-Evolution Book Published by the Whole Earth Catalog with Penguin Books*, ed. Stewart Brand (1977): 47.
103 John Holt in *Space Colonies, A Co-Evolution Book Published by the Whole Earth Catalog with Penguin Books*, ed. Stewart Brand (1977): 62–68; 64.
104 Steve Baer in *Space Colonies, A Co-Evolution Book Published by the Whole Earth Catalog with Penguin Books*, ed. Stewart Brand (1977): 40.
105 Lewis Mumford in *Space Colonies, A Co-Evolution Book Published by the Whole Earth Catalog with Penguin Books*, ed. Stewart Brand (1977): 34.
106 Wendell Berry in *Space Colonies, A Co-Evolution Book Published by the Whole Earth Catalog with Penguin Books*, ed. Stewart Brand (1977): 36–37; 36.
107 Wendell Berry in *Space Colonies, A Co-Evolution Book Published by the Whole Earth Catalog with Penguin Books*, ed. Stewart Brand (1977): 36–37; 36.
108 Wendell Berry in *Space Colonies, A Co-Evolution Book Published by the Whole Earth Catalog with Penguin Books*, ed. Stewart Brand (1977): 36–37; 37.

190 Bounded planet

109 E.F. Schumacher in *Space Colonies, A Co-Evolution Book Published by the Whole Earth Catalog with Penguin Books*, ed. Stewart Brand (1977): 38.
110 Stewart Brand in *Space Colonies, A Co-Evolution Book Published by the Whole Earth Catalog with Penguin Books*, ed. Stewart Brand (1977): 72.
111 Stewart Brand in *Space Colonies, A Co-Evolution Book Published by the Whole Earth Catalog with Penguin Books*, ed. Stewart Brand (1977): 72.
112 Stewart Brand in *Space Colonies, A Co-Evolution Book Published by the Whole Earth Catalog with Penguin Books*, ed. Stewart Brand (1977): 72.
113 Felicity D. Scott, 'Securing adjustable cimate' in *Climates: Architecture and the Planetary Imaginary*, ed. James Graham (Zurich: Lars Müller Publishers, 2016): 90–105; 102.
114 Gerard O'Neill in *Space Colonies, A Co-Evolution Book Published by the Whole Earth Catalog with Penguin Books*, ed. Stewart Brand (1977): 70. The editorial note explains that the text is derived 'from Dr. O'Neill's remarks before the Senate Subcommittee on Aerospace Technology and National Needs on Jan 19, 1977, and his keynote address at the annual national convention of the American Institute of Aeronautics and Astronautics in Washington D.C. on Jan 30, 1976'.
115 Architect Phil Hawes as quoted by John Allen, *Biosphere 2: The Human Experiment* (New York: Penguin Books, 1991): 16.
116 See Biospherics, 'Chronology of Biosphere 2'; www.biospherics.org/biosphere2/chronology/
117 John Allen, *Biosphere 2: The Human Experiment* (New York: Penguin Books, 1991): 147.
118 Peder Anker, 'The ecological colonization of space', *Environmental History* 10.2 (April 2005): 239–268.
119 Christian Schwägerl, *The Anthropocene: The Human Era and How it Shapes Our Planet*, trans. Lucy Renner Jones (Santa Fe & London: Synergetic Press, 2014): 16–17.
120 Frank B. Salisbury *et al.*, 'Bios-3: Siberian experiments in bioregenerative life support', *BioScience* 47 (1997): 575–585.
121 Sabine Höhler, 'The environment as a life support system: The case of Biosphere 2', *History and Technology* 26.1 (2010): 39–58; Sabine Höhler, '"Spaceship Earth": envisioning human habitats in the environmental age', *GHI Bulletin* 42 (2008): 65–85.
122 John Allen and Mark Nelson, *Space Biospheres* (Oracle, AZ: Synergetic Press, 1989): 53.
123 John Allen and Mark Nelson, *Space Biospheres* (Oracle, AZ: Synergetic Press, 1989): 40.
124 Linea Gentry and Karen Liptak, *The Glass Ark: The Story of Biosphere 2* (New York: Viking, 1991): 82.
125 John Allen and Mark Nelson, *Space Biospheres* (Oracle, AZ: Synergetic Press, 1989): 1.
126 John Allen, *Biosphere 2: The Human Experiment* (New York: Penguin Books, 1991): 1; 59.
127 John Allen and Mark Nelson, *Space Biospheres* (Oracle, AZ: Synergetic Press, 1989): 75.
128 John Allen and Mark Nelson, *Space Biospheres* (Oracle, AZ: Synergetic Press, 1989): 52.
129 John Allen and Mark Nelson, *Space Biospheres* (Oracle, AZ: Synergetic Press, 1989): 52.
130 John Allen, Chapter 5: 'Technics', *Biosphere 2: The Human Experiment* (New York: Penguin Books, 1991): 59–68.
131 John Allen and Mark Nelson, *Space Biospheres* (Oracle, AZ: Synergetic Press, 1989): 64.
132 Timothy W. Luke, 'Reproducing Planet Earth? The hubris of Biosphere 2' in *The Ecologist* 25.4 (July/August 1995): 157–162; 157.
133 Timothy W. Luke, Reproducing Planet Earth? The hubris of Biosphere 2' in *The Ecologist* 25.4 (July/August 1995): 157–162; 159.
134 Timothy W. Luke, Reproducing Planet Earth? The hubris of Biosphere 2' in *The Ecologist* 25.4 (July/August 1995): 157–162; 161.
135 John Allen, *Biosphere 2: The Human Experiment* (New York: Penguin Books, 1991): 69–70.
136 John Allen, *Biosphere 2: The Human Experiment* (New York: Penguin Books, 1991): 115.
137 John Allen, *Biosphere 2: The Human Experiment* (New York: Penguin Books, 1991): 115.
138 E.P. Odum, 'Cost of living in domed cities', 'Correspondence', *Nature*, 382 (1996): 18.
139 Nicholas Johnson, Big Dead Place, 'Embracing the experiment: Interview with Abigail Alling of Biosphere 2'; www.bigdeadplace.com/stories-and-interviews/embracing-the-experiment-interview-with-abigail-alling-of-biosphere-2/; accessed 4 September

2013; cf. Mike Hulme, *Can Science Fix Climate Change?* (Cambridge: Polity Press, 2014): 90.
140 Samantha Cole, 'The Strange History of Steve Bannon and the Biosphere 2 Experiment', Motherboard (15 November 2016); motherboard.vice.com/en_us/article/the-strange-history-of-steve-bannon-and-the-biosphere-2-experiment
141 Timothy W. Luke, 'Reproducing Planet Earth? The hubris of Biosphere 2' in *The Ecologist* 25. 4 (July/August 1995): 157–162; 162.
142 John Allen, *Biosphere 2: The Human Experiment* (New York: Penguin Books, 1991); Jayne Poynter, *The Human Experiment: Two Years and Twenty Minutes Inside Biosphere 2* (New York: Basic Books, 2009).
143 See *Biosphere 2 Research Past and Present*, Ecological Engineering Special Issue, 13. 1–4, eds. B.D.V. Marino, H.T. Odum (Elsevier Science, 1999).
144 Jane Poynter, 'Biosphere 2: The experience of being' in *Cosmograms*, eds. Melik Ohanian and Jean-Christophe Royoux (New York: Lukas & Sternberg, 2005): 241–248; 247. Jayne Poynter runs Paragon Space Development Corporation together with her husband Taber McCallum, also a former Biospherian.
145 E.P. Odum, 'Cost of living in domed cities', Correspondence', *Nature* 382 (1996): 18.
146 Donella Meadows, 'Biosphere 2 teaches us another lesson' (23 June 1994); donellameadows.org/archives/biosphere-2-teaches-us-another-lesson/
147 Sabine Höhler, *Spaceship Earth in the Environmental Age, 1960–1990* (London: Pickering & Chatto, 2015): 107.
148 W. Steffen, J. Rockström and R. Costanza, 'How defining planetary boundaries can transform our approach to growth', *Solutions* 2.3 (May 2011) 59–65.
149 J. Rockström *et al.*, 'A safe operating space for humanity', *Nature* 461 (24 September 2009): 472–475; and Will Steffen *et al.*, 'Planetary boundaries: Guiding human development on a changing planet', *Science* 347. 6223 (13 February 2015).
150 J. Rockström *et al.*, 'A safe operating space for humanity', *Nature* 461 (24 September 2009): 472–475.
151 J. Rockström *et al.*, 'A safe operating space for humanity', *Nature* 461 (24 September 2009): 472–475.
152 J. Rockström *et al.*, 'Planetary boundaries: Exploring the safe operating space for humanity', *Ecology and Society* 14.2 (2009): 32–64; 55; www.ecologyandsociety.org/vol14/iss2/art32
153 J. Rockström *et al.*, 'A safe operating space for humanity', *Nature* 461 (24 September 2009): 472–475; 475.
154 Andrew Simms, 'Why did the 400ppm carbon milestone cause barely a ripple?', *The Guardian* (30 May 2013); www.theguardian.com/environment/blog/2013/may/30/carbon-milestone-newspapers
155 T. Nordhaus, M. Schellenberger and L. Blomqvist, *The Planetary Boundaries Hypothesis: A Review of the Evidence* (Washington DC: Breakthrough Institute, 2012): 4.
156 T. Nordhaus, M. Schellenberger and L. Blomqvist, *The Planetary Boundaries Hypothesis: A Review of the Evidence* (Washington DC: Breakthrough Institute, 2012): 37.
157 J. Rockström *et al.*, 'Planetary boundaries: Exploring the safe operating space for humanity', *Ecology and Society* 14.2 (2009): 32–64; 35–36; www.ecologyandsociety.org/vol14/iss2/art32
158 T. Nordhaus, M. Schellenberger and L. Blomqvist, *The Planetary Boundaries Hypothesis: A Review of the Evidence* (Washington DC: Breakthrough Institute, 2012): 5.
159 Kate Raworth, *Planetary and Social Boundaries: Defining a Safe and Just Operating Space for Humanity* (Oxford: Oxfam, 2012).
160 Planetary Boundaries Initiative, 'Sustainable Development Goals Put Planetary Boundaries on the Agenda' (9 October 2015); planetaryboundariesinitiative.org/2015/10/09/sustainable-development-goals-put-planetary-boundaries-on-the-worlds-agenda/
161 Nigel Clark, 'Geo-politics and the disaster of the Anthropocene' in *Disasters and Politics: Materials, Experiments, Preparedness*, eds. Manuel Tironi, Israel Rodríguez-Giralt and Michael Guggenheim (Chichester: John Wiley & Sons, 2014): 19–37.
162 Will Steffen *et al.*, 'The Anthropocene: From global change to planetary stewardship', *Ambio* 40.7 (November 2011): 739–761.

163 E. Lövbrand, J. Stripple and B. Wiman, 'Earth system governmentality: reflections on science in the Anthropocene', *Global Environmental Change* 19 (2009): 7–13.
164 J. Dryzek and H. Stevenson, 'Global democracy and Earth system governance', *Ecological Economics* 70 (2011): 1865–1874; 1873.
165 Future Earth, 'Future Earth launches eight initiatives to accelerate global sustainable development' (6 August 2014); www.futureearth.info/news/future-earth-launches-eight-initiatives-accelerate-global-sustainable-development
166 Johan Rockström, 'Earth Stewardship for World Prosperity', official launch of the Earth League and Inaugural Lecture by Professor Johan Rockström, Stockholm Resilience Centre – hosted by the Grantham Institute for Climate Change, Imperial College, London (7 February 2013); www.youtube.com/watch?v=6mtaSqXVzWE
167 Johan Rockström, 'Earth Stewardship for World Prosperity', official launch of the Earth League and Inaugural Lecture by Professor Johan Rockström, Stockholm Resilience Centre – hosted by the Grantham Institute for Climate Change, Imperial College, London (7 February 2013); www.youtube.com/watch?v=6mtaSqXVzWE
168 Will Steffen *et al.* 'The Anthropocene: From global change to planetary stewardship', *Ambio* 40.7 (November 2011): 739–761.
169 Maarten Hajer, Måns Nilsson, Kate Raworth, Peter Bakker, Frans Berkhout, Yvo de Boer, Johan Rockström, Kathrin Ludwig and Marcel Kok, 'Beyond cockpit-ism: four insights to enhance the transformative potential of the sustainable development goals', *Sustainability* 7 (2015): 1651–1660; www.mdpi.com/2071-1050/7/2/1651
170 Mike Davis, 'Who will build the ark?', *New Left Review* 61 (Jan–Feb 2010): 29–45; newleftreview.org/II/61/mike-davis-who-will-build-the-ark; accessed 20 July 2011.
171 Mike Davis, 'Who will build the ark?', *New Left Review* 61 (Jan–Feb 2010): 29–45; newleftreview.org/II/61/mike-davis-who-will-build-the-ark; accessed 20 July 2011.
172 Garrett Hardin, 'Lifeboat ethics: The case against helping the poor', *Psychology Today* 8 (1974); Garrett Hardin, 'Living on a Lifeboat', *BioScience* 24 (1974): 561–568.
173 Nigel Clark, *Inhuman Nature: Sociable Life on a Dynamic Planet* (London: Sage, 2011): 52.
174 Paul Davies, 'Fly me to Mars. One-way. NASA's given up. But there is no shortage of scientists eager to take the next giant leap: a no-return mission to Mars', *The Guardian* (15 September 2009); www.theguardian.com/commentisfree/2009/sep/15/space-mars-martian-astronaut
175 Robert Pearlman, 'Astronauts snack on space-grown lettuce for first time', Space.com (10 August 2015); www.space.com/30209-astronauts-eat-space-lettuce.html
176 Rory Carroll, 'Elon Musk's missions to Mars', *The Guardian* (17 July 2013); www.theguardian.com/technology/2013/jul/17/elon-musk-mission-mars-spacex
177 Adam Mann, 'The year's most audacious private space exploration plans', Wired (27 December 2012); www.wired.com/2012/12/audacious-space-companies-2012/?pid=5748#slideid-5748
178 Mars One, 'Human Settlement on Mars'; www.mars-one.com
179 National Aeronautics and Space Administration, 'NASA's Journey to Mars: Pioneering Next Steps in Space Exploration' (Washington DC: NASA, October 2015): 21; 'A Home Away from Home: Deep Space Habitat'; www.nasa.gov/sites/default/files/atoms/files/journey-to-mars-next-steps-20151008_508.pdf
180 *Interstellar*, directed by Christopher Nolan (US and UK: Warner Bros and Paramount, 2014)
181 Icarus Interstellar, 'Project Persephone'; www.icarusinterstellar.org/projects/project-persephone/
182 Torah Kachur, 'Ultimate worldship', CBC News (29 May 2014); www.cbc.ca/homestretch/episode/2014/05/29/ultimate-worldship/ (accessed 1 August 2014).
183 Icarus Interstellar, 'Project Persephone'; www.icarusinterstellar.org/projects/project-persephone/
184 Icarus Interstellar, 'Project Persephone'; www.icarusinterstellar.org/projects/project-persephone/
185 National Aeronautics and Space Administration, 'Space Settlements'; settlement.arc.nasa.gov
186 Lifeboat Foundation, 'Ark I Special Report'; lifeboat.com/ex/ark_i
187 Lifeboat Foundation, 'Ark I Special Report'; lifeboat.com/ex/ark_i

188 Alex Leo, 'SurvivaBall: new Yes Men prank focuses on global warming', The Huffington Post (16 November 2009); www.huffingtonpost.com/2009/09/16/survivaball-new-yes-men-p_n_288550.html
189 National Aeronautics and Space Administration, 'NASA's Journey to Mars: Pioneering Next Steps in Space Exploration' (Washington DC: NASA, October 2015): 21; 'A Home Away from Home: Deep Space Habitat'; www.nasa.gov/sites/default/files/atoms/files/journey-to-mars-next-steps-20151008_508.pdf
190 'Meals ready to eat: Expedition 44 crew members sample leafy greens grown on Space Station', NASA (7 August 2015); www.nasa.gov/mission_pages/station/research/news/meals_ready_to_eat
191 Nadia Drake, 'Here's what it feels like to spend a year on Mars', *National Geographic* (29 August 2016); news.nationalgeographic.com/2016/08/nasa-mars-hi-seas-hawaii-human-mission-space-science/
192 National Academies of Sciences, Engineering, and Medicine, *Review of the MEPAG Report on Mars Special Regions* (Washington, DC: The National Academies Press, 2015).
193 Lee Billings, 'Why hunting for life in Martian water will be a tricky task', *Nature* (28 September 2015); www.nature.com/news/why-hunting-for-life-in-martian-water-will-be-a-tricky-task-1.18450?WT.mc_id=TWT_NatureNews; accessed 1 October 2015
194 On the fully integrated Environmental Control and Life Support System (ECLSS), see D. Tito *et al.*, 'Feasibility study for a manned Mars free-return mission in 2018' (2013); inspirationmars.org/Inspiration%20Mars_Feasibility%20Analysis_IEEE.pdf; www.inspirationmars.org
195 Robin McKie, 'Valentina Tereshkova, 76, first woman in space, seeks one-way ticket to Mars', *The Guardian* (17 September 2013); www.theguardian.com/science/2013/sep/17/mars-one-way-ticket
196 Stephen J. Pyne, 'The extraterrestrial Earth: Antarctica as an analogue for space exploration', *Space Policy* 23 (2007): 147–149.
197 Juha Himanka, 'Husserl's argumentation for the pre-Copernican vView of the Earth', *The Review of Metaphysics*, 58.3 (March 2005): 644; 621. See also Nigel Clark, *Inhuman Nature: Sociable Life on a Dynamic Planet* (London: Sage, 2011): 5.
198 Michel Serres, *The Natural Contract* (Ann Arbor: University of Michigan Press, 1995): 123–124.
199 Peter Sloterdijk, Globes: Macrospherology Volume II: Spheres (Semiotext(e) / Foreign Agents) trans. by Wieland Hoban (MIT Press, 2014): 250. First published as Peter Sloterdijk, *Sphären II. Globen* (Frankfurt am Main: Suhrkamp Verlag, 1999).
200 Peter Sloterdijk, *Im selben Boot: Versuch uber die Hyperpolitik* (Frankfurt am Main: Suhrkamp Verlag, 1993). See also Sjoerd van Tuinen, 'Air conditioning spaceship earth: Peter Sloterdijk's ethico-aesthetic paradigm', *Environment and Planning D: Society and Space* 27 (2009): 105–118; 116.
201 Peter Sloterdijk, *Globes: Macrospherology Volume II: Spheres* (Semiotext(e) / Foreign Agents) trans. Wieland Hoban (MIT Press, 2014): 246. First published as Peter Sloterdijk, *Sphären II. Globen* (Frankfurt am Main: Suhrkamp Verlag, 1999). See also Sabine Höhler, '"The real problem of a spaceship is its people" Spaceship Earth as ecological science fiction' in *Green Planets: Ecology and Science Fiction*, eds. Gerry Canavan and Kim Stanley Robinson (Middletown, CT: Wesleyan University Press, 2014): 99–114; 109.
202 Peter Sloterdijk *Im selben Boot: Versuch uber die Hyperpolitik* (Frankfurt am Main: Suhrkamp Verlag, 1993), cf. Sjoerd van Tuinen, 'Air conditioning spaceship earth: Peter Sloterdijk's ethico-aesthetic paradigm', *Environment and Planning D: Society and Space* 27 (2009): 105–118.
203 Peter Sloterdijk, 'How Big is Big?' lecture at COP 15 2009 drawing on his book *You Must Change Your Life* and published at the Collegium International website; www.collegium-international.org/index.php/en/contributions/127-how-big-is-big
204 Mike Davis, 'Who will build the ark?', *New Left Review* 61 (Jan–Feb 2010): 29–45; newleftreview.org/II/61/mike-davis-who-will-build-the-ark; accessed 20 July 2016.
205 Mike Davis, 'Who will build the ark?', *New Left Review* 61 (Jan–Feb 2010): 29–45; newleftreview.org/II/61/mike-davis-who-will-build-the-ark; accessed 20 July 2016.

206 Mike Davis, 'Who will build the ark?', *New Left Review* 61 (Jan–Feb 2010): 29–45; newleftreview.org/II/61/mike-davis-who-will-build-the-ark; accessed 20 July 2016.
207 Mike Davis, 'The imperial city and the city of slums. Green zones and slum sities', A Tomdispatch Interview with Mike Davis (Part 2) (11 May 2006); www.tomdispatch.com/post/82790/tomdispatch_interview_mike_davis_green_zones_and_slum_cities
208 Mike Davis, "Who will build the ark?', *New Left Review* 61 (Jan–Feb 2010): 29–45; newleftreview.org/II/61/mike-davis-who-will-build-the-ark; accessed 20 July 2016.
209 Bruno Latour, 'Forty years later – back to a sub-lunar Earth' in *Ecological Urbanism*, eds. Mohsen Mostafavi and Gareth Docherty (Lars Müller Publishers, 2010): 124–127; 125.

6 Monster Earth

CAUTION: toxic materials

Geoengineering, planet hacking and terraforming are terms that describe global-scale technologically driven interventions in, and management of, the Earth. The fundamental premise is that humans might be competent in Earth-altering. Geoengineering is understood as, 'the intentional large-scale manipulation of the environment, particularly manipulation that is intended to reduce undesired anthropogenic climate change'.[1] This can take many forms, including cloud whitening, space mirrors, carbon capture and storage, with the stated goal of deliberately redesigning, restoring or improving climatic conditions. In a sense, however, the disastrous conditions of the Anthropocene, among them climate change, can already be said to have come about as a result of human planetary-scale manipulation. Geoengineering can be understood, therefore, as both a trigger and ultimate response to the Anthropocene. Geoengineering in the Anthropocene puts questions of human influence on Earth systems into contact with far futures and vast scales difficult to comprehend. It is perhaps the most pointed example of humanity trespassing, intentionally or otherwise, on the thresholds of Earth systems. This is a territory where cautionary tales are particularly useful. Geoengineering unleashes Earth's monstrous twin.

The monstrous effects of human interventions in Earth systems are listed in Paul Crutzen's *Nature* article that signalled the Anthropocene – 'Geology of Mankind': 'the consequences are, among others, acid precipitation, photochemical 'smog' and climate warming.'[2] Humans are understood to have engaged in unintentional large-scale climate engineering since the Industrial Revolution. Entry into a 'managed' Anthropocene hinges on the recognition of a shift from inadvertent to intentional technological interventions in Earth systems. Crutzen has also considered deliberate geoengineering as a possible remedy for the deleterious human impacts on Earth. Perhaps inevitably, the technocratic discourse of the Anthropocene elicits daring technological responses. Geoengineering rests on the possibility that the artificial and purposeful regulation of Earth system processes can avert the onset of dangerous climate change. There is no clear sense, however, that geoengineering can save the day or guarantee the promise of a better future. It is simply a gamble at a less catastrophic one. Or even a futile bid to postpone the inevitable, catastrophic, human-induced transformations of the planetary environment. Some researchers think it a gamble worth the high stakes: 'geoengineering is guided by a promise to attempt, in a situation characterised by despair and uncertainty, but not necessarily to succeed.'[3] They simply feel it is a risk that is worth it.

As commercial interests align with scenarios of a desperate world, many businesses, including oil companies Shell and ConocoPhillips, are funding geoengineering research. There have been numerous patents issued for geoengineering technologies.[4] StratoShield is a system that would disperse sulfate aerosols into the stratosphere for 'solar radiation management'. High-flying blimps in the sky would support a pipe, the thickness of a fire-hose, that would carry sulfur dioxide liquid 30 km up to the stratosphere, where it would be atomised into a fine mist of nanometre-scale aerosol particles that would reflect the sunlight reaching the Earth. 'A Hose is Better than Bombs',[5] its description claims. The strapline announces it to be 'a practical, low-cost way to reverse catastrophic warming of the Arctic – or the entire planet.' The idea, featured in the book *SuperFreakonomics* and inspired by volcanoes, has been put forward by 'Intellectual Ventures', as 'a kind of back-up plan in case human efforts to curb emissions don't succeed fast enough to prevent devastating ecological damage'.[6] Intellectual Ventures has funded research into geoengineering because the company believes it would be 'irresponsible for the technical community to postpone such work until a climate emergency was actually under way'.[7] In 1968 Stewart Brand's dictum in the *Whole Earth Catalog* was: 'We are as Gods and might as well get good at it.' By 2009, responding to the challenges of planetary disaster, the ecopragmatist Brand is more assertive: 'We are as Gods and *have* to get good at it.'[8]

For the most part geoengineering proposals assume that the Earth is an operable system: something that can be controlled and mastered by humans. As the writer and researcher Duncan McLaren has observed of solar radiation management (SRM – the term for the riskier, but also potentially more effective, strand of geoengineering research): 'SRM is arguably the archetypal Anthropocene technology: its signature would be visible globally and it offers both destructive potential and the prospect of management or control, perhaps even the capacity to restore the planet's climate to something more hospitable to human civilisation.'[9] Oliver Morton recounts the history of the term SRM. It was originally proposed by Ken Caldeira 'in partial jest', to assuage concerns at NASA's Ames Research Center of the words 'NASA' and 'geoengineering' being associated in a conference organised there. He suggested that 'they should just replace "geoengineering" with the dreariest management-speak circumlocution they could come up with – something like "solar radiation management".' Morton dislikes the term: 'It sounds like something you'd find stencilled under a stopcock sticking out of a bulkhead on Spaceship Earth. It's no way to talk about the world.'[10]

For the time being, the geoengineering interventions proposed are aimed at keeping things as close to the conditions of the Holocene as possible. The contemplation of planetary-scale engineering is increasingly presented as a necessary evil, as an inevitable response to the emerging threats of global environmental change and the prospect of accelerating climatic chaos. There are many that are convinced that the climate system has the potential for sudden and dangerous shifts, that carbon mitigation efforts are failing or moving too slowly to avert environmental disaster, and that therefore the Earth and sky need to be 'fixed' or controlled in the manner of a planetary thermostat, perhaps, or an air-conditioning unit. Clive Hamilton expresses the opposite position: 'as if we know enough to install and begin to operate a "global thermostat". Truly this qualifies as monstrous hubris.'[11] On the one hand geoengineering is seen as the 'ultimate technological fix', and on the other hand, it has 'unlimited potential for planetary mischief'.[12] In *This Changes Everything*, Naomi Klein imagines a 'Monster Earth'[13] – a toxic patchwork of geoengineering projects gone awry:

> We very likely would not be dealing with a single geoengineering effort but some noxious brew of mixed-up techno-fixes – sulfur in space to cool the temperature, cloud seeding to fix the droughts it causes, ocean fertilisation in a desperate gambit to cope with acidification, and carbon-sucking machines to help us get off the geo-junk once and for all… we might well be dealing with multiple countries launching geoengineering efforts at once, creating unknown and unknowable interactions.[14]

Bernd Scherer's essay 'The Monsters' suggests that the figure of the monster is the 'leitmotif of the Anthropocene'.[15] The monster, or monstrous, originally denoted an aberration from nature. But it has an additional meaning that derives from its root in the Latin word *monstrum*, or 'sign' – as in, for example, the word 'demonstration'. The monster is not just an aberration, but a presentation of this aberration – it thus exists as a kind of explication or warning. From *Frankenstein* to *The Terminator*, stories of technology 'out of control' and 'taking on a life of its own' horrify us *because* they are plausible. The monstrous has its roots in the familiar. The academic Elizabeth Grosz suggests that it is not deformities that make monsters so unsettling, but the blurring of identities: 'Monsters involve all kinds of doubling.' She suggests that the fear of 'ghostly doubles or Doppelgänger' generates 'a horror at the possibility of our own imperfect duplication'.[16] In other words, what is fearsome is the uncanny aspect of these monsters of human making – the possibility that in their distorted features we might discern uncomfortable truths about ourselves.

The Monster Earth of the Anthropocene is a warning. The proposed techno-fixes of geoengineering schemes suppose that the humanity that implements them will be a more prudent, more cooperative species than the beings who created the problem in the first place. This is a large supposition. It seems a repetition – perhaps tragically inevitable – of the hubris that created the mess in the first place. This is geoengineering as humanity's monstrous double. If the Anthropocene is monstrous – a time and place in which drastic mutations of millennia-long changes metastasise and swarm – then the justification for geoengineering is that a monster of our conscious making is better than the one that will arise if we continue to let reason sleep. A number of writers have argued that the persistence of CO_2 in the atmosphere means that past and present human actions may have inadvertently already committed future generations to an irreversibly hostile climate for thousands of years. Steffen, Crutzen and McNeill point out that future *Homo sapiens*, living in altered planetary conditions, may be forced into drastic action to, for example, avert a new ice age, or deflect meteorites and asteroids heading for Earth.[17] With this in mind, they argue, it is best to be prepared. Bonneuil and Fressoz, however, sound a warning, knowing where such trains of thought have led before: 'Still more here than with nuclear tests or the imaginary of Spaceship Earth… the entire Earth is now explicitly reified as object of experimentation and control.'[18] The Earth has already been monsterised, shaped to meet short-term needs and desires. If the monstrous arrival of the Anthropocene provokes questions of what can be done practically and politically to live with a disaster of human making, it does so by coming up against a shifting intransigent domain – the '"monstrously impolitic" reaches of the Earth and cosmos'.[19]

Deliberate planet

The Royal Society defines geoengineering as, 'the deliberate large-scale manipulation of the planetary environment in order to counteract anthropogenic climate change'.[20] In terms of anthropogenic climate change, however, humans have changed the Earth without even trying. So it begs the question, what would it mean if humanity were to *try* to transform the Earth? Those researchers that are giving geoengineering serious thought are also offering words of caution, as exemplified in climatologist Alan Robock's 2008 article, '20 reasons why geoengineering may be a bad idea'.[21] Robock observes that the stated objective of the United Nations Framework Convention on Climate Change (UNFCCC) is to stabilise greenhouse gas concentrations in the atmosphere 'at a level that would prevent dangerous anthropogenic interference with the climate system'. This takes into account the *inadvertent* climate effects of human actions. However, geoengineering needs careful consideration in the context of *deliberate* human interference with the climate system. 'But is this cure worse than the disease?' he asks.[22] There are concerns that a reliance on the promise of geoengineeering could see less public effort to reduce greenhouse gas emissions; reduced attention to political action on carbon mitigation; the differential impact of climate engineering on different regions of the world; the risk of hostile use with the possibility that rogue nations might embark on military appropriation of climate modification programmes; the mammoth, even impossible, task of some kind of global governance and not least a chain of unintended consequences through disastrous and unforeseen changes to the climate system.[23] In spite of all of this, some consider geoengineering as, 'a bad idea whose time has come'.[24] The argument that humans should deliberately manipulate Earth systems and natural processes through geoengineering in order to mitigate the impact of inevitable climate change has in the last decade moved from science fiction and the fringes of scientific research to the mainstream of scientific and policy debate. The story of 21st-century dreams of redesigning the climate through planned technological interventions comes with new proclamations of urgency. According to the historian James Fleming, however, 'This is not, in essence, a heroic saga about new scientific discoveries that can save the planet, as many of the participants claim, but a tragicomedy of overreaching, hubris, and self-delusion'.[25]

Fleming's history of climate engineering and weather modification, *Fixing the Sky*, is an extended cautionary tale of attempting to control the uncontrollable. From Greek mythology to science fiction, manipulating the weather has been a mainstay of the human imagination. Jules Verne's *The Purchase of the North Pole* tells the story of a group of US businessmen who plan to use a giant cannon to alter the Earth's tilt. Their plan is to end the seasons, melt the North Pole, and thus make accessible vast coal deposits under the Arctic. Their scheme initially gains public support because of their promise of an improved climate. However, the plan eventually fails. 'The world's inhabitants could thus sleep in peace. To modify the conditions of the Earth's movement is beyond the power of man.'[26] This fictional scheme, apparently far-fetched, is not so very different from a 1950s Soviet proposal to dam the Bering Strait with a view to redirecting ocean currents, warming the Arctic regions, and giving access to land and resources. The genealogy of geoengineering can be traced to the technoscientific experiments and ambitious research programmes of weather and climate modification undertaken during the Cold War. These programmes were not averse to mobilising the geophysical forces of the Earth system as weapons of mass destruction. They included ideas such as melting polar ice caps in order to create artificial tsunamis to drown coastal cities; producing firestorms in forest areas; altering the temperature of sea currents to disrupt the enemy's climate and therefore food production; and using biological agents to contaminate land, water and atmosphere.[27] Kurt Vonnegut's novel *Cat's Cradle* follows such scheming to its logical conclusion.[28] Felix Hoenikker, the fictional co-inventor of the atom bomb, invents 'ice-nine' as an offshoot of the Manhattan Project. This is a polymorph of water with a special crystalline structure that melts at 48.5°C – below that temperature it turns any water it touches into more ice-nine. The military sees a use for it in crossing boggy terrain. However, its accidental deployment results in a colossal ecological disaster: the freezing of all the world's oceans, rivers and groundwater, and the consequent destruction of all life.

Current geoengineering options fall into two main categories: solar radiation management (SRM) and carbon dioxide removal (CDR). SRM schemes for reflecting sunlight back into space include: releasing sulfate particles into the stratosphere to enhance the Earth's albedo (that is, light-reflecting) effect; 'global dimming' by placing millions of tiny mirrors in near-Earth space orbit; whitening marine layer clouds by spraying seawater into them, and painting dark urban infrastructures such as roads, car parks and rooftops white. CDR schemes to remove CO_2 from the atmosphere include the dumping of pulverised limestone in the oceans to neutralise acidification; the use of ocean fertilisation to promote algae growth; floating vertical pipes in the ocean to aid carbon fixation; and the burial of charred biomass to promote carbon sequestration. The schemes involve bringing experiments hitherto confined to the laboratory and the computer model to the scale of the world, in order to transform the oceans, whiten the clouds, shield the Sun and fix the Earth. While such projects veer between the sublime and ridiculous, feasible and fantastic, depending on one's point of view, they 'typically involve mundane technologies such as mirrors, iron dust, sulphate particles or crumbled rock'.[29] Pushed around a sandbox Earth, these mundane ('of the Earth') materials could bring about massive changes – but would they save us, or destroy us – and is there any way to model this accurately before we lock ourselves into a planet-sized experiment with no off-switch?

Aware of the charge of being audacious, at best, or, at worst, viciously deluded, proponents of geoengineering take pains to acknowledge the complexity of the systems in which they propose to intervene. Their justification is that this may be the only viable alternative left to avert the 'climate catastrophe' – geoengineering offers 'the last chance to save the planet'. Such talk of 'climate emergency' seeks to generate acceptance of geoengineering interventions. The apparently sober conclusion – that society must 'think the unthinkable' – resonates with the same giddy excitement at the opening up of new technological vistas that ran through the Cold War – a time scaffolded by the notion of Mutually Assured Destruction. Geoengineering science often presents a confident front, even though the effects of any deliberate intervention in the climate system are extremely unpredictable. For the academic Melinda Cooper,

> the paradox of this argument is that it calls for a strategic intervention into the atmosphere in order to pre-empt the worst effects of climate change, while acknowledging that such an intervention may itself be indistinguishable from the

process of climate change – that is to say, equally unpredictable, incalculable and turbulent in its unfolding.'[30]

A deliberate planet may thus be a far more unstable prospect than the planet we currently inhabit. Meddling with inherently unpredictable Earth systems in the context of troublesome politics and fragile forms of environmental governance makes for a particularly turbulent mix. Thus, according to Nigel Clark, 'geoengineering promises the worst of all worlds'.[31] Nevertheless, he argues, it is important that geoengineering debates are putting Earth systems on the political agenda:

> In whatever form it might be imagined or applied, then, geoengineering is not a total remaking of the Earth, not the final seal on the 'end of nature'. It can only ever be a negotiation between the forces that humans can conceivably impact upon and those that remain – provisionally or permanently – beyond their practical reach.[32]

Frankenstein world

> Frightful must it be; for supremely frightful would be the effect of any human endeavour to mock the stupendous mechanism of the Creator of the World.[33]

Mary Shelley's *Frankenstein; or, the Modern Prometheus* is a prominent cautionary tale about playing with technological fire. The story brings together the notion of monstrous creatures of human making together with phenomenal disturbances in atmospheric cycles and mutations of climate. The story is iconic enough to lend itself readily to quotation and parody. It serves as a shorthand for all the ways in which nature is out of sorts, modified and aberrant. Genetically modified foods are referred to by their detractors as 'Frankenfood'. More recently, 'Frankenclimate' and 'Frankenstorm' entered the lexicon, via the media coverage of Superstorm Sandy.[34]

Perhaps the most significant thing about this allusion making the jump from, say, GM foods to climate aberrations is that Frankenstein's monster is *human-made*. It may indicate recognition that the freak weather occurrences of recent years are not a whim of volatile nature, but co-created and unpredictable events of human and non-human agency.

Frankenstein was written in 1816, a year that was recorded as 'The Year Without a Summer', or 'Poverty Year'. It was the beginning of several years of major climatic disruptions. In New England, the period was called 'Eighteen-Hundred-and-Froze-to-Death'. Across the Northern hemisphere, plummeting temperatures and rainfall destroyed successive harvests and communities endured famine, disease, dislocation and civil unrest on a catastrophic scale. Europe was at the time still recovering from the aftermath of the Napoleonic wars. Food riots, looting, and the mass displacement of people were all common. The bizarre weather showed no signs of abating; prolonged winter conditions included a persistent 'dry fog'. Snow fell in midsummer and there were unusual optical effects, such as those recorded in the spectacular red sunsets of J.M.W. Turner's paintings. At the time, the loss of seasons and pervasive gloom were mysteries that added to the sense of unease and impending doom. Indeed, many thought that the world was ending. Over a hundred years later, the climatic disruptions were explained as the result of the 1815 eruption of the volcano Mount Tambora on the island of Sumbawa, Indonesia.[35] The colossal eruption had spewed megatons of dust, ash and sulfur particles into the atmosphere. This led to a pronounced cooling of the world's climate: a 'volcanic winter' event. In China, the disruption of the monsoon season had led to overwhelming floods in the Yangtze Valley, while in India late torrential rains aggravated the spread of cholera.

Mary Wollstonecraft Godwin, her future husband Percy Bysshe Shelley, and their companions John Polidori and Lord Byron, had planned to spend the summer of 1816 in Switzerland, near Lake Constance. Trapped indoors by 'incessant rain', they passed the time by reading horror stories and came up with the challenge of writing one themselves.[36] Mary Shelley's *Frankenstein; or, the Modern Prometheus* was published in 1818. Polidori's short story inspired his tale 'The Vampyre', published in 1819. Byron drafted 'Darkness', a poem in which 'the bright sun was extinguish'd'. The monstrosity in the weather, and the creative and destructive forces of storms and lightning that Mary Shelley and her friends witnessed that summer, read in the *Frankenstein* narrative as registers of human terror and awe at non-human agency. But Shelley's story is above all a reminder that monsters can be *made*. In her tale, Dr Victor Frankenstein builds a creature from raw materials supplied by 'the dissecting room and the slaughter-house' and through an unexplained scientific process he somehow brings it to life. Yet he is so terrified of his creation that he disavows the experiment and flees his laboratory as soon as the creature stirs. Later in the story the neglected creature overhears a reading of Milton's *Paradise Lost* and empathises with the role of Satan. A would-be 'Adam', he identifies himself instead as a 'fallen angel'. Adam's lament from *Paradise Lost*, 'Did I request thee, Maker, from my Clay To mould me Man, did I sollicite thee From darkness to promote me?' is the epigraph to Shelley's tale.

As a cautionary tale of unintended consequences and disavowed creations, *Frankenstein; or, The Modern Prometheus* anticipates the dilemmas of the Anthropocene. A fallen Holocene world evokes imaginaries of more desirable, untrammelled and paradisical habitats that bring with them schemes of redesigning or repurposing the Earth. In the face of the results of reckless technological expansionism, humans are revealed to have at once too much and too little power. Shelley's tale warns of the hazards associated with the deliberate alteration of nature, and, as with the story of Prometheus, of 'playing with fire'. In the 19th century, the figure of Prometheus represented human striving and, in particular, the quest for scientific knowledge – but he also personified the risks of overreaching. Percy Bysshe Shelley addressed this theme in his long poem *Prometheus Unbound*. The promethean imperative is expressed with the command at the beginning of Immanuel Kant's *Universal Natural History*: 'Give me only matter and I will build a world out of it for you.'[37] Kant had hailed Benjamin Franklin, known for his experiments with electricity – 'for having robbed thunder of its weapon'– as the 'Prometheus of modern times.' But he had also expressed caution at the promethean feats of geoengineering being considered in the wake of the Lisbon earthquake.

Science has long been associated with promethean hubris – the desire to steal the powers of the gods. The academic and writer Simon Schaffer defines 'promethean science' as 'an experimental enterprise that mixes a vaulting ambition to safeguard humanity against a major threat with the troubling hazards of following this science's recipes'.[38] Since the publication of *Frankenstein*, humanity has achieved forms of mastery over nature that were then unimaginable. The monsters unleashed may yet prove harder to apprehend than was Dr Frankenstein's. Shelley was writing at the dawn of the technological revolutions that have come to define the Anthropocene. The Frankenstein story is often seen as being rooted in a Romantic, anti-industrialist, anti-urbanist philosophy which runs through much of modern environmentalism. To the extent that this is true, the novel is the natural enemy of the hubristic-utopian belief in science's invincibility – the confidence that any problem human thought has created, human thought can also solve. But the novel is not just a warning about scientific overreaching – it is also a plea to take responsibility for mistakes already made. 'Remember, I am thy creature,' Frankenstein's monster rebukes his creator. 'I was benevolent and good; misery made me a fiend.'

Bruno Latour's entreaty to 'love your monsters' makes this point: 'Dr. Frankenstein's crime was not that he invented a creature through some combination of hubris and high technology, but rather that he *abandoned the creature to itself*.'[39] The moral of the story is, perhaps then, that we should not abandon our technological creations, but rather, treat them as we would our children, with care, love, and attention – lest they turn into monsters. Taking responsibility is not only a practical necessity; it could also be a route out of despair. Latour asserts: 'From now on, we should stop flagellating ourselves and take up explicitly and seriously what we have been doing all along at an ever-increasing scale.' Instead of humans neglecting the increasingly monstrous non-human world, 'the environment is exactly what should be even more managed, taken up, cared for, stewarded; in brief, integrated and internalised in the very fabric of the polity'.[40] This is not meant as an exaltation of technology, but as a petition for attachment to the non-human. It arises from the 'normal duty of *continuing* to care for unwanted consequences'.[41] In the Anthropocene, we must learn to love our monsters. Yet serious disagreement remains as to what responsible stewardship should look like. Naomi Klein warns that, 'geoengineering will certainly monsterise the planet as nothing experienced in human history'.[42] Referring to the Frankenstein narrative as well as Bruno Latour's interpretation of Shelley's story, she cautions against the exultant doomsaying of eco-pragmatists and their faith in techno-fixes. They are all too tempting as a rallying cry, drowning out more cautious proposals for mitigation and adaptation. And the large-scale geoengineering projects they are seen to promote could lead, not to safety, but to an eternally sickened 'Frankenstein world'[43]:

> If we sign on to this plan and call it stewardship, we effectively give up on the prospect of ever being healthy again. The Earth – our life-support system – would itself be put on life support, hooked up to machines 24/7 to prevent it from going full-tilt monster on us.[44]

And yet a technologically transformed Earth system is something that humans have already lived with for some time. Moreover, there is no known way of restoring Earth to its former 'healthy' state. The only option, it seems, is to work out a way of adjusting to the monstrosity we have made. Our 21st century affluent, fossil-fuelled lives have demanded a panoply of interventions in Earth systems, including industrial agricultural practices that have redefined the global cycle of nutrients; engineering works that have changed the flow of rivers and processes of erosion; and the introduction of machines and engines whose emissions have altered the composition of the atmosphere. These transformations need to be acknowledged and reckoned with, not recoiled from. Geoengineering promises to find a way forward, free from nostalgia for an unrecoverable 'state of nature'. But should geoengineering be thought of as part of an inevitable redesign whose ambition is to take better care of planetary futures? Or does it speak rather of an impossible and dangerous dream of taking control of the planet? Bruno Latour's promise of redesign yet strikes a warning note: 'Will Prometheus ever be cautious enough to redesign the planet?'[45]

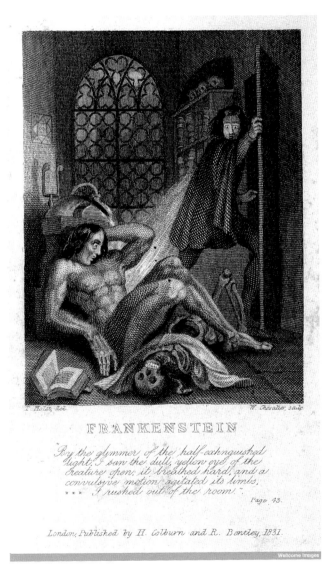

Figure 6.1 Frankenstein observing the first stirrings of his creature; engraving by W. Chevalier after Th. von Holst, 1831; *Frankenstein* by Mary Wollstonecraft Shelley (published by H. Colburn and R. Bentley, London, 1831)

Source: Wellcome Library, London

Optimising climate

> Unless there is a global catastrophe — a meteorite impact, a world war or a pandemic — mankind will remain a major environmental force for many millennia. A daunting task lies ahead for scientists and engineers to guide society towards environmentally sustainable management during the era of the Anthropocene. This will require appropriate human behaviour at all scales, and may well involve internationally accepted, large-scale geoengineering projects, for instance to 'optimise' climate. At this stage, however, we are still largely treading on *terra incognita*.[46]

Paul Crutzen has been a prominent advocate of geoengineering. In 2002, his *Nature* article on the Anthropocene introduced the possibility of geoengineering as a corrective to the destabilising force of anthropogenic climate change. While talk of an optimised climate might involve restoring some semblance of the Holocene, it is also an acknowledgement that the slightest departure from the relatively stable conditions that humanity has got used to could tip the Earth system into a wholly new state that is impossible to anticipate. With growing concern about climate-system tipping points and the feasibility of reductions in emissions that could effectively mitigate the carbon crisis, more scientific research is being conducted into the possibilities of geoengineering. However, the as yet unproven technologies that would be required to effect planetary-scale interventions may bring unintended consequences. The argument is that the severity of climate change justifies the investigation of all possible means to counteract it.

In a controversial editorial for a 2006 issue of *Climatic Change*, Paul Crutzen stated that 'research on the feasibility and environmental consequences of climate engineering of the kind…' which, he continues, 'might need to be deployed in the future, should not be tabooed.'[47] He warned that the 'Earth system is increasingly in the non-analogue condition of the Anthropocene'.[48] The chances of the unexpected therefore, when it comes to the climate system, should not be underestimated. Scientific research into SRM, he argued, needed to be in a position 'to create a possibility to combat potentially drastic climate heating.'[49] Crutzen noted with alarm the failure of political efforts to curb anthropogenic greenhouse gas emissions. His call for 'serious research' into the SRM method of stratospheric sulfur injections was thus presented as a possible techno-fix to avert the 'climate emergency'. In the decade since Crutzen's article, geoengineering has moved from the fringes of scientific research into mainstream discussion. Previously confined to the abstract terrain of computer modelling, experiments in the deliberate shaping of Earth systems are inching closer to possible planetary-scale testing. In part as a result of exasperation at the slow progress of the 'Plan A' of internationally coordinated emissions cuts, geoengineering is emerging as a serious 'Plan B'. The 2009 Royal Society report cautioned, however, that 'none of the methods evaluated in this study offer an immediate solution to the problem of climate change and it is unclear which, if any, may ever pass the tests required for potential deployment'.[50] The 2014 IPCC 5th assessment report, 'Summary for Policymakers', concludes with a terse warning about geoengineering schemes:

> There is insufficient knowledge to quantify how much CO_2 emissions could be partially offset by CDR on a century timescale. Modelling indicates that SRM

methods, if realisable, have the potential to substantially offset a global temperature rise, but they would also modify the global water cycle, and would not reduce ocean acidification. If SRM were terminated for any reason, there is *high confidence* that global surface temperatures would rise very rapidly to values consistent with the greenhouse gas forcing. CDR and SRM methods carry side effects and long-term consequences on a global scale.[51]

In other words, the geoengineering solutions considered thus far are very far from perfect. And it is possible that if implemented, we might find out, too late, that they were worse than doing nothing at all. A growing number of researchers propose to start field trials of these technologies, even in the absence of a globally coordinated regulatory systems to oversee them.[52] To wait for such regulations, they argue, would be to wait forever: 'Governance and experimentation must co-evolve.'[53] Stratospheric aerosol injection, the SRM method favoured by Crutzen, is considered by many to be a cheap, simple and fast-acting technology.[54] It is proposed as the most readily available means to avert the growing sense of a climate emergency in the Anthropocene. But there remains unease, misapprehension, and downright fear when it comes to planetary-scale geoengineering. There is suspicion that we may come to depend on it, rather than taking much-needed action to curb carbon emissions. There is doubt that the proposals can work at all, and concern that if any of the schemes are implemented, a series of negative and unintended consequences might follow, reconfiguring and destabilising regional and local climates in unanticipated and unprecedented ways. There is concern that, rather than diffusing the 'climate emergency', geoengineering technologies might in fact create new political and security emergencies. The difficulties of reaching any agreement through the multilateral United Nations process of the UNFCCC – notably the Kyoto Protocol – with regard to more conventional climate mitigation suggests that governing geoengineering schemes will be even more difficult. Climate change academic Mike Hulme argues that: 'The technology is ungovernable... I find it hard to envisage any scenario in which the world's nations will agree to a thermostat in the sky.'[55]

Oliver Morton argues however that 'leaving geoengineering out of the story'[56] is simply not an option. Geoengineering debates are also putting important questions of how to think about experimentation across thresholds in Earth systems on the political agenda.[57] But it is an impossible task to take into account the differential impact of various untested planet-scale engineering options on different inhabitants and different species in different regions, now and into the future. The related task of convening appropriate and responsive modes of geoengineering governance on a fractious planet is no easier. The stakes are high and we cannot afford to make mistakes. As the familiar activist slogan, adopted recently by Secretary-General of the United Nations Ban Ki Moon, asserts: 'There is no Planet B.'

Under the dome

One approach for cooling the Earth has received more attention than others: the idea of decreasing the amount of sunlight that reaches the Earth through changes in the stratosphere, also called 'albedo modification' or SRM. The interest in this approach stems largely from the fact that it happens naturally during large volcanic eruptions, such as the eruption of Mount Pinatubo in the Philippines. The eruption of Mount Pinatubo in June 1991 threw an enormous cloud of ash, dust and gas into the stratosphere, which spread across the world. While the dust subsided the sulfur dioxide aerosol particles lingered, reflecting sunlight, and the world began to cool. This had happened before with the major eruptions of Tambora in 1815 and Krakatau in 1883, but the global climate emergencies of 'eighteen-hundred-and-froze-to-death' had not been linked to the volcanoes and remained speculative until the 20th century.[58] With the eruption of Pinatubo, computer models of the climate, such as those of James Hansen, finally had 'the opportunity provided by the natural experiment of Pinatubo to test things'.[59] But the stratospheric sulfate aerosols were not just proven to scatter sunlight, they also changed atmospheric chemistry. A year after the eruption, the ozone hole over Antarctica was shown to have excessive thinning because of an ozone-depleting reaction. Pinatubo's changing of the climate occurred in the context of increasing alarm – for the year that Pinatubo cooled the Earth was the year that the UNFCCC was signed at the Rio Earth Summit. Oliver Morton observes, 'It's hardly surprising that some people wondered whether Pinatubo could be more than an experiment – whether it could, instead, be a prototype.'[60]

Proposals for albedo modification schemes range from painting all roofs and roads white to, essentially, placing a roof on the world, made up of small particles of reflective matter – such as sulfate aerosols– sprayed directly into the stratosphere. Naomi Klein has expressed horror at this prospect:

> A grim picture emerges. Nothing on Earth would be outside the reach of humanity's fallible machines, or even fully outside at all. We would have a roof, not a sky – a milky, geoengineered ceiling gazing down on a dying acidifying sea.[61]

Is it worth losing the blue vault of the sky in order to try to stabilise conditions underneath it? Few would argue this was the first desirable course of action. Certainly, it risks many unintended consequences, considering how many of Earth's complex systems could be affected. It is well understood that artificially adjusting reflectivity to counter global warming would merely mask the symptoms of climate change and would do nothing to counter ocean acidification. As Oliver Morton notes, in the case of SRM schemes that use stratospheric aerosols, there are many hard-to-quantify risks or 'unknowns': 'The implications of the predictable effects on the hydrological cycle are unknown. So is the degree of ozone depletion entailed. The direct effects on human health are unquantified. No one knows how to set up a form of governance for such efforts that would be both enduring and equitable.'[62] However, SRM schemes have one crucial thing to recommend them: they promise more significant and more rapid cooling than do atmospheric carbon reduction schemes. Current research indicates 'that a stratospheric geoengineering programme scaled to the task would be able to keep the current increase in global temperature below two degrees over quite a long period and across quite a wide range of emissions scenarios'. Morton goes as far as to say that this is the only 'plausible intervention', for staying under the totemic 2 degrees limit. Paul Crutzen is among the scientists that argue that anthropogenic albedo modification may be the only thing that can possibly outpace and mitigate the damage caused by runaway carbon emissions.

In 2006, Crutzen made the case for more research into SRM, as an urgent response to an urgent problem. 'The issue has come to the forefront,' he argued, 'because of the dilemma facing international policy makers, who are confronted with the task to clean up air pollution, while simultaneously keeping global climate warming under control.'[63] Together with the release of carbon dioxide, the burning of fossil fuels emits sulfur dioxide that concentrates in the smog above large cities. About half of the sulfur dioxide is converted into aerosol sulfate particles that act as enhancers for the albedo effect of the Earth. Greenhouse warming is thus partially compensated by the 'backscattering to space' of solar radiation resultant from the reflecting power of sulfate particles floating in the atmosphere. Whereas the increase of atmospheric concentrations of carbon dioxide leads to an increase in average global warming, sulfur dioxide concentrations in the atmosphere function as a climate cooling system. Crutzen describes a 'Catch-22' scenario: urban air pollution is responsible for more than 500,000 premature deaths a year; and yet pollution keeps global warming at bay. Cleaning up the air – an essential worldwide public health goal – might inadvertently intensify climate change. Crutzen's favoured SRM method of climate engineering counters pollution with more pollution. He tentatively proposes introducing one or two million tons of sulfur into the stratosphere every year, as a way of maintaining the protective albedo effects of sulfate aerosols, while getting rid of them in the lower atmosphere. The feasibility of incremental management of sun-blocking aerosols, even as warming aerosols contributing to conventional air pollution are reduced, needs to be better understood.

While it might well be effective, however, this is *not* a first line of climate defence. Crutzen cautions that albedo enhancement schemes should only be deployed in the event of the onset of rapid global warming, 'paradoxically, in part due to improvements in worldwide air quality'.[64]

But if, under smog, we dream of clearing the air to reveal a blue sky, the SRM dome of Crutzen's scheme would look quite different again: 'some whitening on the sky, but also colourful sunsets and sunrises would occur.'[65] These optical effects recall the murky skies and vivid sunsets of 1816, 'The Year without a Summer' – that masked the more horrific effects of pronounced global cooling. The link between large volcanic eruptions and unseasonal weather with ensuing low crop yields and human crises of famine and food riots is now firmly established. Yet proponents of SRM experiments intentionally emphasise the 'natural' analogue of volcanic activity and the temporary but drastic global dimming that can result. Crutzen's example, the eruption of Mount Pinatubo in the Philippines in 1991, is estimated to have injected 10 million tons of sulfur into the stratosphere. Scientific studies of the event concluded that the albedo effect of the sulfate particles caused a drop in average global surface air temperatures of 0.5°C. This may sound like an extreme effect to attempt to mimic. But, as Crutzen points out, human activity already puts more than 100 million tons of sulfur dioxide into the atmosphere every year — the equivalent of 10 Pinatubos.

SRM technologies could simulate the 'volcano loading effect,' Crutzen argues, 'by burning S_2 or H_2S, carried into the stratosphere on balloons and by artillery guns to produce SO_2'.[66] Crutzen's article also outlines plans for other SRM schemes, which propose to launch tiny mirrors and other nanoparticles into the stratosphere in place of sulfur. Without apparent irony, or direct reference to his research in the 1980s, Crutzen also considers releasing soot particles, to absorb solar radiation and create 'minor nuclear winter conditions'.[67] The Mount Pinatubo eruption was linked to the loss of ozone; the injection of elemental carbon into the stratosphere in place of SO_2 could counter this. All the same, he adds cautiously, 'the consequences of soot deposition on polar glaciers should be checked by model calculations'.[68]

The emphasis on mimicking nature in proposals for possible SRM schemes implies that there is nothing 'unnatural', strange, or hazardous about geoengineering. Also referencing the Mount Pinatubo eruption, Ken Caldeira has argued that 'geoengineering concepts have been tested by nature'.[69] The implication is that, if already tested by nature, then such experiments at the scale of the world should not seem so out of place. Indeed there is no other place for them. As geoengineering researcher Martin Bunzl cautions, 'You can't build a scale model of the atmosphere or tent off part of the atmosphere. As such, you are stuck going directly from a model to full-scale planetary wide implementation.'[70] There is an in-between model of sorts in the sulfur-rich, highly toxic atmospheres of polluted monster cities such as New Delhi, São Paolo and Beijing. These cities act 'as geological counterforces to extreme climatic heating'.[71] Improving atmospheric conditions in tightly packed urban conglomerations around the world could reduce the number of deaths attributed to pollution; but it would also mean the loss of the protective shield of pollutants, allowing higher levels of solar radiation to reach the Earth's surface. Projections of a less polluted but increasingly warmed scenario suggest that the loss of human and non-human life could be far more devastating than that in a smog-shrouded world.

Under the Dome is a documentary about China's air pollution crisis made by a Beijing-based former investigative reporter and author, Chai Jing, released online in February 2015.[72] Jing gives a personal account of her polluted city, tied to the story of her daughter's deteriorating health. Chen Jining, the minister of environmental protection, hailed Jing's work as China's *Silent Spring*: 'Chai Jing deserves our respect for drawing the public's attention to the environment from a unique public health perspective.'[73] The anti-pollution documentary went viral in the People's Republic and was viewed online more than 200 million times before China's so-called 'Great Firewall' removed it from Chinese websites.[74] The title *Under the Dome* was borrowed from a CBS sci-fi mini-series adaptation of a Stephen King novel, in which a mysterious, transparent force field descends on an American town, cutting it off from the outside world. In Jing's documentary this malevolent power is the rampant air pollution generated by China's largely unregulated industries. For the residents of Chinese cities, it is oppressive, a harbinger of death. China's smog, Jing says, 'drifts above us like a ghost'. The immediate danger – to Jing, her young child, and the other residents of Beijing – is all too evident. Yet the failure to deal with the consequences of fossil-fuel burning is a global one. Jing includes studies of London, and Los Angeles, bringing in archival footage of London's 1952 'Great Smog'. For those of us who now live in places where the air has no brown tinge or metallic taste, it is easy to locate the problem of pollution 'elsewhere'.

But in the Anthropocene, all of us live under the dome – trapped in atmospheres of human making, as if in one giant Biosphere experiment. This is not the voluntary sequestering of a few willing 'Biospherians'; ordinary citizens are now living out their days in a vast, polluted laboratory. Climate modification cannot be properly tested without full-scale implementation. So if humans are already living in a full-scale planetary experiment, they are also living with the looming prospect of further, more deliberate intervention. If, for example, China were to follow the rest of the world in cutting sulfate aerosols in a bid to reduce air pollution, the prospect of rising global temperatures through the loss of the cooling effect could result in further calls for geoengineering solutions. And if we baulk at these more deliberate interventions, this neither absolves nor protects us from the incidental effects of continuing as we are – down a path of rapid global industrialisation and rising emissions. The Anthropocene and its monstrosities are the more unsettling for having no 'outside'. We cannot lock the door of laboratory Earth and walk away – we *are* the experiment.

For Crutzen, SRM would be a last resort in response to the climate emergency. He expresses the hope that we can manage to agree to cut emissions; that it will not be necessary to resort to climate engineering. 'Currently,' however, 'this looks like a pious wish.'[75] By framing resistance to SRM as 'piety', Crutzen is casting his lot with the self-proclaimed 'eco-pragmatists', albeit with a flourish of regret. As with so many pragmatisms before it, however, the eco variant raises uncomfortable questions about the fine line between feeling bound to consider an option, and feeling bound to pursue it. The fineness of that membrane can be observed in the history of international tensions during the Cold War: a single moment of crisis, real or imaginary, may be enough to transmute the former feeling into the latter.

The Crutzen project

In their imagined future chronicle *The Collapse of Western Civilization*, written from the perspective of Chinese historians in 2393, Naomi Oreskes and Erik M. Conway describe the catastrophic climatic events of a 21st-century world. They tell a tale of botched attempts to control global climate, accelerating disruptions, and human catastrophe. The story ends badly in more ways then one. The fatalities of pet cats

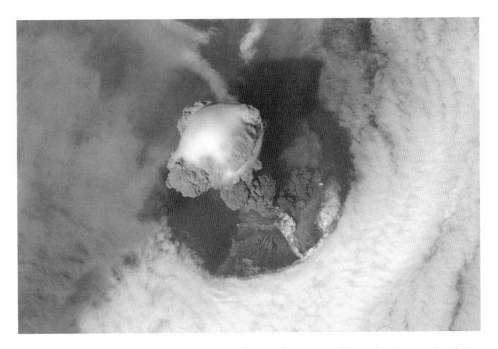

Figure 6.2 Sarychev volcano eruption, Kuril Islands, as seen from the International Space Station, 12 June 2009 (NASA image ISS020-E-9048)
Source: NASA/ISS Expedition 20, Earth Science and Remote Sensing Unit, NASA Johnson Space Center

and dogs, which garners the particular attention of wealthy Westerners in 'the year of perpetual summer' 2023, is only one indication of a cascading series of disasters. Atmospheric doubling of CO_2 from 2001 levels is reached by 2042, causing droughts and heatwaves and leading to a breakdown of social order in 2050. Their future history sounds familiar:

> Many said that the time had come to make the switch to zero-carbon energy sources. Others argued that the world could not wait the ten to 50 years required to alter the global energy infrastructure, much less the 100 years it would take for atmospheric CO_2 to diminish.[76]

A global agreement is hastily put in place – the 'United Nations Convention on Climate Engineering and Protection (UNCCEP)', and blueprints are prepared for the 'International Climate Cooling Engineering Project (ICCEP)'. 2052 sees the launch of the 'International Aerosol Injection Climate Engineering Project (IAICEP)... Sometimes called the Crutzen project after the scientist who first suggested the idea in 2006':

> projects like this engendered heated public opposition when first proposed in the early 21st century but had widespread support by mid-century – from wealthy nations anxious to preserve some semblance of order, from poor nations desperate to see the world do something to address their plight, and from frantic low-lying Pacific Island nations at risk of being submerged by rising sea levels.[77]

However, the geoengineering experiment leads to the shutdown of the Indian monsoon, causing crop failures and famine, and there are calls for its immediate cessation. When IAICEP is stopped in 2063, 'termination shock' ensues: the sudden cessation of sulfate aerosol injection into the stratosphere causes the greenhouse effect to reach a 'tipping point', and global temperatures to escalate rapidly. This precipitates sea level rise, results in the loss of Arctic summer ice by 2060, along with the extinction of the polar bear, and the collapse of the West Antarctica Ice Sheet (the 'ultimate blow'). There follows vast displacement of peoples, along with mass species extinction and the wiping out of the entire populations of Africa and Australia. At the critical moment, neoliberal regimes fail to act in time to avert catastrophe, while the authoritarian state of China is able to coordinate a response to save its population. The 20th century is recalled as the critical era when concerned scientists tried to warn the world – but also as the period in which traditional wisdom was swept away to let neoliberalism dominate utterly. 'Thus, no planning was done, no precautions were taken, and the only management that finally ensued was disaster management.'[78] In Conway and Oreskes' cautionary tale, 'the Crutzen project' turns out to be a bad idea. Their fictional future humanity feels plausible enough, at least to start with – and near enough to hand to warrant serious reflection.

Fixing the Earth

> The acceleration of the human enterprise since the 1950s, particularly the growth of fertiliser use in modern agriculture, resulted in the transgression of the boundary for the rate of human interference with the global nitrogen cycle.[79]

The planetary boundaries hypothesis identifies disturbances in the Earth's phosphorous and nitrogen cycles as among the nine 'planetary boundaries' – transgressions 'may be deleterious or even catastrophic', due to the high risk of triggering abrupt environmental change. Rockström and colleagues explain how to set the nitrogen boundary for a 'safe operating space': 'The simplest and most direct approach is to consider the human fixation of N_2 from the atmosphere as a giant valve that controls a massive flow of new reactive N into the Earth system.' They continue: 'The boundary can then be set by using that valve to control the amount of additional reactive N flowing into the Earth system.' Their 'first guess' is that it should be set at 'approximately 25 per cent of its current value, or to about 35 megatonnes per year'.[80] Thinking in terms of 'planetary boundaries' places humans in the role of fixer of the Earth – as if controlling a 'giant valve' for the flow of reactive nitrogen. As Duncan McLaren has noted, 'Discourses of the "Anthropocene" give a misplaced confidence in the controllability of Earth systems'.[81] A position that maintains that all Earth systems are already irrevocably and irreversibly affected by human activities, leaves little choice but to take control or even enhance them. In such a view, geoengineering could simply be an ongoing project of Earth systems management.

According to Oliver Morton, the 20th century's development of industrial nitrogen fixation, through the Haber-Bosch process, is an important precedent for 21st-century geoengineering schemes. By fixing atmospheric nitrogen and converting it into ammonia, the Haber-Bosch process makes possible the production of artificial fertiliser, gunpowder, and nitroglycerine. The deployment of this technology on a global scale – or 'nitrogen geoengineering' – is a dramatic example of the ways in which humans have already deliberately changed the way the Earth system works. Nitrogen fixation was developed in response to concerns at the end of the 19th century that the world's supply of nitrates – essential for boosting crop production – would not be able to cope with the growing population's demand for food. 'Like climate change today,' Morton observes, 'that threat was seen as being of global significance and to have no easily attainable political solution.'[82]

It was in 1908 that the German chemist Fritz Haber first developed the process of nitrogen fixation. Carl Bosch industrialised the process, just in time for its large-scale use in explosives production during World War I. Aside from his role in making sure the burgeoning global population could be fed (and bombed), Haber was also the 'father of poison gas warfare'.[83] Toxins first developed as weapons found their way into post-war agriculture as pesticides. Industrial agriculture and industrial warfare have been, from the first, inextricably linked. It is estimated that explosives made possible by the Haber-Bosch process have contributed directly to 150 million deaths over the 20th century. In the same period, nitrogen-based fertilisers produced by the process have boosted crop yields to feed the growing human population. The annual global production of artificial nitrogen fertiliser now surpasses 100 million tons. Morton muses, 'By the time the population stabilises somewhere around 10 billion, most of the nitrogen in those people's muscle fibres, nerve cells and DNA will be coming from factories.'[84] Bernd M. Scherer's essay 'The Monsters' equates Fritz Haber with Victor Frankenstein: a 'modern Prometheus… capable of detaching the earthly elements from its course, but leaving his creation to run amok'.[85]

Oliver Morton observes, 'While nitrogen geoengineering has made the world more habitable by humans – more precisely, habitable by more humans – than it could be in a state of nature, it has also done significant damage to biodiversity, human health and ecosystem services in the process.' This particular technological fix is not without controversy, but most people are hardly aware of its impact on their lives. A concerned minority protest at its widespread deployment, arguing that present gains are at the expense of a sustainable future. The majority of us go on buying nitrogen-enriched food products without a murmur. By the same token, although geoengineering is currently seen as a 'fundamental and historic transition', Morton suggests that 'after the fact it might look much less vexatious'.[86] Even though the deliberate alteration of Earth systems by humans is not entirely new, the scale and reach of the geoengineering schemes currently being considered represents an unprecedented degree of anthropogenic manipulation. The potential of these interventions to play havoc with Earth systems will never be understood – that is, unless we try them. Massachusetts Institute of Technology climate scientist Ronald Prinn has asked, 'How can you engineer a system whose behaviour you don't understand?' 'One answer to this question,' Morton suggests, 'is "as carefully and reversibly as you can".'[87]

Examples of more modestly scaled, probably reversible strategies for intervening in Earth systems do exist. These are the so-called 'soft geoengineering technologies', currently under extensive experiment and review.[88] Proposals for localised alterations of the planet's albedo include: brightening water through the creation of hydrosols – inside-out clouds of tiny air bubbles; 'Ice 911', the protection of areas of melting ice with high albedo materials[89]; making roofs and pavements in urban areas more reflective (as promoted by the Global Cool Cities Alliance initiative); transformations of vegetative cover; carbon capture by enhancing the soil with biochar; and a whole range of proposals to protect and enhance ecosystems. Highly urbanised societies can go either way in terms of their impact on climate change. The 20th-century developed world cities tended to lock urban dwellers into lives that depended upon very high levels of consumption of energy. But 21st-century urbanism can take a very different route: reforms to construction standards, integrated transport and land use planning, new approaches to industrial supply chains, infrastructure and transportation networks could all free cities from wasteful energy consumption. The retrofitting, redesign, repurposing and repair of urban infrastructures at scale has long been understood as one of the most effective ways of making a difference to anthropogenic climate change, as an alternative to more radical geoengineering strategies.

Across a range of scales, responses to coastal inundation, drought and other seasonal shortcomings have all been approached with various forms of geoengineering. The geographers Susan Millar and Don Mitchell point out that:

> Walls are built, canals are dug, soils are amended, plants are genetically modified, clouds are seeded, giant piles of snow are stored over the summer months, rivers are dredged (or not), oceans are 'fertilised', power plants are built to supply electricity to ever-greater numbers of air-conditioning units, coal is dug, shale is fracked, and oil wells are sunk into deeper and deeper seas. Geoengineering makes the Earth habitable for humans (and always has): geoengineering simultaneously amplifies the threat from 'nature' (and always has).[90]

This kind of engineering tends to be taken for granted (until those instances where it fails, as with the levees in New Orleans during Hurricane Katrina). This prompts questions about what kind of Earth we have made but also 'how, under what conditions, and to what, decidedly uneven effects'.[91] How might humanity approach Earth-altering in the future? To what extent, for example, can responses to flood inundation pioneered in the Netherlands help much poorer countries such as Bangladesh and Egypt? Such countries are in urgent need but have far more limited capacity for long-term investment in massive engineering projects. Attempts and ambitions for control of the Earth need close scrutiny. This is particularly true within the context of a predominantly capitalist political economy where the legal obligation to return shareholder value, and cultures of target-based reward, can together drive incautious deployment of new technologies and processes.

If we consider the ramifications of the Anthropocene thesis, however, one thing is clear: there is no way of restoring Holocene-like stability. Nor is there any guarantee that we can bring the fluctuations of Earth systems undergoing an Anthropocene transition under human control. There are no strategies that can offer a quick or effective fix to dealing with climate change, or other identified transgressions of planetary boundaries. The very complexity and interdependence of the Earth's systems entails a degree of risk in human climate interventions of any sort, from the vast to the more modest. Continued inhabitation on this fractious planet, requires involvement not only in the scope of any physical and material interventions, but also urgent consideration of the implications of everyday practices in relation to Earth systems dynamics. Steffen, Crutzen and other colleagues have emphasised that: 'humans are not an outside force perturbing an otherwise natural system but rather an integral and interacting part of the Earth system itself'.[92] Humans, however, have historically proved more willing to accept the bad effects of their inadvertent, haphazard and accelerated planetary engineering than to consider renewed purposeful intervention in the climate system.

It seems futile to hope for radical decarbonisation, but dangerous to depend on grand-scale techno-fixes. Interference and intervention in Earth systems can only ever be in an experimental relation to a dynamic and stratified Earth that for the most part is beyond human reach and imagination. There is therefore understandable caution when it comes to 'fixing the Earth'. Time pressure, and our worryingly intransigent habits of carbon consumption, might seem to be driving us inevitably toward drastic high-tech intervention. But there are many obvious advantages for opting instead – and as soon as possible – for a humbler approach of care and repair. Relying on a dream of total control – to be achieved in some unspecified future in which our current excesses will be painlessly, retroactively corrected – seems likely to lead us further into disaster.

Terraforming

It was almost an ice-free planet now, with only Antarctica and Greenland holding on to much, and Greenland going fast. Sea level was therefore 11 metres higher than it had been before the changes. This inundation of the coastline was one of the main drivers of the human disaster on Earth. They had immensely powerful terraforming techniques off-planet, but here they usually couldn't be applied. No slamming comets into it for instance. So they bubbled their ship wakes with surfactants to create a higher albedo, and had tried various levels of sulfur dioxide injected into the stratosphere, imitating volcanoes; but that had once led to disaster and now they couldn't agree on how much sunlight to block ... No, Earth was a mess, a sad place. And yet still the centre of the story.[93]

214   *Monster Earth*

Terraforming, literally 'earth-shaping', encapsulates the idea that worlds can be transformed by deliberate action: slamming comets into planets, for example, as in Kim Stanley Robinson's novel *2312*. The term 'terraforming' was first used in 1940s' science fiction, although the idea of transforming and re-engineering whole planets predates it.[94] It has provided an enduring trope in popular science writing, appearing in the works of Carl Sagan and Isaac Asimov, among others.[95] 'Terraforming' usually implies the alteration of a hostile planetary environment into one that is Earth-like and, by implication, capable of supporting human life. In the Anthropocene, however, the hostile environment we encounter is that of our own home planet – transformed by our past mistakes. A restored Earth-like environment to which we would aspire, in this scenario, is an artificially shaped and maintained Holocene world. For Stewart Brand, terraforming 'to keep this climate something stable like we recognise' is the only option. In a 2011 panel discussion, he insisted:

> We are now in an era called the Anthropocene, an era in which humans are running way too much of the atmosphere and everything else badly. We're in this situation where we don't have a choice of stopping terraforming. We only have a choice of terraforming well. That's the green project for this century.[96]

The notion of 'terraforming well', and the recent surge of research on geoengineering Earth, draws much of its impetus from the promises and possibilities of space exploration, extraterrestrial settlement and, in particular, research on planetary ecosynthesis – or making Mars habitable. Mars is the planet most like Earth in the solar system, and in the past had an approximate Earth environment – a thicker atmosphere and abundant water, lost over hundreds of millions of years. Mars has long been a 'counterpart Earth' in the scientific imaginary – think of Lovelock's studies of Mars that gave rise to his Gaia hypothesis.[97] There have been many terraforming proposals aimed at exploring the steps needed to make Mars fit for life.[98] Projects to warm Mars include Carl Sagan's 1973 idea of depositing low-albedo material such as carbon black dust, or introducing dense plant cover on the Martian polar caps.[99] In 1984, Lovelock and Michael Allaby suggested releasing hundreds of tons of CFC gases into the Martian atmosphere to trigger an artificial greenhouse effect.[100] Moving on from space mirrors, NASA's latest proposals include establishing an ecopoiesis testbed on Mars for the introduction of 'pioneer organisms.'[101]

Proposals for making Mars habitable to humans run parallel to current geoengineering ambitions for 'saving planet Earth'. And in an ironic reversal, climate models that exploit the possibilities for runaway greenhouse scenarios on Mars (aka climate catastrophe on Earth) suggest that relatively modest forcing could push Mars into a quasi-stable high temperature regime more conducive to human life. Keeping pace with terraforming research, Kim Stanley Robinson's *Mars* trilogy, published in the 1990s, speculated on the engineered transformation of the red planet into a human world with a fraught and tangled history. A decade later, his *Science in the Capital* trilogy described a concerned international scientific community embarking on a scheme of Manhattan Project or Apollo Mission scale to reverse severe climate change, with government scientists taking on the role of 'global biosphere managers' tasked with terraforming Earth.[102] The scheme goes badly wrong.

In Robinson's novel *2312*, the difficulties encountered in reshaping Earth, the 'sad place' at the 'centre of the story', are wrapped up in an imaginary of going beyond

Monster Earth 215

the confines of the Earth – of deliberately terraforming other worlds. *2312* imagines a future in which science and technology have continued in an accelerated development of ceaseless innovation. By the 24th century, humanity has escaped its planetary confines and moved into the solar system, refashioning planets and asteroids to establish colonies, mining settlements, laboratories, and wildlife preserves. It is a world in which augmented gender-swapping humans live for hundreds of years, and can choose between a range of space settlements that mimic Earth's biomes, savannahs, and ocean worlds. These are stocked with genetically engineered, hybridised animal and plant species. Like the exocolonies imagined by O'Neill in the 1970s, artificial gravity allows for a range of custom-built cylindrical environments, ranging from New England clapboard villages to cities built with bioceramics to resemble coral reefs. Terraria for endangered species rescued from Earth are crafted in hollowed-out asteroids by self-replicating machines. In short, it is a world where there is plenty of work for designers and engineers, both on and beyond the Earth. Robinson's story enlists a range of geoengineering, terraforming, and paraterraforming techniques for an ingenious array of planetary preserving, redesigning and recomposing projects.

> But clean tech came too late to save Earth from the catastrophes of the early Anthropocene. It was one of the ironies of their time that they could radically change the surfaces of the other planets, but not Earth. The methods they employed in space were almost all too crude and violent. Only with the utmost caution could they tinker with anything on Earth, because everything there was so tightly balanced and interwoven. Anything done for good somewhere usually caused ill somewhere else.[103]

Earth, described as the 'Planet of Sadness', has weathered an accidental Little Ice Age following geoengineering experiments gone awry in the 'early Anthropocene'. In spite of advanced technological know-how, redesigning Earth post-catastrophe has proved a more intransigent problem than making bare space rocks habitable. 'There was no terraforming technique that would help.'[104] Earth remains as the home planet of vast factory cities, drowned coastal cities, huge conurbations and wretched smaller settlements: 'shanty towns in dust bowls or falling apart in tropical downpours and mudslides.'[105] A flooded New York is retrofitted with canals, while planetary built environment regulations specify white photovoltaic roof tiles for all urban constructions: 'these days when seen from space, cities look like patches of snow.'[106] Earth remains home to the usual terrestrial struggles with impossible governance regimes, complex politics, unfair economies and empty promises of poverty alleviation. The recomposing of planets in the story is accompanied by experiments in new economic systems and governance structures. For example, most of the space settlements in the solar system function according to an artificial intelligence-coordinated 'Mondragon Accord'– named after the Basque town whose economy works as a series of nested cooperativess organised for mutual support.[107] A residual capitalism is confined to operating in the margins.

The turning point in Robinson's story is the attempted 'reanimation' of the Earth from a stock of animals preserved in extraterrestrial terraria, a kind of emptying of the ark, with animals ferried back down to Earth in thousands of aerogel bubbles.[108] For Robinson, *2312* is 'a distorted image of present reality'.[109] It is offered as a corrective to what he sees as two pernicious narratives in present-day thinking about humanity's future. These two 'bad stories' – that of Earth as 'humanity's cradle', which originated with Tsiolkovsky; and that of 'the Singularity' – are damaging because they are 'disguised versions of immortality or transcendence'. In Robinson's view, such narratives promote the idea that humanity is destined to escape the confines of the Earth, and perhaps even its own corporeality. They are dangerous in that 'they encourage carelessness toward Earth as our indispensable home, and even toward our own bodies, and our historical project as a species'.[110] Ironically, Robinson's Earth proves more resistant to terraforming than do the barren planets and space rocks that come under human manipulation. Earth's intransigence arises out of its ecological complexity – its many interdependent and unruly systems are impossible to keep in check.

Entry into the Anthropocene requires a responsiveness to both a complex folded and dynamic terrain and the irreversibility of Earth processes. This is a juncture where the limits of human creation come up against a recalcitrant Earth. And in a world already profoundly changed by human actions it brings to the fore the provisional nature of human interventions. Moreover, 'all interventions in Earth systems are matters of trial and error,' and have the capacity to fail, badly, bringing further disaster.[111] The Anthropocene calls for the kinds of improvised adjustments and accommodations that recognise that Earth systems processes will always escape human efforts to control, stabilise or secure them. One of the most worrying consequences of geoengineering and terraforming may prove to be the way adoption of these ideas threatens to alter much more than the physical parameters of a habitable planet. While changing circumstances on Earth drive some to consider ever more audacious acts of Earth shaping and recomposing, they may also provoke a massive redescribing of human and non-human relations. It is the shaping of these relations that are at stake, as well as shifts in the human capacity for restraint, cooperation and respect. Calls to engage in 'thinking like a planet'[112] may yet prompt a sense of humility, rather than a sense of mastery, in the Anthropocene epoch.

The Monster Earth of the Anthropocene is a warning. It suggests the need to follow through with our responsibilities in inhabiting the planet that both supports and surprises us, and to 'continue to care for unwanted consequences'.[113] It is a reminder to pay even closer attention to the limits of human agency, but also the potential for purposeful and ethical action. Restoring a Holocene world is impossible. The question is no longer about how to engage authoritatively with a world that humans might presume to have already made (and unmade), but how to take part with a good deal more precaution in the process of 'remaking the world'. It is also about imagining how to approach such a world with an ethic of taking care instead of a desire to take control.[114]

Handle with care.

Notes

1 D. W. Keith, 'Geoengineering the climate: history and prospect', *Annual Review of Energy and the Environment* 25 (2000): 245–284.
2 Paul J. Crutzen, 'Geology of mankind', *Nature* 415 (2002) 23.
3 Jonas Anshelm and Anders Hansson, 'The last chance to save the planet? An analysis of the geoengineering advocacy discourse in the public debate', *Environmental Humanities* 5 (2014): 101–123; 109.
4 P. Oldham, B. Szerszynski, J. Stilgoe, C. Brown, B. Eacott, A. Yuille, 'Mapping the landscape of climate engineering', *Philosophical Transactions of the Royal Society A* 372.2031 (2014); rsta.royalsocietypublishing.org/content/372/2031/20140065

5 Intellectual Ventures Laboratory, 'The Stratospheric Shield', white paper (2009); www.intellectualventureslab.com/assets_lab/Stratoshield-white-paper-300dpi.pdf
6 Intellectual Ventures Laboratory, 'The Stratospheric Shield', (21 October 2009); www.intellectualventureslab.com/invent/introducing-the-stratoshield
7 Intellectual Ventures Laboratory, 'The Stratospheric Shield', white paper (2009); www.intellectualventureslab.com/assets_lab/Stratoshield-white-paper-300dpi.pdf
8 Stewart Brand, 'We are as gods and we have to get good at it'; 'Stewart Brand talks about his ecopragmatist manifesto', Edge (18 August 2009); www.edge.org/conversation/stewart_brand-we-are-as-gods-and-have-to-get-good-at-it ; author's emphasis.
9 Duncan McLaren, 'Where's the justice in geoengineering?', *The Guardian* (14 March 2015); the post was based on a lecture given at the SRM Science Conference Cambridge, 2015; www.theguardian.com/science/political-science/2015/mar/14/wheres-the-justice-in-geoengineering; accessed 14 March 2015.
10 Oliver Morton, *The Planet Remade: How Geoengineering Could Change the World* (London: Granta, 2015): 156.
11 Clive Hamilton, *Earth Masters: The Dawn of the Age of Climate Engineering* (New Haven and London: Yale University Press, 2013): 181.
12 James Rodger Fleming, *Fixing the Sky: The Checkered History of Weather and Climate Control* (New York: Columbia University Press, 2010): 2.
13 Naomi Klein, *This Changes Everything: Capitalism vs. the Climate* (London: Allen Lane, 2014): 278–280.
14 Naomi Klein, *This Changes Everything: Capitalism vs. the Climate* (London: Allen Lane, 2014): 279–280.
15 Bernd M. Scherer, 'The Monsters', trans. Colin Shepherd in *Textures of the Anthropocene: Grain Vapor Ray*, eds. Katrin Klingan, Ashkan Sepahvand, Christoph Rosol, Bernd M. Scherer (HKW, MIT Press, 2014): 119–133; 127.
16 Elizabeth Grosz, 'Intolerable ambiguity: freaks as/at the limit,' in *Freakery: Cultural Spectacles of the Extraordinary Body*, ed. Rosemarie Garland Thomson (New York: NYU Press, 1996): 55–66; 64–65.
17 Will Steffen, Paul J. Crutzen and John R. McNeill, 'The Anthropocene: Are humans now overwhelming the great forces of nature?', *Ambio* 36.8 (December 2007): 614–621; 620.
18 Christophe Bonneuil and Jean-Baptiste Fressoz, *The Shock of the Anthropocene* trans. David Fernbach, (London: Verso, 2016): 91.
19 Nigel Clark, 'Geo-politics and the disaster of the Anthropocene' in *Disasters and Politics: Materials, Experiments, Preparedness*, eds. Manuel Tironi, Israel Rodríguez-Giralt and Michael Guggenheim (Chichester: John Wiley & Sons, 2014); 19–37; 34. See also Claire Colebrook, 'Matter without bodies', *Derrida Today*, 4.1 (2011): 1–20; 11; Claire Colebrook, 'Not symbiosis, not now: Why anthropogenic change is not really human', *The Oxford Literary Review* 34.2 (2012): 185–209.
20 John Shepherd, Ken Caldeira, Joanna Haigh, David Keith, Brian Launder, Georgina Mace, Gordon MacKerron, John Pyle, Steve Rayner and Catherine Redgwell, 'Geoengineering the Climate. Science, Governance and Uncertainty', (The Royal Society, RS Policy document 10/09, issued September 2009, RS1636). See also Schneider, S.H. 'Earth systems engineering and management', *Nature* 409 (2001): 417–421.
21 Alan Robock, '20 reasons why geoengineering may be a bad idea. Carbon dioxide emissions are rising so fast that some scientists are seriously considering putting Earth on life support as a last resort. But is this cure worse than the disease?', *Bulletin of the Atomic Scientists* 64.2 (May/June 2008): 14–18.
22 Alan Robock, '20 reasons why geoengineering may be a bad idea. Carbon dioxide emissions are rising so fast that some scientists are seriously considering putting Earth on life support as a last resort. But is this cure worse than the disease?', *Bulletin of the Atomic Scientists* 64.2 (May/June 2008): 14–18.
23 Naomi Klein, Chapter 8, 'Dimming the Sun', *This Changes Everything: Capitalism vs. the Climate* (London: Allen Lane, 2014); 256–290.
24 Eli Kintisch, quoted in 'Geoengineering: "A Bad Idea Whose Time Has Come"' (npr books, 29 May 2010); www.npr.org/templates/story/story.php?storyId=127245606
25 James Rodger Fleming, *Fixing the Sky: The Checkered History of Weather and Climate Control* (New York: Columbia University Press, 2010): 2.

26 Jules Verne, The Purchase of the North Pole, cf. James Rodger Fleming, *Fixing the Sky The Checkered History of Weather and Climate Control* (New York: Columbia University Press, 2010): 27.
27 Jacob Darwin Hamblin, *Arming Mother Nature: The Birth of Catastrophic Environmentalism* (Oxford, New York: Oxford University Press, 2013).
28 Kurt Vonnegut, *Cat's Cradle* (New York: Holt, Rinehart & Winston, 1963).
29 Phil Macnaghten and Bronislaw Szerszynski, 'Living the global social experiment: An analysis of public discourse on solar radiation management and its implications for governance', *Global Environmental Change* 23 (2013): 465–474.
30 Melinda Cooper, 'Turbulent worlds: financial markets and environmental crisis', *Theory, Culture and Society* 27.2–3 (2010): 167–190; 184; cf. Nigel Clark, 'Geoengineering and geologic politics', *Environment and Planning A* 45 (2013): 2825–2832; 2827.
31 Nigel Clark, 'Geoengineering and geologic politics', *Environment and Planning A* 45 (2013): 2825–2832.
32 Nigel Clark, 'Geoengineering and geologic politics', *Environment and Planning A* 45 (2013): 2825–2832.
33 Mary Shelley, *Frankenstein; or, The Modern Prometheus* (1818), introduction to 1831 edition (London: Henry Colburn and Richard Bentley, 1831).
34 Clive Hamilton, *Earth Masters: The Dawn of the Age of Climate Engineering* (New Haven and London: Yale University Press, 2013): 83. See, for example, Andrew C. Revkin, 'The #Frankenstorm in climate context', *The New York Times* (28 October 2012); dotearth. blogs.nytimes.com/2012/10/28/the-frankenstorm-in-climate-context/; and also Sarah Laskow, 'Frankenclimate', *The American Prospect* (29 October 2012); prospect.org/article/frankenclimate
35 On the Tambora eruption and its consequences, see Clive Oppenheimer, *Eruptions that Shook the World* (Cambridge: Cambridge University Press, 2011): 295–319.
36 Mary Shelley, *Frankenstein; or, The Modern Prometheus* (1818), introduction to 1831 edition (London: Henry Colburn and Richard Bentley, 1831).
37 Imannuel Kant, *Universal Natural History and Theory of the Heavens* (1755).
38 Simon Schaffer, 'Charged atmospheres: Promethean science and the Royal Society' in *Seeing Further: The Story of Science and the Royal Society*, ed. Bill Bryson (London: HarperPress, 2010): 132–155; 132–133.
39 Bruno Latour, 'Love your monsters: Why we must care for our technologies as we do our children', in *Love Your Monsters: Postenvironmentalism and the Anthropocene*, ed. Michael Schellenberger and Ted Nordhaus (Oakland: Breakthrough Institute, 2011).
40 Bruno Latour, 'Love your monsters: Why we must care for our technologies as we do our children', in *Love Your Monsters: Postenvironmentalism and the Anthropocene*, ed. Michael Schellenberger and Ted Nordhaus (Oakland: Breakthrough Institute, 2011); 25.
41 Bruno Latour, 'Love your monsters: Why we must care for our technologies as we do our children', in *Love Your Monsters: Postenvironmentalism and the Anthropocene*, ed. Michael Schellenberger and Ted Nordhaus (Oakland: Breakthrough Institute, 2011); 26.
42 Naomi Klein, *This Changes Everything: Capitalism vs. the Climate* (London: Allen Lane, 2014): 279.
43 Naomi Klein, *This Changes Everything: Capitalism vs. the Climate* (London: Allen Lane, 2014): 280.
44 Naomi Klein, *This Changes Everything: Capitalism vs. the Climate* (London: Allen Lane, 2014): 279.
45 Bruno Latour, 'A cautious Prometheus? A few steps toward a philosophy of design (with special attention to Peter Sloterdijk)' in *Networks of Design Proceedings of the 2008 Annual International Conference of the Design History Society (UK)*, eds. Jonathan Glynne, Fiona Hackney and Viv Minton (Boca Raton, Florida: Universal-Publishers, 2009): 8.
46 Paul J. Crutzen, 'Geology of mankind', *Nature* 415 (2002): 23.
47 Paul J. Crutzen, 'Albedo enhancement by stratospheric sulfur injections: a contribution to resolve a policy dilemma? An editorial essay', *Climatic Change* 77 (2006): 211–219; 214.
48 Paul J. Crutzen, 'Albedo enhancement by stratospheric sulfur injections: a contribution to resolve a policy dilemma? An editorial essay', *Climatic Change* 77 (2006) :211–219; 217.

49 Paul J. Crutzen, 'Albedo enhancement by stratospheric sulfur injections: a contribution to resolve a policy dilemma? An editorial essay', *Climatic Change* 77 (2006): 211–219; 216.
50 John Shepherd, Ken Caldeira, Joanna Haigh, David Keith, Brian Launder, Georgina Mace, Gordon MacKerron, John Pyle, Steve Rayner and Catherine Redgwell, 'Geoengineering the Climate. Science, Governance and Uncertainty', (The Royal Society, RS Policy document 10/09, issued September 2009, RS1636). See also Schneider, S.H. 'Earth systems engineering and management', *Nature* 409 (2001): 61.
51 IPCC, 'Summary for Policymakers' in *Climate Change 2013: The Physical Science Basis. Contribution of Working Group I to the Fifth Assessment Report of the Intergovernmental Panel on Climate Change*, eds. T.F. Stocker, D. Qin, G.-K. Plattner, M. Tignor, S.K. Allen, J. Boschung, A. Nauels, Y. Xia, V. Bex and P.M. Midgley (Cambridge University Press, Cambridge, United Kingdom and New York, NY, USA, 2013); www.climatechange2013.org/images/report/WG1AR5_SPM_FINAL.pdf : 29.
52 David Keith, *A Case for Climate Engineering* (Boston: MIT Press, 2013).
53 Jane C. S. Long, Frank Loy and M. Granger Morgan, 'Start research on climate engineering', *Nature* 518 (5 February 2015): 29–31; www.nature.com/polopoly_fs/1.16826!/menu/main/topColumns/topLeftColumn/pdf/518029a.pdf
54 John Shepherd, Ken Caldeira, Joanna Haigh, David Keith, Brian Launder, Georgina Mace, Gordon MacKerron, John Pyle, Steve Rayner and Catherine Redgwell, 'Geoengineering the Climate. Science, Governance and Uncertainty', (The Royal Society, RS Policy document 10/09, issued September 2009, RS1636). See also Schneider, S.H. 'Earth systems engineering and management', *Nature* 409 (2001)
55 David Keith and Mike Hulme, 'Climate science: can geoengineering save the world? Climate professors Mike Hulme and David Keith go head to head over whether climate engineering could provide a solution to climate change', *The Guardian* (29 November 2013); www.theguardian.com/sustainable-business/blog/climate-science-geoengineering-save-world
56 Oliver Morton, 'Some of what I think about geoengineering' (11 July 2012); heliophage.wordpress.com/2012/07/11/some-of-what-i-think-about-geoengineering/#more-1354; also, 'On Geoengineering: Oliver Morton reflects on the breakthrough dialogue, geoengineering and climate change' (9 August 2012); thebreakthrough.org/index.php/dialogue/on-geoengineering/
57 Nigel Clark, 'Geoengineering and geological politics', *Environmental Planning A* 45 (2013): 2825–2832.
58 Oliver Morton, *The Planet Remade: How Geoengineering Could Change the World* (London: Granta, 2015): 86–89.
59 Oliver Morton, *The Planet Remade: How Geoengineering Could Change the World* (London: Granta, 2015): 92.
60 Oliver Morton, *The Planet Remade: How Geoengineering Could Change the World* (London: Granta, 2015): 99.
61 Naomi Klein, *This Changes Everything: Capitalism vs. the Climate* (London: Allen Lane, 2014): 260.
62 Oliver Morton, 'Some of what I think about geoengineering' (11 July 2012); heliophage.wordpress.com/2012/07/11/some-of-what-i-think-about-geoengineering/#more-1354
63 Paul J. Crutzen, 'Albedo enhancement by stratospheric sulfur injections: a contribution to resolve a policy dilemma? An editorial essay', *Climatic Change* 77 (2006): 211–219; 217.
64 Paul J. Crutzen, 'Albedo enhancement by stratospheric sulfur injections: a contribution to resolve a policy dilemma? An editorial essay', *Climatic Change* 77 (2006): 211–219; 216.
65 Paul J. Crutzen, 'Albedo enhancement by stratospheric sulfur injections: a contribution to resolve a policy dilemma? An editorial essay', *Climatic Change* 77 (2006): 211–219; 213.
66 Paul J. Crutzen, 'Albedo enhancement by stratospheric sulfur injections: a contribution to resolve a policy dilemma? An editorial essay', *Climatic Change* 77 (2006): 211–219; 212.
67 Paul J. Crutzen, 'Albedo enhancement by stratospheric sulfur injections: a contribution to resolve a policy dilemma? An editorial essay', *Climatic Change* 77 (2006): 211–219; 214.
68 Paul J. Crutzen, "'Albedo enhancement by stratospheric sulfur injections: a contribution to resolve a policy dilemma? An editorial essay', *Climatic Change* 77 (2006): 211–219; 216.

69 Ken Caldeira, 'We need some symptomatic relief', *Earth Island Journal* (Spring 2013); www.earthisland.org/journal/index.php/eij/article/caldeira/
70 Martin Bunzl, 'Geoengineering Research Reservations' presented at AAAS Annual Meeting: 'Can Geoengineering Save us from Global Warming?', San Diego, (20 February 2010); sciencepolicy.colorado.edu/students/envs_5000/bunzl_2011.pdf
71 Paul Tavares, 'Stratoshield' in *Textures of the Anthropocene: Grain Vapor Ray*, eds. Katrin Klingan, Ashkan Sepahvand, Christoph Rosol and Bernd M. Scherer (HKW, MIT Press, 2014): 61–71; 63.
72 Edward Wong, 'China blocks web access to Under the Dome documentary on pollution', *The New York Times* (6 March 2015); www.nytimes.com/2015/03/07/world/asia/china-blocks-web-access-to-documentary-on-nations-air-pollution.html
73 Daniel K. Gardner, 'China's 'Silent Spring' Moment? Why 'Under the Dome' found a ready audience in China', *The New York Times* (18 March 2015); www.nytimes.com/2015/03/19/opinion/why-under-the-dome-found-a-ready-audience-in-china.html?_r=0
74 Ed Rampell, 'The big haze: China's Great Leap Backwards', *Earth Island Journal* (13 March 2015); www.earthisland.org/journal/index.php/elist/eListRead/the_big_haze_chinas_great_leap_backwards
75 Paul J. Crutzen, 'Albedo enhancement by stratospheric sulfur injections: a contribution to resolve a policy dilemma? An editorial essay', *Climatic Change* 77 (2006): 211–219; 217.
76 Naomi Oreskes and Erik M. Conway, *The Collapse of Western Civilization: A View from the Future* (New York: Columbia University Press, 2014): 26.
77 Naomi Oreskes and Erik M., *The Collapse of Western Civilization: A View from the Future* (New York: Columbia University Press, 2014): 26–27.
78 Naomi Oreskes and Erik M. Conway, *The Collapse of Western Civilization: A View from the Future* (New York: Columbia University Press, 2014): 47.
79 J. Rockström, W. Steffen, K. Noone, Å. Persson, F. S. Chapin, III, E. Lambin, T. M. Lenton, M. Scheffer, C. Folke, H. Schellnhuber, B. Nykvist, C. A. De Wit, T. Hughes, S. van der Leeuw, H. Rodhe, S. Sörlin, P. K. Snyder, R. Costanza, U. Svedin, M. Falkenmark, L. Karlberg, R. W. Corell, V. J. Fabry, J. Hansen, B. Walker, D. Liverman, K. Richardson, P. Crutzen, and J. Foley, 'Planetary boundaries: exploring the safe operating space for humanity', *Ecology and Society* 14.2 (2009): 32; www.ecologyandsociety.org/vol14/iss2/art32/
80 J. Rockström, W. Steffen, K. Noone, Å. Persson, F. S. Chapin, III, E. Lambin, T. M. Lenton, M. Scheffer, C. Folke, H. Schellnhuber, B. Nykvist, C. A. De Wit, T. Hughes, S. van der Leeuw, H. Rodhe, S. Sörlin, P. K. Snyder, R. Costanza, U. Svedin, M. Falkenmark, L. Karlberg, R. W. Corell, V. J. Fabry, J. Hansen, B. Walker, D. Liverman, K. Richardson, P. Crutzen, and J. Foley, 'Planetary boundaries: exploring the safe operating space for humanity,' *Ecology and Society* 14.2 (2009): 32; www.ecologyandsociety.org/vol14/iss2/art32/
81 Duncan McLaren, 'Where's the justice in geoengineering?', *The Guardian* (14 March 2015); the post was based on a lecture given at the SRM Science Conference, Cambridge, 2015; www.theguardian.com/science/political-science/2015/mar/14/wheres-the-justice-in-geoengineering; accessed 14 March 2015.
82 Oliver Morton, 'Nitrogen geoengineering', opinion article, Geoengineering Our Climate Working Paper and Opinion Article Series (2013); geoengineeringourclimate.com/2013/07/09/nitrogen-geoengineering-opinion-article/
83 Bernd M. Scherer, 'The Monsters', trans. Colin Shepherd in *Textures of the Anthropocene: Grain Vapor Ray*, eds. Katrin Klingan, Ashkan Sepahvand, Christoph Rosol and Bernd M. Scherer (HKW, MIT Press, 2014): 119–133; 125.
84 Oliver Morton, 'Nitrogen geoengineering', opinion article, Geoengineering Our Climate Working Paper and Opinion Article Series (2013); geoengineeringourclimate.com/2013/07/09/nitrogen-geoengineering-opinion-article/
85 Bernd M. Scherer, 'The Monsters', trans. Colin Shepherd in *Textures of the Anthropocene: Grain Vapor Ray*, eds. Katrin Klingan, Ashkan Sepahvand, Christoph Rosol and Bernd M. Scherer (HKW, MIT Press, 2014): 119–133; 119.
86 Oliver Morton, 'Nitrogen geoengineering', opinion article, Geoengineering Our Climate Working Paper and Opinion Article Series (2013); geoengineeringourclimate.com/2013/07/09/nitrogen-geoengineering-opinion-article/

87 Oliver Morton, 'Climate change: Is this what it takes to save the world?', *Nature* 447 (10 May 2007): 132–136.
88 Robert L. Olson, 'Soft geoengineering: A gentler approach to addressing climate change, environment: science and policy for sustainable development', *Environment: Science and Policy for Sustainable Development* 54:5 (2012): 29–39.
89 Leslie Field, 'Ice 911: Developing an effective response to climate change in the Earth's cryosphere' (16 November 2011); www.ice911.org/Ice911UpdateNov2011.pdf
90 Susan W.S. Millar and Don Mitchell, 'The tight dialectic: The Anthropocene and the capitalist production of nature', *Antipode* 49 (2017): 75–93; 76.
91 Susan W.S. Millar and Don Mitchell, 'The tight dialectic: The Anthropocene and the capitalist production of nature', *Antipode* 49 (2017): 75–93; 76.
92 Will Steffen, Paul J. Crutzen and John R. McNeill, 'The Anthropocene: Are humans now overwhelming the great forces of nature?', *Ambio* 36.8 (December 2007): 614–621; 615.
93 Kim Stanley Robinson, *2312* (London, Orbit, 2013): 90. Copyright © 2012 by Kim Stanley Robinson. Used by permission of Orbit, a division of the Hachette Book Group USA Inc. All rights reserved.
94 J. Williamson, writing as W. Stewart, 'Collision Orbit', *Astounding Science Fiction* XXIX.5 (1942): 80.
95 Author Jack Williamson is credited with coining the term 'terraform', using it in his science fiction novella '*Collision Orbit*', published in *Astounding Fiction Magazine* in July 1942, under the pseudonym Will Stewart. The concept predates the term and is included in works of, for example, Octave Béliard, J.B.Haldane and Olaf Stapledon. Olaf Stapledon's *Last and First Men*, written in the 1930s describes electrolysing a global sea on Venus in order to prepare it for human habitation. Authors such as Arthur C. Clark, Isaac Asimov, Poul Anderson, Carl Sagan, James Lovelock and, most recently, Kim Stanley Robinson have popularised the term.
96 Stewart Brand, Kevin Kelly, George Dyson, 'An Edge Conversation in Munich', introduction: Andrian Kreye, moderator: John Brockman (24 January 2011); *Edge* 338 (7 February 2011); edge.org/documents/archive/edge338.html;
97 Oliver Morton, *Mapping Mars* (London: Fourth Estate, 2002).
98 Martin J. Fogg, 'Terraforming Mars: A review of current research', *Advanced Space Research* 22. 3 (1998): 415–420.
99 Carl Sagan, 'Planetary engineering on Mars', *Icarus* 20.4 (1973): 513.
100 James Lovelock and Michael Allaby, *The Greening of Mars* (New York: Warner, 1984).
101 Eugene Boland, Techshot Inc., 'Mars Ecopoiesis test bed' (NASA, 14 June 2014); www.nasa.gov/content/mars-ecopoiesis-test-bed/#.Vd2YVZVmGfQ
102 Kim Stanley Robinson, *Fifty Degrees Below Zero* (New York: Bantam Books, 2005). The first and third books in the trilogy are *Forty Signs of Rain* (2004) and *Sixty Days and Counting* (2007).
103 Kim Stanley Robinson, *2312* (London: Orbit, 2013): 304. First published in 2012. All quotes copyright © 2012 by Kim Stanley Robinson. Used by permission of Orbit, a division of the Hachette Book Group USA Inc. All rights reserved.
104 Kim Stanley Robinson, *2312* (London: Orbit, 2013): 304.
105 Kim Stanley Robinson, *2312* (London: Orbit, 2013): 315.
106 Kim Stanley Robinson, *2312* (London: Orbit, 2013): 303.
107 Kim Stanley Robinson, *2312* (London: Orbit, 2013): 125–126.
108 Kim Stanley Robinson, *2312* (London: Orbit, 2013): 395.
109 Gerry Canavan and Kim Stanley Robinson, 'Afterword: Still, I'm reluctant to call this pessimism' in *Green Planets: Ecology and Science Fiction*, eds. G. Canavan and K. Stanley Robinson (Middletown, CT: Wesleyan University Press, 2014): 243–260; 246.
110 Gerry Canavan and Kim Stanley Robinson, 'Afterword: Still, I'm reluctant to call this pessimism' in *Green Planets: Ecology and Science Fiction*, eds. G. Canavan and K. Stanley Robinson (Middletown, CT: Wesleyan University Press, 2014): 243–260; 254.
111 Nigel Clark, 'Geo-politics and the disaster of the Anthropocene' in *Disasters and Politics: Materials, Experiments, Preparedness*, eds. Manuel Tironi, Israel Rodríguez-Giralt and Michael Guggenheim (Chichester: John Wiley & Sons, 2014): 19–37; 34.

112 Paul D. Hirsch and Bryan G Norton, 'Thinking like a planet' in *Ethical Adaptation to Climate Change: Human Virtues of the Future*, eds. Allen Thompson and Jeremy Bendik-Keymer (Cambridge, MA: MIT Press, 2012): 317. See also Introduction, *The Future of Nature Documents of Global Change*, eds. Libby Robin, Sverker Sorlin, Paul Warde (New Haven and London: Yale University Press, 2013): 2.
113 Bruno Latour, 'Love your monsters: Why we must care for our technologies as we do our children', in *Love Your Monsters: Postenvironmentalism and the Anthropocene*. eds. M. Shellenberger and T. Nordhaus, (Oakland: The Breakthrough Institute, 2011).
114 Oliver Morton, *The Planet Remade: How Geoengineering Could Change the World* (London: Granta, 2015).

7 Temporary home

WARNING: *trip hazard*

The advent of the Anthropocene lays bare the precariousness that has always characterised human settlement even as it ushers in a period of greater unsettlement than our species has known. Unsettlement usually refers to the displacement of people through migration, urbanisation, environmental catastrophe, and warfare. The word is also used to describe the material, ecological, psychological, social and political shifts engendered by industrial and technological transformations. But there is another kind of unsettlement now occurring. This is the disruption of the Holocene state of the Earth system, which has so far lasted approximately 11,700 years. In other words, this unsettlement refers not only to the fracturing and displacement of human lives but also to the disjunctures and shifts of a dynamic Earth. The geological signature of the new Anthropocene epoch promises to remain as evidence of the irreversible and aggressive impacts on Earth and life processes triggered by human actions. The Anthropocene is defined as a geological boundary crossing. It announces human transformations of the Earth, even as it warns of the limitations of human powers to mitigate these changes once unleashed. It refers to the transgressing of boundaries in Earth systems and a shift into new systemic states that humans have never experienced before. It thus challenges everything about the experience of home – however temporary – on Earth.

The designation of Earth as humanity's home is central to the story of the Anthropocene. And it is on behalf of the home planet that the concept of the Anthropocene has been enlisted. The delineation of 'planetary boundary' conditions that designate 'the safe operating space for humanity' also challenges the established terms of Holocene geopolitics. For a politics of the Earth now needs to address not only conventional political issues of the ownership of resources and the demarcation of territories across the Earth's surface, but also the temporal dynamics and volatility of Earth systems that signal a 'global state of emergency'. However, 'there is no clear-cut or obvious passage from the countenance of planetary disaster to a novel sense of geopolitics'.[1]

The Anthropocene is a warning: that it is no longer the community, the neighbourhood, the city, or even the nation state that is now the primary locus of safety or danger, but the Earth itself. Thinking about issues of 'defence' and 'protection' invokes a planetary scale. Even as this planetary perspective enquires into the condition of the Earth system as a singular whole, it inevitably highlights the unequal effects of anthropogenic damage across the globe. While 'planetary boundaries' thinking has recognised the need for adaptive governance in the face of changing risks, scientific uncertainty and a complex and fragmented policy landscape, it is presented as a risk assessment exercise rather than a set of policy prescriptions.[2] It acknowledges, however, the need for new institutional arrangements and a new international politics to deal with the prospect of myriad unsettlements that accompany the risks of transgressing Earth systems thresholds, intertwined at regional and global scales. The Anthropocene and its 'collateral concept' of planetary boundaries, foregrounds the politicisation of scientific research:

> The concept of the Anthropocene might… become exploited, to a variety of ends. Some of these may be beneficial, some less so. The Anthropocene might be used as encouragement to slow carbon emissions and biodiversity loss, for instance; perhaps as evidence in legislation on conservation measures; or, in the assessment of compensation claims for environmental damage. It has the capacity to become the most politicised unit, by far, of the geologic time scale and therefore to take formal geological classification into uncharted waters.[3]

One of the perils of these 'uncharted waters' is that Anthropocene discourse appears to fit well with a 'politics of emergency' whereby conditions of crisis or catastrophe are mobilised to justify the suspension of established political rights and procedures. Declaring a state of emergency can legitimate certain pre-emptive measures: interventions like increased securitisation, the imposition of martial law, or in the case of a climate emergency, risky geoengineering fixes.[4] Mass migration is inevitable in a world with ever-widening socioeconomic disparities, protracted conflicts, rapid environmental change, and recurring environmental disasters. In 2015, according to the UNHCR (Office of the United Nations High Commissioner for Refugees), the number of displaced people was estimated at 65.3 million.[5] Whether human-induced or not, environmental changes – sea level rise, drought, desertification, deforestation, earthquakes, hurricanes – are major drivers of population displacement.[6] The predictions for climate-induced displacement top 250 million people by 2050. And while most migrations occur within poor regions, they are not confined to them. In 2005, Hurricane Katrina displaced 1.2 million people in the southern United States, and the 2011 Fukushima disaster displaced 470,000 people in Japan. Refugee 'crises' have exposed the problems with national and international emergency responses. The difficulties displaced people subsequently face in achieving documentation, access to basic services, and safe, permanent resettlement, have shown up the shortcomings of a state-based system of population regulation.

The Anthropocene posits humanity as a geologic agent. If a minority of humans (specifically the wealthy elite of industrialised nations) are the main agents of this transformation of the Earth, the result has been to make the Earth increasingly uninhabitable for increasing numbers of humans and non-humans. In *Planet Under Pressure*, Will Steffen and colleagues suggest that the worst is yet to come: 'The human-driven changes to the global environment … may drive the Earth itself into a different state that may be much less hospitable to humans and other forms of life.'[7] Donna Haraway's essay on the Anthropocene draws on Anna Tsing's research to describe the Holocene as the long period when *refugia*, places of refuge or havens for cultural and biological diversity, existed – even abounded. To Haraway the Anthropocene is an 'outrage': the 'destruction of places and times of refuge' for both humans and non-humans. She characterises it as a boundary event, 'like the K-Pg boundary between the Cretaceous and the Paleogene', rather than an epoch. As such it marks 'severe discontinuities' so that 'what comes after will not be like what came before'. She continues:

> I think our job is to make the Anthropocene as short/thin as possible and to cultivate with each other in every way imaginable epochs to come that can replenish refuge. Right now, the Earth is full of refugees, human and not, without refuge.[8]

In the midst of warnings of extreme human mobility and escalating humanitarian crises, an 'Earth full of refugees' is a provocation to our notions of temporary inhabitation – in time and in place. Migrant 'crises' across the world have proliferated unsettlements. These range from the detention zones, tent cities, transit shelters and migrant camps that accrue on Mediterranean shores, to the temporary accommodation that becomes more 'permanent' urban resettlement projects in Europe, the Middle East and North Africa. They include, for example, the temporary-turned-permanent refugee settlements managed by the United Nations Relief and Works Agency for Palestine Refugees in the Near East (UNRWA) in Gaza and the West Bank since 1948,[9] the camp-cities of the Sahrawi population in the border zone of southwestern Algeria founded in 1976,[10] and the migrant 'city' on the outskirts of Calais vying for existence since 2002 and destroyed in October 2016 by French authorities. Such 'makeshift cities' tend to be construed as disaster zones, or zones of exception, fixed in a temporal and territorial limbo. They are spaces of ambiguous jurisdiction that can all too easily become imbued with a rhetoric of illegality and criminality. The Anthropocene boundary event or epoch is a challenge to face the consequences of the changes we are forcing on the world in a spirit of social and environmental justice. As the specialist of environmental geopolitics François Gemenne argues, 'the Anthropocene is first and foremost a matter of keeping the Earth habitable for the most vulnerable'.[11]

In the Anthropocene, after all, the Earth is all of humanity's temporary home. This is a world of cities in crisis, of proliferating camps, of planetary unsettlement. We are inhabiting a planetary state of exception and a planetary temporal condition of *for the time-being*. Fears for this temporary home abound. For how can a home be maintained when its very ground is shifting and rupturing? And if radically changing environmental conditions – flooding, earthquakes, hurricanes, drought – threaten valued ways of living, what does this mean for Earth citizenship? What does exposure to the human-provoked turbulence of Earth systems mean for questions of responsibility or hospitality? The Anthropocene unsettles both familiar modes of planetary consciousness and notions of human agency. Rethinking the meaning of 'temporary home' in the transitional moment of the Anthropocene means imagining a revised geopolitics, or cosmopolitics, that could enable us to co-inhabit an increasingly fractious world.

Habitat

> So whatever is written about our habitat must submit to being incomplete.[12]

'Habitat', the first United Nations Conference on Human Settlements, took place in Vancouver in 1976.[13] 'Habitat is concerned with pulling together the issues faced at the United Nations conferences on the environment, population, food, the status of women and the whole balance of the world economic order,' the Vancouver Declaration stated.[14] 'In the 1970s,' it continued, 'the whole international community started to confront the realities of its planetary life'[15] Barbara Ward's *The Home of Man*, a sequel to *Only One Earth*, established the ideological agenda of the conference in an era filled with anxieties about demographic explosion, rampant urbanisation, resource scarcity and environmental insecurities: 'These overlapping contexts of violent demographic, social and environmental change all meet – one could say collide – in human settlements.'[16] Appropriate management of human settlements, Ward claimed, could solve the mounting problems of planetary life.

In Ward's view the 'explosive growth, explosive aspirations, and potential biophysical limits' of the human species at this critical moment could not be addressed *ad hoc* – they demanded careful analysis and purposeful action.[17] An implicit politics of crisis underpinned notions of the planetary habitat in the 1970's: a limited, bounded and fragile Earth was set at odds with the alarming statistics of rural-to-urban migration, changing population densities, resource consumption, intensifying land use and accumulated industrial stresses and toxicities. Ward's book reads like a world-historical tour of urbanisation – she begins with the earliest cities of Mesopotamia and ranges through empires and civilisations, to arrive at the 'unintended' cities and metropolises of the 19th and 20th centuries. She characterises her own epoch as one of 'staggering creativity and destructiveness – landing men on the Moon and annihilating cities with atom bombs' – and concludes that it is natural that humanity should be reflecting with new intensity on 'its nature, its future, the meaning of its enterprises, the fundamental significance of man himself'.[18]

Ward rejected the 'overloaded lifeboat' model of humanity's precarious situation which was popular among some thinkers of the time. Certainly we are all on the 'same ship', she argued, but the problem is not so much overcrowding as the damage caused by human activity – some aspects of which, such as the development of nuclear weapons, have the potential to sink the 'ship' once and for all. 'Must we then conclude that we are indeed living at the end of time? That our capacity for destruction now far surpasses our powers of control and restraint that shipwreck without survivors is to round off the human voyage?' she asked.[19] For Ward, 'all the world's settlements' are 'irretrievably part of the planetary system that has been in the making in the centuries between Vasco da Gama's first landfall in India, Guglielmo Marconi's first patent for a radio transmitter, and the first mushroom cloud above Los Alamos'.[20] Truly, this was a planet of interconnected cities in the throes of planetary crisis.

> By migration and natural increase, 1,300 million new residents will arrive to crowd into the developing cities – the *callampas* (mushroom cities) of Chile, the *bustees* of India, the *favelas* of Brazil, the *gourbevilles* of Tunisia, the *gecekindu* of Turkey … The names vary but the tarpaper shacks, the unpaved streets and open sewers, the water taken dangerously from open ponds and streams or purchased at monopoly prices from itinerant water carriers – these basic conditions do not much change and it can be argued they make up the most inhuman environments ever endured by man.[21]

Ward's narrative sounded the alarm of unsettlement: 'The demographic flood… an unmanaged, unintended, disorganised rush, pell-mell, into the new urban order.'[22]

In her *Human Settlements: Crisis and Opportunity* of the previous year, Ward had stated: 'The very word "settlement" is in some measure a contradiction.' She continued: 'In many ways modern man is dealing with continuous "unsettlement".'[23] Recognition of this reality demanded a concomitant realisation that a new economic order was necessary, one that Ward called 'planetary housekeeping'. Ward was aware that neither aid nor international law could make a difference if national governments had no commitment to distributive justice. In *The Home of Man* she proposed that, 'Any kind of genuinely social and constructive development in the world's settlements – from village to metropolis – depends upon drawing *all* the people into the process, treating them as resources and not problems, and giving them a decisive part in the creation of their own future.'[24] Ward argued for 'graduated strategies', for 'a full-scale conversion of rich nations to the concept of sharing as a planetary obligation and… to the concept of social justice and citizen involvement as a condition of survival.'[25] She insisted that the bulldozing, clean-up operations and forced evictions of 'resettlement' should be halted, and that such neighbourhoods should instead be redesignated 'settlement' projects, and their infrastructure needs attended to. With the support of the World Bank and the IMF, informal urbanisms in the Third World were to be co-opted into development paradigms, formalised as self-help housing projects, and put to use as a mechanism of social stability or counterinsurgency. The 'established practices of the general welfare' needed to be given 'a planetary dimension'.[26]

Whatever the good intentions – of providing shelter, of meeting aspirations, of restoring dignity, Habitat also invited another agenda. As the architecture academic Felicity Scott observes, self-help strategies 'validated a precarious form of life and located those unsettled citizens and displaced persons, as well as their abodes, within a governing apparatus that could put them to work for profit'.[27] Media reports of the conference helped to establish a new reputation for these hitherto 'unauthorised communities'. *The New York Times* announced, 'Shantytowns of squatters, living on land that does not belong to them, are gaining a new respectability around the world.'[28] From the 1980s on, and in the context of continued inadequate state provision of housing and services for poor urban dwellers, the World Bank, developmental economists and NGOs fell in step with the bootstrap model of urbanisation, which identified practices of shelter and survival as entrepreneurship.

For Buckminster Fuller, Habitat was a 'historical watershed' that marked the 'end of human settlement'.[29] In an article published after the conference, he put it thus: 'Human settlements were inherent to agrarian and mill town ages: now human *unsettlement* is occurring.'[30] Technological innovation had freed humans from rooted dwelling patterns, so that now, 'It was the beginning of the era of local geographical unsettlement and transition into the historically unprecedented and utterly unexpected condition of all humans – successfully-at-home-in-universe.'[31] For Fuller, Habitat was an opportunity to demonstrate his ideal of 'world-around living in the form of electrified and plumbinged campsites and hostels',[32] a nomadic-pastoral application of his Spaceship Earth accounting system of energy and resource inputs and outputs. Fuller's 'camp' at the Habitat Forum exhibition at Jericho Beach[33] consisted of the technological Now House installation: 'a mushroom group of foldable and moveable geodesic domes and modernised Indian tepees.'[34] It was inhabited by ten 'World Gamers', with electricity generated by a windmill, hydroponic tanks for growing vegetables and solar panels for heating water. Now House was presented as an update of Fuller's Dymaxion

228 *Temporary home*

Dwelling Machine, originally conceived in the 1920s and prototyped for use during World War II, an 'air-deliverable, only-rentable, world-around dwelling machine'.[35] It was lightweight, strong, easy to assemble, and fit for all weathers. As Fuller described the smaller 'North Face' domes of the Now House installation: 'An eight-pound home compounded with a sleeping bag permits humans to be very intimate with nature under most hostile conditions.'[36]

Fuller had joined Ward in celebrating informal urbanism, noting with undisguised romanticism shantytown inhabitants' ingenuity and ability to 'improvise something to sleep under that sheds off the rain, whether it's three-ply, corrugated paperboard or rusty corrugated iron'. Fuller mused, 'their way of life is so beautiful that I have always said that if I ever have to retire, it will be into one of those squatter settlements.'[37] Ward and Fuller's pronouncements on *unsettlement* were in many ways both wishful and unsettling. If for Ward 'unsettlement' was both a crisis and an opportunity, Fuller emphatically celebrated it, as an overcoming of obsolete forms of sovereignty and a way of eradicating repressive political boundaries. Both were driven by the notion of a universal humanity and insisted, in different ways, that technical and managerial strategies could replace an incapacitated politics. The stakes of the wager were immense: 'to create a community or risk losing a planet.'[38]

However, this rhetoric of planetary togetherness and Spaceship Earth efficiencies, intended to inform human settlement and development policies, was decidedly at odds with the traumatic and dispersed forms of community experienced in the refugee camps and temporary homes of displaced peoples. At Habitat this was brought into sharp relief by the presence of Palestinians, a group whose concerns were situated at the 'nexus of unsettlement, sovereignty, citizenship, land ownership, and colonial occupation'.[39] The 'Palestinian question' and anxieties about the presence of the Palestine Liberation Organisation (PLO) at the conference dominated media reports and 'implicitly and explicitly disrupted the dominant development narrative, technocratic agenda and rhetoric of human settlement'.[40] As the *Chicago Tribune* lamented, 'The good ship Habitat, a global attempt at improving mankind's living conditions, has run aground on the jagged reef of Arab-Israeli relations'.[41]

With Habitat the urban and the planetary had become synonymous. This was a planetary-scaled problem that demanded global technocratic governance structures of vast scale. In *The Home of Man* the conflation of the planetary and the urban emerges as a litany of violence and despair:

> What the sages once said is now what the nature of the planet exposes. Its fragile mechanisms cannot stand too much pressure. Violent misuse of its life-support system – in the great cities, in the fields and farms – destroys the life of rivers and soils and undermines the integrity of human existence. Violent consumption of its resources will leave nothing to consume. Above all, the resort to man's most destructive civic invention, war between nations, will leave the whole city of man in the plight of his first demolished city, and it is for the planet itself that the cry of lament for Ur will be repeated:
>
> > O my city which exists no longer,
> > my city attacked without cause
> > O my city attacked and destroyed[42]

The vast urban-planetary canvas of crisis is returned to in Mike Davis's *Planet of Slums* (2006), written as a follow-up to the UN Habitat report *The Challenge of Slums*, 2003.[43] According to UN Habitat, sometime around 2050, the human population will achieve its maximum growth, probably at around 10 to 10.5 billion people. Ninety-five per cent of this future growth will occur in cities, overwhelmingly in poor cities, and the majority of it in slums. The one billion people who, according to UN Habitat, live in informal settlements (with insecure forms of tenure), and the additional one billion informal workers, are for Davis a 'planetary deficit of opportunity and social justice'. Davis aligns the crisis of urban poverty with that of climate change, seeing them as twin threats to 'our collective future'.[44] 'If the reports of the Intergovernmental Panel on Climate Change (IPCC) represent an unprecedented scientific consensus on the dangers of global warming,' Davis announces, 'then the *Challenge of Slums* sounds an equally authoritative warning about the worldwide catastrophe of urban poverty.'[45] Davis's *Planet of Slums* is an avowedly apocalyptic vision. He characterises the lives of the majority of the world's urban dwellers, the inhabitants of squatter settlements and peri-urban informal communities, as ones of interminable poverty, violence, and exploitation. It is a bold indictment of capitalist urbanisation: 'Instead of cities of light soaring toward heaven, much of the 21st-century urban world squats in squalor, surrounded by pollution, excrement, and decay.'[46]

Planet of Slums raised the alarm that 'the 'frontier of safe squattable land is everywhere disappearing'.[47] As if fragility of tenure was not enough, squatting had now become an 'increasing wager with disaster'.[48] Slums are only tolerated on land that has no market value – in other words, the most hazardous and unattractive places. The chronically poor cluster in disaster-zones: 'They are the pioneer settlers of swamps, floodplains, volcano slopes, unstable hillsides, rubbish mountains, chemical dumps, railroad sidings, and desert fringes.'[49] The forebodingly named *villa miseria* on the urban periphery of Buenos Aires was built 'over a former lake, a toxic dump, and a cemetery and in a flood zone'.[50] Urban poverty magnifies geological, technological and climatic hazards – these are disasters waiting to happen. Every year brings a rising death toll from urban disasters such as flooding, earthquakes and pollution, the damage concentrating in poor urban areas, demonstrating the uneven global distribution of risk.

The Union Carbide pesticides production plant in Bhopal was surrounded by *bustees* in 1984, the year it released a cloud of methyl isocyanate gas. The accident caused 7,000–10,000 immediate deaths and another 15,000 from related illnesses. Such disasters draw attention to the interconnected terrains of industrial activity, environmental degradation and uneven capital accumulation. The poor are increasingly disconnected from the cultural and political life of what is taken to be the traditional city, and exiled from the formal world economy. The places they live are dangerous, neglected and lack vital infrastructure. They have no choice but to live in and with disaster, with no disaster insurance, no strategies of risk reduction, no finance for repair, no safe zone to evacuate to; no refuge. The poor, desperate and disaster-prone of the world are the inadequately housed or homeless population of this planet of cities – not incidental but essential to a pattern of urbanisation typified as much by surging informal economies as by neoliberal government policies. The proliferation of informal dwellers on the edges and in the gaps of the urban has a counterpart in the exodus of the middle class: 'forsaking its traditional culture, along with the central city, to retreat into off-worlds with themed California lifestyles.'[51] Is it possible that the contours of the future will ever be defined by the struggles and demands of the disenfranchised majority rather than the private desires of powerful elites?

> But if there is no monolitihic subject or unilateral trend in the global slum, there are nonetheless myriad acts of resistance. Indeed the future of human solidarity depends upon the militant refusal of the new urban poor to accept their terminal marginality within global capitalism.[52]

At Habitat III in Quito, Ecuador in 2016, UN nation states agreed on the New Urban Agenda (NUA) meant to guide city development worldwide over the next two decades. The NUA set out the urban dimensions of Agenda 2030 and in particular the eleventh of the 17 Sustainable Development Goals to 'make cities and human settlements inclusive, safe, resilient and sustainable'.[53] The city, however, is increasingly conceived of as a measurable entity, one that is reducible to data streams and controllable through a range of technologies. Sustainable urban development aspirations have become subsumed within the emergent smart city paradigm technocratic approach to urban governance. The efforts of urban planners have little effect on the majority of urban dwellers and for those living and working precariously in informal settlements, access to housing, economic opportunities and social amenities is often impeded by official policies.[54] The NUA's 'cities for all' vision includes a reference to the 'right to the city' – an idea with its origins in the writings of the French Marxist philosopher Henri Lefebvre that seeks to enshrine the equal rights of all citizens at the heart of a city's governance. Writing after Habitat III, Ada Colau, the mayor of Barcelona claimed: 'All the major global challenges – climate change, the economy, inequality, the very future of democracy – will be solved in cities.'[55] But the question remained as to how to translate the NUA's statements into applicable commitments that could address the injustices experienced by many of the world's citizens. Cities in the abstract continue to be paraded as the solution to global social and environmental crises. But referring to the city as a means of inciting planetary consciousness overlooks important questions about a supposedly planetary society.

> Will the electorates of the wealthy nations shed their current bigotry and walled borders to admit refugees from predicted epicentres of drought and desertification like the Maghreb, Mexico, Ethiopia, and Pakistan? Will Americans, the most miserly people when measured by per capita foreign aid, be willing to tax themselves to help relocate the millions likely to be flooded out of densely settled, mega-delta regions like Bangladesh?[56]

Scenarios of climate change from IPCC climate models project dramatically unequal and devastating impacts that will reinforce the present geographies of inequality. For some, the damage is already done, even though many in power have long been aware of the problem. The Anthropocene is a moment of catastrophe that is at once encroaching and already here. The chaos that is ensuing, and is likely to intensify from the convergence of food and energy crises, resource depletion, the effects of climate change and the entanglements of intractable inequality, demands a response. The alternative, according to Davis, is to 'become ourselves complicit in a *de facto* triage of humanity'.[57] He further warns: 'Indeed, there is little hope of mitigating greenhouse emissions or adapting human habitats to the Anthropocene unless the movement to control global warming converges with the struggle to raise living standards and abolish world poverty.'[58] The Anthropocene provocation is about recognising those people that face the most extreme vulnerability to a changing climate and endure a form of dwelling that can only ever be construed as temporary home. Otherwise cities in the Anthropocene will remain consigned to an 'existential ground zero', a planetary 'urbanisation without urbanity'.[59] The planetary city *is* a disaster. However, 'the real danger', Davis warns, 'is that human solidarity itself, like a West Antarctic ice shelf, will suddenly fracture and shatter into a thousand shards.'[60]

Planetary crisis of agency

The Earth has been jolted out of Holocene climatic dependability into an uncontrollable trajectory hazardous to human life. The crisis of the Anthropocene is hard to grasp in its pervasiveness: rising oceans, drowning cities, seasonal disruptions, toxic deserts, species extinctions, forced migrations. It raises the problem of intersecting scales that fold the times of human agency (late capitalism, urbanisation, industrialisation, nuclear age) into the disruptive time of geological agency. Importantly, the notion of the Anthropocene demands reclassifications of agency. It brings up questions of how we can understand temporal and spatial processes that far exceed the usual socio-political ideas of humans' capacity to act in and on the world. In the urgent efforts to understand the pushback that human actions have engendered, agency is shifted not simply to the non-human as a general category, but to the Earth's systems in their present state of long-term human-induced change. A paradox emerges that threatens to defeat thought and paralyse action:

> References to millions of years, which used to make our brief lives seem inconsequential, now endow us with gargantuan agency and an almost unbearable level of responsibility – intuitively beyond our capacities for rational or concerted action. Never mind that climate scientists instruct us that such action, undertaken over the next few years, is the only thing that can possibly avert a catastrophe.[61]

As the authors J.K Gibson-Graham and Gerda Roelvink indicate, the Anthropocene is a critical time in understandings of human agency – and its limitations. What are the possibilities for 'rational or concerted action'? Just at the moment that human capacity to damage Earth's systems is revealed as 'gargantuan', the capacity to reverse that damage starts to look dismayingly limited. As Bruno Latour puts it more bluntly: 'How can we simultaneously be part of such a long history, have such an important influence, and yet be so late in realising what has happened and so utterly impotent in our attempts to fix it?'[62]

Zygmunt Bauman has located the current 'crisis of agency' in a longer history of unresolved issues related to the theme of sovereignty.[63] He defines the crisis as one of governance – the disjunction between power and politics in a globalised world: 'the growing volume of power that matters ... has already turned global; but politics has remained as local as before.'[64] At the same time, trust in the state's capacity to act responsibly to resolve crisis has eroded. There is ample evidence that it only takes the pretext of financial crisis and economic recession for governments and corporations to renege on their promises to reform – or even to roll out more aggressively damaging policies. The convergence of crises – economic, ecological, social – demands nothing less than global geopolitical agreement on the best courses of action. In an inequitable, chaotic world, such agreement proves unattainable. This crisis is not made easier to grapple with by the knowledge of how volatile, unpredictable and unstable planetary conditions really are, nor by the disturbing news that human actions influence these systems far more than had previously been imagined.

The point of the Anthropocene is to announce that the world is not merely a backdrop for human agency: the human inheres in the functioning of Earth systems, and has demonstrated a substantial capacity to disrupt that functioning. The Anthropocene also announces that humans are no longer masters of their own history but have become entangled with dynamic forces beyond their control. The shorthand version of the Anthropocene thesis tends towards implicating humanity as a whole in the precipitation of a new epoch. But this obscures the self-interest, exploitation, energetic compulsions and good or bad luck that makes some the drivers of a new epoch and others its unwitting inhabitants. As Dipesh Chakrabarty writes, 'It is precisely because we are not politically one that histories of intrahuman (in)justice will remain relevant and necessary. But we will probably have to think of them in the much larger context of the history of life, how Earth history connects to it, and where humans figure in it overall.'[65] The Anthropocene raises enormous questions for many human institutions taken for granted in the Holocene. In a world of geopolitical *and* geophysical turbulence, ethical, legal, spatial and environmental norms must all come under fresh scrutiny. The time of the Anthropocene signals a planetary crisis of agency.

Imaginaries of environmental crisis that are out of sync with socioeconomic realities tend to attribute too little or too much agency to humans. Nigel Clark reminds us of the 'radical asymmetry' in experiences of geophysical disruption: 'the impression that deep-seated forces of the Earth can leave on social worlds is out of all proportion to the power of social actors to legislate over the lithosphere.'[66] Thinking about cities and settlements has remained stubbornly focused, in defiance of the emerging facts, on the potential of human action against a stable background. There is a tendency to assume human agency as a given in shaping the future; in transforming, transgressing, subverting, and breaking down barriers; and acting on existing systems and institutions. But the geoclimatic regime change of the Anthropocene has ushered in an entirely new state of affairs. Not only are humans endowed with a geologic agency that is incommensurable with their everyday lives, but this has collided with a more-than-human or planetary agency – neither can be controlled. No amount of hubris, expertise, professionalism or bravado can adequately compensate for human frailty in the face of these forces.

An agency of transformation – of how things could be otherwise – is about inhabiting the politics of crisis and seeking to transform it.[67] But it is also about the potential of transforming with it. As Gibson-Graham and Roelvink observe, 'responding to the challenges of the Anthropocene is not simply about humans finding a technological or normative fix that will control and restore the Earth'.[68] It is a matter of the reciprocal transformation of human beings and the Earth's future. Humans will have to contend with an agency that is anomalous, hybrid and diminished. The entry into the threshold condition of the Anthropocene may yet incite and propel a transformative agency that finds suitably agile accommodations with this more-or-less-than-human agency. Indeed, it may be more useful not to think of human agency at all, but rather of the multiple interactions between humans and non-humans that make up societies: technologies, resources, species, atmospheres. 'The point of living in the Anthropocene,' Latour argues, 'is that all agents share the same shape-changing destiny.' He means all the agents of geostory, for example: 'volcano, Mississippi river, plate tectonics, microbes, or CRF-receptor, just as much as generals, engineers, novelists, ethicists, or politicians.' For Latour, the 'crucial political task' is, 'to *distribute* agency as far and in as *differentiated* a way as possible'.[69] Human geological agency does not put humans in control, acting on the Earth, but neither does the Earth simply act on humans. The geostory is of entanglements. A conjoined, distributed and provisional agency would recognise both the limitations and attachments of human agency and acknowledge a future that can neither be stabilised nor secured but only improvised. The implications are that to enable us to navigate turbulence, we need to be prepared to adapt not only how we approach our policies, practices and technologies, but also our modes of humanity.

Under conditions of intensifying globalisation the most precarious thresholds have long been considered social or political. Imaginaries of spatial mobility, border crossing, and the transgression of boundaries have relied on notions of long-term stability: we tend to imagine humans moving, struggling, surviving on a relatively immobile Earth. But as Nigel Clark asks,

> What if the most crucial borders turn out to be not so much the lines which demarcate one political unit from another across our planet's frenetically criss-crossed surface, as those boundaries which separate one 'regime' or 'state' of the Earth system from another? To put it another way, what if the most critical thresholds are the ones that define strata rather than those which delineate territory?[70]

Even if the collisions of human agency with more-than-human agencies are acknowledged, the entanglements of geoclimatic and geopolitical regime change signal the prospect of intensified upheavals on a planetary scale. 'With both the CIA's coup-making and the military's regime-change traditions in mind, could the United States also overthrow a planet?' asked Tom Engelhardt, writing in the wake of Donald Trump's election in 2016. He warned that if Trump's campaign promises of withdrawing climate science funding, denouncing climate agreements and embarking on fossil-fuelled energy policies were to be upheld, he would 'in effect, be launching a regime-change action against Planet Earth'.[71] International climate change negotiations, already fraught, are likely to become increasingly antagonistic. The entire sum of the political and philosophical techne (laws, rules, treaties, conventions, protocols) that we might bring to bear on this problem was developed in the Holocene period of relative stability. We are still a long way from working out new forums and agreements that might be appropriate for the wholly new and increasingly turbulent conditions of the Anthropocene.

Planetary state of exception

There is a wide acceptance that the present time is one of global emergency: cascading crises of climate change, terrorism, biohazards, political chaos, all have the potential to act unpredictably at global scale, threatening the security of cities, regions and nation states. Emergency situations are defined as both extraordinary and exceptional. Emergency narratives imply, however, that volatile situations can be brought back under human control – through the exercise of political or technological fixes. Critics of current political responses to disaster argue that 'states of emergency' and their associated regulatory practices are being deployed to advance powerful interests at

Figure 7.1 'Where will Hurricane Katrina go?' (29 August 2005); Hurricane Katrina in the Gulf of Mexico; a digitally processed image from the orbiting GOES-12 Weather satellite
Source: GOES 12 Satellite, NASA, NOAA

the expense of the vulnerable.[72] Securitisation measures are often presented as the only viable response, and are becoming normalised. The state of emergency characteristic of Western culture's response to crises (hybrid natural-human catastrophes and political upheavals) is related to the Italian philosopher Giorgio Agamben's 'state of exception'.[73] The state of exception is the paradoxical situation in which the law is legally suspended by a sovereign power in order to safeguard the law against perceived threats (terrorism, immigration). Agamben points out the ways that the state of exception is used to impose new forms of politics, including new modes of political decision-making, changes in law, mobilisation of recovery organisations, the 'safeguarding' of infrastructure through increased securitisation, and the control of the movement of people and goods.[74] According to Agamben, the 'voluntary creation of permanent state of emergency … has become one of the essential practices of contemporary states including so-called democratic ones'.[75] In short, 'the state of exception… has become the rule'.[76] The temporary suspension of the legal order cedes to a new and stable arrangement, and in this generalised condition 'the paradigm of security' has become 'the normal technique of government'.[77]

The Anthropocene thesis acknowledges the exceptional state of the planet insofar as this current situation is unprecedented in human experience. It remains to be seen whether it will be made into a political 'state of exception' as well. In *The Shock of the Anthropocene*, Bonneuil and Fressoz argue 'that war, by creating a state of exception, has justified and encouraged a "brutalising" of relations between society and environment'.[78] They point to nuclear weapons and the 'scorched earth' policy of modern environmental warfare. Al Gore's documentary *An Inconvenient Truth* (2006) – with its subtitle, 'A planetary emergency' – frames climate change as an issue of national security.[79] Its martial and nationalist rhetoric, drawn from Cold War government communiqués, invites the viewer to consent to certain exigencies.

Concerns about the slippage of exceptional circumstances into 'the new normal' are relevant to the martial and highly intrusive actions being proposed in response to the Anthropocene emergency. The possibility of technological intervention at the planetary scale – in the form of geoengineering, for example – has been advanced as an emergency measure that may be necessary to avert the onset of dangerous climate change. Whether we are invited to place our fate in the hands of a few engineers (and their billionaire backers) or under martial law, the threat of climate change is increasingly cast as an exception to democratic process. James Lovelock's description of 'Lifeboat UK', for example, echoes Garrett Hardin's 'lifeboat ethics':

> But what if at some time in the next few years we realise, as we did in 1939, that democracy had temporarily to be suspended and we had to accept a disciplined regime that saw the UK as a legitimate but limited safe haven for civilisation… Orderly survival requires an unusual degree of human understanding and leadership and may require, as in war, the suspension of democratic government for the duration of the survival emergency.[80]

Agamben's study of the state of siege talks of 'gradual emancipation from the wartime situation to which it was originally bound in order to be used as extraordinary police measure to cope with internal sedition and disorder'.[81] And from this presumption of 'sedition and disorder' arises a politics of containment, in which citizens (or non-citizen humans) become a problem to be corralled. For Agamben, the camp is 'the space that is opened up when the state of exception begins to become the rule'.[82] He further argues that it is fundamental to 'recognise the structure of the camp in all of its metamorphoses': 'today it is not the city but rather the camp' that is 'the fundamental biopolitical paradigm of the West'.[83] In other words, the camp – the temporary space of exception that gradually, imperceptibly, becomes abiding – can be understood as an ever-present condition existing in potential within the political order.

In 2005, in the wake of Hurricane Katrina, the city of New Orleans was transformed into a series of camps – poorly equipped emergency refuges at first, and later flood-ravaged homes that the residents had returned to without the means to repair.[84] Over a decade later, many houses are still abandoned and cannot be regenerated because legal title to the buildings cannot be established.[85] Katrina is a story of climate change: a year of record ocean temperatures, the most active hurricane season on record, and storm surges exacerbated by warming seas. It is also a story of abandonment and state failure in a time of emergency, and of a failure of law and policy in the subsequent reconstruction. As Rebecca Solnit notes,

> 'Katrina' is less the name of a storm than it is a shorthand for a series of largely man-made catastrophes: the lack of an evacuation plan for the poorest and most vulnerable people in the city; the regularly predicted failure of the levees maintained by the US Army Corps of Engineers; the inadequate emergency management of city, state, and federal government; and the corruption and bureaucratic delays that hindered the rebuilding process.[86]

Out of a population of 480,000 people, 100,000 could not be evacuated and had to stay to face the storm. There were no competent evacuation plans for the city's poor, and the US government's response to the plight of the city was slow. About 25,000 people managed to get to the city's sports arena, the Superdome, but with no electricity, no air-conditioning, limited supplies of food and water, a failed plumbing system and a police force that could not guarantee the safety of the citizens, they found themselves trapped in an exclusion zone – a refugee population in their own city. Elsewhere in the city, looters were shot with impunity. In the wake of the disaster, the imperative to control the population was given higher priority than assisting the vulnerable. Over 1,500 people died in Louisiana, and the catastrophe revealed just how fragile the city was. Even after so much going wrong, the city has been trying to rebuild itself. Seventy per cent of the population have since returned to the city and embarked on the steady process of reconstruction and recovery. In *A Paradise Built in Hell*, Solnit chronicled the human capacity for solidarity and community building in the wake of disaster that tends to be overlooked in the literature of disaster analysis and planning.[87] But with future catastrophic inundations almost inevitable, the people of New Orleans may need to face refugee status again, and again. New Orleans sits in terrain between 6 and 15 feet below sea level, surrounded on all sides by water. The city is sinking at a rate of about 3 feet per year. According to NASA, various natural and human-produced processes contribute to the sinking, including, 'withdrawal of water, oil and gas; compaction of shallow sediments; faulting; sinking of Earth's crust from the weight of deposited sediments; and ongoing vertical movement of land covered by glaciers during the last ice age'.[88] Even without the problem of intensifying hurricanes and rising sea levels, scientific research suggests that by 2100 the city will be underwater.[89] Louisiana's coastal master plan lists a range of possible projects, including bioengineered oyster barrier reefs, sediment diversion, and ridge and wetland restoration. The challenge is how to create a human-made system that replicates the delta's natural land-building process.[90] In the meantime, the levees have been rebuilt to withstand a Category 3 hurricane, but would be of no use against a direct hit from a Category 5 hurricane – such as Katrina was before it made landfall as a Category 3.

As demonstrated by the flooding of New Orleans and more recently by the European refugee crisis, the announcement of disaster justifies the stripping of democratic rights, the militarisation of emergency response, and the removal of responsibility and agency from the civilian population. With this comes the tendency to value the organised, bureaucratised and militarised work of state organisations over the improvisational skills of ordinary people in response to disaster – leaving community-driven regeneration efforts to languish, and whole populations stuck in the interstices between competing militaristic and bureaucratic orders, supported adequately by none. With the disaster in New Orleans, it has been impossible to distinguish between human-made accident and natural catastrophe. In this sense, it is characteristic of disasters in the Anthropocene. We must hope the chaotic and inadequate human response will not also prove characteristic. Klein observes:

> Although climate change will ultimately be an existential threat to all of humanity, in the short term we know that it does discriminate, hitting the poor first and worst, whether they are abandoned on the rooftops of New Orleans during Hurricane Katrina or whether they are among the 36 million who according to the UN are facing hunger due to drought in Southern and East Africa.[91]

With the Anthropocene, the entire planet has become a disaster zone – one in which, for the time being, the negative effects are concentrated among its most vulnerable inhabitants. With time, however, the territories of risk and safety will be increasingly difficult to demarcate; and the consequences of action and inaction alike will become harder to calculate. The playwright and New Orleans resident John Biguenet reflects:

> In the end, what happened in New Orleans is not about New Orleans. When a country fails to maintain its infrastructure, when it ignores climate change, when it deprofessionalises government service because of ideological contempt for governance itself, when it allows poverty to fester, when it encourages racism through coded speech, when it refuses to hold responsible for the consequences of their policies those leaders who devised them, then what happened in August 2005 is not about the place where it happened. It's about the people who let it happen. And because no one was held accountable, it will happen again. New Orleans is simply where the future arrived first.[92]

The camp is the site *par excellence* of the state of exception that now resonates both with specific cities and across planetary settlement. The camp is a 'temporary' state without end, a 'provisional' community whose terms of inclusion are often unstated, always subject to change. A camp's inhabitants must sustain themselves on the tacit promise of an alternative future. To inhabit a camp is to experience an ongoing, imminent disaster. What shelter is precariously provided may at any point be withdrawn or destroyed; there are multiple, irreconcilable timescales for ameliorative action and no guarantees that the wished-for rescue will happen. The Anthropocene announces an emergency coextensive with planet Earth – 1:1 scale, real time, with no 'outside' and therefore no exclusions. In time, we may all prove to be climate refugees; and then the world will indeed be a camp. Human planetary inhabitation *already* shares the predicaments – the administrative and spatial precarity, the uncertain future, the impossibility of return – of the camp. With several Earth system thresholds already exceeded, the current global condition can be understood as a *planetary state of exception*. The challenge is to develop infrastructures of politics, economics and social relations that might better support human wellbeing through the increasingly frequent disasters of the Anthropocene. The logics of the camp and the lifeboat – the default responses to date to planetary states of emergency – have failed us. It remains to us to find something better.

Makeshift city

The Fertile Crescent, or 'cradle of civilisation,' was an area of comparatively arable land in an otherwise arid region, comprising ancient Mesopotamia and the Levant. The modern-day countries that make up this region include Cyprus, Israel, Jordan, Lebanon, Palestine, Egypt, Iraq, Iran, Turkey, Syria: places now scarred by drought, water scarcity, scorching temperatures and military conflict.[93] The Fertile Crescent is considered to have been the pre-eminent site of socio-technological innovation for most of the 11,700-year-long Holocene epoch. Over ten millennia of intense climatic and ecological reorganisations, this region's development of irrigation, domestication, construction, and urbanisation established radically new ways of living in larger and more settled communities, as an alternative (if not necessarily more prosperous, or healthier) to hunter-gatherer societies. Along with the agricultural transformations that were a prerequisite for the infrastructure we now associate with cities, these places saw many innovations in writing, manufacturing, commerce, democracy, laws, and medicine – in other words, the whole gamut of civilisation. The Fertile Crescent is the region with the oldest city in the world: Jericho, dating from the 10th millennium BC. It is also the site of the largest humanitarian crisis of the 21st century. As a result of just four years of the Syrian conflict, which started in 2011, around 11 million people are in need of humanitarian assistance, with 6.5 million people internally displaced in Syria and over three million refugees in Syria's neighbouring countries.

In the Levant, 1998–2012 was 'likely the driest 15-year period of the last 900 years, well outside the norm of natural variability in the region'.[94] The extreme climatic conditions in Syria in particular are believed to have created instability and exacerbated the conflict, making it, as Rebecca Solnit observes, a 'climate-change war of sorts'.[95] The protracted war in Darfur, western Sudan had also been associated with a 'climate culprit': 'Amid the diverse social and political causes,' Ban Ki Moon writes, 'the Darfur conflict began as an ecological crisis, arising at least in part from climate change.'[96] In 2015 a common media narrative emerged linking climate change not only with the conflict in Syria but with subsequent refugee movements across Europe.[97] Much of the reporting was based on research that argued for a connection between drought in the Fertile Crescent and climate change, and linked the impacts of the drought to patterns of rural to urban migration.[98] Other research noted that the drought aggravated an existing humanitarian crisis, the result of decades of resource mismanagement.[99] However, attempts to establish causal links between climate change and political unrest and conflict have failed to explain the complexity of these interlinked crises. They also tend to misrepresent refugees, migrants and displaced peoples as the source of political chaos and violence. This further entrenches the fear of displaced people as political 'others', and deepens the divide between those whose movement is restricted and those who freely inhabit public space.

The Zaatari refugee camp in the desert landscape of Jordan, 12 km from the Syrian border, was first opened on 28 July 2012. As Killian Kleinschmidt, the UNHCR senior field coordinator of Zaatari from 2012, observes, 'Zaatari is the symbol of the displacement of Syrians. It's where the tragedy of Syria has become visible to everyone'.[100] By 11 March 2013, the camp population was estimated at 156,000 refugees fleeing the violence of the civil war, making it the world's second largest refugee camp (after Daadab in Kenya) and Jordan's fourth largest city. A second refugee camp was opened in Azraq in April 2014 and the numbers of refugees gradually fell in Zaatari to around 80,000 in 2016, about the size of the city of Bath in the UK. The camp is managed jointly by the United Nations High Commission for Refugees (UNHCR), the UN body that is legally mandated to protect and assist refugees, the Jordanian government, and around 30 NGOs. Refugee camps are usually planned by the architects and technical planners of the UNHCR. The standard model for a refugee camp is described in the 'UNHCR Handbook for Emergencies'. It is an abstracted city: its foundation is in the crossing of roads and the basic unit of the tent extended to cluster; block; camp.[101] Dwelling in the camp is organised in emergency zoning according to segregation and health needs, food distribution and waste and energy infrastructures. The processes of the spatialisation of exception reflect the constant negotiation with border politics, juridical justification, humanitarian aid, political agencies, logistics and the basic fact that everything: food, water, materials, people – has to be brought

Temporary home 239

to the desert. Movement in and out of the camp remains restricted. The very harsh climatic conditions in the region have not only made the suffering of those caught up in the conflict across the border in Syria much worse, but have also made it difficult to create good living conditions in the Zaatari camp.[102]

The knowledge that most people have of this 'makeshift city in the desert' is made possible through satellite imagery.[103] It has been possible to monitor the expansion of the camp, locate the camp manager or city 'mayor', take a 'tour of the camp' and zoom in and 'meet the residents'.[104] The camp has its own Twitter feed managed by the UNHCR, @ZaatariCamp, and Google self-driving cars have mapped the streets. On the ground, Zaatari has been described as a 'dismal and edgy place', with a constant military presence: 'the guards of all the inefficiencies.' 'Urban planners have taken a stake' recently because, with no end in sight to the conflict, the camp is being made more permanent.[105] Most of the improvement, however, as Kleinschmidt documents, is thanks to the refugee community taking things into their own hands: 'At Zaatari, the UNHCR never planned to provide electricity for the households. So people took it themselves from the power lines running through the camp.' In addition to hacking the electricity supply to power businesses, refugees erected fountains, built bathing pools, established shops, and set about re-establishing some version of their former lives. The central street in Zaatari was named the 'Champs Élysées' and became a place to buy clothes, wedding dresses and mobile phones, or arrange a pizza delivery – in short, it has come to approximate a city high street. Kleinschmidt reflects on the lesson of Zaatari: that in order for refugees to regain dignity and remake their lives, refugee camps need to be considered as cities – whatever their duration – rather than adhering to the transitory rules of the camp.

> In the Middle East, we were building camps: storage facilities for people. But the refugees were building a city. These are the cities of tomorrow. The average stay today in a camp is 17 years. That's a generation. Let's look at these places as cities.[106]

Kleinschmidt's provocation – that refugee camps *are* the cities of the future – resonates with aspirations to *make shift* the conversation about unsettlement. It is not simply about a recognition that many refugee camps have turned permanent. For while the camp marks the limit of human settlement as well as the limits of human agency it also manifests the provisional foundations of future cities in conditions of uncertainty. The architect Alessandro Petti speaks of the potentiality of the 'anti-city': 'The prolonged exceptional temporality of the refugee camps could paradoxically create the condition for its transformation: from a pure humanitarian space to an active political space, the embodiment and the expression of the right of return.'[107]

This suggests thinking differently about migrant settlements as 'temporary home': as a territory that needs to be better supported in its adjustments and improvisations, rather than foreseen or planned by authorities who don't live there. The dehumanising effects of the biopolitical mechanism of the camp on the human beings they seek to protect, contain, manage, or even coerce, need to be fully absorbed. Provisional cities of the future need to be conceived outside of the constraining terms of exceptionality and embed inclusivity and justice from the outset. Instead of understanding camps as spaces of exception or as the spatialised form of a state of emergency, it is important to acknowledge the everyday urban practices that reproduce 'the city' within the camp.

The challenge is to 'de-exceptionalise the exception'.[108] While not denying the all too frequent examples of horrific deprivations, expulsions and incarcerations, or the sidestepping of political resolution constructed in the name of security, there are still other lessons that can be learnt from places of temporary settlement. For these can also be the places where new practices of urban citizenship are tested and nurtured, and where the camp acts as 'a social and political terrain where rights, entitlements and obligations are reshaped, bended, adjusted, neglected and activated by and through everyday interactions'.[109] The camps of the Sahrawi people displaced in Algeria have been understood as a prefiguration of nation – their borderline urbanity is part and parcel of a proactive and novel political project.[110] The prospect of escalating climate-induced displacement of people and increasing statelessness also presents a challenge to the localised model of nation states and the future of settlements. In other words, the strategies of resistance, cooperation, adaptation and resourcefulness that camp dwellers develop in their everyday lives may prove to be especially important in a fragile and fraught world of both diminished human agency and a more-than-human agency gone awry.

It is anticipated that a warmer planet would bring bigger, more protracted refugee crises in the future. However, it is not possible to predict the scale or direction of human movement in relation to climate change impacts. It may also not be possible to tell the difference between environmental migrants and other kinds of migrants and displaced people. Moreover, much climate-linked migration will not be en masse, but in response to slow onset disasters like drought, desertification and sea level rise. While some movement will need to be immediate, with others it will be part of planned resettlement or seasonal adaptation. Climate impacts will also create more gradual human movement that may be identified as economic migration, since many people's livelihoods, especially in the developing world, are dependent on local climatic conditions which might change. Nevertheless, the recent convulsions of earthquakes, tsunamis, flooding, wildfires, drought and conflict across the world have demonstrated the convergence of two different earthly mobilities: people moving across the Earth's surface through economic or forced migrations, *and* the shifting ground beneath our feet.[111] The complex interweavings of climate, lives, economies, and politics, are likely to force increasingly unpredictable global 'states of emergency'. Their consequences could threaten not only the safety but also the humanity of those displaced. As it becomes harder to distinguish environmental migrants from other kinds of migrants, 'it will become increasingly difficult to… separate the disaster relief camps from the detention centres and other sites of internment'.[112]

Zaatari, the most provisional of cities, is a reminder of the need to develop not only shelters but also new practices of refuge and settlement that have the flexibility to weather frequent catastrophes at multiple scales and over time. Given that humans are changing their habits more slowly than their habits are changing the climate, traumatic unsettlement may well become more common as the so-called Anthropocene epoch unfolds. But if the tendency is to resort to the logic of the camp, to the increased securitisation of the 'state of exception', what will be the approach to unsettlement as both climate and environmental politics get even more chaotic? It might be better to embark now, instead, on a path of greater cooperation, humility and respect. For those who have so far been insulated, this means recognising that unsettlement has already begun – that much of the world's population has already endured scarcity, catastrophe, and the sudden upheavals of environmental change. The local embedded experience of hazard-prone and displaced populations is therefore an essential part of the expert knowledge that will need to be mobilised in order to develop a coordinated, cooperative response to the challenges to come. The turbulent nature of human relations in times of escalating environmental crises indicates the need to be better equipped to cope with experiences of estrangement and deprivation, whether closer to home or further away.

Hospitality

The Anthropocene thesis introduces Earth system regime change to social and political thought. Borders between nation states and within cities have been the most prominent sites of negotiation and conflict. However, the thresholds between one operating state of the Earth system and another will also become significant.[113] This consequential juncture in the history of human societies and their home planet brings to the fore the unstable ground of social existence, and thus the question of *refugia* – sites of relative security and stability in times of environmental disruption. Hannah Arendt's 1943 essay 'We Refugees' noted that refugees were 'the vanguard of their peoples', for they had already experienced the violence, fragility and increasing obsolescence of a territorial understanding of citizenship.[114] It is an observation that is especially relevant to auguries of Anthropocene unsettlement. In the 21st century questions of Earth citizenship have come to the fore along with the challenge to find new forms of politics not bound up with the principle of territoriality. This challenge implies the need to overcome both adherence to the status of the refugee as a temporary condition understood as a deficiency, and the fiction of a necessary relation between citizenship and territoriality. Giorgio Agamben has proposed 'refugium' as a name for such an aterritorial space: 'In this new space, European cities would rediscover their ancient vocation of cities of the world by entering into a relation of reciprocal extraterritoriality.'[115] In the Anthropocene, cultural, political and economic arrangements of settlements or 'refugia' for the poor and vulnerable, as well as the prosperous and protected, touch on not only 'unbearable levels of responsibility' but also on questions of hospitality, one of the most ancient traditions of city dwelling.

The most pressing design challenges of the Anthropocene are about ensuring that cities, architectures, shelters and infrastructures are not only resilient and adaptable but also welcoming to displaced and disenfranchised peoples. Technological advances and improved design can only go so far, and as Nigel Clark points out in his discussion of disaster responses, 'open doors function as the most immediate architectural innovation'.[116] Many of the present-day adaptive strategies of cities and infrastructures will continue to break down in this new epoch: levees will be breached, coastlines will creep, bridges, roads and buildings will be battered by stronger rain and stronger sun. They will not offer solutions. Instead they will be experiments necessarily precarious and provisional: 'If hospitality on an episodically inhospitable Earth presents the most demanding of design problems, it also asks of us, from time to time a hasty redraft of even our best-laid plans.'[117]

Working out a way of dealing with the vulnerability of human habitations to Earth processes is not simply a question of constructing ingenious ways for settlements and infrastructures to be better able to cope with elemental stresses – although this is an important part of the task. The new situation demands adaptable infrastructures of inhabitation and hospitality that can be extended across time and space to those who

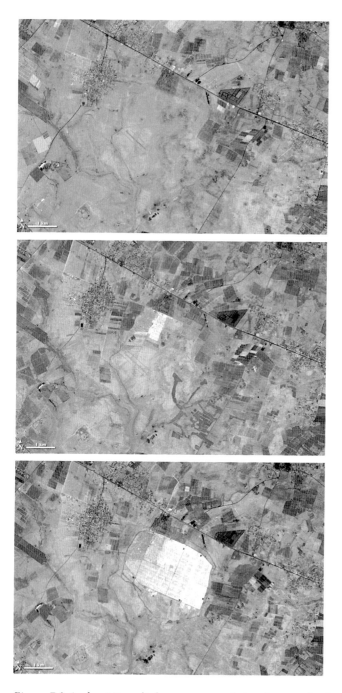

Figure 7.2 (**a, b, c**) 'In a little over a year, it has become Jordan's fourth largest city. Except it is not a city. It is the world's second-largest refugee camp'; Zaatari refugee camp, Jordan (satellite image data acquired 30 May 2009, 27 September 2012, 19 July 2013)

Source: NASA Earth Observatory images by Jesse Allen and Robert Simmon, using data from the NASA/GSFC/METI/ERSDAC/JAROS, and US/Japan ASTER Science Team

need the most help. Hospitality here does not mean simply a gesture of transient welcome. It is an invitation to think beyond conventional conceptions of inclusion and integration. The development of policies of long-term inclusion and integration for the vulnerable of the present and the future may need to adapt to universal aterritoriality as the primary human condition, a condition where Earth citizens are all in the position of seeking refuge. For Derrida, 'there is no culture or social bond without a principle of hospitality'. If 'hospitality is culture', this also requires inventing 'the best arrangements [*dispositions*], the least bad conditions, the most just legislation', it is necessary 'to calculate the risks, yes, but without closing the door on the incalculable, that is, on the future and the foreigner'.[118] He argues that the concepts of hospitality and of 'one's home, the familiar place of dwelling' are inseparable.[119] Hospitality demands empathy – a confrontation with the possibility that any one of us could become estranged at any time.

The idea of the 'city of refuge' has historical and material resonance. It draws on ancient biblical tradition, historical examples of cities offering asylum to the persecuted, and eschews the political calculations associated with state sovereignty. Derrida's 'cities of refuge' is a phrase that 'rings utopian' but refers to the actual institution of a network of 'cities of asylum' by the International Parliament of Writers in 1994.[120] But it also has implications for present-day examples of spaces of hospitality and asylum, such as the City of Sanctuary movement or UNHCR resettlement projects.[121] For even as cities attempt to alleviate the more punitive dimensions of the liminal condition of asylum-seekers, they participate in the apparatus of deferral of rights and citizenship in the increasingly securitised regimes of asylum and immigration at the urban scale. Derrida asks that cities 'reorient the politics of the state' in protection of the 'foreigner in general, the immigrant, the exiled, the deported, the stateless or the displaced person'.[122] He writes of the experience of 'cities of refuge' as allowing for a place for reflection on questions of asylum and hospitality, but also for *testing* a new order of law and democracy. This is not just about evoking an ancient concept to shift exclusionary practices but amounts to an argument that the idea of the 'city of refuge' needs to be reinvented:

> Being on the threshold of these cities, of these new cities that would be other than '*new* cities', a certain idea of cosmopolitanism, *an other*, has not yet arrived, *perhaps*.
> If it has (*indeed*) arrived ...
> ... then, one has perhaps not yet recognised it.'[123]

Cosmopolis

What has happened to the *cosmopolis* – the world as city? Concerns for a planet of cities in planetary crisis have been accompanied by cosmopolitan proclamations of unity. Notions of a common humanity draw on well-established tropes of 'whole Earth' globality, along with attendant expressions of fragility and humility. This cosmopolitan planetary consciousness nevertheless remains 'tethered to an imperial Apollonian gaze'.[124] It risks both normalising humanity and at the same time distinguishing a privileged and hospitable 'we'. In this way as the geographer Tariq Jazeel has pointed out, 'cosmopolitanism itself becomes a "god trick"'.[125] Among expressions of cosmopolitanism are: the Greek architect Constantinos Doxiadis's hierarchy of Anthropos through to the Ecumenopolis that informed Habitat; Derrida's yearning to futures beyond the cosmopolitan; and even its refashioning as urban smart citizenry connected to a big data world. The recent revival of cosmopolitan ideals also has much to do with concerns about the predicament of displaced peoples; it thus provokes important questions about hospitality and responsibility. But the Anthropocene brings with it further challenges to ideas of *cosmopolis*. For it signals the estrangement experienced not just by peoples traversing geopolitical space in times of crisis, but the geophysical stirrings and mobilisations of the Earth itself.

The related ideas of the individual as a citizen of the world, and of the world as city – *cosmopolis* – comes to us from the Stoics via Kant. Cosmopolitanism can be understood as a form of universal citizenship – a view of the Earth as one single place, of which humans are citizens irrespective of nation states or boundaries. Kant's cosmopolitics, as outlined in his 'Idea for a Universal History from a Cosmopolitan Point of View',[126] centred on the enlightened observer, a citizen of the world as city. In *Toward Perpetual Peace*, Kant extrapolated the cosmopolitan right of the 'visitor' to 'universal hospitality' from the notion of the limited nature of the surface of a spherical Earth: 'they have a right to visit, to which all human beings have a claim … by virtue of the right of the common possession of the surface of the Earth. Since it is the surface of a sphere, they cannot scatter themselves on it without limit, but they must ultimately rather tolerate one another as neighbours.'[127] Kant developed the constituent parts of the 'universal cosmopolitan condition' as cosmopolitan rights, international law, and an authoritative international authority – something akin to the contemporary United Nations. The primary aim of the cosmopolitan condition, as Kant saw it, was to put an end to war between states and establish perpetual peace, for 'originally no one has more of a right to be at a given place on Earth than anyone else'.[128] The German sociologist Ulrich Beck has argued for the revival of a 'cosmopolitan vision' or 'outlook' in a radically insecure and globalised world, one where the nation state is 'besieged by a planetary network of interdependencies, by ecological, economic and terrorist risks'. A cosmopolitan vision, according to Beck, allows people to 'view themselves simultaneously as part of a threatened world and as part of their local situation and histories'.[129] But as Bruno Latour observes,

> …whenever cosmopolitanism has been tried out, from Alexandria to the United Nations, it has been during the great periods of complete confidence in the ability of reason and, later, science to know *the one* cosmos whose existence and solid certainty could then prop up all efforts to build the world metropolis of which we are all too happy to be citizens.[130]

There is nothing certain about the cosmos. The implications of the Anthropocene are frightening and unsettling: in the face of unprecedented geophysical upheavals, there is diminishing confidence in the dream of a unified world metropolis or the proper functioning of international relations. As Clark observes, 'Even if its own tensions and inconsistencies could be smoothed out, Kant's dream of "communal possession of the Earth's surface" would fall far short of the politics needed for a stratified planet, for an Earth that destratifies on the spot'.[131] Latour argues that previous definitions of cosmopolis, '(Beck's, Kant's, the Stoics')', are problematic: 'none shows understanding that more than culture is put in jeopardy by conflicts. The cosmos too may be at stake.'[132]

In the 'cosmopolitics' of Isabelle Stengers and Bruno Latour, the Earth and its dynamic physic-materiality are no longer simply a backdrop to human machinations but, rather, are afforded a place in politics. Stengers' book *Cosmopolitics* points to entities and relationships marginalised in an anthropocentric world view.[133] Following Stengers, Latour argues for a redefinition of cosmopolitics which 'must embrace, literally, everything – including all the vast numbers of non-human entities making humans act'.[134] Hurricanes, storms, earthquakes, floods, animals, microbes, viruses, devices, technologies, all the contingent non-human forces capable of taking humans by surprise, as well as the varying responses to them, also require recognition. Stengers' cosmopolitics is a decisive shift from earlier political ideals of cosmopolitanism. Cosmopolitanism designates a world, cosmos, and a way of organising political belonging and citizenship irrespective of boundaries. With cosmopolitics, by contrast, politics is conceived as a transformative activity concerned with how the world is composed – that is, with the entities and relationships that are defined as constitutive actors of a common messy world.

Cosmopolitanism imagines that the only political actors are privileged human subjects capable of clearly defining and articulating their interests, visions and values, as well as morally justifying their preferences and actions. However, cosmopolitics underlines the fragility of human agency and requires reconsidering the role and capacity of non-humans in politics. In other words, it insists that the variability, volatility and unsettling nature of the world – in all its dimensions – needs to be taken into account.

If the Anthropocene as geological 'unconformity' reminds us that we are of a missing time and a ruptured space, it also invokes a constitutive approach to the geophysical and the political. Stengers' 'Cosmopolitical Proposal' is one 'that requires no other verification than the way in which it is able to slow down reasoning and create an opportunity to arouse a slightly different awareness of the problems and situations mobilising us'.[135] Stengers distances her cosmopolitics from both notions of an ancient cosmopolis and the writings of Kant. For her, 'the cosmos… bears little relation either to the world in which citizens of antiquity asserted themselves everywhere on their home ground or to an Earth finally united, in which everyone is a citizen'.[136] Seeking to recast the terms of engagement among science, philosophy and politics, Stengers' cosmopolitics refers to a shift from a position which sees a gulf between science and politics to one which takes the entanglements of the world as a given. Her cosmopolitics vindicates the figure of the 'idiot' – a conceptual character borrowed by Gilles Deleuze from Dostoyevsky.[137] For Stengers the idiot is 'the one who always slows the others down, who resists the consensual way in which the situation is presented and in which emergencies mobilise thought or action'. The idiot's role is to slow down the production of technoscientific certainty by experts, and open up space for the unexpected and uncertain. The cosmopolitical is thus neither an appeal to universality nor a dream of global citizenship, but rather a plea to query – through the figure of the idiot – our assumptions about authority and expertise that result in us '[not] consider[ing] ourselves authorised to possess the meaning of what we know'.[138]

Stengers is suspicious of the adoption of the term Anthropocene, on the basis that its tendency for a human-centring and human-dominated narrative legitimises suspect technologies such as those promoted in geoengineering – 'the mobilisation of technology against the Earth'.[139] The designation carries the potential of swallowing up the mess humanity has made into a grand anthropocentric narrative. This is a caution worth heeding for storytellers of the Anthropocene. For the term harbours a teleological compulsion, one that, although replacing progress, still posits itself as the culmination of defunct stories – perhaps the only possible culmination: it is after all, *the story to end all stories*. Gaia – for Stengers – is the force that moves us all, the source of our nourishment and our calamities, and is certainly powerful enough to interrupt any attempt at a coherent narrative or history. Stengers' cosmopolitical proposal is far from reassuring; it has 'far more to do with a passing fright that scares self-assurance'.[140]

Perhaps the role of the Anthropocene story – like that of Stengers' humble but determined 'idiot' – is neither to focus exclusively on the urgency of the human narrative, nor to produce abyssal perplexity for its own sake, but instead to create a temporary domain in which to address the challenges and complexities of a world in the making. In the face of a rapidly transforming and convulsive Earth, the will to 'slow down' is not about an indifference to urgency. 'Slowing down… is multi-critter thinking, caring for entanglement, learning the art of paying attention.'[141] It invites 'an affair of a process that one must *follow*'.[142] The Anthropocene's entangling of ethics, science and politics puts the human in contact with the non-human in all its frightful variability – and with all the paradoxes that this entails. The Anthropocene has the potential to undo the political, for the magnitude of the changes it signals might be enough to undermine human agency, all its achievements and constructions, even to the point of annihilation. Meanwhile, for Clark:

> We are still a long way from the cosmopolitan thought we need, the kind that might point the way to forms of justice and hospitality fitting for a planet that rips away its support from time to time: for an Earth that is not nearly as human or as homely as we tend to assume.[143]

The Anthropocene rift makes it impossible to speak of a singular composed planetary totality – a one-world-ness – but rather implies an indescribable and incommensurable array of conditions. To respond to the Anthropocene demands both strategic interventions to an encroaching human-made catastrophe as well as support for situations where others are in difficulty and where the ground is literally and metaphorically shifting underfoot. These are scary times. If the sundry cautionary tales for the Anthropocene have more to do with a transformative fright than a paralysing shock, they might yet invite responses to the world-as-city that are practically attuned to the turbulent and chaotic thresholds of time.

Hotel for humanity

> The world, which was properly a home, becomes a global rental, the *Hotel for Humanity*. We no longer own it; we only live here as tenants.[144]

In *Malfeasance*, Michel Serres' account of dealing with the mess humans have made, he questions the limits of ownership when he designates Earth as the 'Hotel for Humanity'. Serres invites us to cast a critical eye on the ways in which humans take ownership of space and the ways in which the Earth is appropriated, befouled, polluted or contaminated as a mark of ownership, so that the physical planet has become a global garbage heap. According to Serres, all political and legal structures have been based on the right to acquire and hold property and territory, usually at the expense of others. Serres' 'Hotel for Humanity' recalls Rousseau's citation from Cicero's *De Senectute*, 'The world is a hotel', when writing of the Lisbon disaster. Cicero writes: 'Nature has given us a hostelry in which to sojourn not to abide.' It also carries echoes of Charles Lyell's identification of the Holocene as the time during which Earth was 'tenanted by man'.[145]

What is it to be a tenant of the world in the unsettling time of the Anthropocene? The Anthropocene geostory is a plea for the world as hotel, with billions of tenants and no landlord; a temporary refuge and a collective asset rather than a private possession or source of profit. Serres proposes that instead of a proprietor the human becomes a '*locataire*', a tenant of a place or locus, a niche, and the world. He advocates the 'de-appropriation' or 'non-ownership' of collective public goods: not only the natural spaces, territories and resources of the Earth, but also those spaces of free and open public discussion. But this is far from a footloose, cosmopolitan 'right of possession of the Earth's surface'. Global rental is an exploration of living in the midst of the spatially and temporally extended dynamics of the world. It demands a change in the emphasis of human inhabitation, from one of appropriation, property management and technologies of exclusion on a planet of boundaries and ultrastructures, to what could be imagined instead as a precarious tenancy – with all its attendant ambiguities and obligations. Staying-a-while in the Hotel for Humanity would also involve an indebtedness to those who came before us and a thought for those that may still seek to inhabit the Earth after us – past and future generations.

As Clark argues, 'a greater sensitivity to the precariousness of past human life in the face of volatile Earth processes might help drive forward the still nascent and fragile commitment to intergenerational justice'.[146] The global rental requires a responsiveness to a complex folded dynamic terrain (politics, economics, ethics), to human histories 'on the ground', and to cosmic temporalities of irreversible Earth processes. It suggests the importance of thinking provisionally in human, more-than-human, and more-than-planetary scales. Being 'at home' is never really safe, and in a less-than-ideal world there are many instances when earthly turbulence leaves Earth-dwellers unsettled, perturbed, traumatised, in need of support.

Camp or hotel? What is the temporary home for our sojourn? The Anthropocene unsettles ideas of global unity and humanity, not simply because humankind is marked by inequality and difference but because we are 'creatures of a shifting, convulsive and cosmically exposed Earth'.[147] The Indian scholar Gayatri Chakravorty Spivak proposes the term 'planetarity' to overwrite the globe, attempting to eschew environmental planet-speak or proclamations of one-world-ness or whole-Earth-ness.[148] Planetarity asks us to reimagine ourselves as planetary subjects or creatures rather than global agents. In place of globalisation or citizenship, 'planetarity demands we work with the indeterminacies and ambivalences of "our planet"'.[149] Spivak's caveat is that, 'It is different from a sense of being the custodians of our very own planet'.[150] Rather, it evokes the planet as that which *exceeds* human control. She writes, 'The planet is in the species of alterity, belonging to another system and yet we inhabit it, on loan.'[151] It is an alterity not derived from the centring impulse of the human. As such it is both home and un-homely, a humbling decentring relation to otherness prompted both by the pace of geological time and by the processes that occur in a differentiated political space.

In the Anthropocene, a time that marks itself by intensified human intervention as much as by a surpassing and decentring of the human, how do cities and the world-as-city change? How might we think differently about human settlement if we add to the usual physical vulnerabilities that humans face, new and surprising earthly dynamics that episodically pull the ground from under our feet? How do we practise cosmopolitics in a turbulent world? A politics for the Anthropocene will need to work across the social and ecological controversies in drought-affected regions, hurricane-battered cities, oceanic garbage patches, nuclear waste repositories. Taking responsibility for the cosmopolis will require a good deal of resourcefulness and readiness for the radical changes to inhabitation that the Anthropocene may yet demand. The alternative means being resigned, as Isabelle Stengers puts it, 'to a planetary New Orleans'.[152] If, as calculations would seem to indicate, planetary boundaries have already been transgressed, then perhaps all that can be hoped for is an equitable means of providing refuge, shelter and support in a turbulent world. This will inevitably require us to find ways of dealing with unsettled and unfamiliar patterns of living in the midst of unforeseen dimensions of change.

What would it mean to be worldly, when the world itself has become extraterrestrial, when we have become so exorbitant?'[153]

Perhaps maintaining a planetary foothold is as much as humans can hope for in the Anthropocene. This is an unstable Earth. We cannot expect it to provide us with a solid, reassuring ground. The social and political worlds of the Holocene have also failed to deliver a yearned-for stability. The incapacity of conventional political institutions to deal with the scale of human catastrophe of present-day refugees has become evident. And it is increasingly displacement and unsettlement rather than conventional citizenship that corresponds to the way in which human beings cohabit in the world. The Anthropocene is a challenge to find ways of living that accommodate the exorbitant: situations that are off-track and unexpected, surprising and frightening. This means acknowledging a human agency that is simultaneously weak and excessive. In this respect, 'worldliness' implies an Earth citizenship that is not about setting ever more stringent boundaries and limits (or worrying about crossing them), but instead about a more provisional, hospitable and generous engagement in Earth processes. It means accommodating ourselves to an increasingly unpredictable temporary home.

Stay safe at home.

Notes

1 Nigel Clark, 'Geo-politics and the disaster of the Anthropocene' in *Disasters and Politics: Materials, Experiments, Preparedness*, eds. Manuel Tironi, Israel Rodríguez-Giralt and Michael Guggenheim (Chichester: John Wiley & Sons, 2014): 19–37; 22.
2 Will Steffen *et al.*, 'Planetary boundaries: Guiding human development on a changing planet', *Science* 347.6223 (2015).
3 J. Zalasiewicz, M. Williams, W. Steffen, and P. Crutzen, 'The New World of the Anthropocene', *Environmental Science and Technology* 44 (2010): 2228–2231; 2231.
4 Nigel Clark, 'Geo-politics and the disaster of the Anthropocene' in *Disasters and Politics: Materials, Experiments, Preparedness*, eds. Manuel Tironi, Israel Rodríguez-Giralt and Michael Guggenheim (Chichester: John Wiley & Sons, 2014): 19–37; 28–29.
5 UNHCR Global Trends 2015, Figures at a Glance; www.unhcr.org/uk/figures-at-a-glance.html

6 The Platform on Disaster Displacement is a follow-up to the Nansen Initiative and seeks to address the challenges of cross-border displacement in the context of disasters and the effects of climate change; disasterdisplacement.org/the-platform/ The term 'climate refugee' is not an officially recognised category under international law. The 1951 UN Convention relating to the Status of Refugees defines a refugee as a person with a genuine fear of being persecuted for membership of a particular social group or class. The environmental refugee – not necessarily persecuted, yet necessarily forced to flee – falls outside this definition. See www.unhcr.org/3d58e13b4.pdf
7 W. Steffen et al., *Global Change and the Earth System: A Planet under Pressure* (Berlin: Springer-Verlag, 2004): 299.
8 Donna Haraway, 'Anthropocene, Capitalocene, Plantationocene, Chthulucene: making kin', *Environmental Humanities* 6 (2015): 159–165; 160.
9 See UNRWA, United Nations Relief and Works Agency for Palestine Refugees in the Near East; www.unrwa.org
10 *From Camp to City: Refugee Camps of the Western Sahara*, ed. Manuel Herz (Lars Muller Publishers, 2012).
11 François Gemenne, 'The Anthropocene and its victims' in *The Anthropocene and the Global Environmental Crisis: Rethinking modernity in a new epoch*, eds. Clive Hamilton, Christophe Bonneuil and François Gemenne (London and New York: Routledge, 2015): 168–174; 173.
12 Barbara Ward, *The Home of Man* (Penguin Books, 1976): 1.
13 The term 'human settlements' was derived from Constantinos Doxiadis paradigm of Ekistics, or the science of human settlements. See Panayiota I. Pyla, 'Planetary home and garden: Ekistics and environmental-developmental politics', *Grey Room* 4 (Summer 2009): 6–35.
14 UN Habitat, 'Declaration of the Vancouver Symposium', *Ekistics* 42.252 (1976): 267–272; 267. The UN World Conferences of the 1970s included: on Human Environment in Stockholm, 1972; on World Population in Bucharest, 1974; on Food in Rome, 1974; on the Law of the Seas in Caracas, Geneva, New York 1974–1976; and International Women's Year in Mexico City, 1975. On the series of UN world conferences see Michael G. Schechter, *United Nations Global Conferences* (New York: Routledge, 2005). See also René Dubos, 'The despairing optimist', *The American Scholar* 46.2 (1977): 152–58.
15 'Declaration of the Vancouver Symposium', *Ekistics* 42.252 (1976): 267–72; 267.
16 Barbara Ward, *The Home of Man* (Penguin Books, 1976): 9.
17 Barbara Ward, *The Home of Man* (Penguin Books, 1976): 9–10.
18 Barbara Ward, *The Home of Man* (Penguin Books, 1976): 60.
19 Barbara Ward, *The Home of Man* (Penguin Books, 1976): 72.
20 Barbara Ward, *The Home of Man* (Penguin Books, 1976): 258.
21 Barbara Ward, *The Home of Man* (Penguin Books, 1976): 57.
22 Barbara Ward, *The Home of Man* (Penguin Books, 1976): 10.
23 Barbara Ward, *Human Settlements: Crisis and Opportunity* (Ottawa, Canada: Ministry of State for Urban Affairs, 1974). See also Barbara Ward, 'United Nations conference-exposition on human settlements', *Ekistics* 38. 227 (1974): 236–39.
24 Barbara Ward, *The Home of Man* (Penguin Books, 1976): 273.
25 Barbara Ward, *The Home of Man* (Penguin Books, 1976): 274–275.
26 Barbara Ward, *The Home of Man* (Penguin Books, 1976): 267.
27 Felicity D. Scott, *Outlaw Territories: Environments of Insecurity/Architectures of Counterinsurgency* (Zone Books, 2016): 241–242.
28 Gladwin Hill, 'View of world's shantytowns less grim', *The New York Times* (9 June 1976): 4; cf. Felicity D. Scott, *Outlaw Territories: Environments of Insecurity/Architectures of Counterinsurgency* (Zone Books, 2016): 244–245.
29 R. Buckminster Fuller, 'Accommodating human unsettlement', *The Town Planning Review* 49.1 (Jan 1978): 51–60.
30 R. Buckminster Fuller, 'Accommodating human unsettlement', *The Town Planning Review* 49.1 (Jan 1978): 57.
31 R. Buckminster Fuller, 'Accommodating human unsettlement', *The Town Planning Review* 49.1 (Jan 1978): 57–58.
32 R. Buckminster Fuller, 'Accommodating human unsettlement', *The Town Planning Review* 49.1 (Jan 1978): 58

33 On the Habitat Forum, fringe event at Jericho Beach, see Felicity D. Scott, *Outlaw Territories: Environments of Insecurity/Architectures of Counterinsurgency* (Zone Books, 2016): 225–229.
34 R. Buckminster Fuller, 'human unsettlement', *The Town Planning Review* 49.1 (Jan 1978): 55.
35 R. Buckminster Fuller, 'Accommodating human unsettlement', *The Town Planning Review* 49.1 (Jan 1978): 57.
36 R. Buckminster Fuller, 'Accommodating human unsettlement', *The Town Planning Review* 49.1 (Jan 1978): 59.
37 R. Buckminster Fuller, 'Accommodating human unsettlement', *The Town Planning Review* 49.1 (Jan 1978): 54–55.
38 Barbara Ward, *The Home of Man* (Penguin Books, 1976): 287.
39 Felicity D. Scott, *Outlaw Territories: Environments of Insecurity/Architectures of Counterinsurgency* (Zone Books, 2016): 265.
40 Felicity D. Scott, *Outlaw Territories: Environments of Insecurity/Architectures of Counterinsurgency* (Zone Books, 2016): 231.
41 Alan Merridew, 'UN's "Habitat" runs afoul of ill will in Middle East', *Chicago Tribune* (13 June 1976): 13; cf. Felicity D. Scott, *Outlaw Territories: Environments of Insecurity/Architectures of Counterinsurgency* (Zone Books, 2016): 265.
42 Barbara Ward, *The Home of Man* (Penguin Books, 1976): 293.
43 United Nations Habitat, *The Challenge of Slums: Global Report on Human Settlements* (UN-Habitat, 2003); unhabitat.org/books/the-challenge-of-slums-global-report-on-human-settlements-2003/. The Global Urban Indicators database used in the report collected information on 237 cities worldwide. For 34 detailed city case studies see University College London Development Planning Unit and UN-Habitat, 'Understanding Slums: Case Studies for the Global Report on Human Settlements 2003'; www.ucl.ac.uk/dpu-projects/Global_Report.
44 Mike Davis, '"Humanity's Ground Zero", a Tomdispatch interview with Mike Davis (Part 1)', TomDispatch (9 May 2006); www.tomdispatch.com/post/82655/
45 Mike Davis, *Planet of Slums* (London and Brooklyn: Verso, 2007): 21.
46 Mike Davis, *Planet of Slums* (London and Brooklyn: Verso, 2007): 19.
47 Mike Davis, *Planet of Slums* (London and Brooklyn: Verso, 2007): 201.
48 Mike Davis, '"Humanity's Ground Zero", a Tomdispatch interview with Mike Davis (Part 1)', TomDispatch (9 May 2006); www.tomdispatch.com/post/82655/
49 Mike Davis, *Planet of Slums* (London and Brooklyn: Verso, 2007): 121.
50 Eileen Stillwaggon, *Stunted Lives, Stagnant Economies: Poverty, Disease and Underdevelopment* (New Brunswick NJ, 1998): 67; cf Mike Davis, *Planet of Slums* (London and Brooklyn: Verso, 2007): 121.
51 Mike Davis, '"The Imperial City and the City of Slums", a Tomdispatch Interview with Mike Davis (Part 2)', TomDispatch (11 May 2006); www.tomdispatch.com/post/82790/tomdispatch_interview_mike_davis_green_zones_and_slum_cities
52 Mike Davis, *Planet of Slums* (London and Brooklyn: Verso, 2007): 202.
53 United Nations, Habitat III, 'The New Urban Agenda'; habitat3.org/the-new-urban-agenda
54 Federico Caprotti, Robert Cowley, Ayona Datta, Vanesa Castán Broto, Eleanor Gao, Lucien Georgeson, Clare Herrick, Nancy Odendaal and Simon Joss, 'The New Urban Agenda: key opportunities and challenges for policy and practice, Urban Research & Practice', *Urban Research and Practice* (2017)
55 Ada Colau, 'After Habitat III: a stronger urban future must be based on the right to the city', *The Guardian* (20 October 2016); www.theguardian.com/cities/2016/oct/20/habitat-3-right-city-concrete-policies-ada-colau
56 Mike Davis, '"Living on the Ice Shelf - Humanity's Meltdown", a Tomdispatch Interview with Mike Davis', TomDispatch (26 June 2008); www.tomdispatch.com/post/174949
57 Mike Davis, 'Who will build the ark?', *New Left Review* 61 (Jan–Feb 2010): 29–45; newleftreview.org/II/61/mike-davis-who-will-build-the-ark;
58 Mike Davis, 'Who will build the ark?', *New Left Review* 61 (Jan–Feb 2010): 29–45; newleftreview.org/II/61/mike-davis-who-will-build-the-ark;
59 Mike Davis, '"Humanity's Ground Zero", a Tomdispatch interview with Mike Davis (Part 1)', TomDispatch (9 May 2006); www.tomdispatch.com/post/82655/

60 Mike Davis, '"Living on the Ice Shelf - Humanity's Meltdown", a Tomdispatch Interview with Mike Davis', TomDispatch (26 June 2008); www.tomdispatch.com/post/174949
61 J. K. Gibson-Graham and G. Roelvink, 'An economic ethics for the Anthropocene', *Antipode: A Journal of Radical Geography* 41 (Supplement 1) (2010): 320–346; 321.
62 Bruno Latour, 'Agency at the time of the Anthropocene', *New Literary History* 45 (2014): 1–18 2.
63 Zygmunt Bauman and Carlo Bordoni, *State of Crisis* (Polity, 2014).
64 Zygmunt Bauman, 'Times of interregnum', *Ethics & Global Politics* 5.1 (2012): 49–56.
65 Dipesh Chakrabarty, 'Human Agency in the Anthropocene' (December 2012); www.historians.org/publications-and-directories/perspectives-on-history/december-2012/the-future-of-the-discipline/human-agency-in-the-anthropocene
66 Nigel Clark, *Inhuman Nature: Sociable Life on a Dynamic Planet* (London: Sage, 2011): xvi.
67 F. Kossak, D. Petrescu, T. Schneider, R. Tyszczuk and S. Walker, *Agency: Working with Uncertain Architectures* (London: Routledge, 2009).
68 J. K. Gibson-Graham and G. Roelvink, 'An economic ethics for the Anthropocene', *Antipode: A Journal of Radical Geography* 41 (Supplement 1) (2010): 320–346; 322.
69 Bruno Latour, 'Agency at the time of the Anthropocene', *New Literary History* 45 (2014): 1–18; 17.
70 Nigel Clark, '400ppm: Regime Change in Geo-Social Formations', '400 ppm', discussion forum convened by Kathryn Yusoff (July 2013); Society and Space – Environment and Planning D; societyandspace.com/material/discussion-forum/400ppm/nigel-clark-400ppm-regime-change-in-geo-social-formations/
71 Tom Engelhardt, 'Was 11/8 a new 9/11? The election that changed everything and could prove history's deal-breaker', TomDispatch (1 December 2016); www.tomdispatch.com/post/176216/tomgram%3A_engelhardt%2C_the_most_dangerous_country_on_earth/#more
72 Bonnie Honig, *Emergency Politics: Paradox, Law, Democracy* (Princeton, NJ: Princeton University Press, 2009).
73 Giorgio Agamben, *State of Exception*, trans. Kevin Attell (Chicago and London: University of Chicago Press, 2005): 11–22.
74 Giorgio Agamben, *State of Exception*, trans. Kevin Attell (Chicago and London: University of Chicago Press, 2005): 1.
75 Giorgio Agamben *State of Exception*, trans. Kevin Attell (Chicago and London: University of Chicago Press, 2005): 2.
76 Giorgio Agamben, *State of Exception*, trans. Kevin Attell (Chicago and London: University of Chicago Press, 2005): 6
77 Giorgio Agamben, *State of Exception*, trans. Kevin Attell (Chicago and London: University of Chicago Press, 2005): 14.
78 Christophe Bonneuil and Jean-Baptiste Fressoz, *The Shock of the Anthropocene*, trans. by David Fernbach (London: Verso, 2016): 129.
79 Jacob Darwin Hamblin, *Arming Mother Nature: The Birth of Catastrophic Environmentalism* (Oxford, New York: Oxford University Press, 2013): 249–250. See also Joe Smith, 'From truth war to a game of risk', *Culture and Climate Change: Narratives*, eds. in J. Smith, R. Tyszczuk, R. Butler (Cambridge: Shed, 2014): 15–24; 16.
80 James Lovelock, *The Vanishing Face of Gaia: A Final Warning* (London: Allen Lane, 2009).
81 Giorgio Agamben, *State of Exception*, trans. Kevin Attell (Chicago and London: University of Chicago Press, 2005): 5.
82 Giorgio Agamben, *Homo Sacer: Sovereign Power and Bare Life*, trans. D. Heller-Roazen (Stanford, CA: Stanford University Press, 1998): 168–169.
83 Giorgio Agamben, *Homo Sacer: Sovereign Power and Bare Life*, trans. D. Heller-Roazen (Stanford, CA: Stanford University Press, 1998): 181.
84 Katy Reckdahl, '10 years after Katrina, some are "homeless in their own homes"', *National Geographic* (13 August 2013); news.nationalgeographic.com/2015/08/150813-homeless-after-katrina-new-orleans/
85 Gillian B. White, 'A housing crisis amid tens of thousands of abandoned homes', *The Atlantic* (20 August 2015); www.theatlantic.com/business/archive/2015/08/new-orleans-blight-hurricane-katrina/401843/
86 Rebecca Solnit, 'In the shadow of the storm', *Harper's Magazine* (August 2015).

87 Rebecca Solnit, *A Paradise Built in Hell: The Extraordinary Communities That Arise in Disaster* (Viking Books, 2009).
88 NASA, 'New Study Maps Rate of New Orleans Sinking' (16 May 2016). The study used data from NASA's Uninhabited Aerial Vehicle Synthetic Aperture Radar (UAVSAR); www.nasa.gov/feature/jpl/new-study-maps-rate-of-new-orleans-sinking
89 Benjamin H. Strauss, Scott Kulp and Anders Levermann, 'Carbon choices determine US cities committed to futures below sea level', *PNAS* 112.44 (3 November 2015): 13508–13513; www.pnas.org/content/112/44/13508.full.pdf
90 Coastal Protection and Restoration Authority (CPRA), 'Louisiana's Comprehensive Master Plan for a Sustainable Coast' (2012); coastal.la.gov/a-common-vision/2012-coastal-master-plan/
91 Naomi Klein, 'Let them drown: The violence of othering in a warming world', *London Review of Books* 38.11 (2 June 2016): 11–14.
92 John Biguenet, *The Rising Water Trilogy Plays* (Baton Rouge: Louisiana State University Press, 2015): 9.
93 Eyal Weizman and Fazal Sheikh, *The Conflict Shoreline: Colonization as Climate Change in the Negev Desert* (Steidl Books, 2015).
94 Benjamin I. Cook, Kevin J. Anchukaitis, Ramzi Touchan, David M. Meko and Edward R. Cook, 'Spatiotemporal drought variability in the Mediterranean over the last 900 years', *Journal of Geophysical Research* 121.5 (16 March 2016): 2060–2074.
95 Rebecca Solnit, 'Bigger than that (the difficulty of) looking at climate change', TomDispatch (6 October 2013); www.tomdispatch.com/blog/175756/tomgram%3A_rebecca_solnit,_the_age_of_inhuman_scale
96 Ban Ki Moon, 'A climate culprit in Darfur', *The Washington Post* (16 June 2007); www.washingtonpost.com/wp-dyn/content/article/2007/06/15/AR2007061501857.html
97 Alex Randall, 'Syria and climate change: did the media get it right?', Climate and Migration Coalition, Climate Outreach interactive site with a summary of the reporting and links to articles; climatemigration.atavist.com/syria-and-climate-change
98 Colin P. Kelley, Shahrzad Mohtadi, Mark A. Crane, Richard Seager and Yochanan Kushnir, 'Climate change in the Fertile Crescent and implications of the recent Syrian drought', *PNAS* 112.11 (17 March 2015): 3241–3246.
99 Francesca de Châtel, 'The role of drought and climate change in the Syrian uprising: Untangling the triggers of the revolution', *Middle Eastern Studies* 50.4 (2014): 521–535.
100 Killian Kleinschmidt, 'Empowering Refugees Q&A with Killian Kleinschmidt', Independent Commission on Multilateralism (ICM); www.icm2016.org/empowering-refugees-q-a-with-kilian-kleinschmidt
101 Manuel Herz, 'Refugee camps – or – ideal cities in dust and dirt' in *Urban Transformation*, eds. I. Ruby and A. Ruby (Ruby Press, 2008).
102 C. E. Werrell, and F. Femia, *The Arab Spring and Climate Change. A Climate and Security Correlations Series* (Stimson, 2013): 24; climateandsecurity.files.wordpress.com/2012/04/climatechangearabspring-ccs-cap-stimson.pdf
103 Martin Chulov, 'Zaatari camp: makeshift city in the desert that may be here to stay', *The Guardian* (25 July 2013); www.theguardian.com/world/2013/jul/25/zaatari-camp-makeshift-city-jordan
104 See, for example, the interactive map on BBC News website: 'Zaatari refugee camp: Rebuilding lives in the desert' (3 September 2013); www.bbc.co.uk/news/world-middle-east-23801200
105 Martin Chulov, 'Zaatari camp: makeshift city in the desert that may be here to stay', *The Guardian* (25 July 2013); www.theguardian.com/world/2013/jul/25/zaatari-camp-makeshift-city-jordan
106 Killian Kleinschmidt, 'Refugee camps are the "cities of tomorrow" says humanitarian-aid expert', interview with Killian Kleinschmidt by Talia Radford, Dezeen (23 November 2015); www.dezeen.com/2015/11/23/refugee-camps-cities-of-tomorrow-killian-kleinschmidt-interview-humanitarian-aid-expert/
107 Alessandro Petti, 'Architecture of Exile'; www.campusincamps.ps/architecture-exile/
108 Bonnie Honig, *Emergency Politics* (Princeton, NJ: Princeton University Press, 2009): 1.
109 N. Sigona, 'Campzenship: reimagining the camp as a social and political space', *Citizenship Studies* 19.1 (2015): 1–15; 1.

110 *From Camp to City: Refugee Camps of the Western Sahara*, ed. Manuel Herz (Lars Muller Publishers, 2012).
111 Nigel Clark, 'Moving and shaking: Mobility on a dynamic planet' in *Atlas: Geography, Architecture and Change in an Interdependent World*, eds. Tyszczuk, *et al.* (London: Black Dog Publishing, 2012): 22–29; 23.
112 Nigel Clark 'Moving and shaking: Mobility on a dynamic planet' in *Atlas: Geography, Architecture and Change in an Interdependent World*, eds. Tyszczuk, *et al.* (London: Black Dog Publishing, 2012): 22–29; 27.
113 Nigel Clark, 'Geopolitics at the threshold', *Political Geography* 37 (2013): 48–50.
114 Hannah Arendt, 'We Refugees', *Menorah Journal* 1 (1943): 77; republished in Altogether Elsewhere: Writers on Exile, ed. Mark Robinson (Boston and London: Faber and Faber, 1994): 110–119.
115 Giorgio Agamben, 'Beyond Human Rights', *Open 2008/No 15/Social Engineering*: 90–95; 95; first published in Giorgio Agamben, 'Means without End. Notes on politics' in: *Theory Out of Bounds*, 20 (Minneapolis/London: University of Minnesota Press, 2000).
116 Nigel Clark 'Moving and shaking: Mobility on a dynamic planet' in *Atlas: Geography, Architecture and Change in an Interdependent World*, eds. Tyszczuk, *et al.*(London: Black Dog Publishing, 2012): 22–29; 28.
117 Nigel Clark, 'Moving and shaking: Mobility on a dynamic planet' in *Atlas: Geography, Architecture and Change in an Interdependent World*, eds. Tyszczuk, *et al.* (London: Black Dog Publishing, 2012): 22–29; 23.
118 Jacques Derrida, 'The principle of hospitality', *parallax*. 11. 1 (2005): 6–9; an interview wih Dominique Dhombres for *Le Monde* (2 December 1997), trans. Ashley Thompson.
119 Jacques Derrida, *On Cosmopolitanism and Forgiveness*, trans.Mark Dooley and Michael Hughes (London: Routledge, 2001): 16–17. See also Jacques Derrida, *Of Hospitality*, 'Anne Dufourmantelle invites Jacques Derrida to respond' (Stanford University Press, 2000).
120 Sean K. Kelly, 'Derrida's cities of refuge: toward a non-Utopian Utopia', *Contemporary Justice Review* 7.4 (December 2004): 421–439.
121 Christine Goodall, *Sanctuary and Solidarity – Urban Community Responses to Asylum Seekers on Three Continents* (UNHCR, September 2011).
122 Jacques Derrida, *On Cosmopolitanism and Forgiveness*, trans. Mark Dooley and Michael Hughes (London: Routledge, 2001): 4.
123 Jacques Derrida, *On Cosmopolitanism and Forgiveness*, trans. Mark Dooley and Michael Hughes (London: Routledge, 2001): 23; emphasis in original.
124 Tariq Jazeel, 'Spatializing difference beyond cosmopolitanism: Rethinking planetary futures' *Theory, Culture & Society* 28.5 (2011): 75–97; 78.
125 Tariq Jazeel, 'Spatializing difference beyond cosmopolitanism: Rethinking planetary futures' *Theory, Culture & Society* 28.5 (2011): 75–97; 84.
126 Immanuel Kant, *Idea for a universal history from a cosmopolitan point of view* (1784) in Immanuel Kant, *On History*, trans. Lewis White Beck (Macmillan, 1963)
127 Immanuel Kant, *Toward perpetual peace and other writings on politics, peace, and history* (1795) in *Rethinking the Western Tradition*, ed. Pauline Kleingeld, trans. David L. Colclasure (New Haven, CT: Yale Universty Press, 2006): 8-358; 82.
128 Immanuel Kant, *Toward perpetual peace and other writings on politics, peace, and history* (1795) in *Rethinking the Western Tradition*, ed. Pauline Kleingeld, trans. David L. Colclasure (New Haven, CT: Yale Universty Press, 2006): 8-358; 82.
129 Ulrich Beck, *Cosmopolitan Vision*, trans. Ciaran Cronin (Cambridge: Polity Press, 2006): 48.
130 Bruno Latour, 'Whose cosmos, which cosmopolitics? Comments on the peace terms of Ulrich Beck', Talking Peace with Gods, Part 1, *Common Knowledge* 10.3 (2004): 450–462.
131 N. Clark, '400ppm: Regime Change in Geo-Social Formations', '400 ppm', discussion forum convened by Kathryn Yusoff (July 2013); Society and Space – Environment and Planning D; societyandspace.com/material/discussion-forum/400ppm/nigel-clark-400ppm-regime-change-in-geo-social-formations/
132 Bruno Latour, "Whose cosmos, which cosmopolitics? Comments on the peace terms of Ulrich Beck', Talking Peace with Gods, Part 1, *Common Knowledge* 10.3 (2004): 450–462; 453.
133 Isabelle Stengers, *Cosmopolitiques*, Volume 1, 'La guerre des sciences' (Paris: La Découverte; Les Empêcheurs de penser en rond, 1996).

134 Bruno Latour, 'Whose cosmos, which cosmopolitics? Comments on the peace terms of Ulrich Beck', Talking Peace with Gods, Part 1, *Common Knowledge* 10.3 (2004): 450–462; 454.
135 Isabelle Stengers, 'The Cosmopolitical Proposal' in *Making Things Public*: *Atmospheres of Democracy*, eds. Bruno Latour and Peter Weibel (Cambridge MA: MIT Press, 2005): 994–1003; 994.
136 Isabelle Stengers, 'The Cosmopolitical Proposal' in *Making Things Public*: *Atmospheres of Democracy*, eds. Bruno Latour and Peter Weibel (Cambridge MA: MIT Press, 2005): 994–1003; 994.
137 See, for example, G. Deleuze, and F. Guattari, *What is Philosophy?* (London: Verso, 1994): 62–63.
138 Isabelle Stengers, 'The Cosmopolitical Proposal' in *Making Things Public*: *Atmospheres of Democracy*, eds. Bruno Latour and Peter Weibel (Cambridge MA: MIT Press, 2005): 994–1003; 995.
139 Isabelle Stengers in conversation with Heather Davis and Etienne Turpin, 'Matters of cosmopolitics: On the provocations of Gaïa' in *Architecture in the Anthropocene: Encounters Among Design, Deep Time, Science and Philosophy*, ed. Etienne Turpin (Ann Arbor, MI: Open Humanities Press, 2013): 171–182; 179.
140 Isabelle Stengers, 'The Cosmopolitical Proposal' in *Making Things Public*: *Atmospheres of Democracy*, eds. Bruno Latour and Peter Weibel (Cambridge MA: MIT Press, 2005): 994–1003; 996.
141 Isabelle Stengers in conversation with Heather Davis and Etienne Turpin, 'Matters of cosmopolitics: On the provocations of Gaïa' in *Architecture in the Anthropocene: Encounters Among Design, Deep Time, Science and Philosophy*, ed. Etienne Turpin (Ann Arbor, MI: Open Humanities Press, 2013): 171–182; 179.
142 Isabelle Stengers, *The Invention of Modern Science* (University of Minnesota Press, 2000): 145.
143 Nigel Clark, *Inhuman Nature: Sociable Life on a Dynamic Planet* (London: Sage, 2011): 219.
144 Michel Serres, *Malfeasance, Appropriation Through Pollution?*, trans. Anne-Marie Feenberg-Dibon (Stanford: Stanford University Press, 2011): 72.
145 Charles Lyell (1830) *Principles of Geology, or The Modern Changes of the Earth and Its Inhabitants, Considered as Illustrative of Geology* (New York; Ninth Edition 1858): 275.
146 N. Clark, V. Chhotray and R. Few, 'Global justice and disasters', *Geographical Journal* 179 2 (2013): 105–113; 112.
147 Nigel Clark, 'Anthropocene incitements: toward a politics and ethics of ex-orbitant planetarity' in *The Politics of Globality since 1945*, eds. Rens van Munster and Caspar Sylvest (London: Routledge, 2016): 126–144; 139.
148 Gayatri Chakravorty Spivak, *Death of a Discipline* (New York: Columbia University Press, 2003): 72.
149 Tariq Jazeel, 'Spatializing difference beyond cosmopolitanism: Rethinking planetary futures', *Theory, Culture & Society* 28.5 (2011): 75–97; 89.
150 Gayatri Chakravorty Spivak, 'Planetarity' in *Dictionary of Untranslatables: A Philosophical Lexicon*, ed. Barbara Cassin (Princeton and Oxford: Princeton University Press, 2014): 1223.
151 Gayatri Chakravorty Spivak, 'Planetarity' in *Dictionary of Untranslatables: A Philosophical Lexicon*, ed. Barbara Cassin (Princeton University Press: Princeton and Oxford, 2014): 1223.
152 Isabelle Stengers, *In Catastrophic Times: Resisting the Coming Barbarism*, trans. Andre Goffey (Open Humanities Press, 2015): 49.
153 Steven Connor, 'I believe that the world' in *Cultural Ways of Worldmaking: Media and Narratives*, eds. Vera Nünning, Ansgar Nünning and Birgit Neumann (Berlin and New York: De Gruyter, 2010): 29–46; 44.

Epilogue
Precautionary tales

The Anthropocene is replete with warnings of imminent dangers to Earth and its inhabitants. Indeed the Anthropocene is made by and with those warnings: the calls of Cassandra scientists, the mutterings of apocalyptic doom-mongers, or the cries of Walter Benjamin's 'fire alarm.'[1] For Paul Crutzen, the 'Anthropocene' is an Earth systems emergency on an unprecedented scale; announcing it, a necessary shock tactic. This epoch-naming gives shape to the sense of human calamity in its full magnitude and dimensions (philosophical, cultural, political, environmental) and yet it resists being pinned down as a blueprint for resolving crisis. Instead the Anthropocene may be understood as a cautionary tale, a way of coming to terms with a runaway human-induced catastrophe. As a *prophecy of doom* – to borrow the German philosopher Hans Jonas's term – it is also a way of apprehending this catastrophe:

> The *prophecy of doom* is made to avert its coming, and it would be the height of injustice to later deride the 'alarmists' because 'it did not turn out to be so bad after all'. To have been wrong may be their merit.[2]

It is not possible to stop the future happening. Instead, Jonas's 'heuristic of fear' was intended to inspire an 'ethics for the future' and awaken the 'imperative of responsibility'. This is a directive *not* to leave the uncertain, distant and precarious future to take care of itself. Jonas's work inspired an important legislative framework in Europe, the 'precautionary principle'. As Jean-Pierre Dupuy, writing on 'enlightened doomsaying', observes:

> All the fears of our age seem to have found shelter in one word: precaution. Yet the conceptual underpinnings of the notion of precaution are extremely fragile.[3]

The Anthropocene story captures the fears of the present day – the condition of *Anthropocenophobia*. It elicits a general mood of anticipation, prognosis and precaution. It is rife with uncertainty and indeterminacy. It is a source of confusion. It transforms the temporal and spatial frames within which human actions are usually measured into entanglements of errant strata and uncommon durations. And it produces anxiety about how to deal with this catastrophe of human making. Dupuy's study of 'enlightened catastrophism', *Pour un catastrophisme éclairé*, tries to makes sense of the human catastrophes of Lisbon, Auschwitz, Hiroshima and New York.[4] He proposes that the only effective way to meet future catastrophes is to imagine worst-case scenarios in order to guide present-day choices. Dupuy's *Short Treatise on the*

Metaphysics of Tsunamis returns to this theme.[5] He quotes Gunther Anders' retelling of the story of Noah, who in this version has grown tired of being a 'prophet of doom' and instead starts to mourn a future catastrophe: 'When he was asked when this catastrophe had taken place, he replied to them: "Tomorrow".' The parable continues with Noah explaining,

> 'The day after tomorrow, the flood will be something that will have been. And when the flood will have been, *everything that is will never have existed*.'… That evening a carpenter knocked on his door and said to him: 'Let me help you build an ark, so that it may become false.'[6]

The thought experiment that underpins the Anthropocene – the vision of tomorrow's forensic geologists looking back on the fossilised remnants of human-induced catastrophe – also collapses the future into the past. It indicates the potential for the very meaning of human history to be destroyed: *everything that is will never have existed*. The Anthropocene – the *story to end all stories* – could be interpreted thus as a strategy of 'enlightened doomsaying'. Accepting catastrophe as inevitable, and mourning the future, is part of it. According to Dupuy, once this is acknowledged, adopting a future standpoint *as if* the calamity had aready happened allows for retroactively contemplating the existence of alternative possibilities – some precipitating the catastrophic event and some preventing it. It is then possible to identify the best course of action. In the case of Noah, the best course is to build the ark – even if he's taking the future flood on faith.

Taking future disaster on faith is the key epistemological challenge of the Anthropocene. No matter how much evidence we accumulate to show that we are bringing it about, we don't believe catastrophe will actually happen. Writing in the aftermath of the World Trade Center attacks of 9/11, Dupuy argues that the worst outcomes are often the least anticipated, and the most unlikely – until they occur.[7] If it is possible, to *work with* future catastrophe, it will certainly require a rigorous prognostic intelligence. One that, according to Peter Sloterdijk, seeks to learn from misfortune before it occurs: 'While to date a large part of human learning was subject to the law of "once bitten, twice shy", prognostic intelligence must seek to be clever before we get bitten.'[8] Sloterdijk, referring to Dupuy's study, points out the 'basal paradox of the prophecies of doom': that the alarm being raised and heard may prompt evasive action, so that the prophesied disaster never comes about. Those who would learn from the worst-case future in order to bring about a better one must not be deterred by the possibility that their strategy may succeed so thoroughly that they end up being ridiculed as paranoid Cassandras. Indeed, perhaps 'only the apocalyptically minded among us can conduct a rational future politics because only they really consider the worst-case as a real possibility.'[9] According to Sloterdijk, the apocalyptic logic within which the Anthropocene is construed suggests that, 'we can only test it through various forms of anticipation – as demonstrated by a series of illustrious simulations, both sublime and profane, ranging from the Egyptian books of the dead to the first report to the Club of Rome'.[10]

Doomsday vault

When it comes to human habitats, our precautionary measures have been exclusionary, defensive, heavy-handed, even idiosyncratic. Attempts at constructing for the unforseen have tended to focus on future-proofing. The Svalbard Global Seed Vault (SGSV), often called a modern-day Noah's Ark, or the 'Doomsday vault', is the largest secure seed storage facility in the world with room for 4.5 million seed samples. It is a repository for Holocene crops, 'on which human civilisation was raised'.[11] The project recalls the nuclear waste containment strategies of WIPP and Onkalo: the same anxieties, the same deficits in imagination and the same fearful domestication of apocalyptic futures, but also the potential for accidents. The 'disaster-proof' vault was built deep into a mountain on Spitsbergen, an island in the Arctic archipelago: out of reach of sea level rise, earthquake- resistant, and insulated by permafrost, to help ensure contents stay safely frozen at -18°C for decades. It was conceived as an emergency measure for an unknown future catastrophe, and aims to 'safeguard the world's crops from future disasters such as nuclear wars, asteroids or dangerous climate change'.[12] Its purpose is to create a genetic 'back-up' of Earth's reserves of plant life in the face of rampant extinctions and climate shifts.

SGSV's imagined distant timescales have been radically curtailed in recent years. Seed stores from Aleppo were moved there when war broke out in Syria, and some samples were withdrawn in 2015 to begin the process of replenishing endangered seeds.[13] The vault has faced a number of challenges, from an electrical malfunction of the refrigeration unit, to funding cuts, to a fundamental dispute about whether the vault is the right strategy for saving diversity. Some argue that the highly centralised approach – 'an overpriced deep freeze' – may not actually help communities cope with climate change 50 or 100 years hence, and encouraging biodiversity works better in the field, particularly in regions where industrial monocultures have not dominated. Seeds are not artefacts for archiving – they have to remain 'viable', and alive: 'diversity cannot be boxed up', but is rather part of constant change. Strategies for ensuring its continuity would need to be 'as diverse and dynamic as plant life itself'.[14] Moreover, the replanting of seeds will always involve the retelling of stories: of growing practices, of food cultures, of cities and settlements.

The repository is not future-proof. 'Thinking in advance' on the deep timescales of the Anthropocene is likely to be interrupted by the here and now. The doomsday future is already here. The question is how to inhabit an increasingly inhospitable world. It is not about rehearsing the end of the world. The lesson from the seed vault is that precaution may also be a way of bringing the not so distant future closer in order to practice taking care of it, rather than consigning a parcelled up present to a doomsday vault.

Precautionary principle

If the Anthropocene is precaution writ large then the 'precautionary principle' may provide a guide. However, it is a guide without guarantee. The term comes from the German *Vorsorgeprinzip*. This legislative framework, developed in environmental policy discourses of the 1970s and 1980s, is also translated as 'responsibility principle' or foresight principle.' The word *vorsorge* means literally 'forecaring'. It thus suggests an imaginative engagement with disaster that allows us to care about it before it happens – that is, before it is too late to care. The precautionary principle owes much to the demotic practice of 'common sense'. The essence of precaution can be traced to Aristotle's treatment of *phronesis*, or 'practical wisdom', in the *Nicomachean Ethics*, which requires skill and the exercise of good judgement to callibrate actions to the circumstances presented. The precautionary principle as common sense also shows up in many popular sayings: '*Better safe than sorry.*' '*Look before you leap.*' '*A stitch in time saves nine.*'

Precautionary measures for the control of CFCs were introduced into the Montreal Protocol in 1987 and the 'precautionary principle' was decisively written into the *geostory* in the Rio Declaration at the 1992 UN 'Earth Summit'. The Rio formulation of the principle, in the context of climate change, states: 'Where there are threats of serious or irreversible damage, lack of full scientific certainty shall not be used as a reason for postponing cost-effective measures to prevent environmental degradation.'[15] From this time, the precautionary principle was enshrined in environmental law throughout the European Union (EU), and is referenced in multiple treaties, including the 1993 charter for the EU, the 1996 Protocol to the Convention on the Prevention of Marine Pollution by Dumping of Wastes and Other Matter, and the Cartagena Protocol on Biosafety, drafted in 2000. In 2005 France inscribed the precautionary principle in its constitution, alongside the 1789 Declaration of the Rights of Man and of the Citizen.[16]

The precautionary principle suggests the obligation to make decisions in situations of uncertainty that are not definitive – a more prospective notion of responsibility based on a 'duty of prudence'.[17] 'At its core lies the idea that decision-makers should act in advance of scientific certainty to protect the environment (and, with it, the well-being of future generations) from incurring harm.'[18] The precautionary principle thus fractures the (often illusory) connection between scientific certainty and political action, asserting that even in the absence of certainty, decisions can be taken. Decisions about, for example, dissemination of new biotechnologies, use of pesticides, geoengineering tests, nuclear waste disposal, or greenhouse effect mitigation, all fall within its scope. The principle is mired in controversy and its history reveals it as 'a rather shambolic concept, muddled in policy advice and subject to whims of international diplomacy and the unpredictable public mood over the true cost of sustainable living'.[19]

Critics of the principle are not against precautionary measures *per se*, but are wary of the suggestion that technological developments that might entail risks could be blocked by invoking the principle until they are deemed absolutely safe – thus missing the window of opportunity in which they might have been put to use. Others warn of last-ditch attempts to counter uncertain catastrophe with technological fixes that could end up making things even worse. The precautionary principle can be used in arguments both for and against geoengineering. On the one hand, the principle can suggest caution against climate engineering so as to avoid the (unknown) risks of proposed irreversible Earth-altering schemes. On the other hand, climate engineering is presented as a precautionary measure mitigating against the (known) risks of climate change. Precaution, it is argued, can uphold both scientific rigour and democratic accountability in conditions of uncertainty. As the academic and writer Andy Stirling points out: 'Precaution does not necessarily mean a ban. It simply urges that time and space be found to get things right.'[20]

In spite of knowledge of the destructive threats to human societies – climate change, environmental degradation, biodiversity loss – the precautionary principle has not led to binding global policies for the substantial actions needed to avert catastrophe – something that the principle was 'supposed to be qualified to adjudicate'.[21] Dupuy observes that the precautionary principle's 'implicit premise is that we do not act in the face of catastrophe because we are not sure of knowing enough to act effectively'.[22] In *The Collapse of Western Civilisation*, Oreskes and Conway's cautionary tale, they also take issue with the 'precautionary principle', describing it as 'moot' at our present stage of advancement into disastrous anthropogenic climate change: 'It's way too late for precaution. Now we are talking about damage control.'[23]

In June 2015 the precautionary principle appeared in the Papal Encyclical (*Encyclical Letter Laudato Si' of the Holy Father Francis On Care For Our Common Home*): 'This precautionary principle makes it possible to protect those who are most vulnerable and whose ability to defend their interests and to assemble incontrovertible evidence is limited.'[24] For Pope Francis, 'care for our common home' is intimately connected with social issues, a case of hearing '*both the cry of the Earth and the cry of the poor*'.[25] The Pope observed that there were environmental issues where a broad consensus is not possible and was keen to stress that the Church 'does not presume to settle scientific questions or to replace politics', but was 'concerned to encourage an honest and open debate so that particular interests or ideologies will not prejudice the common good'.[26] Will Steffen and colleagues also invoked the precautionary principle, in relation to the shift from a destabilised Holocene world to the Anthropocene, in their 2015 update of 'planetary boundaries' thinking:

> The *precautionary principle* suggests that human societies would be unwise to drive the Earth system substantially away from a Holocene-like condition. A continuing trajectory away from the Holocene could lead, with an uncomfortably high probability, to a very different state of the Earth system, one that is likely to be much less hospitable to the development of human societies.[27]

If precaution is the appropriate reaction to partial, uncertain, incomplete and incoherent knowledge of our planetary predicament in the Anthropocene, then the precautionary principle warrants further deliberation. As the political science academic Kerry Whiteside has put it, 'Precaution is this uncertainty made self-conscious'.[28] The precautionary principle also runs counter to overconfident assumptions of human mastery over nature. What makes it the Anthropocene's principle *par excellence* is the growing awareness of both the seriousness of humanity's entanglement in environmental hazards and the limits of understanding of how to manage the risks flowing from them. Recognition of this incomplete knowledge goes hand in hand with the recognition that a shift in political responses is required: 'Precaution is here to stay, but its success may lie in its modesty and preparedness *to be transformed* into various facets of social and political change.'[29]

Precaution as experimentation

> Those who wait for absolute certainty before acting are living in the wrong time. This is the main lesson of the precautionary principle.[30]

Perhaps it is not too late for precaution. Bruno Latour understands precaution as part of his larger project of 'bringing the sciences into democracy'. Researchers working with proxies and models to understand current anthropogenic changes as well as the likely future patterns of human impact on the planet all work with uncertainties – about feedbacks and climate sensitivities in the Earth system. The broader public situation, Latour observes, is one of controversies – in which experts do not necessarily agree, and the decisions to take risks on the basis of 'provisional results' are essentially political:

> Henceforth, public life must get used to cohabiting, not with scientists who settle controversies through the indisputable certainty of their views, but with researchers characterised precisely by the uncertainty and controversial nature of their provisional results.[31]

For Latour, we all inhabit the 'world-wide lab' – the world as laboratory – whether we like it or not. Every course of action *or inaction* is an experiment, and we will have to live with the results. This being the case, 'the precautionary principle is a "protocol" for appropriate laboratory procedures'.[32] Furthermore, for Latour, the principle suggests that 'unexpected consequences are *attached* to their initiators and have to be followed through all the way'.[33] A precautionary approach calls up a duty of care and social responsibility. However, it does not prescribe responsibilities and obligations in advance, but proposes that they be addressed through careful practice, experimentation and democratic debate. Latour argues that the precautionary principle, understood more broadly,

> is a call for experimentation, invention, exploration, and of course risk-taking… For all our actions we consider risk-taking and precaution-taking as *synonymous*: the more risk we take, the more careful we are … Care and caution go together with risk-taking.[34]

There will inevitably be times when experiments fail or fall short. Indeed, the possibility of failure is part of what experimentation is all about.[35] This experimental ethos is echoed by Isabelle Stengers: 'There is no adventure without a risky relation to an environment that has the power to complicate this adventure, or even to doom it to failure.'[36] Stengers' *In Catastrophic Times* calls for 'the art of paying attention' or 'making ourselves pay attention' as a necessary aspect of risk-taking. In the French original, *faire attention* has broader resonance, meaning not only 'to make' or 'to do' but also, as in the command *faites attention*, 'look out' or 'be careful'.[37] While cautionary can mean admonitory, as in giving or serving as a warning, precautionary is the mode of *practising* caution in advance. It is not simply a case of possessing prudent foresight but suggests the engagement of an experimental ethos in taking care of the future. For Latour, 'It is as though we had to combine the engineering tradition with the precautionary principle; it is as though we had to imagine Prometheus stealing fire from heaven in a cautious way!'[38] Perhaps, then, in place of precautionary principles we need *precautionary tales*.

Telling tales

The sundry cautionary tales of the Anthropocene are all concerned with confronting the mess humanity has made. Precautionary tales invite us not to worry so much about foresight or prognostics – there is no telling what the future holds or where it all ends. Instead, these tales might work with an imagination of the future based on the ethics of care and paying attention, rather than solely on the technical management of the predicted risks and hazards associated with anthropogenic Earth system changes. Precautionary tales invite caring as both a practice and an attitude: an attunement and responsiveness to the threshold of an altered Earth and a new, strange reality. Stories are made of and make practices. Stories coalesce into principles, protocols, laws and culture. Precautionary tales, however, might be understood in the manner of prototypes, experiments or improvisations – practices better equipped for approaching an uncertain world. Writing about the lessons learnt from 'volatile worlds', Nigel Clark reflects: 'it's surely as much about the way that extreme conditions condemn us and other creatures to experimentation and improvisation... as it is about the need for precaution and self-restraint. We need more than new curfews.'[39]

If the prospect of Anthropocene rock was intended as a curfew, it is also a provocation to inhabit Earth differently – in a way that acknowledges Earth system shifts occurring as a result of, and in spite of, human actions. This 'negotiation of strata' is not only a matter of urgency but also a question of responsibility and inclusivity. In a fearful situation where all predictions and predictive models are likely to fail, more time could be given to developing our capacity for anticipatory storytelling – not simply as a means of weighing up the risks, but for recalibrating and revising our collective actions in the present. Through the listening and telling of stories to each other, we might become more adept at navigating situations that are dynamic, shifting and contingent. Or as the Australian academic and writer Kate Rigby puts it, more skilful at 'dancing with disaster'.[40] Rather than think of our current predicament as necessitating a series of hedges against an inevitable *future* planetary catastrophe, it might be important to reflect on a more provisional and hospitable engagement with the world we are living in *now*. Uncontrollable calamities, as well as the unintended consequences of human actions, will always threaten the fragile order we create. We inhabit a strange Earth and a fast-changing planetary system doesn't allow for stable conditions.

In a precautionary epoch, characterised as the Anthropocene, there are long-term dangers that are difficult to imagine. These include the altering chemical composition of the atmosphere, the changing distribution and extinctions of flora and fauna across the globe, the reconfigurations of genetic structures, nuclear waste decaying for tens of thousands of years, the destruction of *refugia* and the loss of home for many of Earth's human and non-human inhabitants. If the scale and reach of the environmental predicament is unprecedented, so too are the responses needed to grasp it. Inhabiting an already disrupted present and a restless planet relies on the accumulation of both experience and strategic thinking. This includes indigenous, situated and dynamic understandings of the interconnections between human and non-human, as well as the limits of human knowledge. It is also important to acknowledge that many of the adaptive strategies for present-day cities, settlements and infrastructures are experiments which are necessarily precarious and provisional. They may unravel, require frequent reassembly or continued repair and maintenance. We are, as ever, on unsure ground here. There is another kind of precautionary thinking at stake, where there is no easy or obvious path to follow in an assymetrical, disjointed and convulsive world. Precautionary tales might therefore also be about taking time to learn to tell the story.

The Anthropocene 'posits humanity as a collective oracle'.[41] It also marks a rupture – as crisis, as catastrophe and as unsettlement – whereby the ways humans have always gone about things are no longer safe or dependable. The prophecies of the Delphic Oracle were prompts to action; but they were never straightforward, and it was possible to interpret them amiss and act incorrectly. The temple of Apollo at Delphi was located on the slopes of Mount Parnassus, marking a rift in the Earth, on a site associated with Gaia, Earth-goddess, and Poseidon, the 'Earth-shaker'. It was the site of geological chasm, tectonic jolts and toxic and intoxicating *pneuma*. This was an extraordinary and dangerous site that dispensed extraordinary and dangerous knowledge, in the form of gnomic riddles, across eight centuries. Rather than a signal to rush headlong into the next war, the next crisis, the next tragedy, these *aenigmata* required time and space to ponder over the many aspects of the situation and choose the wisest course of action. They could be the impetus to put more considered plans into effect. However, if things didn't turn out as hoped for, the Oracle was unapologetic: for there was always the possibility that an alternative outcome could have also been far, far worse. The Oracle's caveat therefore, was *gnothi seauton* – 'recognise yourself.' Or, colloquially: 'Be careful what you wish for.'[42]

On ground that is never firm, under a sky that keeps falling, cautionary tales bind us to the travails of a changing, restless Earth. The Anthropocene is about dwelling within a disaster of human making, and yet one that is indifferent to humans. However, it is also one in which 'all agents share the same shape-changing destiny'.[43] Human stories – cautionary tales included – might need to change to accommodate this time of exception. Cautionary tales of the sky-falling and world-ending variety invite us to prepare against impending catastrophe, but also to reflect on the human (in)capacity for world-changing in the Anthropocene – in all its possible manifestations, good and bad. In a fearsome and wonderful world full of surprises, humans can be surprising too. The present turbulent planetary moment requires us to work *with* a catastrophe that is unfolding. It demands that we follow through on responsibilities and go on caring for unwanted consequences – however things turn out.

Among our resources for confronting this challenge is a dynamic repository of stories and prototypes that speak to both our sense of urgency and the need for patience. The telling, listening to, and retelling of stories about anthropogenic environmental changes will continue to be shot through with anxieties – about our lack of foresight; about the ambition that drives our achievements and catastrophes alike; about our constant battle with the elements. There is no knowing how it will end. The Anthropocene story may be messy, halting, incremental, sideways and unfinishable, and it cannot be avoided. What matters is how we respond to what the world throws at us and what enabling stories, cautionary tales included, we continue to tell.

The day after tomorrow the Anthropocene will be something that will have been... Let me help you build an ark...

Figure 8.1 'Noah's Ark'; miniature from Hafiz-i Abru's *Majma al-tawarikh*; Iran (Afghanistan), Herat; c. 1425 (leaf: 42.3 cm x 32.6 cm)
Source: The David Collection, Copenhagen; photograph: Pernille Klemp

Notes

1 Walter Benjamin, *One-Way Street*, trans. Edmund Jephcott (Cambridge MA: The Belknap Press, 2016). See also Michael Löwy, *Fire Alarm: reading Walter Benjamin's 'On The Concept of History'*, trans. Chris Turner (London and New York: Verso, 2005): 16.
2 Hans Jonas, *The Imperative of Responsibility: In Search of Ethics for the Technological Age* (trans. of *Das Prinzip Vernatwortung*) trans. Hans Jonas and David Herr (1979) (Chicago: University of Chicago Press, 1984); my emphasis.
3 Jean-Pierre Dupuy, 'The precautionary principle and enlightened doomsaying: Rational choice before the apocalypse', *Occasion: Interdisciplinary Studies in the Humanities* 1.1 (15 October 2009): 4. See also Jean-Pierre Dupuy, 'Postface: notre dernier sSiecle' in *L'invention de la catastrophe au XVIIIe siècle. Du châtiment divin au désastre naturel*, eds. A.-M. Mercier-Faivre and C. Thomas (Genève: Droz, 2008): 481–494; 483.
4 Jean-Pierre Dupuy, *Pour un catastrophisme éclairé: Quand l'impossible est certain* (Paris: Le Seuil, 2003).
5 Jean-Pierre Dupuy, *A Short Treatise on the Metaphysics of Tsunamis*, trans. M.B. DeBevoise (East Lansing: Michigan State University Press, 2015); originally published as Jean-Pierre Dupuy, *Petite métaphysique des tsunamis* (Paris: Le Seuil, 2005).
6 Jean-Pierre Dupuy, *A Short Treatise on the Metaphysics of Tsunamis*, trans. M.B. DeBevoise (East Lansing: Michigan State University Press, 2015): 2–3; emphasis in Dupuy.
7 Jean-Pierre Dupuy, *A Short Treatise on the Metaphysics of Tsunamis*, trans. M.B. DeBevoise (East Lansing: Michigan State University Press, 2015): 10.
8 Peter Sloterdijk, 'How Big is Big?', lecture at COP 15 (2009) drawing on his book You Must Change Your Life and published at Collegium International website; www.collegium-international.org/index.php/en/contributions/127-how-big-is-big
9 Peter Sloterdijk, 'How Big is Big?', lecture at COP 15 (2009) drawing on his book *You Must Change Your Life* and published at Collegium International website; www.collegium-international.org/index.php/en/contributions/127-how-big-is-big
10 Peter Sloterdijk, 'The Anthropocene: A process-state on the edge of geohistory?, trans. John D. Cochrane in *Textures of the Anthropocene: Grain Vapor Ray*, eds. Katrin Klingan, Ashkan Sepahvand, Chrstoph Rosol, Bernd M. Scherer (MIT Press, 2015): 257–271; 261.
11 Suzanne Goldberg, 'The doomsday vault: the seeds that could save a post-apocalyptic world', *The Guardian* (20 May 2015); www.theguardian.com/science/2015/may/20/the-doomsday-vault-seeds-save-post-apocalyptic-world
12 'Doomsday vault begins deep freeze', BBC News (16 November 2007); news.bbc.co.uk/1/hi/sci/tech/7097052.stm
13 Robin Shulman, 'Sowing the seeds of Syria: farming group rescues plant species threatened by war', *The Guardian* (4 November 2015); www.theguardian.com/environment/2015/nov/04/syria-seeds-experimental-farm-network-plants-biodiversity
14 Suzanne Goldberg, 'The doomsday vault: the seeds that could save a post-apocalyptic world', *The Guardian* (20 May 2015); www.theguardian.com/science/2015/may/20/the-doomsday-vault-seeds-save-post-apocalyptic-world
15 United Nations Environment Programme (UNEP) (1992), 'Rio Declaration on Environment and Development', 'Principle 15.' Declaration made at the United Nations Conference on Environment and Development, Rio de Janeiro, Brazil, 14 June 1992.
16 Kerry H. Whiteside, *Precautionary Politics: Principle and Practice in Confronting Environmental Risk* (Cambridge MA and London, England: The MIT Press, 2006): viii.
17 M. Callon, P. Lascoumes, and Y. Barthe, *Acting in an Uncertain World: An Essay on Technical Democracy* (Cambridge MA: MIT Press, 2009):. 202.
18 Timothy O'Riordan and Andrew Jordan, 'The precautionary principle in contemporary environmental politics and policy' in *Protecting Public Health and the Environment: Implementing the Precautionary Principle*, eds. Carolyn Raffensperger and Joel Tickner (Wasington DC: Island Press, 1999): 23.
19 Timothy O'Riordan and James Cameron, 'The history and contemporay significance of the precautionary principle' in *Interpreting the Precautionary Principle*, eds. Timothy O'Riordan and James Cameron (London: Earthscan, 1994): 12–30; 12.
20 Andy Stirling, 'Why the precautionary principle matters', *The Guardian* (8 July 2013); www.theguardian.com/science/political-science/2013/jul/08/precautionary-principle-science-policy

21 Jean-Pierre Dupuy, *A Short Treatise on the Metaphysics of Tsunamis* trans. M.B. DeBevoise (East Lansing: Michigan State University Press, 2015): 9.
22 Jean-Pierre Dupuy, *A Short Treatise on the Metaphysics of Tsunamis* trans. M.B. DeBevoise (East Lansing: Michigan State University Press, 2015): 3.
23 'Interview with the Authors', Naomi Oreskes and Erik M. Conway, *The Collapse of Western Civilization: A View from the Future* (New York: Columbia University Press, 2014): 75.
24 Pope Francis, Laudato Si (Encyclical Letter Laudato Si' Of The Holy Father Francis On Care For Our Common Home) (Libreria Editrice Vaticana, 2015): 72, paragraph 186.
25 Pope Francis, Laudato Si (Encyclical Letter Laudato Si' Of The Holy Father Francis On Care For Our Common Home) (Libreria Editrice Vaticana, 2015): 22, paragraph 49; emphasis in original.
26 Pope Francis, Laudato Si (Encyclical Letter Laudato Si' Of The Holy Father Francis On Care For Our Common Home) (Libreria Editrice Vaticana, 2015): 73, paragraph 188.
27 Will Steffen, Katherine Richardson, Johan Rockström, Sarah E. Cornell, Ingo Fezer, Elena M. Bennet *et al.*, 'Planetary boundaries: guiding human development on a changing planet', *Science* 347.6223 (13 February 2015): 736–47; author's emphasis.
28 Kerry H. Whiteside, *Precautionary Politics: Principle and Practice in Confronting Environmental Risk* (Cambridge MA and London: The MIT Press, 2006): 27.
29 Timothy O'Riordan and James Cameron, 'The history and contemporary significance of the precautionary principle' in *Interpreting the Precautionary Principle*, eds. Timothy O'Riordan and James Cameron (London: Earthscan, 1994): 12–30; 28; author's emphasis.
30 Bruno Latour, *Politics of Nature: How to Bring the Sciences into Democracy*, trans. Catherine Porter, (Cambridge MA: Harvard University Press, 2004): 263, note 17.
31 Bruno Latour, 'Prenons garde au principe de précaution par Bruno Latour, rubrique Horizons-Débats', *Le Monde* (4 January 2000); cf. Kerry H. Whiteside, *Precautionary Politics: Principle and Practice in Confronting Environmental Risk* (Cambridge MA and London: MIT Press, 2006): 101.
32 Kerry H. Whiteside, *Precautionary Politics: Principle and Practice in Confronting Environmental Risk* (Cambridge MA and London: The MIT Press, 2006):109.
33 Bruno Latour, 'Love your monsters: Why we must care for our technologies as we do our children', in *Love Your Monsters: Postenvironmentalism and the Anthropocene*, eds. Michael Schellenberger and Ted Nordhaus (Oakland: Breakthrough Institute, 2011): 27.
34 Bruno Latour, 'From multiculturalism to multinaturalism: What rules of method for the new socio-scientific experiments?', *Nature and Culture* 6.1 (Spring 2011): 1–17; 12–13; emphasis in original.
35 Nigel Clark, 'Geo-politics and the disaster of the Anthropocene' in *Disasters and Politics: Materials, Experiments, Preparedness*, eds. Manuel Tironi, Israel Rodríguez-Giralt and Michael Guggenheim (Chichester: John Wiley & Sons, 2014): 19–37.
36 Isabelle Stengers, *Thinking with Whitehead: A Free and Wild Creation of Concepts* (Cambridge MA: Harvard University Press, 2011): 18.
37 Isabelle Stengers, *In Catastrophic Times: Resisting the Coming Barbarism*, trans. Andre Goffey (London: Open Humanities Press, 2015): 62.
38 Bruno Latour, 'A cautious Prometheus? A few steps toward a philosophy of design (with special attention to Peter Sloterdijk)' in *Networks of Design Proceedings of the 2008 Annual International Conference of the Design History Society (UK)*, eds. Jonathan Glynne, Fiona Hackney and Viv Minton (Boca Raton FL: Universal-Publishers, 2009): 3.
39 Nigel Clark, 'Volatile worlds, vulnerable bodies: Confronting abrupt climate change', *Theory, Culture & Society* 27.2–3 (2010): 31–53.
40 Kate Rigby, *Dancing with Disaster: Environmental Histories, Narratives, and Ethics for Perilous Times* (Charlottesville and London: University of Virginia Press, 2015).
41 Ashkan Sepahvand, Christoph Rosol, Katrin Klingan, 'MUD: All worlds, all times!' in *Textures of the Anthropocene: Grain Vapor Ray*: Manual, eds. Katrin Klingan, Ashkan Sepahvand, Christoph Rosol, Bernd M. Scherer (HKW, MIT Press, 2014): 8.
42 James Davidson, 'Delphi: A History of the Centre of the Ancient World by Michael Scott – review', *The Guardian* (31 May 2014); www.theguardian.com/books/2014/may/30/delphi-history-centre-ancient-world-michael-scott-review
43 Bruno Latour, 'Agency at the time of the Anthropocene', *New Literary History* 45 (2014): 1–18; 17.

Bibliography

Adorno, Theodor, *Negative Dialectics* (London: Routledge, 1973)

Agamben, Giorgio, *Homo Sacer: Sovereign Power and Bare Life*, trans. D. Heller-Roazen (Stanford CA: Stanford University Press, 1998)

Agamben, Giorgio, *State of Exception*, trans. Kevin Attell (Chicago and London: University of Chicago Press, 2005)

Agamben, Giorgio, 'Beyond Human Rights', *Open 2008/No 15/Social Engineering*: 90–95

Alberti, Marina, Correa, Cristian, Marzluff, John M., Hendry, Andrew P., Palkovacs, Eric P., Gotanda, Kiyoko M., Hunt, Victoria M., Apgar, Travis M. and Zhou, YuYu, 'Global urban signatures of phenotypic change in animal and plant populations', *Proceedings of the National Academy of Sciences of the United States of America (PNAS)* (2017)

Allen, John, *Biosphere 2: The Human Experiment* (New York: Penguin Books, 1991)

Allen, John and Nelson, Mark, *Space Biospheres* (Oracle AZ: Synergetic Press, 1989)

Alley, R.B., *The Two Mile Time Machine: Ice Cores, Abrupt Climate Change and Our Future* (Princeton NJ: Princeton University Press, 2000)

Alvarez, L.W., Alvarez, W., Asaro, F. and Michel, H.V., 'Extraterrestrial cause for the Cretaceous-Tertiary extinction', *Science* 208.4448 (1980): 1095–1108

Alvarez, Robert, 'The WIPP problem, and what it means for defense waste disposal', *Bulletin of the Atomic Scientists* (23 March 2014)

Anders, Gunther, *Burning Conscience: The Case of the Hiroshima Pilot Claude Eatherley, told in his Letters to Gunther Anders* (New York: Monthly Review Press, 1961)

Angus, Ian, *Facing the Anthropocene: Fossil Capitalism and the Crisis of the Earth System* (New York: Monthly Review Press, 2016)

Anker, Peder, 'The ecological colonization of space', *Environmental History* 10.2 (April 2005): 239–268

Anker, Peder, *From Bauhaus to Ecohouse: A History of Ecological Design* (Baton Rouge: Louisiana State University Press, 2010)

Anshelm, Jonas and Hansson, Anders, 'The last chance to save the planet? An analysis of the geoengineering advocacy discourse in the public debate', *Environmental Humanities* 5 (2014): 101–123

Arendt, Hannah, 'The conquest of space and the stature of man' (1963), *The New Atlantis* 18 (Autumn 2007): 43–55; www.thenewatlantis.com/docLib/TNA18-Arendt.pdf

Arendt, Hannah, 'We refugees', *Menorah Journal*, 1 (1943): 77; republished in *Altogether Elsewhere: Writers on Exile*, ed. Mark Robinson (Boston and London: Faber and Faber, 1994): 110–119

Armiero, Marco, 'Of the Titanic, the Bounty, and other shipwrecks', *intervalla* 3 (2015)

Armstrong, Rachel, 'Transitioning towards the Ecocene', in *Built to Grow: Blending Architecture and Biology*, eds. Barbara Imhof and Petra Gruber (Basel: Birkhauser, 2016): 11–13

Asimov, Issac, (and Richard F. Babcock, Edmund N. Bacon, Buckminster Fuller, Gerard Piel), 'Five noted thinkers explore the future', *National Geographic* 150.1 (July 1976): 68–74

Asimov, Isaac, 'The next frontier?', *National Geographic* 150.1 (July 1976): 76–89
Asimov, Isaac, *Earth: Our Crowded Spaceship* (Greenwich, Connecticut: Fawcett Publications, 1974)
Atwood, Margaret, 'Chicken Little goes too far', *The Tent* (London: Bloomsbury, 2006)
Barnes, Julian, 'A candid view of Candide', *The Guardian* (1 July 2011) www.theguardian.com/books/2011/jul/01candide-voltaire-rereading-julian-barnes
Barnosky, Anthony D. et al., 'Has the Earth's sixth mass extinction already arrived?', *Nature* 471 (2011): 51–57
Bataille, Georges, *The Accursed Share*, 1 (New York: Zone Books, 1991)
Bauman, Zygmunt, '*City of Fears, City of Hopes*' (London: Goldsmiths College, Centre for Urban and Community Research, 2003)
Bauman, Zygmunt, *Collateral Damage Social Inequalities in a Global Age* (Cambridge: Polity Press, 2011)
Bauman, Zygmunt, 'Times of interregnum', *Ethics & Global Politics* 5.1 (2012): 49–56.
Bauman, Zygmunt and Bordoni, Carlo, *State of Crisis* (Cambridge: Polity Press, 2014)
Beck, Ulrich, *Cosmopolitan Vision*, trans. Ciaran Cronin (Cambridge: Polity Press, 2006)
Belloc, Hillaire, *Cautionary Tales for Children: Designed for the Admonition of Children between the Ages of Eight and Fourteen Years* (London: Eveleigh Nash, 1907)
Benford, Gregory, Kirkwood, Craig W., Otway, Harry and Pasquatelli, Martin J., '*Ten Thousand Years of Solitude? On Inadvertent Intrusion into the Waste Isolation Pilot Project Repository*' (Los Alamos National Laboratory New Mexico, 1990)
Benjamin, Walter, 'The Lisbon earthquake', trans. Rodney Livingstone, in *Selected Writings*, 2, eds. Michael W. Jennings, Howard Eiland and Gary Smith (Cambridge MA: Belknap/Harvard University Press, 1999)
Benjamin, Walter, *One-Way Street*, trans. Edmund Jephcott (Cambridge MA: The Belknap Press, 2016)
Bennett, Jane, 'Afterword: Earthling, now and forever?' in *Making the Geologic Now: Responses to Material Conditions of Contemporary Life*, eds. Elizabeth Ellsworth and Jamie Kruse (Brooklyn NY: Punctum Books, 2012): 244–246
Bennett, Jane, *Living in the Anthropocene*, No 53 100 Notes-100 Thoughts dOCUMENTA 13 (Hatje Cantz Verlag, 2012)
Biermann, Frank, *Earth System Governance: World Politics in the Anthropocene* (Cambridge MA: MIT Press, 2013)
Biguenet, John, *The Rising Water Trilogy Plays* (Baton Rouge: Louisiana State University Press, 2015)
Billings, Lee, 'Why hunting for life in Martian water will be a tricky task', *Nature* 28 (September 2015); www.nature.com/news/why-hunting-for-life-in-martian-water-will-be-a-tricky-task-1.18450?WT.mc_id=TWT_NatureNews
Blanchot, Maurice, *The Writing of Disaster*, trans. Ann Smock (Lincoln: University of Nebraska Press, 1986)
Bonneuil, Christophe and Fressoz, Jean-Baptiste, *The Shock of the Anthropocene* trans. David Fernbach (London: Verso, 2016):79–80.
Boland, Eugene, Techshot, Inc, '*Mars Ecopoiesis Test Bed*' (NASA, 14 June 2014); www.nasa.gov/content/mars-ecopoiesis-test-bed/#.Vd2YVZVmGfQ
Boulding, Kenneth E., 'The economics of the coming Spaceship Earth' in *Environmental Quality in a Growing Economy*, Essays from the Sixth RFF Forum on Environmental Quality held in Washington DC, 8-9 March 1966, ed. Henry Jarrett (Baltimore: Johns Hopkins University Press, 1966)
Bowcott, Owen, 'Britain to claim more than 1m sq km of Antarctica,' *The Guardian* (17 October 2007); www.theguardian.com/news/2007/oct/17/antarctica.sciencenews
Brand, Stewart (ed.), *Space Colonies A Co-Evolution Book Published by the Whole Earth Catalog with Penguin Books* (London: Penguin, 1977)

Brand, Stewart, Kelly, Kevin and Dyson, George, 'An Edge Conversation in Munich', introduction: Andrian Kreye, moderator: John Brockman (24 January 2011); *Edge* 338 (7 February 2011) ; ww.edge.org/documents/archive/edge338.html

Brand, Stewart, 'We are as gods and we have to get good at it', 'Stewart Brand talks about his ecopragmatist manifesto', *Edge* (18 August 2009); www.edge.org/conversation/stewart_brand-we-are-as-gods-and-have-to-get-good-at-it

Brenner, Neil and Schmid, Christian, 'Planetary urbanization', in *Urban Constellations*, ed. Matthew Gandy (Berlin: Jovis, 2012): 10–13

Brenner, Neil, (ed.), *Implosions/Explosions: Towards a Study of Planetary Urbanization* (Berlin: Jovis, 2013)

Bridge, Gavin, 'The Hole world: Scales and spaces of extraction', *New Geographies 2: Landscapes of Energy* (Graduate School of Design, Harvard University, 2009): 43–48

Broderick, Mick and Jacobs Robert, 'Nuke York, New York: Nuclear holocaust in the American imagination from Hiroshima to 9/11', *The Asia-Pacific Journal* 10.11.6 (12 March 2012)

Broecker, Wallace S., 'Ice cores: Cooling the Tropics', *Nature* 376 (20 July 1995): 212–213

Broecker, Wallace S., 'Unpleasant surprises in the greenhouse?', *Nature* 328 (1987): 123–126

Bryson, Bill (ed.), *Seeing Further: The Story of Science and the Royal Society* (London: HarperPress, 2010)

Buell, Frederick, *From Apocalypse to Way of Life: Environmental Crisis in the American Century* (London: Routledge, 2003)

Bunzl, Martin, 'Geoengineering Research Reservations' presented at AAAS Annual Meeting: 'Can Geoengineering Save us from Global Warming?', San Diego, (20 February 2010); sciencepolicy.colorado.edu/students/envs_5000/bunzl_2011.pdf

Burdett, Ricky and Sudjic, Deyan (eds.), *The Endless City* (London: Phaidon Press, 2008)

Burdett, Ricky and Sudjic, Deyan (eds.), *Living in the Endless City* (London: Phaidon Press, 2011)

Byrd, Richard E., *Little America* (New York and London: G. P. Putnam's Sons, 1930)

Byrd, Richard E., *Alone* (London: George Putnam and Sons, 1938)

Byrd, Richard E., 'The conquest of Antarctica by air', *National Geographic* 58 (1930): 127–225

Caldeira, Ken, 'We need some symptomatic relief', *Earth Island Journal* (Spring 2013); www.earthisland.org/journal/index.php/eij/article/caldeira/

Callon, M., Lascoumes, P. and Barthe, Y., *Acting in an Uncertain World: An Essay on Technical Democracy* (Cambridge MA: MIT Press, 2009)

Canavan, Gerry and Robinson, Kim Stanley (eds.), *Green Planets: Ecology and Science Fiction* (Middletown, CT: Wesleyan, 2014)

Canavan, Gerry and Robinson, Kim Stanley, 'Afterword: Still, I'm reluctant to call this pessimism' in *Green Planets: Ecology and Science Fiction* (Middletown CT: Wesleyan University Press, 2014): 243–260

Caprotti, Federico *et. al.*, 'The New Urban Agenda: key opportunities and challenges for policy and practice', *Urban Research and Practice* (2017)

Carrington, Damian, 'The Anthropocene epoch: scientists declare dawn of human-influenced age', *The Guardian* (29 August 2016); www.theguardian.com/environment/2016/aug/29/declare-anthropocene-epoch-experts-urge-geological-congress-human-impact-earth?CMP=Share_iOSApp_Other

Carroll, Rory, 'Elon Musk's missions to Mars', *The Guardian* (17 July 2013); www.theguardian.com/technology/2013/jul/17/elon-musk-mission-mars-spacex

Carson, Rachel, *Silent Spring* (London: Hamish Hamilton, 1963)

Chakrabarty, Dipesh, 'The climate of history: four theses,' *Critical Inquiry* 35 (Winter 2009): 219–20.

Chakrabarty, Dipesh, 'Human agency in the Anthropocene' (December 2012); www.historians.org/publications-and-directories/perspectives-on-history/december-2012/the-future-of-the-discipline/human-agency-in-the-anthropocene

Chatterton, Paul, 'The urban impossible: A eulogy for the unfinished city', *City*, 14.3 (2010): 234–244

Chester, Frederick M. *et al.*, 'Structure and composition of the late-boundary slip zone for the 2011 Tohoku-Oki Earthquake', *Science* 342.6163 (2013)

Cherry-Garrard, Apsley, *The Worst Journey in the World* (London: Chatto and Windus, 1922)

Chulov, Martin, 'Zaatari camp: makeshift city in the desert that may be here to stay', *The Guardian* (25 July 2013); www.theguardian.com/world/2013/jul/25/zaatari-camp-makeshift-city-jordan

Clark, Nigel, 'Anthropocene incitements: toward a politics and ethics of ex-orbitant planetarity' in *The Politics of Globality since 1945*, eds. Rens van Munster and Caspar Sylvest (London: Routledge, 2016): 126–144

Clark, Nigel, 'Politics of strata', *Theory, Culture & Society* 34.2–3 (2017): 211–231

Clark, Nigel, 'Geo-politics and the disaster of the Anthropocene' in *Disasters and Politics: Materials, Experiments, Preparedness*, eds. Manuel Tironi, Israel Rodríguez-Giralt and Michael Guggenheim (Chichester: John Wiley & Sons, 2014): 19–37

Clark, Nigel, 'Geoengineering and geological politics', *Environmental Planning A* 45 (2013): 2825–2832

Clark, Nigel, 'Geopolitics at the threshold', *Political Geography* 37 (2013): 48–50

Clark, Nigel, 'Rock, Life, Fire: Speculative Geophysics and the Anthropocene', *Oxford Literary Review* 34.2 (December 2012)

Clark, Nigel, 'Moving and shaking: mobility on a dynamic planet' in *Atlas: Geography, Architecture and Change in an Interdependent World*, eds. R. Tyszczuk (London: Black Dog Publishing, 2012): 22–29

Clark, Nigel, *Inhuman Nature: Sociable Life on a Dynamic Planet* (London: Sage, 2011)

Clark, Nigel, 'Volatile worlds, vulnerable bodies: Confronting abrupt climate change', *Theory, Culture & Society* 27.2–3 (2010): 31–53

Clark, Nigel, 'Ex-orbitant globality', *Theory, Culture and Society* 22.5 (2005): 165–185

Clark, Nigel, 'Turbulent prospects: Sustaining urbanism on a dynamic planet' in *Urban Futures: Critical Commentaries on Shaping the City*, eds. Malcolm Miles and Tim Hall (London and New York: Routledge, 2003): 182–193

Clark, N., '400ppm: Regime Change in Geo-Social Formations', '400 ppm', discussion forum convened by Kathryn Yusoff (July 2013); Society and Space – Environment and Planning D; societyandspace.com/material/discussion-forum/400ppm/nigel-clark-400ppm-regime-change-in-geo-social-formations/

Clark, N., Chhotray V. and Few, R., 'Global justice and disasters', *Geographical Journal* 179. 2 (2013): 105–113

Coastal Protection and Restoration Authority (CPRA), 'Louisiana's Comprehensive Master Plan for a Sustainable Coast' (2012); coastal.la.gov/a-common-vision/2012-coastal-master-plan/

Coen, Deborah, *The Earthquake Observers: Disaster Science from Lisbon to Richter* (Chicago: University of Chicago Press, 2013)

Cohen, Jeffrey Jerome, *Stone: An Ecology of the Inhuman* (Minneapolis and London: University of Minnesota Press, 2015)

Colau, Ada, 'After Habitat III: a stronger urban future must be based on the right to the city', *The Guardian* (20 October 2016); www.theguardian.com/cities/2016/oct/20/habitat-3-right-city-concrete-policies-ada-colau

Cole, Samantha, 'The strange history of Steve Bannon and the Biosphere 2 experiment', Motherboard (5 November 2016); motherboard.vice.com/en_us/article/the-strange-history-of-steve-bannon-and-the-biosphere-2-experiment

Colebrook, Claire, *Death of the PostHuman, Essays on Extinction, Vol. 1* (Ann Arbor: Open Humanities Press with Michigan Publishing – University of Michigan Library, 2014)

Colebrook, Claire, 'Not symbiosis, not now: Why anthropogenic change is not really human', *The Oxford Literary Review* 34.2 (2012): 185–209

Colebrook, Claire, 'Matter without bodies', *Derrida Today* 4.1 (2011): 1–20

Colgan, William *et al.*, 'The abandoned ice sheet base at Camp Century, Greenland, in a warming climate', *Geophysical Research Letters* 43 (2016): 8091–8096

Collis, Christy and Dodds, Klaus, 'Assault on the unknown: the historical and political geographies of the International Geophysical Year (1957–8)', *Journal of Historical Geography* 34.4 (2008): 555–573

Connor, Steven, 'I believe that the world', in *Cultural Ways of Worldmaking: Media and Narratives*, eds. Vera Nünning, Ansgar Nünning and Birgit Neumann (Berlin and New York: De Gruyter, 2010): 29–46

Cook, Benjamin I., Anchukaitis, Kevin J., Touchan, Ramzi, Meko, David M., Cook, Edward R., 'Spatiotemporal drought variability in the Mediterranean over the last 900 years', *Journal of Geophysical Research* 121.5 (16 March 2016): 2060–2074

Cook, Frederick A., *Through the First Antarctic Night 1898–1899: A Narrative of the Voyage of the "Belgica" Among Newly Discovered Lands and Over an Unknown Sea About the South Pole* (New York: Doubleday, Page and Company, 1909)

Cook, James, *A Voyage Towards the South Pole and Round the World: Performed in His Majesty's Ships the Resolution and Adventure, in the Years 1772, 1773, 1774 and 1775* (London, 1777)

Cooper, Melinda, 'Turbulent worlds: financial markets and environmental crisis', *Theory, Culture and Society* 27.2–3 (2010): 167–190

Cosgrove, Ben, 'The haunted desert: aftermath of a Nevada A-bomb test', *Time magazine* (30 May 2012); time.com/3675016/nevada-a-bomb-test/

Cosgrove, Denis, *Apollo's Eye: A Cartographic Genealogy of the Earth in the Western Imagination* (Baltimore MD: John Hopkins University Press, 2001)

Costanza, Robert, Graumlich, Lisa J. and Steffen, Will (eds.), *Sustainability or Collapse?: An Integrated History and Future of People on Earth* (Cambridge MA and London: MIT Press, 2007)

Crist, Eileen, 'On the poverty of our nomenclature', *Environmental Humanities* 3 (2013): 129–147

Crutzen, Paul J., 'Estimates of possible variations in total ozone due to natural causes and human activities', *Ambio* 3.6 (1974): 201–210

Crutzen, Paul J., 'Geology of mankind', *Nature* 415 (January 2002): 23

Crutzen, Paul J., 'Albedo enhancement by stratospheric sulfur injections: a contribution to resolve a policy dilemma? An editorial essay', *Climatic Change* 77 (2006): 211–219

Crutzen, Paul J. and Birks, John W., 'The atmosphere after a nuclear war: Twilight at noon', *Ambio* 11 (1982): 114–125

Crutzen, Paul J. and Steffen, Will, 'How long have we been in the Anthropocene era? An editorial comment', *Climatic Change* 61: (2003): 251–257 Crutzen, Paul J. and Stoermer, Eugene, 'The Anthropocene', *International Geosphere-Biosphere Programme Newsletter* 41 (2000): 17–18

Davidson, James, '*Delphi: A History of the Centre of the Ancient World* by Michael Scott – review', *The Guardian* (31 May 2014); www.theguardian.com/books/2014/may/30/delphi-history-centre-ancient-world-michael-scott-review

Davies, Jeremy, *The Birth of the Anthropocene* (Oakland CA: University of California Press, 2016)

Davies, Paul, 'Fly me to Mars. One-way', *The Guardian* (15 September 2009); www.theguardian.com/commentisfree/2009/sep/15/space-mars-martian-astronaut

Davis, Mike, *Dead Cities and Other Tales* (New York: The New Press, 2002)

Davis, Mike, 'Cosmic dancers on history's stage? The permanent revolution in the Earth sciences', *New Left Review* 217 (1996): 48–84

Davis, Mike, 'Living on the ice shelf: Humanity's meltdown', TomDispatch (26 June 2008); www.tomdispatch.com/post/174949

Davis, Mike, 'Who will build the ark?', *New Left Review* 61 (Jan–Feb 2010): 29–45; newleftreview.org/II/61/mike-davis-who-will-build-the-ark

Davis, Mike, 'Humanity's ground zero: A Tomdispatch interview with Mike Davis (Part 1)', TomDispatch (9 May 2006); www.tomdispatch.com/post/82655/

Davis, Mike, 'The imperial city and the city of slums. Green zones and slum cities: A Tomdispatch interview with Mike Davis (Part 2)', TomDispatch (11 May 2006); www.tomdispatch.com/post/82790/tomdispatch_interview_mike_davis_green_zones_and_slum_cities

Davis, Mike, *Planet of Slums* (London and Brooklyn: Verso, 2007)

Davis, Tracy C., *Stages of Emergency: Cold War Nuclear Civil Defense* (Durham NC: Duke University Press, 2007)

de Châtel, Francesca, 'The role of drought and climate change in the Syrian uprising: Untangling the triggers of the revolution', *Middle Eastern Studies* 50.4 (2014): 521–535

Deleuze, G. and Guattari, F., *What is Philosophy?* (London: Verso, 1994)

DeLoughrey, Elizabeth, 'Satellite planetarity and the ends of the Earth' in *Public Culture* 26.2 (2014): 73; 257–280.

Denizen, Seth, 'Three holes in the geological present' in *Architecture in the Anthropocene: Encounters Among Design, Deep Time, Science and Philosophy*, ed. E. Turpin (Ann Arbor: Open Humanities Press, 2013): 29–46

Der Derian, James (ed.), *The Virilio Reader* (Malden MA: Blackwell, 1998)

Derrida, Jacques, 'No apocalypse, not now (Full speed ahead, seven missiles, seven missives)', trans. Catherine Porter and Philip Lewis, *Diacritics* 14.2 (Summer, 1984): 20–31

Derrida, Jacques, *The Gift of Death (Second Edition) & Literature in Secret*, trans. David Wills (Chicago: University of Chicago Press, 2008)

Derrida, Jacques, *On Cosmopolitanism and Forgiveness*, trans. Mark Dooley and Michael Hughes (London: Routledge, 2001)

Derrida, Jacques, 'The principle of hospitality,' *parallax* 11. 1 (2005): 6–9. An interview wih Dominique Dhombres for *Le Monde* (2 December 1997), trans. Ashley Thompson

Dibley, Ben, 'The shape of things to come: Seven theses on the Anthropocene and attachment', *Ecological Humanities* 52 (May 2012); www.australianhumanitiesreview.org/archive/Issue-May-2012/dibley.html

Diemberger, Hildegard, Hastrup, Kirsten, Schaffer, Simon *et al.*, 'Communicating climate knowledge: Proxies, processes, politics', *Current Anthropology*, 53.2 (April 2012): 226–244

Drake, Nadia, 'Here's what it feels like to spend a year on Mars', *National Geographic* (29 August 2016); news.nationalgeographic.com/2016/08/nasa-mars-hi-seas-hawaii-human-mission-space-science/

Drake, Nick, *Farewell Glacier* (Hexham, Northumberland: Bloodaxe Books, 2012)

Dryzek, J. and Stevenson, H., 'Global democracy and Earth system governance', *Ecological Economics* 70 (2011): 1865–1874

Dubos, René, 'The despairing optimist', *The American Scholar* 46. 2 (1977): 152–58

Dupuy, Jean-Pierre, *A Short Treatise on the Metaphysics of Tsunamis*, trans. M.B. DeBevoise (East Lansing, MI: Michigan State University Press, 2015)

Dupuy, Jean-Pierre, 'Postface: Notre dernier siècle' in *L'invention de la catastrophe au XVIIIe siècle. Du châtiment divin au désastre naturel*, eds. A.-M. Mercier-Faivre and C. Thomas (Genève: Droz, 2008): 481–494

Dupuy, Jean-Pierre, 'The precautionary principle and enlightened doomsaying: Rational choice before the apocalypse', *Occasion: Interdisciplinary Studies in the Humanities* 1.1 (15 October 2009)

Dupuy, Jean-Pierre, *Pour un catastrophisme éclairé: Quand l'impossible est certain* (Paris: Le Seuil, 2003)

Dynes, Russell, 'The dialogue between Voltaire and Rousseau on the Lisbon earthquake: The emergence of a social view', *International Journal of Mass Emergencies and Disasters* 18.1 (March 2000): 97–115

Dynes, Russell R., 'The Lisbon earthquake in 1755: the first modern disaster', in *The Lisbon Earthquake of 1755. Representations and Reactions*, eds. Braun, Theodore E. D. and Radner, John B. (Oxford: SVEC, The Voltaire Foundation, 2005): 34–49.

Eden, Lynn, *Whole World on Fire: Organizations, Knowledge, and Nuclear Weapons Devastation* (Ithaca NY: Cornell University Press, 2004)

Edgeworth, Matt, Richter, Dan deB, Waters, Colin, Haff, Peter, Neal, Cath and Price, Simon James, 'Diachronous beginnings of the Anthropocene: The stratigraphic bounding surface between anthropogenic and non-anthropogenic deposits', *The Anthropocene Review* 2.1 (2015): 33–58

Edwards, Monica, Antarctica provides ICE to study behavior effects in astronauts', (19 December 2016); blogs.nasa.gov/analogsfieldtesting/2016/12/19/antarctica-provides-ice-to-study-behavior-effects-in-astronauts/

Edwards, Paul N., *A Vast Machine: Computer Models, Climate Data, and The Politics of Global Warming* (Cambridge: MIT Press, 2010)

Engelhardt, Tom, 'Was 11/8 a New 9/11? The election that changed everything and could prove history's deal-breaker', TomDispatch (1 December 2016); www.tomdispatch.com/post/176216/tomgram%3A_engelhardt%2C_the_most_dangerous_country_on_earth/#more

Ehrlich, Paul R., *The Population Bomb* (1968; New York: Ballantine, 1969)

Ehrlich, Paul *et al.*, 'Long-term biological consequences of nuclear war', *Science* 222.4630 (23 December 1983)

Ehrlich, Paul R. and Harriman, Richard L., *How to be a Survivor: A Plan to Save Spaceship Earth* (London: Ballantine Books Ltd., 1971)

Eisenberg, Evan, *The Ecology of Eden: Humans, Nature and Human Nature* (London: Picador, 1998)

Ellsworth, Elizabeth and Kruse, Jamie (eds.), *Making the Geologic Now: Responses to Material Conditions of Everyday Life* (New York: Punctum Books, 2013)

Farman, J. C., Gardiner, B.G., and Shanklin, J.D., 'Large losses of total ozone layer in Antarctica reveal seasonal ClO_x/NO_x interaction', *Nature* 315 (May 1985): 207–210

Field, Leslie, 'Ice 911: Developing an effective response to climate change in the Earth's cryosphere' (16 November 2011); www.ice911.org/Ice911UpdateNov2011.pdf

Figueiredo, Antonio Pereira de, *A narrative of the earthquake and fire of Lisbon by Antony Pereira, of the Congregation of the Oratory, an eye-witness thereof. Illustrated with notes. Translated from the Latin* (London: G. Hawkins, 1756)

Fischer, H. *et al.*, 'Where to find 1.5 million yr old ice for the IPICS "Oldest Ice" ice core', *Climate of the Past Discussions* 9.3 (2013): 2771

Fleming, J. R., *Fixing the Sky: The Checkered History of Weather and Climate Control* (New York: Columbia University Press, 2010)

Fogg, Martin J., 'Terraforming Mars: A review of current research', *Advanced Space Research* 22.3 (1998): 415–420

Foley, Stephen F. I 'The Palaeoanthropocene – The beginnings of anthropogenic environmental change', *Anthropocene* 3 (2013): 83–88

Frazer, Heather, 'Icy demands: Coring, curating and researching the GISP2 ice core' in *Bipolar*, ed. Kathryn Yusoff (London: the Arts Catalyst, 2007): 40.

Fuller, R. Buckminster (1969), *Operating Manual for Spaceship Earth* (Zurich: Lars Müller Publishers, 2008)

Fuller, R. Buckminster (1969), *Utopia or Oblivion the Prospects for Humanity* (Zurich: Lars Müller Publishers, 2008)

Fuller, R. Buckminster, *Your Private Sky R. Buckminster Fuller: Discourse*, eds. Joachim Krausse and Claude Lichtenstein (Zurich: Lars Müller Publishers, 2001)

Fuller, R. Buckminster, *Your Private Sky R. Buckminster Fuller: the Art of Design Science*, eds. Joachim Krausse and Claude Lichtenstein (Zurich: Lars Müller Publishers, 1999)

Fuller, R. Buckminster, 'Accommodating human unsettlement', *The Town Planning Review* 49.1 (January 1978): 54–55

Future Earth, 'Future Earth launches eight initiatives to accelerate global sustainable development' (6 August 2014); www.futureearth.info/news/future-earth-launches-eight-initiatives-accelerate-global-sustainable-development

Gabrynowicz, Joanne Irene, 'The International Space Treaty Regime in the Globalization Era', *Ad Astra, The Magazine of the National Space Society* 17.3 (Autumn 2005)

Gaffney, Owen, '15 ways you know you're in the Anthropocene', *The Huffington Post* (9 August 2016); www.huffingtonpost.com/owen-gaffney/15-ways-you-know-youre-in_b_9764330.html

Gaffney, Owen and Steffen, Will, 'The Anthropocene equation', *The Anthropocene Review* (February 2017): 1–9

Gaffney, Owen and Steffen, Will, 'Introducing the terrifying mathematics of the Anthropocene', *The Conversation* (10 February 2017); theconversation.com/introducing-the-terrifying-mathematics-of-the-anthropocene-70749

Gannon, Megan, 'Doomsday Clock set at 3 minutes to midnight', *Scientific American* (24 January 2015); www.scientificamerican.com/article/doomsday-clock-set-at-3-minutes-to-midnight/

Gardner, Daniel K., 'China's 'Silent Spring' moment? Why 'Under the Dome' found a ready audience in China', *The New York Times* (18 March 2015); www.nytimes.com/2015/03/19/opinion/why-under-the-dome-found-a-ready-audience-in-china.html?_r=0

Gemenne, François, 'The Anthropocene and its victims' in *The Anthropocene and the Global Environmental Crisis: Rethinking modernity in a new epoch*, eds. Clive Hamilton, Christophe Bonneuil and François Gemenne (London and New York: Routledge, 2015): 168–174

Gentry, Linea and Liptak, Karen, *The Glass Ark: The Story of Biosphere 2* (New York: Viking, 1991)

Ghamari-Tabrizi, Sharon, *The Worlds of Herman Kahn: The Intuitive Science of Thermonuclear War* (Cambridge MA and London: Harvard University Press, 2005)

Gibson-Graham, J. K. and Roelvink, G., 'An economic ethics for the Anthropocene', *Antipode: A Journal of Radical Geography* 41(Supplement 1) (2010): 320–346

Glasberg, Elena, *Antarctica as Cultural Critique: The Gendered Politics of Scientific Exploration and Climate Change* (New York: Palgrave Macmillan, 2012)

Goaman-Dodson, Toby, 'Zone of exclusion' in *Anticipatory History*, eds. Caitlin de Silvey, Simon Naylor and Colin Sackett (Axminster: Uniform Books, 2011): 71

Goldberg, Suzanne, 'The doomsday vault: the seeds that could save a post-apocalyptic world', *The Guardian* (20 May 2015); www.theguardian.com/science/2015/may/20/the-doomsday-vault-seeds-save-post-apocalyptic-world

Goldsmith, Edward and Allen, Robert, *A Blueprint for Survival* (London: Penguin Books, 1972)

Goodall, Christine, *Sanctuary and Solidarity – Urban Community Responses to Asylum Seekers on Three Continents* (UNHCR, September 2011)

Gould, Steven Jay, *Time's Arrow, Time's Cycle* (Cambridge MA: Harvard University Press, 1987)

Graham, James (ed.), *Climates: Architecture and the Planetary Imaginary* (Zurich: Lars Müller Publishers, 2016)

Griggs, David, *et al.*, 'Sustainable development goals for people and planet', *Nature* 495 (21 March 2013): 305–307

Grosz, Elizabeth, 'Intolerable ambiguity: Freaks as/at the limit' in *Freakery: Cultural Spectacles of the Extraordinary Body*, ed. Rosemarie Garland Thomson (New York: NYU Press, 1996): 55–66

Hache, Émilie and Latour, Bruno, 'Morality of moralism?: An exercise in sensitization', trans. Patrick Camilier, in *Common Knowledge* 16.2 (Spring 2010): 311–330.

Hajer, Maarten *et al.* (Måns Nilsson, Kate Raworth, Peter Bakker, Frans Berkhout, Yvo de Boer, Johan Rockström, Kathrin Ludwig and Marcel Kok), 'Beyond Cockpit-ism: Four insights to enhance the transformative potential of the sustainable development goals', *Sustainability* 7 (2015): 1651–1660; www.mdpi.com/2071-1050/7/2/1651

Hamblin, Jacob Darwin, *Arming Mother Nature: The Birth of Catastrophic Environmentalism* (Oxford and New York: Oxford University Press, 2013)

Hamilton, Clive, *Earth Masters: The Dawn of the Age of Climate Engineering* (New Haven and London: Yale University Press, 2013)

Hamilton, Clive, 'The Anthropocene as rupture', *The Anthropocene Review* 3. 2 (2016): 93–106

Hamilton, Clive, 'The theodicy of the "good Anthropocene"', *Environmental Humanities* 7 (2015): 233–238

Hamilton C., and Grinevald, J., 'Was the Anthropocene anticipated?', *The Anthropocene Review* 2.1 (2015): 59–72

Hamilton, Clive, Bonneuil, Christophe and Gemenne, François (eds), *The Anthropocene and the Global Environmental Crisis: Rethinking modernity in a new epoch* (London and New York: Routledge, 2015)

Hansen, James *et al.*, (J., D. Johnson, A. Lacis, S. Lebedeff, P. Lee, D. Rind and G. Russell), 'Climate impact of increasing atmospheric carbon dioxide', *Science* 213 (1981): 957–966

Hansen, James *et al.*, 'Ice melt, sea level rise and superstorms: evidence from paleoclimate data, climate modelling, and modern observations that 2 °C global warming is highly dangerous', *Atmospheric Chemistry and Physics*, Discussion paper 15 (2015): 20059–20179

Hansen, James *et al.*, 'Ice melt, sea level rise and superstorms: evidence from paleoclimate data, climate modeling, and modern observations that 2 °C global warming could be dangerous', *Atmospheric Chemistry and Physics* 16 (2016): 3761–3812

Haraway, Donna, 'Anthropocene, Capitalocene, Plantationocene, Chthulucene: making kin', *Environmental Humanities* 6 (2015): 159–165

Hardin, Garrett, 'Lifeboat ethics: The case against helping the poor', *Psychology Today* 8 (1974)

Hardin, Garrett, 'Living on a lifeboat', *BioScience* 24 (1974): 561–568

Hardin, Garrett, *Exploring New Ethics for Survival: The Voyage of the Spaceship Beagle* (New York: The Viking Press, 1972)

Harman, Graham, *Guerilla Metaphysics Phenomenology and the Carpentry of Things* (Chicago and La Salle IL: Open Court, 2005)

Harries, Karsten, *Infinity and Perspective* (Cambridge MA: The MIT Press, 2001)

Hayward, Bronwyn, 'Rethinking resilience: reflections on the earthquakes in Christchurch, New Zealand, 2010 and 2011', *Ecology and Society* 18.4 (2013)

Henley, Jon, 'Greenland's receding icecap to expose top-secret US nuclear project', *The Guardian* (27 September 2016); www.theguardian.com/world/2016/sep/27/receding-icecap-top-secret-us-nuclear-project-greenland-camp-century-project-iceworm

Hennessy, Selah, 'Chernobyl zone –Europe's largest wildlife refuge?' *Russia Watch Voice of America* (25 April 2011); blogs.voanews.com/russia-watch/2011/04/25/nuclear-zone-turns-into-wildlife-refuge/

Herring, David, 'Time on the Shelf', NASA Earth Observatory (12 July 2005); earthobservatory.nasa.gov/Features/TimeShelf/time_shelf4.php

Hersey, John, *Hiroshima* (New York: Knopf, 1946)

Herz, Manuel (ed.), *From Camp to City: Refugee Camps of the Western Sahara* (Lars Muller Publishers, 2012)

Himanka, Juha, 'Husserl's argumentation for the pre-Copernican view of the Earth', *The Review of Metaphysics* 58.3 (March 2005): 621–644

Höhler, Sabine, '"The real problem of a spaceship is its people" Spaceship Earth as ecological science fiction' in *Green Planets: Ecology and Science Fiction*, eds. Gerry Canavan and Kim Stanley Robinson (Middletown CT: Wesleyan University Press, 2014): 99–114

Höhler, Sabine, *Spaceship Earth in the Environmental Age, 1960–1990* (London: Pickering & Chatto, 2015)

Höhler, Sabine, '"Spaceship Earth": envisioning human habitats in the environmental age', *GHI Bulletin* 42 (2008): 65–85

Höhler, Sabine, 'The environment as a life support system: The case of Biosphere 2', *History and Technology* 26.1 (2010): 39–58

Honig, Bonnie, *Emergency Politics* (Princeton NJ: Princeton University Press, 2009)
Huet, Marie-Hélène, *The Culture of Disaster* (Chicago and London: The University of Chicago Press, 2012)
Hulme, Mike, 'On the origins of the greenhouse effect: John Tyndall and the interrogation of nature', *Weather* 64.5 (2009): 121–123
Hulme, Mike, *Can Science Fix Climate Change?* (Cambridge: Polity Press, 2014)
Hutton, James, 'Theory of the Earth; or an investigation of the laws observable in the composition, dissolution and restoration of land upon the globe', *Transactions of the Royal Society of Edinburgh* (1788)
Icarus Interstellar, 'Project Persephone'; www.icarusinterstellar.org/projects/project-persephone/
IPCC: Summary for Policymakers. In: *Climate Change 2013: The Physical Science Basis. Contribution of Working Group I to the Fifth Assessment Report of the Intergovernmental Panel on Climate Change*, eds. Stocker, T.F., D. Qin, G.-K. Plattner, M. Tignor, S.K. Allen, J. Boschung, A. Nauels, Y. Xia, V. Bex and P.M. Midgley (Cambridge and New York: Cambridge University Press, 2013); www.climatechange2013.org/images/report/WG1AR5_SPM_FINAL.pdf
Jacob, Sam, 'High tech primitive: The architecture of Antarctica' in *Ice Lab: New Architecture and Science, Arts Catalyst exhibition catalogue*, ed. Sandra Ross (London: The British Council, 2013): 54–75
Jazeel, Tariq, 'Spatializing difference beyond cosmopolitanism: Rethinking planetary futures', *Theory, Culture & Society* 28.5 (2011): 75–97
Johnson, Elizabeth et al., 'After the Anthropocene: Politics and geographic inquiry for a new epoch', *Progress in Human Geography* (2014): 1–18
Johnson, Nicholas, *Big Dead Place: Inside the Strange And Menacing World of Antarctica* (Los Angeles: Feral House, 2005)
Jonas, Hans, *The Imperative of Responsibility: In Search of Ethics for the Technological Age*, trans. Hans Jonas and David Herr (1979) (University of Chicago Press, 1984)
Interstellar, directed by Christopher Nolan (Los Angeles and London: Warner Bros and Paramount, 2014)
Kahn, Herman, *On Thermonuclear War* (New Brunswick NJ: Transaction Publishers, 2007)
Kahn, Herman, *World Economic Development: 1979 and beyond* (London: Croom Helm, 1979)
Intellectual Ventures Laboratory, 'The Stratospheric Shield', white paper (2009); www.intellectualventureslab.com/assets_lab/Stratoshield-white-paper-300dpi.pdf
Kant, Immanuel, 'On the causes of earthquakes on the occasion of the calamity that befell the Western countries of Europe towards the end of last year', trans. Olaf Reinhardt in *Natural Science, The Cambridge Edition of the Works of Immanuel Kant*, ed. Eric Watkins (Cambridge: Cambridge University Press, 2012): 327–336
Kant, Immanuel, 'History and natural description of the most noteworthy occurrences of the earthquake that struck a large part of the Earth at the end of the year 1755' (1756), trans. Olaf Reinhardt in *Natural Science, The Cambridge Edition of the Works of Immanuel Kant*, ed. Eric Watkins (Cambridge: Cambridge University Press, 2012): 337–364
Kant, Immanuel, 'Continued observations on the earthquakes that have been experienced for some time' (1756), trans. Olaf Reinhardt in *Natural Science, The Cambridge Edition of the Works of Immanuel Kant*, ed. Eric Watkins (Cambridge: Cambridge University Press, 2012): 365–373
Kant, Imannuel, *Universal Natural History and Theory of the Heavens* (1755)
Kant, Immanuel, '*Toward perpetual peace and other writings on politics, peace, and history* (1795), trans. David L. Colclasure in *Rethinking the Western Tradition*, ed. Pauline Kleingeld (New Haven CT: Yale University Press, 2006)
Kant, Immanuel, 'Idea for a universal history from a cosmopolitan point of view' (1784) in Immanuel Kant, *On History*, trans. Lewis White Beck (Basingstoke: Macmillan, 1963)
Karacs, Sarah, 'Doomsday Clock: humanity might be edging closer to its end', CNN (1 February 2017); edition.cnn.com/2017/01/26/world/doomsday-clock-2017/index.html
Kearney, Richard, *On Stories* (Abingdon: Routledge, 2002)

Keeling, Charles David, 'The concentration and isotopic abundances of carbon dioxide in the atmosphere', *Tellus* 12 (1960): 200–203

Keith, David and Hulme, Mike, 'Climate science: can geoengineering save the world? Climate professors Mike Hulme and David Keith go head to head over whether climate engineering could provide a solution to climate change', *The Guardian* (29 November 2013); www.theguardian.com/sustainable-business/blog/climate-science-geoengineering-save-world

Keith, David, *A Case for Climate Engineering* (Boston: MIT Press, 2013)

Keith, D. W., 'Geoengineering the climate: history and prospect', *Annual Review of Energy and the Environment* 25 (2000): 245–284

Kelly, Sean K., 'Derrida's cities of refuge: Toward a non-Utopian Utopia', *Contemporary Justice Review* 7.4 (December 2004): 421–439

Kelley, Colin P., Mohtadi, Shahrzad, Crane, Mark A., Seager, Richard, Kushnir, Yochanan, 'Climate change in the Fertile Crescent and implications of the recent Syrian drought', *PNAS* 112.11 (17 March 2015): 3241–3246

Kendrick, Thomas Downing, *The Lisbon Earthquake* (London: Methuen & Co., 1956)

Kennedy, John F., 'If the Soviets control space – they can control the Earth', from 'Missiles and Rockets' (10 October 1960): 12–13; www.jfklink.com/speeches/joint/app17_missilesandrockets.html

Kerr, R. A., 'Hansen vs. the world on the greenhouse threat: Scientists like the attention the greenhouse effect is getting on Capitol Hill, but they shun the reputedly unscientific way their colleague James Hansen went about getting that attention', *Science* 244.4908 (1989): 1041–1043

Ki Moon, Ban, 'A climate culprit in Darfur', *The Washington Post* (16 June 2007); www.washingtonpost.com/wp-dyn/content/article/2007/06/15/AR2007061501857.html

Kinver, Mark, 'Chernobyl not a wildlife haven', BBC News (14 August 2007); news.bbc.co.uk/1/hi/sci/tech/6946210.stm

Kirsch, Scott L., *Proving Grounds: Project Plowshare and the Unrealized Dream of Nuclear Earthmoving* (New Brunswick: Rutgers University Press, 2005)

Klein, Naomi, *This Changes Everything Capitalism vs. the Climate* (London: Allen Lane, 2014)

Klein, Naomi, 'Let them drown: The Violence of othering in a warming world', *London Review of Books* 38.11 (2 June 2016): 11–14

Kleinschmidt, Killian, 'Refugee camps are the "cities of tomorrow" says humanitarian-aid expert', interview with Killian Kleinschmidt by Talia Radford, Dezeen (23 November 2015); www.dezeen.com/2015/11/23/refugee-camps-cities-of-tomorrow-killian-kleinschmidt-interview-humanitarian-aid-expert/

Kleinschmidt, Killian, Empowering Refugees Q&A with Killian Kleinschmidt', Independent Commission on Multilateralism (ICM); www.icm2016.org/empowering-refugees-q-a-with-kilian-kleinschmidt

Kolbert Elizabeth, 'The climate of man – I', *The New Yorker* (25 April 2005); www.newyorker.com/magazine/2005/04/25/the-climate-of-man-i

Kolbert, Elizabeth, *Field Notes from a Catastrophe: A Frontline Report on Climate Change* (London: Bloomsbury, 2007)

Kolbert, Elizabeth, *The Sixth Extinction: An Unnatural History* (London: Bloomsbury Publishing, 2014)

Kolbert, Elizabeth, 'Enter the Anthropocene – age of man', *National Geographic Magazine* (March 2011): ngm.nationalgeographic.com/2011/03/age-of-man/kolbert-text

Kolbert, Elizabeth, 'OutlLoud: The Misanthropocene', podcast on *The New Yorker* online (29 December 2013); www.newyorker.com/culture/culture-desk/out-loud-the-misanthropocene

Kopenawa, Davi and Albert, Bruce, *The Falling Sky: Words of a Yanomami Shaman*, trans. Nicholas Elliott and Alison Dundy (Cambridge MA: Harvard University Press, 2013)

Kossak, F., Petrescu, D., Schneider T., Tyszczuk R. and Walker, S., *Agency: Working with Uncertain Architectures* (London: Routledge, 2009)

Krauss, Lawrence M. and Titley, David, 'Thanks to Trump, the Doomsday Clock advances towards midnight', *The New York Times* (26 January 2017); www.nytimes.com/2017/01/26/opinion/thanks-to-trump-the-doomsday-clock-advances-toward-midnight.html?partner=IFTTT&_r=0

Laskow, Sarah, 'Frankenclimate', *The American Prospect* (29 October 2012); prospect.org/article/frankenclimate

Latour, Bruno, 'War and peace in an age of ecological conflicts', lecture prepared for the Peter Wall Institute, Vancouver (23 September 2013), published in *Revue Juridique de l'Environnement* 1 (2014): 51–63

Latour Bruno, '*Anthropology at the Time of the Anthropocene—A Personal View of What Is to Be Studied*', lecture, Washington DC (December 2014); www.bruno-latour.fr/sites/default/files/139-AAA-Washington.pdf

Latour, Bruno, 'Agency at the time of the Anthropocene', *New Literary History* 45 (2014): 1–18

Latour, Bruno, '*Facing Gaia, six lectures on the political theology of nature*', The Gifford Lectures on Natural Religion (Edinburgh, 2013)

Latour, Bruno, 'War and Peace in an age of ecological conflicts', *Revue Juridique de l'Environnement* 1 (2014): 51–63

Latour, Bruno, 'Love your monsters: Why we must care for our technologies as we do our children', in *Love Your Monsters: Postenvironmentalism and the Anthropocene*, eds. Michael Schellenberger and Ted Nordhaus (Oakland: Breakthrough Institute, 2011)

Latour, Bruno, *We have never been modern*, trans. Catherine Porter (Cambridge MA: Harvard University Press, 1993)

Latour, Bruno, *Politics of Nature: How to Bring the Sciences into Democracy*, trans. Catherine Porter (Cambridge MA: Harvard Universuty Press, 2004)

Latour, Bruno, 'From multiculturalism to multinaturalism: What Rules of Method for the New Socio-Scientific Experiments?', *Nature and Culture* 6 (Spring 2011): 1–17

Latour, Bruno, 'A cautious Prometheus? A few steps toward a philosophy of design (with special attention to Peter Sloterdijk)' in *Networks of Design Proceedings of the 2008 Annual International Conference of the Design History Society (UK)*, eds. Jonathan Glynne, Fiona Hackney and Viv Minton (Boca Raton, FL: Universal-Publishers, 2009)

Latour, Bruno, 'Forty years later – Back to a sub-lunar Earth' in *Ecological Urbanism*, eds. Mohsen Mostafavi and Gareth Docherty (Zurich: Lars Müller Publishers, 2010): 124–127

Latour, Bruno, 'Whose cosmos, which cosmopolitics? Comments on the peace terms of Ulrich Beck', Talking Peace with Gods, Part 1, *Common Knowledge* 10.3 (2004): 450–462.

Lear, John, 'Hiroshima USA: Can anything be done about it?', *Collier's* (5 August 1950): 11–15

Leo, Alex, 'SurvivaBall: New Yes Men prank focuses on global warming', *The Huffington Post* (16 November 2009); www.huffingtonpost.com/2009/09/16/survivaball-new-yes-men-p_n_288550.html

Lewis, Simon L. and Maslin, Mark A., 'Defining the Anthropocene', *Nature* 519 (12 March 2015): 171–180.

Lifeboat Foundation, 'Ark I Special Report'; lifeboat.com/ex/ark_i

Long, Jane C. S., Loy, Frank and Granger Morgan, M., 'Start research on climate engineering', *Nature* 518 (5 February 2015): 29–31

Lovecraft, H.P, *At the Mountains of Madness* (1931) (CreateSpace Independent Publishing Platform, 2016)

Lovelock, James, *The Ages of Gaia* (New York: W.W. Norton & Co., 1988)

Lovelock, James, *The Vanishing Face of Gaia: A Final Warning* (London: Allen Lane, 2009)

Lovelock, James and Allaby, Michael, *The Greening of Mars* (New York: Warner, 1984)

Lovelock, J.E. Maggs R. J. and Wade R.J., 'Halogenated hydrocarbons in and over the Atlantic', *Nature* 241 (1973): 194–96

Lövbrand, E., Stripple J. and Wiman B. 'Earth system governmentality: reflections on science in the Anthropocene', *Global Environmental Change* 19 (2009): 7–13

Löwy, Michael, *Fire Alarm: reading Walter Benjamin's 'On The Concept of History'*, trans. Chris Turner (London and New York: Verso, 2005)

Lucas Jr., George, et al. (eds.), *Lifeboat Ethics: The Moral Dilemmas of World Hunger* (New York: Harper & Row, 1976)

Luke, Timothy W., 'Urbanism as Cyborganicity: Tracking the materialities of the Anthropocene', *New Geographies 06: Grounding Metabolism*, eds. in Daniel Ibenez and Nikos Katsikis (Harvard University Press, 2014): 38–51

Luke, Timothy W., 'Reproducing Planet Earth? The hubris of Biosphere 2', *The Ecologist* 25.4 (July/August 1995): 157–162

Lyell, Charles, *Principles of Geology, Being an Attempt to Explain the Former Changes of the Earth's Surface, by Reference to Causes Now in Operation*, Volume I (London: John Murray, 1830)

Lyell, Charles, *Principles of Geology, or The Modern Changes of the Earth and Its Inhabitants, Considered as Illustrative of Geology* (1830) (New York: D. Appleton and Co, Ninth Edition, 1858)

Lynas, Mark, 'Global warming: the final warning. According to yesterday's UN report, the world will be a much hotter place by 2100. This will be the impact …', *The Independent* (3 February 2007)

Lynas, Mark, "How a nuclear disaster can be good for ecology' (7 June 2011); www.marklynas.org/2011/06/how-a-nuclear-disaster-can-be-good-for-ecology/

Mann, Adam, "The year's most audacious private space exploration plans', Wired (27 December 2012); www.wired.com/2012/12/audacious-space-companies-2012/?pid=5748#slideid-5748

Mars One, 'Human Settlement on Mars'; www.mars-one.com

Masco, Joseph, 'Terraforming planet Earth: the age of fallout' in *The Politics of Globality since 1945: Assembling the Planet*, eds. Rens van Munster and Caspar Sylvest, (London and New York: Routledge, 2016): 44–70

Masco, Joseph, *The Nuclear Borderlands: the Manhattan Project in Post-Cold War New Mexico* (Princeton and Oxford: Princeton University Press, 2006)

Maogoto, Jackson N., 'The Military ascent into space: from playground to battleground – the new uncertain game in the heavens', bepress Legal Series. Working Paper 1347 (5 May 2006)

McNeill, John R., *Something New Under the Sun: An Environmental History of the Twentieth Century* (London: Penguin Books, 2000)

McNeill, J. R. and Engelke, Peter, *The Great Acceleration: An Environmental History of the Anthropocene since 1945* (Cambridge MA: Harvard University Press, 2016)

Macfarlane, Robert, 'Generation Anthropocene: How humans have altered the planet for ever', *The Guardian* (1 April 2016); www.theguardian.com/books/2016/apr/01/generation-anthropocene-altered-planet-for-ever

Maddox, John, *The Doomsday Syndrome* (New York: McGraw-Hill, 1972)

Margulis, Lynn and Sagan, Dorion, *Slanted Truths: Essays on Gaia, Symbiosis and Evolution* (New York: Copernicus, Springer-Verlag, 1997)

Marino B.D.V., Odum, H.T. (eds.), *Biosphere 2 Research Past and Present*, Ecological Engineering Special Issue, 13.1–4 (Elsevier Science, 1999)

Massey, Doreen, 'Landscape as a provocation: reflections on moving mountains', *Journal of Material Culture* 11.1–2 (2006): 33–48

McCarthy, Cormac, *The Road* (New York: Alfred A. Knopf, 2006)

Macnaghten, Phil and Szerszynski, Bronislaw, 'Living the global social experiment: An analysis of public discourse on solar radiation management and its implications for governance', *Global Environmental Change* 23 (2013): 465–474

McKie, Robin, 'Chernobyl 25 years on: a poisoned landscape', *The Guardian* (27 March 2011); www.theguardian.com/world/2011/mar/27/chernobyl-disaster-anniversary-japan

McKie, Robin, 'Valentina Tereshkova, 76, first woman in space, seeks one-way ticket to Mars', *The Guardian* (17 September 2013); www.theguardian.com/science/2013/sep/17/mars-one-way-ticket

McLaren, Duncan, 'Where's the justice in geoengineering?', *The Guardian* (14 March 2015); www.theguardian.com/science/political-science/2015/mar/14/wheres-the-justice-in-geoengineering;

McNeill, David, 'Google Street View sends cameras into Namie, an abandoned town in Fukushima where once 21,000 people lived', *The Independent* (27 March 2013); www.independent.co.uk/news/world/asia/google-street-view-sends-cameras-into-namie-an-abandoned-town-in-fukushima-where-once-21000-people-lived-8552039.html

McNeill J. R. and Engelke, Peter, *The Great Acceleration: An Environmental History of the Anthropocene since 1945* (Cambridge MA: Harvard University Press, 2016)

Meadows, Donella, 'Biosphere 2 Teaches Us Another Lesson' (23 June 1994); donellameadows.org/archives/biosphere-2-teaches-us-another-lesson/

Meadows, Donella H., Meadows, Dennis L., Randers, Jorgen and Behrens III, William W., *The Limits to Growth: A Report for the Club of Rome's Project on the Predicament of Mankind* (New York: Universe Books, 1972)

Meillassoux, Quentin, *After Finitude: An Essay on the Necessity of Contingency* (London: Continuum, 2008)

Mehlman, Jeffrey, *Walter Benjamin for Children: An Essay on his Radio Years* (Chicago and London: University of Chicago Press, 1993)

Melville, Herman, *Moby-Dick; or the Whale* (New York: Harper & Brothers, 1851)

Millar, Susan W.S. and Mitchell, Don, 'The tight dialectic: The Anthropocene and the capitalist production of nature', *Antipode* 49 (2017): 75–93

Molina Mario J. and Rowland, F. S., 'Stratospheric sink for chlorofluoromethanes: chlorine atomc-atalysed destruction of ozone', *Nature* 249 (1974): 810–812

Moore, Kathleen Dean, 'Anthropocene is the wrong word', *Earth Island Journal* (Spring 2013); www.earthisland.org/journal/index.php/eij/article/anthropocene_is_the_wrong_word/

Morton, Oliver, 'The Anthropocene: A man made world; Science is recognizing humans as a geological force to be reckoned with', *The Economist* (26 May 2011)

Morton, Oliver, 'Some of what I think about geoengineering' (11 July 2012); heliophage.wordpress.com/2012/07/11/some-of-what-i-think-about-geoengineering/

Morton, Oliver, *The Planet Remade: How Geoengineering Could Change the World* (London: Granta, 2015)

Morton, Oliver, *Mapping Mars* (London: Fourth Estate, 2002)

Morton, Oliver, 'Climate change: Is this what it takes to save the world?', *Nature* 447 (10 May 2007): 132–136

Morton, Oliver, 'Nitrogen geoengineering', opinion article, Geoengineering Our Climate Working Paper and Opinion Article Series (2013); geoengineeringourclimate.com/2013/07/09/nitrogen-geoengineering-opinion-article/

Morton, Timothy, *Hyperobjects: Philosophy and Ecology after the End of the World* (Minneapolis and London: University of Minnesota Press, 2013)

Morton, Timothy, 'Ecology without the present', *The Oxford Literary Review* 34.2 (2012): 229–238

Moss, Sarah, *Scott's Last Biscuit. The Literature of Polar Exploration* (Oxford: Signal Books, 2006)

Mullin, John R., 'The reconstruction of Lisbon following the earthquake of 1755: a study in despotic planning', *Planning Perspectives* 7.2 (April 1992): 157–179

Murteira, Helena, 'City-making in the Enlightenment: the rebuilding of Lisbon after the earthquake of 1755', *E.A.R. Edinburgh Architecture Research* 29 (2004): 19–22

Nabokov, Vladimir, *Speak, Memory: An Autobiography Revisited* (London: Vintage International, 1989)

National Academies of Sciences, Engineering, and Medicine, *Review of the MEPAG Report on Mars Special Regions* (Washington DC: The National Academies Press, 2015)

National Aeronautics and Space Administration (NASA), 'NASA study solves two mysteries about wobbling Earth' (8 April 2016); www.nasa.gov/feature/nasa-study-solves-two-mysteries-about-wobbling-earth

National Aeronautics and Space Administration (NASA), '*NASA's journey to Mars: Pioneering next steps in space xxploration*' (Washington, DC: NASA, October 2015); www.nasa.gov/sites/default/files/atoms/files/journey-to-mars-next-steps-20151008_508.pdf

National Aeronautics and Space Administration (NASA), 'Space Settlements'; settlement.arc.nasa.gov

National Aeronautics and Space Administration (NASA), 'New Study Maps Rate of New Orleans Sinking' (16 May 2016); www.nasa.gov/feature/jpl/new-study-maps-rate-of-new-orleans-sinking

Neiman, Susan, *Evil in Modern Thought: An Alternative History of Philosophy* (Princeton and Oxford: Princeton University Press, 2002)

Nietzsche, Friedrich, 'On the uses and sisadvantages of history for life', in *Untimely Meditations*, trans. R.J. Hollingdale (Cambridge: Cambridge University Press, 1983)

Nirei, Hisashi et al., 'Classification of man made strata for assessment of geopollution', *Episodes* 35.2 (2012): 333–336

Nixon, Rob, 'The Anthropocene: the promise and pitfalls of an epochal idea', The Edge Effects (6 November 2014); edgeeffects.net/anthropocene-promise-and-pitfalls/

Nordhaus, T., Schellenberger, M. and Blomqvist, L., *The Planetary Boundaries Hypothesis: A Review of the Evidence* (Washington DC: Breakthrough Institute, 2012)

Nozes, Judite (ed.), *The Lisbon Earthquake of 1st November 1755: Some British Eye-Witness Accounts* (Lisbon: British Historical Society of Portugal, 1987)

Oakes, Guy, *The Imaginary War: Civil Defense and American Cold War Culture* (New York and Oxford: Oxford University Press, 1994)

Oates, David, *Earth Rising: Ecological Belief in an Age of Science* (Corvallis OR: Oregon State University Press, 1989)

Odum, E.P., 'Cost of living in domed cities', Correspondence, *Nature* 382 (1996): 18

Odum, Eugene P., *Ecology and our Endangered Life-support Systems* (Sundarland MA: Sinauer Associates, 1989)

Odum, H.T., *Environment, Power and Society* (New York: Wiley Interscience, 1971)

Ohanian, M. and Royaux, J.C. (eds.), *Cosmograms* (New York: Lukas and Sternberg, 2005)

Oldham, P., Szerszynski, B., Stilgoe, J., Brown, C., Eacott, B. and Yuille, A., 'Mapping the landscape of climate engineering', *Philosophical Transactions of the Royal Society A* 372. 2031 (2014); rsta.royalsocietypublishing.org/content/372/2031/20140065

Olson, Robert L., 'Soft geoengineering: A gentler approach to addressing climate change,', *Environment: Science and Policy for Sustainable Development* 54.5 (2012): 29–39

Oppenheimer, Clive, *Eruptions that Shook the World* (Cambridge: Cambridge University Press, 2011)

Oreskes, Naomi and Conway, Erik M., *The Collapse of Western Civilization: A View from the Future* (New York: Columbia University Press, 2014)

O'Neill, Dan, 'How Alaska escaped nuclear excavation', *Bulletin of Atomic Scientists* 45.10 (December 1989)

O'Neill, Dan, *The Firecracker Boys: H-Bombs, Inupiat Eskimos, and the Roots of the Environmental Movement* (New York: Perseus, 2007)

O'Neill, Gerard K., *The High Frontier: Human Colonies in Space* (London: Jonathan Cape, 1977)

O'Neill, Gerard K., 'Space Colonization and Energy Supply to the Earth. Testimony of Dr Gerard K. O'Neill, Professor of Physics, Princeton University, Princeton New Jersey Before the Sub-Committee on Space Science and Applications of the Committee on Science and Technology United States House of Representatives. July 23, 1975'; see settlement.arc.nasa.gov/ONeill1975Testimony.pdf

O'Neill, Gerard K., 'A-III. The colonization of space', Appendix A (Proceedings of the Princeton Conference on the Colonization of Space, 10 May 1974) in *Space Manufacturing Facilities (Space Colonies), Proceedings of the Princeton/AIAA/NASA Conference May 7–9, 1975 and the Princeton Conference on the Colonization of Space, May 10, 1974*, ed. Jerry Grey

(New York: American Institute of Aeronautics and Astronautics, 1977); www.nss.org/settlement/manufacturing/spacemanufacturing01.htm

O'Riordan, Timothy and Jordan, Andrew, 'The precautionary principle in contemporary environmental politics and policy' in *Protecting Public Health and the Environment: Implementing the Precautionary Principle*, eds. Carolyn Raffensperger and Joel Tickner (Wasington DC: Island Press, 1999)

O'Riordan Timothy and Cameron, James, 'The history and contemporary significance of the precautionary principle' in *Interpreting the Precautionary Principle*, eds. Timothy O'Riordan and James Cameron (London: Earthscan, 1994): 12–30

Page, Max, *The City's End: Two Centuries of Fantasies, Fears and Premonitions of New York's Destruction* (New Haven: Yale University Press, 2008)

Patel, Raj, 'Misanthropocene', *Earth Island Journal* (sp 2013); www.earthisland.org/journal/index.php/eij/article/misanthropocene/

Pearlman, Robert, 'Astronauts snack on space-grown lettuce for first time', Space.com (10 August 2015); www.space.com/30209-astronauts-eat-space-lettuce.html

Peterson, Jeannie (ed.), *The Aftermath: The Human and Ecological Consequences of Nuclear War* (Oxford: Pergamon, 1983)

Petit, J.R., Jouzel, J., Raynaud, D. et al., 'Climate and atmospheric history of the past 420,000 years from the Vostok Ice Core, Antarctica', *Nature* 399 (1999): 429–436; reprinted in *The Future of Nature*, eds Libby Robin, Sverker Sörlin and Paul Warde (New Haven and London: Yale University Press, 2013): 348–358

Petti, Alessandro, 'Architecture of Exile'; www.campusincamps.ps/architecture-exile/

Planetary Boundaries Initiative, 'Sustainable Development Goals Put Planetary Boundaries on the Agenda' (9 October 2015); planetaryboundariesinitiative.org/2015/10/09/sustainable-development-goals-put-planetary-boundaries-on-the-worlds-agenda/

Playfair, John, 'Hutton's Unconformity', *Transactions of the Royal Society of Edinburgh* V.III (1805)

Poirier, Jean-Paul, *Le Tremblement de terre de Lisbonne* (Paris: Odile Jacob, 2005)

Poynter, Jane, 'Biosphere 2: The experience of being' in *Cosmograms*, eds. Melik Ohanian and Jean-Christophe Royoux (New York: Lukas & Sternberg, 2005): 241–248

Poynter, Jayne, *The Human Experiment: Two Years and Twenty Minutes Inside Biosphere 2* (New York: Basic Books, 2009)

Pope Francis, Laudato Si (Encyclical Letter Laudato Si' Of The Holy Father Francis On Care For Our Common Home) (Vatican City: Libreria Editrice Vaticana, 2015)

Price, S. J. Ford, J.R. Cooper A. H. and Neal, C., 'Humans as major geological and geomorphological agents in the Anthropocene: the significance of artificial ground in Great Britain', *Philosophical Transactions of the Royal Society A* 369 (2011): 1056–1084

Pyla, Panayiota I., 'Planetary home and garden: Ekistics and environmental-developmental politics', *Grey Room* 4 (Summer 2009): 6–35

Pyne, Stephen J., *The Ice* (London: Weidenfeld & Nicolson, 2003)

Pyne, Stephen J., 'The extraterrestrial Earth: Antarctica as analogue for space exploration', *Space Policy* 23 (2007): 147–149

Pynchon, Thomas, *Gravity's Rainbow* (London: Vintage, 2013)

Rampell, Ed, 'The big haze: China's Great Leap Backwards', *Earth Island Journal* (13 March 2015); www.earthisland.org/journal/index.php/elist/eListRead/the_big_haze_chinas_great_leap_backwards

Randall, Alex, 'Syria and climate change: did the media get it right?', Climate and Migration Coalition; climatemigration.atavist.com/syria-and-climate-change

Raworth, Kate, *Planetary and Social Boundaries: Defining a Safe and Just Operating Space for Humanity* (Oxford: Oxfam, 2012)

Ray, Gene, 'Reading the Lisbon earthquake: Adorno, Lyotard, and the contemporary sublime', *The Yale Journal of Criticism* 17.1 (2004): 1–18

Reckdahl, Katy, '10 years after Katrina, some are "homeless in their own homes"', *National Geographic* (13 August 2015); news.nationalgeographic.com/2015/08/150813-homeless-after-katrina-new-orleans/

Reed, Christina, 'Plastic Age: How it's reshaping rocks, oceans and life', *New Scientist* (28 January 2015); www.newscientist.com/article/mg22530060-200-plastic-age-how-its-reshaping-rocks-oceans-and-life/

Rees, Martin, *Our Final Hour. A Scientist's Warning: How Terror, Error, and Environmental Disaster Threaten Humankind's Future in This Century – On Earth and Beyond* (New York: Basic Books, 2003)

Revelle, R. and Suess, H.E., 'Carbon dioxide exchange between atmosphere and ocean and the question of an increase of atmospheric CO_2 during the past decades', *Tellus* 9 (1957): 18–27

Revkin, Andy, *Global Warming: Understanding the Forecast* (New York: Abbeville Press, 1992)

Revkin, Andrew C., 'The #Frankenstorm in climate context', *The New York Times* (28 October 2012); dotearth.blogs.nytimes.com/2012/10/28/the-frankenstorm-in-climate-context/

Revkin, Andy, 'An Anthropocene journey', *Anthropocene* (October 2016); www.anthropocenemagazine.org/anthropocenejourney/

Richardson, Robert S., 'Rocket blitz from the Moon', *Collier's* (23 October 1948): 24–25, 44–46

Rigby, Kate, *Dancing with Disaster: Environmental Histories, Narratives, and Ethics for Perilous Times* (Charlottesville and London: University of Virginia Press, 2015)

Roan, Sharon, *Ozone Crisis: The 15-year Evolution of a Sudden Global Emergency* (New York: John Wiley, 1990)

Robinson, Kim Stanley, *Red Mars* (New York: Bantam Books, 1993)

Robinson, Kim Stanley, *Green Mars* (New York: Bantam Books, 1995)

Robinson, Kim Stanley, *Blue Mars* (New York: Bantam Books, 1996)

Robinson, Kim Stanley, *Fifty Degrees Below Zero* (New York: Bantam Books, 2005)

Robinson, Kim Stanley, *Antarctica* (New York: Bantam Books, 2002)

Robinson, Kim Stanley, *2312* (London: Orbit, 2013)

Robin, Libby Sörlin, Sverker, Warde, Paul (eds.), *The Future of Nature* (New Haven and London: Yale University Press, 2013)

Robin, Libby and Steffen, Will, 'History for the Anthropocene', *History Compass* 5.5 (2007): 1694–1719.

Robock, Alan, '20 reasons why geoengineering may be a bad idea. Carbon dioxide emissions are rising so fast that some scientists are seriously considering putting Earth on life support as a last resort. But is this cure worse than the disease?', *Bulletin of the Atomic Scientists* 64. 2 (May/June 2008): 14–18.

Rockström, Johan, 'Earth Stewardship for World Prosperity', official launch of the Earth League and Inaugural Lecture by Professor Johan Rockström, Stockholm Resilience Centre – hosted by the Grantham Institute for Climate Change, Imperial College, London (7 February 2013); www.youtube.com/watch?v=6mtaSqXVzWE

Rockström, Johan, *et al.*, 'A safe operating space for humanity', *Nature* 461 (September 2009): 472–75

Rockström Johan, *et al.*, 'Planetary boundaries: Exploring the safe operating space for humanity', *Ecology and Society* 14.2 (2009): 32–64

Romero, Simon, 'Antarctic life: no dogs, few vegetables and a 'little intense" in the winter', *International New York Times* (6 January 2016)

Rose, Hilary, 'Doomsday gloom and optimism', *The Times* (3 September 1971)

Ross, Sandra (ed.), *Ice Lab: New Architecture and Science*, Arts Catalyst exhibition catalogue (The British Council, 2013)

Rousseau, Jean-Jacques, 'Letter to Voltaire on optimism', 18 August 1756 in *Candide and Related Texts*, ed. David Wootton (Indianapolis: Hackett Publishing Company, 2000): 108–122

Ruby, I. and Ruby, A., *Urban Transformation* (Berlin: Ruby Press, 2008)

Ruddiman, W. F., 'The Anthropogenic greenhouse era began thousands of years ago', *Climatic Change* 61 (2003): 261–293

Ruddiman, W. Crucifix, M.C. and Oldfield, F., 'The early-Anthropocene hypothesis', *The Holocene* 21.5 (2011): 713–879

Ruddiman, W., 'The Anthropocene', *Annual Review of Earth & Planetary Science* 41 (2013): 45–68

Saada, Anne, 'Le désir d'informer: le tremblement de terre de Lisbonne, 1755' in *L'invention de la catastrophe au XVIIIe siècle. Du châtiment divin au désastre naturel*, eds. A.-M. Mercier-Faivre and C. Thomas (Genève: Droz, 2008): 208–230

Saada Anne and Sgard, Jean, 'Tremblements dans la presse' in *The Lisbon Earthquake of 1755: Representations and Reactions*, eds. E.D. Braun and John B. Radner (Oxford: Voltaire Foundation, 2005): 208–224

Sachs, Wolfgang, *Planet Dialectics: Explorations in Environment and Development* (London: Zed Books, 1999)

Sagan, Carl, 'Nuclear War and climate catastrophe: Some policy implications', *Foreign Affairs* 62.2 (1983): 257–292

Sagan, Carl, 'Nuclear winter', *Parade* (30 October 1983)

Sagan, Carl, 'Planetary engineering on Mars', *Icarus* 20.4 (1973): 513

Salisbury, Frank B. *et al.*, 'Bios-3: Siberian experiments in bioregenerative life support', *BioScience* 47 (1997): 575–585

Sample, Ian and Garside, Juliette, 'Some Virgin Galactic seatholders ask for refund on tickets after crash', *The Guardian* (5 November 2014); www.theguardian.com/science/2014/nov/05/virgin-galactic-seatholders-ask-for-refund-on-tickets

Schechter, Michael G., *United Nations Global Conferences* (New York: Routledge, 2005)

Scherer, Bernd M., 'The Monsters', trans. Colin Shepherd in *Textures of the Anthropocene: Grain Vapor Ray*, eds. Katrin Klingan, Ashkan Sepahvand, Christoph Rosol, Bernd M. Scherer (HKW, MIT Press, 2014): 119–133

Schneider, S.H., 'Earth systems engineering and management', *Nature* 409 (2001): 417–421

Scott, Felicity D., 'Securing adjustable climate' in *Climates: Architecture and the Planetary Imaginary*, ed. James Graham (Zurich: Lars Müller Publishers, 2016): 90–105

Scott, Felicity D., *Outlaw Territories: Environments of Insecurity/Architectures of Counterinsurgency* (Zone Books, 2016)

Schwägerl, Christian, *The Anthropocene: The Human Era and How it Shapes Our Planet*, trans. Lucy Renner Jones (Santa Fe & London: Synergetic Press, 2014)

Sebald, W. G., *On the Natural History of Destruction* (New York: Random House, 2003)

Sepahvand, Ashkan, Rosol, Christoph, Klingan, Katrin, 'MUD: All worlds, all times!' in *Textures of the Anthropocene: Grain Vapor Ray: Manual*, eds. Katrin Klingan, Ashkan Sepahvand, Christoph Rosol, Bernd M. Scherer (HKW, MIT Press, 2014)

Serres, Michel, *Malfeasance, Appropriation Through Pollution?*, trans. Anne-Marie Feenberg-Dibon (Stanford: Stanford University Press, 2011)

Serres, Michel, *The Natural Contract* (Ann Arbor: University of Michigan Press, 1995)

Serres, Michel, *Rome: The Book of Foundations* (1983), trans. Felicia Mc Carren (Stanford: Stanford University Press, 1991)

Shelley, Mary (1818), *Frankenstein; or, The Modern Prometheus* (London: Henry Colburn and Richard Bentley, 1831)

Shepherd, John *et al.*, 'Geoengineering the Climate. Science, Governance and Uncertainty', (The Royal Society, RS Policy document 10/09, issued September 2009, RS1636).

Shulman, Robin, 'Sowing the seeds of Syria: farming group rescues plant species threatened by war', *The Guardian* (4 November 2015); www.theguardian.com/environment/2015/nov/04/syria-seeds-experimental-farm-network-plants-biodiversity

Sigona, N., 'Campzenship: reimagining the camp as a social and political space' *Citizenship Studies* 19.1 (2015): 1–15

Simms, Andrew, 'Why did the 400ppm carbon milestone cause barely a ripple?', *The Guardian* (30 May 2013); www.theguardian.com/environment/blog/2013/may/30/carbon-milestone-newspapers

Simone, AbdouMaliq, 'Ghostly cracks and urban deceptions: Jakarta' in *In the Life of Cities*, ed. Mohsen Mohstafavi (Zurich: Lars Muller Publishers, 2012): 105–119;

Smith, Bradon, 'Words after things: narrating the ends of worlds' in *Culture and Climate Change: Narratives*, eds. J. Smith, R. Tyszczuk and R. Butler (Cambridge: Shed, 2014): 58–68

Soja, Edward W., *Postmetropolis: Critical Studies of Cities and Regions* (London: Blackwell, 2000)

Solnit, Rebecca, *Savage Dreams: A Journey into the Landscape Wars of the American West* (Berkeley and Los Angeles: University of California Press, 1999)

Solnit, Rebecca, *Hope in the Dark: Untold Histories, Wild Possibilities* (New York: Nation Books, 2004)

Solnit, Rebecca, *A Paradise Built in Hell: The Extraordinary Communities That Arise in Disaster* (New York: Viking Books, 2009)

Solnit, Rebecca, 'Bigger than that (the difficulty of) looking at climate change', TomDispatch (6 October 2013); www.tomdispatch.com/blog/175756/tomgram%3A_rebecca_solnit,_the_age_of_inhuman_scale

Solnit, Rebecca, 'In the shadow of the storm', *Harper's Magazine* (August 2015)

Sloterdijk, Peter, *Globes: Macrospherology Volume II: Spheres* (Semiotext(e) / Foreign Agents), trans. Wieland Hoban (Cambridge MA: MIT Press, 2014)

Sloterdijk, Peter, How Big is Big?' lecture at COP 15 2009 drawing on his book *You Must Change Your Life* and published at the Collegium International website; www.collegium-international.org/index.php/en/contributions/127-how-big-is-big

Sloterdijk, Peter, 'The Anthropocene: A process-state on the edge of geohistory?', trans. John D. Cochrane in *Textures of the Anthropocene: Grain Vapor Ray: Ray*, eds. Katrin Klingan, Ashkan Sepahvand, Chrstoph Rosol, Bernd M. Scherer (Cambridge, MA: MIT Press, 2015): 257–271

Sloterdijk, Peter, 'Foreword to the theory of spheres', in *Cosmograms*, eds. M. Ohanian and J.C. Royaux (New York: Lukas and Sternberg, 2005): 223–240

Smith, Joe, 'From truth war to a game of risk', in *Culture and Climate Change: Narratives*, eds. J. Smith, R. Tyszczuk, R. Butler (Cambridge: Shed, 2014): 15–24

Spivak, Gayatri Chakravorty, 'Planetarity' in *Dictionary of Untranslatables: A Philosophical Lexicon*, ed. Barbara Cassin (Princeton and Oxford: Princeton University Press, 2014)

Spivak, Gayatri Chakravorty, *Death of a Discipline* (New York: Columbia University Press, 2003)

Spufford, Francis (ed.), *The Ends of the Earth: An Anthology of the Finest Writing on the Arctic and the Antarctic*, Volume 2, 'The Antarctic' (London: Granta Books, 2007)

Stengers, Isabelle, *The Invention of Modern Science* (Minneapolis: University of Minnesota Press, 2000)

Stengers, Isabelle, *Thinking with Whitehead: A Free and Wild Creation of Concepts* (Cambridge MA: Harvard University Press, 2011)

Stengers, Isabelle, *In Catastrophic Times: Resisting the Coming Barbarism*, trans. Andre Goffey (Ann Arbor MI: Open Humanities Press, 2015)

Stengers, Isabelle, 'The Cosmopolitical Proposal' in *Making Things Public: Atmospheres of Democracy*, eds. Bruno Latour and Peter Weibel (Cambridge MA: MIT Press, 2005): 994–1003

Stengers, Isabelle, Isabelle Stengers in conversation with Heather Davis and Etienne Turpin: 'Matters of Cosmopolitics: On the Provocations of Gaïa' in *Architecture in the Anthropocene: Encounters Among Design, Deep Time, Science and Philosophy* (Ann Arbor MI: Open Humanities Press, 2013): 171–182

Stengers, Isabelle, 'History through the middle: between macro and mesopolitics – an interview with Isabelle Stengers, 25 November 2008', with Brian Massumi and Erin Manning, *INFLeXions* 3 – Micropolitics: Exploring Ethico-Aesthetics (October 2009); www.inflexions.org/n3_stengershtml.html

Stengers, Isabelle, *Cosmopolitiques*, Volume 1, '*La guerre des sciences*' (Paris: La Découverte; Les Empêcheurs de penser en rond, 1996)

Steffen, Will, 'Commentary: Paul J. Crutzen and Eugene F. Stoermer, '"The Anthropocene" (2000)' in *The Future of Nature*, eds. Libby Robin, Sverker Sörlin, Paul Warde (New Haven and London: Yale University Press, 2013): 486–490

Steffen, Will, Richardson, Katherine, Rockström, Johan, Cornell, Sarah E., Fezer, Ingo, Bennet Elena M. *et al.*, 'Planetary boundaries: Guiding human development on a changing planet', *Science* 347.6223 (13 February 2015)

Steffen, W., Rockström, J. and Costanza, R., 'How defining planetary boundaries can transform our approach to growth', *Solutions* 2.3 (May 2011): 59–65

Steffen, Will *et al.*, 'The Anthropocene: From global change to planetary stewardship', *Ambio* 40 (2011): 739–761

Steffen, Will, Grinevald, J. Crutzen, P. and McNeill, J., 'The Anthropocene: Conceptual and historical perspectives', *Philosophical Transactions of the Royal Society A* 369 (2011): 842–867

Steffen, Will *et al.*, *Global Change and The Earth System: A Planet Under Pressure*, The IGPB Series (Berlin, Heidelberg, New York: Springer, 2004)

Steffen W. *et al.*, 'Stratigraphic and Earth system approaches to defining the Anthropocene', *Earth's Future* 4 (2016): 324–345

Steffen, W., Crutzen P.J. and McNeill J.R., 'The Anthropocene: Are humans now overwhelming the great forces of nature? *Ambio* 36.8 (2007): 614–621

Sterling, Bruce and Lebkowsky, John, 'State of the World' (2012); www.well.com/conf/inkwell.vue/topics/430/Bruce-Sterling-and-Jon-Lebkowsky-page01.html

Stewart, W., 'Collision orbit', *Astounding Science Fiction* 29.5 (1942)

Stirling, Andy, 'Why the precautionary principle matters', *The Guardian* (8 July 2013); www.theguardian.com/science/political-science/2013/jul/08/precautionary-principle-science-policy

Stoppani, Antonio, 'First period of the Anthropozoic era', an excerpt from *Corso di Geologia* (1873), trans. Valeria Federighi; Etienne Turpin and Valeria Federighi (eds.); 'A new element, a new force, a new input: Antonio Stoppani's Anthropozoic', in *Making the Geologic Now: Responses to Material Conditions of Everyday Life*, eds. Elizabeth Ellsworth and Jamie Kruse (New York: Punctum Books, 2013): 34–41

Strauss, Michael and Strong, Maurice, *Only One Earth: The Long Road via Rio to Sustainable Development* (London and New York: Routledge, 2012)

Strauss, Benjamin H., Kulp, Scott and Levermann, Anders, 'Carbon choices determine US cities committed to futures below sea level', *PNAS* 112.44 (3 November 2015): 13508–13513; www.pnas.org/content/112/44/13508.full.pdf

Sullivan, Walter, *Assault on the Unknown: The International Geophysical Year* (London: Hodder and Stoughton Limited, 1961)

Sullivan, Walter, *Quest for a Continent: The Story of the Antarctic* (New York: McGraw Hill, 1963)

Szerszynski, Bronislaw, 'The end of the end of nature; The Anthropocene and the fate of the human', *Oxford Literary Review* 34.2 (2012): 165–184

Tavares, Paul, 'Stratoshield' in *Textures of the Anthropocene: Grain Vapor Ray*, eds. Katrin Klingan, Ashkan Sepahvand, Christoph Rosol, Bernd M. Scherer (Cambridge MA: MIT Press, 2014): 61–71

Taylor Victor E. and Kearney, Richard, 'A conversation with Richard Kearney', *Journal for Cultural and Religious Theory* 6.2 (Spring 2005): 17–26

Thompson, Allen and Bendik-Keymer, Jeremy (eds.), *Ethical Adaptation to Climate Change: Human Virtues of the Future* (Cambridge MA: MIT Press, 2012)

Thoreau, Henry D., *Walden; or, Life in the Woods* (Boston: Ticknor and Fields, 1854)

Tironi, Manuel, Rodríguez-Giralt, Israel and Guggenheim, Michael, *Disasters and Politics: Materials, Experiments, Preparedness* (Chichester: John Wiley & Sons, 2014)

Tito, D. et al., 'Feasibility study for a manned Mars free-return mission in 2018' (2013); inspirationmars.org/Inspiration%20Mars_Feasibility%20Analysis_IEEE.pdf

Trauth, Kathleen M, Hora, Stephen C. Guzowski and Robert V., *Expert Judgment on Markers to Deter Inadvertent Intrusion into the Waste Isolation Pilot Plant* (DOE, Sandia National Laboratories, 1993)

Tsiolkovsky, Konstantin, *The Call of the Cosmos*, trans. by X. Danko, ed. V. Dutt (Moscow: Foreign Languages Publishing House, 1960)

Turco, R.P et al., 'Nuclear winter: Global consequences of multiple nuclear explosions', *Science* 222 (1983): 1283

Turpin, Etienne, 'Who does the Earth think it is, now?' in *Architecture in the Anthropocene: Encounters Among Design, Deep Time, Science and Philosophy*, ed. Etienne Turpin (Ann Arbor, MI: Open Humanities Press, 2013)

Turpin, Etienne, (ed.), *Architecture in the Anthropocene: Encounters Among Design, Deep Time, Science and Philosophy* (Ann Arbor MI: Open Humanities Press, 2013)

Tyndall, John, 'On the transmission of heat of different qualities through gases of different kinds', *Proceedings of the Royal Institution* 3 (London, 1859): 155–158

Tyndall, John, 'The Bakerian Lecture: On the absorption and radiation of heat by gases and vapours, and on the physical connexion of radiation, absorption, and conduction', *Philosophical Transactions of the Royal Society of London* 151 (1861): 1–36

Tyszczuk, Renata, 'Mappa Mundi', in *Atlas: Geography, Architecture and Change in an Interdependent World*, eds. Renata Tyszczuk, Joe Smith, Nigel Clark and Melissa Butcher, (London: Black Dog Publishing, 2012): 10–14

Tyszczuk, Renata, 'Anthropocenophobia. The stone falls on the city', *Harvard Design Magazine* 42 (2016)

Tyszczuk, Renata, 'Architecture of the Anthropocene: The crisis of agency', *Scroope* 23 (Summer 2014): 67–73

Tyszczuk, Renata, 'Cautionary tales: The sky is falling! The world is ending!' in *Culture and Climate Change: Narratives*, eds. Joe Smith, Renata Tyszczuk, and Robert Butler (Cambridge: Shed, 2014): 45–57

Tyszczuk, Renata, 'On constructing for the unforeseen' in *Culture and Climate Change: Recordings*, eds. Robert Butler, Eleanor Margolies, Joe Smith and Renata Tyszczuk (Cambridge: Shed, 2011): 23–27

Tyszczuk, Renata, 'Future worlds – to-ing and fro-ing', in *Atlas: Geography, Architecture and Change in an Interdependent World*, eds. R. Tyszczuk, J. Smith, N. Clark and M. Butcher, (London: Black Dog Publishing, 2012): 132–139

Tyszczuk, R. Smith, J. Clark N. and Butcher, M., eds. *Atlas: Geography, Architecture and Change in an Interdependent World* (London: Black Dog Publishing, 2012)

UN Habitat, *State of the World's Cities 2012/2013: Prosperity of Cities* (New York: Earthscan, Routledge, 2013)

UN Habitat, 'Declaration of the Vancouver Symposium', *Ekistics* 42. 252 (1976): 267–72

United Nations, Habitat III, 'The New Urban Agenda'; habitat3.org/the-new-urban-agenda

United Nations Environment Programme (UNEP) (1992), 'Rio Declaration on Environment and Development', 'Principle 15.' Declaration made at the United Nations Conference on Environment and Development, Rio de Janeiro, Brazil, 14 June 1992

United Nations Habitat, *The Challenge of Slums: Global Report on Human Settlements* (UN-Habitat, 2003); unhabitat.org/books/the-challenge-of-slums-global-report-on-human-settlements-2003/

UN World Commission on Environment and Development: Our Common Future (1987)

Vanderbilt, Tom, *Survival City: Adventures Among the Ruins of Atomic America* (New York: Princeton Architectural Press, 2002)

van Tuinen, Sjoerd, 'Air conditioning spaceship earth: Peter Sloterdijk's ethico-aesthetic paradigm', *Environment and Planning D: Society and Space* 27 (2009): 105–118.

Van Wyck, Peter C., *Signs of Danger: Waste Trauma and Nuclear Threat* (Minneapolis MN: University of Minnesota Press, 2005)

Vernadsky, V., 'The biosphere and the noosphere', *American Scientist* 33 (1945): 1–12

Vidas, Davor, 'The Anthropocene and the International Law of the Sea', *Philosophical Transactions of the Royal Society A* 369 (2011): 909–925

Voltaire, *Candide and Other Stories*, trans. Roger Pearson (London: Everyman's Library, 1992)

Voltaire, 'Poem on The Lisbon Disaster' in *Candide and Related Texts*, ed. David Wootton (Indianapolis: Hackett Publishing Company, 2000): 99–108

Vonnegut, Kurt, 'Excelsior! We're going to the Moon! Excelsior!', *The New York Times Magazine* (13 July 1969): 9–11; reprinted in *Wampeters, Foma and Granfalloons (Opinions) (1974)* (New York: Dell, 1985): 77–89

Vonnegut, Kurt, *Cat's Cradle* (New York: Holt, Rinehart & Winston, 1963)

Walker, Mike *et al.*, 'Formal definition and dating of the GSSP (Global Stratotype Section and Point) for the base of the Holocene using the Greenland NGRIP ice core, and selected auxiliary records', *Journal of Quaternary Science* 24 (2009): 3–17

Walsh, Lynda, *Scientists as Prophets: A Rhetorical Genealogy* (New York: Oxford University Press, 2013)

Ward, Barbara, *Spaceship Earth* (New York: Columbia University Press, 1966)

Ward, Barbara, *The Home of Man* (London: Penguin Books, 1976)

Ward, Barbara and Dubos, René, *Only One Earth: the Care and Maintenance of a Small Planet* (Middlesex: Penguin Books, 1972)

Ward, Barbara, *Human Settlements: Crisis and Opportunity* (Ottawa, Canada: Ministry of State for Urban Affairs, 1974).

Ward, Barbara, 'United Nations Conference-Exposition on human settlements', *Ekistics* 38.227 (1974): 236–39

Waters, C.N., Zalasiewicz, J.A., Williams, M., Ellis M.A., and Snelling A.M., *A Stratigraphical Basis for the Anthropocene*, Geological Society, London, Special Publications, 395 (2014)

Waters, Colin N. *et al.*, 'The Anthropocene is functionally and stratigraphically distinct from the Holocene', *Science* 351.6269 (8 Jan 2016)

Waters, Colin N., Zalasiewicz Jan A., Williams, Mark, Ellis Michael A. and Snelling, Andrea M., 'A stratigraphical basis for the Anthropocene?' in *A Stratigraphical Basis for the Anthropocene*, eds. C.N. Waters, J.A. Zalasiewicz, M. Williams, M.A. Ellis and A.M. Snelling, Geological Society, London, Special Publications, 395 (2014)

Weart, Spencer, *The Discovery of Global Warming* (Cambridge MA: Harvard University Press, 2003)

Weizman, Eyal, 'Forensic architecture: notes from fields and forums', '100 Notes – 100 Thoughts' *dOCUMENTA* 13.62

Weizman, Eyal, 'Matters of calculation: the evidence of the Anthropocene', Eyal Weizman in conversation with Heather Davis and Etienne Turpin in *Architecture in the Anthropocene: Encounters Among Design, Deep Time, Science and Philosophy* (Ann Arbor MI: Open Humanities Press, 2013): 63–81

Weizman, Eyal and Sheikh, Fazal, *The Conflict Shoreline: Colonization as Climate Change in the Negev Desert* (Göttingen: Steidl Books, 2015)

Werrell, C. E. and Femia, F., *The Arab Spring and Climate Change. A Climate and Security Correlations Series* (Washington DC: Stimson, 2013)

White, Tony, *Shackleton's Man Goes South* (London: Science Museum, 2013)

White, Gillian B., 'A housing crisis amid tens of thousands of abandoned homes', *The Atlantic* (20 August 2015); www.theatlantic.com/business/archive/2015/08/new-orleans-blight-hurricane-katrina/401843/

Whiteside, Kerry H., *Precautionary Politics: Principle and Practice in Confronting Environmental Risk* (Cambridge MA and London: MIT Press, 2006)

288 Bibliography

Wilkes, Owen and Mann, Robert, 'The story of Nukey-Poo', *Bulletin of the Atomic Scientists* (October 1978): 32–36

Williams, M. and Zalasiewicz, J., 'Enter the Anthropocene: an epoch of geological time characterised by humans', *Open University Geological Society Journal* 30 (2010): 31–34

Williams, M., Zalasiewicz, J.A Waters, C.N. and Landing, E. 'Is the fossil record of complex animal behaviour a stratigraphical analogue for the Anthropocene?', in *A Stratigraphical Basis for the Anthropocene*, eds. C.N. Waters, J.A. Zalasiewicz, M. Williams, M.A. Ellis and A.M. Snelling, Geological Society, London, Special Publications, 395 (2014): 143–148

Williams, M., Zalasiewicz, J., Haywood, A. and Ellis, M. (eds.), theme issue 'The Anthropocene: a new epoch of geological time?', *Philosophical Transactions of the Royal Society A* 369.1938 (2011): 833–1112; rsta.royalsocietypublishing.org/content/369/1938

Wills, John, *US Environmental History: Inviting Doomsday* (Edinburgh: Edinburgh University Press, 2013)

Wolfe, Cary and Colebrook, Claire, "Is the Anthropocene… a doomsday device?', (12 January 2013), in conversation for the Anthropocene Project HKW; www.hkw.de/en/programm/projekte/veranstaltung/p_83894.php

Wolff, Eric W., 'Ice sheets and the Anthropocene', in *A Stratigraphical Basis for the Anthropocene*, eds. C.N. Waters, J.A. Zalasiewicz, M. Williams, M.A. Ellis and A.M. Snelling, Geological Society, London, Special Publications, 395 (2014): 255–263

Wolin, Richard, *The Heidegger Controversy: A Critical Reader* (Cambridge MA: MIT Press, 1993)

Wong, Edward, 'China blocks web access to *Under the Dome* documentary on pollution', *The New York Times* (6 March 2015); www.nytimes.com/2015/03/07/world/asia/china-blocks-web-access-to-documentary-on-nations-air-pollution.html

Wooley, Agnes, '"There's a storm coming!": Reading the threat of climate change in Jeff Nichols's *Take Shelter*', *Interdisciplinary Studies in Literature and Environment* 21.1 (Winter 2014)

World Economic Forum, 'The new plastics economy: rethinking the future of plastics' (January 2016)

Yusoff, Kathryn (ed.), *Bipolar* (London: The Arts Catalyst, 2007)

Yusoff, Kathryn, 'Navigating the Northwest Passage', in *Envisioning Landscapes, Making Worlds: Geography and the Humanities*, eds. S. Daniels, D. DeLyser, J.N. Entrikin and D. Richardson (New York and London: Routledge, 2011): 299–310

Yusoff, Kathryn, 'Excess, catastrophe, and climate change', *Environment and Planning D: Society and Space* 27 (2009): 1010–1029

Zalasiewicz, Jan, 'Buried treasure', *New Scientist* 158.2140 (27 June 1998)

Zalasiewicz, Jan, *The Earth After Us: What Legacy will Humans Leave in the Rocks?* (Oxford: Oxford University Press, 2009)

Zalasiewicz, Jan, *The Planet in a Pebble: A Journey into Earth's Deep History* (Oxford: Oxford University Press, 2010)

Zalasiewicz Jan et al., 'The geological cycle of plastics and their use as a stratigraphic indicator of the Anthropocene,' *Anthropocene* 13 (2016): 4–17

Zalasiewicz, Jan, Williams, Mark, Smith, A., Barry T. L., Coe, A. L., Bown, P. R., Brenchley P., et al. 'Are we now living in the Anthropocene?', *GSA Today* 18.2 (2008): 4–8

Zalasiewicz, Jan, Williams, Mark, Haywood, Alan and Ellis, Michael, 'The Anthropocene: A new epoch of geological time?', *Philosophical Transactions of the Royal Society A: Mathematical, Physical and Engineering Sciences* 369.1938 (13 March 2011): 835–41

Zalasiewicz, J. et al., 'Stratigraphy of the Anthropocene', *Philosophical Transactions of the Royal Society A* 369 (2011): 1036–1055

Zalasiewicz J. et al, 'Colonization of the Americas, "Little Ice Age" climate, and bomb-produced carbon: Their role in defining the Anthropocene', *The Anthropocene Review* 2.2 (2015): 117–127

Zalasiewicz, Jan *et al.*, 'When did the Anthropocene begin?' A mid-twentieth century boundary level is stratigraphically optimal', *Quaternary International* 383 (2015): 196–203

Zalasiewicz J., Williams M. and Waters C.N., 'Can an Anthropocene Series be defined and recognized?' in *A Stratigraphical Basis for the Anthropocene*, eds. C.N. Waters, J.A. Zalasiewicz, M. Williams, M.A. Ellis and A.M. Snelling, Geological Society, London, Special Publications, 395 (2014)

Zalasiewicz J., Williams, M. Steffen, W. and Crutzen, P. 'The New World of the Anthropocene', *Environmental Science and Technology* 44 (2010): 2228–2231

List of illustrations

Cover image
Interior view, Toroidal Colony; population: 10,000; 'Stanford Torus' based on the 1975 NASA Ames/Stanford University Summer Study (art work by Don Davis, 1975; NASA ID Number AC75-2621)
Source: NASA Ames Research Center

0.0 The Comet of 1618 over Augsburg; from *Iudicium Astrologicum*, by Elias Ehinger (publisher: Johann Schultes, ca. 1621?)
Source: Beinecke Rare Book & Manuscript Library, Yale University   xvii

0.1 'Night Lights 2012'; the image of the Earth at night is a composite assembled from data acquired by the Suomi National Polar-orbiting Partnership (Suomi NPP) in April 2012 and October 2012
Source: NASA Earth Observatory image by Robert Simmon, using Suomi NPP VIIRS data provided courtesy of Chris Elvidge (NOAA National Geophysical Data Center)   5

1.1 Hutton's Unconformity; engraving after a drawing by John Clerk of Eldin (1787) of the unconformity at Jedburgh in James Hutton, *Theory of the Earth*, Volume I, Plate III (1795)
Source: Cambridge University Library   25

1.2 Construction of the Metropolitan Railway, the world's first underground railway. Illustration shows the trench and partially completed cut-and-cover tunnel close to King's Cross Station, London. The railway opened in 1863. (Photographed by Topical Press, January 1862 – December 1862; 2 February 1861. *The Illustrated London News*, page 99; author: Percy William Justyne)
Source: London Transport Museum collection   35

1.3 Cut-and-cover construction at Praed Street, Paddington, London, during the building of the Metropolitan Railway's Kensington extension. A steam crane or 'steam navvy', with vertical boiler, complex gearing and crude shelter, stands midground left. The workmen seem to have stopped work to pose for the camera (unknown photographer, circa 1866)
Source: London Transport Museum collection   39

1.4 Building the District Railway in front of Somerset House, London, in 1869. Construction of a cut-and-cover cutting; most of the workmen are staring at the photographer. Victoria Embankment was opened on 13 July 1870; the railway from Westminster to Blackfriars on 30 May 1870 (unknown photographer, 1869)
Source: London Transport Museum collection — 40

2.1 Lisbon 1756 (*Lissabon / Das ruinirte Lissabon / Untergang der Stadt Mequinetz*; print of original etching and engraving; published by Paul Emanuel Richter, Stolpe, 1756). Design in three compartments; the upper a view of Lisbon from the river Tagus; lower left: Lisbon in ruins after the earthquake of 1755, agitated figures by tents in the foreground, a double hanging in the background at centre; lower right: the fall of Meknes from the effects of the Lisbon earthquake, buildings, figures and camels toppling into the ground
Source: © The Trustees of the British Museum — 51

2.2 'An Attempt to assign the Cause of the late, most Dreadful Earthquake & Fiery Irruption at Lisbon Or Suppression of Superstition & Idolatry & Persecution for Conscience sake the most probable means of averting National Calamities'; 'A goose of old did save a State'; etching and engraving of a satirical print published by Thomas Kitchin, London, 29 November 1755
Source: © The Trustees of the British Museum — 57

2.3 'Ruins of Lisbon as appeared immediately after the Earthquake and Fire of the 1st Novbr 1755'; 'The Patriarchal Square'; print of an etching and engraving after Jacques Philippe Le Bas, published by Robert Sayer, London, 1757–1760
Source: © The Trustees of the British Museum — 61

2.4 'Ruins of Lisbon as appeared immediately after the Earthquake and Fire of the 1st Novbr 1755'; 'St Roch's Tower commonly call'd the Patriarch's Tower'; print of an etching and engraving after Jacques Philippe Le Bas, published by Robert Sayer, London, 1757–1760
Source: © The Trustees of the British Museum — 62

2.5 A Topographical Plan of Lisbon ruined by the earthquake of 1755 with superimposed reconstruction project of Eugénio dos Santos Carvalho and Carlos Mardel, 12 June 1758 (Coloured lithograph by João Pedro Ribeiro, 1947)
Source: Museu de Lisboa — 68

3.1 Project for a geodesic dome over Manhattan, R. Buckminster Fuller, with Shoji Sadao, 1960
Source: Estate of R. Buckminster Fuller — 81

3.2 Manhattan Shelter Study, by Guy B. Panero Engineers, 1958 (image by Federal Civil Defense and Preparedness Agency under contract No. CD-SR-58-42)
Source: FEMA US Fire Administration, National Emergency Training Center Library — 82

292 List of illustrations

3.3 'Operation Doorstep'; four mannequins in damaged living room, Nevada Test Site
Source: Nevada Test Site; National Nuclear Security Administration (NNSA), DOE ... 88

3.4 'Operation Doorstep'; damaged wooden bedroom with mannequin, Nevada Test Site
Source: Nevada Test Site; National Nuclear Security Administration (NNSA), DOE ... 88

3.5 'Operation Doorstep'; vehicle No. 40, and other vehicles at the Nevada Test Site
Source: Nevada Test Site; National Nuclear Security Administration (NNSA), DOE ... 89

3.6 (a, b, c, d, e, f, g, h) 'Operation Doorstep'/'Upshot-Knothole Annie'; Nevada Proving Grounds, 17 March 1953; complete destruction of House No 1 located 3,500 feet from ground zero. The time from the first to last picture was 2.33 seconds. The camera was completely enclosed in a 2-inch lead sheath as a protection against radiation. The only source of light was that from the bomb
Source: Nevada Test Site; National Nuclear Security Administration (NNSA), DOE ... 93

4.1 View looking towards the Discovery Hut, with sailing ship *Discovery* moored behind; British National Antarctic Expedition, 1901–04 (photographer: Herbert Ponting)
Source: Scott Polar Research Institute, University of Cambridge ... 119

4.2 The 'Tenements' – bunks in Winterquarters Hut of Lt Henry Bowers, Apsley Cherry-Garrard, Captain Oates, Cecil Meares and Dr Atkinson; 9 October 1911; British Antarctic Expedition 1910–13 (photographer: Herbert Ponting)
Source: Scott Polar Research Institute, University of Cambridge ... 122

4.3 Little America IV, Austral Summer 1946–1947; an aerial view of Little America IV, established at the Bay of Whales, during Operation Highjump, a US Navy operation that commenced August 1946 and ended in late February 1947 (photograph by: US Navy, NSF)
Source: United States Antarctic Program, National Science Foundation (NSF) ... 127

4.4 Ozone Hole, 1983; first space-based view of the ozone hole, data from TOMS (Total Ozone Mapping Spectrometer)
Source: NASA Goddard Space Flight Center ... 137

5.1 'Earthrise' (24 December 1968); astronaut photograph from Apollo 8 mission (NASA image AS08-14-2383)
Source: Earth Science and Remote Sensing Unit, NASA Johnson Space Center ... 151

List of illustrations 293

5.2 'The Blue Marble' or 'Whole Earth' (7 December 1972); astronaut photograph from Apollo 17 mission (NASA image AS17-148-22727)
Source: Earth Science and Remote Sensing Unit, NASA Johnson Space Center   152

5.3 'Free Space' (9 March 1883); manuscript: sketch of cross-section of jet-propelled spaceship. Right: Cannon firing spherical projectiles and propelling the vehicle through space with its recoil (reaction). Centre: Gyroscopes, the revolving of which can change the position (orientation) of the spaceship in space
Source: KE Tsiolkovsky Archive; Russian Academy of Sciences   156

5.4 Drawing of people and objects floating around weightless in space; from Konstantin Tsiolkovsky's 1933 paper 'Album of Space Travel'
Source: KE Tsiolkovsky Archive; Russian Academy of Sciences   157

5.5 Toroidal Colony, population: 10,000; construction along the Torus rim; 'Stanford Torus' based on the 1975 NASA Ames/Stanford University Summer Study (art work by Don Davis, 1975; NASA ID Number AC75-1886)
Source: NASA Ames Research Center   169

5.6 Interior view, Toroidal Colony, population: 10,000; 'Stanford Torus' based on the 1975 NASA Ames/Stanford University Summer Study (art work by Don Davis 1975; NASA ID Number AC75-2621)
Source: NASA Ames Research Center   170

5.7 Bernal Sphere Colony, population: 10,000; construction crew at work on the colony; the Bernal Sphere is a point design with a spherical living area (art work by Don Davis, 1976; NASA ID Number AC76-1288)
Source: NASA Ames Research Center   171

5.8 Apollo 1 astronaut pre-flight training, Ellington Air Force Base Houston, Texas (June 1966; NASA image: S66-51583)
Source: NASA Johnson Space Center   183

6.1 Frankenstein observing the first stirrings of his creature; engraving by W. Chevalier after Th. von Holst, 1831; *Frankenstein* by Mary Wollstonecraft Shelley (published by H. Colburn and R. Bentley, London, 1831)
Source: Wellcome Library, London   203

6.2 Sarychev volcano eruption, Kuril Islands, as seen from the International Space Station, 12 June 2009 (NASA image ISS020-E-9048)
Source: NASA/ISS Expedition 20, Earth Science and Remote Sensing Unit, NASA Johnson Space Center   209

7.1 'Where will Hurricane Katrina go?' (29 August 2005); Hurricane Katrina in the Gulf of Mexico; a digitally processed image from the orbiting GOES-12 Weather satellite
Source: GOES 12 Satellite, NASA, NOAA   234

7.2 (a, b, c) 'In a little over a year, it has become Jordan's fourth largest city. Except it is not a city. It is the world's second-largest refugee camp'; Zaatari refugee camp, Jordan (satellite image data acquired 30 May 2009, 27 September 2012, 19 July 2013)
Source: NASA Earth Observatory images by Jesse Allen and Robert Simmon, using data from the NASA/GSFC/METI/ERSDAC/JAROS, and US/Japan ASTER Science Team   242

8.1 'Noah's Ark'; miniature from Hafiz-i Abru's *Majma al-tawarikh*; Iran (Afghanistan), Herat; c. 1425 (leaf: 42.3 cm x 32.6 cm)
Source: The David Collection, Copenhagen; photograph: Pernille Klemp   263

Acknowledgements

This book was made possible by the award of a British Academy Mid-Career Fellowship 2013–2014 for the project 'Provisional Cities'.

In the same academic year I was a Visiting Scholar at the University of Cambridge School of Architecture, which provided me with a quiet place to work as well as the opportunity to share research in progress with staff and students through a Martin Centre seminar, 'Architecture of the Anthropocene'. Early on in the project I also presented the research to the 2013 Architectural Humanities Research Association conference.

The origins of the project go back to themes around architecture, environmental change and provisionality, explored in Masters in Architecture design studios I have led at the University of Sheffield since 2006, and also the paired Postgraduate Taught Masters modules I developed there: *Histories of Sustainability* and *Future Climates*. I am enormously grateful to the students that have challenged my thinking over the years.

The idea for a book on the Anthropocene took shape whilst working on the *Interdependence Day Project* and some of the early sketches (both text and drawing) on the themes I was interested in, around the 'unconformities' of this proposed epoch are also included in publications that emerged from that project, notably the 2012 publication *Atlas*, coedited with Joe Smith, Nigel Clark and Melissa Butcher. I am extremely grateful to Peter Carl for being supportive of the 'Provisional Cities' project in its earliest stages. During the British Academy Fellowship year I further tested and honed some of my thinking with Joe Smith, Robert Butler and Hannah Bird, while we were working on *Culture and Climate Change: Narratives*. The writing of the book also coincided with research on the AHRC *Stories of Change* project and I am particularly grateful to all my colleagues on the *Stories* team, especially Joe Smith, Bradon Smith and Julia Udall, for their commitment to testing new forms of storytelling in and about difficult times.

In the last two years I have completed the book round the edges of other research and teaching commitments and I have been glad of the opportunities to share my thinking about living in the Anthropocene in varied venues. Two very different events that stand out were TRANSform > (re) Imagine- a pop-up exhibition in London curated by Dale and Steve Russell in 2015, which was a spur to make more of the art work that has informed the project. Also the 'Sharing the Anthropocene' Doreen Massey 2016 Event, convened by the OUs OpenSpace Research Centre, where I presented my anxieties about this new geological epoch, with a paper titled, 'Cautionary Tales for the Anthropocene'.

I am grateful to the many libraries and institutions that gave access to documents and images and permission to reproduce them, and I extend my thanks to the archivists and librarians that have helped me. My colleagues at Sheffield, Doina Petrescu and Stephen Walker, and also Mark Brandon and Joe Smith of the Open University, all gave their time and attention by reading and commenting on parts of the book. Thanks particularly to Katrina Zaat who read and commented on the whole text. I would also like to acknowledge the editors at Routledge.

Some of the material in the book has previously been published in fragments in the following: 'Future Worlds: to-ing and fro-ing' in Tyszczuk *et al.* (eds.), *Atlas: Geography, Architecture and Change in an Interdependent World* (London: Black Dog Publishing, 2012): pp. 132–139; 'Cautionary Tales: The sky is falling! The world is ending!' in Smith *et al.* (eds.), *Culture and Climate Change: Narratives* (Cambridge: Shed, 2014) pp. 45–57; 'The fly and the satellite: transgressing planetary boundaries in the Anthropocene' in D. Littlefield and L. Rice (eds.), *Transgression: Towards an Expanded Field of Architecture* Critiques series (London: Routledge, 2014): pp. 19–39; 'Architecture of the Anthropocene: the crisis of agency', *Scroope* 23, *Cambridge Architecture Journal* (July 2014): pp. 66–73; 'Anthropocenophobia. The Stone Falls on the City', *Harvard Design Magazine* 42 (2016); 'Anthropocene Unconformities; on the aporias of geological space and time' *Space and Culture*, 2016.

I am very grateful to colleagues, friends and family for their support and encouragement during the long development of this project. My deepest thanks for their love and patience go to my mother Krystyna, my sons Tomasz, Łukasz and Staś, and my ally in everything, Joe.

Index

acts of god 49, 59
adaptation x, 6, 8, 91, 105, 179, 202, 230, 240
Adorno, Theodor 66–7, 79
After London 11
aftershocks 52–5, 63; cultural, philosophical and political 50, 68
Agamben, Giorgio 234–5, 241
Agassiz, Louis 124
agency: heroic 127; improvisatory 184; of stories 1; political 177, 236; provisional 233; transformative 232; *see also* geological agency; human agency; planetary agency
Alamogordo 29; *see also* Los Alamos; Manhattan Project; Trinity test
albedo modification 50, 199, 205–7, 212, 214; *see also* solar radiation management (SRM)
Allen, John P. 169–70
Alley, Richard 132, 163
analogue missions 120; *see also* Antarctica; Biosphere 2
Anders, Gunther 77, 79–80, 256
Antarctica: as analogue for outer space and space exploration 115, 120, 129 182
Antarctic Treaty 114, 117, 138–40
Anthropocene: as catastrophe xvi, 1, 3, 6, 10, 24, 34, 134, 230, 255–7, 262; as disaster of human-making xi, xiii, 8, 9, 65, 67, 183, 197, 262; as warning ix, x, xiii, 7–8, 14, 15, 16, 38, 50, 92, 105, 134, 137, 197, 216, 223, 255
Anthropocene equation xv
Anthropocene rock ix, xvi, 33, 34, 37, 261
anthropocene unconformity 14, 23, 24, 41, 245
Anthropocene Working Group (AWG) ix, 20, 21, 27–30, 32, 33, 50, 114
anthropoceneries 7–8
Anthropocenophobia viii, ix, x, xvi, 255
anthropos ix, xiii, 16, 41, 125, 244
Anthropozoic era 16, 21, 30, 32

apocalypse viii, 8, 11, 55, 77, 87, 91, 102–4, 124, 181
Apollo mission 148, 178, 180, 214; Apollo 1 183; Apollo 8 148, 151, 162; Apollo 11 155, 163; Apollo 13 155, 160, 162–3, 175; Apollo 17 148, 152
Arendt, Hannah 153, 241
Asimov, Isaac 4, 164, 214
Asterix the Gaul xv
asteroids: impacts viii, xii, xiv, xv, 1, 7, 10, 21, 26, 34, 37, 77, 98, 150, 152, 180, 197, 257; mining 164, 180, 181; space habitats 164, 165, 168, 215
astronautics 150–5, 172
astronoetics 154–5
atomic age 86, 105; *see also* nuclear age
Atwood, Margaret xv–xvi
Auschwitz 66, 67, 79, 255
auto-da-fé 55, 58, 79

Ballard, J.G. 11
Bataille, Georges 7
Bauman, Zygmunt 8, 80, 231
being-quake 9–10
Belgica 118–19
Benjamin, Walter 50, 64, 255
Biguenet, John 237
biosphere 6, 7, 21, 141, 148, 168, 169, 170, 172–6, 179, 208, 214
Biosphere 2 169–175, 182; as analogue for Earth 169–70, 173
Biospherians 172–5, 208
Blanchot, Maurice 66
Bloch, Ernst 184
Blue Marble 148, 152
Blueprint for Survival 12, 91
Blumenberg, Hans 154
Boulding, Kenneth 159
Brand, Stewart 164, 166–8, 196, 214
Broecker, Wallace S. 132
Brundtland Report 137, 149, 150
Bulletin of the Atomic Scientists xiv, 101
Byrd, Admiral Richard 125–7

Index

Caldeira, Ken 196, 208
Camp Century 131
camps 53, 67, 95, 120, 123, 225, 227–228, 238–40; New Orleans 235; space of exception 235, 237; world as camp 237, 247; *see also* refugees; Zaatari refugee camp
Candide 57–8
Capitalocene x
Captain Nemo 117
carbon dioxide (CO_2): concentration as possible signal for Anthropocene 27; emissions 3, 29, 37, 129, 130, 133, 177, 197, 204; measurements 129, 177; *see also* carbon dioxide removal (CDR)
carbon dioxide removal (CDR) 199; *see also* geoengineering
carrying capacity 15, 149, 156, 159, 160, 161, 166, 176, 177, 179
Carson, Rachel xiv, 11, 96–7
Cassandra scientists xiii, 255, 256
catastrophes: anthropogenic 135, 137, 234–6, 246, 255–6; averting or avoiding 163, 175–6, 180–1, 199, 204, 210, 215, 231, 258; global climate catastrophe 114, 134, 140, 240; living with 7–8, 12–13, 21, 32, 41, 124, 130, 184, 236, 259–62; marking transition to new epoch 26, 134; predictions of x–xiv, 6, 141, 161, 255–7; rehearsals for 87, 89–91; Spaceship Earth 155, 159, 162–3, 175–6, 184; *see also* Anthropocene as catastrophe; triple-disaster
catastrophe fatigue 177
catastrophe narratives 98, 177, 209–10
catastrophism 6, 25–6, 91, 255
cautionary tale viii–xviii, 1–2, 7, 10, 11–13, 15–17, 24, 50, 57, 60, 67, 91, 95, 96, 102, 104, 135, 175, 177, 197, 198, 200–1, 210, 246, 255, 259, 260–262
Cenozoic-Anthropozoic (C-A) boundary 30
Cenozoic Era ix, 27, 30
Chakrabarty, Dipesh ix, 30, 232
Chernobyl 67, 104
Chicken Licken, Chicken Little xi, xv–xvi
chlorofluorocarbons (CFCs) xiii, 135–6, 214, 258
Christchurch earthquakes 60
chronostratigraphy 28, 36
Cicero 61, 247
citizenship 60, 139, 225, 228, 240, 241, 243–5, 247–8
city of refuge 243
civil defence rehearsals 87
Clark, Nigel 6, 41, 50, 60, 69, 70, 134, 179, 200, 232–3, 241, 244, 246–7, 261
climate catastrophe 114, 163, 199, 214

climate change xii, xiv–xv, 2, 4, 6, 8–12, 31, 67, 77, 97, 114, 125, 127, 131–3, 137, 140, 176–9, 195, 198–200, 204, 206–7, 211–14, 229–30, 233, 235–8, 240, 257–9
climate emergency 196, 199, 204, 205, 209, 224
climate engineering 4, 195, 198, 204, 207, 209–10, 258; *see also* geoengineering
climate refugees 237–238, 240
Club of Rome 91, 161, 256
coastal cities xiv, 37, 114, 199, 215
CoEvolution Quarterly 164, 166
Cold War xi, 10, 13, 14, 67, 76, 77, 81, 85, 86, 94, 96, 98, 121, 128, 130, 131, 138, 140, 198, 199, 209, 235
Collapse of Western Civilisation 209–10, 259
comet xii, xv, xvi, 52, 55, 64, 65, 154, 172, 180, 213–14; *see also* asteroid
concept-quake- (*Begriffsbeben*) 8–10
Cook, Captain James 115, 117, 139
Cook, Frederick 118–19
Cosgrove, Denis 117, 148
Cosmopolitanism 4, 243–5
cosmopolitical proposal 245–6
cosmopolitics 4, 225, 244–6, 248
cradle of civilisation 237
cradle of humanity (humanity's cradle) 150–1, 155, 216
Cretaceous-Paleogene (K-Pg) boundary 225
Cretaceous-Tertiary (K-T) boundary 21, 30, 37, 65, 98
crisis of agency ix, 231–2; *see also planetary crisis of agency*
Crutzen, Paul xiii, 21, 28, 29, 30, 96, 97, 133, 135, 136, 195, 197, 204–7, 209–10, 213
Cuban Missile Crisis 96
cybernetic 158, 173, 179, 184

Davis, Mike 6, 10, 28, 77, 79, 130, 179, 184–5, 229–31
Day after Tomorrow 12, 132
deep time 1, 7, 14, 24, 26–7, 30, 36, 38–9, 41, 130, 257
deficit of imagination 80
Deleuze, Gilles 58, 245
Derrida, Jacques 9, 102–3, 243–4
disasters xii, xv, xviii, 7, 10, 12, 14, 21, 23–4, 31, 49–50, 51, 66, 97, 116, 132, 152, 155, 157, 160, 177, 196, 199, 210, 213, 216, 223–4, 229, 231, 233, 236–7, 240–1, 247, 256, 257, 261; *see also* Anthropocene as disaster; catastrophe; disaster zone; earthquake; Hurricane Katrina; Lisbon disaster; natural disaster; nuclear disaster
dis-astered 65–7
dis-astron, 'fallen star' 65, 67

disaster zone 2, 14, 48, 50, 60, 70, 225, 229, 237
Discovery Hut 119, 120, 123
Dome over Manhattan 81
Doomsday Clock xiv
doomsday device xii, 90, 92
Doomsday Machine 90–2
doomsday scenarios 87–92, 99
doomsday vault *see* Svalbard Global Seed Vault (SGSV)
Doom Town 82–6
Doxiadis, Constantinos 4, 244
Dr Strangelove 11, 90, 98
Dry Valleys, Antarctica 140, 182
Dugway Proving Ground 77, 79, 83
Dupuy, Jean-Pierre 80, 255–6, 258
dynamic Earth xv, 16, 39, 65, 148, 159, 223

Earth as an ark, Earth-ark 49, 183–5
Earth citizenship 225, 241, 248
earthquake xiv, 7–10, 13, 15, 23, 50, 65, 68–9, 95, 104, 152, 159, 224, 225, 229, 240, 245, 257; *see also* Christchurch earthquakes; Lisbon earthquake; Sichuan earthquake; Tōhoku earthquake and tsunami
Earthrise 148, 151
Earth system ix, xii–xiii, xv, 1, 3, 5, 10, 13, 20–3, 27–9, 30–1, 37, 41, 60, 103, 129–32, 134–7, 141, 148–9, 159, 169, 176–9, 195, 198, 200, 202, 204; intervening in 211–16; transgressing boundaries of 223–5, 232, 233, 237, 241, 255, 259–61
Earth system governance 136, 178–9, 200
eco-pragmatist 202, 209
Ecumenopolis 4, 244
Ehrlich, Paul 91, 160, 166, 179
emergency scenarios 14, 76, 81, 86–7, 91, 160
Encounters at the End of the World 123–4
enemy villages 78, 83
environmental crisis 15, 156, 183, 232, 241
environmentalism 76, 91, 103, 141, 202
environmental migrants 240; *see also* climate refugees
erosion 3, 27, 36–7, 202
exocolonies 161, 215; *see also* space colonies
experimental ethos 16, 27, 260
extinction event ix, 3, 37, 38, 65, 98; *see also* mass extinction

FAD (first occurrence datum) 37
Fear and Trembling 9
Fertile Crescent 237–8
fossil assemblages 27, 37
fossilization 21, 37, 103, 114, 159
fossil record 38, 98

fossil traces 14, 20, 22, 33, 37–9
Frankenstein 197, 200–2, 211
Franklin, Benjamin 64, 201
Fukushima 67, 224; Daiichi Power Plant 104–5; *see also* Tōhoku earthquake and tsunami
Fuller, R. Buckminster 81, 156–9, 162, 166, 172, 184, 227–8

Gagarin, Yuri 154
Gaia 12, 31, 148, 173, 214, 246, 262
gaiola seismic protection 56
Gazeta de Lisboa 52, 54
geoengineering x, xii, xiii, 4, 12, 15, 64, 94, 195–216, 224, 235, 245, 258; *see also* terraforming
geological agency (of humans) xiii, 20, 23, 41, 231–33
Geologic Time Scale (GTS) 3, 20, 26, 28, 30, 224
geopolitics 2, 223, 225
geophysical experiment 129, 175
geostory xii, 1–2, 22, 233, 247, 258
Gherman, Titov 154
glaciation 3, 28, 125
Global Boundary Stratotype Section and Point (GSSP) 27, 28, 38, 133; *see also* golden spike
global observatory 128, 130; *see also* International Geophysical Year (IGY)
god trick 243
golden spike 20, 28, 37–8
Google Street View 105, 117, 239
governance 60, 94, 140–1, 161, 167–8, 184, 215, 228, 230, 231, 237; in Antarctica 140–1; of geoengineering 205–6; *see also* Earth-system governance
Great Acceleration 21, 29, 37, 38, 76
Greenland xiv, 6, 28, 130, 131, 132, 133, 213

Haber-Bosch process 211
Habitat, UN Conference on Human Settlements, Vancouver 225–228, 244
Habitat III, Quito 2016 230
Halley VI 121, 123
Hamilton, Clive 22, 29, 32, 196
Hansen, James xiv, 206
Hardin, Garrett 160–1, 166, 173, 175, 179, 235
Hashimoto, Isao 76–7
Heidegger, Martin 153
Herzog, Werner 123–4
Hiroshima 79, 80, 81, 82, 92, 96, 98, 104, 105, 255
Hiroshima 80, 96
HMS *Endeavour* 115, 128
HMS *Erebus* 116

HMS *Terror* 116
Holocene viii, ix, xii, xvi, 2–4, 8–9, 11, 14–16, 20, 22, 24, 27–30, 41, 100, 114, 124, 125, 127, 133, 134, 141, 175–6, 179, 184, 185, 196, 201, 204, 213–14, 216, 223–4, 231–33, 237, 247–8, 257, 259
High Frontier: Human Colonies in Space 165
Home of Man 226–28
hospitality 15, 225, 241–244, 246
Hotel for Humanity 246–7
Huet, Marie-Helene 56, 59, 65–66, 116
human agency 22–3, 32, 66, 179, 200, 225, 231–3; limits of 6–7, 15, 32, 216, 231, 239–40, 245–6, 248; *see also* geological agency (of humans)
Human Event Stratum 33
Hurricane Katrina 60, 212, 224, 234–236
Husserl, Edmund 49, 183
Hutton, James 24–6, 30
Hutton's unconformity 25–6
Hyper-Anthropocene xiv
hyperobjects 9

Icarus Interstellar 180
ICE (Isolated Confined Environment) 120, 174, 182
ice age viii, 21, 113, 124–7, 131–3, 197, 215, 236
ice core 28, 29, 113, 114, 130–4, 137
improvisation 8, 70, 163, 184, 216, 228, 233, 236, 239, 261
Inconvenient Truth 235
Industrial Revolution 21, 28, 29, 37, 116, 164, 177, 195
informal urbanism 227–30
inside-out planets 164, 168
Intergovernmental Panel on Climate Change (IPCC) 11–12, 204, 229–30
International Commission on Sratigraphy (ICS) 20, 28
International Geophysical Year (IGY) 113, 117, 121, 128–30, 131, 135, 138, 140, 152
International Space Station (ISS) 154, 180
International Union of Geological Sciences 20
Interstellar 180
Into Eternity 34
inverted astronomy 150, 153, 154, 164, 185

Jerusalem 13
jinji unconformity or *jinji* discontinuity 24; *see also* unconformity
Jonas, Hans 255

Kahn, Herman 11, 13, 87–91
Kant, Immanuel 4, 48–9, 61–5, 66, 201, 244–5

Keeling Curve 129
Klein, Naomi 197, 202, 206, 236
Kolbert, Elizabeth 12, 37, 132
Kyoto Protocol 137, 205

Laika 153, 154
Larsen B ice shelf collapse 114, 132
Latour, Bruno xii, xiii, 4, 9, 22, 134, 175, 185, 202–3, 231–3, 244–5, 259–60
Lawrence Livermore Radiation Laboratory 92, 100
Leibniz, Gottfried Wilhelm 51, 58, 66
lifeboat ethics 127, 161, 179, 235
Lifeboat Foundation 181
Lifeboat UK 235
life-support system 15, 121, 148, 150, 151, 154, 157–8, 160, 162–3, 168, 169, 174–5, 182, 202, 228
Limited Test Ban 1963; 83, 92
Limits to Growth 12, 91, 161, 162, 176
Lisbon disaster 48–70, 247; *see also* Lisbon earthquake; Poem on the Lisbon Disaster
Lisbon earthquake xi, 14, 48–70, 104, 201
Lisbon Earthquake 49–50
Lisbon as first modern disaster 49, 56
Lisbon, and understandings of catastrophe 49, 54, 58, 60–2, 66–8, 70, 104
Little America 125–7
living in an earthquake 9, 68–9
living with uncertainty 6
London Underground 38
Los Alamos 100, 226
Lovecraft, H.P. 116
Lovelock, James 12, 31, 135, 148, 173, 179, 214, 235
Lyell, Charles 26, 27, 32, 33, 124, 247

MAD (Mutually Assured Destruction) 87, 199
made ground 36, 41
Madrid Protocol 1991; 139, 140
Malagrida, Gabriel 55
Manhattan 35, 81, 82, 90
Manhattan Project xiv, 79–81, 199, 214
Manhattan Shelter Study 82, 90
Mare Liberum 138
Mars: as counterpart Earth 214; in relation to Antarctica 118, 140; missions to 172, 180, 181, 182–3; life on 148, 182
Mars trilogy 140, 214
mass extinction xii, 10, 21, 26, 30, 37, 77, 98, 134
Mauna Loa 129, 177, 182
McMurdo Station 116, 121–3
megacities 2, 5, 8, 22, 37, 69, 181
meteors, meteorites xv, xvi, 65, 69, 131, 172, 181, 182, 197, 204; *see also* comets; asteroids

migration 6, 124, 166, 182, 223–4, 226, 231, 238, 240
Misanthropocene x
missing time 23, 24–7, 245
Monster Earth 197, 216
monsters: as human-made 197, 201–202; geoengineering effects as monstrous 195, 197, 200, 202
Montreal Protocol 136–7, 258
Moon 98, 115, 148, 153, 154, 155, 162, 163, 164, 165, 168, 175, 180, 181, 226
Moon, Ban Ki 205, 238
Morton, Oliver 4, 135, 149, 196, 205, 206, 211–12
Morton, Timothy 9, 26, 67, 99
Mount Pinatubo 136, 205–8
Mount Tambora 201
Mumford, Lewis 166–7

Nagasaki 79, 105
Namie, Fukushima Prefecture 104–5
National Aeronautics and Space Administration (NASA) xiv, 114, 120, 128, 135, 136, 140, 148, 149, 153, 155, 164, 165, 172, 180, 181, 182, 196, 214, 236
NASA's Hi-Seas (Hawaii Space Exploration Analog and Simulation) 182
NASA's Mars programme 120, 182
natural disaster 7, 21, 57, 59, 63, 67
Neiman, Susan 55, 56, 66, 79
Nelson, Mark 170
Nevada Test Site 77, 82–6, 94–6, 100
New Orleans 9, 37, 60, 89, 212, 235–7, 248
NewSpace 180
New Urban Agenda (NUA) 230
New York 11, 37, 80–1, 86, 89–90, 158, 215, 255
Nietzsche, Friedrich 9
nitrogen cycle 36, 176, 210–11
nitrogen fixation *see* Haber-Bosch process
Noah 11, 25; Noah's Ark 158, 165, 172, 184, 256–7
no-analogue state of the Earth system 3, 20, 127; non-analogue condition of the Anthropocene 204
Now House 227–8
nuclear age 14, 29, 37, 76, 85, 87, 92, 99, 102–3, 105, 231
nuclear deterrence 76–7, 87, 90, 92, 102–3
nuclear disaster 76–7, 80, 86–7, 102, 104–5
nuclear explosion xiii, 76, 80–4, 86, 92, 92, 94–6, 98
nuclear winter xiii, 96–9, 134, 172, 207

Odum, Eugene P. 163, 173, 174, 175
Odum, Howard 148
Oldest Ice 131

O'Neill, Gerard 163–8, 173, 215
Onkalo, Finland 34, 257
On the Beach 89
On Thermonuclear War 13, 87–90
Only One Earth 162, 226
Operating Manual for Spaceship Earth 155–9; *see also* Spaceship Earth
Operation Alert (OPAL) 86
Operation Argus 129
Operation Cue 84, 87
Operation Deep Freeze 117
Operation Doorstep 83–4, 86, 88–9, 93
Operation Gomorrah 78
Operation Plowshares 76 92–5
optimising climate 96, 204
oracle xiv, 262
Our Common Future 149; *see also* Brundtland Report
Outer Space Treaty 138–9, 182
ozone crisis 134–6
ozone depletion 118, 135–7, 176, 206
Ozone Hole xiii, 15, 114, 134–7, 206

Palaeoanthropocene 29
Papal Encyclical 259
Paradise Lost 201
peaceful purposes 138–40
Persephone project 181
phronesis or 'practical wisdom' 257
planet of cities 4–6, 21, 37, 229, 243
Planet under Pressure 224
planetarity 247
planetary agency 232; cosmic 7; more-than-human 185, 232–3; non-human xvii, 200–1
planetary boundaries 3, 15, 114, 150, 175–9, 180, 211, 213, 223–4, 248, 259
planetary crisis of agency 9, 231–2
planetary emergency 4, 235
planetary force (humans as) 16, 20
planetary housekeeping 227
planetary settlement 1, 237; *see also* unsettlement
planetary shipwreck 183, 185; *see also* shipwreck
planetary state of emergency 8
planetary state of exception 225, 233–7
planetary urbanization 5
Playfair, John 25
Pleistocene 3, 28, 124–7, 131, 133
Pleistocene-Holocene boundary 133
Poem on the Lisbon Disaster 48, 51
politics of emergency 224; *see also* state of emergency
Pombal, Marquis of 53–7
Population Bomb 91, 160
Poynter, Jane 174, 182

precautionary principle 255, 257–9, 260
precautionary tale 260–2
preparedness 6, 14, 54, 56, 76, 80, 86, 90, 259; *see also* rehearsals; civil defense rehearsals
Principles of Geology 26–7, 32–3
Pripyat, Ukraine 104
Project Chariot 94–5
Project Sedan 95
Prometheus 64, 201, 203, 211, 260
prophecy of doom 255
prophet xiii, 11, 91, 256
prophetic narrative xiii
prototype 172, 206, 228, 261, 262
Providencias 54
proving ground 14, 76–9, 84–5, 105, 128, 180
provisional cities 1–2, 8, 10, 14, 239
provisionality xvii 2 183
proxy 15, 113–14, 140, 169, 182
Pyne, Stephen 115, 124, 128, 140, 182

radioactive 9, 23, 33–4, 76, 83, 85, 86, 94–6, 99 100 102, 104, 121, 131, 138
RAND Corporation 11, 76, 90–1
Reagan administration 98, 102
Rees, Martin xiv
refugees, 53–4, 224–5, 230, 237–9, 241, 248; *see also* camps
refugia 224, 241, 261
rehearsal 8, 15, 76, 77, 80, 83, 86–7; *see also* civil defense rehearsals; preparedness
resilience 6, 60, 91, 176
right to the city 230
RMS Titanic 6
Road xii, 11, 103
Robinson, Kim Stanley 13, 140, 214–6
Rockström, Johan 176, 178, 211
Ross, James Clark 116–7
Rousseau, Jean-Jacques 49, 59–61, 247
rupture (Anthropocene as) 22, 23, 26–7, 29, 41, 67, 245, 262

safe operating space ix, 176, 211, 223; *see also* planetary boundaries
Sagan, Carl 97–8, 166, 214
scenarios xii, xiv, 1, 11–13, 14, 32, 76–7, 86–7, 91–2, 99, 101, 140, 161, 196, 206, 214, 230, 255
Scheherazade 12–13
Schumacher, E.F. 166, 168
Scott, Captain Robert Falcon 116–17, 120
Sebald, W.G. 78
securitization 76, 224, 234, 240
sedimentation 3, 27, 37
seismic imaginary 50
Serres, Michel xvi, 5, 9–10, 27, 40–1, 50, 69, 137, 155, 184, 246–7

Shackleton, Ernest 116, 120, 123, 125
Shelley, Mary 200–2
shipwreck alert 184–5
Shock of the Anthropocene xiii, 29, 31, 234
Siccar Point 24, 26
Sichuan earthquake 69
Silent Running 163
sky-falling xv-xvii 13, 50, 65, 68, 98, 262
Sloterdijk, Peter 121, 150, 184, 256
solar radiation management (SRM) 196, 199, 204–9; *see also* geoengineering
Solnit, Rebecca xiii, 83, 85, 235, 236, 238
South Polar Times 125
South Pole 115–17, 121, 124, 125
sovereignty 138–9, 158, 228, 231, 234, 243
Space Biosphere Ventures 169, 174
Space Colonies 166–8
space colonies, space colonisation 15, 151, 161, 164–8, 172, 180–1, 215
space mirrors 195, 214
space race 76, 128, 140
space settlements *see* space colonies
Spaceship Beagle 161, 166, 175
Spaceship Earth 15, 149, 155–63, 169, 173, 175–6, 184–5, 196, 197, 227, 228
SpaceX 180
Spivak, Gayatri Chakravorty 247
Spufford, Francis 120
Sputnik 128, 151–4
state of emergency 8, 56, 223–4, 234, 239
state of exception 225, 233–5, 237, 240
Steffen, Will xiii, xv, 28, 29, 30, 32, 132, 133, 178, 197, 213, 224, 259
Stengers, Isabelle 4, 17, 31–2, 245–6, 248, 260
stewardship xii, 113, 138, 150, 158, 160–3, 176–9, 185, 202
Stockholm Resilience Centre 150, 176
Stoermer, Eugene 21, 29, 133, 135
Stoppani, Antonio 21, 32
story to end all stories xii, 12, 66, 77, 103, 246, 256
storytellers, storytelling 1, 10, 13, 33, 66, 91, 246, 261; *see also* cautionary tale
Strangelove ocean 98
strata machine 33
stratigraphy 16, 22, 28, 30, 32, 34, 36
Stratigraphy Commission of the Geological Society of London 20, 28, 33
stratosphere 135–6, 196, 199, 205–7, 210, 213
Strontium-90 95, 96, 102, 104
sustainable, sustainability 2, 8, 172, 178–80, 182, 212, 230, 258
sustainable development 149–50
Sustainable Development Goals 178, 230
sustainable management 96, 204

Svalbard Global Seed Vault (SGSV) 256–7
Syria 237–9, 257

technofossil ix, 3, 27, 28, 34, 37
technological fix, techno-fix 127, 196–7, 202, 204, 212–13, 233, 258
Teller, Edward, 92, 95
temporary home 15, 225, 228, 231, 239, 247–8
Ten Thousand Years of Solitude 34, 101
tent cities 2, 15, 53, 225
Tereshkova, Valentina 154, 182
terra australis 115
terra firma 152, 168
terra incognita 113–18, 134, 141, 180, 182, 204
Terra Nova expedition 116, 125, 126
terra nullius 115
terraforming 95, 195, 213–6; *see also* geoengineering
test cities 14, 77–82, 84, 86–7; *see also* Doom Town; enemy villages; proving ground
Theory of the Earth 24
thermonuclear war 83, 89
tipping points x, 3, 127, 132, 137, 204, 210
Tōhoku earthquake and tsunami 23, 24, 69, 104
Tokyo, Japan 37, 69, 79
Treaty of Tordesillas 138–9
Trim-Tab 158 184
Trinity test 79
triple-disaster 24, 69, 104; *see also* Tōhoku earthquake and tsunami
Trump, Donald J. xiv, 233
Tsiolkovsky, Konstantin 150–2, 153, 155, 164, 165, 216
tsunami xi, 7, 23, 24, 48, 49, 50, 63, 65, 69, 104
TTAPS group 98
Tyndall, John 113–4

UN Climate Change Conference COP 15 184
UN Climate Change Conference COP 21 xiv
UN Convention on the Law of the Sea (UNCLOS) 138, 141
UN Framework Convention on Climate Change (UNFCCC) 198, 205, 206
UN High Commission for Refugees (UNHCR) 224, 238, 239, 243
UN Rio conference 'Earth Summit' 137, 206, 258
UN Rio+20 conference 177
UN Stockholm conference, 'Earth Summit' 91, 161–2

unconformity 14, 23–6, 41, 245; *see also* Anthropocene unconformity; *jinji* unconformity
Under the Dome 208
uniformitarianism 26
Union of Concerned Scientists xiv
unsettlement: Anthropocene as condition of 1, 2, 7, 10–11, 14–16, 42, 223–5, 240, 241, 248, 262; displacement of people 223–8, 239, 240, 248
urban age 5, 125
urban disturbances 5
urban fossils 2, 125
urban stratum 36–9
urbanisation ix, xv, 3–5, 7, 14, 36, 38, 60, 76, 100, 122, 223, 226–7, 229, 231, 237
urbanthropocene 5, 7, 36

Vernadsky, Vladimir 21, 173
Verne, Jules 116, 117, 198
volcanoes, volcanic eruptions xii, 7, 8, 21, 33, 34, 50, 58, 63, 69, 116, 122, 130–1, 135–6, 159, 196, 201, 205–7, 213, 233; volcanic activity as analogue for SRM 207
Voltaire 33, 48–9, 51, 52, 57–8, 59, 61, 66
Vonnegut, Kurt 155, 199
Vorsorgeprinzip 257; *see also* precautionary principle
Vostok ice core 133

Ward, Barbara 159–60, 162, 226–8
Waste Isolation Pilot Plant (WIPP) 34, 99–103, 257
West Antarctic Ice Sheet 37, 114, 140, 210, 231
Whole Earth Catalog 148, 164, 166, 196
WORLD3 161–2
World Dynamics 91, 161
world-ending: threats and phenomena 50, 65, 92, 98, 170; tales and scenarios 13, 77, 262
World War II 13, 21, 29, 30, 76, 86, 135, 138, 162, 228
world-wide lab 260
World Without Us 12, 104
worst-case scenario xii, 7, 11, 12, 77, 161, 180; *see also* scenarios

Year without a Summer 200, 207

Zaatari refugee camp 238–40
Zalasiewicz, Jan 20–3, 29–30, 33, 36–7, 65, 114, 125

Taylor & Francis eBooks

Helping you to choose the right eBooks for your Library

Add Routledge titles to your library's digital collection today. Taylor and Francis ebooks contains over 50,000 titles in the Humanities, Social Sciences, Behavioural Sciences, Built Environment and Law.

Choose from a range of subject packages or create your own!

Benefits for you
- Free MARC records
- COUNTER-compliant usage statistics
- Flexible purchase and pricing options
- All titles DRM-free.

Benefits for your user
- Off-site, anytime access via Athens or referring URL
- Print or copy pages or chapters
- Full content search
- Bookmark, highlight and annotate text
- Access to thousands of pages of quality research at the click of a button.

REQUEST YOUR FREE INSTITUTIONAL TRIAL TODAY

Free Trials Available
We offer free trials to qualifying academic, corporate and government customers.

eCollections – Choose from over 30 subject eCollections, including:

Archaeology	Language Learning
Architecture	Law
Asian Studies	Literature
Business & Management	Media & Communication
Classical Studies	Middle East Studies
Construction	Music
Creative & Media Arts	Philosophy
Criminology & Criminal Justice	Planning
Economics	Politics
Education	Psychology & Mental Health
Energy	Religion
Engineering	Security
English Language & Linguistics	Social Work
Environment & Sustainability	Sociology
Geography	Sport
Health Studies	Theatre & Performance
History	Tourism, Hospitality & Events

For more information, pricing enquiries or to order a free trial, please contact your local sales team:
www.tandfebooks.com/page/sales

Routledge
Taylor & Francis Group

The home of Routledge books

www.tandfebooks.com